# Innovative CSR

# Innovative CSR

## FROM RISK MANAGEMENT TO VALUE CREATION

EDITED BY CÉLINE LOUCHE, SAMUEL O. IDOWU
AND WALTER LEAL FILHO

Greenleaf
PUBLISHING

© 2010 Greenleaf Publishing Limited

Published by Greenleaf Publishing Limited
Aizlewood's Mill
Nursery Street
Sheffield s3 8GG
UK
**www.greenleaf-publishing.com**

Printed in Great Britain on acid-free paper by
CPI Antony Rowe, Chippenham, Wiltshire

Cover by LaliAbril.com

British Library Cataloguing in Publication Data:
    A catalogue record for this book is available from the British Library.

    ISBN–13: 9781906093358

# Contents

# Foreword

**Professor Dr Philippe Haspeslagh**
Dean, Vlerick Leuven Gent Management School, Belgium

Corporate social responsibility (CSR) has gone mainstream; an increasing number of companies are realising not only that CSR is their franchise to operate sustainably but also that their ability to establish trust with a new generation of consumers and citizens depends on how the company is perceived as an actor in society. Sustainability is thus increasingly becoming a core ingredient of companies' strategies for competitive advantage.

Now that the case for CSR has been made, the time has come to further clarify the mechanisms through which CSR affects stakeholders, in order to enable companies to shape effective sustainable strategies. Much can also be learned from the forerunners in this field about the pitfalls in implementation, and the organisational learning that is required to implement effective CSR strategies throughout the organisation.

In this coherent collection of essays edited by Céline Louche, Samuel O. Idowu and Walter Leal Filho, the new landscape of CSR is clearly coming into focus. While the authors report that there are still environments, such as Japan, where most CSR efforts are focusing on minimising risks, the studies of most authors in this volume illustrate a landscape where CSR is being used resolutely as a focal point of strategy, with its competitive advantage stemming not only from the perception of stakeholders but also from real economic advantages created in the value chain.

Some of the chapters in this volume focus on the former and illustrate how CSR can create non-economic value in the consumer's mind, and hence become a great brand-building tool. The majority of the chapters, however, focus on economic value added and illustrate through case examples how firms can benefit strategically.

As in any sound academic work, the various authors are raising some puzzles and linking CSR to mainstream theory. For example, if the search for competitive advantage is usually based on differentiating factors, why then is it that so many companies' CSR efforts tend to converge on the same well-worn recipes?

Truly implementing and benefiting organisation-wide also raises two implementation issues dealt with in some of the chapters. One is the resistance to change that must be overcome. The other is the importance of the processes of innovation and learning which are central to refining the CSR approach in practice. Even the role of consultants as catalysts is critically examined in this volume.

Some chapters also debunk the myth that CSR is for large firms, illustrating how SMEs can greatly benefit. Actually, smaller firms stand to benefit as a result of many factors: for example, changing customers' attitude, which opens new opportunities, and changing buying behaviour of the now CSR-conscious large firms and public authorities.

This volume also points to some of the challenges ahead both for management and for authorities. Managers will have to progress in measuring and monitoring the value that CSR brings. And regulators will have to become adept at creating a context that allows CSR initiatives to soar beyond the traditional regulatory compliance effort.

This book not only offers researchers an overview of where the research on CSR stands, but it is also an eye-opener for the curious manager. As Chapter 6 by Barbara Del Bosco points out, in the end the role of the entrepreneur is crucial, as any proactive organisational change requires an act of leadership. Lest we want to be left behind, as leaders of our organisations we are challenged by the speed of what is happening in the CSR arena to take the lead in our organisations and commit to change.

# Preface

The general acceptance of the field of corporate social responsibility (CSR) world-wide continues to improve the relationship between business and society. There is now a general understanding that they are interwoven; neither the business nor society can function effectively without the other. The ethos and principles encompassed in the field of CSR coupled with innovative practices emerging on the corporate scene have mandatorily created a congenial environment for this mutual respect and understanding between the two sides to flourish.

It is generally believed that any business that wishes to survive and prosper must innovate. If it fails to innovate this could result in serious consequences. How does CSR lead to, contribute to, or stimulate innovation in terms of new products, services and technologies but also new organisational and institutional systems, structures and new business models? And how can such innovations on the one hand empower organisations to advance strategically in an ever competitive business world and on the other hand respond to sustainability challenges? It was curiosity about these questions that spawned the idea for this book on *Innovative Corporate Social Responsibility*.

The current challenging global economic climate has made it more important than ever for corporate entities of all shapes, forms and sizes to weave CSR into their core strategies. There are, similarly, some unimaginably serious consequences that could befall any corporate entity that fails to do so. The 'do no harm' type of CSR is not sufficient to respond to the sustainability challenges faced by our societies; at best, it serves to avoid scandals. But the time has come to shift the CSR focus away from risk management towards a more progressive and entrepreneurial approach that seeks to create value for both companies and society and identify sustainable opportunities for strategic innovation. This is a necessary step for CSR to reach its full potential.

This book is a contribution to move CSR from risk management to value creation. Integrating CSR as a strategic component will lead to the fundamental changes necessary to move towards more sustainable patterns of consumption and production, create value, generate new ideas and open up new opportunities.

The purpose of this book is to explore different dimensions of innovative and strategic practice on the part of corporate entities around the globe, and to discuss innovation-specific and general issues on corporate social responsibility. It therefore provides insights on innovative and strategic CSR, CSR in SMEs, cases in CSR and general issues in CSR.

Each chapter was written with the primary objective of satisfying the information needs of stakeholders, researchers, practitioners and corporate managers, international organisations, governments and all those that are enthusiastic about the field of CSR and new developments in the field.

*Céline Louche, Samuel O. Idowu and Walter Leal Filho*
*Spring 2010*

# Acknowledgements

We would like to thank a host of individuals for their kind support and assistance in ensuring the successful completion of the third book in a series of books on corporate social responsibility by these three editors.

Our first 'thank you' goes to all the authors who submitted so many suggestions, proposals and papers; without their hard work this volume would never have got off the drawing board.

We want to thank the numerous networks, institutions and individuals who have kindly advertised our call for papers and especially the European Academy for Business in Society (EABIS), the International Association for Business and Society (IABS), CSR Europe and SSRNet.

Many thanks to our institutions, Vlerick Leuven Gent Management School, London Metropolitan University Business School and Hamburg University of Applied Sciences, for giving us the opportunity to write the book in the first place. We would especially like to thank Lutgart Van den Berghe and Philippe Haspeslagh, respectively Partner and Dean of Vlerick Leuven Gent Management School, for their support and contribution to the book.

We would like to thank John Stuart at Greenleaf Publishing for his dedication, patience and openness. We also extend our thanks to the staff at Greenleaf for their professionalism and support throughout the editing process.

We are also grateful to many friends and colleagues who have helped us to shape the book. Their encouragements and suggestions throughout the project have been hugely appreciated. We would like to thank some people individually for their support, insights, challenging questions and generosity in time and ideas: Bieke Dewulf, Vickie Dekocker, Katinka C. van Cranenburgh, Michael A. Idowu, Elizabeth A.A. Lawal, Olufunmilola O. Idowu, Rachael T. Idowu, Mary T. Idowu, Abigail O. Idowu, Olaniyi J. Idowu, Christopher Soyinka, Denis Haffner, Andrea Dunhill,

Richard Ennals, Timothy Cleary, Anthony Brabazon and David Crowther.

Incalculable thanks go to those whose names we've forgotten to mention and to the numerous people who have, intentionally or unintentionally, contributed to the book, including our families.

Finally, the team of editors would like to thank the lead editor, Céline Louche, for managing the project to the highest possible standards despite her many life roles including coping with a pregnancy at the start of the project and her young family.

We believe that we have taken all possible steps to ensure that the facts presented in this book are error-free. However, as it is impossible to completely avoid errors in any book, we therefore wish to apologise for any error or omission that may appear anywhere in this book. No harm was intended either directly or indirectly to anyone.

# Innovative corporate social responsibility

## An introduction

**Samuel O. Idowu**
London Metropolitan Business School, UK

**Céline Louche**
Vlerick Leuven Gent Management School, Belgium

**Walter Leal Filho**
Hamburg University of Applied Sciences, Germany

By and large, corporations of the 21st century have come to realise that their obligations to societies in terms of corporate social responsibility are fourfold: namely, economic, ethical, altruistic and strategic (Levitt 1958; Carroll 1979; Lantos 2001). Meeting these four responsibilities is crucial to their survival in their various markets and industries; it also requires them to rewrite their previously less socially responsible business models in order to accommodate meeting these obligations. All indications continue to suggest that it is those organisations that are perceived to be socially responsible by stakeholders in modern markets that will survive and prosper (Tilt 1997; Katsoulakos and Katsoulacos 2007). Corporate entities of this era have equally realised that, by being innovative in all ramifications including their CSR activities and initiatives, they will certainly add value not only to the so-called bottom line, but also to the positive contributions they make to society and the natural environment and how they are perceived by their key stakeholders; in other words, how they are rated in terms of the now generally accepted triple-bottom-line (economic, social and environment) league table. In addition, they are more likely to avoid taking unnecessary reputational risks which could result in serious financial and non-financial consequences.

These entities are equally aware that several of their many stakeholder groups—for example, governments, NGOs and the media to name but three—are watching them and are ready to hold them to account for the social consequences of their operational activities (Porter and Kramer 2006), and to judge them in terms of their environmental performance (Idowu 2009). Besides, there are several organisations with sustainability indices which institutional investors and some private investors now consider before making their investment decisions: for instance, the Dow Jones Sustainability Index and FTSE4Good Index. Modern environmental movements are suggesting that a considerable number of today's social and environmental problems are traceable to some of the previous strategies followed by corporations. These strategies have been criticised for failing to weave into them socially responsible initiatives and actions which would have either removed or at least ameliorated the adverse impact of these organisations' actions. These adverse impacts have been manifested in terms of the ecological, social and economic problems which have recently been exacerbated around the world. A few of these are depicted in the form of environmental pollution and degradation, global warming and climate change, human rights abuses, irresponsible employment practices in so-called sweatshops, unequal opportunities in workplaces in some parts of the world, depletion of natural resources, the food crisis and of course the current global financial meltdown. These are perhaps problems that would have been considered to be far too remote to be laid at the door of corporations some 50 or so years ago.

Corporate social responsibility as a field that is concerned with what some advocates of CSR have referred to as the 3Ps (People, Planet and Profit), which perhaps is another approach of expressing the triple-bottom-line model mentioned above. If this is so, then it is reasonable to assume that corporate entities of all shapes and forms should consider issues that relate to the 3Ps as important to them for various reasons. *People* are the lifeblood of a corporate entity; without people, corporate entities will not exist. The *planet* also is the abode of people and corporate entities. If the planet is made uninhabitable because of corporate actions, then enterprises and people will similarly be wiped off the face of the Earth. And finally *profit* is a necessary condition as it enables companies to expand their activities and hopefully behave responsibly.

Before the issue of CSR became topical around the world, it was the interest of the shareholders/owners (the providers of capital) that was wrongly perceived as being of paramount importance by corporate managers who were and are still their appointed agents (Jensen and Meckling 1976). This was before the era of

**stakeholder theory** which was popularised in the 1980s (see for example Freeman 1984; Donaldson and Preston 1995). Initially, eminent scholars such as Levitt (1958) and Friedman (1962, 1970) had posited that organisations owe no responsibility to the larger publics but only to their owners—the shareholders—and that their responsibility has only one element, which is to make as much profit as possible while conforming to the basic rules of society. Anything other than that, Friedman (1970) concludes, is *pure socialism* which is not what *capitalism* is all about. Friedman (1962, 1970) argues that what CSR requires corporate entities to do is actually the responsibility of governments; these corporations like other citizens pay their taxes and should therefore expect governments to expend the revenues they receive from taxes in the provision of social benefits for all taxpayers. But Clarkson (1995) notes that organisations do not operate for the sole benefit of one stakeholder group; there are two classes of stakeholders. The first class he refers to as **primary stakeholders**: shareholders, employees, customers, suppliers, governments and communities. He argues that members of this class are so important in the life of a business entity that the firm would cease to exist without their continuing support. The second class he refers to as **secondary stakeholders**: they influence or are influenced by the entity's activities but are not engaged directly in transactions with it and are therefore not so important for its survival but could still be a source of unwanted bad publicity. A few corporations which were criticised for encouraging sweatshop practices in some South-East Asian countries discovered this to their cost a few years ago. It would therefore be futile for the entity in question to ignore the interests of all but one of its stakeholders as advocated by Levitt (1958) and Friedman (1962, 1970).

Halal (2000) suggests that three models of governance have been practised at different times by corporate managers over the last 100 years or so. The first model he refers to as the **profit-centred model** (PCM), which was practised between 1900 and 1950. This model erroneously assumed that profit was the only objective of the firm. It failed abysmally because it ignored the fact that corporate entities have several stakeholders whose interests and expectations must be considered in order to function effectively. The model was then replaced with a more socially responsible model which Halal (2000) describes as the **social responsibility model** (SRM), which was practised between 1950 and 1980. This period falls during the hot debate on the desirability of CSR by corporate entities following Howard Bowen's (1953) book on *Social Responsibilities of the Businessman*, which hypothesised that business owes a responsibility to society and should pursue strategies that are desirable in meeting societal objectives and values. The SRM was an attempt to rectify some of the mistakes inherent in the PCM. It soon became apparent that, even though the SRM was a marked advance on the PCM, it still fell short of the expectations of society; there were still some missing links between what society desires and what the model offered. Halal (2000) notes that it was inevitable that the **corporate community model** (CCM), which is a more socially responsible and progressive model, was going to replace the SRM from the 1980s to the present period. Society and business appear to have an understanding of what business must do in order to make our world a better place. The story has not ended there; there is still room to explore how the art of innovation could be used to elicit how the field of CSR could be practised worldwide; hence the need for a book on *Innovative Corporate Social Responsibility*.

This book provides an insight into how scholars in 12 different countries around the world perceive innovative and strategic actions of corporate entities as they continue to drive forward developments on corporate social responsibility. Society now demands that we should all behave responsibly by demonstrating that those issues that are at the core of CSR are equally important to us in the same way as those traditional issues which earlier scholars had identified as falling within the domain of CSR. Academics in this discipline have an opportunity to drive innovation by formulating concepts that can have immediate practical application.

This book is divided into three parts. Part I, 'CSR and competitive advantage', encompasses six chapters, with each addressing the strategic dimensions of CSR. This section provides a combination of theoretical contributions and case studies exploring the relationship between CSR and competitiveness, not only for large companies but also for small and medium-sized enterprises.

Jeremy Galbreath and Kim Benjamin, in 'An action-based approach for linking CSR with strategy: framework and cases', argue that modern firms must face the reality that CSR is a new battleground the importance of which for competitive advantage cannot be ignored. It is also a focal issue for corporate strategy, they note. The chapter provides a theoretical framework for linking CSR with strategy as well as three mini case studies to illustrate the implementation of the framework.

David Williamson, Gary Lynch-Wood and Rilka Dragneva-Lewers, in 'Exploring the regulatory preconditions for business advantage in CSR', focus on the regulatory dimension and how it can provide competitive advantage. They argue that CSR is intrinsically linked to regulation basically because the field requires a corporate entity to extend its moral duties to its stakeholders beyond what the law requires. The association between CSR and regulation goes deeper than a simplistic interrelationship because, they claim, innovative CSR is a form of regulatory compliance which the market reacts to and consequently affects bottom-line results. Nation states also need to provide an environment for innovative CSR to flourish through regulatory pressures, they note.

Nicola Misani, in 'Convergent and divergent corporate social responsibility', argues that two types of CSR, namely convergent and divergent, co-exist. For CSR to offer competitive advantage, firms should concentrate their efforts on divergent CSR. However, according to Misani, many firms maintain a focus on non-differentiating practices—in other words, convergent CSR—and thereby fail to fulfil the potential of CSR as a source of competitive advantage. In this chapter Misani explores the reasons why such a large number of firms choose convergent CSR instead of divergent CSR.

Denise Baden, in 'CSR: an opportunity for SMEs', examines the opportunities of CSR for small and medium-sized enterprises (SMEs). The chapter explores the effects of inculcating CSR strategies by firms in the buying decisions of their customers—individuals, multinational corporations (MNCs) and public sector organisations—and their implications for SMEs.

Malcolm F. Arnold, in 'Competitive advantage from corporate responsibility programmes', examines how four CSR programmes of large multinational organisations have helped to increase their market competitiveness while 'doing good' for their stakeholders. Arnold applies the Porter–Kramer (2006) model to identify what competitive advantages are offered by their CSR programmes.

Barbara Del Bosco, in 'A strategic approach to CSR: the case of Beghelli', discusses the case of an Italian company that has adopted a strategic approach to embedding CSR principles into its activities. Focusing on how CSR could be used to derive competitive advantage in the market, the chapter explores the role played by the firm's resources. It also uses the five strategic dimensions of CSR projects in Burke and Logsdon 1996 as its frame of reference to explore these issues.

Part II, 'CSR and value creation', examines the ways in which CSR can create value for a firm, its stakeholders and society. It comprises six chapters proposing frameworks, cases and an empirical study. Each of the chapters has a different focus and perspective: some examine value creation for the firm as a whole while others focus on specific issues or stakeholders. This section of the book highlights the potential of CSR to create value but it also underlines some of the difficulties in understanding where and how it can do so.

Karen Maas and Frank Boons, in 'CSR as a strategic activity: value creation, redistribution and integration', explore how CSR can provide value for a firm, society and ecosystems. According to the authors, there are three ways CSR can add value: namely, through value creation, value integration and value distribution. The authors propose a framework for assessing the strategic potential of CSR (illustrated by examples) and examine the consequences for measuring the impact of CSR activities.

Alejandro Alvarado-Herrera *et al.*, in 'Does corporate social responsibility really add value for consumers?', study the relationship between CSR, perceived value and satisfaction by consumers. The authors note that companies would be encouraged to strategise on CSR if they perceive it as a source of value. The study is based on a theoretical model to empirically test the impact of non-economic aspects on value, cognitive satisfaction and affective satisfaction.

Francisco Guzmán and Karen L. Becker-Olsen, in 'Strategic corporate social responsibility: a brand-building tool', argue that integrating CSR into a company's core value proposition is a powerful tool for building brands. The authors explore the core business versus broader goals perspective in light of a strategic CSR framework, and explain when and how it makes sense for a brand to adopt each of these perspectives according to the level of development of CSR in a determined market. They also provide a CSR life-cycle model for strategic CSR decision-making and multiple international examples of CSR programmes.

Jyoti Navare, in 'Corporate social responsibility: risk managing for value creation in the housing sector in the UK', looks at a not-for-profit sector, more specifically housing associations (HAs) in the UK. HAs are facing a series of roadblocks in their attempts to provide affordable sheltered housing. The author argues that having to manage a wide stakeholder group in the sector has made the risk management activity much more difficult. The chapter uses a case study approach to create a risk scorecard in order to determine the correlation between risk and value outputs.

Katinka C. van Cranenburgh, Daniel Arenas and Laura Albareda, in 'Healthcare provision of a multinational company operating in emerging markets: ethical motivations, benefits of healthcare investment and the impact on socially responsible investors', analyse Heineken's healthcare programmes in sub-Saharan Africa. The chapter provides insights into the benefits of healthcare investment for the company and its employees and more especially investigates the impact of such programmes on the firm's valuation by the investment community.

Karla Duarte and Maeve Houlihan, in 'A rose by any other name? The case of HIV/AIDS interventions among South African SMEs', examine the practice of CSR among eight South African SMEs with regard to their participation in the fight against the spread of HIV/AIDS in the workplace. The chapter notes that these SMEs use either ad hoc initiatives or well-structured programmes to reduce the spread of the deadly disease in the workplace. It notes that South African SMEs are CSR-active even though the term 'CSR' may not necessarily be used by them. The authors also highlight how crucial contextualisation is when implementing, managing and researching the field of CSR.

Part III, 'CSR and innovation', focuses on the innovative aspect of CSR. This section consists of six chapters, which consider several aspects of the relationship between CSR and innovation, including the barriers to innovative CSR. In these chapters, the reader will be able to investigate innovative CSR in very different contexts in terms of geography, sector and company size.

Céline Louche, Samuel O. Idowu and Walter Leal Filho, in 'Innovation in corporate social responsibility: how innovative is it? An exploratory study of 129 global innovative CSR solutions', analyse 129 CSR solutions implemented by companies around the world. Through an evaluation framework designed by the authors, this chapter makes an attempt to capture and understand the innovative dimensions, the sustainability aspects addressed and the degree of innovation of each of the CSR solutions.

Steven P. MacGregor, Joan Fontrodona and Jose Hernandez, in 'Towards a sustainable innovation model for small enterprises', examine the link between CSR and innovation in European SMEs. They note that, even though the uptake of CSR activities was good, it was often informal and consequently failed to produce real value. The study also notes that the most successful companies in different industries are often the largest adopters of the concept of CSR.

Lutz Preuss, in 'Barriers to innovative CSR: the impacts of organisational learning, organisational structure and the social embeddedness of the firm', discusses what barriers companies are likely to experience on their journey towards innovative forms of CSR. The author develops an integrated framework on innovation using the innovative literature.

Magnus Frostenson, in 'How consultants contribute to CSR innovation: combining competences and modifying standards', notes that consultants as intermediaries involved in the field of CSR have played an important role in promoting innovative practices in the field. The chapter examines how consultants have translated their knowledge of CSR into useful services which their clients buy in. The chapter argues that consultants in various disciplines—for example, accounting and auditing, IT and PR—have been able to innovate in order to offer useful products to clients. The chapter notes that consultants create CSR instruments alongside the existing business models to help their clients.

Scott Davis, in 'Strategic CSR in the Japanese context: from business risk to market creation', argues that an increasing number of Japanese corporations are joining the CSR bandwagon but a considerable number of the resulting CSR initiatives are designed to legitimise their strategic objectives using some traditional management theories of the role of business in society. This has led some proponents of CSR principles by corporate entities to suggest that they implement value-creation CSR. The author notes in a Japanese study that the majority of the current CSR initiatives used by these corporations are risk-reduction initiatives instead of value-creation ones.

Ciaran O'Faircheallaigh, in 'CSR, the mining industry and indigenous peoples in Australia and Canada: from cost and risk minimisation to value creation and sustainable development', notes that those companies that operate in the mining industry face unimaginable levels of competition and are simultaneously exposed to enormous levels of risk. It is therefore necessary for them to use CSR to reduce the risk levels at the lowest possible cost, one would imagine. Unfortunately, notes this author, operators in this industry are in a no-win situation as their attempts at cost reduction exercises often expose them to even greater levels of risk. Several scholars have argued that there are various opportunities to be derived from embarking on CSR activities. To realise the opportunities of CSR for these mining companies, a more positive approach to CSR is required. The chapter argues that operators in the industry are required to embed a more strategic approach to CSR. The chapter examines the benefits of innovation in CSR by mining companies among the indigenous peoples of Australia and Canada.

It is hoped that our readers will find the articles in this book relevant to their needs. We would like to thank all our readers spread across the globe for their continued support.

# References

Bowen, H.R. (1953) *Social Responsibilities of the Businessman* (New York: Harper & Row).

Burke, L., and J.M. Logsdon (1996) 'How Corporate Social Responsibility Pays Off', *Long Range Planning* 29.4: 495-502.

Carroll, A.B. (1979) 'A Three-dimensional Conceptual Model of Corporate Social Performance', *Academy of Management Review* 4.4: 497-505.

Clarkson, M.B.E. (1995) 'A Stakeholder Framework for Analyzing and Evaluating Corporate Social Performance', *Academy of Management Review* 20: 92-117.

Donaldson, T., and L.E. Preston (1995) 'The Stakeholder Theory of the Corporation: Concepts, Evidence and Implications', *Academy of Management Review* 20.1: 65-91.

Freeman, R.E. (1984) *Strategic Management: A Stakeholder Approach* (Boston, MA: Pitman).

Friedman, M. (1962) *Capitalism and Freedom* (Chicago: University of Chicago Press).

—— (1970) 'The social responsibility of business is to increase its profits', *New York Times Magazine*, 13 September 1970.

Halal, W.E. (2000) 'Corporate Community: A Theory of the Firm Uniting Profitability and Responsibility', *Strategy & Leadership* 28.2: 10-16.

Idowu, S.O. (2009) 'Corporate Social Responsibility from the Perspective of Corporate Secretaries', in S.O. Idowu and W.L. Filho (eds.), *Professionals' Perspectives of CSR* (Berlin: Springer).

Jensen, M.C., and W.H. Meckling (1976) 'The Theory of the Firm: Managerial Behavior, Agency Cost and Ownership Structure', *Journal of Financial Economics* 3.4: 305-60.

Katsoulakos, T., and Y. Katsoulacos (2007) 'Integrating Corporate Responsibility Principles and Stakeholder Approaches into Mainstream Strategy: A Stakeholder-Oriented and Integrative Management Framework', *Corporate Governance* 7.4: 355-69.

Lantos, G.P. (2001) 'The Boundaries of Strategic Corporate Social Responsibility', *Journal of Consumer Marketing* 18.7: 595-632.

Levitt, T. (1958) 'The Dangers of Social Responsibility', *Harvard Business Review* 36: 41-50.

Porter, M.E., and M.R. Kramer (2006) 'Strategy and Society: The Link between Competitive Advantage and Corporate Social Responsibility', *Harvard Business Review*, December 2006: 78-92.

Tilt, C.A. (1997) 'Environmental Policies of Major Companies: Australian Evidence', *British Accounting Review* 29: 367-94.

# Part I
## CSR and competitive advantage

# 1

# An action–based approach for linking CSR with strategy
## Framework and cases

**Jeremy Galbreath**

Graduate School of Business, Curtin University of Technology, Western Australia

**Kim Benjamin**

Curtin Business School, Curtin University of Technology, Western Australia

Although the call from academics and consultants to integrate CSR with corporate strategy has been established, there is concern that many firms seem to lack direction on how to address CSR in an innovative way and, importantly, strategically. By way of example, while CEOs acknowledge that addressing stakeholder expectations for CSR is an important consideration for competitive success, they appear to be struggling with just how to link CSR with corporate strategy (Hirschland 2005; McKinsey & Company 2006; PricewaterhouseCoopers 2007; IBM 2008). Recent reports reveal that a majority of organisations have no defined strategy for CSR, while many companies are unclear about how to adequately anticipate which social issues will affect their overall strategy (Work Foundation 2002; McKinsey & Company 2006; IBM 2008).

In an effort to explore innovative ways of addressing CSR, this chapter seeks to develop a couple of key themes and insights. First, we seek to identify how to view CSR strategically. To do this, an argument is made that firms need to take an 'issues' perspective of CSR by identifying social issues that are prevalent to stakeholders. According to Aguilera and colleagues (2007), CSR is best defined as actions designed to improve social conditions. By identifying prevailing social issues, firms place themselves in a position to improve social conditions. However, not all social issues are relevant—let alone strategic—across all industries. We develop a means to strategically address the matter. Second, once firms identify social issues that are strategic, action must be taken. Strategy is about tough choices and trade-offs and our framework explains three means of action with respect to CSR. The main objective of the chapter is not to offer a pure theoretical treatment, but rather to discuss a sensible approach to CSR and strategy, and to highlight what the use of the framework might look like pragmatically.

To proceed, the chapter first offers an overview of our framework; we discuss the logic behind the framework, including theoretical and practical aspects. Next, three short cases are elaborated which expound the framework. The companies are Aveda, Herman Miller and Toyota. Lastly, implications and conclusions are offered.

## Linking CSR and strategy: an action-based framework

Our research suggests that many firms appear to be struggling with how to create a dynamic link between CSR and strategy. This struggle is exacerbated by the fact that many firms seem to equate CSR with 'cheque-book' philanthropy, codes of ethics or public relations efforts, which are too far removed from strategy (Davis 2005). To move beyond such approaches and to view CSR strategically, firms should consider five key aspects: (1) the social issues perspective; (2) strategic issues; (3) industry context; (4) issues prioritisation; and (5) strategic actions (Figure 1.1).

The five aspects are rooted in social issues management (Mahon and Waddock 1992; Lamertz *et al.* 2003), industrial organisation economics (Bain 1959; Porter 1981), stakeholder theory (Clarkson 1995; Mitchell *et al.* 1997) and the strategy literature (Ansoff 1980; Porter 1980, 1996). Although there are many potential aspects that could be important to linking CSR and strategy, we make the argument that the five aspects outlined above are most critical.

First, although CSR has been elevated to one of the most widely accepted concepts in business in the last 20 years, multiple definitions and theoretical treatments create confusion regarding precise meaning (Min-Dong 2008). In simplest terms, we believe that CSR is best defined as actions designed to improve social conditions (Wood and Jones 1995; Waddock and Bodwell 2004; Aguilera *et al.* 2007). What this definition suggests is that, if firms are going to demonstrate CSR through a given set of actions, they need to understand what social 'conditions' need to be improved. Understanding social conditions is perhaps best framed within the

**Figure 1.1** Proposed framework

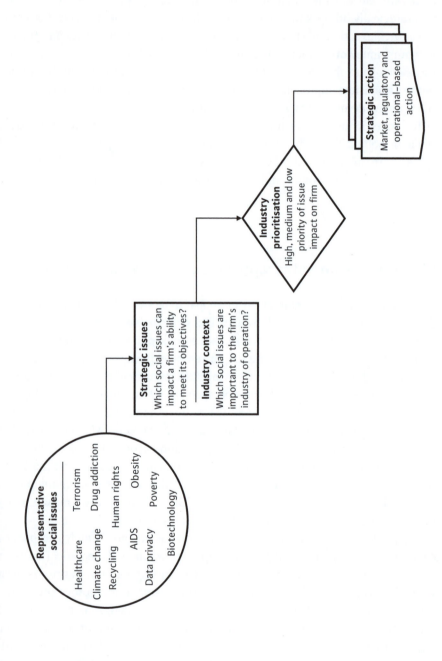

**Representative social issues**

Healthcare   Terrorism   Drug addiction
Climate change   Human rights
Recycling   AIDS   Obesity
Data privacy   Poverty
Biotechnology

**Strategic issues**
Which social issues can impact a firm's ability to meet its objectives?

**Industry context**
Which social issues are important to the firm's industry of operation?

**Industry prioritisation**
High, medium and low priority of issue impact on firm

**Strategic action**
Market, regulatory and operational–based action

'social issues' perspective (Mahon and Waddock 1992; Lamertz *et al.* 2003). More specifically, a social issue is one deemed problematic to society through the actions of stakeholders capable of influencing governmental or corporate response and policy (Mahon and Waddock 1992). Many social issues exist: HIV/AIDS, climate change, human rights, terrorism, pollution, obesity, information privacy and so on. However, not all social issues are important to a given firm and, thus, firms need to consider which ones are *strategic*.

Understanding social issues in light of the **strategic issue** concept is important. Ansoff (1980: 133) suggests that 'a strategic issue is a forthcoming development, either inside, or outside the organisation, which is likely to have an important impact on the ability of the enterprise to meet its objectives'. What Ansoff suggests is that, while firms might face a variety of issues (including those that are social), only certain ones could be considered significant enough to have an impact on the ability to fulfil corporate objectives. For example, a local symphony orchestra that is under threat of closure because of a lack of funding is not likely to be a social issue that is going to have a major impact on the ability of a given firm to compete effectively. On the other hand, when consumers begin buying a green alternative laundry detergent from a rival because of a growing social issue such as concern for the environment, then a leading firm that does not address environmental quality in its products could be under threat of losing market share and failing to meet its growth objectives. This example raises another closely related factor in our framework: namely, industry context.

Industrial organisation economists and strategy scholars alike argue that industry context is one of the most important considerations for strategy development and for understanding the determinants of firm performance (e.g. Bain 1959; Porter 1980, 1981). Industry sector, for example, comprises many structural characteristics such as intensity of competition and number of competitors, capital requirements, access to distribution channels and the degree to which suppliers or buyers have bargaining power, among others. By taking an issues perspective in relation to strategy, we argue that the importance of some social issues is greater than others in a given industry. For example, in the apparel industry, safe working conditions and fair pay are key social issues. Mining firms must address air and water pollution. Alternatively, producers and retailers in the food industry face intense pressure over the obesity issue. Given industry context and the fact that some issues are more pressing than others, managers should first understand the 'hot button' social issues that are specific to their industry of operation. This requires the ability to understand stakeholder demands and pressures (Clarkson 1995; Mitchell *et al.* 1997), and to identify which social issues stakeholders view as most critical.

While addressing all known social issues might be a noble goal, strategy is about tough choices and trade-offs (Porter 1996). To address CSR in the context of strategy, firms must prioritise social issues. To do so, we recommend the following approach. First, by studying industry context and asking questions related to stakeholder demands and pressures, several social issues will be identified. These (potentially many) issues can be assessed by placing them within a prioritisation matrix (Figure 1.2). One dimension of this matrix looks at stakeholder salience: the degree to which stakeholders demonstrate power, legitimacy and urgency (Mitchell *et al.* 1997). Stakeholders have power when they hold a firm responsible for a given social issue and can organise and take action if it is not addressed. They have legitimacy if they have a claim on the firm, such as a legal or contractual obligation, a moral right or an at-risk status.

**FIGURE 1.2** Representative prioritisation matrix

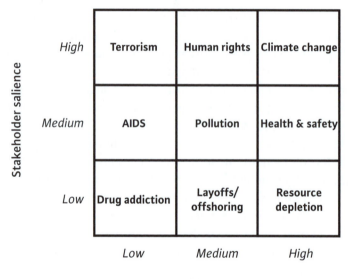

## Oil producer

Stakeholder urgency refers to the degree to which a stakeholder claim requires immediate attention. Because stakeholder demands can often be varied and conflicting, firms can have trouble identifying the range of relevant social issues they must address. Examining stakeholder salience is a good means to develop sensemaking.

The other dimension looks at the degree to which the issue is expected to affect the firm's ability to meet its objectives. That is, in light of stakeholder salience, if a firm does not address a given issue, will its ability to meet corporate objectives be constrained? Studying the impact of social issues on the firm, within industry context and via stakeholder salience, enables issues to be placed into low, medium and high priority (Figure 1.2). The result helps firms to better prioritise those social issues that are strategic, versus those that are non-strategic. Evidence suggests that this type of assessment is critical. For example, Hillman and Keim (2001) found that firms who addressed social issues that were not related to their core strategy were punished financially. Thus, to respond to stakeholder demands for social responsibility and to allocate resources, social issues must be prioritised. After prioritisation, firms can develop their strategic agenda. Specifically, firms need to consider the types of strategic action that need to be taken.

According to one scholar (Galbreath, in press), there are three types of action that firms can take to address CSR strategically: (1) market-based; (2) regulatory or standards-based; and (3) operational-based. Market-based actions include those that are market-driven. Market-based can include actions such as entering a new market or market segment that directly addresses a social issue, introducing new products that are oriented towards social responsibility, or redesigning existing products to offer features or characteristics that address a social issue. For example, McDonald's initially approached the rising concern over obesity (a social issue) mainly by defending its menu as nutritious through PR campaigns—a risk management approach. Now, McDonald's approaches obesity as an opportunity for developing and selling new products, including salads and other types of fresh, healthy food.

Second, governments can require firms to address social issues by enacting laws and regulatory frameworks. In the 1960s, for example, the rights of workers in the US was an unmet social need before it became a social issue, eventually enforced through labour laws (Dobbin and Sutton 1998). On the other hand, in the absence of regulatory mandates, a firm such as Whole Foods Market voluntarily created its own set of standards to meet specifications for certification of organically grown foods—standards that were eventually incorporated by the United States Department of Agriculture (USDA) in 2002 (Greene and Kremen 2003). Therefore, regulatory or standards-based actions include those that bolster reputation, mitigate risk or otherwise give the firm some level of advantage.

Third, according to Porter (1996), operational excellence is necessary for competitive strategy. Operational effectiveness largely refers to the degree to which a firm demonstrates exemplary performance in the way it conducts business. Perhaps the best way to determine operational-based actions is to examine the value chain. Exploring the value chain is a common approach to understanding the activities that firms carry out in day-to-day business. The value chain consists of activities such as finance and accounting, research and development, human resources management, procurement, production, logistics, sales and service. According to Porter and Kramer (2006), virtually all value chain activities can be viewed in light of issues related to social responsibility (Figure 1.3). Thus, operational-based

**FIGURE 1.3  Value chain and issues related to social responsibility**

Source: Porter and Kramer 2006

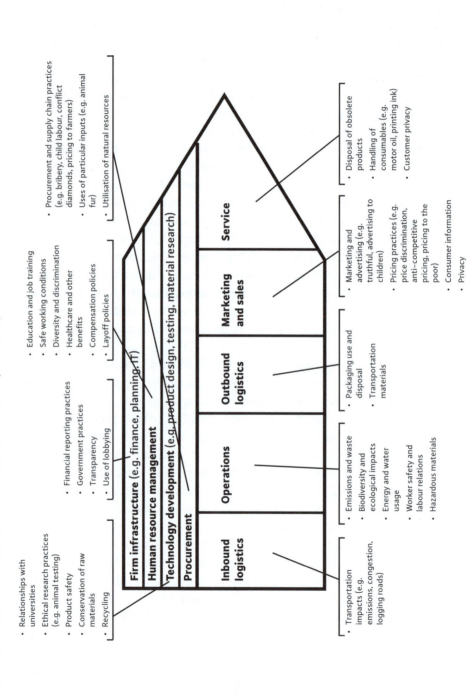

actions include those that enable the firm to capture or internalise the benefits of operational activities specifically related to a given social issue. For example, food retailers, particularly large retailers, consume considerable amounts of energy and produce significant carbon emissions in the construction of new facilities and in ongoing operations (Royal Institute of Chartered Surveyors 2005), which is directly related to a social issue such as climate change. Whole Foods Market, in its new store construction, addresses many environmental issues by reducing the amount of virgin material used and the toxic waste produced (Porter and Kramer 2006). Construction material includes recycled steel, biodegradable linoleum and tiles made from recycled glass bottles.

In sum, three forms of action are proposed to explore CSR strategy options: (1) market-based; (2) regulatory/standards-based; and (3) operational-based. The reality is there is no consensus, either theoretical or empirical, that implies that one type of action is more important than others or results in higher value benefits to the firm—or society. Research simply does not exist at this point to empirically verify how firms should prioritise their actions, nor what an optimal mix of actions looks like. Practically, firms can probably address all three strategic actions in order to proactively address CSR. However, in certain contexts, in certain industries and under certain conditions, one form of action may be more of a priority than others for a firm at any given point in time. The skill of the strategist, therefore, is required to prioritise response.

## Applying the framework: case studies

So far, this chapter has described a framework that can be used to more tightly link CSR with strategy. In this section, we develop three mini case studies to examine how the framework might be applied pragmatically. Three companies are explored: Aveda, Herman Miller and Toyota. These three companies were chosen after reviewing several sources (e.g. 'scorecard CSR lists' such as those produced by the Coalition for Environmentally Responsible Economies and the Dow Jones Sustainability Index; companies listed in the Global Reporting Initiative on sustainability reporting) to identify exemplar and innovative firms—firms that demonstrate social responsibility to their stakeholders. Further, we believe these firms offer a good mix of diversity in terms of industry and products and the social issues they face, making them ideal for comparative purposes. Data were primarily collected through annual reports and supplemental reports (e.g. CSR reports), corporate websites and other published information generated outside the organisations but dealing directly with them, such as scholarly articles and media reports.

What the cases are designed to demonstrate is a representative application of the framework, such as issues prioritisation and how each firm's strategy reveals market-based, regulatory/standards-based and operational-based action. While the cases do not detail the technicalities of implementation, they do provide examples and guidance on how the framework might be applied to link CSR with strategy.

## Aveda Corporation

Aveda Corporation ('Aveda') operates in the personal care products industry. Established in 1978 by world renowned stylist Horst Rechelbacher, Aveda offers a full line of premium professional and consumer, plant-derived personal care products. Today, the company is a network of approximately 7,000 salons, day spas and retail outlets located in America, Canada, Europe, Asia and Australia. The company has also established Concept Schools to prepare students for cosmetology licensing, while its Institutes and Advanced Academies teach seasoned pros new techniques. Approximately 3,000 people are directly employed by Aveda, while another 45,000 are connected to the Aveda spa and salon network.

Aveda was acquired for US$300 million in 1997 by the cosmetics giant Estée Lauder, although it operates as an independent entity. As part of the Estée Lauder family of brands, Aveda has contributed substantially to corporate growth, particularly in hair care products. According to research firm Datamonitor, one in three consumers sought cosmetic products, for example, with natural and organic credentials more frequently over the 2005–2006 period (Datamonitor 2007), suggesting the growing interest in the market for products offered by Aveda.

## Industry context and prioritisation of issues

Aveda conducts business in the personal care products industry, an industry estimated at US$180 billion plus globally. However, even within broad industries, sub-groups exist in the form of strategic groups, which face their own unique set of competitive rules (Porter 1980). In the case of Aveda, the firm operates in the natural and organic personal care market, a US$14 billion niche group of the broader personal care product industry. Within this context, while several issues related to CSR confront the industry, a few are particularly important.

Most personal care products contain petrochemicals which are potentially toxic to humans and the environment during their entire life-cycle. Further, in the continual pursuit for ingredients in the production of personal care products, rare plants are often over-harvested, important ecosystems such as rainforests plundered and indigenous cultures robbed of their botanical knowledge (Marinova and Raven 2006). In the 1980s and 1990s, however, a new generation of consumers who were environmentally and socially conscious began to elevate concerns over personal care product ingredients and sustainable development, placing the problem on the radar screens of manufacturers in the industry.

Beyond ingredients and sustainable production concerns, other key issues have also been the focus of stakeholders in the industry. For example, there has been growing ethical concern over product testing on animals. In order to pass safety standards, personal care product manufacturers test products and ingredients on live animals, including eye, skin and oral toxicity tests. Such tests can lead to skin irritations, sickness or even death. In recent years, many stakeholders—especially well-informed consumers—have rejected purchases because of animal testing. Other issues include packaging, standards and energy use. Packaging, for example, is one of the main components of a personal care product, representing a massive waste footprint for the industry. Recent stakeholder concern has arisen calling on manufacturers to invest in biodegradable and recyclable packaging, as well as offering refillable products. On the other hand, in the absence of government-mandated standards for natural and organically certified personal care products, stakeholders have also expressed concern over the validity and truthfulness of manufacturer claims. Lastly, as with most industries, electrical energy use is a key contributor to greenhouse gas emissions and climate change. The personal care products industry is no exception and stakeholders increasingly appear to be concerned about brands that can demonstrate carbon neutrality and sensitivity to the natural environment in their operations.

## Aveda: strategic action

### Market-based action

In many ways, Aveda's value proposition to sell organic, natural and healthy personal care products addressed a social issue long before it was recognised as a social 'issue'. For example, upon Aveda's founding in 1978, Horst Rechelbacher drew on his knowledge of herbal medicine to create products from pure plant and flower-based ingredients using sustainable practices, such as renewable sourcing, economic development of indigenous communities and no over-harvesting. By introducing the concept of 'aromatherapy', Aveda became one of the first companies to use botanically based beauty products. Thus, Aveda addressed ingredients and sustainable production issues in the personal care products industry long before they were recognised as being potentially problematic to society. Bonini and colleagues (2006) suggest that addressing unmet social needs affords firms opportunities to be first-movers, which can lead to a competitive advantage.

With respect to market-based action, Aveda has helped to build an entire market around natural and organic personal care products. The firm offers one of the largest ranges in the industry including hair care, styling, skin care, body, makeup and perfumes; all products must meet strict, natural/organic ingredient standards. In the process, Aveda has carved out a market which appeals to consumers who are concerned about natural and healthy personal care products. Currently number two in the US professional product market, Aveda has focused on its core competences to increase its product range, improve product performance and gain market dominance, while at the same time addressing social issues such as sustainable agriculture and healthy product ingredients.

## Regulatory/standards-based action

Aveda's founder, Horst Rechelbacher, and current president, Dominique Conseil, are acutely aware of what biodiversity means for their business: if new plant species and indigenous knowledge are lost through habitat destruction and displacement, so too are the potential healing properties they may hold. Rooted in the belief that individuals can make a difference, and have a responsibility to educate others, Aveda has been an industry leader in environmental sustainability for 30 years. Aveda adheres closely to the 10 Ceres principles it adopted in 1989: protection of the biosphere, sustainable use of natural resources, waste minimisation, energy conservation, risk reduction, safe products and services, environmental restoration, informing the public, management commitment, and assessment and reporting.

Committed to sustainable agricultural techniques, Aveda has set industry standards that form the foundation of OASIS (Organic and Sustainable Industry Standards) and the Organic Trade Association, which promotes organic and sustainable production for the beauty industry. The company has achieved these standards by forming close business partnerships with its supply chain—often community-based farmers and indigenous communities. The rose and lavender oil farmers of Bulgaria, for example, were offered long-term contracts and supported financially during the transition from conventional to organic farming practices.

Lastly, Aveda has recently received, from the Environmental Protection and Encouragement Agency (EPEA), cradle-to-cradle (C2C) certification (Braungart and McDonough 2002) for sandalwood, lavender, rose oils and uruku ingredients, which must meet stringent ecological and health criteria. Aveda was also the first beauty company to receive C2C accreditation for any of its products. With over 80% of its botanical ingredients certified organic in 2007, Aveda is well on the way to achieving its aim of having all its products and packaging C2C accredited, demonstrating its proactive stance with respect to industry standards.

## Operational-based action

As a company Aveda focuses on continual improvement and social responsibility, and its operational-based actions are driven by a 'Green Ingredients Policy' and the closely related C2C philosophy. For example, every step of the manufacturing process, from soil to bottle, has been designed and refined to minimise toxic waste and maximise energy efficiency. Concerned about the toxicity of petrochemicals since its inception, Aveda's innovation has made it an industry leader in the replacement of petrochemical surfactants with organic and biodegradable substitutes. In the manufacturing of products, the company has successfully replaced nearly 50% of its petrochemical surfactants with glucose and compounds derived from coconut and babassu oils. In 2007, less than 20% of Aveda beauty products contained petrochemicals. These will be phased out as suitable, high-performing alternatives are identified (Conseil 2008).

Aveda has also revised its manufacturing processes, based at its Minnesota facilities, to minimise the use of inorganic compounds and the production of toxic wastes, for which it received ISO 14000 certification (Aveda 2008a). Herb sterilisation using gamma-irradiation, a technique widely used in the US food industry, has been replaced by neo-autoclave and other greener alternatives. Plastic derivatives used in styling products have been substituted with pine resin, and plant-derived acids including salicylic acid from oil of wintergreen have eliminated the need for many inorganic preservatives including formaldehyde. Energy consumption during every step of the production and manufacturing process is also scrutinised and improved upon. Energy consumption has increased by just 30% despite an 80% increase in production between 1996 and 2006 (Aveda 2006).

Another concern among stakeholders in the personal care products industry is the issue of packaging and recycling. Aveda, like any corporation, lacks control over how much of its packaging, if any, will be recycled once a product has been purchased. To address the situation, Aveda has focused on minimising packaging while using post-consumer recycled materials. Nevertheless, packaging must be appealing to consumers, comply with safety standards and provide product protection during transport, storage and use. Materials containing high post-consumer recycled content are given preference over virgin plastics and forest products. In 2007, over 80% of Aveda packaging was obtained from recycled PET and HDPE bottles and jars, reducing the need for virgin high-density polyethylene by 300 tonnes (Aveda 2008b).

Lastly, as in its manufacturing processes, Aveda attempts to address stakeholder concerns over the environment and sustainable development in its on-the-ground operations, such as buildings. Building materials and fixtures that are non-toxic, rapidly renewable, biodegradable or easily recyclable—such as sustainably harvested and recycled timbers—are used in the construction of new retail outlets. Aveda is currently investigating ways of incorporating agricultural and timber wastes in construction materials as well. In Aveda retail outlets, the need for artificial lighting is reduced by the use of skylights that track the sun and direct natural light into buildings. Energy consumption is offset by investing in wind farms; the company has become the first in the industry with 100% certified wind power. Aveda also assists third-party owners to green their own businesses, and works with the US Green Building Council to develop green standards in the operation of retail buildings (Aveda 2006).

## Herman Miller

Herman Miller is an internationally acclaimed furniture design house for office, healthcare, educational and residential use. Since its purchase from the Michigan Star Furniture Company in 1923 by D.J. DePree, the Herman Miller brand has become synonymous with classic, high-quality designs recognised and housed by Cooper Hewitt, National Design Museum, Smithsonian Institution. The company's award-winning products include seating, furniture systems, storage and material handling solutions, freestanding furniture and case goods, which are complemented by furniture management and strategic consulting services. Primary products are sold through wholly owned subsidiaries in the US, Canada, South America, Europe, Australia and Asia. These products are also sold through independent dealerships, extending Herman Miller's market reach to over 100 countries across the globe.

A relentless pursuit of innovative solutions coupled with a strategy to diversify into new and emerging markets, both in the US and internationally, has enabled Herman Miller to grow despite slowing economic activity in key markets (Herman Miller 2008). Herman Miller is one of the top four suppliers of office furniture in the US, representing an approximate 16% share of a US$9 billion-dollar industry (Lee and Bony 2008). The firm's domestic and international sales, in fiscal 2008, generated just over US$2 billion in revenue.

## Industry context and prioritisation of issues

Herman Miller operates in the office furniture manufacturing industry, a multiple-billion-dollar global market. As with most manufacturing firms, climate change, $CO_2$ emissions, worker safety and the environmental impact of the supply chain are social issues facing Herman Miller. However, with international markets becoming increasingly important to Herman Miller's net income, especially in Europe, furniture design and manufacturing must comply with international guidelines and standards and a broadening range of stakeholder concerns. For example, office furniture typically contains over 50% polyvinyl chloride (PVC) because it is durable, versatile and cost-effective (Lee and Bony 2008). Unfortunately, the high chlorine content in PVC forms the potent carcinogen dioxin as a by-product of its manufacture and incineration. PVC-based products entered into landfill, as opposed to incineration, still pose environmental problems. PVC is not biodegradable, and both PVC and its associated softening agent DEHP release toxins which leach into the soil and waterways. These toxins have been linked with asthma, birth defects, childhood brain cancers, leukaemia and male infertility (Lee and Bony 2008). Public outrage during the 1990s in the US, Europe and Japan has seen governments in both developed and developing countries strictly regulate the use and incineration of PVC, creating institutional pressures from key stakeholders for furniture manufacturers to develop PVC-free alternatives.

Other issues facing the industry and Herman Miller include health-related concerns. For example, health risks associated with the slow release of volatile organic compounds (VOCs), such as formaldehyde, from furniture and soft furnishings, ranks indoor air pollution as one of the top five major environmental public health risks (Herman Miller 2007a). 'Sick building syndrome' is particularly acute in people with respiratory problems such as asthma and allergies and people with depressed immune systems, making it especially problematic in hospitals where VOC emissions may actually hinder patient recovery. Increasingly, public and private institutions are seeking low- or no-VOC furniture and fittings.

Lastly, a social issue facing the industry is sustainable design—from the supply chain through to disposal. As society generates larger volumes of waste, more and more land is dedicated to the disposal of non-biodegradable, and often toxic, waste. Government agencies urge everyone to reduce, re-use or recycle, yet over 30 tonnes of waste is generated for every one tonne of product that reaches the consumer, who throws away 98% of those products within the first six months of purchase (Herman Miller 2003). With respect to furniture manufacturers, a growing social issue is ensuring that product designs are eco-effective and sustainable, so that they can be quickly and easily modified for re-use, rather than creating more disposable product that increases toxic waste and landfill footprints.

## Herman Miller: strategic action

### Market–based action

An important component of the Herman Miller business strategy is to actively pursue a programme of new product research, design and development. The company generously funds its research and development unit to the tune of US$40 million per annum. By focusing R&D on customer needs and problems to enhance working life, Herman Miller has been able to provide innovative solutions that address social issues related to the furniture industry. The ergonomic chair is one such example. The company employed a designer with a deep understanding of how poor furniture design impacted on musculoskeletal health. Launched in 1976, Herman Miller's iconic Ergon chair, with easily adjustable settings to suit individual needs, was one the first of its kind to address health issues in the workplace through furniture design. Now ergonomic design is the norm in office furniture rather than the exception, demonstrating that Herman Miller's status as a first-mover has been beneficial not only to its own success, but to the broader industry.

Herman Miller has also innovatively targeted the market by developing its own Design for Environment (DfE) guidelines, which were used to address sustainable design through the introduction of the Mirra chair, an eco-efficient product. Specifically, eco-effectiveness offers a truly sustainable industrial system that does not deplete natural resources or generate pollution because it mimics the cyclical nature of biological systems. Detailed assessment of all materials used in product manufacturing is essential under the McDonough Braungart Design Chemistry (MBDC) or C2C protocol. Materials are classified as biological or technical nutrients and the two should be kept separate to assist ease of recyclability at the end of the product life-cycle. Biological nutrients such as water and natural fibre can be safely returned to the natural environment, while technical nutrients such as plastic and metal alloys are continuously recycled to produce new products. In addition, chemical selection and product manufacturing processes must have little or no impact on the environment.

By using their DfE guidelines, Herman Miller made environmentally informed decisions about material selection, product disassembly at the end of its life-cycle and material recyclability. Over time an inventory of C2C suitable chemicals and materials has been compiled and used in the design and manufacture of the Mirra chair, the first highly engineered product to receive C2C certification. The DfE guidelines resulted in a less costly, more elegant, PVC-free design that has since been patented (Herman Miller 2003), and has added to Herman Miller's credentials as an innovator when it comes to market-based social responsibility. In fact, the Herman Miller brand is synonymous with quality and socially responsible business practices, so much so that the company was named the 'Most Admired' company in its industry by *Fortune* magazine for the 20th time in 22 years in March 2008.

## Regulatory/standards-based action

Herman Miller's founder D.J. De Pree was an environmental visionary, establishing corporate values in the 1950s that led the company to be 'a good corporate neighbor by being a good steward to the environment' (Rossi *et al.* 2006: 194). These core values form the basis of the company's 'Perfect Vision' programme which was developed by its Environmental Quality Action Team (EQAT). EQAT started as a voluntary team formed in 1989 and later became a formal steering committee to set the company's environmental direction and priorities, and to monitor progress in the early 2000s. In developing the company's Perfect Vision guidelines the EQAT has set a target date of 2020 for: (1) 100% reductions in VOC emissions to air, its use of process water, hazardous waste, waste to landfill; and (2) 100% increases in the use of renewable energy, sales from DfE-approved products, and leased or owned buildings which meet or exceed the US Green Building Council (USGBC)'s Silver certification standard (Herman Miller 2007b).

With the company's Perfect Vision goals in sight and convinced that the strict environmental standards emerging in Europe will become global practice, Herman Miller is determined to develop its own standards to stay ahead of its competitors and provide market-ready products before tighter industry standards emerge. This vision has enabled Herman Miller to obtain GREENGUARD certification for about 50 products. GREENGUARD is an industry-independent, third-party testing programme for low-emitting products and materials. Companies already offering furniture with GREENGUARD certification appear to have a strategic advantage over those that have yet to come on board, given stakeholder concerns over sustainable design. Lastly, Herman Miller's Perfect Vision guidelines have also assisted the company in obtaining ISO 14001 and ISO 9000 certification, demonstrating that the firm takes seriously its approach to regulatory frameworks and other standards in the industry.

## Operational–based action

While Herman Miller is keen to address sustainable design, much of the effort involves how the firm manages its operations, particularly its supply chain operations. For example, the success of the Herman Miller Production System and DfE protocol is critically dependent on developing synergistic relationships with suppliers (Rossi *et al.* 2006). One way in which this is demonstrated is in materials selection. Herman Miller asks its material suppliers to provide the chemical constituents, down to 100 parts per million, for each of the components planned for a product so that the environmental safety of the nutrients can be assessed (Rossi *et al.* 2006). However, some suppliers are understandably reluctant to enter into the process because this means that they must endeavour to address environmental concerns in their *own* operations—and in the raw materials and inputs they supply to Herman Miller. Thus, Herman Miller does give its suppliers the option to decline participation; if one declines, the company finds another supplier that is willing to meet its stringent requirements.

Supply chain matters are not the only operational focus of Herman Miller. As with any manufacturing firm, employee health and safety has long been a social issue of major importance. Herman Miller takes employee health and safety seriously. For example, in its Van Wagoner, Michigan, manufacturing facility, the firm introduced an innovative workplace safety programme that reduced on-the-job injuries by 40%. The programme focuses on alignment/extension body movements and eyes on path/work, among others. This has helped Herman Miller to maintain an incident rate per 100 employees of about 2.5 since 2005, with no fatalities.

Lastly, with respect to something basic to operations—buildings—Herman Miller has long recognised the importance of 'green' buildings. As such, the company was an early pioneer in developing environmentally sound and aesthetically pleasing manufacturing and office spaces. By using green design techniques, such as energy efficiency, grey water usage, natural lighting, use of recycled materials in construction and low-VOC paints and carpets, Herman Miller became a pilot study for the development of the LEED (Leadership in Energy and Environmental Design) Green Building Rating System, now in force throughout the world. Given that buildings consume more than 40% of total annual US energy use and emit more than 100 million tonnes of carbon dioxide, Herman Miller demonstrates commitment not only to a social issue such as sustainable design in its products, but also to a social issue such as climate change through the way it operates buildings and office space to produce those products.

## Toyota Motor Corporation

Toyota Motor Corporation is Japan's largest vehicle manufacturer and one of the largest automotive companies in the world. Established in 1937, the automobile manufacturer grew rapidly during Japan's economic boom, gaining market dominance over its closest rivals Nissan and Honda during the 1980s. Toyota's strategic expansion into offshore markets during the 1980s and 1990s saw it surpass Ford as the world's second largest manufacturer of automobiles in 2004 (Reinhardt *et al.* 2006). A truly global enterprise, Toyota had 53 production sites and manufactured automobiles in 27 countries and regions in March 2008, employing approximately 300,000 people worldwide. A total of 8.9 million vehicles were sold in more than 170 countries and regions under the Toyota, Lexus, Daihatsu and Hino brands at the end of March 2008. Toyota aims to reach 15% world market share over the next decade (Reinhardt *et al.* 2006).

## Industry context and prioritisation of issues

The automobile industry has long been critical to nations around the world as a source of jobs, economic growth and simply moving people and goods around. It is an industry that defines societies, communities and other industries. Indeed, automakers are one of the biggest consumers of steel, aluminium, copper, glass, zinc, leather, plastic, platinum and rubber. As an indication of size, forward estimates predict that private vehicle ownership will increase from just under 500 million vehicles in 1996 to as many as 3 billion vehicles across the globe by 2050 (Saperstein and Nelson 2003), while the global market size for the auto industry is over

US\$1 trillion, making it one of the largest of any industries. In terms of production, for years, the US 'Big Three'—General Motors, Ford and Chrysler—dominated global market share. However, Japanese firms, including Honda and Toyota, have steadily made inroads in the global market, and especially in the US. Given its size and scope, many social issues face the industry.

In an industry employing such massive numbers, health and safety for workers is an issue that has certainly confronted automobile manufacturers for years, and continues to be a major stakeholder concern. Safety of automobiles is a similar concern. Given that motor vehicle accidents are the leading cause of death and injury to 5–45 year olds in the industrialised world, auto-makers are constantly under pressure to build safer vehicles—those that fail here risk being labelled irresponsible. In the wake of intense stakeholder concern over high petrol prices, auto-makers also need to address the fuel efficiency issue. Here, in the US, regulatory pressure forced improvements in the average miles per gallon (mpg) of a vehicle from 13–14 mpg to 28 mpg. However, in recent years, perhaps one of the most pressing social issues with respect to the automobile industry is climate change.

Despite improvements in fuel efficiency, petrol accounts for a third of the world's fossil fuel consumption (Reinhardt *et al.* 2006), and is set to increase as China and India become the economic powerhouses of the 21st century. Predicted increases in private vehicle ownership will increase the level of carbon dioxide ($CO_2$) emitted when fuel is burnt in a traditional combustion engine. In Europe, for example, fossil fuel consumption accounted for 80% of all greenhouse gas (GHG) emissions in 2006/7. Of particular concern, however, if one accepts the science and projections behind climate change, is that a cost of up to 3% of global GDP annually is predicted if no efforts are made to reduce $CO_2$ emissions (Llewellyn 2007). Climate change is also predicted to lead to increased social problems, such as health issues, diseases, infrastructure degradation and high unemployment (Research Australia 2007). Thus, as stakeholders become increasingly savvy about the impact of climate change on their future and that of their children, their expectations for cleaner automobiles clearly have a direct impact on the automotive industry. In an industry that is often seen as one of the leading contributors to global warming, 'sustainable motoring' is perhaps the key issue facing automobile manufacturers.

## Toyota Motor Corporation: strategic action

### Market-based action

For much of its history, Toyota was comfortable selling 'look-alike', reliable cars, but its lack of innovation dissuaded younger drivers, who were more concerned about the aspirational value of their purchase than mature drivers. Recognising growing concerns of younger drivers over social issues such as fuel efficiency and climate change, Toyota saw an opportunity to manufacture the ultimate eco-car. Believing that competitors would produce eco-efficient vehicles once government regulations were in force, Toyota put in place a strategy to be first to market by offering a new, innovative product before it was legitimised by consumer demand, and in the process gambled that its technology would drive future government policy.

As part of the process, Toyota sought to build an eco-car by combining the luxury features of existing vehicles with a technology that accommodated new energy sources, which had low exhaust emissions. Hybrid technology showed the most promise. Hybrids combined existing technology with environmentally conscious technology, offering 100% improvement in fuel economy, while demonstrating adaptability to new energy sources as they became available. Toyota aggressively focused research efforts on releasing its first hybrid car, the Prius, in 1997, in the hope that competitors would not have the infrastructure, technology or product plans to be able to compete effectively in this emerging market (Saperstein and Nelson 2003).

The consensus seems to be that Toyota's gamble is paying off. The firm had sold 1 million hybrid cars by the first quarter of 2008, capturing two-thirds of the global hybrid car market, with 80% market share in the US. However, in the quest to tap into—if not build—a new market segment, Toyota had to endure losses on each Prius produced as variable costs were US$3,000–4,000 more relative to a comparable gasoline-powered car (Reinhardt *et al.* 2006). The company was taking an enormous risk, but was also making a clear statement about a commitment to environmental protection and combating climate change. Toyota aims to sell 1 million hybrid cars per month during the next decade and has committed to expand hybrid technology in all vehicle series by 2020 (Toyota Motor Corporation 2008a). With respect to market-based action, although Toyota is by no means the first to offer an eco-friendly car (zero-emissions electric cars existed long before the Prius), the firm has demonstrated that a commitment to innovation, sustainable motoring and market needs is resulting in first-mover advantages in the hybrid car segment.

## Regulatory/standards–based action

Given the groundswell in stakeholder concern about climate change and dwindling oil reserves, Toyota predicted stringent environmental regulations in the future. For example, the US state of California has consistently initiated aggressive environmental regulations that have been adopted by other states and the federal government. In 1990 the Californian Air Resources Board adopted a Zero Emission Vehicle programme, mandating that 10% of cars would need to have zero exhaust and zero evaporative emissions by 2003 (Saperstein and Nelson 2003). Similarly, at the federal level, the US government was legislating for greater fuel economy, and the EU was aggressively implanting policies to cut GHG emissions by 2020. It was in Toyota's strategic interest to become an industry leader in developing new technologies that would satisfy society's expectations for sustainable motoring, and set industry standards. By relying on its guiding principles, which include a commitment 'to provide clean and safe products' (Reinhardt *et al.* 2006), Toyota is not simply practising 'greenwashing' for public relations benefit; rather, the firm clearly demonstrates care for the environment through the Prius model and technology that is far exceeding industry standards for fuel efficiency and $CO_2$ emission reductions.

Another way that Toyota has addressed standards relates directly to the Japanese market. In 1999, the Japanese government first established fuel economy standards under the 'Top Runner' energy efficiency programme. Fuel economy targets are based on weight class, with automakers allowed to accumulate credits in one weight class for use in another and, if targets are not met, penalties apply. The effectiveness of the standard is enhanced by the fact that highly progressive taxes are levied on the gross vehicle weight and engine displacement of automobiles when purchased and registered, which is designed to promote the purchase of lighter vehicles with smaller engines. In December 2006, the government revised the fuel economy targets upward, from 13.6 km/l (kilometres per litre) in 2004 to 16.8 km/l in 2015, under the new 2015 Fuel Efficiency Standards initiative. Through the Prius model, Toyota was the first automobile manufacturer in the world to not only meet the 2015 Fuel Efficiency Standards, but exceed them (delivering 35.5 km/l compared with the standard of 16.8 km/l). According to Carroll (1979), firms have the option of doing nothing with respect to standards (essentially reject or ignore them) or meet the minimal requirement. However, they can also be proactive and exceed given standards. In the case of Toyota, the firm demonstrates a proactive response to standards, further bolstering its reputation as a firm committed to social responsibility and to sustainable motoring.

## Operational–based actions

For any automobile manufacturer, making cars (i.e. manufacturing) is the most basic and fundamental aspect of its operations. Part and parcel with the groundswell of concern over climate change, manufacturing facilities, like automobiles, have come under increased pressure from stakeholders to become 'cleaner'. Toyota has responded to the challenge and demonstrates action against climate change, not only in the vehicles it sells, but in how it produces those vehicles. Specially, Toyota demonstrates commitment to the climate change issue in its operations through the sustainable plant concept.

In order to incorporate the concept of sustainability into manufacturing operations, Toyota plants in Japan, USA, Europe and Asia are being built or modified to incorporate greener technologies. In the Tsutsumi Plant in Japan, for example, the company has installed an innovative gas engine cogeneration system which translates into a reduction of approximately 140,000 tonnes of $CO_2$ emissions annually (Toyota Motor Corporation 2008b). The plant also has a polysilicon-type photovoltaic power generation system, one of the largest in the world, which is capable of supplying approximately half the electricity needed for the assembly process (Toyota Motor Corporation 2008b). Part of the generated electricity is also stored in batteries and is used for powering the streetlights surrounding the plant. However, Toyota extends sustainable practices beyond just manufacturing plants.

The company's South Campus expansion of its headquarters in Torrance, California, was the largest facility in the US to earn LEED-gold rating in 2003. The building was a pivotal project for the green building movement because it dispelled the myth that LEED-certified buildings were more expensive to operate than conventional buildings. Each building has long narrow wings with north–south orientation so nearly 90% of offices enjoy natural light and views. Rooftop photovoltaic panels combined with highly efficient air handling units and gas-powered chillers contribute to a 31% reduction in energy consumption. Recycled water is used for watering, toilet flushing and cooling, saving 78.4 million litres of potable water per annum. The South Campus enjoys high employee retention rates, greater productivity and less absenteeism (Lockwood 2006), demonstrating that attention to social issues such as climate change and 'sustainability' in operational-based actions can benefit firms beyond the manufacturing floor.

## Conclusions

If an assumption is made that CSR is important to competitiveness, and if strategy serves as a foundation for a business firm's creation, while establishing its position in the market, its competitiveness and its ongoing existence, then placing CSR within the context of strategy seems vital. Thus, as highlighted in this chapter, an attempt at elaborating this relationship surfaces a few important implications.

First, as firms seek to move CSR from a peripheral to a core activity, they need to frame the effort from an issues perspective. This will probably uncover many issues as stakeholders within the industry will have a broad range of expectations regarding a firm's social responsibilities. Second, to address CSR strategically, a firm will have to narrow its focus. The closer a given social issue is to a firm's mission and objectives and the greater its stakeholder salience, the more strategic the issue is likely to be. Lastly, firms have to make choices about how they will address social issues. What we have suggested is that firms focus efforts in three areas, including market-based, regulatory/standards-based and operational-based actions. While

**TABLE 1.1** Summary of case studies

| Company | Key social issues | Strategic actions |
| --- | --- | --- |
| Aveda | • Sustainable agriculture<br>• Use of harmful ingredients<br>• Animal testing<br>• Recycling/ product disposal<br>• Climate change | *Market-based:*<br>• One of the first firms to produce organic and natural personal care products<br>*Regulatory/standards-based:*<br>• Set industry standards that form the foundation of OASIS (Organic and Sustainable Industry Standards) and the Organic Trade Association which promotes organic and sustainable production for the beauty industry<br>• Cradle-to-cradle (C2C) certification for sandalwood, lavender, rose oils and uruku ingredients, which must meet stringent ecological and health criteria<br>• Over 80% of its botanical ingredients certified organic in 2007<br>*Operational-based:*<br>• Every step of the manufacturing process, from soil to bottle, has been designed and refined to minimise toxic waste and maximise energy efficiency<br>• 80% of product packaging is obtained from recycled materials<br>• Develops 'green' retail outlets<br>• First company in their industry with 100% certified wind power |
| Herman Miller | • Sustainable design<br>• Use of PVC in products<br>• Indoor air pollution ('sick building syndrome')<br>• Toxic waste<br>• Health and safety<br>• Climate change | *Market-based:*<br>• Developed first ergonomic chair, the Ergon, which addressed worker health through furniture design<br>• Produces the eco-efficient chair Mirra, which addresses sustainable design<br>*Regulatory/standards-based:*<br>• Has obtained GREENGUARD certification for about 50 products<br>• ISO 14001 and ISO 9000 certification<br>• In-house environmental quality action team develops regulatory/standards strategy<br>*Operational-based:*<br>• Suppliers must meet strict sustainable design requirements for raw material inputs or else jeopardise relationship with Herman Miller<br>• Employee health and safety programmes<br>• Green building design and techniques (pilot company for development of the LEED Green Building Rating System) |
| Toyota | • Sustainable motoring<br>• Climate change<br>• Fuel efficiency<br>• Sustainable production | *Market-based:*<br>• Developed and markets most successful, eco-efficient, hybrid vehicle in the world<br>*Regulatory/standards-based:*<br>• Exceed government requirements for fuel economy and emissions reductions through the Prius model, particularly in Japan (2015 Fuel Efficiency Standards) and the US (Californian Air Resources Board's Zero Emission Vehicle programme)<br>*Operational-based:*<br>• Sustainable plant concept for manufacturing facilities<br>• Torrance, California, headquarters largest facility in the US to earn LEED-gold rating and was pivotal for the green building movement |

the optimal mix of actions is context specific, firms that can address all three are likely to expand options to address CSR strategically.

In conclusion, firms acknowledge the increasing importance of CSR and are concerned about its impact on their ability to compete. However, there does appear to be some confusion over how to address CSR strategically. What this chapter represents is a pragmatic approach to link strategy and CSR. By drawing on the strategy and issues management literature, we have developed a framework that addresses the task of creating strategies for CSR. Three mini cases were developed that highlight how the framework might be applied. The cases reveal which social issues are important in the context of industry and the types of action taken that demonstrate strategic social responsibility (Table 1.1). Our hope is that this chapter offers meaningful guidance to scholars and practitioners on the subject of strategy and CSR, and that the work will stimulate further research and development on innovative ways to address firms' social responsibilities.

# References

Aguilera, R.V., D.E. Rupp, C.A. Williams and J. Ganapathi (2007) 'Putting the S Back in Corporate Social Responsibility: A Multi-level Theory of Social Change in Organizations', *Academy of Management Review* 32.3: 836-63.

Ansoff, H.I. (1980) 'Strategic Issues Management', *Strategic Management Journal 1.2:* 131-48.

Aveda (2006) *Aveda Corporation: Living the Company Mission. Biennial Scorecard from the Coalition for Environmentally Responsible Economies* (Blaine, MN: Aveda Corporation).

—— (2008a) *History of Aveda since 1978* (Blaine, MN: Aveda Corporation, aveda.aveda.com/aboutaveda/history.asp).

—— (2008b) *Responsible Packaging* (Blaine, MN: Aveda Corporation, aveda.aveda.com/aboutaveda/responsible_packaging.asp).

Bain, J.S. (1959) *Industrial Organization* (New York: John Wiley).

Bonini, S.M.J., L.T. Mendonca and J.M. Oppenheim (2006) 'When Social Issues Become Strategic', *McKinsey Quarterly* 2: 20-31.

Braungart, M., and W. McDonough (2002) *Cradle to Cradle: Remaking the Way We Make Things* (New York: North Point Press).

Carroll, A.B. (1979) 'A Three-dimensional Conceptual Model of Corporate Performance', *Academy of Management Review* 4.4: 497-505.

Clarkson, M.B.E. (1995) 'A Stakeholder Framework for Analysing and Evaluating Corporate Social Performance', *Academy of Management Review* 20.1: 92-117.

Conseil, D. (2008) *Aveda Corporation: Key Achievements Since 2000* (Blaine, MN: Aveda Corporation).

Datamonitor (2007) *Natural Personal Care Consumers: Unlocking Future Potential* (London: Datamonitor).

Davis, I. (2005) 'What is the Business of Business?', *McKinsey Quarterly* 3: 105-13.

—— and E. Stephenson (2006) 'Ten Trends to Watch in 2006', *McKinsey Quarterly* 1: 1-5.

Dobbin, F., and R.C. Sutton (1998) 'The Strength of a Weak State: The Rights Movement and the Rise of the Human Resources Management Divisions', *American Journal of Sociology* 104.2: 441-76.

Galbreath, J. (in press) 'Strategy in a World of Sustainability: A Developmental Framework', in M.A. Quaddus and M.A.B. Siddique (eds.), *The Handbook of Corporate Sustainability: Frameworks, Strategies and Tools* (Cheltenham, UK: Edward Elgar Publishers).

Greene, C., and A. Kremen (2003) *US Organic Farming in 2000–2001: Adoption of Certified Systems* (Washington, DC: United States Department of Agriculture).

Herman Miller (2003) *Sustainable Products for a Sustainable Planet* (Zeeland, MI: Herman Miller).

—— (2007a) *Healthier Planet, Healthier People: Hospitals Go Green to 'First Do No Harm'* (Zeeland, MI: Herman Miller).

—— (2007b) *Our Journey towards a Better World: A Report from Herman Miller, Inc.* (Zeeland, MI: Herman Miller).

—— (2008) *Herman Miller, Inc., and Subsidiaries: 2008 Annual Financial Statements* (Zeeland, MI: Herman Miller).

Hillman, A.J., and G.D. Keim (2001) 'Shareholder Value, Stakeholder Management, and Social Issues: What's the Bottom Line?', *Strategic Management Journal* 22.2: 125-39.

Hirschland, M. (2005) *Taking the Temperature of CSR Leaders* (San Francisco: Business for Social Responsibility).

IBM (2008) *The Enterprise of the Future: Global CEO Study* (Armonk, New York: IBM Institute for Business Value).

Lamertz, K., M. Martens and P.P.M.A.R. Heugens (2003) 'Issue Evolution: A Symbolic Interactionist Perspective', *Corporate Reputation Review* 6.1: 82-93.

Lee, D., and L. Bony (2008) *Cradle-to-Cradle Design at Herman Miller: Moving toward Environmental Sustainability* (Case No. 9-607-003; Boston, MA: Harvard Business Publishing).

Llewellyn, J. (2007) *The Business of Climate Change* (New York: Lehman Brothers).

Lockwood, C. (2006) 'Building the Green Way', *Harvard Business Review* 84.6: 129-37.

Mahon, J.F., and S.A. Waddock (1992) 'Strategic Issues Management: An Integration of Issue Life Cycle Perspectives', *Business and Society* 31.1: 19-33.

Marinova, D., and M. Raven (2006) 'Indigenous Knowledge and Intellectual Property', *Journal of Economic Surveys* 20.4: 587-605.

McKinsey & Company (2006) 'Global Survey of Business Executives', *McKinsey Quarterly*, January 2006: 1-10.

Min-Dong, P.L. (2008) 'A Review of the Theories of Corporate Social Responsibility: Its Evolutionary Path and the Road Ahead', *International Journal of Management Reviews* 10.1: 53-73.

Mitchell, R., B. Agle and D. Wood (1997) 'Toward a Theory of Stakeholder Identification and Salience: Defining the Principle of Who and What Really Counts', *Academy of Management Review* 22.4: 853-86.

Porter, M.E. (1980) *Competitive Strategy* (New York: The Free Press).

—— (1981) 'The Contributions of Industrial Organization to Strategic Management', *Academy of Management Review* 6.4: 609-21.

—— (1996) 'What is Strategy?', *Harvard Business Review* 74.6: 61-78.

—— and M.R. Kramer (2006) 'Strategy and Society: The Link between Competitive Advantage and Corporate Social Responsibility', *Harvard Business Review* 84.12: 78-92.

PricewaterhouseCoopers (2007) *10th Annual Global CEO Survey* (New York: PricewaterhouseCoopers).

Reinhardt, F.L., D.A. Yao and M. Egawa (2006) *Toyota Motor Corporation: Launching Prius* (Case No. 9-706-458; Boston, MA: Harvard Business Publishing).

Research Australia (2007) *Healthy Planet, Places and People* (Melbourne: Research Australia Limited).

Rossi, M., S. Charon, G. Wing and J. Ewell (2006) 'Design for the Next Generation: Incorporating Cradle-to-Cradle Design into Herman Miller Products', *Journal of Industrial Ecology* 10.4: 193-210.

Royal Institute of Chartered Surveyors (2005) *Green Value* (Coventry, UK: Royal Institute of Chartered Surveyors).

Saperstein, J., and J. Nelson (2003) *Toyota: Driving the Mainstream Market to Purchase Hybrid Electric Vehicles* (Case No. 904A03; London, Ontario: Richard Ivey School of Business).

Toyota Motor Corporation (2008a) *Toyota Annual Report 2008* (Toyota City, Japan: Toyota Motor Corporation).

—— (2008b) *Sustainability Report 2008* (Toyota City, Japan: Toyota Motor Corporation).

Waddock, S., and C. Bodwell (2004) 'Managing Responsibility: What Can Be Learned from the Quality Movement', *California Management Review* 47.1: 25-38.

Wood, D.J., and R.E. Jones (1995) 'Stakeholder Mismatching: A Theoretical Problem in Empirical Research on Corporate Social Performance', *International Journal of Organizational Analysis* 3.3: 229-67.

Work Foundation (2002) *Managing Best Practice: Corporate Social Responsibility* (London: The Work Foundation).

# 2
# Exploring the regulatory preconditions for business advantage in CSR

**David Williamson, Gary Lynch–Wood**
**and Rilka Dragneva–Lewers**
University of Manchester, UK

This chapter explores and develops the argument that corporate social responsibility (CSR) is a regulation-dependent construct. This means, among other things, that explanations of how firms gain business advantage through CSR should consider the role of regulation. To substantiate this, the chapter first outlines the causal link between regulation and business advantage and why CSR has no meaning when removed from a regulatory context. The implication is that gaining business advantage from socially responsible behaviour can occur only when a firm complies with, or exceeds, regulatory requirements. If this is the case, then the structure and form of regulation can likewise determine when a firm can gain business advantage. An important aspect of this part of the analysis is the distinction made between primary and non-primary CSR behaviour. These, as we show, are distinct but conflated terms in CSR discourse and, as such, have the potential to influence how regulation is perceived and drafted. Following this, the analysis then focuses on the impact of regulation, particularly civil regulation, on CSR. In considering this form of regulation, special attention is given to non-compliance, compliance and beyond-compliance behaviour and how these are related to the response capacity of firms. Indeed, it is argued that regulatory preconditions for business advantage in CSR can be understood and developed only when regulatory forms and the response capacity of firms are considered jointly. This, too, is posited to be the case for states at different stages of economic development, as demonstrated in our analysis of CSR pressure in Central and Eastern European (CEE) states. Overall, the analysis suggests that regulatory strategies for business advantage in CSR are more nuanced and important than previously thought. In particular, it requires that we move beyond the rhetoric of regulation of CSR being good or bad for business to a more informed consideration of how different regulatory forms support CSR and improve business performance across firms and states.

## Regulation and competitive advantage

It is worth restating that firms provide goods, services and employment that under-pin societal well-being. In providing these, however, they create negative impacts, such as pollution, which potentially harm well-being. We therefore use regulation to balance these positive and negative impacts—an essential component of over-all well-being. That said, the problem for policy-makers lies in determining what level and type of regulation is appropriate. Regulating too much to reduce nega-tive impacts may constrain the strategic choices available to firms to maintain or increase levels of economic production. Also, in diverting finances away from other more productive investments, regulation can be seen as a burden on business by requiring ever more management attention, capital and technical resources. These concerns are well acknowledged in both academe and policy (Pethig 1976; Siebert 1977; McGuire 1982; Jorgenson and Wilcoxen 1990; Makower 1993; Wally and Whitehead 1994; Gardiner and Portney 1994; Palmer *et al.* 1995; Hart and Ahuja 1996; Xing and Kolstad 2002; European Commission 2002; Gray and Shadbegian 2003; Shadbegian and Gray 2005; Better Regulation Task Force 2005). However, these views are countered by alternative perspectives: that well-crafted regula-tion can stimulate innovation and performance to increase competitiveness (Por-ter 1991; Westley and Vredenburg 1991; van der Linde 1993; Shrivastava 1995; Klassen and McLaughlin 1996; Russo and Fouts 1997; Albrecht 1998; Sharma and Vredenburg 1998; Berman and Bui 1998; Orlitzky *et al.* 2003; Mackey *et al.* 2005) and that regulation protects business interests through the provision of subsidies, tariffs, price controls and entry barriers (see Stigler 1971; Mitnick 1981; Shaffer 1995).

As well as these views, there are studies suggesting that regulation has both nega-tive and positive impacts. For example, Jaffe *et al.* (1995) say there is no noticeable adverse relationship between environmental protection and international competitiveness, though regulation does impose costs on society. Conversely, Guasch and Hahn (1997) identify regulation as having a negative impact on growth and economic wealth but a positive effect on consumer welfare. More recently, a review of the literature by Defra (2005) showed that regulation was unlikely to improve overall competitiveness but that there was evidence that it stimulated innovation in the longer term and that for some firms it creates possibilities for increased productivity.

Alongside—and perhaps resulting from—the perceived negative and positive impact of regulation on competitiveness, there has been a reported evolution of the relationship between firms and regulation. With respect to the firm–environment relationship, Berry and Rondinelli (1998) describe the 1960/70s as a period when firms responded to environmental crises as they occurred. This then progressed to a compliance orientation in the 1980s and to more proactive environmental strategies in the 1990s, where firms start to seek competitive advantage by anticipating future legislative changes. The aligning of a firm's resources and strategy to external demands to achieve competitive advantage is consistent with much of the strategic management literature (Porter 1980, 1985; Ansoff 1987; Peteraf 1993; Bowman 1997; Jenkins 2005; Johnson *et al.* 2007; Barney and Hesterly 2008) and with arguments and evidence that environmental regulation provides unforeseen opportunities by, among other things, forcing the upgrading of technologies that lead to increased efficiency (Vandermere and Oliff 1990; Porter 1991; Cairncross 1992; Porter and van der Linde 1995a, b; Nehrt 1996).

Associated with why firms might align their resources to external demands is the question of why regulation and societal pressure leads to competitive advantage in some firms and not others. Two distinct, though not exclusive, explanations have been presented to explain the gaining of competitive advantage. According to Grant (1995), the first relates to the type of business a firm should be in (i.e. strategic choice perspective), while the second focuses on how a firm competes within that business (i.e. a resource-based perspective). The strategic choice perspective of Porter (1980, 1985) says the basis of competitive advantage is above-average performance, gained either through a cost leadership or a differentiation strategy. It is assumed that appropriate corporate strategies can be derived from an analysis of the external environment, with managers having freedom of movement in directing the firm and thus identifying successful strategies before delivering success. From this perspective, Porter and van der Linde (1995a, b) argue that strict environmental regulation can provide competitive advantage for firms and nation states. A similar conclusion is stated in the resource-based view of competitive advantage, where firms vary in their ability to attain competitive advantage because their capacity to control resources for implementing successful strategies varies (Foss 1997). Consequently, the focus for understanding competitive advantage shifts to how firms build and/or acquire superior resource endowments. In this context, resources refer to anything that can be thought of as a strength or weakness (Wernerfelt 1984), or as stocks of available factors that are owned or controlled (Amit and Schoemaker 1993), or as a bundle of assets, capabilities, organisational processes, firm attributes, information and knowledge (Barney 1991). They can broadly be categorised as tangible and intangible, and consisting of financial, physical, legal, human, organisational, relational, technological and informational assets, skills and competences.

Developing this further, Peteraf (1993) argues that sustained competitive advantage requires resources meeting four sets of criteria. The first of these is the heterogeneity argument, which states that unless there are differences across resources there cannot be differences in the ability to earn rents. The second criterion is *ex ante* limits to competition. This states that resources have to be acquired at a price below their discounted net present value in order to yield rents, as otherwise future rents will be fully absorbed in the price paid for the resource. The third criterion, *ex post* limits to competition, says that it has to be difficult for competitors to imitate or substitute rent-yielding resources. Fourth, resources should be specific to the firm such that they cannot be traded. Since these resources remain bound to the firm and are available for use over the long run they become a source of sustained competitive advantage. The implications for CSR-based business advantage are as follows: the heterogeneity argument suggests that it may be possible to gain superior rents by being socially responsible because it creates an efficiency difference; *ex ante* limits to competition implies that CSR resources must exceed their discounted net present value rents, otherwise the cost of the investment cannot be repaid; the *ex post* limits to competition argument indicates that if CSR resources are to be linked to sustained competitive advantage then they must be difficult to copy; and that competitive advantage through CSR can be enhanced if it has imperfect mobility properties.

Each criterion can also be enhanced through regulation. For example, when regulation specifies that firms have to comply with minimum animal welfare practices or with environmental labelling requirements, it accentuates compliance capacity differences across firms and the concomitant ability to utilise these differences to be more competitive and earn higher rents. Likewise, when firms have already acquired these capacities they avoid *ex ante* costs. Indeed, it is better that regulation increases the stringency or technical difficulty associated with the task as this enables firms with extant resources and capabilities to increase *ex post* limits to competition rents. Finally, when these resources and capabilities are specific to the firm because they have been built up over a long period of time and are intangible then they cannot be easily copied. This, in turn, protects their longer-term competitive position.

In line with this reasoning, research by Judge and Douglas (1998) shows that, for the environment, tacit (hard-to-imitate) environmental capability can mitigate external threats, and that the more embedded the integration is, the greater and more sustainable the competitive advantage. These arguments and examples are also broadly supportive of Hart's (1995) natural-resource-based argument, which posits that an increasing awareness of the constraints imposed by the natural environment makes it possible to gain and sustain competitive advantage via pollution prevention, product stewardship and sustainable development. Pollution prevention, in this context, is driven by regulatory requirements to minimise emissions and so forth, with the key organisational resource (capability) being continuous improvement that lowers costs; product stewardship minimises life-cycle costs of products and is associated with stakeholder integration so that the firm can pre-empt its competitors; while sustainable development minimises the environmental burden associated with organisational growth. Although this has yet to be fully substantiated, there is empirical support for the argument that a proactive environmental strategy leads to the development of unique, competitively valuable organisational resources (Russo and Fouts 1997; Sharma and Vredenburg 1998; Klassen and Whybark 1999).

A similar argument can be applied to CSR-based advantage in nation states. To demonstrate this, we draw on the concept of dynamic capabilities, where the process of corporate learning and new skills acquisition is as important as the bundles of resources themselves (Teece and Pisano 1994). In this context, Nelson (1991) argues that learning and innovation are associated with the three interrelated criteria: strategy, structure and core capabilities. Core capabilities originate and are shaped by the firm's strategy and structure, strategy provides guidance regarding the capabilities a firm needs to protect, enhance or acquire if it is to be effective in innovation-driven competition, while structure guides and supports the building and sustaining of core capabilities needed to undertake the strategy. The inference is that CSR strategies for competitive advantage will require appropriate organisational structures to guide and support the building of core CSR capabilities. This process, as Dosi and Malerba (1996) observe, will be influenced by the macro-level co-evolution of sector-specific knowledge bases and country-specific institutions. Consequently, strategies for business success are affected by the cognitive frames and capabilities that accumulate over time (i.e. they build on what has already been learnt). Oliver (1997) develops a similar view by attributing common structures and activities among firms to their tendency to conform to prevailing norms, traditions and social influences in their institutional and sector environment. Empirical support for this view is evident in studies that have identified differences in CSR behaviour that arise from differences in national institutional and cultural contexts (Maignan 2001; Maignan and Ralston 2002). It is also interesting to note, as these authors point out, that shared technological bases within sectors and institutional frameworks within countries (e.g. legal, educational, political, financial) prevent the emergence of complete heterogeneity of learning and core capabilities.

From the perspective of CSR, it is thus important to understand the social context within which resource selection decisions are embedded (e.g. firm traditions, network ties, regulatory pressure) and how this context might affect variations in CSR performance. This would include an analysis of the attributes of firm resources (e.g. their rarity, uniqueness or non-substitutability) and how these are developed, managed and diffused. In addition, as Oliver (1997) points out, given normative rationality and institutional barriers to resource change, we should also consider the speed with which new capabilities (such as being socially responsible) are embedded or integrated into the firm's existing knowledge base, and the frequency with which capabilities, once integrated into the firm, are re-evaluated and realigned for competitive advantage. Moreover, given that cognitive frames and capabilities evolve over time (Dosi and Malerba 1996) we need to accommodate the possibility that firms develop a path dependency that both directs and limits how they develop (Teece and Pisano 1994). Thus, the study of CSR-based corporate change for competitive advantage should focus on the firm and the institutional structure within which it is embedded.

The above framework for analysis also needs to include and take cognisance of innovation as a form of competitive advantage (Schumpeter 1934; Freeman 1982; von Hippel 1988; Utterback 1994). Regulation in this context is important because it can incentivise innovation which then stimulates new markets, or help shape how innovation is developed and brought to market (Rothwell and Zegveld 1985). Once an innovation is brought to market it can follow what Nelson and Winter (1983) call a natural trajectory. Firms that might benefit from adopting the new approach must therefore become aware of the trajectory and decide whether to follow it. Likewise, if there is more than one trajectory then the firm must select which one to follow. Factors that affect this include cost advantages, product differentiation possibilities, regulations, ethical considerations and so forth.

In summary, although evidence that regulation improves competitiveness is inconclusive, there is a view that regulation influences and shapes how firms respond to issues. This is because regulation affects the micro and macro institutional environment of the firm and how it then perceives and responds to opportunities and threats. Indeed, Irwin and Vergragt (1989) argue that regulation and innovation are both facets of the same overall process of change, so they must be analysed together. Also, both the strategic choice and resource-based schools of the strategic management literature indicate that some firms will respond to institutionally bounded opportunities and threats by aligning strategies and developing capabilities to gain competitive advantage in the market place. Consequently, we argue that regulation is an essential ingredient to the development of CSR strategies and capabilities which can produce business benefit in the short and long term.

## Regulation and CSR

When considering how regulation supports CSR-based business advantage, it is necessary to distinguish between primary and non-primary CSR behaviour (Lynch-Wood and Williamson 2007; Lynch-Wood *et al.* 2009). Primary CSR behaviour occurs when a firm does not seek a payback on its CSR activity (Manne and Wallich 1972). Examples include anonymous contributions to good causes, fixed percentage contributions from profits, withdrawing from activities deemed unethical even when this may affect financial well-being, and seconding staff to community projects. In contrast, non-primary CSR activities are undertaken as part of a firm's normal commercial operation, and include producing wind turbines as part of a product portfolio, childcare facilities to attract and retain working parents, and so forth. Firms may engage in both types of CSR behaviour simultaneously, and have multiple motives: for example, when they engage in cause-related marketing to attract new customers and at the same time commit to implementing procedures to comply with the Global Compact (Manne and Wallich 1972; Weaver *et al.* 1999; Aguilera *et al.* 2007). Although we are not aware of data that distinguishes these types of CSR activity, we anticipate that most CSR activity is of a non-primary kind, followed by a smaller number of firms that engage in non-primary and primary CSR activities, and a few firms that engage purely in primary CSR behaviour.

Before considering how these different forms of CSR behaviour relate to regulation and competitive advantage, we must first outline the general relationship between regulation and CSR. The fundamental premise that we seek to establish in doing this is that regulation determines CSR activity. By this we mean that CSR cannot exist independently of CSR regulation because a firm always operates within a regulatory space (Hancher and Moran 1989). This space includes state regulation in the form of command-and-control, economic and voluntary instruments (Gunningham and Grabosky 1998; Baldwin and Cave 1999), and civil pressure in the form of a granting of a social licence to operate (Gunningham *et al.* 2004; Vogel 2005). From this perspective, firms always require the sanction of state or society, which firms satisfy by complying with, or going beyond, state and civil society requirements. Such a view is consistent with the following definitions of CSR and corporate philanthropy: 'It refers to the obligations of businessmen to pursue those policies, to make those decisions, or to follow those lines of action which are desirable in terms of the objectives and values of our society' (Bowen 1953: 6, cited in

Carroll 1999); 'Social responsibilities mean that businessmen should oversee the operation of an economic system that fulfills the expectations of the public' (Frederick 1960: 60, cited in Carroll 1999); 'social responsibility in business . . . takes place within a socio-cultural system that outlines through norms and business roles particular ways of responding to particular situations and sets out in some detail the prescribed ways of conducting business affairs' (Johnson 1971: 51, cited in Carroll 1999); and in Porter's (2003) claim that CSR is obeying the letter and spirit of the law, mitigating harm caused, using resources to support sustainable development, and donating money and corporate resources to social causes.

Examples of how firms respond to this form of regulatory—CSR—pressure can be demonstrated by looking at how firms innovate to produce a market-conditioned response. Consider Barclays Bank (Barclays Bank 2009). Concern over poor banking facilities and access to affordable credit in less prosperous neighbourhoods and in developing nations has led Barclays to introduce an entry-level basic bank account. Following its pilot in the UK it intends to extend the service to countries such as Ghana, India, South Africa and Uganda. The new bank account facilitates regular payment and encourages responsible financial behaviour by not allowing customers to go overdrawn. It also supports well-being by providing credit. By doing this Barclays has responded to regulatory pressure (the bank consulted with government, industry and consumer groups) by providing an innovative bank account (market response) that supports the banks global competitive aspirations (it increases its potential source of customers). A further example is provided by the construction supply company, Wolseley (Article 13 2007). As a global distributor of heating, plumbing, construction and insulation materials, the company was aware of the potential impact that concern for more sustainable patterns of living could have on its business. Specifically, it was aware that impending mandatory sustainability targets in the UK would significantly affect the construction sector. Seeing this as a business opportunity the company decided to build a Sustainable Building Centre to showcase how buildings could operate in harmony with the environment. The target audience was the construction supply chain as this contained the key players in the market. By inviting supply chain representatives to the Sustainable Building Centre, and by promoting it more generally, Wolseley was able to both promote its own products to existing customers and generate new demand more generally.

The general relationship between regulation and CSR is demonstrated in Figure 2.1. This shows that there is an increase in CSR activity as the amount of regulation increases. For the purposes of this model we define CSR regulation as the body of regulation (which includes formal and civil regulation) that specifies minimum CSR requirements in areas such as health and safety, product and environmental performance, corporate disclosure, collective bargaining rights, and corporate corruption and bribery. In a similar fashion, we can broadly define CSR activity to include, as outlined above, non-primary, primary and combinations of non-primary and primary behaviours.

**FIGURE 2.1** Regulation and CSR relationship

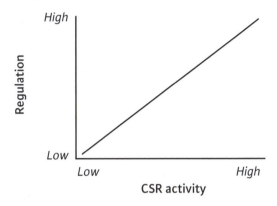

The justification for this relationship is best explained by considering the following four regulation–CSR combinations:

- **Regulation (low)–CSR activity (low).** A lack of CSR regulation means there is no mechanism for stimulating or requiring CSR activity among firms. Firms that engage in CSR therefore do so despite their institutional and cultural context, and as a result are true pioneers (in the UK, examples of early corporate paternalists include William Lever, George Cadbury and Robert Owen). This situation is evident, as we demonstrate later, in CEE states such as Hungary and Bulgaria

- **Regulation (high)–CSR activity (high).** In this position there is a well-developed and embedded framework of CSR regulations and CSR activity. This situation is most evident in countries such as Sweden and Denmark and for highly visible firms

- **Regulation (low)–CSR activity (high).** Unlikely to exist in market economies as there is no institutional context to support such widespread CSR behaviour

- **Regulation (high)–CSR activity (low).** Unlikely to exist in market economies as a firm's mandate to operate is at odds with customer and stakeholder expectations

The question of how firms gain competitive advantage from CSR is therefore most relevant to those firms and nations that operate towards the top right-hand corner of Figure 2.1. This is demonstrated in the following analysis of civil regulation.

# Forms of regulation and CSR–based competitive advantage

In considering how regulation supports CSR-based competitive advantage, it is first necessary to distinguish between soft and hard law instruments (e.g. command-and-control regulation, economic instruments and self-regulation) and the context for their application. This is because a particular regulatory regime may be effective in one circumstance but not another (Sinclair 1997). From our standpoint, this means that what is appropriate in the bottom left-hand corner of Figure 2.1 may not be appropriate for the top right-hand corner, and vice versa. For example, a governance approach to regulation, which seeks reflexivity through self-learning (Orts 1995), is only feasible in the top right-hand corner of Figure 2.1. In this location it is thus possible to build on traditional command-and-control regulations, in the realisation that these are too restrictive to achieve deep-seated change, by adopting a more pluralistic approach that facilitates alternative systems of rule. This frequently involves the use of civil or social licence regulatory pressure, which mainly draws on markets and norms and assumes a quasi-contractual relationship in that the offerings of the firm have to be implicitly accepted by society or groups in society (Lynch-Wood and Williamson 2007). The role of law in this context is 'to catalyze the processes of self-regulation by which other individuals, organisations, and social systems coordinate themselves with the rest of the world' (Parker 2008: 358). Firms can therefore be regulated by diverse actors, including shareholders, public authorities, inter-governmental bodies, trade unions, NGOs and consumer groups.

In their analysis of the social licence as a form of regulatory pressure, Lynch-Wood and Williamson (2007) noted that primary and non-primary behaviour was pivotal to the driver, impact and response aspects of regulatory pressure. The driver characteristic relates to those factors that form the framework which determines the extent to which a firm needs to retain the approval of external—and non-regulatory—stakeholders; the impact characteristic concerns the consequences for a firm's reputation capital if it behaves in a way that is potentially harmful; while the response characteristic focuses on the firm's strategic reaction to its interpretation of the first two characteristics that leads to behaviour with respect to CSR.

These characteristics influence business advantage and competitive advantage more generally as follows. The driver characteristic posits that a firm will continue to trade in a particular way unless its behaviour contravenes regulation or disregards the expectations of its stakeholders—a firm that disregards stakeholder expectations may therefore be in breach of its social licence. In practice the CSR expectations of stakeholders will be at their most influential when they are channelled through a firm's customers (Spar and La Mure 2003) as their expectations create a market pressure that has been called a market for virtue (Vogel 2005). As previously indicated, the market for virtue has two overlapping markets. The first, the market for **non-primary virtuous products**, relates to the demand for products such as recycled or energy-efficient goods and has grown significantly. In contrast, the market for **primary virtuous CSR behaviour** requires firms to act responsibly regardless of economic opportunity. Unlike the market for non-primary virtuous products, this market is not uniformly powerful and is less likely to influence small firms and non-sensitive sectors. In these sectors, consumers will place a greater emphasis on issues such as price, quality and availability than they do on CSR, thereby reducing the potential for business advantage by engaging in primary virtuous behaviour.

The impact characteristic is the value or damage to the firm's reputation capital that can derive from meeting or not meeting stakeholder expectations (Gunningham *et al.* 2004; Graafland and Smid 2004). Evidence that positive reputations produce financial and strategic benefits and that socially responsible practices improve a firm's market valuation, and conversely that negative reputations damage firms, is evident in a number of studies (Podolny 1993; McIntosh *et al.* 1998; Brammer and Pavelin 2006). Research also indicates that the reputation mechanism is enhanced in markets where there is a greater need for trust and where firms are larger and more visible (Milgrom and Roberts 1992)—features we would expect to find in the top right-hand side of Figure 2.1. The response characteristic, the firm's strategic reaction to its interpretation of the driver and impact characteristics, can include non-compliance, compliance or beyond compliance behaviour. By responding positively firms can legitimise their activities and in doing so help secure their long-term survival (Maurer 1971; Suchman 1995). Evidence suggests that firms are most likely to justify their actions when they are highly visible and operate in sensitive areas (Deegan *et al.* 2002; Guében and Skerratt 2007).

## Regulatory capacity of firms and nation states

The ability of firms to respond to different regulatory instruments and to gain competitive advantage is strongly influenced by factors that change as firm size, sector and nation state vary. This is because firm size, sector and nation state act as a proxy for resource availability within firms and for how they are perceived by, and how they react to, external factors (Williamson *et al.* 2008). As a consequence the ability of firms to move from non-compliance to leading-edge compliance-plus behaviour and to secure competitive advantage from such behaviour parallels the ability and willingness of firms to respond to substantive and reflexive policy tools.

A brief examination of how this operates at the firm and nation state level is provided below.

## Firms

The internal and external drivers of CSR behaviour in firms vary in their intensity and impact as firm size increases or decreases. For example, compliance with legislation is frequently cited as the main driver of behaviour in SMEs (Baylis *et al.* 1998; Chittenden *et al.* 2005; Worthington and Patton 2005). Though legislative compliance is essential for large firms—for the obvious reason that non-compliance can impact on their legitimacy—it is not, of itself, the primary driver of CSR and environmental compliance or beyond compliance behaviour (Arora and Cason 1996; Gunningham *et al.* 2004). Firms are also affected by the actions of stakeholders such as NGOs, neighbours, local communities, employees, customers and investors (Freeman 1984). Although these groups can affect firms' behaviour, their influence has been shown to vary across firms. Research indicates that external stakeholders have little interest in, and insufficient power to influence, the environmental practices of SMEs (Rowe and Enticott 1998). The consequence of this is a lessening of the environment as a priority for smaller firms (Revell and Blackburn 2004) and a view that they have little to gain from developing their environmental reputations (Graafland and Smid 2004). In contrast, because larger firms tend to be more visible and have more prominent brand identities to protect, their stakeholders are proportionally more active and powerful (Lynch-Wood and Williamson 2007). This is supported by Weber and Wasieleski (2003), who show that pressure from corporate stakeholders is strongly correlated with firm size. We therefore conclude that, since a firm's visibility increases with its size, it is more likely that large firms will be more vulnerable to attention from interested parties and augmented institutional pressures (Oliver 1991) than smaller firms.

Likewise, the perceived economic opportunity from being proactive in CSR increases as firms become larger in size. This is because many small-firm owner-managers believe their firms have a negligible environmental and CSR impact (Williamson *et al.* 2006) and that, for the environment, economic opportunities appear limited and tend to revolve around making cost reductions and small efficiency gains (Baylis *et al.* 1998). With limited spare resources and a failure to see potential commercial benefits (Hutchinson and Chaston 1994; Gerstenfeld and Roberts 2000; Hitchens *et al.* 2004) there is also a reduced likelihood that smaller firms will capitalise on green opportunities if this involves significant capital outlay (Tenon Forum 2008) or participate in improvement programmes (Petts *et al.* 1999; Hitchens *et al.* 2005). The ability of larger firms to reduce costs and to see strategic opportunities, however, is different because of their greater willingness and capacity to invest in innovative technology to achieve cost reductions and to exploit emerging markets (Russo and Fouts 1997; Judge and Douglas 1998). Ethical pressures arising from social legitimacy expectations (DiMaggio and Powell 1991; Wood 1991) are also greater for large firms because they are more visible to those pressures that induce ethical behaviour. This, together with their greater capacity to exploit green market opportunities, makes it strategically more rational for them to adopt beyond-compliance measures. Also, as previously indicated, the resource endowments of firms influence how they respond to opportunities and threats (Barney 1991; Peteraf 1993). Indeed, in a resource-based analysis of environmental performance, Russo and Fouts (1997) demonstrate that firms that tend towards compliance will differ in their resources than those that tend towards prevention. Likewise, Nooteboom's (1994) study of innovation shows that differences in firm resources result in small firms having comparative advantage in the earlier stages of inventive work because it is less expensive, and large firms having the advantage in the later stages because they have the resources to scale up innovative products and processes.

## Nation states

The view that firms and society can benefit from CSR is so strong it can be said to drive policy and corporate practice in many countries (Frynas 2005). Evidence that this 'business case' argument is seen in this way and that it now acts as the main mechanism for delivering new forms of business practice is provided in EU policy on CSR (European Commission 2001; MacLeod 2005; De Schutter 2008). This supports and promotes organisational self-governance and self-regulation in social and environmental matters on the implicit assumption that the business case acts as a form of civil regulation that has the power to steer and control corporate behaviour (Lynch-Wood *et al.* 2009). To understand the appropriateness of this policy, we examine the role of institutions in explaining social and firm behaviour (DiMaggio and Powell 1991; Scott 2001) by outlining the systemic-level determinants and institutional requirements that influence the effectiveness of the business case.

The majority of institutionalist research on CSR focuses on the institutional preconditions for firms to act in a socially responsible manner and seeks to explain the variations in cross-state CSR activities (Aguilera and Jackson 2003; Brammer and Pavelin 2005; Campbell 2007; Matten and Moon 2008). Maignan and Ferrell (2003) have shown that consumer attitudes to CSR vary across states. Aguilera *et al.* (2007) develop this by offering a model of the motives of various actors for exerting pressure for social responsibility initiatives. To develop this further, we draw on frameworks inspired by new institutionalism (Tempel and Walgenbach 2007) cross-fertilised by research on national business systems (Matten and Moon 2008), comparative corporate governance (Aguilera and Jackson 2003) and comparative political economy (Campbell 2007). By adopting such a broad sociological definition of institutions we attempt to capture the 'culture-cognitive, normative, and regulative elements that, together with associated activities and resources, provide stability and meaning to social life' (Scott 2001: 48). These spheres, we posit, overlap in producing particular institutional features that determine the strength of civil regulation in nation states. In particular, we argue that nine institutional features influence the power of civil regulation in states, which in turn influence the ability of firms within those states to secure business benefit and competitive advantage from CSR.

The first institutional feature is freedom of association and other legal preconditions. Generally, the civil regulation mechanism relies on the activities of non-state actors, or organisational intermediaries, to formulate public and/or consumer interest and mobilise societal pressure. What matters is the ease with which such intermediaries can be set up. This feature relies particularly on a set of political and constitutional institutions, underpinning the freedom of association and being conducive to the emergence of a developed NGO and other types of civil organisation sector. In addition to the right to entry, civil society organisations need to be free from barriers to their operational activity, to speech and advocacy, and from legal barriers in their ability to raise financial resources (World Movement for Democracy 2008). A second institutional feature is independence. The value of an independent civil society sector is widely recognised as important in the literature and is secured by political and legal institutions guaranteeing freedom from political (state) interference. The third institutional feature, financial resources, underpins the ability of non-state actors to engage in effective action. Threatening a firm with harm through direct public action or consumer mobilisation has important costs, which are particularly high in the context of global business (Spar and La Mure 2003). In this sense, this feature relies on important economic institutions affecting the availability of financial resources and the mechanisms for raising them.

Fourth, mechanisms for the distribution of information are a critical precondition for the activism of organisational intermediaries and consumers. In the environmental field, for example, this entails contemporary information on pollution levels and other forms of harmful impact, as well as historical information on potential polluters. In this sense effective regulatory provisions for monitoring and prevention of pollution are of great importance. Fifth, societal values and expectations regarding the ethical behaviour of companies create the ideational context in which societal actors and consumers are placed. The sixth institutional feature relates to needs (income), in that in line with Maslow's hierarchy of needs, income levels and general state of poverty affect individual choices. The seventh institutional feature, uncertainty, has been widely identified as an important factor affecting systemic processes and individual choices. At the level of consumer behaviour, for example, uncertainty may drive more short-term decisions regarding basic needs. Similarly, historical contingencies or disasters may distract the attention from more principled, longer-term ethical concerns. Eighth, continuity provides an historical opportunity to accumulate experience, information, tradition and skill. For example, it applies also to the level of development of various market intermediaries, such as consumer and shareholder associations. The ninth and final institutional feature is openness. Openness has a positive impact on civil regulation by allowing cross-fertilisation of NGO and business best practices.

When we look at civil society development in CEE states we see that rights of association are guaranteed by post-1989 constitutions and that civil society organisations are generally free from administrative and other forms of interference (USAID 2007; Freedom House 2008a). However, despite the generally free legal context, a key problem for civil society engagement is financial insecurity. This is related to the decline in concern for CSR following the fall of communism. There is a range of reasons for this: economic difficulties, public fatigue accompanying the transition process, and prevalence of a neo-liberal ideology (Pavlínek and Pickles 2004; Hicks 2004). As a result of this, civil society organisations largely rely on external or government funding, which undermines their independence (Freedom House 2008b). The mechanisms for distributing CSR information also limit the effectiveness of civil society pressure. For example, the EU Directive 96/61 on Integrated Pollution Prevention and Control, which sets out common rules for permitting and monitoring risks, requires significant administrative oversight (Carmin and Vandeveer 2004). However, as many of the pre-accession progress reports of the European Commission indicate, this has proved to be difficult in most countries because of a lack of administrative capacity. The use of official databases to monitor and disclose environmental impacts has also proved difficult (even though the European Commission's Decision 2000/479 requires member states to compile data on emissions and discharges).

In addition to this information deficiency, the active 'grey' sector in CEE countries obscures corporate practices more generally. Moreover, the structural legacy of their planned economies makes Western-style consumer activism a relatively new phenomenon. The process of Europeanisation is therefore seen as being important in fostering CSR consciousness: 'at the moment consumers lack clear information on the social and environmental performance of goods and services, including information on the supply chain' (European Commission 2006: 7). This lack of information is compounded by communism's effect on consumer values, which fostered a reliance on the state. In terms of the perceptions of their own power, only 38% of Polish consumers believed that pressure for CSR behaviour could come from them; most pointed to the importance of local authorities and central government. Surveys also show that consumers tend to choose products and services on the basis of traditional commercial factors (price, sales advice) rather than by virtue of their ethical image (IFHR 2006; Mazurkiewicz and Crown 2006). As a consequence, while firms are conscious of their reputation, they tend to engage in ethical behaviour less as a response to consumer pressure and more out of the owner's personal values and interests. A study on Bulgaria, for example, shows that smaller firms tend to engage in sporadic acts of seasonal charity or reflect paternalistic care about the extended family around the firm (Alpha Research 2006).

Collectively, the evidence suggests that institutional factors in CEE countries weaken the power of civil regulation and the associated business case argument for CSR. In general, the strength of state institutions, the level of progress in the process of Europeanisation, the extent of market development (and its reflection in income levels), and the degree of development of civil society, combine to weaken business case pressures compared with more established EU states.

## Discussion

The proposition that CSR is a regulation-dependent construct has been developed using strategic management, regulatory and institutional literatures. By drawing on the strategic management literature it was possible to show that successful firms regularly monitor their socioeconomic environment (Johnson *et al.* 2007). In doing this it is also apparent that CSR awareness is affected by managers' cognitive frames of reference. However, research indicates that managers are implicitly aware of this and therefore try to focus on issues they deem important (Quinn 1978; Hough and White 2004). Equivalent processes, we argue, operate in the CSR sphere. Firms whose products or processes are perceived as potentially harmful will therefore monitor change more rigorously than firms whose products and processes are perceived as benign. As Jenkins (2004) points out, consumers purchase on the basis of the benefits and costs they incur. Consequently, firms that supply to CSR-sensitive customers are more likely to provide more CSR-sensitive products and services (Lynch-Wood *et al.* 2009). The strategic management literature also suggests that successful firms will try to maintain a fit between their resources and their industry's macroeconomic, sociological, technological and ecological environments in order to satisfy the needs of their stakeholders (Johnson *et al.* 2007). A strategically aware firm therefore regularly monitors its commercial environments as part of its business planning process. As such, an integral part of its strategy-making processes is being aware of and seeking to influence its industry's response to pressures from those who perceive the firm as a community member.

The regulation literature parallels these findings to the extent that different forms of regulation produce different types of organisational response. This was demonstrated by considering the determinants of civil regulation and how this form of regulatory pressure affects firms of different size in different sectors and nation states. An important feature of this analysis was consideration of the rational choice perspective, which focuses on the interests or identities that motivate stakeholder groups (Rowley and Moldoveanu 2003). This showed that civil regulation (i.e. social licence) pressure was most effective in influencing CSR behaviour in large and highly visible firms. Building on this we then looked at systemic-level determinants and institutional requirements (Hancher and Moran 1989; DiMaggio and Powell 1991; Scott 2001) that influence the effectiveness of civil regulation in CEE countries. This approach is consistent with the increasing efforts to examine the role of institutions in explaining social and organisational behaviour.

The evidence is used to support our central thesis that CSR activity increases as the amount of CSR-related regulation increases. In light of this, it is argued that the scope for CSR-based business benefit and competitive advantage increases as CSR regulation increases, as shown above in Figure 2.1, and as elaborated in Figure 2.2.

**FIGURE 2.2** Regulatory form and scope for CSR business advantage

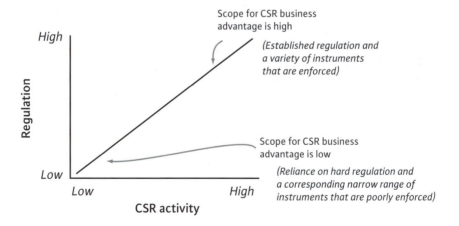

Regulation, from this perspective, provides the necessary conditions from which business and competitive advantage can be gained. It does this by increasing the scope for the development and accumulation of strategic competences in line with resource-based theory (e.g. Toyota's expertise in hybrid car technology; Brand Neutral 2007). Likewise, it enables firms to make strategic product/service offerings to differentiate themselves in the market and, in doing so, protect and enhance their reputations (e.g. Xerox's commitment to 'product design for energy efficiency and innovative remanufacturing and recycling practices' to cut greenhouse gas emissions from its worldwide operations by 10% from the baseline year 2002 to the end of 2012; Xerox Corporation 2005). Yet it also means that firms will find it very difficult to gain a business benefit or secure competitive advantage when the regulatory frameworks, and the underpinning institutional conditions, are absent (e.g. the commercial disaster of the Sinclair C5 battery electric car; Cartype 2009). This suggests that the extensive research and debate concerning whether regulation, and CSR regulation in particular, provides opportunities for business success or damages competitiveness is misplaced in the sense that CSR regulation has to be in place for CSR to exist. What is important is whether the institutional and market conditions for firms to gain business advantage and competitive advantage are in place, which itself is dependent on regulation being in place.

The view that innovative CSR for business advantage is a manifestation of regulatory compliance through the medium of the market is likely to be controversial. However, in addition to the evidence presented here, the argument is consistent with the work of social theorists such as Habermas (1984, 1987). Although a detailed justification for this argument is not possible (given the necessary restrictions imposed on a book such as this) the central point is that economic systems have to be anchored into the moral and normative fabric of society. This is achieved through communication in the sense that this enables mutual understanding, which is necessary for a shared interpretation of the world (i.e. without a shared understanding you cannot have society). Regulation, as defined in this chapter, facilitates this by communicating societal expectations to firms. Some firms will be proactive in responding to this expectation by innovating, with society rewarding such behaviour through the provision of enhanced legitimacy. The innovation also has to be commercially viable in that it must support profitability. In market economies innovative CSR is therefore necessary and risky since it requires that firms satisfy both requirements—although the benefits are potentially great for successful firms. Likewise, if firms exceed CSR expectations so that the activity incurs costs that society is not prepared to pay for, then their actions are likely to go unrewarded.

# References

Aguilera, R., and T. Jackson (2003) 'The Cross-national Diversity of Corporate Governance: Dimensions and Determinants', *Academy of Management Review* 28.3: 447-65.

——, V. Ruth, D. Rupp, C. Williams and J. Ganapathi (2007) 'Putting the S Back in Corporate Social Responsibility: A Multilevel Theory of Social Change in Organizations', *Academy of Management Review* 32.3: 836-63.

Albrecht, J. (1998) *Environmental Regulation, Comparative Advantage and the Porter Hypothesis* (Ghent, Belgium: Faculty of Economics and Applied Economics, University of Ghent).

Alpha Research (2006) 'Corporate Social Responsibility within the Bulgarian Context', www.unglobalcompact.bg/publication/files/en/CSR%20ENG.pdf, accessed 2 December 2009.

Amit, R., and P. Schoemaker (1993) 'Strategic Assets and Organisational Rent', *Strategic Management Journal* 14.1: 33-46.

Ansoff, H. (1987) *Corporate Strategy* (London: Penguin).

Arora, S., and T. Cason (1996) 'Why do Firms Volunteer to Exceed Environmental Regulations? Understanding Participation in EPA's 3/50 Program', *Land Economics* 72.4: 413-32.

Article 13 (2007) 'Wolseley: The Development of an Innovative New Centre for the Building and Construction Sector to Showcase Technology and Products that are Designed to Address Sustainability Concerns' www.article13.com/A13_ContentList.asp?strAction= GetPublication&PNID=1369, accessed 3 December 2009.

Baldwin, R., and M. Cave (1999) *Understanding Regulation: Theory, Strategy and Practice* (Oxford, UK: Oxford University Press).

Barclays Bank (2009) 'Reducing the Number of Unbanked and Providing Access to Affordable Credit through its Growing Financial Inclusion Programme', www.article13.com/ CBI/CSR_case_study_Barclays_January_2009.pdf, accessed 2 December 2009.

Barney, B. (1991) 'Firm Resources and Sustained Competitive Advantage', *Journal of Management* 17.1: 99-120.

Barney, J., and W. Hesterly (2008) *Strategic Management and Competitive Advantage: Concepts and Cases* (Upper Saddle River, NJ: Pearson Education).

Baylis, R., L. Connell and A. Flynn (1998) 'Company Size, Environmental Regulation and Ecological Modernization: Further Analysis at the Level of the Firm', *Business Strategy and the Environment* 7.5: 285-96.

Berman, E., and L. Bui (1998) *Environmental Regulation and Productivity: Evidence from Oil Refineries* (WP 6776; Cambridge, MA: National Bureau of Economic Research).

Berry, M., and D. Rondinelli (1998) 'Proactive Corporate Environmental Management: A New Industrial Revolution', *Academy of Management Executive* 12.2: 38-50.

Better Regulation Task Force (2005) 'Regulation—Less is More: Reducing Burdens, Improving Outcomes, A BRTF Report to the Prime Minister', www.berr.gov.uk/files/file22967. pdf, accessed 2 December 2009.

Bowen, H. (1953) *Social Responsibilities of the Businessman* (New York: Harper & Row).

Bowman, C. (1997) 'Interpreting Competitive Strategy', in C. Bowman and D. Faulkner (eds.), *Competitive and Corporate Strategy* (London: Irwin).

Brammer, S., and S. Pavelin (2005) 'Corporate Community Contributions in the UK and the US', *Journal of Business Ethics* 56.1: 15-26.

—— and S. Pavelin (2006) 'Corporate Reputation and Social Performance: The Importance of Fit', *Journal of Management Studies* 43.3: 435-55.

Brand Neutral (2007) 'The Prius Effect: Learning from Toyota: Engaging Consumers, Driving Profit, and Avoiding Risk through Environmental Strategy', www.brandneutral.com/ documents/Prius_Effect.pdf, accessed 3 December 2009.

Cairncross, F. (1992) *Costing the Earth* (Boston, MA: Harvard Business School Press).

Campbell, J. (2007) 'Why Would Corporations Behave in Socially Responsible Ways?', *Academy of Management Review* 32.3: 946-67.

Carmin, J., and S. Vandeveer (2004) 'Enlarging EU Environments: Central and Eastern Europe from Transition to Accession', *Environmental Politics* 13.1: 3-24.

Carroll, A. (1999) 'Corporate Social Responsibility: Evolution of a Definitional Construct', *Business & Society* 38.3: 268-95.

Cartype (2009) 'Sinclair C5: 1985', www.cartype.com/pages/3521/www.c5alive.co.uk, accessed 3 December 2009.

Chittenden, F., S. Kauser and P. Pourziouris (2005) 'PAYE-NIC Compliance Costs: Empirical Evidence from the UK SME Economy', *International Small Business Journal* 23.6: 635-56.

Deegan, R., M. Rankin and J. Tobin (2002) 'An Examination of the Corporate Social and Environmental Disclosures of BHP from 1983–1997: A Test of Legitimacy Theory', *Accounting, Auditing and Accountability Journal* 15.3: 312-43.

Defra (UK Department for Environment, Food and Rural Affairs) (2005) 'Exploring the Relationship between Environmental Regulation and Competitiveness: A Literature Review', report for Department for Environment, Food and Rural Affairs, SQW Ltd; www.sqw.co.uk/file_download/7, accessed 3 December 2009.

De Schutter, O. (2008) 'Corporate Social Responsibility European Style', *European Law Journal* 14.2: 203-36.

DiMaggio, P., and W. Powell (eds.) (1991) *The New Institutionalism in Organizational Analysis* (Chicago: University of Chicago Press).

Dosi, G., and F. Malerba (eds.) (1996) *Organization and Strategy in the Evolution of the Enterprise* (London: Macmillan).

European Commission (2001) *Green Paper: Promoting a European Framework for CSR* (COM[2001]366 final; Brussels: European Commission).

—— (2002) *Simplifying and Improving the Regulatory Environment: Action Plan* (COM[2002]278; Brussels: European Commission).

—— (2006) *Implementing the Partnership for Growth and Jobs: Making Europe a Pole of Excellence on CSR* (COM[2006]136 final; Brussels: European Commission).

Foss, N. (ed.) (1997) *Resources, Firms, and Strategies. A Reader in the Resource-Based Perspective* (Oxford, UK: Oxford University Press).

Frederick, W. (1960) 'The Growing Concern over Business Responsibility', *California Management Review* 2: 54-61.

Freedom House (2008a) 'Nations in Transit 2008', www.freedomhouse.hu/index.php?option=com_content&task=view&id=196, accessed 24 March 2010.

—— (2008b) 'Nations in Transit, Hungary', www.freedomhouse.hu/images/fdh_galleries/NIT2008/NT-Hungary-final.pdf, accessed 3 December 2009.

Freeman, C. (1982) *The Economics of Industrial Innovation* (London: Francis Pinter).

Freeman, R. (1984) *Strategic Management: A Stakeholder Approach* (Boston, MA: Pitman Publishing).

Frynas, J. (2005) 'The False Developmental Promise of Corporate Social Responsibility: Evidence from Multinational Oil Companies', *International Affairs* 81.3: 581-98.

Gardiner, D., and P. Portney (1994) 'Does Environmental Policy Conflict with Economic Growth?', *Resources* 115: 21-23.

Gerstenfeld, A., and H. Roberts (2000) 'Size Matters: Barriers and Prospects for Environmental Management in Small and Medium-sized Enterprises', in R. Hillary (ed.), *Small and Medium-sized Enterprises and the Environment: Business Imperative* (Sheffield, UK: Greenleaf Publishing).

Graafland, J., and H. Smid (2004) 'Reputation, Corporate Social Responsibility and Market Regulation', *Tijdschrift voor Economie en Management* 49.2: 271-308.

Grant, R.M. (1995) *Contemporary Strategy Analysis* (Cambridge, MA: Blackwell Business).

Gray, W., and R. Shadbegian (2003) 'Plant Vintage, Technology, and Environmental Regulation', *Journal of Environmental Economics and Management* 46.3: 384-402.

Guasch, J., and R. Hahn (1997) 'The Costs and Benefits of Regulation: Implications for Developing Countries', The World Bank, Policy Research Working Paper 1773; www-wds.worldbank.org/servlet/WDSContentServer/WDSP/IB/1997/06/01/000009265_3971126124256/Rendered/PDF/multi_page.pdf, accessed 3 December 2009.

Guében, C., and G. Skerratt (2007) 'SMEs and Environmental Communications: Motivations and Barriers to Environmental Reporting', *International Journal of Environment and Sustainable Development* 6.1: 1-16.

Gunningham, N., and P. Grabosky (1998) *Smart Regulation: Designing Environmental Policy* (Oxford, UK: Clarendon Press).

——, R. Kagan and D. Thornton (2004) 'Social License and Environmental Protection: Why Businesses Go Beyond Compliance', *Law & Social Inquiry* 29.2: 307-41.

Habermas, J. (1984) *The Theory of Communicative Action: Reason and the Rationalization of Society* (trans. T. McCarthy; vol. 1; Boston, MA: Beacon).

—— (1987) *The Theory of Communicative Action: Lifeworld and System: A Critique of Functionalist Reason* (trans. T. McCarthy; vol. 2; Boston, MA: Beacon).

Hancher, L., and M. Moran (eds.) (1989) *Capitalism, Culture, and Economic Regulation* (Oxford, UK: Oxford University Press).

Hart, S. (1995) 'A Natural Resource-Based View of the Firm', *Academy of Management Review* 20.4: 986-1,014.

—— and G. Ahuja (1996) 'Does it Pay to be Green? An Empirical Examination of the Relationship between Emission Reduction and Firm Performance', *Business Strategy and the Environment* 5.1: 30-37.

Hicks, B. (2004) 'Setting Agendas and Shaping Activism. EU Activism: EU Influence on Central and Eastern European Environmental Movements', *Environmental Politics* 13.1: 216-33.

Hitchens, D., J. Clausen, M. Trainor and S. Thankappan (2004) 'Competitiveness, Environmental Performance and Management of SMEs', *Greener Management International* 44 (Winter 2004): 45-57.

——, S. Thankappan, M. Trainor, J. Clausen and B. de Marchi (2005) 'Environmental Performance, Competitiveness and Management of Small Businesses in Europe', *Tijdschrift voor Economische en Sociale Geografie* 96.5: 541-57.

Hough, J., and M. White (2004) 'Scanning Actions and Environmental Dynamism: Gathering Information for Decision Making', *Management Decision* 42.6: 781-93.

Hutchinson, A., and I. Chaston (1994) 'Environmental Management in Devon and Cornwall's Small and Medium-sized Enterprise Sector', *Business Strategy and the Environment* 4.1: 15-22.

IFHR (2006) *An Overview of Corporate Social Responsibility in Hungary* (Report No. 458/2; Paris: IFHR).

Irwin, A., and P. Vergragt (1989) 'Re-thinking the Relationship between Environmental Regulation and Industrial Innovation: The Social Negotiation of Technological Change', *Technology Analysis & Strategic Management* 1.1: 57-70.

Jaffe, A., S. Peterson, P. Portney and R. Stavins (1995) 'Environmental Regulation and the Competitiveness of US Manufacturing: What Does the Evidence Tell Us?', *Journal of Economic Literature* 23.1: 132-63.

Jenkins, W. (2004) 'Towards a Strategic Framework for Competition in Multi-product Consumer Markets', *International Journal of Management and Decision Making* 5.2–3: 117-34.

—— (2005) 'Competing in Times of Evolution and Revolution: An Essay on Long-Term Firm Survival', *Management Decision* 43.1: 26-37.

Johnson, G., K. Scholes and R. Whittington (2007) *Exploring Corporate Strategy, Text and Cases* (London: Prentice Hall Europe).

Johnson, H. (1971) *Business in Contemporary Society: Framework and Issues* (Belmont, CA: Wadsworth).

Jorgenson, W., and P. Wilcoxen (1990) 'Environmental Regulation and US Economic Growth', *RAND Journal of Economics* 21.2: 314-40.

Judge, W., and T. Douglas (1998) 'Performance Implications of Incorporating Natural Environmental Issues into the Strategic Planning Process: An Empirical Assessment', *Journal of Management Studies* 35.2: 241-62.

Klassen, R., and C. McLaughlin (1996) 'The Impact of Environmental Management on Firm Performance', *Management Science* 42.8: 1,199-214.

—— and D. Whybark (1999) 'The Impact of Environmental Technologies on Manufacturing Performance', *Academy of Management Journal* 42.6: 599-615.

Lynch-Wood, G., and D. Williamson (2007) 'The Social Licence as a Form of Regulation for Small and Medium Enterprises', *Journal of Law and Society* 34.3: 321-41.

——, D. Williamson and W. Jenkins (2009) 'The Over-reliance on Self-regulation in CSR Policy', *Business Ethics: A European Review* 18.1: 52-65.

Mackey, A., T. Mackey and J. Barney (2005) 'Corporate Social Responsibility and Firm Performance: Investor Preferences and Corporate Strategies', *Academy of Management Review* 32.1: 817-35.

MacLeod, S. (2005) 'Corporate Social Responsibility within the European Union Framework', *Wisconsin International Law Journal* 23: 541-51.

Maignan, I. (2001) 'Consumers' Perception of Corporate Social Responsibilities: A Cross-cultural Comparison', *Journal of Business Ethics* 30.1: 57-72.

—— and O.C. Ferrell (2003) 'Nature of Corporate Responsibilities Perspectives from American, French, and German Consumers', *Journal of Business Research* 56.1: 55-76.

—— and D. Ralston (2002) 'Corporate Social Responsibility in Europe and the US: Insights from Businesses' Self-presentations', *Journal of International Business Studies* 33.3: 497-515.

Makower, J. (1993) *The E-factor: The Bottom-Line Approach to Environmentally Responsible Business* (New York: Random House).

Manne, H., and H. Wallich (1972) *The Modern Corporation and Social Responsibility* (Washington, DC: American Enterprise Institute for Public Policy Research).

Matten, D., and J. Moon (2008) ' "Implicit" and "Explicit" CSR: A Conceptual Framework for a Comparative Understanding of Corporate Social Responsibility', *Academy of Management Review* 33.2: 404-24.

Maurer, J. (1971) *Readings in Organization Theory: Open System Approaches* (New York: Random House).

Mazurkiewicz, P., and R. Crown (2006) 'Public Expectations for Corporate Social Responsibility in Poland', The World Bank Development Communication Division and the World Bank Warsaw Country Office; siteresources.worldbank.org/EXTDEVCOMSUSDEVT/Resources/csrpublicexpectationsinpoland.pdf, accessed 24 March 2010.

McGuire, M. (1982) 'Regulation, Factor Rewards and International Trade', *Journal of Public Economics* 17.3: 335-55.

McIntosh, M., D. Leipziger, K. Jones and G. Coleman (1998) *Corporate Citizenship: Successful Strategies for Responsible Companies* (London: FT Pitman).

Milgrom, P., and J. Roberts (1992) *Economics, Organization and Management* (Upper Saddle River, NJ: Prentice Hall).

Mitnick, B.M. (1981) 'The Strategic Uses of Regulation and Deregulation', *Business Horizons* 24.2: 71-83.

Nehrt, C. (1996) 'Timing and Intensity Effects of Environmental Investments', *Strategic Management Journal* 17.7: 535-47.

Nelson, R. (1991) 'Why Do Firms Differ, and How Does It Matter?', *Strategic Management Journal* 12.2: 61-74.

—— and S. Winter (1983) *An Evolutionary Theory of Economic Change* (Cambridge, MA: Harvard University Press).

Nooteboom, B. (1994) 'Innovation and Diffusion in Small Firms: Theories and Evidence', *Small Business Economics* 6.5: 985-1010.

Oliver, C. (1991) 'Strategic Responses to Institutional Processes', *Academy of Management Review* 16.1: 145-79.

—— (1997) 'Sustainable Competitive Advantage: Combining Institutional and Resource-based Views', *Strategic Management Journal* 18.9: 697-713.

Orlitzky, M., F. Schmidt and S. Rynes (2003) 'Corporate Social and Financial Performance: A Meta-analysis', *Organization Studies* 24.3: 403-41.

Orts, E. (1995) 'Reflexive Environmental Law', *Northwestern University Law Review* 89: 1227-339.

Palmer, K., W. Oates and P. Portney (1995) 'Tightening Environmental Standards: The Benefit-cost or the No-cost Paradigm?', *Journal of Economic Perspectives* 19.4: 119-32.

Parker, C. (2008) 'The Pluralization of Regulation', *Theoretical Inquiries in Law* 9.2: 349-69.

Pavlínek, P., and J. Pickles (2004) 'Environmental Pasts/Environmental Futures in Post-socialist Europe', *Environmental Politics* 13.1: 237-65.

Peteraf, M. (1993) 'The Cornerstones of Competitive Advantage: A Resource-Based View', *Strategic Management Journal* 14.3: 179-91.

Pethig, R. (1976) 'Pollution, Welfare, and Environmental Policy in the Theory of Comparative Advantage', *Journal of Environmental Economics and Management* 2.3: 160-69.

Petts, J., A. Herd, S. Gerrard and C. Horne (1999) 'The Climate and Culture of Environmental Compliance within SMEs', *Business Strategy and the Environment* 8.1: 14-30.

Podolny, J. (1993) 'A Status-Based Model of Market Competition', *American Journal of Sociology* 98.4: 829-72.

Porter, M. (1980) *Competitive Strategy: Techniques for Analysing Industries and Competitors* (New York: The Free Press).

—— (1985) *Competitive Advantage: Creating and Sustaining Superior Performance* (New York: The Free Press).

—— (1991) 'America's Green Strategy', *Scientific American* 264 (April 1991): 168.

—— (2003) 'Corporate Philanthropy: Taking the High Ground', Foundation Strategy Group; earthmind.net/ngo/docs/philanthropy-high-ground.pdf, accessed 3 December 2009.

—— and C. van der Linde (1995a) 'Green and Competitive: Breaking the Stalemate', *Harvard Business Review* 73 (September/October 1995): 120-34.

—— and C. van der Linde (1995b) 'Toward a New Conception of the Environment–Competitiveness Relationship', *Journal of Economic Perspectives* 9.4: 97-118.

Quinn, J. (1978) 'Strategic Change: Logical Incrementalism', *Sloan Management Review* 20.1: 7-21.

Revell, A., and R. Blackburn (2004) *SMEs and their Response to Environmental Issues in the UK* (London: Small Business Research Centre, Kingston University).

Rothwell, R., and W. Zegveld (1985) *Reindustrialisation and Technology* (Harlow, UK: Longman).

Rowe, J., and R. Enticott (1998) 'Evaluating the Links between Locality and Environmental Performance of SMEs: Some Observations from Survey and Partnership Programmes in the Greater Bristol Area', *Eco-Management and Auditing* 5.3: 112-25.

Rowley, T., and M. Moldoveanu (2003) 'When Will Stakeholder Groups Act? An Interest- and Identity-Based Model of Stakeholder Group Mobilization', *Academy of Management Review* 28.2: 204-19.

Russo, M., and P. Fouts (1997) 'A Resource-Based Perspective on Corporate Environmental Performance and Profitability', *Academy of Management Journal* 40.3: 534-59.

Schumpeter, J. (1934) *The Theory of Economic Development* (New York: Oxford University Press).

Scott, W. (2001) *Institutions and Organizations* (Thousand Oaks, CA: Sage).

Shadbegian, R., and W. Gray (2005) 'Pollution Abatement Expenditures and Plant-Level Productivity: A Production Function Approach', *Ecological Economics* 54.2-3: 196-208.

Shaffer, B. (1995) 'Firm-level Responses to Government Regulation: Theoretical and Research Approaches', *Journal of Management* 21.3: 495-514.

Sharma, S., and H. Vredenburg (1998) 'Proactive Corporate Environmental Strategy and the Development of Competitively Valuable Organizational Capabilities', *Strategic Management Journal* 19.8: 729-53.

Shrivastava, P. (1995) 'The Role of Corporations in Achieving Ecological Sustainability', *The Academy of Management Review* 20.4: 936-60.

Siebert, H. (1977) 'Environmental Quality and the Gains from Trade', *Kyklos* 30.4: 657-73.

Sinclair, D. (1997) 'Self-regulation versus Command and Control? Beyond False Dichotomies', *Law & Policy* 19.4: 529-59.

Spar, D., and L. La Mure (2003) 'The Power of Activism: Assessing the Impact of NGOs on Global Business', *California Management Review* 45.3: 78-101.

Stigler, G. (1971) 'The Theory of Economic Regulation', *Bell Journal of Economics and Management Science* 2.1: 3-21.

Suchman, M. (1995) 'Managing Legitimacy: Strategic and Institutional Approaches', *Academy of Management Review* 20.3: 571-610.

Teece, D., and G. Pisano (1994) 'The Dynamic Capabilities of Firms: An Introduction', *Industrial and Corporate Change* 3.3: 537-56.

Tempel, A., and P. Walgenbach (2007) 'Global Standardization of Organizational Forms and Management Practices? What New Institutionalism and the Business-Systems Approach Can Learn from Each Other', *Journal of Management Studies* 44.1: 1-24.

Tenon Forum (2008) 'Tenon Forum Report: January 2008', www.tenongroup.com/Forum?Published%20Reports.asp, accessed 3 December 2009.

USAID (2007) '2007 NGO Sustainability Index', www.usaid.gov/locations/europe_eurasia/dem_gov/ngoindex/2007, accessed 3 December 2009.

Utterback, J. (1994) *Mastering the Dynamics of Innovation: How Companies Can Seize Opportunities in the Face of Technological Change* (Cambridge, MA: Harvard Business School Press).

Van der Linde, S. (1993) 'The Micro-economic Implications of Environmental Regulation: A Preliminary Framework', in *Environmental Policies and Industrial Competitiveness* (Paris: OECD): 69.

Vandermere, S., and M. Oliff (1990) 'Customers Drive Corporations Green', *Long Range Planning* 23.6: 10-16.

Vogel, D. (2005) *The Market for Virtue: The Potential and Limits of Corporate Social Responsibility* (Washington, DC: Brookings Institution Press).

Von Hippel, E. (1988) *The Sources of Innovation* (New York: Oxford University Press).

Wally, N., and B. Whitehead (1994) 'It's Not Easy Being Green', *Harvard Business Review* 72.3: 46-52.

Weaver, G., L. Trevino and P. Cochran (1999) 'Integrated and Decoupled Corporate Social Performance: Management Commitments, External Pressures, and Corporate Ethics Practices', *Academy of Management Review* 42.5: 539-52.

Weber, J., and D. Wasieleski (2003) 'Managing Corporate Stakeholders: Subjecting Miles's 1987 Data-collection Framework to Tests of Validation', *Journal of Corporate Citizenship* 9.1: 133-53.

Wernerfelt, B. (1984) 'The Resource Based View of the Firm', *Strategic Management Journal* 5.2: 171-80.

Westley, F., and H. Vredenburg (1991) 'Strategic Bridging: The Collaboration between Environmentalists and Business in the Marketing of Green Products', *Journal of Applied Behavioral Science* 27.1: 65-90.

Williamson, D., G. Lynch-Wood and J. Ramsay (2006) 'Drivers of Environmental Behaviour in Manufacturing SMEs and the Implications for CSR', *Journal of Business Ethics* 67.3: 317-30.

——, G. Lynch-Wood, A. Prochorskaite, C. Abbot and A. Ogus (2008) *Better Regulation: Rethinking the Approach for SMEs* (Edinburgh: Scottish and Northern Ireland Forum for Environmental Research).

Wood, D. (1991) 'Corporate Social Performance Revisited', *Academy of Management Review* 16.4: 691-718.

World Movement for Democracy (2008) 'Defending Civil Society', www.wmd.org/documents/Defending%20Civil%20Society%20-%20English.pdf, accessed 24 March 2010.

Worthington, I., and D. Patton (2005) 'Strategic Intent in the Management of the Green Environment within SMEs: An Analysis of the UK Screen-printing Sector', *Long Range Planning* 38.2: 197-212.

Xerox Corporation (2005) 'Xerox Pledges to Trim Greenhouse Gas Emissions from Worldwide Operations by 10 percent by 2012', Xerox press release, 5 May 2006; www.xerox.com.

Xing, Y., and C.D. Kolstad (2002) 'Do Lax Environmental Regulations Attract Foreign Investment?', *Environmental and Resource Economics* 21.1: 1-22.

# 3
# Convergent and divergent corporate social responsibility

**Nicola Misani**[1]

Bocconi University, Italy

> The current issues go beyond just differentiation and competitive advantage—this is a moral issue. The industry could do far more if rivals worked together instead of turning 'being green' into a competition (Andy Bond, chief executive of Asda, quoted in Bell and Sanghavi 2007: 6).

During recent years corporate social responsibility (CSR) has come to be accepted as central to modern economy. This growth in importance of CSR has been accompanied by a proliferation of new concepts and definitions of the responsibilities of firms, but here I follow the simple notion of CSR formulated by Davis (1973: 312): 'the firm's considerations of, and response to, issues beyond the narrow economic, technical, and legal requirements of the firm to accomplish social [and environmental] benefits along with the traditional economic gains which the firm seeks' (see also Aguilera *et al.* 2007: 836-37).

It has long been clear that CSR has strategic implications for firms adopting it. When Milton Friedman launched his oft-quoted attack *against* CSR (Friedman 1970), one of his arguments was that managers disguise as a moral duty what in reality is often a set of practices that create value for the firm. In the subsequent decades, the idea that a business case exists for being socially responsible has been

1 I thank Stela Bejenari and Karen Maas for helpful comments on earlier drafts of this chapter.

a stimulus that has pushed firms to embrace CSR, along with increased societal expectations and stakeholder pressures (McWilliams *et al.* 2006).

In their review of the research on the link between CSR and the financial performance of firms, Margolis *et al.* (2007) identified two main theoretical accounts of how CSR is expected to pay off. In one account, CSR is conceptualised as a resource that generates benefits or reduces costs. The benefits may come from the heightened efforts by employees who react to being treated well, or by the innovative products that the firm develops in collaboration with non-market partners. The decreased costs include the avoidance of penalties and the efficiency gains from reduced pollution and waste. Examples of this account are Hart 1995, where the resource-based view (RBV) of the firm is applied to environmental responsibility, or McWilliams and Siegel 2001, where firms invest in CSR to add 'social' features to their products. In the second theoretical account, it is the appearance of doing good that generates demand or commitment by stakeholders to the stock, the products, or the jobs offered by the firm. Even though this appearance is supposed to be based on actual CSR practices, followers of this account theorise that appearance improves financial performance independently of the possible effects of these practices on the products or the processes of the firm. Examples of this account are Siegel and Vitaliano 2007, where CSR is presented as a type of advertising that makes experience goods more appealing to consumers, or Mackey *et al.* 2007, where the market value of firms is modelled as a function of the investor demand for CSR.

Scholars have also tried to determine empirically whether the business case holds. About 180 studies have been published since 1972 on the link between the social performance and the financial performance of firms. Three major meta-analyses have been conducted on these studies (Margolis and Walsh 2003; Orlitzky *et al.* 2003; Margolis *et al.* 2007), all of them concluding that the link exists but is relatively small. The most recent and complete of these meta-analyses obtained a mean $r$ of only 0.132, and found that the association varies greatly across categories of social performance. Moreover, questions about the causal direction of the association are still substantially unresolved. The authors of this meta-analysis conclude that scholars should concentrate less on looking for a direct measurable link between social and financial outcomes and more on the conditions that allow some firms (and not necessarily all of them) to create value through CSR. In the words of Barnett (2007: 795), the suggested direction for research is to 'make the business case firm specific, not universal'.

In order to understand whether and when firms earn financial returns from CSR, the strategic implications of being socially responsible need to be spelled out. It is a central tenet of the strategic management literature that above-average financial returns are obtained only by the firms that enjoy a sustainable competitive advantage. In turn, a competitive advantage depends on being different (and better) than rivals in satisfying customer needs, through better quality, reduced costs or niche products and services (Porter 1985). The competitive advantage is sustainable when a firm succeeds in achieving and preserving a unique position, based on a distinctive set of resources (Barney 1991).

Therefore, the first requirement for a firm that aims to get a financial return from CSR is to differentiate itself from rivals in its CSR practices, developing innovative and non-imitable solutions. Porter and Kramer (2006: 88) state this requirement very clearly:

> [Strategy] is about choosing a unique position—doing things differently from competitors in a way that lowers costs or better serves a particular set of consumer needs. These principles apply to a company's relationship to society as readily as to its relationship with customers and rivals.

Reinhardt (1998) underscored that a firm investing in environmental protection or other CSR-based strategies obtains above-average returns only if the firm can prevent rivals from replicating these strategies.

As a consequence, we should see the firms that engage in CSR trying to differentiate themselves from rivals. The evidence points in the opposite direction: it seems that only a small number of firms, such as Ben & Jerry's or The Body Shop, actively differentiate their CSR practices from those of their rivals. In general, competition on the basis of CSR appears to be rare (Aguilera *et al.* 2007). Most socially responsible firms seem content to adhere to codes of conduct, standards and other practices that have many adopters and cannot guarantee a unique position. One way to synthesise this evidence is to distinguish two types of CSR.

- **Convergent CSR**. Firms adopt practices that have already been adopted by rivals in the industry, or are within their reach, or collaborate with these rivals (and with stakeholders) to develop new practices that will be open to other adopters

- **Divergent CSR**. Firms try to use social performance to obtain competitive advantage; these firms want to be unique in their CSR practices and build barriers to imitation by rivals in order to protect the profits they expect from their position

While divergent CSR can be seen as an attempt by firms to harvest the financial promises of being socially responsible, convergent CSR is in need of explanation. If the CSR practices of a firm are convergent, the firm is not trying to achieve a competitive advantage but it is pursuing some other objective.

In this chapter I try to answer this question: why do a large number of socially responsible firms engage in convergent CSR instead of exploring unique ways to deal with stakeholders? In some cases managers may prefer convergent CSR because they want to respect ethical principles or are forced to be socially responsible by external coercion, and do not see CSR as a source of competitive advantage. But in other cases, which will be the focus of the chapter, convergent CSR can be strategically motivated: managers believe in the business case but they choose to share the benefits from CSR with rivals in the industry. In particular, I will describe six causes at the industry level that are able to produce convergent CSR; these causes appeal both to institutional factors and to organisational agency (Heugens and Lander 2009). Then I compare the distinction between divergent and convergent CSR with other typologies that have been proposed in the literature. I show that the distinction has an impact on the societal benefits of CSR, since divergent and convergent CSR practices are associated with different private incentives to invest in social innovation. I also suggest that the widespread adoption of convergent CSR practices helps to explain why studies have not found a stronger link between the social and the financial performance of firms, since firms that adopt a convergent CSR approach are unlikely to obtain extra returns. In the conclusions, I outline the implications for future research and for management.

## Why does convergent CSR exist?

When compared with the pile of studies on the empirical link between social and financial performance, the literature on the strategic implications of CSR is relatively thin. Husted and Allen (2007: 595) recently complained that there is still not 'a compelling framework for the strategic management of CSR'. However, a number of scholars have provided suggestions about how such a framework could be built. For example, Hillman and Keim (2001) hypothesise that socially responsible firms can achieve competitive advantage through **relational** interactions with primary stakeholders. Relational interactions involve investments by both parties, include a time dimension, are sensitive to reputation and are enhanced by fair dealing and principled behaviour. In contrast, the **transactional** interactions (which operate at arm's length) can be easily duplicated and thus offer little potential for competitive advantage.

Recently, Tetrault Sirsly and Lamertz (2008) argued that socially responsible firms can build unique capabilities in the domains of environmental assessment, stakeholder management and social issues management. These capabilities are not easily imitable by rivals and allow these firms to launch 'strategic CSR initiatives'. A firm that excels in the assessment of the environment may be able to detect shifts in stakeholder interests, changes in the regulatory setting, technological developments, or new CSR niches before its rivals and take immediate action to pre-empt them. If a firm is strong in managing stakeholders, it can achieve a central position in the stakeholder network and gain the reputation of a leader in the field; this position will pre-empt the effectiveness of similar responses by rivals because they will be judged to be mere followers. When the firm capabilities are in the domain of the management of social issues, the firm will be better than its rivals in diagnosing the issues and anticipating the implications for business; as a result, the firm will implement relevant initiatives before rivals and obtain reputation credits for identifying the importance of the issue.

All the attempts at pre-empting rivals or at capturing other types of first-mover advantage described by Tetrault Sirsly and Lamertz (2008) presuppose divergent CSR: that is, an approach in which a firm tries to build a unique position. However, convergent CSR seems more common among socially responsible firms. Waddock (2008) portrays a 'CSR infrastructure' that includes NGOs, investors, public agencies, philanthropists, certification bodies, consultants, and other profit and non-profit institutions. Through pressures, dialogue or soft regulation, this CSR infrastructure tries to redefine the rules of the modern economy and to foster change in the practices of firms. Convergent CSR coincides largely with the choice by a firm to adopt a practice recommended by the CSR infrastructure or, alternatively, to ally with it and other firms to negotiate new practices that will subsequently be shared with other potential adopters.

In contrast, a firm that engages in divergent CSR develops its own practices, or uses the recommended practices as mere starting points for building its own specific initiatives. By 'practices', I refer strictly to business processes and activities that have a direct impact on stakeholders or social issues. I exclude reporting, which is a means to communicate to stakeholders the practices a firm is following and the outcomes it is obtaining. The reason for excluding reporting from the practices I will be concerned with is that divergence in social or environmental reporting schemes would obviously be costly for the audience of the reports. Conflicting reporting schemes make cross-company or cross-industry comparisons impossible or time-expensive; converging on de facto standards such as GRI (Global Reporting Initiative) permits socially responsible firms to make their communications more transparent and easily readable.

Most of the practices on which socially responsible firms converge fall into four groups, outlined below.

## Codes of conduct and principles

Codes of conduct and principles provide guidance to firms about how to conduct business responsibly. While some firms have written their own specific codes or principles (this is a case of divergent CSR), most of the firms adhere to codes and principles that have been developed by international organisations, industry associations or other parts of the CSR infrastructure. Examples are the United Nations Global Compact (a scheme for advancing ten responsibility principles in the areas of human rights, environment, labour and anti-corruption) or the OECD Guidelines for Multinational Enterprises (a set of recommendations for firms operating in global markets).

## Certified managerial standards

Certified managerial standards (CMS) are more detailed than codes or principles and define exact technical requirements or management practices. CMS are written by a standard setter and are usually assisted by a certification process that allows firms to be officially recognised as adherents after they accept monitoring by accredited third-party certifiers. Examples are EMAS (Eco-Management and Audit Scheme, a standard for environmental management created by the European Union, which grants an official EMAS logo to certified participants) or ISO 14001 (an international management standard that helps firms minimise their impact on the environment; complying firms are awarded a ISO 14001 certificate after being audited by an accredited external body).

## Ethical labels

Ethical labels are applied on the product or its package to make known to consumers that the product meets certain social or environmental standards. Examples are the Fairtrade certification (which identifies products that meet environmental, labour and developmental standards established by FLO International, as certified by a system of auditors overseen by FLO International's certification body) and Forest Stewardship Council (a multi-stakeholder coalition that manages a standard to ensure that forests are managed sustainably and grants adherents an FSC Certification Label). For both CMS and ethical labels, the convergent CSR approach is followed by the firms that adhere to the standard or request the label without going beyond the recommended practices. The divergent CSR approach is compatible with adopting a standard or a label, but it involves attempts by firms to differentiate themselves from rivals. An example is IKEA, which, while being an FSC adherent, has its own environmental standards and tries to associate the values of sustainability directly with the IKEA brand; as a signal of this divergent approach, IKEA does not usually display the FSC certification on its products (*Buyer Be Fair* 2009).

## Alliances or coalitions

Alliances or coalitions of firms (with the possible inclusion of stakeholders) develop practices to share data, information, knowledge, experiences and other resources. The purpose of these initiatives is to improve the social performance of all the participants. While alliances or coalitions allow firms to collectively address serious issues, the best that each participant can expect from these initiatives is to align itself with the best practices of the industry. The best-known example is the Responsible Care programme, a voluntary international initiative of the chemical industry with the aim of improving the health, safety and environmental perform- ance of members (King and Lenox 2000). Another example is the $CO_2$ emissions data collection programme recently launched by the World Steel Association, which aims at identifying technical benchmarks and allows transfers of technol- ogy among steel-makers to revamp and improve the energy efficiency of outdated plants (World Steel Association 2008).

While codes of conduct and principles, CMS, ethical labels, and industry alliances and coalitions for improving social performance are praiseworthy, usually they do not allow a participating firm to be unique. In fact, the aim of these initiatives is the opposite: spreading sets of recommended practices among the firms in an industry or in a group. Therefore, a firm that adopts these practices probably does not hope to obtain a competitive advantage, unless it is deluded into thinking it can outper- form its rivals without differentiating itself from them.

Thus, the question is: why do many socially responsible firms converge on shared CSR practices instead of trying to be unique and achieve competitive advantage? It is possible that some of them are coerced into CSR by external pressures (Husted and De Jesus Salazar 2006), in which case they may want to minimise efforts and limit themselves to adhere to the initiatives sponsored by the CSR infrastructure. Other firms may be led to CSR by the altruistic preferences of their managers or their shareholders (Baron 2001) and adopt the practices that they think satisfy some fundamental ethical requirements; since these firms do not conceive CSR as an avenue to competitive advantage, there is no immediate reason they should want to differentiate their CSR practices from their rivals.

Both external coercion and altruistic considerations can be a powerful motiva- tion for firms to engage in CSR, but in many cases convergent CSR can also be stra- tegically motivated. The literature on strategic management acknowledges that in some situations firms should not differentiate too much from rivals and converge instead on intermediate levels of strategic similarity (Deephouse 1999). One rea- son for limiting differentiation has been advanced in institutional theory, where it is suggested that firms resort to mimetism in order to preserve legitimacy. This is the first possible cause of convergent CSR that I analyse in the next section ('Insti- tutional isomorphism'). The subsequent causes are deduced from various streams of research that have dealt with strategic firm interactions in industries: studies on imitation ('Environmental uncertainty', 'Rivalry mitigation'), on competition ('Low barriers to imitation'), and on collaboration ('Economies of scale', 'Reputation interdependences'). The resulting six-cause list is not intended as exhaustive, but is presented as a demonstration of the variety of strategic reasons that can push socially responsible firms to converge in their CSR practices.

# Causes of convergence in CSR activities

## Institutional isomorphism

Institutional theory (Meyer and Rowan 1977; DiMaggio and Powell 1983) asserts that the choices of firms are constrained by pressures coming from institutions such as public regulators, interest groups, public opinion and so on. These pressures take the form of expectations of the firms' activities. A central concept in institutional theory is **legitimacy**, which is the generalised social perception that the actions of an organisation are appropriate, given a system of beliefs and norms (Suchman 1995). Firms need legitimacy in order to attain their ends; therefore, firms will try to be isomorphic to these beliefs and norms.

The consequences of institutional theory for CSR are straightforward: firms engage in CSR to be seen as legitimate. Recently, many scholars have focused on how institutions shape CSR (e.g. Campbell 2007; Teerlak 2007; Matten and Moon 2008). In this framework, convergent CSR can be explained as homogeneity owing to the fact that firms in an industry are exposed to approximately the same institutional pressures (Bansal 2005). Institutional theory includes three mechanisms that may force firms to adapt to their institutional environment (DiMaggio and Powell 1983); all of them seem to contribute to pushing firms to converge on CSR practices.

- **Coercive isomorphism**. Direct prescriptions (such as rules and norms) supported by economic or social sanctions. As we have seen, principles, codes of conduct and standards are used by institutions to specify prescriptions in the areas of CSR

- **Mimetic isomorphism**. The attempts by organisations to model themselves on other organisations perceived as legitimate. The mechanism is different from information cascades or bandwagons (which I will examine below) because it is activated by a quest for social approval, not by lack of information or by risk-avoiding. In the areas of CSR, mimetic isomorphism explains why firms with excellent social performance and solid reputation become role models in their industries and attract imitation by rivals seeking legitimacy

- **Normative isomorphism**. Ideas spread by professions, educational institutions and authoritative observers. These ideas are presented as the right way of doing things and over time they come to be taken for granted. In the areas of CSR, normative isomorphism is evident where some practices achieve the status of 'non-choice behaviour', such as the ban on forced labour

While early versions of institutional theory presented firms as passively conforming to the institutional environment, the so-called 'new institutional theory' gives them some freedom in deciding how to react to institutional pressures (Oliver 1991). This is why I am treating institutional isomorphism as a different cause of convergent CSR from mere external coercion. The new institutional theory emphasises that firms in general can avoid, defy, manipulate or try to reach compromises on the institutional requests they receive. Correspondingly, socially responsible firms can try to negotiate the practices that are recommended by the institutional environment and bargain with stakeholders in order to arrive at balanced solutions. In these bargaining efforts, firms in the same industry will have an incentive to join forces to increase their contractual power. This mechanism can be a further driver of convergence. Studies have shown that often the bargaining process is started by powerful stakeholders that put an issue on the public agenda and request changes in the behaviour of firms; after an initial resistance, firms form coalitions and try to negotiate the requests and define the exact content of the practices to be adopted. An example is Bartley 2007, which describes the historical origins of Forest Stewardship Council and shows that the process leading to the new standard was started by timber boycotts by Friends of the Earth and other environmentalist groups. Subsequently, Austria and other European countries imposed restrictions on the import of tropical timber; then, these countries and private foundations such as the Ford Foundation and Pew Charitable Trust financed and supported the creation of FSC. Eventually the timber industry accepted negotiations, entered FSC and participated in writing the standard for the sustainable management of forests.

## Environmental uncertainty

Research on the diffusion of innovations shows that the adoption of managerial practices in a population of firms often follows a two-stage model: a first group of early innovators adopts the practice because of its intrinsic perceived benefits; a second group of latecomers adopts it because they imitate the first group (Abrahamson and Rosenkopf 1993). Various mechanisms explain why the second group imitates the first. One is **information cascades** (Bikhchandani *et al.* 1992). Information cascades happen because choices made by individuals reveal useful information to observers. Suppose that a group of people wants to decide whether to invest in real estate or in stocks. The first two persons to speak have favoured investment in real estate, but the third person's private information suggests to her that investing in stocks is better; even in this case, she may think the first two persons had good reasons for their choice. If she discards her own information and follows their lead, she is in a cascade; the cascade will grow stronger and stronger if subsequent persons follow suit (Sunstein 2008). Researchers have used information cascades to explain stock market bubbles, fads in fashion, waves in mergers and acquisitions, and other self-sustaining phenomena (Bikhchandani *et al.* 1992).

A second mechanism is **bandwagons**: firms adopt a practice because of the sheer number of rivals that have already adopted it. While information cascades derive from information externalities, bandwagons are the result of risk-avoiding. Abrahamson and Rosenkopf (1993) describe two kinds of pressure that can start bandwagons: **institutional pressures**, which happen when non-adopters fear the risk of looking different from the growing number of peers that are adopting the practice; and **competitive pressures**, where non-adopters fear the risk of finding themselves at a loss if the practice gives advantages to the early adopters.

Institutional pressures are a source of institutional isomorphism, which I discussed above. Here I focus on information cascades and bandwagons driven by competitive pressures. As argued by Lieberman and Asaba (2006), both mechanisms are more frequent when the environment is uncertain and managers cannot confidently foresee the consequences of actions. In such environments, managers will be more receptive to information revealed by others and more sensitive to the risks of deviating from the consensus.

Environmental uncertainty characterises many areas of CSR. What is ethical or unethical in corporate behaviour is often ambiguous and subject to the vagaries of media scrutiny and political interpretations; whether or not a given practice will satisfy stakeholder requests is not always predictable; accidents can change the public perceptions of a firm in unexpected ways. Therefore, responsible firms may be tempted to seek safety in numbers and emulate the practices adopted by their rivals. For example, consider a firm that finds out that a supplier in Indonesia employs 14-year-old workers. It is ethically debatable what the firm should do: on one hand, asking the supplier to fire the teenage workers would mean wiping out their incomes and forcing them to find probably worse jobs elsewhere; on the other, keeping them in the factory would mean profiting from child labour (Frank 2008). The safest solution for the firm is to look at its rivals' behaviour and fire or keep the teenage workers according to the labour standards usually followed in that region by the industry.

## Rivalry mitigation

Socially responsible firms may not want to be *too* responsible. Like in other business areas, there may be an optimal level of social performance beyond which the economic benefits of investments in CSR are surpassed by costs (McWilliams and Siegel 2001). Rivalry among firms that compete for stakeholder favour risks leading rivals beyond this optimal level of CSR. The problem is similar to price competition. Lowering prices lets a firm attract customers and enlarge market share but it may initiate a price war at the end of which all the rivals lose (Besanko *et al.* 2000). Since firms are aware of this risk, they try to avoid price wars and converge on a collusive equilibrium; for the same reasons, they may want to avoid costly 'CSR wars'.

Tit-for-tat strategies are a typical way of avoiding wars (Lieberman and Asaba 2006): by matching the moves of rivals, a firm signals that it is ready to use the same lever. The signal tells the rivals that the benefits of further actions will be eroded by competition. In this way, imitation is helpful in discouraging rivalry and enforcing implicit collusion.

It is not easy to find direct evidence of rivalry mitigation in the areas of CSR, but there are some behaviours by firms that can be interpreted as signals to rivals to avoid aggressive competition on CSR. For example, Fairtrade is currently only a niche in the coffee market but, were it to become a 'non-choice' requirement for the firms importing coffee from developing countries, it could raise the prices paid to local producers and damage the profitability of the industry. Large multinationals such as Nestlé would suffer the most from such developments. One could expect these multinationals to ostracise Fairtrade; instead, Nestlé entered the niche by launching its own Fairtrade-certified coffee, Partners' Blend, in the UK (Dawar and Mitchell 2006). It can be reasonably speculated that this move serves, among other purposes, to signal that Nestlé is able to compete in the niche and to discourage rivals that may think of investing aggressively in the Fairtrade market. More direct evidence of rivalry mitigation is provided by Bansal and Roth (2000), who argue that firms can be limited in their efforts to practise environmental protection by the fear of 'persecution' by peers for going beyond industry standards.

## Low barriers to imitation

When a socially responsible firm adopts a practice that can have positive impacts on its relationships with stakeholders, rivals can imitate that practice in order to harvest the same benefits. In this case imitation is not driven by uncertainty: rivals predict a probable positive reaction by stakeholders to the practice and act on this prediction.

In a competitive industry, any practice with clear benefits gets replicated by rivals unless there are barriers to imitation, such as property rights, causal ambiguity and so on (Barney 1991). Therefore, convergent CSR can be the consequence of the fact that many CSR practices may not be protected from imitation. CSR practices are typically highly transparent, with little causal ambiguity (McWilliams *et al.* 2006). For a firm, telling stakeholders what it does is an essential part of being responsible (Vogel 2008): patent protection or 'secret formulas' are not usually an option for CSR practices. Moreover, sometimes disclosure itself is a way of being socially responsible. For example, in 2008 pharmaceutical producer Eli Lilly announced that it will start to disclose the payments made to doctors for various services. Eli Lilly will provide details of each payment above US$500 for advice and speaking; in the future, Eli Lilly will extend the policy to travel, entertainment and gifts. This decision was made in response to mounting suspicion that pharmaceutical firms influence medical choices through payments made to doctors (*Business Respect* 2008b). Of course, there is no barrier to imitation of Eli Lilly's policy by other pharmaceutical firms should they see that the policy is going to reward Eli Lilly in terms of goodwill and reputation.

## Economies of scale

If we assume that socially responsible firms want to be beneficial to society, convergent CSR can be motivated by the need for them to achieve the scale required to address some issues effectively. There are economies of scale in CSR when the marginal contribution of a firm's effort in a given cause increases with the number of firms that contribute to it, or with the total amount of resources they are investing. When there are these economies, a socially responsible firm may prefer to coordinate its efforts with its peers in order to maximise the outcome. For example, in August 2008 a coalition formed by major US retail and clothing producers called on the Uzbekistan government to take action against the use of child labour in the country's cotton industry. Participants included the National Retail Federation, the American Apparel and Footwear Association, and the Association of Importers of Textiles and Apparel; individual firms in the US and UK, including Gap, Marks & Spencer, Target and Tesco, are also contributing to the initiative. Of course, each of these firms could have decided unilaterally to avoid sourcing from Uzbekistan (this would have been a case of divergent CSR), but concerted action is clearly a more effective way to obtain the desired changes in countries plagued by the use of child labour (*Business Respect* 2008a).

Another example is the effort launched in February 2009 by the Groupe Spéciale Mobile Association (GSMA), an industry group representing all the major mobile handset producers, which announced a commitment to develop a universal charger for all the new handsets by 2012. This re-usable charger is expected to dramatically reduce waste from discarded chargers and save millions of tonnes of greenhouse gases annually as demand for new chargers decreases. Of course, the amount of these benefits will be a more-than-linear function of the number of manufacturers that adhere to the initiative, which has already been signed by Nokia, Samsung, Motorola, Sony Ericsson, and 13 of their technological or commercial partners (Sustainable Life Media 2009).

## Reputation interdependences

Stakeholder theory (Freeman 1984) focuses on the relationships between stakeholders and a single firm. Nonetheless, sometimes stakeholders form opinions and take action against groups of firms. In this case, the fate of a firm depends not only on its own CSR practices, but also on the practices of its peers: if they behave irresponsibly, they can attract stakeholder reactions against the whole industry. A firm in such an industry could be punished even when its individual social performance is faultless. Where there are such interdependences among firms, divergent CSR can be futile: a socially responsible firm will sustain all the costs of investing in CSR but risk being 'tarred with the same brush' as its irresponsible peers.

One source of interdependences is **reputation externalities**. In general, reputation is important when observers are not fully informed about a firm's 'type' (Weigelt and Camerer 1988). Observers try to judge the type of a firm on the basis of the available signals. The literature on reputation has usually assumed that observers look at information that directly concerns the particular firm to be judged; more recently, scholars have acknowledged that observers may also look at information about other firms, if they think these firms are similar to the focal firm in the relevant respects (Barnett and Hoffman 2008). Reputation externalities arise when the observable traits of firm A are used by observers to infer the type of firm B.

Reputation externalities are frequent in CSR, because stakeholders are often unable to observe the actual social performance of a firm (King *et al.* 2002). Therefore, they will try to determine the 'social responsibility type' of a firm (that is, whether the firm is socially responsible or not) on the basis of clues, which include the observable performance of the peers of that firm. As a matter of fact, the reputations of many industries have been hurt by the 'sins' of single members. The Union Carbide disaster in Bhopal damaged the reputation of the whole chemical industry; the Three Mile Island accident created public suspicion about all nuclear energy plants; the *Exxon Valdez* oil spill was bad publicity for the other major oil companies.

To avoid reputation externalities, socially responsible firms can try to develop a unique reputation, distancing themselves from rivals; another option is to exert pressure and help peers to improve their performances, ensuring that good CSR practices are shared across the industry (King *et al.* 2002). A leading role in the process will be taken by the firms that have the most to lose from damage to the industry's reputation. These may be the firms with large specific investments in the industry or the most publicly visible ones, which are the preferred targets of stakeholder backlash (Spar and La Mure 2003).

Another source of interdependences is **common sanctions**: stakeholder interventions against an industry because of the irresponsible behaviour of single members. In particular, public regulation is a sanction that is feared by industries. Reputation externalities can originate common sanctions, because the accidents of single members can lead stakeholders to believe that all the firms in the industry are the same and deserve punishment or regulation. But common sanctions can be inflicted even when the stakeholders are aware of differences in behaviour among the firms: it is the intrinsic nature of laws and regulation that forces public authorities or other agencies to intervene against the firms as a group. Again, socially responsible firms that want to avoid common sanctions have a vested interest in helping sub-performing peers to improve their practices.

Both reputation externalities and the fear of common sanctions can push firms to converge on a shared set of practices. These practices will be enforced at the industry level through codes of conduct, standards or other forms of private regulation. These initiatives will also allow firms to avoid the risk of finding themselves at a cost disadvantage, because a private regulation scheme forces all the industry peers to sustain the same investments.

This process involves explicit cooperation among firms and therefore it differs from the type of convergence predicted by institutional isomorphism. The practices will be defined by the firms, not by the stakeholders. For example, both reputation externalities and regulatory risk are evident in the efforts of the diamond industry to solve the issue of 'conflict diamonds'. The issue was brought up by NGOs at the end of the 1990s, when some African paramilitary groups began to extract rough diamonds to finance their violent operations against legitimate governments. After being cut and polished, these diamonds would enter the normal distribution channels. The NGOs directed their campaign mainly against De Beers, the most visible player in the industry. As a matter of fact, De Beers did not import diamonds from conflict regions and had introduced a certificate of origin to ensure that its diamonds were not from these regions. Anyway, the campaign risked destroying the reputation of products—diamonds and the related jewellery—that depend on symbolic values; conflict diamonds are also called 'blood diamonds', which is probably not good advertising for an engagement ring. Instead of ignoring the NGOs' campaign or trying to distance itself further from rivals that purchased diamonds from illegal traffickers, De Beers choose to use its structural power to push for a political solution to the conflict diamonds issue (Kantz 2007). De Beers persuaded the South African government to convene a workshop on conflict diamonds in 2000 in Kimberley. De Beers also financed the creation of the World Diamond Council, an institution that represented the industry at the workshop and in the subsequent negotiations with African governments and NGOs. In 2003, the negotiations gave birth to the Kimberley Process Certification Scheme, an industry programme that includes a code of conduct, a system of detailed records for all the trades of rough diamonds, third-party monitoring, and warranties on the sale of cut and polished diamonds to guarantee that they have been purchased from legitimate sources.

## Consequences of convergent CSR

The distinction between convergent and divergent CSR refers to how socially responsible firms shape their practices in respect of their rivals. While there is a large literature on the antecedents of the CSR policies of firms, this literature has concentrated on internal factors (such as organisational culture or ethical climate; e.g. Crilly *et al.* 2008) or factors external to the competitive context (institutional pressures at the national or the transnational level; e.g. Matten and Moon 2008). In this chapter, I suggest that the actual and predicted behaviour of industry rivals is also an antecedent of the CSR practices of firms, because one of the most important choices that a responsible firm has to make is whether it wants to be like its peers (convergent CSR) or to differentiate itself from them (divergent CSR).

The six causes of convergent CSR that I presented are not exhaustive. Besides, more than one of these causes can concur to activate particular instances of convergence. For example, both fear of reputation externalities and institutional pressures coming from NGOs have clearly contributed to De Beers' decision to support the Kimberley Process. The aim of the chapter was not to analyse when, in what forms, or under what conditions convergent CSR happens, but to show that there are multiple and cogent reasons for socially responsible firms to renounce developing their own ways to deal with stakeholder issues.

The convergent/divergent CSR distinction differs from two other distinctions that have been recently introduced in the CSR literature and that apparently deal with similar problems. Matten and Moon (2008) distinguish between **explicit** and **implicit** CSR. Explicit CSR is deliberate: firms engaging in this type of CSR may be under pressure from stakeholders or may collaborate with them, but pursue CSR objectives through their own discretional decisions. These firms explicitly use the language of CSR (or 'responsibility', 'sustainability' and the like) in communicating their policies to the public. In contrast, implicit CSR is compulsory: firms engage in it because they are embedded in a system of formal and informal institutions that represent the concerns of society. Firms that engage in implicit CSR do not even consider the possibility of rejecting these concerns; they do not try to build individual versions of the requirements expressed by institutions; they do not communicate their actions to the public under the label of 'CSR' (or, again, of related concepts). According to Matten and Moon, explicit and implicit CSR are, respectively, representative of the US and European social traditions.

Implicit CSR overlaps with convergent CSR, because firms engaging in implicit CSR renounce any attempt to differentiate their actions from those of other firms. However, we have seen that institutional pressures are only one of the causes that push firms to converge on the same practices; convergent CSR due to rivalry mitigation or reputation externalities is the result of strategic thinking and deliberate actions, which belong to explicit CSR in Matten and Moon's distinction. Therefore, convergent CSR covers much more ground than implicit CSR.

Moreover, implicit CSR can result in divergent practices. Even if a firm accepts the institutional pressures as non-negotiable, there can be room for firm-specific adaptations. Many responsible firms build their particular connections to society over time and, while lacking an explicit commitment to CSR, they develop idiosyncratic cultures and peculiar projects. For example, US firm General Mills is known for focusing its CSR programmes on issues of crime prevention and the quality of city life in Minneapolis (Minnesota), where the firm is headquartered. General Mills' approach is local, low-profile and different from the explicit CSR agenda of other large US firms; at the same time, General Mills' CSR approach is divergent, because the firm looks at solutions in tune with the special needs of the community, not at general best practices (Guthrie and Durand 2008).

In summary, the implicit/explicit CSR distinction is useful in analysing how firms conceive of their responsibilities to society, what forms their decision processes take, and how policies are communicated to the public, but it has little to say about whether a firm will have a distinctive set of practices or align itself with its rivals.

Porter and Kramer (2006) distinguish between **responsive** and **strategic** CSR. Firms adopt responsive CSR when their only objective is to mitigate the adverse societal effects of their business operations and improve relationships with stakeholders. Firms that follow the responsive CSR approach address generic social issues that are not directly related to their business (such as poverty in developing countries where the firms do not have operations) or, if they intervene in their own value chain, their purpose is only to reduce harm. Firms adopt strategic CSR when they want to achieve unique positions and look for business opportunities that create value (for themselves and for society). These firms do not stop at mitigating harm, but try to transform the value chain in ways that contribute to competitive advantage; alternatively, they invest in social causes that are directly relevant to their competitive arena and could add to the profitability of the industry in the long term.

While it is tempting to assimilate responsive CSR into convergent CSR, and strategic CSR into divergent CSR, the two distinctions are different. The main reason is that Porter and Kramer's distinction reduces strategic behaviour to the quest for uniqueness, whereas responsible firms can be strategically motivated (that is, their intent can be to do more than mitigate harm) but choose not to be unique. An example is given by the firms that fear reputation externalities or common sanctions and help rivals to improve their CSR practices: these firms want to contribute to industry profitability and therefore their behaviour counts as strategic CSR in Kramer and Porter's distinction; at the same time, they renounce being unique (which is convergent CSR). A firm can even avoid adopting an efficient practice that could lead to competitive advantage precisely because it would be beyond the reach of its industry peers and risk disbanding a private regulatory scheme. Responsive CSR can also be divergent, because firms that focus on mitigating harm or addressing general social issues can look for an individual way to do so and diverge from rivals (General Mills is, again, a pertinent example).

The distinction between convergent and divergent CSR has implications both at the societal and at the firm level. At the societal level, the implications are about the contribution of firms to social innovation. At first sight, divergent CSR seems more promising, since firms that adopt divergent CSR try to create new ways of satisfying stakeholder needs. In the convergent CSR approach the private incentives for social innovations are lower, because firms do not expect to obtain extra returns from their practices and may want to minimise costs by adopting well-established solutions. Moreover, convergent CSR can stifle competition, as is the case where rivalry mitigation is the primary motivation. However, in other cases convergent CSR can facilitate social innovation, especially when it takes the form of industry collaborations (such as in the case of the new universal charger for mobile handsets), or when it allows cross-firm fertilisation of ideas through exchange of knowledge between peers (or within broader coalitions involving firms and stakeholders).

The social actors may need to appreciate the different private incentives associated with divergent and convergent CSR. While governments and NGOs tend to applaud the adoption of standards or codes of conduct by firms, the lack of proper incentives to innovate associated with certain forms of convergent CSR can damage society's best interests in the long term. Policy-makers should consider whether the active promotion of divergent CSR, even through antitrust measures, would not sometimes be preferable to industry self-regulation and other forms of convergent CSR. The current debate about how to address climate change is an example of the tension between the two approaches: on one side there are entrepreneurs that invoke public support for research on new energy sources or carbon-absorbing technologies, which could disrupt markets and create huge opportunities for private profits; on the other side there are incumbents that invoke gradualism and favour collective industry improvements that do not alter the competitive status quo.

At the same time, divergent CSR has its own problems. When firms follow this approach they expect a competitive advantage; thus, they will focus their innovation efforts on outcomes that they can appropriate, for example through distinctive product brands. These firms could not invest enough in innovations that add to social welfare but cannot be protected from imitation.

At the firm level, the convergent/divergent CSR distinction helps to explain the shortage of conclusive empirical evidence for the business case for CSR. An extensive literature has tried to ascertain a measurable link between the social performance of firms and their financial performance. As we have seen, the results have been partially unsatisfactory: the link seems to be weaker than expected (Margolis *et al.* 2007). Some scholars have hypothesised, and tried to prove empirically, that CSR impacts positively on financial performance only in certain circumstances. For example, Hillman and Keim (2001) suggested that the CSR activities that are concerned with the management of stakeholders have a positive correlation with financial performance, while the CSR activities that address generic social issues have a negative impact. Barnett and Salomon (2006) showed that certain issues (relationships with employees, relationships with the community, protection of natural environment) seem to be more instrumental to a firm's success than others. Hull and Rothenberg (2008) provided evidence that CSR activities are more likely to improve the financial performance of the firms operating in low-differentiation industries and of the firms that invest the least money in R&D.

Divergent and convergent CSR practices are two types of CSR that could impact differently on the bottom line; while (successful) divergent CSR can lead to competitive advantage and extra returns, convergent CSR does not allow firms to outperform their peers and should have no effect on stock performance or profit differentials. Studies about the link between social and financial performance could arrive at clearer results if they focused on firms with divergent CSR approaches.

## Conclusions

In this chapter I tried to answer the question: why do many firms that make costly investments in CSR choose to converge on practices that cannot create competitive advantage? Such a convergence is difficult to reconcile with the widely shared idea that there is a business case for CSR, since profits require that a firm differentiate itself from rivals. I identified six different causes for this convergence and suggested that the CSR policies of firms are shaped not only by institutional factors or by internal culture, as is largely acknowledged in the literature, but also by strategic reasoning: firms compare their policies with those of their rivals in the industry. This means that, while the benefits associated with the business case (such as reduced transaction costs or improved reputation) are real, firms may be forced to share them with their rivals or simply find it more prudent not to compete on CSR.

In trying to explain why many firms adopt convergent CSR practices, I take part in the line of enquiry suggested, among others, by Aguilera *et al.* (2007: 837), which is to find out 'what catalyzes organisations to engage in increasingly robust CSR initiatives and consequently impact social change' and, correlatively, what can block organisations from engaging in such robust CSR initiatives. While divergent CSR does not necessarily equal 'robust CSR', the convergence in CSR practices has the potential to weaken innovation and to push firms to limit their investments.

While the six causes are conceptually independent, it is necessary to formulate criteria to discriminate empirically among them. Some criteria have been mentioned in the chapter: for example, looking at the player who starts a given initiative helps separate processes due to institutional isomorphism (guided by stakeholders) from processes due to reputation externalities or fear of common sanctions (guided by firms). Research is required to formulate other criteria and to test the different empirical predictions.

The effects of convergent and divergent CSR on social innovation are also in need of research. Here I stopped at the suggestion that convergent CSR can stifle innovation and that firms applying divergent CSR can selectively look at opportunities for social innovation that are appropriable, discarding others that could possibly have greater beneficial impacts on society. Research should analyse the different outcomes of the two types of approach in more detail and take into consideration situational factors, such as the particular social issue to be addressed, the state of industry rivalry, the traits of the institutional environment and so on.

Finally, the convergent/divergent distinction has managerial implications, because firms need to establish what type of CSR best fits their needs. Many of the advantages that supporters of CSR tend to associate with being socially responsible, such as the ability to attract and retain customers, are probably associated only with divergent CSR. The choice between the two types of CSR should depend on conditions such as the firm's resources and the expected moves of rivals. Divergent CSR in today's firms is relatively rare, which suggests that these conditions may be restrictive, but continuous changes in the global economy, technologies and the institutional environment could open up opportunities to be seized.

# References

Abrahamson, E., and L. Rosenkopf (1993) 'Institutional and Competitive Bandwagons: Using Mathematical Modeling as a Tool to Explore Innovation Diffusion', *Academy of Management Review* 18.3: 487-517.

Aguilera, R., D.E. Rupp, C.A. Williams and J. Ganapathi (2007) 'Putting the S Back in Corporate Social Responsibility: A Multilevel Theory of Social Change in Organizations', *Academy of Management Review* 32.3: 836-63.

Bansal, P. (2005) 'Evolving Sustainability: A Longitudinal Study of Corporate Sustainable Development', *Strategic Management Journal* 26: 197-218.

—— and K. Roth (2000) 'Why Companies Go Green: A Model of Ecological Responsiveness', *Academy of Management Journal* 43: 717-36.

Barnett, M.L. (2007) 'Stakeholder Influence Capacity and the Variability of Financial Returns to Corporate Social Responsibility', *Academy of Management Review* 32.3: 794-816.

—— and A.J. Hoffman (2008) 'Beyond Corporate Reputation: Managing Reputational Interdependence', *Corporate Reputation Review* 11.1: 1-9.

—— and R.M. Salomon (2006) 'Beyond Dichotomy: The Curvilinear Relationship between Social Responsibility and Financial Performance', *Strategic Management Journal* 27: 1,106-22.

Barney, J. (1991) 'Firm Resources and Sustained Competitive Advantage', *Journal of Management* 17: 99-120.

Baron, D.P. (2001) 'Private Politics, Corporate Social Responsibility, and Integrated Strategy', *Journal of Economics & Management Strategy* 10.1: 7-45.

Bartley, T. (2007) 'Institutional Emergence in an Era of Globalization: The Rise of Transnational Private Regulation of Labor and Environmental Conditions', *American Journal of Sociology* 113.2: 297-351.

Bell, D., and N. Sanghavi (2007) *A Differentiation Strategy at Asda* (Case 507-047; Boston, MA: Harvard Business School).

Besanko, D., D. Dranove and M. Shanley (2000) *Economics of Strategy* (New York: Wiley, 2nd edn).

Bikhchandani, S., D. Hirshleifer and I. Welch (1992) 'A Theory of Fads, Fashion, Custom and Cultural Change as Informational Cascades', *Journal of Political Economy* 100.5: 992-1,026.

*Business Respect* (2008a) 'Uzbekistan: Major Retailers Call for End of Child Labour in Cotton', 15 August 2008; www.mallenbaker.net/csr/CSRfiles/page.php?Story_ID=2186, accessed 24 October 2008.

—— (2008b) 'US: Eli Lilly Payments to Doctors to be Reported', 24 September; www.mallenbaker.net/csr/CSRfiles/page.php?Story_ID=2243, accessed 24 October 2008.

*Buyer Be Fair* (2009) 'Frequently Asked Questions', www.buyerbefair.org/faq.html, accessed 17 April 2009.

Campbell, J.L. (2007) 'Why Would Corporations Behave in Socially Responsible Ways? An Institutional Theory of Corporate Social Responsibility', *Academy of Management Review* 32.3: 946-67.

Crilly, D., S.C. Schneider and M. Zollo (2008) 'Psychological Antecedents to Socially Responsible Behavior', *European Management Review* 5: 175-90.

Davis, K. (1973) 'The Case for and against Business Assumption of Social Responsibilities', *Academy of Management Journal* 16: 312-23.

Dawar, N., and J. Mitchell (2006) *Nestle's Nescafe Partners' Blend: The Fairtrade Decision (A and B)* (London, Canada: Richard Ivey School of Business, Ivey Publishing).

Deephouse, D.L. (1999) 'To be Different, or to be the Same? It's a Question (and Theory) of Strategic Balance', *Strategic Management Journal* 20: 147-66.

DiMaggio, P.J., and W.W. Powell (1983) 'The Iron Cage Revisited: Institutional Isomorphism and Collective Rationality in Organizational Fields', *American Sociological Review* 48.2: 147-60.

Frank, T.A. (2008) 'Confessions of a Sweatshop Inspector', *The Washington Monthly*, 4 August 2008; www.washingtonmonthly.com/features/2008/0804.frank.html, accessed 23 October 2008.

Freeman, R.E. (1984) *Strategic Management: A Stakeholder Approach* (Boston, MA: Pitman/ Ballinger).

Friedman, M. (1970) 'The social responsibility of business is to increase its profits', *New York Times Magazine*, 13 September 1970.

Guthrie, D., and R. Durand (2008) 'Social Issues in the Study of Management', *European Management Review* 5: 137-49.

Hart, S. (1995) 'A Natural Resource-Based View of the Firm', *Academy of Management Review* 20: 986-1,014.

Heugens, P.P., and M.W. Lander (2009) 'Structure! Agency! (and Other Quarrels): A Meta-analysis of Institutional Theories of Organization', *Academy of Management Journal* 52.1: 61-85.

Hillman, A.J., and G.D. Keim (2001) 'Shareholder Value, Stakeholder Management, and Social Issues: What's the Bottom Line?', *Strategic Management Journal* 22: 125-39.

Hull, C.E., and S. Rothenberg (2008) 'Firm Performance: The Interactions of Corporate Social Performance with Innovation and Industry Differentiation', *Strategic Management Journal* 29: 781-89.

Husted, B.W., and D.B. Allen (2007) 'Strategic Corporate Social Responsibility and Value Creation among Large Firms: Lessons from the Spanish Experience', *Long Range Planning* 40: 594-610.

—— and J. De Jesus Salazar (2006) 'Taking Friedman Seriously: Maximizing Profits and Social Performance', *Journal of Management Studies* 43.1: 75-91.

Kantz, C. (2007) 'The Power of Socialization: Engaging the Diamond Industry in the Kimberley Process', *Business and Politics* 9.3; www.bepress.com/bap/vol9/iss3/art2, accessed 23 October 2008.

King, A., and M.J. Lenox (2000) 'Industry Self-regulation without Sanctions: the Chemical Industry's Responsible Care Program', *Academy of Management Journal* 43.4: 698-716.

——, M.J. Lenox and M.J. Barnett (2002) 'Strategic Responses to the Reputation Commons Problem', in A.J. Hoffman and M.J. Ventresca (eds.), *Organizations, Policy, and the Natural Environment* (Stanford, CA: Stanford University Press): 393-406.

Lieberman, M.B., and S. Asaba (2006) 'Why Do Firms Imitate Each Other?', *Academy of Management Review* 31.2: 366-85.

Mackey, A., T.B. Mackey and J.B. Barney (2007) 'Corporate Social Responsibility and Firm Performance: Investor Preferences and Corporate Strategies', *Academy of Management Review* 32: 817-35.

Margolis, J.D., and J.P. Walsh (2003) 'Misery Loves Companies: Rethinking Social Initiatives by Business', *Administrative Science Quarterly* 48: 268-305.

——, H.A. Elfenbein and J.P. Walsh (2007) 'Does it Pay to be Good? A Meta-analysis and Redirection of Research on the Relationship between Corporate Social and Financial Performance', www.unglobalcompact.org/NewsandEvents/articles_and_papers/margolis_november_07.pdf, accessed 11 April 2009.

Matten, D., and J. Moon (2008) ' "Implicit" and "Explicit" CSR: A Conceptual Framework for a Comparative Understanding of Corporate Social Responsibility', *Academy of Management Review* 33.2: 404-24.

McWilliams, A., and D. Siegel (2001) 'Corporate Social Responsibility: A Theory of Firm Perspective', *Academy of Management Review* 33.2: 404-24.

——, D. Siegel and P.M. Wright (2006) 'Corporate Social Responsibility: Strategic Implications', *Journal of Management Studies* 43.1: 1-18.

Meyer, J.W., and B. Rowan (1977) 'Institutional Organizations: Formal Structure as Myth and Ceremony', *American Journal of Sociology* 26.1: 117-27.

Oliver, C. (1991) 'Strategic Responses to Institutional Processes', *Academy of Management Review* 16.1: 145-79.

Orlitzky, M., F.L. Schmidt and S.L. Rynes (2003) 'Corporate Social and Financial Performance: A Meta-analysis', *Organization Studies* 24.3: 403-41.

Porter, M.E. (1985) *Competitive Advantage: Creating and Sustaining Superior Performance* (New York: The Free Press).

—— and M.R. Kramer (2006) 'Strategy and Society: The Link between Competitive Advantage and Corporate Social Responsibility', *Harvard Business Review* 84.12: 78-92.

Reinhardt, F. (1998). 'Environmental Product Differentiation: Implications for Corporate Strategy', *California Management Review* 40.4: 43-73.

Siegel, D.S., and D.F. Vitaliano (2007) 'An Empirical Analysis of the Strategic Use of Corporate Social Responsibility', *Journal of Economics & Management Strategy* 16.3: 773-92.

Spar, D., and L. La Mure (2003) 'The Power of Activism: Assessing the Impact of NGOs on Global Business', *California Management Review* 45.3: 78-101.

Suchman, M.C. (1995) 'Managing Legitimacy: Strategic and Institutional Approaches', *Academy of Management Review* 20: 571-610.

Sunstein, C.R. (2008) 'Wall Street's Lemmings', *The New Republic*, 11 October 2008; www.tnr.com/article/politics/wall-streets-lemmings, accessed 24 March 2010.

Sustainable Life Media (2009) 'Cellphone Makers Pledge Universal Charger by 2012', www.sustainablelifemedia.com/content/story/strategy/cellphone_makers_to_develop_universal_cellphone_charger, accessed 11 April 2009.

Teerlak, A. (2007) 'Order without Law? The Role of Certified Management Standards in Shaping Socially Desired Firm Behaviours', *Academy of Management Review* 32.3: 968-85.

Tetrault Sirsly, C.A., and K. Lamertz (2008) 'When Does a Corporate Social Responsibility Initiative Provide a First-Mover Advantage?', *Business & Society* 47.3: 343-69.

Vogel, D. (2008) 'The Private Regulation of Global Corporate Conduct: Achievements and Limitations', paper presented at the *Transatlantic Business Ethics Conference*, Milan, 2–3 October 2008.

Waddock, S. (2008) 'Building a New Institutional Infrastructure for Corporate Responsibility', *Academy of Management Perspectives* 22.3: 87-108.

Weigelt, K., and C. Camerer (1988) 'Reputation and Corporate Strategy: A Review of Recent Theory and Applications', *Strategic Management Journal* 9.5: 443-54.

World Steel Association (2008) 'World Steel Association Sets Target for Data Collection', www.worldsteel.org/?action=newsdetail&id=252, accessed 23 October 2008.

# 4

# CSR
## An opportunity for SMEs

**Denise Baden**
University of Southampton, UK

Corporate social responsibility (CSR) can encompass a whole range of perspectives and activities. What comes under the banner of CSR for any given company will depend in part on the issues of the day. For example, fears regarding climate change are increasing focus on environmental issues and carbon management. Also it will depend on the nature of the organisation and the sector—labour issues may be prominent in companies that outsource much of their work to factories in the developing world, for example, and environmental issues will be more pertinent to a mining company than a retailer. How CSR is perceived and responded to will also depend on firm size. Whereas multinational corporations (MNCs) need to protect their reputations and their brand image, small and medium-sized enterprises (SMEs) are more reliant on their reputation within a smaller network of contacts.

SMEs are defined within Europe as any business with fewer than 250 employees. SMEs are an important part of the national and global economy, accounting for 99.8% of European enterprises, and 66% of total employment. Alongside their economic impact, SMEs have a social and environmental impact. It has been estimated that SMEs are the largest contributors to pollution, carbon dioxide ($CO_2$) emissions and commercial waste (NetRegs 2003). SMEs are therefore crucial in helping to deliver local and national targets set by government. For example, the UK government's Climate Change Act (2008) makes the UK the first country in the world to have a legally binding long-term framework to both cut $CO_2$ emissions and adapt to climate change. At present the target is to reduce emissions by at least 26% by 2020, and 80% by 2050, against the 1990 baseline.

Attention is thus beginning to be paid to ways in which SMEs can be encouraged to engage in the CSR agenda. The UK government's CSR website (www.csr.gov. uk) defines CSR as: 'the voluntary actions that business can take, over and above compliance with legal requirements, to address both its own competitive interests and the interests of wider society'. The International Strategic Framework for CSR was launched in 2005, and sets out the overall objectives and priorities of the UK government's approach towards the international dimension of CSR and defines its vision for CSR, which is: 'to see UK businesses taking account of their economic, social and environmental impacts, and acting to address the key sustainable development challenges based on their core competences wherever they operate—locally, regionally and internationally'.

A proliferation of agencies and organisations to promote and facilitate CSR has emerged at the regional, national, European and global levels. For example Business in the Community (BITC), CSR Academy and the United Nations Global Compact all aim to provide support and incentives for businesses large and small to demonstrate social and environmental responsibility. Several organisations focus specifically on SMEs. In the UK, the Small Business Consortium was set up in 2002 to provide resources for SMEs, such as advice on how they can enhance both their reputation and their bottom line. One useful initiative has been their website (www.smallbusinessjourney.com), which provides case studies and examples of firms that have made a difference, and also benefited as a result. The UK government has published numerous reports and handbooks, such as the handbook produced by the Small Business Service entitled *Encouraging Responsible Business* (2002). Furthermore, a social responsibility module has been added to the SME Benchmark Index, and a new international standard in CSR (ISO 26000) is due for release in 2010.

So how are SMEs responding to the challenge of CSR and what are the key issues they face? A common finding is that most SMEs are unfamiliar with CSR terminology and do not see any connections between these concepts and their business (Toyne 2003; FSB 2007; Baden *et al.* 2009). Furthermore, the term 'corporate' in CSR leads many to perceive CSR as the domain of big business. This is partly due to their sheer size and influence: for example, of the world's 100 largest economic entities, 51 are corporations and 49 are countries, and thus their behaviour is more subject to scrutiny. Although MNCs have dominated the CSR discourse, their visibility makes them more vulnerable to reputational damage, and thus MNCs tend to make every effort to publicise their CSR credentials: most FTSE 100 companies have dedicated CSR reports available on their websites.

This approach to CSR is in stark contrast to that of SMEs. Research into SMEs suggests that many are not realising the strategic advantages of their CSR activities. While large companies are very canny about promoting their social and environmental credentials, SMEs rarely publicise their CSR activities. For example, in a recent survey of UK SMEs, only a quarter recognised the benefits of demonstrating social or environmental responsibility to their customers (FSB 2007). However, the same research also indicated that most SMEs were engaged in CSR-type activities, even if they were not being categorised as such. These include environmental policies, waste reduction through recycling, community support, positive working environments and support for conservation areas.

In comparison with large companies, SMEs have characteristics that mean they are well placed to engage in CSR. Although SMEs may be less reliant on brand image than MNCs, they are more reliant on the nature of their personal relationships with their immediate stakeholders: that is, how are they perceived by their staff, their creditors, the local regulators, their suppliers and their key customers. In contrast to large companies, the small entrepreneur experiences first-hand the territory in which he or she operates, and shares with the local community both results and worries (Longo *et al.* 2005). SMEs can thus be particularly sensitive to the problems surrounding social responsibility. Rather than couching such an attitude in terms of CSR, though, the SME approach tends to be more rooted in common sense and experience: for example, by appreciating the tenet that when you are rooted within a local community 'what goes around, comes around'.

In addition, as many SMEs are owned and managed by the same person, the owner-manager has the freedom and power to implement CSR strategies without having to answer to a board of directors or shareholders. This can allow SMEs to be flexible and speedy in their response to changing market conditions. The new business environment with increased focus on environmental and social factors presents opportunities for entrepreneurial SMEs to apply their creativity and flexibility to adopt innovative processes and/or products that fulfil, or even anticipate, the developing CSR agenda. The less hierarchical, less bureaucratic and more personal culture of SMEs also allows for easier transmission of values throughout the organisation, which results in CSR-type policies being both more readily communicated and more immediately realised in terms of their effect on organisational culture and employee motivation.

SMEs are also valued for being the source of much innovation. Jenkins (2006) interviewed 24 SMEs in the UK known for their social responsibility. Most revealed that they began by looking at how they can demonstrate responsibility in the areas where they as a business had the most impact. Some of these activities were quite innovative: for example, a construction company that developed and promoted sustainable timber construction, and a property development company that uses its position to stimulate urban regeneration. Also, necessity can be the mother of invention, and SMEs, through their lack of time and resources, are often driven to find new and innovative ways of doing things for less.

It could be argued that, if SMEs are engaged with CSR, albeit without realising it, then it does not really matter that the terminology and the issues are not fully understood. This argument has some merit, especially when contrasted with the 'greenwashing' activities of some MNCs who have been accused of putting their energies into publicising rather than practising CSR. However, by understanding the real drivers behind the CSR agenda, SMEs can position themselves to use their innovative capacity to address these issues, and realise sustained competitive advantage in the long term. Consideration of the current challenges faced by governments such as sustainable development and waste management can thus enable businesses to anticipate where future regulation or other pressures may come into force that may have an impact on their business. It is likely to become more difficult to dispose of waste as the cost of waste disposal increases and landfill sites become fewer, for example. Businesses are then likely to be pressured into adopting waste-minimisation policies or face large costs.

## Business case for CSR

The notion of strategic or 'instrumental CSR', which focuses on the complementarity of a company's economic and social/environmental goals, has gained increasing currency in recent years. Increases in energy prices and in social and environmental regulation have meant that those companies that proactively pursued CSR activities have been able to reap the reward. Jenkins's (2006) research with UK SMEs revealed that, although CSR activities were generally undertaken for their own sake, all of the SMEs talked about the business benefits of CSR. In some cases these were quantifiable in terms of reduced costs, for example for environmental initiatives, but in many cases they were more intangible, such as increased employee motivation, improved image or better market position. These findings are in accordance with much of the literature that focuses on the business case for CSR.

One can distinguish between internal benefits and external benefits accruing to a firm from their CSR activities. Internal benefits may be experienced as decreased operating costs. Often firms that decide to take on environmental initiatives (e.g. recycling, waste reduction, pollution prevention, water conservation) will be able to obtain grants and assistance, in addition to the cost savings resulting from waste minimisation and energy efficiency (Branco and Rodrigues 2006). A more subtle, but no less potent outcome can be that the mere act of considering CSR strategically and engaging with stakeholders in a proactive manner in itself generates skills that are crucial to good management and firm success. Thus greater management expertise is a potential resource arising from CSR. The processes involved in taking a strategic approach to CSR could be viewed as a form of in-house management training, which can constitute a managerial competence that can have far-reaching effects. External benefits can include better relations with external stakeholders, such as customers, creditors, regulators, suppliers, investors and even competitors. There are also many recent studies demonstrating benefits of CSR in terms of attracting and retaining staff, and improved motivation and organisational commitment (Branco and Rodrigues 2006).

## Ethical purchasing

One of the business benefits of CSR for SMEs is its potential to increase sales. There has been a vast growth in ethical consumption by individual consumers over the last decade. This includes expenditure on any product or service where ethical decisions come into play, such as free-range eggs, fair-trade goods, renewable energy, ethical investments, decision to buy from local shops and so on. According to the *Ethical Consumerism Report* (November 2007), published by The Co-operative Bank, household expenditure on ethical goods and services has almost doubled in the past five years. The average rate of growth for ethical consumerism is 15% per annum since 2002, which compares with 5% pa for overall household expenditure. Simon Williams, Director of Corporate Affairs at CFS, said in 2007:

> The market share for ethical food and drink appears to have broken through the 'green' glass ceiling of 5 per cent, and factoring in the effect of consumer boycotts, this market share could be as high as 7 per cent. Potentially, we could see market share hit ten per cent in the next year or two (Co-operative Bank 2007).

Despite growth in the ethical market being triple that of overall average growth, there has been some cynicism about this trend; some point out that ethical consumption is still a niche market, with most consumers still purchasing on price. However, another increasing trend is that of sustainable procurement by governmental organisations. The European Union (EU) for example has looked at the power of procurement strategies that include CSR-type criteria alongside value for money variables as a means to promote CSR among their suppliers. The EU, alongside many national governments, is beginning to include CSR criteria into its purchasing strategies, with CSR, in most cases, being treated as a qualifier for tendering to supply (Harwood and Humby 2008).

MNCs are also starting to recognise that their own exposure to environmental matters is directly linked to that of their suppliers. Companies have used supply chain auditing to provide bottom-line benefits for decades. It is now being extended to protect the triple bottom line, by including social and environmental factors alongside economic factors, helping smaller businesses prepare to respond through innovation, and improving the overall carbon efficiency of the end product. Another compelling reason for MNCs to include CSR criteria in their purchasing decisions is to mitigate reputational damage. The reputational damage suffered by Nike when conditions in its suppliers' factories became known is a good example. Instead of symbolising sport and achievement, the Nike logo symbolised sweatshops and exploitation and Nike had to invest a lot of resources before that began to change.

Suppliers chosen for their CSR credentials can offer a competitive edge to large companies tendering for huge government contracts. For example, in the UK, Bovis recently won a £2.4 billion schools contract, with the head of supply chain management at Bovis claiming that the work done on improving the sustainability of suppliers and contractors gave his company the edge: 'we won that bid based on the supply chain management and diversity policies because we had all of this in place and could demonstrate it' (see Rae 2009). SMEs wanting to supply Bovis needed to satisfy the company on their environmental policies, waste management practices, codes of conduct and ethical policies, and carbon footprint, as well as their own procurement polices (i.e. whether fair trade, sustainably sourced, etc.).

A report by the UK Department of Trade and Industry claimed that

> CSR is likely to become an increasingly important business issue for many SMEs in future. This is partly because of the increasing take-up of ethical codes of practice by their large customers, which is creating a pressure for demonstrably responsible behaviour back down the supply chain (DTI 2002: 31).

Over half of UK retailers in 2005 had codes of conduct for their suppliers (Starcher 2005). Interviews with nine large UK businesses from a variety of sectors on their procurement strategies revealed that CSR-type criteria were generally not used as a decision variable alongside the usual value for money variables, but did tend to be used as a qualifier for submitting a tender (Harwood and Humby 2008). However, there was evidence that CSR-type criteria were used in the selection process in marginal cases. The trend now is increasingly for large companies to share information about the CSR performance of potential suppliers, to reduce duplication of assessment and monitoring (Tuppen, cited in Harwood and Humby 2008). This reduces costs of supply chain management for the large buyers, but it also means that it raises the stakes for the SME suppliers. Suppliers may find that if they are rejected by one buyer for failing to meet CSR criteria, they may find to their shock that they do not get another chance with other buyers who have pooled knowledge.

A study of the perceptions of UK firms indicated that many SMEs were worried about being excluded from large contracts because of CSR criteria. Many of the businesses questioned had noticed an increase in the demand from large organisations for suppliers to include social issues in the tendering process, in addition to increases in regulations relating to health and safety and the environment (Roberts *et al*. 2006). Similarly an online survey of its readers by *Strategic Risk* online magazine in 2006 found that 20% of firms reported that environmental/CSR issues were their biggest supply chain risk, and 25% of firms required their suppliers to adhere to CSR in order to mitigate supply chain risk (Anon 2006 cited in Harwood and Humby 2008). These finding are not confined to the UK. In a Danish study, 60% of SMEs reported being asked to comply with requirements from buyers; some buyers asked about CSR issues in general, and others required compliance with specific criteria such as health and safety or environmental criteria (Jørgensen and Knudsen 2006).

A comparison of research on CSR and SMEs carried out in 2007 with research carried out in 2002 indicates that buyer pressure with respect to CSR-type criteria is on the increase. In the 2007 sample, 67% of the respondents said they had to satisfy customers with respect to health and safety criteria compared with 60% in 2002; 55% on environmental issues in 2007, compared with 43% in 2002; and 43% on employee issues and 35% on community issues in 2007, compared with 16% on social community commitment in 2002 (Baden *et al*. 2009). Thus one of the risks of not engaging in CSR expressed by SMEs is exclusion from supply chains.

## Risk management versus value creation

The response of SMEs to the increasing pressures on business to demonstrate social and environmental responsibility can vary from avoidance of such criteria by refusing to supply where such requirements exist, to compliance, all the way through to a proactive strategic stance towards CSR. Among those firms that do engage in CSR, there is similarly a distinction between those who take predominantly a risk-management approach, designed to avoid risk of not engaging in CSR, and those who take a proactive strategic approach, seeing CSR as an opportunity for value creation. Fombrun *et al*. (2000) classed these perspectives as 'safety nets' and 'opportunities', respectively. An opportunity perspective focuses on ways in which the firm can achieve a competitive advantage through its social and environmental practices: for example, through improved reputation, employee motivation, customer loyalty, creditor or regulator flexibility, favourable media coverage, more efficient use of resources and attaining preferred supplier status for CSR-aware buyers. On the other hand, the safety net perspective aims to avoid fines and penalties from non-compliance with social or environmental regulations, avoid reputation damage from poor practice, avoid defection of partners, threats of legal action or negative media exposure, threats to value from investors and so on.

It is argued by Porter and Kramer (2006) that companies should take a strategic approach to CSR, based on the premise of interdependence between society and business. This involves both addressing any negative social impacts and seeking opportunities to distinguish themselves by strategic social engagement that focuses on issues that build on the businesses' particular strengths. CSR can thus be seen as enlightened self-interest if companies look for opportunities to attain competitive advantage by identifying social initiatives that provide the greatest shared value to both the business and society. This positive view of CSR is echoed by Grayson and Hodges (2004: 9) who make the case that drivers for business success are linked to 'a willingness to look for creativity and innovation from non-traditional areas— including CSR'.

So do SMEs take a reactive stance, limiting themselves to legislative compliance, or do they take a strategic approach, looking for ways to increase their competitive advantage through their social and environmental practices? Many small businesses see CSR as relating to large organisations, and view attempts to inflict CSR on SMEs as a cost burden and external threat. Often such attitudes are based on a view of CSR as externally imposed regulation relating to social and environmental issues, in contrast to the EU definition of CSR as voluntary (Baden *et al.* 2009). The literature on SMEs' responses to environmental legislation is revealing in this respect. Findings indicate that many SMEs are not fully aware of the environmental legislation that affects them and that most action to improve environmental performance is driven by a fear of prosecution (Taylor *et al.* 2003). For example, a study of environmental initiatives in the UK screen-printing sector found that improvements in environmental performance tended to be driven by and limited to legislative compliance, particularly for the smaller firms (Worthington and Patton 2005). Few managers had the vision to anticipate future threats or opportunities, and thus did not consider the opportunities to exploit these environmental developments to gain a competitive advantage, to access new markets or to differentiate their products. While many companies identified benefits from their environmental improvements, the predominantly reactive approach meant that innovative responses to regulation such as seeking out ways to eliminate environmental damage at source, or develop first-mover advantages, were not considered.

Another reason to be proactive rather than reactive to factors such as increasing environmental regulation is that findings demonstrate that it is easier to implement sustainable systems in advance, rather than after external stakeholders require it (Andersen and Skovgaard 2008). Without a good environmental track record it is becoming harder to obtain insurance and financial backing as the relevant bodies will see the company as risky to insure or to finance. Regulation and fiscal instruments also put pressure on companies to respond to the need to make environmental improvements. Businesses face the risk of being outside the law and being fined if they do not comply.

Many SMEs thus take a fire-fighting approach, focusing on tasks that appear urgent, but may not be important, rather than those that are important but not urgent. This is understandable when struggling for survival on a day-to-day basis, but SMEs risk losing out unless they make time to take a strategic, long-term view of where their business is going, how it is getting there, and what future issues may become more prominent. One piece of advice for SMEs suggested by the UK Small Business Consortium is to make the effort to identify parts of their existing business aims and policies that show social responsibility and build on these. Doing this in a structured way as you go along, and building on this to develop statements of values, mission statements, environmental policies or whatever is pertinent to the type of company will provide a useful document to refer to when faced with buyers who may ask for such documentation (UK Small Business Consortium 2006).

## Meeting the challenge of sustainable development

One look at the targets set by the EU and by the UK government in particular should alert any future-oriented company to the possibility of radical changes in the business environment, and priorities given to CSR factors. The key challenge is that of sustainable development, which is defined as: 'Development that meets the needs of the present without compromising the ability of future generations to meet their own needs' (Brundtland Commission 1987). It is generally accepted that our present way of life does not meet this criteria of sustainability. If everyone in the world were to consume natural resources and generate $CO_2$ at the rate we do in Europe, we'd need three planets to support us, or five planets if we consumed at the level of the US.[1] One-third of diversity has been lost in the last 35 years, in part because we now consume resources 30% faster than the world can replenish them. In other words, we are no longer living off the interest; we are eating into natural capital. Add to this the prospect of population growth: world population was 3 billion in 1960, 6 billion in 1999 and projected to be 9 billion in 2050, and we are facing severe resource constraints (WWF website). This then gives rise to the necessity to be much more efficient in our use of resources.

There is also the issue of climate change. A full discussion of the research is beyond the scope of this chapter, but sufficient to say that increases in global temperatures mirror growth in GDP, greenhouse gas emissions and in oil consumption, and decline in glacier thickness (IPCC 2007). This raises the necessity to reduce our carbon dependence and limit our emissions of greenhouse gases, which have

1 WWF website: www.wwf.org.uk/what_we_do/about_us/building_a_one_planet_future. cfm, accessed 2 April 2009.

been demonstrated to be the key controllable factor in global warming. We already have solutions to these issues, and know what we should be doing or not doing, but the problem is behavioural change. For example, we are aware that taking the train is more sustainable than flying, and walking or cycling is more environmentally friendly than driving, and that driving a small car generally consumes less fuel than driving a big car. The issue is encouraging people to choose the more sustainable options. This is where governments are using a mixture of economic incentives and legislation to encourage more sustainable lifestyles.

The EU's carbon trading scheme is one attempt to incentivise carbon minimisation. The idea is to set a cap on carbon by setting national allocations, and allowing organisations to sell surpluses, or buy the extra they need on the carbon market. The initial phase of the project was accused of offering overly generous carbon allowances that resulted in the price of carbon being too cheap to provide an incentive to invest in low-carbon processes and technologies. In the second phase, however, more stringent allocations have been set that have raised the cost of carbon. The aim is to meet the goals set at the 1997 Kyoto climate change conference to reduce greenhouse gas emissions to 5.5% below 1990 emissions. There are plans to expand the scheme to include more sectors and more gases, such as nitrous oxide.

It is only relatively recently therefore that the carbon trading scheme has offered any real economic incentive to reduce $CO_2$ emissions; however, now this cap-and-trade scheme is in its second phase, this will start to affect the business landscape in a more visible way. Signs of the increased weight put on carbon can be seen in the plethora of agencies, websites and software available to help individuals and businesses calculate their carbon footprint. In addition, a number of companies have made a start on introducing carbon labelling. For example, Tesco, the UK's biggest retailer, has said it would put new labels on every one of the 70,000 products it sells so that shoppers can compare carbon costs in the same way they can compare salt content and calorie counts.

Adjusting to this new business environment is a must for those businesses who hope to gain custom from public sector organisations. The UK government, for example, has begun working with the Carbon Disclosure Project in its initiative to analyse supplier emissions to help create more sustainable supply chains. UK government organisations including Defra, Office of Government Commerce, the Foreign and Commonwealth Office and the V&A Museum will be studying the carbon footprints within each of their supply chains.

Going even further is the proposal put forward by the former UK Environment Secretary, David Miliband, to issue personal carbon 'credit cards'. Miliband commissioned a five-year study in 2006 into the feasibility of allocating an annual allowance of carbon, with the card being swiped on items such as travel, energy or food. Clearly as carbon labelling becomes more widespread, there are more opportunities for such a scheme to be a reasonably comprehensive carbon rationing scheme. As with the carbon trading scheme, the initial idea is that those who used less than their allowance could sell any surplus to those who wanted more.

In the face of issues such as climate change and resource constraints, one has to wonder how far the governmental response will go, and what that may mean for business. Will carbon become the new currency? Are we seeing a new model for business that goes beyond the traditional self-interest model, but instead requires businesses to take a hand in meeting these important challenges? Certainly there are signs that some of the large MNCs seem to be moving in new directions. One unprecedented move has been for a consortium of technology companies to forfeit their intellectual property rights by joining an eco-patent commons. For example, Bosch, DuPont and Xerox have pledged to publicly provide the patent for their environmentally friendly technologies, which include Xerox's method for hazardous waste removal, DuPont's technology to convert non-recyclable plastics into fertiliser, and Bosch's automotive technologies that reduce fuel consumption and emissions.

Clearly as consumers of resources and providers of the world's products and services, businesses, both large and small, will be expected to play their part in meeting these challenges. This makes it an exciting time to be in business. Businesses that take a defensive, reactive approach that focuses on compliance will experience these changing times as a seemingly non-stop proliferation of regulation and changing goalposts, as customers, large MNCs and policy-makers alike try to reconcile economic, social and environmental requirements. However, going on the offensive, looking forward to the challenges ahead and positioning yourself to be part of the solution, rather than part of the problem, will engender a more creative, innovative and rewarding frame of mind. Kramer and Kania (2006: 23) suggest that, rather than viewing CSR as a 'vulnerability—an external risk to be managed with the least possible investment', businesses would benefit from seeing CSR as 'an opportunity for valuable social impact or competitive differentiation'. A number of writers have commented on the strategic potential of taking a proactive stance towards CSR.

> If problems are only opportunities in work clothes, could climate change turn into the snappiest dresser in town? It's time the UK's smallest businesses had a good look in the mirror, and opened up a whole new wardrobe of potential (McLachlan 2005).

One of the qualities that SMEs are prized for is their innovative capacity, and it is in the hugely growing green market that innovation is most strongly sought after. One example of green innovation is B9 Energy, a wind farm development and maintenance business. Managing director David Surplus turned his headquarters into a low-carbon showcase, using thorough insulation, special Pilkington K glass, photovoltaic panels, a 6 kW wind turbine and sophisticated solar water heating.

Willow trees for the wood-burning stove are grown in the grounds. 'By showing it is possible for an office building to be almost self-sufficient,' says Surplus, 'we are raising our own profile, as well as that of renewable energy.' A £75,000 grant from the (now defunct) NI Energy Demonstration Scheme helped with the cost.

Similarly the French shipping company CTMV decided to save nearly 125 g of carbon per bottle of wine, by shipping wine using barges and sailing boats. Frédéric Albert, founder of the shipping company said: 'My idea was to do something for the planet and something for the wines of Languedoc. One of my grandfathers was a wine-maker and one was a sailor.' The green nature of the project attracted publicity, investment and customers. The growing ethical investment market made the project easy to fund, with seven private investors contributing 70% of the business's start-up costs; in an interview about the business (see *Observer* 2008) Albert said some 250 producers in Languedoc alone were keen to use his ships.

With increasing energy prices and likelihood of increased regulation in the field of carbon management, any company that can get ahead of the game by taking action to improve its environmental credentials stands to gain, both in terms of reduced costs and in terms of becoming preferred suppliers, both to CSR-focused buyers from the public sector with commitments to further Millennium Development Goals, and to buyers from large organisations looking to preserve their social and environmental credentials. As several large UK companies such as National Grid and DHL are now incorporating carbon-related performance targets into the bonus structures of their managers and CEOs, the pressure to demonstrate carbon savings is likely to increase even further (see Murray 2009). Those SMEs that are proactive in demonstrating they meet buyers' requirements in these areas will attain a competitive advantage over other companies that are slower to react.

In its consultation paper on sustainable development, for example, the former UK Department of the Environment, Transport and the Regions (DETR 1998) suggested that the provision of 'greener' products can enable business to create new markets, increase business competitiveness and build customer trust. The success of the Toyota Prius and other hybrid cars is a well-known example. Similarly the Aeron chair made by Herman Miller is an example of eco-design: 62% of the chair is made from recycled material and 94% of it can be recycled. Parts are easy to disassemble and components are clearly marked to help in the recycling stream. Thomas Friedman (2008) coined the term 'out-greening', claiming that this will be the winning strategy for the future as old strategies such as out-performing or out-consuming that rely on diminishing resources become less viable. Friedman claims that companies that out-green their competitors do so generally via efficiency (or conservation) and innovation.

Thus SMEs who do take a strategic stance towards CSR have the potential to develop innovative responses to the new challenges, which can offer them a first-mover advantage and enable them to gain cost advantages, to access new markets and to differentiate their products. For example, in preparations for the 2012 Olympic Games in London, contracts are being awarded based on much more than price. Construction firms that can demonstrate eco-friendly trucks, waste minimisation and recycling policies will gain an edge when pitching to the Olympic Delivery Authority which is aiming for the greenest possible games.

SMEs wanting a slice of this rapidly growing pie need to ask themselves how their particular business is responding to these changing priorities. Can more environmentally friendly materials be used? Can better products that incorporate full life-cycle analysis be designed? How can these be designed to either last longer or be re-usable or recyclable? Firms that take the initiative to incorporate these environmentally friendly features into the design stage will find that sales will kick off as more large organisations are under pressure to consider, not only their own environmental practices, but also those of their suppliers. In particular the government and the EU have made commitments to encourage sustainable design through their purchasing power.

One inspiring example is that of Kresse Wesling[2] who applied her entrepreneurial talents to a number of environmental problems:

> I was working at a venture capital company in Hong Kong, an exciting city that had and still has some serious environmental issues; there was no recycling and no sewage treatment and also no shortage of waste. I was 24 when I had the opportunity to set up my first company, Bio-Supplies, which makes and sells environmental packaging alternatives. I thought, if I'm going to work from 5 am–10 pm everyday, I might as well do something that excites me!
>
> Two years later I relocated to the UK to expand Bio-Supplies and also started Babaloo, a company that produces a range of ethical and environmental products for parents and babies. Then last year I encountered another environmental problem. The London Fire Brigade was sending its decommissioned fire hose to landfill, after several years of active duty. My partner and I founded EAKO to take on this hose and other commercial and industrial wastes so that they could be transformed. We make a range of incredibly beautiful lifestyle products and 50% of our profits go to charities affiliated with the waste; from the fire hose line, 50% of our profits go to the Fire Brigade's Benevolent Fund.
>
> Days after starting the business we were asked by the team behind Live Earth to make 500 belts in three weeks. Supplying our very cool carbon free belts for the London concert was our first big challenge and took us from cottage industry to full-scale production literally overnight.

2 socialenterpriseambassadors.org.uk/content/view/106/74, accessed 2 April 2009.

# Certifications and awards

Developing competences in environmental management, and attaining certification is another way of opening doors to large orders, more customers, and may also enable premium prices to be charged. For example large organisations that require their suppliers to conform to CSR-type criteria often do so by specifying certain certifications such as ISO 14001 (environmental sustainability) or OHSAS 18001 (Health and Safety); SA8000 (social accountability); ISO 9001 (quality management), and upcoming specific CSR certification ISO 26000. Some SMEs are very aware of the competitive advantage such certifications can provide: for example, a Catalan company interviewed on its CSR practices responded: 'we not only sell parts, we also sell certifications' (Murillo and Lozano 2006). Similarly many of the companies interviewed by Jenkins (2006) on their CSR practices had followed the route of certification. For example, a printing company realised its greatest impact was environmental, and thus went for ISO 14001 accreditation as a systematic means of improving its environmental performance: for example, by switching to water-based inks, using recycled paper and reducing its waste and emissions.

Organisations such as the EU, the Department for Business, Enterprise and Regulatory Reform (now called Department for Business, Innovation and Skills), CSR Europe and BITC are keen to recognise any company that exhibits good CSR practices, often publicising case studies as an example to other businesses. Several of the companies interviewed by Jenkins (2006) found that entering awards, such as the BITC award, both helped to publicise their efforts, and helped them to think about their activities in a more systematic fashion, enabling the development of a specific CSR strategy. Any company that proactively seizes the initiative on social and environmental issues and proactively publicises its stance can find that exposure snowballs from there as NGOs keen to encourage such practices distribute awards and accolades freely; researchers keen for case studies, businesses keen to follow suit and CSR-related agencies refer to the company in articles, quoting it as an example of best practice, or innovation. The company may find very quickly that its CSR credentials are its biggest asset.

For example, a UK company, Ormiston Wire, gained public recognition when it received the Queen's Award for Sustainable Development in 2002, for its activities in terms of enhancing the company's impact on the local community and wider environment. Managing Director Mark Ormiston admitted that the initial motivation was looking for cost savings during the recession of the 1990s:

> That's when we realised that we were very wasteful with our energy, heating the factory after we'd gone home, and leaving lights on all night. We invested in automated systems to minimise energy use and maximise efficiency, such as fans to blow hot air back to the factory floor (McLachlan 2005).

The company implemented a wide range of initiatives that included ISO 14001 certification, the purchase of electricity from renewable sources and the installation of efficiency measures, including higher-efficiency lighting, occupancy detectors, water-saving devices, and high rates of packaging recycling via a customer deposit scheme. Encouraged by the award, the company went on to install 220 solar panels and a wind turbine. Ormiston can now claim that his business has 'one of the lowest carbon footprints in the UK' and that his green policies save in the region of £20,000 a year. He believes that these savings are easily available to all SMEs but that 'whilst a lot of British business people know about their products, they don't know how to run the operations side, nor are they prepared to be innovative'. Similarly, Reed Paget, the MD of Belu Water, which launched the UK's first 'carbon neutral' bottled water, recently won the *Independent* newspaper's Social Entrepreneur of the Year Award, as profits are used to fund clean water projects around the world. Reed also developed the 'Penguin Approved' consumer product certification stamp which is for goods and services that have reduced and offset all their emissions measured over their entire life-cycle.

## Conclusion

This chapter presented an overview of some of the distinctive challenges and opportunities open to SMEs as a result of the increasing focus on CSR: for example, when large organisations include CSR-type criteria in their purchasing decisions. This trend, whether it is known as ethical consumption or sustainable procurement, has implications for SMEs that are only just beginning to be felt. However, the flurry of organisations, research, conferences and policy papers pertaining to this topic suggest that those SMEs that can anticipate these changes in procurement criteria and position themselves to take advantage of them may find they have a sustainable competitive advantage over those who have failed to adapt.

Some companies have taken a defensive approach to CSR, including opposition, ignorance or seeing CSR as a risk to be managed. The risk management approach, for example, tends to involve a reactive stance to community and legal requirements, compliance with current regulation and standards, and focuses on reducing the risk of sanctions or lack of business for failing to meet minimum standards. This is fine as far as it goes, but the focus is mostly negative, avoiding rather than striving. A more positive approach is to see CSR as an opportunity to access new markets and increase efficiency. The concept of eco-efficiency (Schmidheiny 1992) is based on the concept of creating more goods and services while using fewer resources and creating less waste and pollution. This is one of the win–win strategies open to business, because, while achieving eco-efficiency can result in short-term costs as processes and equipment may need to be changed, there are cost savings that will benefit the business in the long term, and also lead to the potential attraction of new business, and positive employee and customer responses.

There is now an emerging trend which views CSR as a means of gaining long-term strategic advantage. The term 'corporate social opportunity' (e.g. Grayson and Hodges 2004) has been proposed in order to capture the more proactive stance that many forward-thinking companies are now adopting. It also captures the point that it is much more empowering to be motivated by the positive than by the negative. It is hoped that this chapter, by presenting examples of some businesses that have used their innovative capacity to meet the challenges of the future head on, has not only demonstrated the value of a strategic proactive approach to CSR to the business, but has also provided inspiration to any who want to achieve success and make a positive contribution to society at the same time.

# References

Andersen, M., and R.G. Skovgaard (2008) *Small Suppliers in Global Supply Chains* (Copenhagen: Danish Commerce and Companies Agency).

Baden, D., I. Harwood and D. Woodward (2009) 'The Effect of Buyer Pressure on Suppliers to Demonstrate CSR: An Added Incentive or Counterproductive?' *European Journal of Management* 27.6: 429-41 (dx.doi.org/10.1016/j.emj.2008.10.004).

Branco, M.C., and L.L. Rodrigues (2006) 'Corporate Social Responsibility and Resource-Based Perspectives', *Journal of Business Ethics* 69.2: 111-32.

Brundtland Commission (1987) 'Report of the World Commission on Environment and Development', General Assembly Resolution 42/187, 11 December 1987; www.un-documents.net/a42r187.htm, accessed 4 December 2009.

Co-operative Bank (2007) *Ethical Consumer Report*; www.goodwithmoney.co.uk/ethical-consumerism-report-07, accessed 24 March 2010.

DETR (UK Department of the Environment, Transport and the Regions) (1998) *Sustainable Development: Opportunities for Change* (consultation paper on a revised UK strategy; London: DETR).

DTI (UK Department of Trade and Industry) (2002) 'Business and Society: Corporate Social Responsibility Report 2002'.

Fombrun, C., N. Gardberg and M. Barnett (2000) 'Opportunity Platforms and Safety Nets: Corporate Citizenship and Reputational Risk', *Business and Society Review* 105.1: 85-106.

Friedman, F. (2008) *Hot, Flat and Crowded: Why We Need a Green Revolution and How it Can Renew America* (New York: Farrar, Straus & Giroux).

FSB (Federation of Small Businesses) (2007) *Social and Environmental Responsibility and the Small Business Owner* (Blackpool, UK: FSB).

Grayson, D., and A. Hodges (2004) *Corporate Social Opportunity! Seven Steps to Make Corporate Social Responsibility Work for your Business* (Sheffield, UK: Greenleaf Publishing).

Harwood, I.A., and S. Humby (2008) 'Embedding Corporate Responsibility into Supply: A Snapshot of Progress', *European Management Journal* 26.3: 166-74.

IPCC (Intergovernmental Panel on Climate Change) (2007) 'Summary for Policymakers', in S. Solomon, D. Qin, M. Manning, Z. Chen, M. Marquis, K.B. Averyt, M. Tignor and H.L. Miller (eds.), *Climate Change 2007: The Physical Science Basis. Contribution of Working Group I to the Fourth Assessment Report of the Intergovernmental Panel on Climate Change* (Cambridge, UK: Cambridge University Press).

Irwin, D. (2002) *Encouraging Responsible Business* (UK Department of Trade and Industry Small Business Service, March 2002).

Jenkins, H.M. (2006) 'Small Business Champions for Corporate Social Responsibility', *Journal of Business Ethics* 67.3: 241-56.

Jørgensen, I.L., and J.S. Knudsen (2006) *Sustainable Competitiveness in Global Value Chains: How do Danish Small Firms Behave?* (Copenhagen: The Copenhagen Centre).

Kramer, M., and J. Kania (2006) 'Changing the Game: Leading Corporations Switch from Defense to Offense in Solving Global Problems', *Stanford Social Innovation Review*, Spring 2006.

Longo, M., M. Mura and A. Bonoli (2005) 'Corporate Social Responsibility and Corporate Performance: The Case of Italian SMEs', *Corporate Governance* 5.4: 28-42.

McLachlan, M.E. (2005) 'Just how hard is it to . . . reduce the carbon footprint of a small business?', *Green Futures*, 22 June 2005.

Murillo, D., and J.M. Lozano (2006) 'SMEs and CSR: An Approach to CSR in their Own Words', *Journal of Business Ethics* 67.3: 227-40.

Murray, J. (2009) 'National Grid Launches Carbon Remuneration Scheme', Busi-nessGreen;         www.businessgreen.com/business-green/news/2238989/national-grid-launches-carbon, accessed 2 April 2009.

NetRegs (2003) 'SME-nvironment 2003', Environment Agency; www.environment-agency. gov.uk/netregs/links/63809.aspx, accessed 4 December 2009.

*Observer* (2008) 'Eco-friendly French to ship their wine under sail', *The Observer*, 24 February 2008; www.guardian.co.uk/environment/2008/feb/24/food.carbonemissions.

Porter, M., and M. Kramer (2006) 'Strategy and Society: The Link between Competitive Advantage and Corporate Social Responsibility', *Harvard Business Review* 84: 78-92.

Rae, D. (2009) 'Sustainability earns Bovis £2.4bn schools contract', Sustainable Sourcing; www.sustainable-sourcing.com/2009/02/26/sustainability-earns-bovis-24bn-schools-contract, accessed 4 December 2009.

Roberts, S., R. Lawson and J. Nicholls (2006) 'Generating Regional-Scale Improvements in SME Corporate Responsibility Performance: Lessons from Responsibility Northwest', *Journal of Business Ethics* 67.3: 275-86.

Schmidheiny, S. (1992) *Changing Course: A Global Business Perspective on Development and the Environment* (World Business Council for Sustainable Development; Cambridge, MA: MIT Press).

Starcher, G. (2005) *Responsible Entrepreneurship: Engaging Small and Medium Sized Enterprises in Socially and Environmentally Responsible Practices* (Paris: European Bahá'í Business Forum).

Taylor, N., K. Barker and M. Simpson (2003) 'Achieving "Sustainable Business": A Study of Perceptions of Environmental Best Practice by SMEs in South Yorkshire', *Environment and Planning C: Government and Policy* 21.1: 89-105.

Toyne, P. (2003) 'Corporate Social Responsibility: Good Business Practice and a Source of Competitive Edge for SMEs?', paper presented at the *48th World Conference International Council for Small Business: Advancing Entrepreneurship and Small Business*, Belfast, Northern Ireland, 15–18 June 2003.

UK Small Business Consortium (2006) 'Better Business Journey: Helping Small and Medium Sized Businesses to Increase their Profitability and Responsibility', www.smallbusiness-journey.com/files/pdf/BITC%20SME_final%20low%20res.pdf, accessed 4 December 2009.

Worthington, I., and D. Patton (2005) 'Strategic Intent in the Management of the Green Environment within SMEs: An Analysis of the UK Screen-printing Sector', *Long Range Planning* 38.2: 197-212.

# 5
# Competitive advantage from CSR programmes

**Malcolm F. Arnold**
Cranfield University, UK

There has been a steady decline in the belief, argued in the 1970s by Milton Friedman (1970), that business should only be engaged in the pursuit of profit and that concern with wider social responsibility by business was fundamentally wrong. It is now considered entirely possible that corporate social and environmental responsibility programmes are not only compatible with business success, but they also offer managers new ways of creating additional corporate value through strengthening their competitive position.[1] Evidence of this changing management view can be found in the growing number of businesses now running corporate social and environmental responsibility programmes, shortened in this chapter to corporate social responsibility (CSR) programmes.

Both business managers and the investment community need to know what economic effects CSR programmes are having on a business. While it is possible to state the benefits of a particular programme in terms of its social, environmental or

---

1 In this chapter the use of the term **corporate value** specifically means the monetary value of an enterprise. This is the value that the seller of a private enterprise might realise if the enterprise was sold, but is often estimated when a sale is an impractical way of determining value of a privately owned enterprise. It also refers to the enterprise value of a company which has shares traded on a public stock exchange. Use of the word **value** alone is limited to more general concepts of value and benefits. For a discussion of corporate value see a financial management text: for example, Arnold 2005: Part 5.

wider economic outcomes, it is often more difficult to see how a CSR programme would impact on financial performance and corporate value.

Researchers have attempted for some time to identify any direct relationships between CSR performance and financial performance, as a measure of the economic effectiveness of CSR programmes. However the findings have been complex and mixed, and no clear direct link has been identified. Overall CSR programme performance appears to give an improved financial performance, or at worst no improvement, and there is little evidence of CSR programmes worsening financial performance (for an overview of financial studies see Griffin and Mahon 1997; Roman *et al.* 1999; Margolis and Walsh 2003; Orlitzky *et al.* 2003; Allouche and Laroche 2005).

The creation of corporate value in a business results from a firm's operational, marketing and financial performance. This performance is heavily influenced by the firm's competitive position in an industry. CSR programmes often have complex multiple relationships with these areas of business activity, and it is not surprising that attempts to find direct links between CSR performance and financial performance have been so difficult and elusive. However CSR programmes can be considered as an additional opportunity area in the mix of corporate activities which can enhance competitive advantage and complement existing business initiatives.

Grayson and Hodges (2004) outlined how to seize opportunities to deliver the unique business and social benefits offered by CSR programmes in their book *Corporate Social Opportunity!* Further work on competitive strategy by Porter and Kramer (2006) has indicated that CSR activities can be used to improve the competitive advantage and strategic position of a business in an industry. By assessing the improved competitive opportunities offered by CSR activities, we can better judge the potential contributions from CSR to corporate value creation. This chapter applies the Porter–Kramer model to the work of four well-respected CSR leaders and their companies to identify what competitive advantages are offered by their CSR programmes. This model gives a unique view of a CSR programme, identifying its ability to change competitive advantage, and opening a direct path to being able to estimate its contribution to corporate value.

## Theoretical background

Programmes of CSR activities are usually complex and involve many elements which are usually presented to conform to standard reporting practices, such as the

Global Reporting Initiative (GRI).[2] While this is an excellent format for reporting the social, environmental and economic benefits of a CSR programme, it is often difficult to compare the value contribution of one CSR element or programme against another. A common currency of 'value exchange' does not exist, even with so-called 'triple-bottom-line reporting' (TBL). It is also difficult to establish the importance and significance of the interrelationships with other business activities, and to identify a programme's combined influence on a company's competitive position.

Porter and Kramer (2006) propose classification of the CSR activities within a programme.[3] This classification helps identify which CSR activities contribute the most to improving competitive advantage and ultimately to corporate value creation. They identified the four current, main drivers of CSR programmes as 'moral obligation', 'sustainability', 'licence to operate' and 'reputation', while Milliman *et al.* (2008) listed six current drivers: 'bolster the organisation's public image', 'meet needs or pressures from key external stakeholders', 'be in alignment with industry or community expectations', 'protect itself from legal threats', 'provide a source of motivation for employees' and 'achieve a marketing advantage or other direct economic impact'. Whichever list is used, most of the drivers are essentially about acting as good corporate citizens and responding to the expectations or pressure of stakeholders. Only the 'reputation' and 'achieve a marketing advantage or other economic impact' drivers can be considered as strategic.

Business strategists argue that creation of corporate value arises out of developing the strategic position of the firm through improvements to competitiveness. A company has a competitive advantage over its competitors when it can produce greater profitability from sales of its products and services. This increased profitability arises from a combination of lower cost and a higher perceived value for its products. The higher perceived value allows a company to charge higher prices compared with its competitors. Reduced costs and increased customer value produce a higher profit margin on products leading to improved company profits and ultimately increased corporate value.

The financial link between competitive advantage and corporate value arises through the valuation of the forecast future cash flows. The incremental value of a CSR programme can be estimated by using either discounted cash flow (DCF) valuation, or the Rappaport value driver approach (for a financial discussion see, for example, Arnold 2005: 814-28).

---

2   The Global Reporting Initiative (GRI) website contains further information and can be found at www.globalreporting.org (accessed 7 December 2009).
3   Porter and Kramer (2006) were published in the *Harvard Business Review* (HBR), and as such the paper has not undergone the normal academic peer review process. Nevertheless the HBR is a highly respected business journal. The authors were the winners of the 2006 McKinsey Award for their paper.

Porter and Kramer (2006) argue that elements of CSR programmes can be categorised in a way that relates to their strategic nature and importance to a business. They present a classification model for CSR activities which is based on the power of a CSR programme element to change competitive advantage by delivering one or more of four benefits:

- Cost reduction

- Differentiation of products and services from competitors' offerings

- Increased perceived value by customers

- Add some degree of proprietary protection

An in-depth discussion of competitive advantage can be found in Porter 1980.

Porter and Kramer (2006) argue that CSR activities should be considered to be just one component in the business mix, and elements of CSR programmes should be classified in a way that relates to their strategic importance to a business. They present the following classification model (Porter and Kramer 2006: 85-88) and introduce the concept of **responsive CSR** and **strategic CSR** which is further subdivided and defined as outlined below.

## Responsive CSR activities

These are activities that companies undertake in response to the *reasonable expectations of society*. They comprise acting as a good corporate citizen (i.e. being aware of evolving social and environmental concerns of stakeholders) and mitigating existing or anticipated adverse effects from business activities.

### Good citizenship activities

Good citizenship is an essential prerequisite for a credible CSR programme and it needs to be done well if the company is to project a sound image of being genuinely concerned about social and environmental issues. Often it involves community involvement and possibly some philanthropy. If done well the firm creates goodwill and improves relations with key stakeholders and constituencies, but it remains *incidental to the firm's business* and the effects may be only modest.

### Mitigate adverse effects from a firm's value chain activities

These activities mainly occur in the operational areas of the firm and are concerned with achieving best practice with respect to any adverse effects arising out of the firm's value chain activities. The activities follow from an analysis of products and the value chain to identify or anticipate where there may be adverse CSR effects from its operations. Activity programmes can then be devised to overcome the adverse effects. Effective programmes will remove adverse effects of operations or the risk of adverse events and effects occurring. This reduces the risk of future enforcement actions or adverse publicity from vocal stakeholders or activists. The GRI reporting standard can be used as a checklist of issues and concerns, which can guide the creation of a programme and allows for compatible public reporting. While these activities can provide definite advantages for a firm to reduce the risk from adverse social and environmental effects, any competitive advantages bestowed may be short-lived as competitors quickly catch up with current practices. Often these activities lack uniqueness and may be easily copied. Nevertheless they are usually complementary to strategic CSR elements and needed to establish the creditability of the overall CSR programme.

## Strategic CSR activities

This group of activities comprises CSR initiatives that go beyond best practice or simply responding to anticipated future social and environmental concerns and issues. They are part of moving the firm to a unique position which differentiates the firm and its products and services from its competitors, reduces costs, increases benefits and value to customers, and extends protection of a proprietary nature from competitive pressures. These activities are likely to be fewer in number than responsive CSR activities but can create large and distinctive social, environmental and business benefits when implemented well.

### Transforming the value chain to benefit society and strategy

Transformation of the value chain involves going beyond the simple mitigation of adverse effects referred to above. The approach is innovative and focuses on doing things differently from that done by competitors, rather than just applying best industry practice. The activities are more likely to demonstrate a firm's leadership in an industry and set new standards for other to follow. While the act of transforming the value chain is technically complex and likely to require significant investment, there are real opportunities to establish an enduring competitive advantage while delivering social and environmental benefits. For example, product leadership gives a competitive advantage until the competitors catch up, while development of improved products and processes offers opportunities for innovation which may be protected by patents. Social and environmental benefits become design objectives for the transformed value chain creating the opportunity to deliver greater benefits than are currently possible by adopting industry best practice alone.

## Philanthropy to improve the salient areas of the competitive context

Again the focus is on doing things differently from that done by competitors, and to use corporate philanthropy in a way that goes beyond the philanthropy of being a good corporate citizen. By focusing on key social and environmental issues, which are of mutual concern to both the firm and targeted stakeholders, a strong, self-reinforcing symbiotic relationship can be formed that delivers significant benefits to both the firm and society. Examples of social and environmental programmes that offer great opportunities of this type lie in healthcare and education in developing-world economies. Often disease in a community surrounding an operational site is a real barrier to efficient operation causing a significant amount of sickness-related absence. A public healthcare programme to reduce the levels of the disease (e.g. supplying medicines and public health measures) can improve the health of the local community and provide an improved source of healthy workers who are less troubled by their ill health or that of their family. Similarly improved education can help provide a better life and greater opportunities for the community while developing a more educated pool of local people from which the firm can recruit. In these ways philanthropy aimed at serious social issues can deliver significant mutual benefits to a community and the firm. If successful, the relationship that develops between the firm and the community becomes self-reinforcing and symbiotic in nature.

Strategic CSR opportunities are potentially more capable of enhancing the competitive position and context of the business than the responsive CSR activities, and should offer ways of differentiating the firm from competitors. Responsive CSR activities alone only offer ways of being a good citizen and adopting best practice, which can lead to 'me-too' policies and risk reduction approaches; the company then falls short of becoming a value-creating leader in the industry. Strategic CSR activities offer better opportunities for the firm to reinvent the way things are done, and introduce innovative approaches which can deliver both substantial social benefits and genuine enduring competitive advantage. It is this enduring improvement in the competitive context that will lead to the creation of corporate value for the firm. Of course, like all strategic plans, they need to be well implemented for value to be realised.

While strategic CSR activities are very important to corporate value creation, in practice a real CSR programme being run by a firm will be likely to employ a mix of both responsive and strategic CSR elements in their CSR programme. While the responsive CSR activities alone may not have the same value creating potential as strategic CSR activities, they can be an essential adjunct, or prerequisite, to strategic CSR activities by establishing a firm's CSR credibility and public image. For example, without a reputation for being a good corporate citizen, or after receiving critical publicity about adverse effects from operations, more grandiose strategic CSR activities may not be fully recognised by stakeholders and some of the value-creating potential may be lost. Responsive and strategic CSR activities can be used to complement each other and reinforce the strength of the firm's CSR programme in the eyes of stakeholders.

Competitive advantage may not endure well over time in a strong competitive environment. As competitors strive to keep up and fight for a leading position in an industry, any competitive advantage is continually under attack and becomes eroded. What was yesterday's innovative, unique scheme becomes adopted more widely and may ultimately become industry best practice, yielding less and less contribution to competitive advantage as time progresses. If competitive advantage is to be sustained the CSR element must be difficult to imitate. The more difficult it is to imitate the longer its strategic importance will endure. For example, patents can give protection against imitation over many years, while holding on to key staff and managers with unique knowledge and experience is likely to give protection from imitation for significantly shorter periods. Ultimately the competition will catch up and therefore any CSR element classified as strategic CSR will inevitably be 'downgraded' to responsive CSR over time as it is imitated, its uniqueness disappears and its contribution to competitive advantage is eliminated. Read and DeFillippi (1990) discuss barriers to imitation and sustaining competitive advantage through the resource-based view of the firm.

## Methodology

Four companies and their leaders were selected for examination to determine the strategic benefits created by their CSR programmes. The chosen companies were led by enthusiastic leaders who publicly advocated CSR as well as promoting these CSR programmes within their organisations, and motivating employees and managers. This choice represents a small sample of large multinational corporations in different industries which have substantial CSR programmes. There is no attempt to suggest that they are the best or the only companies that fit these criteria. The companies chosen and their CSR leaders/advocates are:

- **Anglo American**: Sir Mark Moody-Stuart
- **Standard Chartered Bank**: Mervyn Davies
- **E.ON**: Wolf Bernotat
- **IKEA**: Marianne Barner

Publicly available information on each company was collected where possible in the form of press interviews, press articles and profiles, transcripts of speeches by the leaders, and corporate CSR reports. This data is summarised in a short narrative in the following section. Then the four programme strategies are assessed and summarised in Tables 5.1–5.4.

To use the Porter–Kramer model involves categorising the firm's CSR activities as discussed above. Corporate programmes as reported need to be summarised, reformatted and categorised in line with the Porter–Kramer model before the mix of responsive CSR and strategic CSR elements can be clearly seen.

The approach used in this chapter is to construct a table in which activities within the firm's CSR programme are grouped into several key elements (i.e. an element is a group of similar and related activities). Each programme element is then categorised as:

- Good citizenship actions

- Mitigating harm that can arise from the value chain

- Elements transforming the value chain for the benefit of society and which also improve the competitive context

- Philanthropic elements that also improve the competitive context (e.g. by developing a symbiotic relationship with a key stakeholder group)

In addition, the issue being addressed, the target stakeholder group, and the expected benefit or contribution from each element is identified. A table of all the CSR programme elements is constructed showing their benefits, from which the strategic elements can be readily identified.

In this chapter the programme elements have been categorised using my judgement of the current level of industry best practice for that type of CSR element. The categorisation requires an assessment of whether the element constitutes industry best practice (responsive CSR) or goes well beyond what is currently best practice for the industry, demonstrating originality, innovation and leadership (strategic CSR). It is possible for opinions to vary from assessor to assessor on these categories. In addition industry best practices develop over time resulting in changed assessments between responsive and strategic CSR as time goes by.

In some cases, some CSR elements appear to have both responsive and strategic characteristics, and it is not possible to separate the two from the detail in the publicly available data. This is particularly evident when trying to classify some value chain development related elements, and where this is the case columns have been combined in the assessment tables shown below.

It is often the case in attempts to value corporate activities that there can be some variations between the judgements applied by different valuers. Valuation is not a precise science. The approach used in this methodology attempts to reduce possible judgemental variations by providing a framework of definitions, but it cannot entirely eliminate such differences.

## Some CSR leaders and their programmes

This section collects and examines data from press interviews and articles, profiles, speeches and corporate CSR reports that give an insight into CSR leaders' views and their implementation in their organisations. It aims to highlight the principal approaches adopted, objectives and CSR activities for these leaders and their companies. The resulting CSR elements form from a leader's vision, inspiration and motivation. These elements are the combined result of the leader's work within his or her organisation and with external stakeholders in convincing them of the importance of the CSR programme. The data collected in the form of speech transcripts is evidence of the leader acting as an advocate of the programme. London (2008) discusses the importance of this dual behavioural role of advocate and leader in relation to the work of leaders of CSR programmes.

### Anglo American led by Sir Mark Moody-Stuart

Sir Mark Moody-Stuart has been a key figure and promoter of CSR over many years. He became chairman of Anglo American, a multinational company in the mineral extraction industry, in December 2002. Prior to this he held senior positions with Shell and has lived and worked in many countries. As such he has significant experience at senior levels in business and of international operations in the oil and mineral extraction industries. He is at the helm of a company that has a considerable impact on the environment and society of the countries in which it operates, and is acutely aware of the realities such operations can bring. From interviews and addresses since 2002 (for example, see Macalister 2003; Potter and Balfour 2005; Moody-Stuart 2006) and the corporate CSR report, it is possible to form a picture of the salient points that guide Sir Mark Moody-Stuart as he leads the business forward.[4]

In his keynote address to the International Institute for Sustainable Development (IISD), 'People, Planet and Profits' (Moody-Stuart 2006), he identified that the three strands of sustainable development—economic, environmental and social—are not the sole responsibility of any one company, government, labour organisation or

---

4 The Anglo American Sustainable Development Report can be found at www. angloamerican.co.uk/aa/development (accessed 7 December 2009).

NGO, but demand cooperation from different sectors of society working together responsibly within society with shared purpose. He acknowledges, however, that if the economic strand is not under control it very quickly rises to the top of the priorities, and some stakeholders consider this often places overriding emphasis on the economic strand. Cooperation on activities is a key enabler, rather than the adversarial position often traditionally adopted between some social groups, governments and business. When there isn't a common, shared social or environmental purpose (for example, where corruption is endemic), sustainable development becomes very difficult to achieve, and he compares examples of development in Nigeria with examples in Malaysia and Oman. Moody-Stuart questions what social and environmental activities corporations should, and should not, become involved in, and what principles should guide their selection. His main principle for choosing which social and environmental activities to adopt is whether they are mutually beneficial to the company and the community where the company operates. In this way both the company and the community it depends on for skilled people develop together.

However, he finds more difficulty with the decision on whether his company should be involved in wider human rights activities by bringing pressure on some governments. He feels this could be too wide a subject for involvement even where his company operates within a country of concern. He believes that, for cooperation to be effective, trust must be built between the social groups involved. Very open reporting is central to building that trust. In this sense widely adopted metrics such as GRI are extremely valuable tools for monitoring and communicating progress. In interviews with *BusinessWeek Online* (Potter and Balfour 2005) and the *Guardian* (Macalister 2003) he also discusses his view on when and where he may become involved in activities to fight HIV/AIDS. Moody-Stuart sees health and education as being two major areas where local cooperation between corporations and society can be mutually beneficial. These themes are clearly evident among wider CSR activity reported in the corporate CSR report and assessed in more depth below.

## Standard Chartered led by Mervyn Davies

Mervyn Davies has spent most of his professional life in banking and is CEO of Standard Chartered. The banking sector may not have the obvious direct impact on society and environment as have some other industries. However Standard Chartered, registered in London, mainly operates in developing countries in Asia and Africa and the Middle East. It has identified that blindness and HIV/AIDS have a massive negative impact on the economic development of the societies in which Standard Chartered operates. Davies explained his approach in his speech (Davies 2006) to the British Chamber of Commerce in Pudong, China, on 3 November 2006. He has embedded CSR values in the business and developed two major CSR activities to help cure blindness and reduce the impact of HIV/AIDS through improved medical attention in these countries. His 2007 Sustainability Review also indicates a number of educational initiatives focused on financial literacy and developing better local understanding towards economic development.[5]

Davies also has concerns about climate change, particularly with the need to provide energy for the economic growth required for political stability in countries such as China, and is keen to encourage cooperation on tackling climate change. Davies sees CSR as part of a management philosophy (Davies 2007), and he points to the increased enthusiasm and interest young people have in working for Standard Chartered; 50% of graduates employed cited Standard Chartered's reputation for CSR as their reason for choosing to join Standard Chartered rather than competitors. These themes are evident among wider CSR activities in Standard Chartered's CSR report and are discussed further below.

## E.ON led by Wulf Bernotat

Energy companies have an obvious impact on the environment. In addition, the security of energy supplies is crucial for the long-term sustainable economic development of our society. Bernotat (2007) is CEO of German electricity producer E.ON and discusses his views on strategic issues for sustainable energy development. He takes the view that renewable energy sources (e.g. wind and solar) and increased energy efficiency by consumers can play an important part in our future energy plans. However, improved efficiency and carbon reduction in conventional electrical generation, and careful examination of the role for nuclear generation will also be essential developments. Bernotat asserts that the size of electricity generators is a strategic issue, as they need to have sufficient scale both to deliver the technological improvements necessary to move to a reduced carbon society and to have sufficient negotiating power to deal with the extremely large gas and oil producers.

It is interesting to note that Bernotat's CSR perspective on dealing with environmental issues largely depends on implementing strategic technological change, although energy security is more dependent on sociopolitical issues. As the infant market develops for the EU Emissions Trading System (ETS), introduced in 2005, it becomes possible to price $CO_2$ emission costs and allow more conventional financial appraisal tools to be used in business planning. In theory this should make it easier to handle the massive capital investment decisions needed to deal with climate change issues. The ETS should also help ensure that lower $CO_2$ emissions

---

5 The Standard Chartered Sustainability Review can be found at www.standardchartered. com/sustainability/en/index.html (accessed 7 December 2009).

will lead to a competitive advantage. These issues and activities are discussed fully in the E.ON CSR Report.[6]

## IKEA led by Marianne Barner

Barner (2007) is Director of Corporate Communications and Ombudsman for the Child at IKEA and she identifies salient CSR strategic issues for the Swedish furniture manufacturer. The company has banned use of certain chemicals from its production and product range, and is making stringent attempts to eliminate child labour from its global supply chain. It has a clear corporate policy on eliminating child labour from its supply chain, forming partnerships with NGOs such as Save the Children, UNICEF and WWF. IKEA holds the support of the family as one of its main values. It has a strong CSR focus on its supply chain, auditing suppliers for compliance and reducing the number of suppliers to allow better control over product specification adherence, while developing long-term relationships with its suppliers. IKEA is also designing energy saving into its distribution stores, and looking at improvements to reduce $CO_2$ produced by its products and in home delivery transport. On energy usage IKEA intends to reduce consumption by 25% and buy entirely from renewable energy sources.

Barner admits the hardest task in becoming a socially responsible company has been communication to employees and the realisation that it takes longer to become a socially responsible company than managers usually expect. This emphasises the importance of advocacy in the dual advocate/leader role of CSR leaders (London 2008). The CSR issues and activities are discussed fully in the IKEA Social and Environmental Responsibility Report.[7]

## Strategic assessment of programmes

Tables 5.1–5.4 summarise the assessments of the corporate CSR programmes made using the approach discussed above. They show programmes in summary form, boiling down many pages of published press interviews, transcripts of speeches, press articles and corporate CSR reports into a short table of the salient elements. Although details of individual CSR activities are very limited, the tables clearly show the elements that provide the greatest strategic contributions.

---

6  The E.ON Corporate Responsibility Report can be found at www.eon.com/responsibility (accessed 7 December 2009).
7  The IKEA Social and Environmental Responsibility Report 2008 can be found at www.ikea.com/ms/en_GB/about_ikea/pdf/ikea_se_report_2008.pdf (accessed 7 December 2009).

**TABLE 5.1  Sir Mark Moody–Stewart: Anglo American**

| Primary stakeholder addressed | Social or environmental issue addressed | CSR approach applied | | | | Benefit or contribution produced |
|---|---|---|---|---|---|---|
| | | Responsive CSR | | Strategic CSR | | |
| | | Good citizenship | Mitigating harm from value chain activities | Transforming value chain to benefit society and strategy | Strategic philanthropy to improve salient areas of the competitive context | |
| | Poor levels of public health and education in some parts of developing countries | | | | Provision of healthcare and education to communities around global operational sites' HIV/AIDS programmes | • Provides a healthier and better–educated society around operations, giving greater recruitment potential for a more productive local workforce<br>• Reduces dependence on migrant employees |
| Communities local to the company's operations in developing countries | Potentially hazardous working environments lead to illness, injury and death of workforce | | Working environments are safe, healthy and free from occupational diseases | | | • Maintains health, productivity and motivation of the workforce, reducing sickness, absenteeism and recruitment costs |
| | Improving economic opportunities | | | Local procurement and economic development | | • Provides increased economic development opportunities for community<br>• Stronger local supplies |

| | | CSR approach applied | | |
| --- | --- | --- | --- | --- |
| | | Responsive CSR | Strategic CSR | |
| Communities local to the company's operations in developing countries *(continued)* | Diversity | | Increased opportunities for women in mining | • Provides better employment opportunities for women from the local community<br>• Increases employee loyalty |
| | Corruption prevention | | 'Speak up' programme to identify corrupt practices | • Business with corrupt organisations is limited<br>• Fair competition is fostered between suppliers |
| In country suppliers and authorities | Human rights | Company policy and guidelines on rights issues | | • Creates loyalty with workforce and suppliers through fair treatment |

| | | CSR approach applied | | |
|---|---|---|---|---|
| | | Responsive CSR | Strategic CSR | |
| Global society | $CO_2$ emissions and climate change | Improved energy utilisation and travel management | | • Reduced $CO_2$ emissions<br>• Reduced operating costs |
| | Improved water utilisation | Improved water usage, recycling and efficiency | | • Reduced demand on finite local resources<br>• Possible reduced costs |
| | Waste management | Improved waste reduction and recycling management | | • Reduced demand for waste disposal and use of spoil tips and landfill sites<br>• Lower environmental impact<br>• Better relationship between company and community |
| Other local community resource users | Air pollution | Targeted local reductions in $SO_2$ and $NO_X$ | | • Improved air quality around operations<br>• Less impact on community health<br>• Improved relationship between company and community |

**TABLE 5.2 Mervyn Davies: Standard Chartered**

| Primary stakeholder addressed | Social or environmental issue addressed | CSR approach applied | | | | Benefit or contribution produced |
|---|---|---|---|---|---|---|
| | | Responsive CSR | | Strategic CSR | | |
| | | Good citizenship | Mitigating harm from value chain activities | Transforming value chain to benefit society and strategy | Strategic philanthropy to improve salient areas of the competitive context | |
| | Provision of bank funding for sustainable investments | | | Provides funding for renewable energy projects in Asia, Africa and the Middle East | | • Provides funding for projects that meet environmental standards (Equator Principles)<br>• Provides green product development support<br>• Introduces new products to new markets |
| Citizens local to the company's operations in developing counties | Availability of small packets of development funding for communities and businesses in developing countries | | | Support for the starting up of microfinancing institutions (MFIs) to act as independent financial intermediaries in India | | • Develops responsible funding for small business start-ups in India<br>• Accelerates community economic development<br>• Increases the number of start-up businesses<br>• Introduces new products to new markets |
| | Providing banking consistent with shariah principles for Muslim customers | | | Development of Islamic banking products and services | | • Provides funding for Islamic businesses<br>• Improves community economic development<br>• Accelerates economic development in Islamic countries<br>• Introduces new products to new markets |

| | | CSR approach applied | | |
|---|---|---|---|---|
| | | Responsive CSR | Strategic CSR | |
| Citizens local to the company's operations in developing counties (continued) | High levels of blindness and HIV/AIDS causing debilitating personal, social and economic effects | | Health programmes implemented in communities around global operational sites for treatment and prevention of blindness and HIV/AIDS | • Provides a healthier and better-educated society around operations<br>• Provides more productive local workforce<br>• Less time off work due to sickness or caring for others |
| Global society | Reduce the impact of climate change | Reduced $CO_2$ emissions<br>Reduced paper usage | | • Contribution to reduced climate change<br>• Increases sustainability<br>• Strong CSR reputation attracts graduates |

| | | CSR approach applied | |
| --- | --- | --- | --- |
| | | Responsive CSR | Strategic CSR | |
| **Customers** | Development of financial understanding | | Financial literacy programmes in conjunction with central banks, government and education authorities | • Provides financially literate communities<br>• Improves economic development<br>• Reduces risk of customers over-borrowing |
| | Protection from mis-selling of financial products | Proactive assessment of customer creditworthiness | | • Reduces risk of over-borrowing<br>• Customers protected from being sold unsuitable products<br>• Reduces risk of bad debt |
| | Financial crime | Processes to detect money laundering and fraud | | • Reduces losses due to fraud<br>• Limits the possibilities for crime<br>• Protects customers from fraud |
| **Employees** | Diversity | | Equal opportunities policies implemented and monitored | • Develops reputation of fairness<br>• Increases recruitment pool |

**TABLE 5.3  Wulf Bernotat: E.ON**

| Primary stakeholder addressed | Social or environmental issue addressed | CSR approach applied | | | | Benefit or contribution produced |
|---|---|---|---|---|---|---|
| | | Responsive CSR | | Strategic CSR | | |
| | | Good citizenship | Mitigating harm from value chain activities | Transforming value chain to benefit society and strategy | Strategic philanthropy to improve salient areas of the competitive context | |
| | Education about energy supply technology and $CO_2$ | Education programmes for schools about energy supplies | | | | • Raising understanding of energy issues and climate change<br>• Positioning E.ON as a responsible provider |
| Global society | Need for sustainable energy production considering energy security and climate change | | | • Innovative reduction of $CO_2$ emissions from existing power generation plants by improved efficiency and carbon reduction<br>• Redesigning the power production capacity to include renewable sources (i.e. wind and solar power)<br>• Considering the role for nuclear generation in the 'energy mix'<br>• Ensuring adequate scale of operations is essential to be able to support the technology and deal with large oil and gas suppliers | | • Reduced carbon footprint can enhance competitive position through the EU Emissions Trading Scheme<br>• Increased use of renewable and nuclear sources of energy can improve energy supply security, leading to improved competitive position with more stable pricing |

| | | CSR approach applied | | |
|---|---|---|---|---|
| | | *Responsive CSR* | *Strategic CSR* | |
| **Vulnerable customers and members of the community** | Protection from escalating energy costs while keeping warm | | • Discounted insulation schemes for vulnerable customers: 'Caring Energy' | • Differentiates E.ON as a caring supplier<br>• Reduces total energy needed and $CO_2$ emissions<br>• Increases customer loyalty |
| **Employees** | Development of specialist employee skills | | • Programme for employee development, education and training<br>• Vocational training for young people | • Develops staff to their full potential<br>• Allows focus on developing specific skills needed by business<br>• Increases staff loyalty<br>• Overall improves staff productivity and reduces turnover |

**TABLE 5.4  Marianne Barner: IKEA**

| Primary stakeholder addressed | Social or environmental issue addressed | CSR approach applied | | | | Benefit or contribution produced |
|---|---|---|---|---|---|---|
| | | Responsive CSR | | Strategic CSR | | |
| | | Good citizenship | Mitigating harm from value chain activities | Transforming value chain to benefit society and strategy | Strategic philanthropy to improve salient areas of the competitive context | |
| | Abolishing the use of child labour in its global supply chain | | Specific code of practice relating to the use of child labour and young workers | Reduction in number of suppliers, combined with mandatory compliance and audit to IKEA child labour code of practice | Formed partnerships with key NGOs (Save the Children and UNICEF) aimed at reducing child labour globally | • Established IKEA's strong family values (product differentiation) • Eliminates child labour in the supply chain |
| Communities around global suppliers' operations | Child health and education | | | | • Supports UNICEF to help children access quality education • Supports research into child health in Indian subcontinent | • Strengthens health and education in communities where global suppliers operate (increases educational ability of workforce) • Improved health leads to higher workforce productivity |

| | | CSR approach applied | | |
|---|---|---|---|---|
| | | Responsive CSR | Strategic CSR | |
| Global society | CO₂ emissions impacting climate change | Reducing CO₂ emissions from home delivery transport | | • Reduces carbon footprint<br>• Shows concern for the future and sustainability of operations (differentiation) |
| | Need for sustainable future energy supplies | Reducing energy consumption in buildings by 25% and moving to entirely renewable energy source suppliers | | • Move towards sustainable energy supplies for the company (differentiation) |
| | Improving lighting product efficiency to reduce CO₂ emissions | | Replacing inefficient tungsten lighting products with fluorescent and LED technologies | |
| Customers | Manufactured household goods and furniture use environmentally hazardous chemicals | Elimination of environmentally hazardous chemicals in electrical and electronic equipment, furniture and coatings | | • Protects customers and environment<br>• Creates reputation for responsible business<br>• Differentiates IKEA products in the marketplace |

The assessments in this chapter are based on published information only. They are more limited than the assessments that may be undertaken by a firm's managers with access to additional internal data: for example, costs or budgets. Nevertheless the categorisation exercise is a powerful tool which forces activities into the responsive CSR or strategic CSR groupings. This exercise is an essential precursor to further quantitative valuation work.

Table 5.1 covers the CSR programme of Anglo American. Their operations around the globe are located around mineral deposits often in remote areas of the world with distinct social problems. The sustainable development section of the Anglo American website gives a significant volume of data on CSR and sustainability activity. The essential elements of the programme show the role played by strategic philanthropy in improving the competitive context. In particular, programmes at local operational sites provide health and education to the surrounding communities, improving lives and opportunities. In the locally recruited workforce, improved health and education reduces sickness absence, delivers improved productivity, and reduces operational costs and the dependence on employees from outside the locality. Higher employment and induced employment deliver further economic development to the local community.

Table 5.1 shows that the majority of activities are categorised as strategic CSR elements and are mainly targeted at the stakeholders' local community at operational locations. However on wider social issues of preventing corruption and human rights the stakeholders are at a national level as this begins to involve the supply chain and possibly government cooperation. The table shows the CSR programme is heavily weighted towards activities that transform the value chain or strategic philanthropy. These focus largely on stakeholders local to the company's operational sites, aiming at solving mutual problems affecting community and company.

Table 5.2 covers the CSR programme of Standard Chartered which provides financial services mainly in Asia, Africa and the Middle East. It shows the majority of CSR elements are targeted at stakeholders local to the bank's operations. It also indicates that a considerable amount of the CSR activity has been focused on transforming the value chain through the development of new products and services appropriate for the countries in which the bank operates. Strategic philanthropy is strongly represented, mainly in the form of health programmes and educational initiatives. These activities form a strong bond with local communities, strengthening their well-being, education and economic development. In turn this benefits Standard Chartered by giving access to a healthy, educated, local workforce and by having well-informed and financially aware customers who have access to financial products matched to their needs. This confers improvements on Standard Chartered's strategic position through cost reduction, improved value for customers and differentiated products.

Table 5.3 assesses the CSR programme of E.ON, which is a large multinational energy company with significant electricity generation capacity, operating mainly in Europe and the USA. The salient problem that E.ON shares with society is production of $CO_2$ from its operations and its impact on global warming. E.ON needs to substantially reduce its $CO_2$ emissions and is keen to be part of the solution to global warming, rather than part of the problem. By contrast to Anglo American and Standard Chartered, the primary stakeholder is the global community, rather than the smaller local communities surrounding its operations.

E.ON has adopted a CSR approach that involves the transformation of its value chain. It has concentrated heavily on using improved and innovative technology to reduce $CO_2$ emissions from its existing conventional thermal electricity generating operations, and increasing the role of renewable energy sources and nuclear generation in the mix. In addition there has been support for improved energy efficiency and better insulation to reduce energy usage.

The main group of CSR elements are categorised as transforming the value chain, with some further strategic philanthropy to provide discounted energy saving schemes for vulnerable energy users. Again, as in Tables 5.1 and 5.2, there is a large emphasis on strategic CSR activities which improve E.ON's competitive position through increasing product value ('green electricity'), possible cost savings and security of energy source supplies, differentiation of E.ON products in the marketplace, and possible protection for some proprietary developments from the innovative work being carried out.

Table 5.4 summarises the CSR programme of IKEA, European and North American retailer of furniture with a Scandinavian flavour to its products and designs. The original primary social problem encountered by IKEA was that child labour was commonly used in the Far East where many of IKEA's suppliers were based. The use of child labour was contrary to IKEA's and Swedish values. IKEA wanted to be part of a solution to eradication of child labour, rather than being an economic cause of it by using goods produced in this way. IKEA is also concerned about the use of environmentally damaging chemicals in the manufacture of its products, and the $CO_2$ emissions from the company's products, premises and transport contributing to global warming.

Table 5.4 shows a majority of strategic CSR elements classified as transforming the value chain or strategic philanthropy. The target stakeholders for child welfare issues are communities around the global suppliers' operational sites. For $CO_2$ emission issues the target stakeholder is global society. IKEA's programme potentially has an impact on the wider use of child labour, rather than simply on IKEA's direct suppliers and the obvious direct stakeholders. It sets an example of what can be done in regions and is supported by the work of NGOs who can spread the work further afield. In this regard the programme is ambitious and capable of creating the desired market positioning of IKEA as a socially responsible organisation. However, from the literature available it is difficult to detect how tight any symbiotic relationship between targeted stakeholders and the company might be, and how strong are the mutual benefits. Nevertheless the majority of programme elements are strategic CSR activities, consistent with the view that the key target stakeholder is the prospective customer globally. This should significantly strengthen IKEA's global strategy by differentiating the company and its products from the competition.

## Discussion and conclusions

This chapter has examined the CSR programmes of four large, well-respected, multinational companies through the lens of the Porter–Kramer model and identified CSR approaches for potentially creating corporate value through improved competitive advantage. The four complex CSR programmes operated in different industries, dealt with a range of different social issues, and they contain both responsive CSR and strategic CSR elements. The programmes were characterised as having a majority of strategic CSR elements which potentially improve competitiveness.

CSR programmes are usually large, complex and very difficult to evaluate comparatively, particularly with respect to their corporate value creation capability. The template approach used in this chapter allows large and complex CSR programmes to be distilled into the key elements, to which the Porter–Kramer model is applied. The power of this approach is that virtually any CSR programme can be summarised and categorised into the key elements, allowing it to be assessed for strategic contributions. These strategic CSR elements go beyond best practice and potentially improve the competitive context in which the company is operating. Such an approach allows a CSR programme to be evaluated with regard to its fit with the overall business strategy.

Owing to the absence of numerical and financial data in this assessment, the method could not be extended to deliver a financial valuation of the competitive advantages identified. However, this template approach can be extended to include financial data for the elements where available, allowing the identified competitive advantages to be valued financially.

Turning to the four programmes, we find a mix of CSR elements in each one, but simple, responsive good citizen philanthropy features in relatively small amounts. In contrast the main elements of the programmes are focused on transforming the value chain to benefit society and strategy, and on strategic philanthropy to improve salient areas of the competitive position. It is difficult to separate some CSR activities between mitigation of the effect of the value chain and transformational activities. Some CSR elements contain both activities and it is difficult for an external assessor to identify the balance. Where this has occurred the two columns are merged in Tables 5.1–5.4. For example, reduction of $CO_2$ emissions often involves both activities that improve performance by adopting current best practice (e.g. insulation of buildings) and those transforming value chain operations, going beyond best practice by redesigning operational processes (e.g. using electric delivery vehicles and reorganising customer order delivery arrangements to better match this form of transport). In the case of philanthropy the decision is much clearer whether it is of a responsive good citizen form or whether it goes further by improving strategic position.

Common themes run through the strategic CSR elements found in this chapter. First, they are focused on an important problem that is shared by the business and the targeted stakeholder group. Second, the solutions involving philanthropy often work through the development of a symbiotic relationship between the company and the stakeholder group, where delivery of mutual benefits to both parties creates a long-term, self-reinforcing relationship between the company and the target stakeholders.

Anglo American and Standard Chartered both perceive the health and education of the local communities around their operations as very important to their ability to operate efficiently in developing economies. Endemic health problems often reduce the work output from locally sourced staff, but with HIV/AIDS the long-term debilitating effects on family members contribute to increased time off and serious worries about future prospects for those affected or their dependants. The social effects of blindness are similar to HIV/AIDS in this respect. The countries in which these two companies operate have a high incidence of these diseases. So far many national governments have not been able to afford the mass healthcare programmes to make a significant improvement to this situation. The productivity and wider economic benefits of improving the health of the population are highly significant. This presents a significant challenge to these companies to introduce sufficient healthcare programmes to significantly reduce the social impacts of these diseases, while controlling costs to ensure some corporate value is created.

Social benefits arising from improved education give the company a better-educated community from which to choose employees. Developing training opportunities for employees also improves overall educational standards. Standard Chartered extends its education approach to teaching of financial principles to the communities it serves, producing a financially aware and literate community that better understands the basic principles involved in economic development.

Overall the local community benefits from health and educational programmes through local economic development from increased direct and induced employment. For the company, improved health and education combine to make local operations more productive and reduce the dependence on 'imported' staff from outside the local community. This reduces the specific costs of operating at a location and develops a loyal relationship with the community, working well where the company is a major local employer.

In contrast E.ON faces a key problem relating to $CO_2$ emissions which it shares with the global community. This requires a radically different approach and one that involves governments and national populations. E.ON sees a number of possible routes to reducing $CO_2$ emissions in the energy industry which include improved efficiency of generating plant, carbon capture and sequestration, use of renewable energy sources (i.e. wind, solar and wave), nuclear generation and more efficient insulation and energy usage. These technologies are at various stages of development and deployment and the long-term answer to $CO_2$ reduction lies in adopting the optimal mix to achieve the $CO_2$ emission targets. The adoption of these new and more sustainable technologies is central to E.ON's programme to transform its value chain. Also represented in its CSR programme is philanthropy in the provision of discount insulation for residential customers who are vulnerable to price increases. This helps protect more vulnerable customers from escalating fuel costs by reducing their energy needs, $CO_2$ emissions, and by delivering mutual benefits to target stakeholders and the company. The combined effect of transforming the value chain and some strategic philanthropy can help to improve the strategic position of E.ON by potentially reducing costs and improving the value to customers (less $CO_2$ per kWh). The company also differentiates itself from others that are slower to adopt more sustainable methods. Opportunities for using innovative technology and novel ideas also provide more enduring elements of competitive advantage if patents can be secured.

IKEA has clear values centred on the family which influence its product range and company ethos. The use of child labour by its suppliers is clearly incompatible with these values. To find suppliers in other parts of the world where child labour is not used could reduce IKEA's cost advantages and weaken its competitive position. IKEA therefore followed a route of standard setting and compliance audits for its suppliers, changing the approaches used by its suppliers. Through its support of NGOs it has been able to influence views on child labour over much greater areas than simply dealing with its suppliers. IKEA has turned an earlier threat of being accused of profiting from the proceeds of goods manufactured by child labour, into a position of strength where its values and policies are clearly stated and compatible with its practice and behaviour. This allows the company to use low-cost suppliers around the world and proclaim its family values, leading to competitive advantages of cost reduction, increased customer value and differentiation. For employers and their communities supplying IKEA, child labour has been eliminated and educational programmes developed in collaboration with NGOs, benefiting the communities and promising improved economic development for the future.

The approach used in this chapter using the Porter–Kramer model has identified the strategic elements in four large CSR programmes which should create long-term value for the companies if the programmes are well executed. The model was reasonably easy to use. Managers inside a company, and possibly investors, could add quantitative information to the assessment tables to improve further their understanding of how their CSR programme can create corporate value for their enterprises. As in any valuation the assessor will inevitably need to apply his or her judgement. However, the framework of the Porter–Kramer model helps to limit the judgemental freedom. In addition, assessor judgements will change over time, as unique competitive advantages obtained though novel and innovative approaches are gradually lost as competitors catch up and imitate. As with any assessment of strategic position, it is valid for a limited period only and a competitive advantage should not be expected to endure indefinitely.

In summary, the Porter–Kramer model helps to identify the competitive advantages arising from a company's CSR programme. This understanding complements other methods of reporting CSR programmes such as TBL. It enhances CSR reporting similarly to the way that the knowledge of assets on a financial balance sheet complements the profit and loss statement in an annual financial report. The Porter–Kramer model is relatively easy to use, and provides an additional view of a CSR programme which can help managers and the investment community to understand more fully where the corporate value-creating potential of a CSR programme lies.

# References

Allouche, J., and P. Laroche (2005) 'A Meta-analytical Investigation of the Relationship between Corporate Social and Financial Performance', *Revue de Gestion des Ressources Humaines* 57 (July/September 2005): 18-41.

Arnold, G. (2005) *Corporate Financial Management* (Harlow, UK: Pearson Education).

Barner, M. (2007) 'Be a Socially Responsible Corporation', *Harvard Business Review* 85.7–8: 59-60.

Bernotat, W. (2007) 'Take Responsibility for Climate Change', *Harvard Business Review* 85.7–8: 58-59.

Davies, M. (2006) 'Speech by Mervyn Davies, British Chamber of Commerce, Pudong, China, 3 November 2006', www.standardchartered.com/_documents/british-chamber-of-commerce-pudong/sc_bccPudong_031106.pdf, accessed March 2009.

—— (2007) 'Interview: Mervyn Davies, Group CEO of Standard Chartered', *The Banker*, 4 September 2006.

Friedman, M. (1970) 'The social responsibility of business to increase its profits', *New York Times Magazine*, 13 September 1970: 32.

Grayson, D., and A. Hodges (2004) *Corporate Social Opportunity! Seven Steps to Make Corporate Social Responsibility Work for your Business* (Sheffield, UK: Greenleaf Publishing).

Griffin, J.J., and J.F. Mahon (1997) 'The Corporate Social Performance and Corporate Financial Performance Debate', *Business and Society* 36.1 (March 1997): 5-31.

London, M. (2008) 'Leadership and Advocacy: Dual Roles for Corporate Social Responsibility and Social Entrepreneurship', *Organisational Dynamics* 37.4: 313-26.

Macalister, T. (2003) 'Angel's Angle: Interview with Sir Mark Moody-Stuart', *The Guardian*, 11 January 2003.

Margolis, J.D., and J.P. Walsh (2003) 'Misery Loves Companies: Rethinking Social Initiatives by Business', *Administrative Science Quarterly* 48.2 (June 2003): 268-305.

Milliman, J., J. Ferguson and K. Sylvester (2008) 'Implementation of Michael Porter's Strategic Corporate Social Responsibility Model', *Journal of Global Business Issues*, April 2008 (conference edition): 29-33.

Moody-Stuart, M. (2006) 'People, Planet and Profits: A Keynote Address by Sir Mark Moody-Stuart', IISD Commentary; www.iisd.org/pdf/2006/commentary_general_3.pdf, accessed March 2009.

Orlitzky, M., F.L. Schmidt and S.L. Rynes (2003) 'Corporate Social and Financial Performance: A Meta-analysis', *Organization Studies* 24.3 (March 2003): 403-11.

Porter, M.E. (1980) *Competitive Strategy: Techniques for Analysing Industries and Competitors* (New York: The Free Press).

—— and M.R. Kramer (2006) 'Strategy and Society: The Link between Competitive Advantage and Corporate Social Responsibility', *Harvard Business Review* 84.12 (December 2006): 78-92.

Potter, J.L., and F. Balfour (2005) 'Anglo American AIDS Initiative . . . Sir Mark Moody-Stuart . . . Discusses Industry's Role in Tackling the Disease', *BusinessWeek Online*, 2 December 2005.

Read, R., and R.J. DeFillippi (1990) 'Causal Ambiguity, Barriers to Imitation, and Sustainable Competitive Advantage', *Academy of Management Review* 15.1 (January 1990): 88-102.

Roman, R.M., S. Hayibor and B.R. Agle (1999) 'The Relationship between Social and Financial Performance', *Business & Society* 38.1 (March 1999): 109-25.

# 6
# A strategic approach to CSR
## The case of Beghelli

**Barbara Del Bosco**
University of Bergamo, Italy

An important recent stream of literature on corporate social responsibility (CSR) focuses on the relationship between CSR and strategy, and asserts the possibility and the importance for companies to engage in strategic or 'profit-maximising' CSR (Burke and Logsdon 1996; Baron 2001; McWilliams and Siegel 2001; Porter and Kramer 2006; Siegel and Vitaliano 2007). Strategic CSR aims explicitly to benefit both society and the firm by realising opportunities created by social issues (Grayson and Hodges 2004). In this chapter a broad concept of social issue is adopted, which includes the environmental issue.

Studies on strategic CSR have focused on the potential competitive and economic benefits of an approach to CSR that integrates social issues into corporate strategy and business processes (Zadek 2004; Porter and Kramer 2006). The literature has also emphasised the need to start the integration between CSR and other business activities at the strategic level, and has presented examples of companies engaging successfully in profit-maximising CSR by differentiating products, serving unsupplied markets, building new business models or investing in social aspects of context that strengthen company competitiveness (Grayson and Hodges 2004; Porter and Kramer 2006; Jenkins 2009).

In spite of the interesting contributions, the literature has not yet 'provided a compelling framework for the strategic management of CSR' (Husted and Allen 2007: 595). In particular, limited attention has been devoted to how to realise this integration between CSR and strategy, both in terms of identification and evaluation of 'corporate social opportunities' (Grayson and Hodges 2004) and as regards the mechanisms and processes through which the firm can realise these opportunities and integrate CSR into business strategies and activities.

This chapter focuses on *how* the integration of strategy and CSR can be concretely executed. In particular, it investigates the mechanisms, conditions and processes through which CSR can be progressively integrated into business strategies and activities, focusing on the role played by firm resources and resource management. The reference frame used is the model developed by Burke and Logsdon (1996), who suggested five strategic dimensions of CSR projects—centrality, specificity, proactivity, voluntarism and visibility—that may contribute to improving the impact of these projects on value creation. In this chapter their model is applied to the analysis of a reference case regarding a company that adopts a strategic approach to CSR: the Beghelli Group, an Italian firm producing emergency and energy-saving lighting, electronic safety and security systems and renewable energy products. The objective is to try to better understand how it is possible to identify and develop corporate social initiatives characterised by these dimensions.

Findings reveal how this company has created a link between competitive advantage and corporate social responsibility, by focusing on a specific social issue (environmental protection), finding business opportunities related to this issue and exploiting them by leveraging its firm-specific resources and through a process of innovation and resource development.

## Theoretical background and research questions

CSR is strategic 'when it yields substantial business-related benefits to the firm' (Burke and Logsdon 1996: 496). The strategic approach to CSR is focused on the opportunity of 'reinforcing corporate strategy through social progress' (Porter and Kramer 2006: 84) and adding a social dimension to the value proposition of the company. In this perspective, corporate social involvement aims to create shared value: a benefit for society that is also valuable to the business.

A company undertakes a strategic CSR approach when it identifies and exploits an opportunity based on a societal issue (Milliman *et al.* 2008). Grayson and Hodges (2004: 11) define corporate social opportunities as 'commercially viable activities which also advance environmental and social sustainability'. According to these authors, firms, in order to create value, should become able to capitalise on corporate social opportunities instead of regarding CSR only as a tool to minimise risks. CSR, in fact, provides opportunities for innovation (Husted and Allen 2007) and, by combining social responsibility and competitive objectives, it is possible to pioneer CSR innovations that benefit society and are valuable for the business too (Bansal and Roth 2000).

Thus, the shift to strategic CSR implies the capacity to face social issues and trends with an eye on potential opportunities instead of focusing only on potential threats. In fact, interpreting an issue as either a threat or an opportunity demonstrates important differences in organisational responses (Dutton and Jackson 1987). Empirical evidence suggests that companies with high social performance tend to be those that see social and environmental challenges as drivers for innovation: that is, as market opportunities (Response Project 2008).

The adoption of a strategic approach to CSR also requires a shift of corporate responsibility from a tactical to a strategic level of management and an integration of social issues into corporate strategy and business processes (Zadek 2004; Porter and Kramer 2006). The link with strategies and day-to-day organisational activities allows companies to respond to societal demands in an organisationally integrated way, instead of a decoupled fashion (Weaver *et al.* 1999). Managing CSR at the strategic level can imply benefits both in terms of coherence of a firm's CSR activities and as regards their efficacy. When CSR is managed only at the tactical level, it risks delivering uncoordinated activities whose substantial social impact is conditioned by the high fragmentation of the firm's effort.

Another important characteristic of a strategic approach to CSR regards the choice of societal issues to focus on and corporate social activities to develop. Not all CSR issues and activities provide opportunities for value creation. Each firm has to identify which social issue has points of intersection with its activities and can be better served by the firm (Porter and Kramer 2006). Therefore, the analysis of stakeholder needs and claims has to be combined with the analysis of firm activities, resources and competences. The allocation of resources to meet social needs is not only based on stakeholder salience (Mitchell *et al.* 1997), but also oriented to strengthen and expand CSR activities in those areas where competitive advantage can be created (Husted and Allen 2007).

In this perspective, the strategic analysis of CSR is a focal point because it is fundamental to understanding which CSR activities provide the potential for gain. In this regard, Burke and Logsdon (1996) have developed an interesting framework, which identifies five variables that the authors suggest as 'dimensions of corporate strategy which are . . . useful in relating CSR policies, programmes and processes to value creation by the firm' (Burke and Logsdon 1996: 496): centrality, specificity, proactivity, voluntarism and visibility.

- **Centrality** is 'a measure of the closeness of fit between a CSR policy or programme and the firm's mission and objectives' (Burke and Logsdon 1996: 496). According to the authors, CSR initiatives that are consistent with the mission and strategic objectives of the firm are expected to receive priority because they can contribute to fulfilling the firm's objective and thus to yielding business-related benefits and value creation. In a resource-based perspective, centrality is associated with 'the firm's ability to provide a coherent focus to a portfolio of firm resources and assets' (Husted and Allen 2007: 596)

- **Specificity** 'refers to the firm's ability to capture or internalise the benefits of a CSR programme' (Burke and Logsdon 1996: 497). Many CSR initiatives create collective goods that reap only public benefits and no private benefit for the company. The 'appropriability' (Husted and Allen 2007) of the added value created is related to the ability to realise CSR initiatives that also deliver benefits that are specific to the firm. An example is product differentiation on the basis of CSR attributes related to product or process innovation

- **Proactivity** 'reflects the degree to which behaviour is planned in anticipation of emerging economic, technological, social or political trends and in the absence of crisis condition' (Burke and Logsdon 1996: 498). The ability to identify changes in competitive and socioeconomic environment is crucial in order to define strategies that take advantage of opportunities and counter threats, and the ability to anticipate these changes can create an advantage over competitors. CSR issues and changes in the needs of stakeholders provide opportunities and threats for firms. Thus, the ability to recognise and respond to them in advance can contribute to value creation

- **Voluntarism** is linked to proactivity. It corresponds to 'the absence of externally imposed compliance requirements' (Burke and Logsdon 1996: 498). According to the authors, voluntarism of CSR projects increases the potential for value creation through these projects. In contrast, Husted and Allen (2007) hypothesise an uncertain relationship between voluntarism and value creation since it is also possible that legal constraints can stimulate innovation. These authors, in their study on large Spanish companies, also find empirical evidence of a perceived positive influence of non-voluntarism on value creation

- **Visibility** depends on the extent to which social activities may be observed by stakeholders and the firm's ability to gain recognition from these stakeholders. Positive visibility may affect the reputation of the firm and improve its relationship with key internal and external stakeholders. Thus, CSR activities with a positive visibility can yield economic benefits for the firm because of its improved reputation

Burke and Logsdon (1996) suggest these dimensions as useful criteria for assessing when CSR initiatives are strategic. I distinguish the five key factors identified by the authors into two categories. The first includes centrality, specificity and visibility. These dimensions, in part, are determined by the choice of which CSR activities to undertake (and, thus, are related to the ability to identify corporate social opportunities) and, in part, depend on how these activities are concretely executed. The other category includes voluntarism and proactivity. These variables are strictly related to the decision to address a specific societal issue and, in particular, they concern the motivation and timing of this decision.

Regarding these two categories, the research questions addressed in this chapter are the following:

- In which way is it possible to select and manage CSR initiatives in order to improve their centrality, specificity and visibility?

- Which factors can lead to the adoption of strategic CSR initiatives?

## Methodology

The chapter is based on an in-depth analysis of a single relevant case. The case selected for analysis is Beghelli Group, an Italian firm that adopts a strategic approach to CSR. This company has integrated environmental issues into its competitive strategies by developing a portfolio of energy-saving lighting products (for consumer, industrial and public use) and, then, entering into the renewable energy industry. Moreover, this company has been selected because it has become the market leader in the Italian energy-saving lighting industry through its strategic approach to the environmental issue.

Regarding data collection, several information sources were used. Primary information was collected through semi-structured interviews with Beghelli's management. Secondary data came from annual reports, quarterly reports, the code of ethics, the corporate website, press releases and other archival data from the firm, magazine and financial newspaper articles, industry reports and reports by financial analysts. The use of such different types of data and sources is aimed at providing greater triangulation, validity and robustness to the findings (Eisenhardt 1989).

For the primary data collection, I undertook in-depth interviews with two key contacts: Luca Beghelli—marketing director, son of the founder and minority shareholder—and a corporate communication manager not belonging to the

Beghelli family.[1] Interviews were based on open-ended questions regarding the profile and history of the company, CSR in Beghelli and its relationship with strategy, the path that has conduced to the present level of integration between strategy and environmental commitment, motivation and antecedents of this integrated approach to CSR and the role of the entrepreneur.

## Company profile: Beghelli Group

Founded in 1982, Beghelli has always had its core business in the emergency lighting sector, in which it is the Italian market leader with a market share exceeding 50%.[2] Nonetheless, over the years it has expanded its activity to related businesses: electronic safety and security systems, energy-saving lighting and renewable energies. Business activities in the lighting sector (including emergency and energy-saving lighting) are dominant: in 2007 they generated 91.4% of consolidated turnover.

The Beghelli Group operates through the parent company, Beghelli SpA, and its subsidiaries: five manufacturing companies (one in Italy and four abroad); a service company that offers remote assistance services (Beghelli Servizi); a service company that manages the first Italian vertical portal completely dedicated to safety and energy conservation (Sicurweb); a research and development company (Becar); and local commercial companies devoted to market penetration in different foreign countries. The Beghelli Group employs more than 1,800 staff and its 2007 turnover amounted to €167.6 million, 32.3% of which was provided by exports. Despite the process of internationalisation, Beghelli maintains an important link with its original territory and local community; 30% of employees operate in Italy. Four out of eight manufacturing plants are located in Italy; more precisely, in a narrow mountain zone in the Emilia Romagna region around Monteveglio, the home village of the founder where he and his family still live. Discussing the creation of new plants in this area, the founder said: 'I decided to invest here and to recruit in disadvantaged zones in order to help citizens and, especially, local young people to remain in their home village without having to emigrate elsewhere.'[3,4] The investment in training young people has benefited the firm. Employees have developed expertise and specific skills and the firm has also obtained very positive results in terms of employee loyalty.

1   These interviews were undertaken in the second half of 2008 and at the beginning of 2009.
2   Beghelli press kit, April 2008.
3   Interview with Gian Pietro Beghelli published by *Il Sole 24 ore* (Bonicelli 1997).
4   All the citations from documents regarding Beghelli and interviews are translated from the original Italian version.

Beghelli SpA has been listed on the Italian Stock Exchange since June 1998. Nevertheless, it remains a family business, with the founder's family retaining 73% of its equity. Gian Pietro Beghelli has a pivotal role in the company. He is the founder, the president, the chief executive officer and he personally owns 58% of company equity. The history of the company is directly related to the personal history of the founder, his competences, attitude to innovation and entrepreneurship. These characteristics allowed him to receive the 1997 Ernst & Young award for 'Entrepreneur of the Year' in the category of technological research and innovation.

## A strategic and social opportunity: energy saving and environmental protection

As mentioned above, the field of emergency lighting represents the original activity and core business of Beghelli. In 1993 Beghelli diversified its activities through the launch of its first product in the telerescue field (the popular 'Telesalvalavita Beghelli'), followed by several other innovative electronic safety and security systems for both the consumer and the business market. This process of diversification is characterised by the fact that the new business areas have two important points of contact with the core business. First, they are areas in which the company may benefit from the competences developed in the electronics field and its related innovative capacity. Second, these new business activities have been developed around safety and security needs.

Another important step in the history of Beghelli was its entrance into the energy-saving lighting industry in 1999. Beghelli launched new products for the business market that allowed companies to obtain energy savings of 50% compared with traditional lighting systems.

In this way, the company has identified a societal issue that has points of intersection with its strategies, activities and resources, and has integrated it into its competitive strategy. The firm even highlights the strategic relevance of environmental issues in its Code of Ethics:

> The environmental policy of Beghelli also finds support in the knowledge that the environment can provide a competitive advantage in a market that is increasingly broad and demanding as regards quality and behaviours. The Group's strategy is based on investments and activities that meet the principles of sustainable development; in particular: allocating a significant share of investment to the production of environmentally friendly products; and within national and international agencies and programmes, promoting actions and behaviours that consider the environment as a strategic variable.[5]

5  Beghelli's Code of Ethics; www.beghelli.it.

Over the years, environmental protection has become an important focal point for Beghelli's innovation processes. The company has developed a group of projects called 'SalvaPianeta (Save the Planet) Beghelli' aimed at energy saving and reducing the environmental effects of both consumption and production processes. These initiatives concern different areas and have assisted its entrance into new markets and business sectors. Currently, the company operates in three business areas related to energy saving and environmental protection:

- Energy-saving lighting for commercial, industrial and public use

- Energy-saving lighting for the consumer market

- Renewable energies

With regard to these areas, it is interesting to analyse the major current projects to understand how the company has exploited market opportunities related to environmental sustainability through technological and marketing innovation.

## Energy–saving lighting for the business market

The main current project in this field, labelled 'A world of light at zero cost', assumes the burden of investment and risk by offering business clients the replacement of their obsolete light installations at zero cost. Beghelli replaces old lighting fixtures at zero cost and installs in their place its patented lighting systems that produce energy savings of up to 70% compared with traditional lighting fixtures. After installation, Beghelli measures real energy savings thanks to a patented and certified system; 90% of the verified energy saving is used to pay Beghelli's service fees over the following seven years. The customer benefits from the remaining 10% of energy savings. Moreover, for the entire duration of the contract, the client receives a cost-free maintenance service covering the installation of all new parts and eventual replacement of the fluorescent tubes. At the end of the contract, the customer may renew the contract (increasing its savings to 30%) or buy the installation outright and enjoy total energy savings.

In this way, Beghelli invests directly in more efficient lighting solutions for their clients, both bearing the related risks and providing an incentive for the adoption of environmentally friendly solutions by potential customers.

The same commercial formula has recently been used to offer energy-saving street-lighting systems to public entities, since the absence of initial investment and risk represents an important incentive to the adoption of energy-saving solutions, even by these types of customer. Even in this case, this commercial formula is used to offer products that incorporate several patented innovations.

## Energy–saving lighting for the consumer market

In this field, Beghelli has launched a line of energy-saving lamps, called 'Immediately Dual', which boast an innovative technology patented by the company. These lamps incorporate a halogen bulb, which is switched on only during the first seconds of operation. This feature provides all the advantages typical of incandescent lamps, which light up instantly, and also facilitates a rapid warming-up of the fluorescent tubes, which avoids the sensation of 'dim light' during the first minutes of operation. This line of products combines energy saving (up to 80%) with the advantages of traditional incandescent lamps. The innovation aims to both increase the use of energy-saving lamps and differentiate the firm's products from its competitors.

## Renewable energies

Beghelli has recently entered into the renewable energy industry. This strategic decision is seen by the company as 'the natural evolution of the Group, which has gained considerable experience in the field of energy saving';[6] and 'the step from efficient use of energy to intelligent production of energy'.[7] Even this new business area has points of contact with the other business areas of the firm, regarding both the focus on the environmental issue and technological competences (even if these competences must be integrated with others).

Beghelli has presented two products in the field of renewable energies: 'Pianeta Sole' (Planet Sun) in the photovoltaic field and 'Albero dell'Energia' (Energy Tree) regarding the use of solar and geothermal energy.

Pianeta Sole is an innovative photovoltaic array that 'follows' the sun. It incorporates a micro-movement system that moves photovoltaic modules during the day in order to follow sun movements and maximise the quantity of energy stored. It is possible for this system to increase energy production up to 25%, compared with traditional static modules. This innovation leads to both product differentiation and energy efficiency.

Albero dell'Energia is a product that combines two sources of energy: solar and geothermal. It uses solar energy to extract geothermal energy for domestic heating and cooling. The name of the product comes from its shape: it looks like a tree, with photovoltaic modules as branches, vertical geothermal probes as roots and a wooden curvilinear structure as its trunk. This product integrates different factors of differentiation. It combines innovative 'green' technologies with a distinctive design that provides a good visual integration with the environment.

6 Beghelli, First-Half Report (30 June 2008); www.beghelli.it.
7 Interview with Luca Beghelli.

Although the firm entered into this market only in 2008, it is investing significantly in it.[8] Beghelli is already able to offer a complete catalogue of photovoltaic components and systems, and produces 'the first photovoltaic system entirely realised by a single producer' (Pianeta Sole) thanks to previously developed expertise.[9]

Moreover, at the end of 2008, the firm signed an agreement for the creation of a joint venture with ErgyCapital, an investment company specialising in investing in the field of energy saving and renewable energies, aimed at projecting, producing, installing and managing large photovoltaic plants. The new venture will be 49% owned by Beghelli and 51% by ErgyCapital. In this joint venture, Beghelli will exploit its know-how by focusing on the technological, production and commercial aspects, while ErgyCapital will focus on energy management and financing.

# Discussion: the five CSR strategic variables in Beghelli

In this section, company initiatives related to environmental protection are analysed with regard to the five CSR strategic variables suggested by Burke and Logsdon (1996): centrality, specificity, visibility, proactivity and voluntarism. In the following pages, I analyse the case study in order to verify the presence of these characteristics and investigate *how* the firm has developed and implemented CSR activities with such characteristics.

## Centrality

Beghelli's activities related to the environmental issue show very high centrality because the firm has integrated environmental sustainability into its strategies and value proposition. Luca Beghelli said in this regard:

> The issues of energy saving and renewable energy are central to our business strategy and around these we are developing new projects addressed to the final consumer, firms and public bodies. Thanks to available technologies, individuals, companies and institutions really can do something to reduce carbon dioxide emissions and their oil bill, and do it immediately.

The firm's environmental commitment has influenced the characteristics of its product offering and the choice of market segments and industries in which it

---

8  Planned investment for the project 'Pianeta Sole' amounts to about €15 million over five years (Beghelli press release, 15 June 2007).

9  Beghelli press release, 26 January 2009.

operates. By realising a broad portfolio of energy-saving lighting and renewable energy products, the firm gives centrality to the environmental issue because the same resources sustain both the firm's competitive advantage and its social responsiveness. Innovations that improve the energy efficiency of the firm's products contribute to environmental protection and allow the firm to differentiate its products from those offered by competitors.

This centrality has been reached through a process of gradual integration. The starting point was the vision to interpret the environmental issue as an opportunity and see the sustainability challenge as a driver for innovation. Facing an increase in awareness and sensitivity to sustainability issues, the entrepreneur (Gian Pietro Beghelli) understood that resources and competences accumulated by his company could be leveraged to exploit specific sustainability and business opportunities related to the rational use of energy.

The company has seized these opportunities by means of innovation. Strategic, technological and marketing innovation has, in turn, contributed to the development of resources and competences within the firm, enhancing its ability to recognise and exploit other corporate social opportunities. This has gradually increased the centrality of the environmental issue. Figure 6.1 illustrates the virtuous circle in which resources and competences (including those related to the personal values and capabilities of the entrepreneur) are at the origin of the ability to identify corporate social opportunities (that benefit both society and the company). These resources and competences are developed and improved by the processes of innovation, learning and resource development aimed at exploiting the opportunities identified. The new resources developed then allow the firm to recognise and better exploit other corporate social opportunities.

**FIGURE 6.1** Firm resources and corporate social opportunities

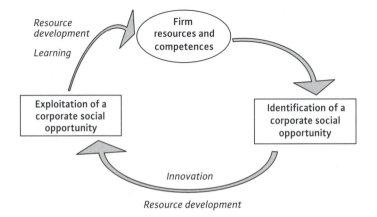

Beghelli has leveraged both its upstream (technological) and downstream (marketing) resources and competences (Anand and Delios 2002). Regarding upstream competences, R&D activities have always had a central role in company strategy; Beghelli's investment in R&D accounted for over 3% of consolidated sales in 2007. The societal issue selected—energy saving—was the most suitable to be served through the technological competences developed by the firm in the electronics and lighting fields. As already shown, the focus on energy-saving lighting for the business market aided the development of competences that allowed the firm to offer energy-saving products for consumer use and, then, enter the renewable energies sector.

Regarding downstream competences, Beghelli has leveraged its marketing competences and benefited from its previous experience in emergency lighting and in the development of several innovative safety and security products for both the business and the consumer market.

The firm has also leveraged an important intangible asset: its brand. Massive advertising campaigns have helped Beghelli reach a high level of brand awareness (92.9% of the Italian population recognises the brand)[10] and has created an association between the Beghelli brand and an image of 'safety and security' products. The company has used its brand to enter into new businesses related to energy saving and has emphasised the link with previous activities, calling this group of projects 'SalvaPianeta' (Save the Planet). The use of the word *salva* (to save) to create this name represents a clear reference to the names of different popular products launched by the company in the field of safety and security.

The company has leveraged its brand image through a massive communication activity focused on energy-saving and renewable-energy products. In this way, the company has concretely communicated its environmental commitment. Consequently, other companies have chosen Beghelli as a qualified partner in initiatives aimed at environmental protection, contributing further to the improvement of its reputation. For example, the Whirlpool Group launched its new line of energy-efficient appliances using a promotion offering a free kit of Beghelli energy-saving products.

Over the years, the focus on energy saving has oriented and given coherence to product and process innovation, growth processes (entrance into new business areas and creation of a joint venture) and resource development (Husted and Allen 2007).

---

10 According to the results of market research conducted by Doxa and cited on Beghelli's website (visited on 20 April 2009).

## Specificity

As mentioned above, specificity consists of a firm's ability to obtain a private benefit from a CSR programme. In the case of Beghelli, specificity is due to the interrelation between competitive and sustainability objectives. Its environmental commitment has stimulated the creation of new products. R&D investments leading to more energy-efficient, patented products were highly specific and enabled the firm to capture private economic benefits while benefiting society.

From a resource-based perspective, it is important to underline that specificity has been obtained by developing resources and competences based on existing firm-specific competences. To a question regarding the creation of new energy-saving products, Luca Beghelli answered: 'These are not sudden insight. They come from resources developed during more than 30 years of work, research and studies on materials and technologies in the field of emergency lighting, before, and in energy-saving lighting, after.' Thus, specificity is related to resource accumulation and the effects of time compression diseconomies that characterise R&D investments (Dierickx and Cool 1989).

Another aspect that has contributed to increase specificity is the capability of combining different factors of differentiation: those factors relating to environmental sustainability and those responding to other customer needs. In particular, the company has focused on attributes that may contribute to overcoming obstacles to the adoption of environmentally friendly products by potential customers.

An example is the 'Immediately Dual' line of energy-saving lamps that light up instantly, overcoming one of the typical disadvantages of these kinds of product. Another example is the 'Energy Tree' that is characterised by innovative technologies for using both renewable energies and design to meet customer aesthetic needs. Even the commercial formula 'A world of light at zero cost' combines energy-saving attributes with a financing, installation and maintenance service that encourages the adoption of energy-saving solutions by eliminating initial investments and risks for the customer.

This kind of product differentiation may contribute to overcoming some obstacles to using energy-saving products and alternative energy sources, ultimately enlarging the market and directly contributing to actual energy saving and environmental protection. At the same time, this product differentiation increases specificity, contributing to the firm's competitiveness.

Specificity is testified by the positive competitive and economic results obtained by Beghelli. The company entered into the energy-saving lighting industry in 1999. As shown in Figure 6.2, it was a difficult period for the firm, which recorded significant economic losses for four years (1999–2002), in part due to important long-term investments. However, since 1999, the firm has grown significantly and recently obtained positive financial and economic performances.

**FIGURE 6.2** Beghelli's consolidated turnover and net profit, 1999–2007

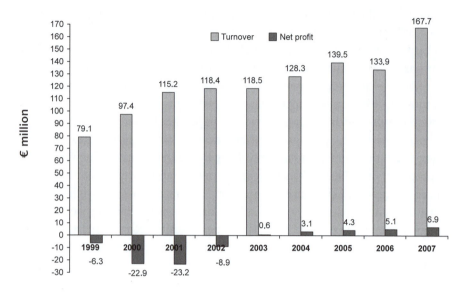

Source: Beghelli's annual reports

Data can contribute to our understanding of the role played by those business areas related to energy saving in determining recent positive competitive and economic performances.

The first important result is the fact that Beghelli has become 'the Italian leader in the energy-saving lighting industry'.[11] Second, the majority of Beghelli's consolidated turnover (91.4% in 2007) is derived from the lighting business area. In this area, the group's revenues have grown significantly, in particular in the period 2005–2007 when Beghelli's turnover increased by 28% while the rate of turnover growth in the Italian lighting industry was just 16.3%.[12]

According to the firm, these positive results are mainly due to its activities in the energy-saving area. The press release regarding Beghelli's third-quarter results in 2008 highlighted this sales trend:

> In the first nine months of 2008, the Group recorded a significant increase in net revenues (+15%) due largely to the good performance of sales in the lighting industry (+14.2%), in particular the project 'A world of light at zero cost', and the increase in revenues of photovoltaic products.[13]

11 Beghelli press release, 13 November 2008.
12 Source: Beghelli's annual reports and ANIE (Italian Federation of Electrotechnical and Electronics Industries).
13 Beghelli press release, 13 November 2008.

## Visibility

By integrating sustainability into company strategy, investing in business areas related to energy saving and developing innovations aimed at energy efficiency, Beghelli has given visibility to its environmental commitment by means of its business activity and its products. To improve this visibility, the company has invested significantly in corporate communication regarding energy saving and renewable energies, using different media and communication tools such as TV, radio and billboard advertising, advertising in cinemas, the company website and participation in fairs and exhibitions.

More precisely, the current focus of all corporate communication is on the promotion of products and projects that may contribute to energy saving. In 2007, the company used television advertising for the launch of the project 'A world of light at zero cost', of the line of energy-saving lamps and of photovoltaic products. In 2008, TV advertising campaigns were focused on environmentally friendly products. Moreover, the founder personally participated in five lengthy commercial spots broadcast by national Italian television during 'Festival di Sanremo', the most important Italian singing competition and one of the most popular television programmes (sponsored by Beghelli since 2003). All five commercials (presented during the same week) were focused on the company's activities on environmental protection and the promotion of both business and consumer products from the line 'Save the Planet'.

This communication activity played an important role in the relationship with potential customers and other stakeholders because it contributed to different objectives:

- Increasing interest in environmental protection and energy saving

- Increasing the adoption of energy-saving lighting systems and renewable energies

- Improving the company's market position in these fields

- Communicating the commitment of the company on environmental issues

Increasing interest and knowledge on environmental issues and increasing the adoption of energy-efficient solutions are important objectives for both the company and society. Thus, there is a shared benefit. The company promotes its products for commercial objectives and, at the same time, contributes to attracting attention to the environmental issue and on the possibilities of saving energy.

From the point of view of visibility of CSR initiatives, focusing on communicating the products and projects related to environmental protection allows the company to combine commercial advertising with its CSR-related messages. In fact, important advertising campaigns and the sponsorship of a popular event such as 'Festival di Sanremo' enable the company to communicate to several stakeholders at once. Those products presented are the tangible results of R&D investment oriented to sustainability. The innovative project 'A world of light at zero cost' is another concrete example of what the entrepreneur and the company do to help other companies and public entities save energy. From this perspective, it may be useful to present it to all stakeholders, not only those directly interested in it. This justifies the choice of using far-reaching TV campaigns for the promotion not only of consumer products but also for business products.

However, it is important to consider that, regarding visibility, the credibility of the source is an important factor. In this perspective, purchased advertising attracts the attention of stakeholders, but may lead to stakeholder scepticism and risks appearing as 'greenwash' (Tetrault Sirsly and Lamertz 2008). In the case of Beghelli, this problem is mitigated by the fact that the company does not describe its generic environmental commitment, but instead presents the concrete results of this commitment (i.e. its products and services). Nevertheless, the choice to focus almost exclusively on advertising as a tool for communicating CSR-related messages represents a limit of Beghelli's approach to CSR. The company does not recognise any form of reporting activity regarding the social and environmental dimensions of its performance, limiting the possibility for adequate evaluation by stakeholders. One of the reasons for this absence of reporting activity on CSR seems to be related to a cultural problem. Regarding this aspect, Beghelli continues to act 'informally' as do many family businesses and small and medium-sized companies.[14] In SMEs, this may be justified by the direct and personal relationship of the entrepreneur (and his or her family) with the relevant stakeholders (Fassin 2008). But it seems inadequate in the case of a company such as Beghelli with subsidiaries and customers in several foreign countries and a duty to report to all shareholders (including socially responsible investors) and the financial market, being listed on the Italian Stock Exchange.

## Proactivity and voluntarism

Proactivity and voluntarism are analysed jointly since they are strictly related. Beghelli's projects on energy saving are characterised by voluntarism because the company is not subject to externally imposed compliance requirements (Burke and Logsdon 1996).

---

14 On the other hand, Beghelli has developed important forms of codification of its corporate social involvement, in particular the Group Code of Ethics and ISO 14001 certification of its environmental management system.

Regarding proactivity, Beghelli has not developed new products and commercial formulas as a consequence of explicit stakeholder requests. On the contrary, some developments are aimed at creating an incentive or removing an obstacle to the adoption of energy-efficient products and renewable energies. The company provides a response to the social issue by encouraging more energy-efficient behaviour in potential customers. An interesting example is represented by the decision to offer energy-saving street-lighting systems through the commercial formula 'A world of light at zero cost'. The focus on this target is an example of proactivity because in Italy the attention on energy saving by public entities is still limited.

On the other hand, it is worth pointing out that one of the drivers of the focus on energy efficiency is the evolution of regulatory and public incentives, and expectations about future trends. From this point of view, the company responds to a social trend and, at the same time, tries to anticipate future developments that may represent corporate social opportunities. In this regard, it should also be noted that, during development of energy-saving and renewable-energy products, the firm has benefited from previous R&D investment regarding the rational use of energy that has been realised even before the entrance into business areas strictly related to energy saving and conservation.

Focusing on the background of voluntarism and proactivity, Beghelli's case identifies the central role of the entrepreneur, his values, his ability to identify opportunities and his attitude towards innovation. Luca Beghelli's response to a question on the origin of his business strategies and the activities related to energy saving was as follows:

> It is a characteristic of my own father: the ability to interpret the needs of the market, sometimes anticipating them, and the propensity for technological innovation. It was in a TV commercial with Robert De Niro in 2000 when we presented the claim 'Every penny saved is a penny earned'. By then his conviction was already that in the lighting industry the future would depend on a key phrase: energy saving—benefiting environmental quality and with a substantial reduction in expenditure on electricity. On the one hand, the rational use of energy obeys a principle of responsibility towards the environment and future generations; on the other hand, it also has an economic advantage for those who adopt it. After a decade, both these issues are proving to be extremely topical and relevant.

The entrepreneur has a decisive influence on corporate culture and strategy. Thanks to his commitment, his personal values have become corporate values and he has championed CSR throughout the firm and integrated it into competitive strategy. With regard to the evolution of his firm and its product portfolio, Gian Pietro Beghelli said: 'Despite dealing with different industries and products, the philosophy has always remained the same: to realise socially useful and technologically advanced products.'[15]

---

15 Interview with Gian Pietro Beghelli published by *Il Giorno* (Perego 2008).

Ownership concentration and the centrality of the entrepreneur in corporate governance have favoured strategic flexibility: that is 'the degree to which firms react to opportunities and threats within their competitive environments' (Zahra et al. 2008: 1,036). The entrepreneur's values and aspirations have played a central role in the identification of corporate social opportunities and in the choice of which opportunities to pursue (Chrisman et al. 2003). Moreover, the possibility of exploiting corporate social opportunities related to energy saving has also benefited the long-term orientation of the entrepreneur. He decided to invest in the exploitation of such opportunities regardless of the time required to break even and with the perspective typical of 'patient capital' (Gallo and Vilaseca 1996). The entrepreneur is also at the origin of the creation of several new products and services that have been developed from his personal ideas and intuitions.

From the point of view of the factors that facilitate the adoption of strategic CSR, this case testifies to the possibility for a family business to adopt a strategic approach to CSR. Better still, it reveals a central role of the entrepreneur in the identification of a corporate social opportunity and in the decision to try to realise it.

More generally, the analysis of this case reveals that the firm's approach to CSR has several characteristics in common with other family businesses and SMEs (Spence 1999, 2007; Uhlaner et al. 2004; de la Cruz Déniz-Déniz and Cabrera Suárez 2005; Jenkins 2009), even if Beghelli is a large firm listed on the stock exchange. Besides the strong link with the entrepreneur's values and his personal motivations, Beghelli's approach to CSR is characterised by its roots in the local community and the importance it places on primary stakeholders, particularly employees. In this regard, Luca Beghelli described the peculiarities and the origin of corporate social involvement in his firm as follows:

> The social responsibility of Beghelli originates primarily from its strong link with the region and the communities where the company has its headquarters and where my father, the three of us children and our families live. This translates into a clear and strong will to continue to grow here, using the workforce here. And it is the love for our hills that drove us for years towards environmental protection.

This approach has positively contributed to integrating CSR into business strategy and activities.

## Conclusions

This chapter sought to increase knowledge of strategic CSR by investigating how the integration between CSR and strategy can be concretely executed. The five strategic dimensions of CSR identified by Burke and Logsdon (1996) have been used as a frame of reference and two research questions have been defined based on this model. The chapter tried to address these questions through the analysis of a relevant case: Beghelli.

The first research question focused on how CSR initiatives can be selected and managed in order to improve their centrality, specificity and visibility. In the case of Beghelli, centrality, specificity and visibility have been obtained by focusing on a specific societal issue (the environmental issue) and creating products with attributes and intrinsic functionalities that contribute to addressing this issue: energy-saving lighting systems and renewable energy products. In this way, the firm's efforts towards energy saving and conservation assume centrality because they are oriented to both environmental sustainability and the company's competitive objectives. The same resources sustain both the firm's competitive advantage and its social responsiveness. The energy-efficient products developed and the technological innovations they incorporate are highly specific and, hence, allow the company to gain a private benefit, while contributing to environmental protection. Moreover, these products give visibility to the environmental commitment of the firm and, by focusing corporate communication on products and projects related to environmental protection, the company combines commercial advertising and CSR-related messages.

The case shows the importance of leveraging existing firm-specific resources. Beghelli has leveraged different categories of resources and competences: technological and marketing competences, as well as its corporate image and reputation derived from its well-known brand. Based on these resources, the firm has developed new resources and competences through the processes of innovation and resource development in order to exploit corporate social opportunities related to the production of energy-saving systems. The resources developed are firm-specific and difficult to imitate. For example, R&D investment aimed at developing energy-efficient products are highly specific and, being based on the knowledge previously developed by the firm, lead to the creation of resources and competences that are difficult to replicate since they are the result of a process of resource accumulation and are characterised by time compression diseconomies.

The case also shows how the integration of strategy and CSR issues can be gradually increased through a process of resource development. Beghelli entered the energy-saving lighting industry by exploiting the know-how previously developed in the emergency lighting industry. Then, by operating in the energy-saving lighting industry, it has developed competences regarding the efficient use of energy that it has subsequently leveraged to enter the renewable energies industry. This has gradually increased the centrality of the firm's commitment on energy saving and conservation. In this, it is also possible to identify a virtuous circle. When the business activities and competitive strategies of a company address sustainability issues, the company develops resources that allow it to recognise and better exploit other corporate social opportunities.

Regarding innovation, the analysis of the case reveals that the exploitation of corporate social opportunities does not necessarily require radical innovation. It can be executed through incremental innovation of both technological and marketing aspects.

This case also reveals how Beghelli has improved the specificity of its activities aimed at energy saving by offering products that combine different factors of differentiation: factors related to environmental sustainability (high energy efficiency) and factors that respond to other customer needs (such as comfort, design, financing and accessory services). In particular, the company in several cases has identified factors of differentiation that may contribute to overcoming obstacles to the adoption of environmentally friendly products by potential customers and, hence, may increase the diffusion of such products. This contributes to actual energy saving and, at the same time, increases the appropriability of the wealth created by the company.

The second research question concerned the factors behind the adoption of strategic CSR initiatives. From this perspective, Beghelli is characterised by the central role of the entrepreneur. His values, propensity for innovation, long-term orientation, ability to identify business opportunities and intuitions are at the basis of the focus of the company on energy saving and conservation and of the integration between the environmental issue and Beghelli's competitive strategy.

Beghelli is a family firm with a concentrated ownership structure and corporate governance that attributes a pivotal role to the founder. In this specific case, these characteristics have not been an obstacle to the adoption of a strategic approach to CSR, but, on the contrary, have allowed it. In this regard, it is important to point out that, in companies characterised by high centrality of the entrepreneur, critical factors are his or her values and ability to identify corporate social opportunities, which requires a prerequisite of a positive attitude towards societal issues and a readiness to interpret them as an opportunity (and not only as a threat). Unfortunately, this is rare among entrepreneurial and family firms, which frequently focus on the costs of CSR and refraining from actions that could be regarded as socially irresponsible (de la Cruz Déniz-Déniz and Cabrera Suárez 2005; Dyer and Whetten 2006; Wiklund 2006). In these cases, a change of attitude towards societal issues and CSR is necessary as a first step.

# References

Anand, J., and A. Delios (2002) 'Absolute and Relative Resources as Determinants of International Acquisitions', *Strategic Management Journal* 23: 119-34.

Bansal, P., and K. Roth (2000) 'Why Companies Go Green: A Model of Ecological Responsiveness', *Academy of Management Journal* 43.4: 717-36.

Baron, D. (2001) 'Private Politics, Corporate Social Responsibility and Integrated Strategy', *Journal of Economics and Management Strategy* 10.1: 7-45.

Bonicelli, E. (1997) 'Beghelli fattura 250 miliardi con le idee studiate "in casa" ', *Il Sole 24 ore*, 2 December 1997.

Burke, L., and J.M. Logsdon (1996) 'How Corporate Social Responsibility Pays Off', *Long Range Planning* 29.4: 495-502.

Chrisman, J.J., J.H. Chua and S.A. Zahra (2003) 'Creating Wealth in Family Firms through Managing Resources: Comments and Extensions', *Entrepreneurship Theory and Practice* 27.4 (Summer 2003): 359-65.

De la Cruz Déniz-Déniz, M., and M.K. Cabrera Suárez (2005) 'Corporate Social Responsibility and Family Business in Spain', *Journal of Business Ethics* 56.1: 27-41.

Dierickx, I., and K. Cool (1989) 'Asset Stock Accumulation and Sustainability of Competitive Advantage', *Management Science* 35.12: 1,504-11.

Dutton, J.E., and S.E. Jackson (1987) 'Categorizing Strategic Issues: Links to Organizational Action', *Academy of Management Review* 12.1: 76-90.

Dyer, W.G., and D.A. Whetten (2006) 'Family Firms and Social Responsibility: Preliminary Evidence from the S&P 500', *Entrepreneurship: Theory & Practice* 30.6 (November 2006): 785-802.

Eisenhardt, K.M. (1989) 'Building Theories from Case Study Research', *Academy of Management Review* 14.4: 532-50.

Fassin, Y. (2008) 'SMEs and the Fallacy of Formalising CSR', *Business Ethics: A European Review* 17.4: 364-78.

Gallo, M.A., and A. Vilaseca (1996) 'Finance in Family Business', *Family Business Review* 9.4: 387-401.

Grayson, D., and A. Hodges (2004) *Corporate Social Opportunity! Seven Steps to Make Corporate Social Responsibility Work for your Business* (Sheffield, UK: Greenleaf Publishing).

Husted, B.W., and D.B. Allen (2007) 'Strategic Corporate Social Responsibility and Value Creation among Large Firms: Lessons from the Spanish Experience', *Long Range Planning* 40.6: 594-610.

Jenkins, H. (2009) 'A "Business Opportunity" Model of Corporate Social Responsibility for Small- and Medium-sized Enterprises', *Business Ethics: A European Review* 18.1: 21-36.

McWilliams, A., and D.S. Siegel (2001) 'Corporate Social Responsibility: A Theory of the Firm Perspective', *Academy of Management Review* 26.1: 117-27.

Milliman, J., J. Ferguson and K. Sylvester (2008) 'Implementation of Michael Porter's Strategic Corporate Social Responsibility Model', *Journal of Global Business Issues: Conference Edition 2008*, April 2008: 29-33.

Mitchell, R.K., B.R. Agle and D.J. Wood (1997) 'Toward a Theory of Stakeholder Identification and Salience: Defining the Principle of Who and What Really Counts', *Academy of Management Review* 22.4: 853-86.

Perego A. (2008) '8 domande a Gian Pietro Beghelli', *Il Giorno*, 15 September 2008.

Porter, M.E., and M.R. Kramer (2006) 'Strategy and Society. The Link between Competitive Advantage and Corporate Social Responsibility', *Harvard Business Review* 84.12 (December 2006): 78-92.

Response Project (2008) 'Understanding and Responding to Societal Demands on Corporate Responsibility (RESPONSE)', Final Report (draft), Sixth Framework Programme, Priority 7, Citizens and Governance in a Knowledge Based Society; www.insead.edu/v1/ibis/response_project/documents/Response_FinalReport.pdf, accessed 24 March 2010.

Siegel, D.S., and D.F. Vitaliano (2007) 'An Empirical Analysis of the Strategic Use of Corporate Social Responsibility', *Journal of Economics & Management Strategy* 16.3 (Fall 2007): 773-92.

Spence, L.J. (1999) 'Does Size Matter? The State of the Art in Small Business Ethics', *Business Ethics: A European Review* 8.3: 163-74.

—— (2007) 'CSR and Small Business in a European Policy Context: The Five "C"s of CSR and Small Business Research Agenda 2007', *Business and Society Review* 112.4: 533-52.

Tetrault Sirsly, C.A., and K. Lamertz (2008) 'When Does a Corporate Social Responsibility Initiative Provide a First-mover Advantage?', *Business & Society* 47.3 (September 2008): 343-69.

Uhlaner, L.M., H.J.M. van Goor-Balk and E. Masurel (2004) 'Family Business and Corporate Social Responsibility in a Sample of Dutch Firms', *Journal of Small Business and Enterprise Development* 11.2: 186-94.

Weaver, G.R., L.K. Treviño and P.L. Cochran (1999) 'Integrated and Decoupled Corporate Social Performance: Management Commitments, External Pressures, and Corporate Ethics Practices', *Academy of Management Journal* 42.5 (October 1999): 539-52.

Wiklund, J. (2006) 'Commentary: "Family Firms and Social Responsibility: Preliminary Evidence from the S&P 500" ', *Entrepreneurship Theory and Practice* 30.6 (November 2006): 803-808.

Zadek, S. (2004) 'The Path to Corporate Responsibility', *Harvard Business Review* 82.12 (December 2004): 125-32.

Zahra, S.A., J.C. Hayton, D.O. Neubaum, C. Dibrell and J. Craig (2008) 'Culture of Family Commitment and Strategic Flexibility: The Moderating Effect of Stewardship', *Entrepreneurship Theory and Practice* 32.6 (November 2008): 1,035-54.

# Part II
# CSR and value creation

# 7
# CSR as a strategic activity
## Value creation, redistribution and integration

**Karen Maas and Frank Boons**

Erasmus University Rotterdam, The Netherlands

In recent years corporate social responsibility (CSR) has become increasingly important as the concept that frames the business contribution to sustainable development (Commission of the European Communities 2002). Building on generic definitions of sustainable development (WCED 1987) it denotes a situation in which firms combine their economic goals with taking responsibility for their ecological and social impact.

CSR has received a lot of attention from researchers and practitioners. In both fields we find advocates as well as critics. The latter believe CSR is about enlightened self-interest, PR and greenwashing and will not provide any value for society (Keim 1978; Frankental 2001; Margolis and Walsh 2003; Matten *et al.* 2003) and perhaps not even for businesses (Friedman 1970; Bragdon and Marlin 1972; Vance 1975). Advocates of CSR believe that CSR will provide value for business, society and ecosystems, and is a source of innovation (Freeman 1984; Hart and Milstein 2003; Husted and Salazar 2006; Porter and Kramer 2006). These mixed qualifications are at least partially a consequence of the fact that a wide range of activities are subsumed under the umbrella term of CSR, ranging from philanthropy to CSR reporting and from pollution prevention to sustainable purchasing.

In our view, CSR has potential to become a strategic activity adding value on different dimensions—business, society and ecosystems—if two conditions are met. The first condition for strategic CSR is that CSR needs to become integrated with the strategy of the firm. As long as CSR activities are 'bolt-on', companies engage in socially beneficial spot-initiatives and extra activities which are disconnected from their core business operations (Wolff and Barth 2005). Examples of this are financial or material donations, and sponsoring or volunteering activities of employees. 'Built-in' CSR constitutes an integral part of business strategy and operations (Grayson and Hodges 2004). This includes efforts to integrate economic, ecological and social values into business processes, make production processes more sustainable and to improve the ecological and social properties of the products, services or goods, either by improving existing products or by creating new products.

The second condition for strategic CSR is to have the means to measure and monitor these new or additional values. The reason for this is twofold. On the one hand, given the public interest in CSR, CSR is closely related to transparency, accountability and legitimacy and requires some form of validation. On the other hand, if CSR is to become a strategic activity, the firm itself will have a need to monitor the impact of its activities. Strategic CSR urges firms to assess their value added (or destroyed) across ecological, social and economic dimensions and to incorporate those impacts into management decisions.

Thus, in order to provide insight into the strategic potential of CSR, two questions need to be answered:

- How can the value of business activities for a firm, society and ecosystems be defined?

- How can the contribution of activities of the firm to such value be measured?

The answer to the first question is difficult as 'value' eventually is a judgement made by individuals and communities: there is no objective way of defining it. For this reason, we will draw on literature from various sources to explore what is actually meant by 'providing value'. The answer to the second question will build on this. Interestingly, it will show that current practice tends to focus on measuring a limited part of the value that is generated by CSR. Management scholars have focused mainly on the financial gains for the firm. In practice, management and reporting standards such as ISO 14000 and the Global Reporting Initiative (GRI) assess CSR procedures rather than performance in terms of impacts on society and ecosystems.

In this chapter we propose a framework for assessing the strategic potential of CSR. This framework consists of two parts. First, based on distinct bodies of literature, we distinguish three ways in which CSR may provide value to a firm, society and ecosystems. These are illustrated by examples. Building on this distinction, we explore the consequences for measuring the impact of CSR activities in the second part of the framework.

## Defining the value of firm activities

Before we go into the question of how value can be created through strategic CSR we will explore how the concept of value creation is framed in strategic management literature. In general, the primary pursuit of firms is to create and maintain value (Conner 1991). How to create and appropriate[1] value are central concepts in the (strategic) management and organisational literature (Lepak *et al.* 2007; Verwaal *et al.* 2008). However, what actually constitutes value is often left unaddressed in these theories.

Strategic management theories explore the question of why one strategy is more successful in creating and maintaining value than another, given product, firm and industry characteristics. Those theories basically boil down to two general types: competence-based theories and governance-based theories. Competence-based theories—including evolutionary economics and the resource-based view—focus on value creation by explaining the emergence and sustainability of economic rents (Barney 1991; Conner 1991; Barney *et al.* 2001). Governance-based theories—including agency theory, transaction-cost economics and property rights theory—mainly focus on value appropriation by explaining the existence and boundaries of economic institutions, such as firms, and employment relations (Williamson 1985, 1999; Makadok 2003). In both cases, value is—implicitly—defined in terms of immediate or future financial gains for firm owners.

Financial profit remains an important standard for optimal functioning in the private sector (March and Simon 1993) and it is more or less accepted that the main target of for-profit firms is to maximise, in the long run, the wealth of the shareholders of firms (Friedman 1970; Jensen 1998). From this perspective, CSR is received with great scepticism as a zero-sum game where the impact on companies mainly adds costs and limits the freedom of firms through additional regulatory demands (Haigh and Jones 2006).

This view was already being challenged in the 1970s in a public and academic debate about the social responsibility of business (Ackerman 1975; Vink 1986). With the rise of the concept of CSR this debate has been revitalised. Firms adopting CSR also take actions that are intended to further social good and which are beyond their economic interest and what is required by law (McWilliams and Siegel 2001: 117).

The management perspective of value as financial profit is also challenged by insights from economic sociologists. They have shown that economic value is not an objective fact, but rather the result of judgements of individual consumers, producers and other societal actors (e.g. financial institutions, government, environ-

---

1 Value appropriation refers to the distribution of the value created (Klein 2008). Value appropriation is in literature labelled variously as value capture, allocation, realisation, dispersion or distribution (Priem 2007).

mental and social groups). Cars can be valued for their speed, range, reliability, fuel efficiency, comfort, or as a signifier of social status. Depending on what value is dominant, financial profits are accrued based on this value. More generally, the measurement of economic value has been institutionalised in accounting practices (Callon 1998). This insight builds on the sociological perspective of social constructivism which holds that actors base their decisions and actions not on an objective reality, but rather on their beliefs and norms about that reality (Berger and Luckman 1966). Understanding economic activities is thus only possible if we analyse the beliefs and norms that guide economic actors.

Given the socially constructed nature of value it is not possible to provide specific definitions: these emerge in the context of interactions among economic actors and those that seek to influence them. Together they enact the specific value provided for the firm, society and ecosystems. It is possible though to reflect on different ways in which such value is constructed. For this we draw from literature on innovation, global commodity chains and stakeholder theory.

## New value creation

Firms derive profit from value-adding activities. If such activities are performed more efficiently, the value-added increases. In addition to such efficiency improvements, firms may develop product innovations. This consists of creating new value: the firm develops a new object, service or activity which is perceived as valuable by some social group. This may be the creation of a new market, or the development of a new product based on the recognition of a new problem field. Such innovations usually require collaborations with other firms, knowledge institutes and governments, especially when they are aimed to reduce the ecological and social impact of the firm or be more sustainable than the product that is replaced (Weber and Hemmelskamp 2005). Such innovations may be considered as the core of a strategic approach to CSR as they move the firm and its core activities towards a redefined balance between economic revenues for the firm, reduced impact on ecosystems and improved value for society. To the extent that products are more systemic (Prencipe 2003), such innovations often require an approach such as transition management (Loorbach 2008). Moving from the internal combustion engine towards electric or fuel cell vehicles requires innovations not only in car technology and design, but also in the supporting infrastructure and servicing. In addition, such systemic innovations replace to some extent existing firms, a process referred to by Schumpeter as 'creative destruction' (Schumpeter 1975 [1942]). CSR as new value creation is thus a process of collaborative innovation with winners and losers. A key characteristic is that, at the level of the firm, but often also at the level of the larger production and consumption system, a new balance is struck between economic, ecological and social value.

An example of CSR as new value creation is the rising trend of firms developing strategies targeting the so-called 'bottom of the pyramid' (BoP). These firms distinguish themselves in that they seek to create new markets involving customers, employees, suppliers and/or distributors who have an average daily purchasing power of US$2 or less (Prahalad 2005). These initiatives can lead to profitable businesses and economic development for people living at the bottom of the pyramid as well as the multinational corporations that serve them. We describe two examples where people at the BoP fulfil different roles.[2] In the first case, increased access to affordable life-saving medicines for South Africans, the people at the BoP are consumers. In the second case, using straw for district heating, the people at the BoP are the suppliers.

Five and half million South Africans are infected with HIV/AIDS, and more than 837,000 individuals urgently require access to life-prolonging antiretroviral medicines. According to the World Health Organisation only an estimated 21% of people living with HIV have access to the needed treatment in public clinics and hospitals. The founder of Aspen Pharmacare translated the need to supply South Africans with the essential medicines required for the treatment of life-threatening diseases such as HIV/AIDS, tuberculosis and malaria into a business opportunity by developing a pharmaceutical manufacturer capable of supplying the South African market with brand name, generic and over-the-counter medicines at affordable prices. In ten years, Aspen Pharmacare has become one of the largest drug companies in South Africa. Initially worth US$7 million, Aspen has grown at a rate of 40% per year. By building the largest manufacturing plant in the country, Aspen Pharmacare is now in a position to supply South Africa's national antiretroviral treatment programme with approximately 60% of its current requirements. In 2005, Aspen had annual revenues of US$467 million and net profits of US$75 million. Aspen's efforts provide increased access to affordable life-saving medicines for South Africans.

A second example shows how people at the BoP can act as suppliers. PEC Luban, a company providing district heating in the town of Luban, Poland, began using straw for heat generation in the late 1990s. This allowed for significant reductions of harmful emissions from the combustion of traditional fuels (mostly coal). The use of straw also created demand for straw from local farmers—straw is a locally produced and renewable source of biomass energy. The straw-fired boilers were constructed as an upgrade and extension to the existing coal-fired boiler plant. The Luban facility is Poland's largest boiler plant fired with straw, offering a good example of overcoming technical challenges to meet energy needs in a sustainable way and avoiding dependence on polluting sources of energy that also contribute

---

2 Both cases are based on information from the 'Growing Inclusive Markets' initiative of UNDP; www.growinginclusivemarkets.org (accessed 9 December 2009).

to climate change. PEC Luban was able in recent years to reduce its use of coal by 2,500 tonnes per year. The use of waste straw instead of coal has lowered $CO_2$ emissions by 2,000 tonnes per year, $SO_2$ emissions by 6,000 kilograms per year, and $NO_2$ emissions by 2,500 kilograms per year. The wide-scale use of biomass energy is likely to stimulate the development of rural areas and agriculture and to increase employment and incomes for smaller farmers. In addition, the sustainable use of biomass energy sources helps to manage the local environment. Previously most of the surplus straw was burned in the fields, which constituted a serious health hazard for the population and caused environmental damage. One of the main obstacles was that the farmers lacked knowledge about the benefits of selling straw for energy purposes and about how to comply with strict and costly technical requirements. This example shows how the development of new products can benefit both the firm and the local communities.

## Value integration

A second type of CSR concerns the integration of stakeholder concerns into the firm's strategy. Stakeholders are those individuals and organisations that are influenced by, or are able to influence, the activities of a firm (Freeman 1984). The concept of CSR builds on the idea that the interest of all stakeholders should not be sacrificed to the interest of the shareholders and it is a firm's task to create value with and for its stakeholders. The purpose of the organisation is thus to create value for its stakeholders (or the interests they represent, such as those of ecosystems), bringing into focus different targets, including earnings for owners, satisfaction for employees, product benefits for customers and taxes for society (Post *et al.* 2002). The mutual dependence of firms and society implies that any business decision, as well as any policy decision, influences society and other stakeholders as well as businesses (Emerson 2003). Therefore, the main challenge is to maximise value in win–win situations or to optimise value in win–lose or lose–win situations. This is one of the main theoretical and practical problems around CSR as a strategic activity. Different stakeholders may have different views of what is valuable because of differing knowledge, goals and context. Stakeholders can even have competing interests and viewpoints of what is valuable (Lepak *et al.* 2007: 191).

Value integration implies the effort of a firm to integrate values espoused by stakeholders into its activities and organisational routines that were previously disregarded. As a result, firms no longer strive for financial benefits in isolation but adopt a broader view including environmental and social values. The voice of the stakeholder is inserted into the business processes through interaction with external parties such as suppliers, customers, communities, governmental and non-governmental organisations or the media. Incorporation of stakeholder views may result in optimisation of existing products and processes by pollution prevention or product stewardship. Pollution prevention comprises activities that reduce the amount of pollution generated by a process or product. This can be achieved either by reducing the source or input, or by reducing emissions and waste during the production process. Whereas pollution prevention focuses on internal operations, product stewardship extends beyond organisational boundaries to include the entire product life-cycle, from raw material access through production processes, to product use and disposal of used products (Hart and Milstein 2003).

An example of CSR as value integration is the initiative of the Dutch regional platform for nuisance and safety to set up a residential advisory board (RAB) in Pernis, Rotterdam.[3] The RAB was designed as an organised form of stakeholder consultation with the local community. After a trial period of two years, the board was positively evaluated by the firm and by the local residents, and has been run successfully for more then ten years. Shell is a global group of energy and petrochemical companies, with 104,000 employees in more than 110 countries. Shell Pernis, a joint oil refinery/chemicals manufacturing site, is the largest refinery in Europe. In the direct vicinity of the Shell Pernis refinery over 450,000 people live permanently in the local communities, leading to a large potential for nuisance or risk situations. In 1998 a residential advisory board (RAB) was initiated. The board includes representatives of the local community, Shell Pernis and an independent facilitator, enabling local residents to discuss with the firm anything that may directly or indirectly affect them as neighbours of the firm. The main reason for initiating the RAB was that it could facilitate and support open and direct communication between the firm and the local residents which is in the interest of both the firm and the neighbours. The RAB meets four times a year. The emphasis in these meetings is on environmental and social aspects such as nuisance, environmental, health and safety aspects.

Within the RAB, agreements have been reached about reduction of large-scale flaring and water pollution in the harbour area, as well as improved communication about nuisance. The RAB provides a means for such agreements, and is a way to show accountability towards the people living in the immediate area and for the quality of life in that area. Besides this, the RAB is a vehicle for Shell to be made aware of the concerns of the local residents and their perceptions and to encourage Shell to incorporate those perceptions in their operations. Furthermore, feedback is obtained for the preparation of external communication material which helps to maintain or even improve Shell's image (Shell Pernis Residential Advisory Board 2003). This example shows how stakeholder consultation can be used to identify

---

3  The case description is based on information from the Shell Pernis website (www.shell. com/home/content/nld/aboutshell/shell_businesses/pernis, accessed 9 December 2009) and on the model for a residential advisory board published by the Shell Pernis Residential Advisory Board (2003).

stakeholder value and indicators to be measured, reported on and incorporated in strategic management decisions.

## Value redistribution

A third type of strategic CSR activity can be drawn from the literature on global commodity chains. Such chains refer to the globally linked stages of a product's life-cycle from the extraction of raw materials through production, consumption, to recycling and waste disposal (Gereffi 1999a, b). This approach focuses on the international dimension of power and dependence relationships, often between developing and developed countries. Second, it addresses the issue of relative power in the chain, identifying lead firms that control crucial resources and generate most of the profits. Third, it views mechanisms of coordination throughout the chain as a source of competitive advantage. Lead firms choose coordination mechanisms (varying from market transactions to network forms and hierarchical relationships) that allow them to achieve their goals. Finally, organisational learning is viewed as the central mechanism through which firms consolidate or improve their relative position towards other actors in the chain.

Based on the analysis of global commodity chains of food products, apparel, electronics and automobiles, two distinct types of commodity chain have been identified (Gereffi 2001). Producer-driven commodity chains (automobiles, computers), are led by large transnational corporations that coordinate production and distribution into vertical networks. Buyer-driven commodity chains (food products, apparel, toys) are led by large retailers, marketers and branded manufacturers that coordinate the development of decentralised production networks in developing countries based on trade rather than direct coordination.

The global commodity chain approach provides an analysis of what in debates about CSR is often construed as a social issue: the dependence of farmers and workers in developing countries on Western firms. Firms in consuming countries hold power over producers of commodities such as coffee and cacao, but also apparel and consumer electronics, and are thus able to appropriate most of the value-added. Moreover, Clift (2003; see also Clift and Wright 2000) finds that such inequalities correlate with ecological impact. For example, in the commodity chains of mobile phones, producing countries combine low value appropriation with a disproportionately high ecological impact.

Based on this analysis, a third type of strategic CSR takes the shape of value redistribution as relationships among commodity chains are altered to strike a more equal balance among economic actors in producing and consuming countries in terms of ecological, economic and social value. Over the years, various initiatives have developed to forge such a change in relationships, of which fair-trade programmes are the most well known.

A case of structural redistribution of value has occurred in the last decade in the product chain of coffee. Before 1990, coffee-producing countries operated under a relatively successful price agreement which was upheld by the International Coffee Organisation (ICO) (Bates 1997). When this cartel collapsed, prices dropped dramatically, leaving many farmers in South American and African countries with almost no income. The social problems resulting from that were an incentive to members of several Western countries to develop programmes where coffee was bought from farmers at a price exceeding world market levels, and then sold to consumers that were willing to pay this extra price. Over time, such initiatives were institutionalised in an international standard organisation under the Fairtrade label. For the people involved in these programmes, value (in terms of monetary compensation) redistribution was their main aim: the purpose was to establish links from coffee farmers to Western producers outside the mainstream coffee product chain. For firms, carrying the Fairtrade label implies that they are involved in value redistribution in monetary terms. The principles behind this suggest that monetary improvement for farmers is a prerequisite for improving other qualities, including improved environmental performance.

After a period in which Fairtrade existed as a small market niche alongside the mainstream coffee chain, in recent years several roasting firms have started to include in their product line products that carry the Fairtrade label, or a label that has similar purposes. In the Dutch market, a large retailer developed its own standard for its in-house brand, seeking to capture part of the market that Fairtrade initiatives were taking. More recently, the market leader in coffee products, Douwe Egberts, a Sara Lee subsidiary, has announced that it aims to have fulfilled the major competing certification programme to Fairtrade, UTZ CERTIFIED, for its total product line.

At least on the Dutch market, there is thus a competition emerging among firms based on their definitions of social value as exemplified by the standards to which they adhere. During the beginning of 2008, this competition became manifest in a legal suit by Douwe Egberts against the province of Groningen. This governmental body had formulated criteria for a new contract for coffee suppliers that could only be fulfilled by firms adhering to fair-trade standards. Douwe Egberts fought these criteria, stating that this amounted to market distortion. The judge decided that the governmental agency had the freedom to set criteria in this way. This example shows how value redistribution, in terms of monetary units, can be successful and lead to competition among firms (Boons 2009).

# Measurement

If CSR is to become a strategic activity, two conditions have to be met. The first condition for strategic CSR was the integration of CSR within the strategy of the firm, which can be distinguished in the three types outlined above. The second condition for firms is to measure and monitor not only their financial returns but also the value added (or destroyed) across the environmental and social dimension. Current practice tends to focus on measuring only a limited part of the value that is generated by CSR. Management scholars have focused mainly on performance measurement measuring the financial gains for the firm. The question about what impacts those corporate CSR actions have, not only on the bottom line but also on society and ecosystems, remains largely unexplored (Margolis and Walsh 2003).

**FIGURE 7.1** Developments over time in the focus of performance measurement and value creation

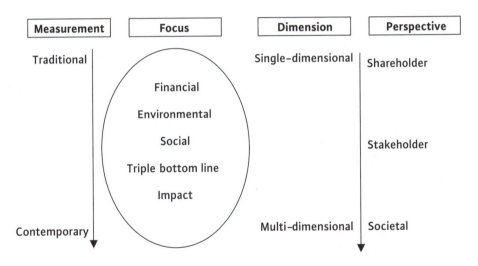

To be able to measure the impact of CSR on different dimensions, a shift is needed from output thinking, focusing on a single-dimensional firm perspective, to impact thinking, which includes a social and ecosystem perspective (see Figure 7.1). Performance measurement, traditionally used to measure companies' efficiency, profit and competitive advantage, builds on output thinking. Measuring output does not enable firms to assess their value added (or destroyed) across environmental, social and economic dimensions. This indicates that new methods capable of measuring impact are needed.

In this chapter we use the definition of impact as developed by Clark *et al.* (2004): 'By impact we mean the portion of the total outcome that happened as a result of the activity of an organisation, above and beyond what would have happened any-way'.

This definition is based on the so-called impact value chain (see Figure 7.2) and is developed to differentiate outputs from outcomes and impact.

**FIGURE 7.2** Impact value chain

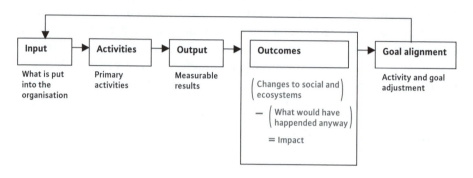

Source: adapted from Clark *et al.* 2004

By doing this we borrow from evaluation theory that conceptualises the idea that impacts are different from outputs (Rossi and Freeman 1993). While outputs and outcomes are related to the provider of the product, activity or service, impacts are associated with the user (Kolodinsky *et al.* 2006) and other stakeholders.

In business, generally accepted principles of accounting and an international legal infrastructure have been established over the years to help measure and report on financial impact. Life-cycle assessment provides a framework and indicators for the measurement of ecological impacts.[4] For social impact measurement, however, general accepted standards do not yet exist. Nevertheless, social and ecological impacts are often not explicitly included in measurement or are even ignored. Next to this the impact and the dimension of the impact (economic, environmental and social) vary on a case-by-case basis depending on the CSR activity.

## Different measurement for different purposes

Impact measurement is not an end in itself. Neither the act of measuring impact nor the resulting data accomplishes anything itself; only when someone uses these

---

4 LCA is a 'cradle-to-grave' approach—from extraction of raw materials to end-of-life—used to evaluate or compare the overall ecological impacts of alternative products or processes.

measures in some way do they accomplish something (Behn 2003). Besides this, only if managers know what they want to do with the measurement results can they select a collection of impact measures with the characteristics necessary to help them achieve these purposes (Maas 2009). Managers should therefore begin by deciding on the managerial purposes to which impact measurement may contribute. Managers might want to answer questions from several perspectives:

- How is value distributed in the supply chain?
- How do stakeholders see us?
- How can we continue to improve?
- How can we create value?
- How do shareholders see us?

A measurement approach should be selected based on the CSR activity undertaken by the firm—value redistribution, value integration or new value creation—and the corresponding impact. Measuring the impact of CSR can be difficult because any meaningful measurement needs a reference point in terms of accepted criteria.

In our typology of strategic CSR activities we distinguish three ways in which CSR may provide value to a firm, society and ecosystems. Each of these requires different impact measures. Impact measurement in the case of value redistribution should focus on the global commodity chain perspective and answer the question: how is impact, on different dimensions, distributed in the supply chain and how could this be optimised in view of sustainable development? Impact measurement in case of value creation through the development of new products or new markets should focus on a financial shareholder perspective and a societal perspective and answer the question: how can we increase positive impact on the different dimensions? Impact measurement in the case of value integration should focus on the stakeholder perspective and answer the question: how do stakeholders see and value the firm?

## Measuring value creation

Value creation for the firm through the development of new products or new markets or by bottom-of-the-pyramid strategies are comparable with general innovation activities. CSR as new value creation is a process of collaborative innovation. A key characteristic is that, at the level of the firm, but often also at a system level, a new balance is struck between economic, ecological and social impact.

The difficulty of measuring the impact of new value creation is dependent on whether the innovation constitutes a departure from the existing technological paradigm: that is, the current accepted frame of reference on which firms and knowledge institutes base their search for new technologies (Dosi 1982). When new value creation takes the shape of efficiency improvements of processes and products, impact can be measured by comparing the old with the new situation: a TV set that uses less energy during the consumption phase, or substituting a hazardous substance which results in less water pollution. However, it has been argued that sustainable development requires more fundamental innovations that require new technological paradigms, such as the shift from car-based mobility to alternative modalities. This also has consequences for behavioural patterns of consumers: for instance, by working at home rather than at an office. Taken together, these shifts in activities are too complex to be compared with the old situation; as with scientific paradigms, the impacts are incommensurable (Kuhn 1962). In the BoP examples, involving people at the bottom of the pyramid as consumers and producers might be measured in terms of their monetary income, but this fails to measure the social impact in terms of introducing new behavioural patterns.

Thus, measuring new value creation is difficult especially when it involves a shift in technological paradigms. Besides this, new value creation by entering new markets or by launching new products could cause unforeseen external effects or rebound effects might occur. The difficulty with such effects is the time-frame in which they can occur. Only after market introduction can value for all stakeholders be defined in a meaningful way.

If companies want to include social and environmental impact next to the financial impact for the firm, they can use the so-called social return on investment (SROI) method (Lingane and Olsen 2004). SROI is a methodology pioneered by the Roberts Enterprise Development Fund (REDF) in 1996. More recently the approach has been used to assess the multi-dimensional impacts of CSR activities.

## Measuring value integration

Value integration implies the effort of a firm to integrate values espoused by stakeholders into its activities and organisational routines that were previously disregarded. Problems, solutions and impacts, whether intended or unintended, are often the subject of ambiguity, uncertainty and disputes (Roome 2001). Measuring such impacts has to be a collective activity; the firm cannot measure impacts without taking the perspective of the stakeholder into account. The impacts to address have to be selected by the firm and its stakeholders. To be valid, they need the kind of public acceptance that can only be achieved through well-structured participatory decision processes (Clift 2003). For each stakeholder, it is important to have insight into the way in which, for them, the relevant impacts are addressed by the firm. Therefore, the firm and its stakeholders have to interact and continuously learn, take action and change. This process can be viewed as a multi-party, learning-action network that spans business organisations and stakeholders in society (Clarke and Roome 1999).

Indicators for value measurement can be selected directly through stakeholder consultation, as in the case of Shell's residential advisory board, by building learning-action networks or indirectly by using different guidelines, frameworks, standards and rating schemes which provide information on potentially useful indicators.[5] These guidelines, such as the GRI G3, are developed based on a multi-stakeholder, consensus-seeking approach which is a valuable way to produce indicators that appropriately respond to stakeholders' needs. The different impact can be measured in their own metrics or can be integrated into one 'grade'. The relevance of aggregating across the dimensions, for example by expressing environmental impacts in monetary terms, depends on the interests and information need of the stakeholders and the firm.

## Measuring value redistribution

Value redistribution includes the effort of a firm to change the distribution of impact over the system actors. Redistribution builds on the accepted definition of what is valuable. Often redistribution efforts focus on redistributing the financial impact. Successful impact redistribution would, in this case, mean that producers and workers in the supply chain obtained a better price for their work or product. What should be measured is how impact is distributed in the global commodity chain. In addition to measuring the distribution of ecological impact, it should be assessed how much of the value is obtained by the producers and workers in the value chain. This can be done by looking at the prices paid or obtained at every step in the supply chain and making a comparison of the initial situation and the situation after the redistribution effort. Again, this is problematic as changes in practices of actors, constituting social impact, are difficult to measure. In the case of organic coffee, increased income for farmers is combined with an increased demand for labour, as organic coffee requires much more intensive farming practices throughout the year. The consequence is that people growing coffee have to focus on this as their main activity whereas previously they often grew coffee as one of several activities. In addition, harvesting requires the input of additional labour, for which people from the community are hired. Thus, organic coffee farming involves a change in practices and monetary benefits for other people besides the principal farmer, who becomes more like a Western entrepreneur (Jaffee

---

5 Some examples are the Social Accountability 8000 standard (SA8000), International Labour Organisation (ILO convention), World Resource Institute (WRI indicators), OECD guidelines, rating schemes from the Dow Jones Sustainability Index and FTSE4Good, and the Global Reporting Initiative (GRI 2006).

2007). Such impacts are difficult to capture by measuring the monetary part of redistribution of value.

Previous research used an extended version of the overall business impact assessment (OBIA), originally developed by Unilever (Taylor and Postlethwaite 1996), to analyse the environmental and economic impact of supply chains (Jackson and Clift 1998; Clift and Wright 2000). These authors observed that the primary resource industries, often located in developing countries, incur disproportionately high environmental impact but receive disproportionately low economic benefit. Clift (2003) concludes that, in view of sustainability, the ratio between environmental and financial impact along the global commodity chain should be equivalent. Results from this kind of measurement can be used to produce a more equal distribution of economic and environmental impact along supply chains.

## Conclusion

CSR has potential to become a strategic activity adding value on different dimensions—business, society and ecosystems—if two conditions are met. The first condition for strategic CSR is that CSR needs to become integrated with the strategy of the firm through value creation, value integration and value redistribution. Whenever a firm engages in activities of one or more of these types, it connects CSR to its core activities, making it more than a 'bolt-on' exercise. The second condition for CSR as strategic activity is to measure and monitor its impact across environmental, social and economic dimensions and, ideally, to incorporate those impacts into management decisions.

Measuring the impact of CSR is difficult because any meaningful measurement needs a reference point in terms of accepted criteria. Criteria have to be selected by taking the perspective of the stakeholder into account. However, current developments in measurement instruments focus mainly on output measurement and emphasise the payback results of CSR initiatives for companies instead of the impact along the dimensions of the firm as well as the societies and ecosystems on which its activities have an impact. A shift is needed from output thinking, focusing on a single-dimensional firm perspective, to impact thinking which includes a social and ecosystem perspective. New measurement methods capable of measuring impact are needed.

A measurement approach should be selected based on the CSR activity undertaken by the firm—value redistribution, value integration or new value creation—and the corresponding impact. Managers should begin by deciding on the managerial purposes to which impact measurement may contribute. Value redistribution in a way is the easiest in terms of criteria. As redistribution builds on an accepted definition of what is valuable, CSR initiatives that fall into this category can look at the relative equality of distribution of this value across actors in the product chain. But as redistribution can also involve changes in social practices, it mingles with the creation of new value, complicating the measurement of impact. Value integration brings more sets of values to those previously espoused by the firm, and involves stakeholders in the strategic process. In such instances of CSR, measurement may best proceed through an assessment as part of the stakeholder dialogue. For this to work, scores on different values do not necessarily need to be integrated into one 'grade'; for each of the stakeholders, it is important to have insight into the way in which their value is addressed by the firm. Value creation is perhaps the most difficult to measure. As it involves the creation of new products and/or services, it is embedded in a process in which value of the activity of the firm at first is uncertain. (Will consumers, governmental agencies and other stakeholders accept the product/service?) Only after market introduction is it possible to define value in any meaningful way.

There is general agreement in literature that organisations until now have done little work in evaluating the impact of their CSR activities, specifically on a social and ecosystem level (Margolis and Walsh 2003; Clark *et al.* 2004). There is also consensus that organisations are beginning to express greater interest in their impact (Young 2002). The SROI methodology could be a useful approach to include social and environmental impacts in measurement.

Future research might assess actual impact measurement behaviour of firms. Besides this, it might be interesting to look in more detail at existing impact measurement methods. Methods may differ in approach, perspective and metrics and might be useful for specific situations. Finally, it would be interesting to actually measure the impact of CSR for several cases capturing the different ways in which CSR may provide value to a firm, society and ecosystems.

# References

Ackerman, R.W. (1975) *The Social Challenge to Business* (Cambridge, MA: Harvard University Press).

Barney, J.B. (1991) 'Firm Resources and Sustained Competitive Advantage', *Journal of Management* 17.1: 99.

——, M. Wright and D.J. Ketchen Jr (2001) 'The Resource-Based View of the Firm: Ten Years after 1991', *Journal of Management* 27.6: 625-41.

Bates, R. (1997) *Open-Economy Politics: The Political Economy of the World Coffee Trade* (Princeton, NJ: Princeton University Press).

Behn, R.D. (2003) 'Why Measure Performance? Different Purposes Require Different Measures', *Public Administration Review* 63.5: 586-606.

Berger, P., and T. Luckman (1966) The Social Construction of Reality (New York: Anchor Books).

Boons, F. (2009) *Creating Ecological Value: An Evolutionary Approach to Business Strategies and the Natural Environment* (Cheltenham, UK: Edward Elgar).

Bragdon, J.H., and J. Marlin (1972) 'Is Pollution Profitable?', *Risk Management* 19.4: 9-18.

Callon, M. (ed.) (1998) *The Laws of the Market* (Oxford, UK: Blackwell Publishers).

Clark, C., W. Rosenzweig, D. Long and S. Olsen (2004) 'Double Bottom Line Project Report: Assessing Social Impact in Double Bottom Line Ventures. Methods Catalog', www.shidler.hawaii.edu/Portals/1/resources/DoubleBottomLine.pdf, accessed 9 December 2009.

Clarke, S., and N. Roome (1999) 'Sustainable Business: Learning–Action Networks as Organizational Assets', *Business Strategy and the Environment* 8.5: 296-310.

Clift, R. (2003) 'Metrics for Supply Chain Sustainability', *Cleaner Technology and Environmental Policy* 5: 240-47.

—— and L. Wright (2000) 'Relationships between Environmental Impacts and Added Value along the Supply Chain', *Technological Forecasting and Social Change* 65: 281-95.

Commission of the European Communities (2002) *Corporate Social Responsibility: A Business Contribution to Sustainable Development* (COM[2002]347 final; Brussels: CEC).

Conner, K.R. (1991) 'A Historical Comparison of Resource-Based Theory and Five Schools of Thought within Industrial Organization Economics: Do We Have a New Theory of the Firm?', *Journal of Management* 17.1: 121-54.

Dosi, G. (1982) 'Technological Paradigms and Technological Trajectories: A Suggested Interpretation of the Determinants and Directions of Technical Change', *Research Policy* 11: 147-62.

Emerson, J. (2003) 'The Blended Value Proposition: Integrating Social and Financial Returns', *California Management Review* 45.4: 35-51.

Frankental, P. (2001) 'Corporate Social Responsibility: A PR Invention?', *Corporate Communications* 6.1: 18-23.

Freeman, R.E. (1984) *Strategic Management: A Stakeholder Approach* (Boston, MA: Pitman).

Friedman, M. (1970) 'The social responsibility of business is to increase its profits', *New York Times Magazine*, 13 September 1970: 32-33, 122, 126.

Gereffi, G. (1999a) 'International Trade and Industrial Upgrading in the Apparel Commodity Chain', *Journal of International Economics* 48.1: 37-70.

—— (1999b) 'A Commodity Chains Framework for Analysing Global Industries' (mimeo; Durham, NC: Department of Sociology, Duke University).

—— (2001) 'Shifting Governance Structures in Global Commodity Chains, with Special Reference to the Internet', *American Behavioral Scientist* 44.10: 1,616-37.

Grayson, D., and A. Hodges (2004) *Corporate Social Opportunity! Seven Steps to Make Corporate Social Responsibility Work for Your Business* (Sheffield, UK: Greenleaf Publishing).

GRI (2006) *Sustainability Reporting Guidelines (G3)* (Amsterdam: Global Reporting Initiative).

Haigh, H., and M.T. Jones (2006) 'The Drivers of Corporate Social Responsibility: A Critical Review', *The Business Review* 5.2: 245-52.

Hart, S.L., and M.B. Milstein (2003) 'Creating Sustainable Value', *Academy of Management Executive* 17.2: 56-67.

Husted, B.W., and J. de Jesus Salazar (2006) 'Taking Friedman Seriously: Maximising Profits and Social Performance', *Journal of Management Studies* 43.1: 75-91.

Jackson, T., and R. Clift (1998) 'Where's the Profit in Industrial Ecology?', *Journal of Industrial Ecology* 2.1: 3-5.

Jaffee, D. (2007) *Brewing Justice: Fair Trade Coffee, Sustainability, and Survival* (Berkeley, CA: University of California Press).

Jensen, M.C. (1998) *Foundations of Organizational Strategy* (Cambridge, MA: Harvard University Press).

Keim, G.D. (1978) 'Corporate Social Responsibility: An Assessment of the Enlightened Self-interest Model', *Academy of Management Review* 3.1: 32-39.

Klein, M.H. (2008) *Poverty Alleviation through Sustainable Strategic Business Models: Essays on Poverty Alleviation as a Business Strategy* (Rotterdam: ERIM).

Kolodinsky, J., C. Stewart and A. Bullard (2006) 'Measuring Economic and Social Impacts of Membership in a Community Development Financial Institution', *Journal of Family and Economic Issues* 27.1: 27-47.

Kuhn, T. (1962) *The Structure of Scientific Revolutions* (Chicago: University of Chicago Press).

Lepak, D.P., K.G. Smith and M.S. Taylor (2007) 'Value Creation and Value Capture: A Multi-level Perspective', *Academy of Management Review* 32.1: 180-94.

Lingane, A., and S. Olsen (2004) 'Guidelines for Social Return on Investment', *California Management Review* 46.3: 116-35.

Loorbach, D. (2008) *Transition Management: New Mode of Governance for Sustainable Development* (Utrecht, Netherlands: International Books).

Maas, K.E.H. (2009) 'Social Impact Measurement: A Classification of Methods' (working paper; Rotterdam, Netherlands: Erasmus University Rotterdam).

Makadok, R. (2003) 'Doing the Right Thing and Knowing the Right Thing to Do: Why the Whole is Greater than the Sum of the Parts', *Strategic Management Journal* 24.10: 1,043-55.

March, H.A., and J.G. Simon (1993) *Organizations* (New York: Wiley, 2nd edn).

Margolis, J.D., and J.P. Walsh (2003) 'Misery Loves Companies: Rethinking Social Initiatives by Business', *Administrative Science Quarterly* 48.2: 268-305.

Matten, D., A. Crane and W. Chapple (2003) 'Behind the Mask: Revealing the True Face of Corporate Citizenship', *Journal of Business Ethics* 45.1: 109-20.

McWilliams, A., and D. Siegel (2001) 'Corporate Social Responsibility: A Theory of the Firm Perspective', *Academy of Management Review* 26.1: 117-27.

Porter, M.E., and M.R. Kramer (2006) 'Strategy and Society: The Link between Competitive Advantage and Corporate Social Responsibility', *Harvard Business Review* 84.12: 78-92.

Post, J., L. Preston and S. Sachs (2002) *Redefining the Corporation: Stakeholder Management and Organizational Wealth* (Stanford, CA: Stanford University Press).

Prahalad, C. (2005) *The Fortune at the Bottom of the Pyramid* (Upper Saddle River, NJ: Wharton School Publishing).

Prencipe, A. (2003) 'Corporate Strategy and Systems Integration Capabilities: Managing Networks in Complex Systems Industries', in A. Prencipe (ed.), *The Business of Systems Integration* (Oxford, UK: Oxford University Press): 114-32.

Priem, R.L. (2007) 'A Consumer Perspective on Value Creation', *Academy of Management Review* 32.1: 219-35.

Roome, N. (2001) 'Conceptualizing and Studying the Contribution of Networks in Environmental Management and Sustainable Development', *Business Strategy and the Environment* 10.2: 69-76.

Rossi, P., and H. Freeman (1993) *Evaluation: A Systematic Approach* (Newbury Park, CA: Sage Publications).

Schumpeter, J. (1975) *Capitalism, Socialism and Democracy* (New York: Harper, first published 1942).

Shell Pernis Residential Advisory Board (2003) *Model for a Residential Advisory Board* (Pernis, Netherlands).

Taylor, A.P., and D. Postlethwaite (1996) 'Overall Business Impact Assessment (OBIA)', paper presented at the *4th LCA Case Studies Symposium: SETAC-Europe*, Brussels, 3 December 1996: 181-87.

Vance, S. (1975) 'Are Socially Responsible Firms Good Investment Risks?', *Management Review* 64: 18-24.

Verwaal, E., H.R. Commandeur and W. Verbeke (2009) 'Value Creation and Value Claiming in Strategic Outsourcing Decisions: A Resource-Contingency Perspective', *Journal of Management* 35.2: 420-44.

Vink, N. (1986) *Macht en kultuur in marketing. een studie over de responsiviteit bij besluitvorming van ondernemingen in de jaren 1965–1980* (Delft, Netherlands: Delftse Universitaire Pers, in Dutch).

WCED (World Commission on Environment and Development) (1987) *Our Common Future* (Oxford, UK: Oxford University Press).

Weber, M., and J. Hemmelskamp (eds.) (2005) *Towards Environmental Innovation Systems* (Berlin: Springer).

Williamson, O.E. (1985) *The Economic Institutions of Capitalism* (New York: The Free Press).

—— (1999) 'Strategy Research: Governance and Competence Perspectives', *Strategic Management Journal* 20.12: 1,087-108.

Wolff, F., and R. Barth (2005) *Corporate Social Responsibility: Integrating a Business and Societal Governance Perspective: The RARE Project's Approach* (EU project contract No. CIT2-CT-2004-506043); www.rare-eu.net/fileadmin/user_upload/documents/RARE_Background_Paper.pdf, accessed 12 December 2009.

Young, J. (2002) *Community Impact of Health Philanthropy, 1995–2000* (Memphis, TN: University of Tennessee Health Science Center).

# 8

# Does corporate social responsibility really add value for consumers?

**Alejandro Alvarado-Herrera**
University of Quintana Roo, Mexico

**Enrique Bigné-Alcañiz, Rafael Currás-Pérez and Joaquín Aldás-Manzano**
University of Valencia, Spain

Companies are becoming increasingly interested in associating their brand with corporate social responsibility (CSR) principles. Increased competition in markets has saturated the possibility of brand differentiation based on traditional attributes such as price and quality (Aaker 2005; Marín and Ruiz 2007); in this context, CSR has proved to be a very effective positioning strategy giving the brand symbolic value, and becoming an attribute of competitive differentiation (Kotler and Lee 2005; Brammer and Millington 2006; Du *et al.* 2007). Thus, internationally recognised brands such as Coca-Cola, Apple and Nike have developed promotional campaigns that strategically link them with various social causes such as, respectively, the fight against climate change, the fight against AIDS in Africa, and the fight against child labour, as they seek to generate a socially responsible brand image.

This favourable context has encouraged marketing academics to examine these types of socially responsible initiative, developing a line of research that attempts to analyse how consumer information on companies' social responsibility practices influences consumer behaviour. Actually, consumers are one of the most influential groups of stakeholders for marketing managers, so, if consumers perceive corporate social responsibility as a source of value, this would be a powerful reason for including sustainable development principles in firms' business strategies.

However, the consumer perspective on CSR has been, with some exceptions, largely neglected and little is known about this issue. Despite the fact that some researchers have found that CSR perception significantly influences different consumer responses, such as consumer–company identification (Sen and Bhattacharya 2001; Lichtenstein *et al.* 2004), attitude towards the brand, purchase intentions (Bigné *et al.* 2006) and consumer response to the product (Brown and Dacin 1997), recent studies show the still evident lack of research into the relational effects of CSR actions on these stakeholders' perceptions (Bigné *et al.* 2006; Du *et al.* 2007; Sen and Bhattacharya 2001). Particularly scarce are works that analyse how a company's CSR initiatives can generate value and satisfaction for the consumer.

Although consumers positively evaluate socially responsible firms, they often appear initially sceptical about these types of initiative (Forehand and Grier 2003), since they tend to believe that firms' CSR initiatives are mainly motivated from egoistic interests (Webb and Mohr 1998). In this context, from a consumer point of view, CSR innovations could be considered 'risky' initiatives, as the firm appears in the public arena associated with social and environmental issues, and the organisation's credibility can be called into question (Polonsky and Wood 2001). Marketing managers therefore need in-depth knowledge of the mechanisms that lead CSR to influence positively consumer responses. Understanding the effects of CSR on consumer relational outcomes, particularly perceived value and satisfaction, could be a first step to shift CSR thinking from a risk management approach to a value creation one.

In this regard, the literature notes that CSR is a very useful tool for developing and consolidating stable relationships with customers; as Marín and Ruiz (2007) point out, consumers of socially responsible brands feel closely linked to them, promote a good image of the company, recommend it to their acquaintances, and defend it from possible opponents. It is therefore striking that such important relational variables for the study of consumer behaviour such as satisfaction and perceived value have barely been tested empirically in the CSR and consumer behaviour literature, and to the best of our knowledge they have never been considered simultaneously in this area. This gap is particularly marked in view of the fact that marketing is responsible for creating, communicating and delivering value to consumers (AMA 2004) and that 'customer satisfaction plays an important mediating role in the relationship between CSR and firm market value' (Luo and Bhattacharya 2006:16).

In addition, the few studies that have empirically tested CSR-consumer satisfaction have tended to base the analysis on economic criteria (e.g. Luo and Bhattacharya 2006) and so examination of this relationship based on criteria other than economic utilities is likely to be a potential source of contributions to the marketing literature. This is so, although, according to Brown and Dacin (1997), corporate social responsibility (CSR) associations are not related to company ability in the production of goods and services, or corporate ability (CA) associations.

Furthermore, literature suggests a fuller explanation for the causes of consumer satisfaction may emerge if explanations other than the traditional one based on the disconfirmation of expectations stance are taken into account, such as a cognitive and affective processes stance (Swan and Trawick 1981; Oliver 1997; Cronin *et al.* 2000). This study therefore differentiates between cognitive and affective satisfaction to provide more in-depth information on the impact of company CSR initiatives on consumer satisfaction.

Finally, this research proposes that it is possible to obtain a more sophisticated explanation for the influence of CSR initiatives on consumer behaviour by taking into account not only consumer perceptions of the socially responsible nature of the brand (CSR perceptions), but also what individuals expect the company's social commitment to be (CSR expectations) (Swaen 2003). It is logical to think that, as a consequence of consumers' own values, personality characteristics, experiences, desires and interests, each individual will have specific expectations of what a company should do to be considered socially responsible; based on the classical disconfirmation of expectations notion, this study proposes that what really influences consumer responses (particularly perceived value and satisfaction) is not simply the perception that a brand is socially responsible, but the gap between this perception and consumer expectations (CSRp–CSRe gap). Nevertheless, it is striking that this gap between consumer CSR perceptions and expectations, to our knowledge, has not yet been studied empirically in marketing, especially in view of the fact that this analysis will become increasingly important while CSR strategies, policies and their communications continue to grow and to be more widespread among firms—as seems to be the case. In such conditions, consumer CSR perceptions would tend to be a constant and, therefore, the whole influence of CSR activities on consumer responses would arise from consumer expectations. Hence, it is necessary to determine, first, if the CSRp–CSRe gap does really (and effectively) influence consumer perceived value and satisfaction.

Consequently, taking into account these calls, and with the intention of contributing to the marketing literature by partially remedying the gaps in the body of knowledge, the general aim of this work is to determine the degree to which the gap between consumer CSR perceptions and CSR expectations (CSRp–CSRe) influences perceived value and the cognitive and affective dimensions of consumer satisfaction. A quantitative study was designed and carried out with an empirical application between consumers of tourist services and, more specifically, of hotel accommodation.

The methodology, results and main conclusions of this study are described in the sections below, which are organised as follows. First, based on the relevant literature review, the theoretical elements for the studied variables are presented, and the hypotheses and the proposed theoretical model are formulated. This is followed by a description of the research methodology, and analysis and discussion of the results. Finally, the conclusions are presented, identifying the managerial and academic implications of the findings, the main limitations of the study, and some possible lines for further research.

## Literature review

In recent decades various conceptual models have been developed, based on different theoretical approaches, to attempt to capture the CSR domain and its dimensions. Three of these models have gained the most support in the academic community: Carroll's pyramid (1979, 1991, 1999), the model based on sustainable development (Linnanen and Panapanaan 2002; van Marrewijk 2003) and Brown and Dacin's (1997) approach.

The first of these, Carroll's model (1979, 1991, 1999), considers CSR to have four, successively dependent dimensions, covering society's economic, legal, ethical and discretional (or philanthropic) expectations of organisations at a given point in time (Carroll 1991). The sustainable development model is based on the triple-bottom-line approach—that is, economic, social and environmental considerations (van Marrewijk 2003)—and understands CSR in the terms presented by the European Commission (2001: 7), as the integration by companies of 'social and environmental concerns in their business operations and in their interaction with their stakeholders on a voluntary basis'. Finally, Brown and Dacin (1997: 68) propose distinguishing two types of association perceived by stakeholders with regard to the company (or corporate associations): corporate ability (CA) associations refer to the company's experience in producing and delivering products and services, which is mainly technical and economic in nature; and corporate social responsibility (CSR) associations which 'reflect the organization's status and activities with respect to its perceived societal obligations', and correspond to non-economic issues.

Although each of the above models has its advantages and drawbacks, they are all valuable contributions to the literature and have been used in CSR research in consumer behaviour field. However, Brown and Dacin's model (1997) was chosen for this study because it allowed us to clearly discriminate between two factors—(i) consumers' economic perceptions of companies and (ii) consumers' non-economic perceptions of companies—and associate the second one to CSR uni-dimensionally. Hence, it showed the best fit of the three analysed models in relation to the aims of this study.

In effect, in their seminal work on corporate associations and CSR, Brown and Dacin (1997) propose a distinction between two basic types of cognitive association that stakeholders may have about a company: CA and CSR. According to their postulates, the importance of this discrimination lies in the fact that, although both types of association can influence consumer evaluations of the company and its products, each one does so in a different way. In fact, the authors' empirical results show that the associations concerning technical and economic matters (e.g. CA) have more influence than those concerning non-economic aspects (e.g. CSR) in consumer evaluations of the company and the product; although CSR associations do not directly affect product evaluations, they do provide information on which to judge the organisation as a whole and, through this framework, evaluate the company's products or services.

Now, it is possible to deduce, on the basis of previous work based on Carroll's model (e.g. Sethi 1979; Maignan and Ferrell 2003), that the common denominator for the four CSR dimensions proposed by the author is the consistency between society's expectations of business behaviour and the real or perceived way business acts. We consider that this common denominator would be equally valid for the model based on the sustainable development paradigm, and for the corporate associations model (Brown and Dacin 1997), since the idea of comparing consumers' perceptions and expectations of company CSR activities (CSRp and CSRe, respectively), has already been stated in marketing literature (Swaen 2003). In particular, a disconfirmation stance based on the gap model of Parasuraman *et al.* (1985) has been proposed for this, since it seems logical to consider that consumers compare their expectations of CSR activities with what they receive, and, as with satisfaction, when CSRp is greater than CSRe they will presumably tend to react favourably towards the company (Swaen 2003) and vice versa.

As this is the point of view assumed in this chapter, CSRe, CSRp and disconfirmation should be understood in a similar vein as in the satisfaction literature, but with CSR as the object of study. Building on Sasser *et al.* (1978), Grönroos (1982) and Lehtinen and Lehtinen's (1982) research, Parasuraman *et al.* (1988: 16) offer the following definitions: consumers' expectations 'as desires or wants of consumers, i.e. what they feel a service provider *should* offer' [emphasis added]; consumers' perceptions as consumer's judgements 'of the performance of firms providing the services'; and disconfirmation as the degree and direction of *discrepancies between those two* prior notions. Accordingly, consumer's CSRe can be defined as consumer desires or wants with regard to firms' CSR activities; consumer CSRp can be understood as consumer judgements on the performance of firms' CSR activities; and disconfirmation as the CSRp–CSRe gap.

The literature review is therefore the basis for proposing a theoretical model that relates the CSRp–CSRe gap to consumer perceived brand value and satisfaction. This model is shown in Figure 8.1; it can be seen that the CSRp–CSRe gap directly influences perceived brand value (PV) and the cognitive (CS) and affective (AS) dimensions of consumer satisfaction, and indirectly influences these dimensions through the mediator effect of perceived value.

**FIGURE 8.1 Proposed theoretical model**

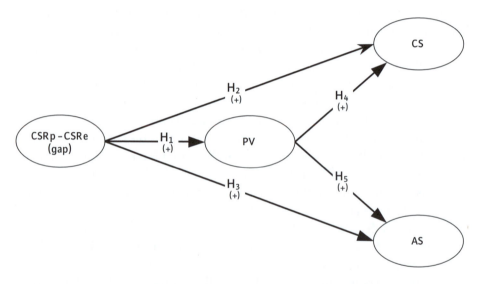

First, a significant number of researchers consider that CSR actions and programmes can be a source of sustainable competitive advantage for companies and their brands, as they improve the proposed value offered to the consumer (McEnally and de Chernatony 1999; Porter and Kramer 2002; Garriga and Melé 2004). Perceived value is a first-order element in relational marketing (Peterson 1995; Ravald and Grönroos 1996; Oh 2003), a basic result of marketing activities (Holbrook 1994) and a direct determinant of behavioural intentions and consumer loyalty (Sirdeshmukh *et al.* 2002; Yang and Peterson 2004). Although it is true that no definition of perceived value has obtained unanimous support, one of the most general definitions with the greatest explanatory power is that proposed by Zeithaml (1988), which understands perceived value as 'the consumer's overall assessment of the utility of a product based on perceptions of what is received and what is given' (Zeithaml 1988: 14). This is the notion followed in this study.

Conceptually, perceived value has been considered as the consequence of consumer CSR perceptions (Webb and Mohr 1998; Maignan *et al.* 1999, 2005; García de los Salmones *et al.* 2005; Polonsky and Jevons 2006) to the extent that the information emerging from CSR actions can make them believe that the satisfaction of their individual needs, materialised through the purchase of a product from a socially responsible brand also helps to satisfy society's needs (Polonsky and Wood 2001). According to McEnally and de Chernatony (1999), in the advanced stages of brand evolution it is possible to associate, in addition to instrumental values, symbolic and end values which transcend utilitarianism. A socially responsible brand not only provides value to the consumer because of its intrinsic functional or utility attributes, but also because it becomes a very strong symbolic element which allows consumers to demonstrate to others the type of person they are and the world they aspire to and want (Sen and Bhattacharya 2001), since 'a brand is designed to embody and reflect the core values and attributes of the "product" ' (Polonsky and Jevons 2006: 342). In accordance with this logic, it is possible to propose that, as the difference between the degree to which a consumer really perceives what a company is doing to be socially responsible and the expectations about what it should be doing grows, the brand value perceived by the individual will increase. Therefore:

> $H_1$: The higher the degree to which CSRp exceeds CSRe, the higher the positive influence of the CSRp–CSRe gap on perceived brand value

Second, it can also be considered that the CSRp–CSRe gap will influence consumer satisfaction with the brand (Swaen 2003; Luo and Bhattacharya 2006). According to institutional theory (Handelman and Arnold 1999), when a company projects itself as socially responsible, it is satisfying consumers' needs for socialisation, conceiving the individual as more than just an agent for economic transaction, but also as a member of a community, a society, and as a citizen; as a result the company becomes a satisfier of self-definitional needs (Sen and Bhattacharya 2001; Lichtenstein *et al.* 2004). Thus CSR generates a favourable context around the brand which, thanks to a halo effect, causes more favourable judgements to be emitted regarding the service experience (Brown and Dacin 1997), and more understanding over any failures in service provision (Klein and Dawar 2004), thereby improving consumer satisfaction.

As is well known, satisfaction is a core variable for marketing and consumer behaviour research (Churchill and Surprenant 1982), and, although a significant part of this research has been based on the disconfirmation of expectations, some research suggests that a fuller explanation of its origin must embrace not only the disconfirmation process but also other cognitive and affective processes (Swan and

Trawick 1981; Oliver 1997; Cronin *et al.* 2000), which is why Westbrook and Oliver (1991: 89) suggested that 'satisfaction measurement might be enhanced by distinguishing between these alternative experiential bases'.

In this sense, some definitions and measures consider satisfaction to be the result of a cognitive process (Howard and Sheth 1969; Churchill and Surprenant 1982; Zeithaml and Bitner 2002) and others consider it to be the result of an emotional process (Day 1983; Cadotte *et al.* 1987; Oliver 1997). This two-dimensional approach to consumer satisfaction is used in this research, as currently even researchers who defended the disconfirmation paradigm to explain satisfaction, insist on the need to contemplate new approaches (Churchill and Surprenant 1982; Westbrook and Oliver 1991; Mano and Oliver 1993). A similar approach was taken by Cronin *et al.* (2000) who developed specific scales for each of the aspects in question (cognitive and affective satisfaction), considering the concept as a two-dimensional hybrid. In view of the above discussion, we can posit:

> $H_2$: The higher the degree to which CSRp exceeds CSRe, the higher the positive influence of the CSRp–CSRe gap on the cognitive dimension of consumer satisfaction

> $H_3$: The higher the degree to which CSRp exceeds CSRe, the higher the positive influence of the CSRp–CSRe gap on the affective dimension of consumer satisfaction

Finally, the literature has considered perceived value to be a direct antecedent of consumer satisfaction (Spreng *et al.* 1993; Anderson *et al.* 1994; Ravald and Grönroos 1996; McDougall and Levesque 2000). Obviously individuals who perceive that they have received a greater value proposal in the service provision will experience a greater degree of cognitive and affective satisfaction (Oh 1999; Gallarza and Gil 2006). Furthermore, it has been found that perceived value is not just another antecedent of customer satisfaction but one of its most important drivers (Spreng *et al.* 1993), which is why 'perceived value should be incorporated into models designed to understand the determinants of customer satisfaction' (McDougall and Levesque 2000: 407). Therefore:

> H4: Consumer perceived value of a brand through CSR activities has a direct, positive influence on the cognitive dimension of consumer satisfaction

> H5: Consumer perceived value of a brand through CSR activities has a direct, positive influence on the affective dimension of consumer satisfaction

# Methodology

As presented above, the basic research line in this work focuses on studying the role of the gap between consumer perceptions and expectations of non-economic aspects of CSR in the formation of perceived value and satisfaction. The proposed model was tested with a quantitative, empirical cross-section study using a structured questionnaire and estimation of the structural relationships. The estimation procedure used covariance structure analysis assisted by EQS 6.1 (Bentler 1985–2005).

The tourist industry and, in particular, accommodation services were chosen for three main reasons. First, in the Spanish market there are various corporate social responsibility initiatives in this industry; the association of this type of company with social causes is perceived positively as the industry is not socially stigmatised; this therefore eliminated any *a priori* adverse effects due to social de-legitimisation of the industry (Dean 2002). Second, this research area meant the characteristic limitations of laboratory experiments could be avoided, as information was obtained on real consumption conditions. Third, it was considered that this area reasonably satisfied both the intrinsic evolutionary conditions for the studied brands and product categories (McEnally and de Chernatony 1999), and the extrinsic conditions of homogeneity of brand (Barone *et al.* 2000), product (Mohr and Webb 2005) and offer.

Thirteen four-star hotels were chosen for the research, belonging to three Spanish hotel chains of recognised quality and prestige. The study population consisted of hotel accommodation tourists from Spain and abroad, over the age of 18 who stayed in various Spanish Mediterranean resorts between 7 January and 2 February 2008. Sampling was multi-stage, consisting of three consecutive stages. The first one established the quotas for tourist percentages by city (33.3%) and by origin (50% from Spain and 50% from abroad), while the sampling units (hotel) and sampling elements (tourists) in the second and third stages, respectively, were randomly selected. Total sample size was 462 consumers for a confidence level of 95% ($z = 1.96$) and estimation error below 5% for an infinite population in the most unfavourable case of $p = q = 50\%$.

## Measures

As mentioned above, this research considers CSR associations in accordance with Brown and Dacin's (1997) model and accordingly original items of this seminal work were used once they were adapted to measure respondents' expectations (CSRe1 to CSRe3) and perceptions (CSRp1 to CSRp3). Perceived value of the brand was measured with the scale proposed by Oh (2003) in the context of tourism services. Finally the cognitive and affective dimensions of satisfaction were measured adapting the scales developed by Cronin *et al.* (2000). All the scales items were seven-point Likert-type questions. Before carrying out the fieldwork, the questionnaire was pretested to assure the correct interpretation of the questions.[1] The whole set of questions is shown in more detail in the Appendix on pages 194-95.

## Reliability and validity assessment

To assess measurement reliability and validity, a confirmatory factor analysis (CFA) containing all the multi-item constructs in our framework was estimated with EQS 6.1 (Bentler 1985–2005) using the maximum likelihood method. Raw data screening showed evidence of non-normal distribution (Mardia's coefficient normalised estimate = 45.9) and, although other estimation methods have been developed for use when the normality assumption does not hold, the recommendation of Chou *et al.* (1991) and Hu *et al.* (1992) of correcting the statistics rather than using a different estimation model have been followed. So, robust statistics (Satorra and Bentler 1988) will be provided.

A CFA did not lead to the deletion of any item based on non-significant or low loading estimates (below 0.50), patterns of residuals and Lagrange multiplier tests (Anderson and Gerbing 1988; Hatcher 1994). The results of this CFA are reported in Table 8.1 and suggest that our final measurement model provides a good fit to the data on the basis of a number of fit statistics (S-B$\chi^2$ = 216.38, $df$ = 71, $p$ < 0.01; root mean square error of approximation (RMSEA) = 0.07; normed fit index (NFI) = 0.93; non-normed fit index (NNFI) = 0.94; comparative fit index (CFI) = 0.95). As evidence of convergent validity the CFA results indicate that all items are significantly ($p$ < 0.01) related to their hypothesised factors, and the size of all the standardised loadings are higher than 0.60 (Bagozzi and Yi 1988) and the average of the item-to-factor loadings are higher than 0.70 (Hair *et al.* 1998).

Table 8.1 also demonstrates the high internal consistency of the constructs. In each case, Cronbach's alpha exceeded Nunnally and Bernstein's (1994) recommendation of 0.70. Composite reliability represents the shared variance among a set of observed variables measuring an underlying construct (Fornell and Larcker 1981). Generally, a composite reliability of at least 0.60 is considered desirable (Bagozzi and Yi 1988). This requirement is met for every factor. Average variance extracted (AVE) was also calculated for each construct, resulting in AVEs greater than 0.50 (Fornell and Larcker 1981).

Evidence for discriminant validity of the measures was provided in two ways (Table 8.2). First, none of the 95% confidence intervals of the individual elements

---

1 Owing to the study population characteristics, the final version of the questionnaire was in English and Spanish, and was produced with the support of native professional translators, in collaboration with a member of the research team, with particular emphasis on maintaining semantic equivalence.

of the latent factor correlation matrix contained a value of 1.0 (Anderson and Gerbing 1988). Second, the shared variance between pairs of constructs was always less than the corresponding AVE (Fornell and Larcker 1981). On the basis of these criteria, we concluded that the measures in the study provided sufficient evidence of reliability, convergent and discriminant validity.

**TABLE 8.1** CFA results and measurement model psychometric properties

| Factor | Item | Reliability | | | Convergent validity | |
|---|---|---|---|---|---|---|
| | | α | CR | AVE | λ (stand.) | Average λs |
| CSRp–CSRe | CSRp–CSRe1 | 0.81 | 0.82 | 0.60 | 0.839** | 0.77 |
| | CSRp–CSRe2 | | | | 0.837** | |
| | CSRp–CSRp3 | | | | 0.633** | |
| PV | PV1 | 0.88 | 0.88 | 0.70 | 0.802** | 0.84 |
| | PV2 | | | | 0.832** | |
| | PV3 | | | | 0.883** | |
| CS | CS1 | 0.88 | 0.89 | 0.73 | 0.877** | 0.85 |
| | CS2 | | | | 0.921** | |
| | CS3 | | | | 0.761** | |
| AS | AS1 | 0.93 | 0.93 | 0.73 | 0.818** | 0.85 |
| | AS2 | | | | 0.870** | |
| | AS3 | | | | 0.840** | |
| | AS4 | | | | 0.863** | |
| | AS5 | | | | 0.874** | |

**Goodness of fit indicators**

| S-B $\chi^2$ (71gl) = 2160.38** | NFI | | NNFI | CFI | IFI | | RMSEA |
|---|---|---|---|---|---|---|---|
| | 0.93 | | 0.94 | 0.95 | 0.95 | | 0.07 |

** $p < 0.01$

**TABLE 8.2** Discriminant validity, AVE, corr² and confidence intervals

| | CSRp–CSRe | PV | CS | AS |
|---|---|---|---|---|
| **CSRp–CSRe** | **0.75** | [0.20 ; 0.43] | [0.22 ; 0.41] | [0.14 ; 0.35] |
| **PV** | 0.10 | **0.78** | [0.53 ; 0.69] | [0.60 ; 0.74] |
| **CS** | 0.10 | 0.37 | **0.73** | [0.74 ; 0.85] |
| **AS** | 0.06 | 0.45 | 0.63 | **0.73** |

Note: The diagonal shows the values of the variance extracted indexes, above the diagonal the confidence intervals for each pair of factors and below the diagonal the squares of the inter-factor correlation coefficients.

## Hypothesis testing and theoretical discussion

We tested the proposed conceptual model (Figure 8.1) using structural equation modelling (SEM). The empirical estimates for the main-effects model are shown in Table 8.3. The results indicate that the data fit our conceptual model acceptably (S-B$\chi^2$ = 216.35, $df$ = 71, $p$ = 0.01; RMSEA = 0.06; NFI = 0.94; NNFI = 0.95; CFI = 0.96).

**TABLE 8.3** SEM results and hypothesis fulfilment

| Hypotheses | Proposed structural relationship | $\lambda$ (stand.) | Result |
|---|---|---|---|
| $H_1$ | CSRp–CSRe → Perceived brand value | 0.31** | Accepted |
| $H_2$ | CSRp–CSRe → Cognitive satisfaction | 0.14** | Accepted |
| $H_3$ | CSRp–CSRe → Affective satisfaction | 0.04$^{NS}$ | Rejected |
| $H_4$ | Perceived value of a brand through CSR activities → Cognitive satisfaction | 0.56** | Accepted |
| $H_5$ | Perceived value of a brand through CSR activities → Affective satisfaction | 0.66** | Accepted |

| Goodness of fit indicators | | | | | |
|---|---|---|---|---|---|
| S–B $\chi^2$ (71gl) = 216.351** | NFI | NNFI | CFI | IFI | RMSEA |
| | 0.94 | 0.95 | 0.96 | 0.96 | 0.06 |

** $p$ < 0.01    $^{NS}$ = not significant

As can be seen from Table 8.3, data analysis suggests that the structural relationships established in four of the five hypotheses are significant ($H_1$, $H_2$, $H_4$ and $H_5$ for $p$ < 0.01) and therefore must be accepted. The direct influence of the CSRp–CSRe gap on affective satisfaction ($H_3$) did not prove to be significant and was rejected. Figure 8.2 shows the final model described in Table 8.3, including the items for each factor and the standardised loads.

First, acceptance of hypothesis $H_1$ corroborates the assumption that the CSRp–CSRe gap has a direct, positive influence on perceived brand value. This influence, in addition to being statistically significant ($p$ < 0.01), has an important magnitude ($\lambda_{CSRp–CSRe(gap)VP}$ = 0.31) and is therefore in keeping with proposals in previous research that CSR actions and programmes can be a source of competitive advantage for the company, as they provide the brand with a greater symbolic load which has the benefit of providing greater value for the consumer (e.g. Brown and Dacin 1997; Maignan *et al.* 1999, 2005; Polonsky and Wood 2001; García de los Salmones *et al.* 2005).

**FIGURE 8.2** Final estimated model

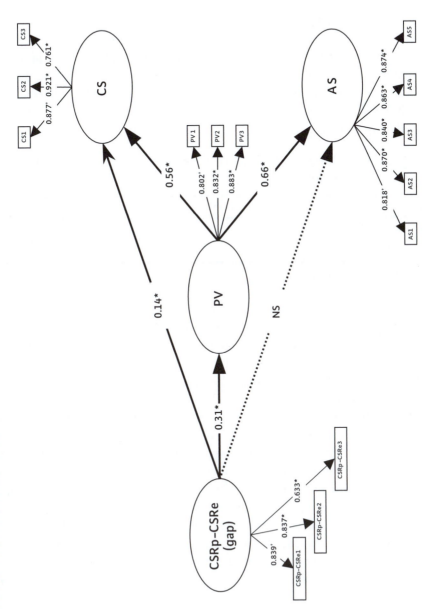

*p < 0.01    NS= not significant    †= not estimated because it was used to identify the model

Second, as to be expected according to Luo and Bhattacharya (2006) and Swaen (2003), the results show that the CSRp–CSRe gap also has significant impact on consumer satisfaction, but does so in different degrees and ways based on cognitive and affective satisfaction. As Table 8.4 shows, where the direct and indirect effects of the CSRp–CSRe gap break down into the two dimensions of consumer satisfaction, the total effect of the impact of the CSRp–CSRe gap on the cognitive component of satisfaction ($\lambda_{CSRp-CSRe(gap)CS(Total)}$ = 0.32; $p < 0.01$) is greater than on the affective component ($\lambda_{CSRp-CSRe(gap)AS(Total)}$ = 0.20; $p < 0.01$). This is because the direct effects of the CSRp–CSRe gap were found to be significant only in the case of cognitive satisfaction, as shown by the acceptance of $H_2$ and the rejection of $H_3$, despite the fact that the indirect effects, mediated by perceived brand value, were slightly lower in the first case ($\lambda_{CSRp-CSRe(gap)CS(Indirect)}$ = 0.18; $p < 0.01$) than in the second ($\lambda_{CSRp-CSRe(gap)AS(Indirect)}$ = 0.20; $p < 0.01$).

**TABLE 8.4** Breakdown of CSRp–CSRe gap effects on cognitive and affective satisfaction

| Direct effect | Indirect effect | Total effect |
| --- | --- | --- |
| CSRp–CSRe $\rightarrow$ CS = 0.14* | CSRp–CSRe $\rightarrow$ PV $\rightarrow$ CS = 0.18* | 0.32* |
| CSRp–CSRe $\rightarrow$ AS = 0.04[NS] | CSRp–CSRe $\rightarrow$ PV $\rightarrow$ AS = 0.20* | 0.20* |

*$p < 0.01$; [NS] = not significant

This result suggests that the influence of CSR on consumer satisfaction has more to do, in global terms, with cognitive processes; this finding is in keeping with the studies that postulate that CSR initiatives persuade the consumer following an associative learning process, based on the classical conditioning paradigm (Dean and Biswas 2001; Hoeffler and Keller 2002). CSR programmes and activities tend to follow the same logic as other brand endorsement strategies, although firms associate with a social cause to produce in their publics an associative learning process so that a transfer of meanings takes place; associations that the individual makes with the social cause are transferred to the brand's identity, which becomes characterised for assuming a social commitment (McCracken 1986, 1989). In this context, the very interactivity demanded by consumers when the brand projects itself as being socially responsible in advanced evolutionary stages (McEnally and de Chernatony 1999) involves more active learning on their part and consequently a more systematic processing of information; that is, CSR may play a rather more cognitive role in strengthening consumers' memory networks, influencing satisfaction more intensely thanks to improved beliefs about the brand, and not through improved affects towards the brand.

Third, this study has confirmed that perceived brand value is a powerful antecedent to consumer satisfaction, both in its cognitive ($\lambda_{PV-CS}$ = 0.56; $p < 0.01$) and affective ($\lambda_{\text{PV-AS}} = 0.65$; $p < 0.01$) dimensions; the intensity of said relations shows that perceived brand value in a service provision is a key indicator of consumer satisfaction (Anderson *et al.* 1994; Ravald and Grönroos 1996; Oh 1999; McDougall and Leveske 2000). Moreover, the very significance of the indirect effects (through perceived value) of the CSRp–CSRe gap on the two satisfaction dimensions corroborates that it is necessary to include perceived value in any model that attempts to understand the antecedents of consumer satisfaction (Spreng *et al.* 1993).

Finally, a last contribution concerns the determination of discriminant validity among the variables in the studied model, which gives empirical support to the idea that consumer satisfaction can be understood and measured as a two-dimensional construct, which, in accordance with the stance in this study, is composed of cognitive and affective dimensions (Swan and Trawick 1981; Oliver 1997; Cronin *et al.* 2000). We consider that this is a contribution to the marketing literature as it represents a second-level inference which externally validates previous findings (Lykken 1968; Yin 2003), in particular, those reported by Cronin *et al.* (2000).

# Conclusions, managerial implications, limitations and future lines of research

## Conclusions

With the intention of contributing to the line of work that investigates the relationship between CSR and consumer behaviour and shedding some light on the issue of whether corporate social responsibility really does add value for consumers, this work proposed to determine the degree to which the difference between consumer CSR perceptions and CSR expectations (CSRp–CSRe gap) influences two key relational variables, such as perceived value and satisfaction, with the latter conceived as a two-dimensional construct comprising a cognitive and an affective component. An empirical study was designed and carried out which, based on a literature review, proposed a theoretical model which was tested by covariance structure analysis (CFA and SEM) and data from a sample of 462 consumers of tourist services in three cities in the Spanish Mediterranean.

Three main conclusions have been drawn from this research. First, that the CSRp–CSRe gap directly influences perceived value for the individual; this study demonstrated, with a real sample of customers of hotel accommodation services, that the degree of compliance with expectations about a company's social commitment is an indicator that individuals use to determine the perceived value of their service experience. In this regard, thanks to the inclusion of the disconfirmation of expectations paradigm in the analysis of the influence of CSR initiatives as a value generation mechanism, it was possible to identify that merely perceiving a company to be socially responsible may not be sufficient for CSR to add value for the consumer and be considered a source of competitive advantage for the company. The results of this research show that CSR perceptions can really add value for consumers when they exceed or satisfy CSR expectations.

Second, this research highlights the CSRp–CSRe gap which is capable of significantly influencing consumer satisfaction, directly in the cognitive dimension and indirectly (by improving perceived value) in the affective dimension. This study therefore provides information on how CSR influences consumer satisfaction because analysis of the breakdown of CSR effects on both satisfaction components suggests that, overall, the satisfaction generated by CSR information is more closely related to cognitive processes than affective processes. It can be stated that the analysis of consumers' CSR expectations and perceptions gap is a useful method to determine the value added by CSR initiatives and their effects on consumer satisfaction.

Third, as far as our findings suggest that non-economic aspects of CSR play a key role in value creation in the consumer's mind, and that the impact of CSR programmes and activities on consumer satisfaction depends—to some extent—on such added value, it can also be settled, at a more general level, that innovative CSR tools and methods can help firms to shift from seeing CSR as a risk management issue to a value creation one. This is the case only if the designed and performed innovations on CSR programmes and activities exceed consumers' expectations; otherwise, CSR innovations could raise consumer and public scepticism, calling the organisation's credibility into question.

Hence, as explained above, understanding the effects of CSR on consumer perceived value and satisfaction has proved to be a useful first step to shift CSR thinking from a risk management approach to a value creation one. These main research conclusions have relevant implications for marketing managers.

## Managerial implications

The findings of the research raise some interesting managerial implications. First, as has been shown above, when perceived CSR exceeds consumer expectations it is capable of generating greater perceived value and consumer satisfaction with the service experience and can, therefore, be a source of competitive advantages for the company. In this sense, this study provides powerful reasons for brand managers to address the construction of brand identity characterised by innovative CSR associations, especially among those interested in obtaining more positive relational consequences of their marketing and branding strategies.

In this context, CSR must be managed as part of the consumer value chain, although if said CSR actions and programmes are incapable of fulfilling consumer expectations, they can become a source of disadvantage for the company as they have a negative impact on perceived value. In our opinion, there are four main reasons for non-fulfilment of CSRe: (1) not addressing CSR aspects; (2) inadequate planning, introduction and management of CSR; (3) inefficient communication of these efforts to stakeholders; or (4) ignorance of consumers' real expectations with regard to the company's social responsibility.

Second, as the disconfirmation-based stance has been demonstrated to be a good analytical framework with which to gain valuable information on the degree to which CSR initiatives respond to consumer demands in a company-specific context, it could be used as an effective tool to assist marketing managers' decisions on their firm's CSR innovations, commitment and target alignment. In other words, this stance would allow managers to take CSR into consideration more effectively during strategic planning, and therefore to contribute to the sustainable development of the firm and society.

Furthermore, the evidence provided by this research is also useful for marketing managers interested in managing and controlling the actions and programmes for communicating CSR initiatives and innovations more effectively. This work therefore invites managers not only to investigate the outputs of these campaigns in terms of brand image, knowledge and awareness, for example, but also to monitor their publics' expectations concerning the degree of commitment to social and environmental matters, so that the company may know the result of the consumer perceived CSRp–CSRe; this in turn will provide them with a very effective control instrument for their CSR communications strategies.

## Research limitations

The findings reported here can only be generalised with caution because of the limitations of this research. First, although the sample is considered sufficiently broad and representative of the population of tourist service consumers in major cities on the Spanish Mediterranean coast, obviously this does not necessarily represent another type of consumer of another class of services. Second, although special attention was paid to the choice of sector, type of product and the companies studied to guarantee that they largely satisfied the desired conditions of homogeneity of brand, product and offer, we acknowledge that absolute compliance with these conditions is difficult. Third, as Swaen (2003) noted, it is likely that both CSRe and CSRp are influenced not only by CSR activities and company communication, but also by communications from other groups and consumers' own values and CSR expectations, which further reduces the capacity to generalise these results.

## Future lines of research

Finally, the findings, conclusions and limitations of this work suggest the need to address new lines of research and study the topics dealt with here in greater depth. First, the proposed theoretical model must be replicated in other activity sectors for goods and services in order to be able to generalise the influence of the CSRp–CSRe gap on perceived value, and above all on the dimensions of satisfaction. Second, it would be interesting to identify and test other variables which may intervene to shape CSR-based perceived value and satisfaction, such as consumer identification with the company or the individual's involvement with the domain supported by the company in its CSR initiatives. In addition, it would be interesting to extend the model by including behavioural responses such as return intention or intention to recommend the brand. Third, given the power of the two-dimensional conception of consumer satisfaction for the study of consumer behaviour, more in-depth study is required on the discriminant validity of the cognitive and affective dimensions of satisfaction by replicating this study in different geographical contexts and markets. Finally, it is assumed that our understanding of CSR influence on consumer behaviour could be improved by including the disconfirmation of expectations paradigm in the other two models of CSR dimensions (Carroll's pyramid and the model based on sustainable development principles).

## References

Aaker, D. (2005) *Strategic Market Management* (New York: John Wiley, 7th edn).

AMA (American Marketing Association) (2004) 'Marketing Redefined: Nine Top Marketers Offer their Personal Definitions', *Marketing News* 38: 16.

Anderson, E.W., E. Fornell and D. Lehmann (1994) 'Customer Satisfaction, Market Share, and Profitability: Findings from Sweden', *Journal of Marketing* 58.3: 53-66.

Anderson, J.C., and D.W. Gerbing (1988) 'Structural Equation Modelling in Practice', *Psychological Bulletin* 103.3: 411-23.

Bagozzi, R., and J. Yi (1988) 'On the Evaluation of Structural Equation Models', *Journal of the Academy of Marketing Science* 16.2: 74-94.

Barone, M.J., A.D. Miyazaki and K.A. Taylor (2000) 'The Influence of Cause-Related Marketing on Consumer Choice: Does One Good Turn Deserve Another?', *Journal of the Academy of Marketing Science* 28.2: 248-62.

Bentler, P.M. (1985–2005) *EQS (Version 6.1)* (Multivariate Software, Inc.).

Bigné, E., L. Andreu, R. Chumpitaz and V. Swaen (2006) 'La influencia de la responsabilidad social corporativa en el comportamiento de compra de estudiantes universitarios', *ESIC Market* 6.597: 163-89.

Brammer, S., and A. Millington (2006) 'Firm Size, Organizational Visibility and Corporate Philanthropy: An Empirical Analysis', *Business Ethics: A European Review* 15.1: 6-18.

Brown, T.J., and P.A. Dacin (1997) 'The Company and the Product: Corporate Associations and Consumer Product Responses', *Journal of Marketing* 61.1: 68-84.

Cadotte, E.E., R.B. Woodruff and R.L. Jenkins (1987) 'Expectations and Norms in Models of Consumer Satisfaction', *Journal of Marketing Research* 24.3: 305-14.

Carroll, A.B. (1979) 'A Three-dimensional Conceptual Model of Corporate Performance', *Academy of Management Review* 4.4: 497-505.

—— (1991) 'The Pyramid of Corporate Social Responsibility: Toward the Moral Management of Organizational Stakeholders', *Business Horizons* 34.4: 39-48.

—— (1999) 'Corporate Social Responsibility: Evolution of a Definitional Construct', *Business & Society* 38.3: 268-95.

Chou, C., P. Bentler and A. Satorra (1991) 'Scaled Test Statistics and Robust Standard Errors for Non-normal Data in Covariance Structure Analysis: A Monte Carlo Study', *British Journal of Mathematical and Statistical Psychology* 44.2: 347-57.

Churchill, G.A. Jr, and C. Surprenant (1982) 'An Investigation into the Determinants of Customer Satisfaction', *JMR: Journal of Marketing Research* 19.4: 491-504.

Cronin, J.J., M.K. Brady and G.T.M. Hult (2000) 'Assessing the Effects of Quality, Value, and Customer Satisfaction on Consumer Behavioral Intentions in Service Environments', *Journal of Retailing* 76.2: 193-218.

Day, R.E. (1983) 'The Next Step: Commonly Accepted Constructs for Satisfaction Research', in R.E. Day and H.K. Hunt (eds.), *International Fare in Consumer Satisfaction and Complaining Behavior* (Bloomington, IN: Indiana University): 113-17.

Dean, D. (2002) 'Associating the Corporation with a Charitable Event through Sponsorship: Measuring the Effects on Corporate Community Relations', *Journal of Advertising* 34.4: 77-87.

—— and A. Biswas (2001) 'Third Party Organization Endorsement of Products: An Advertising Cue Affecting Consumer Prepurchase Evaluation of Goods and Services', *Journal of Advertising* 30: 41-57.

Du, S., C.B. Bhattacharya and S. Sen (2007) 'Reaping Relational Rewards from Corporate Social Responsibility: The Role of Competitive Positioning', *International Journal of Research in Marketing* 24.3: 224-41.

European Commission (2001) *European Parliament Resolution on the Commission Green Paper on Promoting a European Framework for Corporate Social Responsibility* (Brussels: European Parliament).

Forehand, M., and S. Grier (2003) 'When is Honesty the Best Policy? The Effect of Stated Company Intent on Consumer Skepticism', *Journal of Consumer Psychology* 13.3: 349-56.

Fornell, C., and D.F. Larcker (1981) 'Evaluating Structural Equation Models with Unobservable Variables and Measurement Error', *Journal of Marketing Research* 18.1: 39-50.

Gallarza, M.G., and I. Gil (2006) 'Value Dimensions, Perceived Value, Satisfaction and Loyalty: An Investigation of University Students' Travel Behaviour', *Tourism Management* 27.3: 437-52.

García de los Salmones, M.d.M., Á. Herrero Crespo and I. Rodríguez del Bosque (2005) 'Influence of Corporate Social Responsibility on Loyalty and Valuation of Services', *Journal of Business Ethics* 61.4: 369-85.

Garriga, E., and D. Melé (2004) 'Corporate Social Responsibility Theories: Mapping the Territory', *Journal of Business Ethics* 53.1–2: 51-71.

Grönroos, C. (1982) *Strategic Management and Marketing in Service Sector* (Helsingfors, Finland: Swedish School of Economics and Business Administration).

Hair, J.F., R.E. Anderson, R.L. Tatham and W.C. Black (1998) *Multivariate Data Analysis* (Englewood Cliffs, NJ: Prentice Hall, 4th edn).

Handelman, J.M., and S.J. Arnold (1999) 'The Role of Marketing Actions with a Social Dimension: Appeals to the Institutional Environment', *Journal of Marketing* 63.3: 33-48.

Hatcher, L (1994) *A Step-by-Step Approach to Using the SAS System for Factor Analysis and Structural Equation Modeling* (Cary, NC: SAS Publishing).

Hoeffler, S., and K.L. Keller (2002) 'Building Brand Equity through Corporate Societal Marketing', *Journal of Public Policy and Marketing* 21.1: 78-89.

Holbrook, M.B. (1994) 'The Nature of Customer Value: An Axiology of Services in the Consumption Experience', in R. Rust and R.L. Oliver (eds.), *Service Quality: New Directions in Theory and Practice* (Newbury Park, CA: Sage): 21-71.

Howard, J.A., and J.N. Sheth (1969) *The Theory of Buyer Behavior* (New York: John Wiley).

Hu, L., P. Bentler and Y. Kano (1992) 'Can Test Statistics in Covariance Structure Analysis Be Trusted?', *Psychological Bulletin* 112: 351-62.

Klein, J., and N. Dawar (2004) 'Corporate Social Responsibility and Consumers' Attributions and Brand Evaluations in a Product-Harm Crisis', *International Journal of Research in Marketing* 21.3: 203-17.

Kotler, P., and N. Lee (2005) *Corporate Social Responsibility: Doing the Most Good for Your Company and Your Cause* (New Jersey: John Wiley).

Lehtinen, A., and J.R. Lehtinen (1982) 'Service Quality: A Study of Quality Dimensions' (unpublished working paper; Helsinki, Finland: Service Management Institute).

Lichtenstein, D.R., M.E. Drumwright and B.M. Braig (2004) 'The Effect of Corporate Social Responsibility on Customer Donations to Corporate-Supported Nonprofits', *Journal of Marketing* 68.4: 16-32.

Linnanen, L., and V.M. Panapanaan (2002) *Roadmapping CSR in Finnish Companies* (Helsinki: Helsinki University of Technology).

Luo, X., and C.B. Bhattacharya (2006) 'Corporate Social Responsibility, Customer Satisfaction, and Market Value', *Journal of Marketing* 70.4: 1-18.

Lykken, D.T. (1968) 'Statistical Significance in Psychological Research', *Psychological Bulletin* 70.3 (Pt 1): 151-59.

Maignan, I., and O.C. Ferrell (2003) 'Nature of Corporate Responsibilities: Perspectives from American, French, and German Consumers', *Journal of Business Research* 56.1: 55-67.

——, O. Ferrell and G.T.M. Hult (1999) 'Corporate Citizenship: Cultural Antecedents and Business Benefits', *Journal of the Academy of Marketing Science* 27.4: 455-69.

——, O. Ferrell and L. Ferrell (2005) 'A Stakeholder Model for Implementing Social Responsibility in Marketing', *European Journal of Marketing* 39.9–10: 956-77.

Mano, H., and R.L. Oliver (1993) 'Assessing the Dimensionality and Structure of the Consumption Experience: Evaluation, Feeling and Satisfaction', *Journal of Consumer Research* 20.3: 451-66.

Marín, L., and S. Ruiz (2007) 'I Need You Too! Corporate Identity Attractiveness for Consumers and the Role of Social Responsibility', *Journal of Business Ethics* 71: 245-60.

McCracken, G. (1986) 'Culture and Consumption: A Theoretical Account of the Structure and Movement of the Cultural Meaning of Consumer Goods', *Journal of Consumer Research* 13.1: 71-84.

—— (1989) 'Who is the Celebrity Endorser? Cultural Foundations of the Endorsement Process', *Journal of Consumer Research* 16:3: 310-23.

McDougall, G.H., and T. Levesque (2000) 'Customer Satisfaction with Services: Putting Perceived Value into the Equation', *Journal of Services Marketing* 14.5: 392-410.

McEnally, M.R., and L. de Chernatony (1999) 'The Evolving Nature of Branding: Consumer and Managerial Considerations', *Academy of Marketing Science Review* 1999/2: 1-26.

Mohr, L.A., and D.J. Webb (2005) 'The Effects of Corporate Social Responsibility and Price on Consumer Responses', *Journal of Consumer Affairs* 39.1: 121-47.

Nunnally, J., and I. Bernstein (1994) *Psychometric Theory* (New York: McGraw-Hill).

Oh, H. (1999) 'Service Quality, Customer Satisfaction and Customer Value: An Holistic Perspective', *International Journal of Hospitality Management* 18: 67-82.

—— (2003) 'Price Fairness and its Asymmetric Effects on Overall Price, Quality, and Value Judgments: The Case of an Upscale Hotel', *Tourism Management* 24.4: 387-99.

Oliver, R. L. (1997) *Satisfaction a Behavioral Perspective on the Consumer* (New York: McGraw-Hill).

Parasuraman, A., V.A. Zeithaml and L.L. Berry (1985) 'A Conceptual Model of Service Quality and its Implications for Future Research', *Journal of Marketing* 49: 41-50.

——, V.A. Zeithaml and L.L. Berry (1988) 'Servqual: A Multiple-Item Scale for Measuring Consumer Perceptions of Service Quality', *Journal of Retailing* 64.1: 12-40.

Peterson, R.A. (1995) 'Relationship Marketing and the Consumer', *Journal of the Academy of Marketing Science* 23.4: 278-81.

Polonsky, M.J., and C. Jevons (2006) 'Understanding Issue Complexity when Building a Socially Responsible Brand', *European Business Review* 18.5: 340-49.

—— and G. Wood (2001) 'Can the Overcommercialization of Cause-Related Marketing Harm Society?', *Journal of Macromarketing* 21.1: 8-22.

Porter, M.E., and M.R. Kramer (2002) 'The Competitive Advantage of Corporate Philanthropy', *Harvard Business Review* 80.12: 56-68.

Ravald, A., and C. Grönroos (1996) 'The Value Concept and Relationship Marketing', *European Journal of Marketing* 30.2: 19-30.

Sasser, W.E., P.R. Olsen and D.D. Wickoff (1978) *Management of Service Operations: Text and Cases* (Boston, MA: Allyn & Bacon).

Satorra, A., and P. Bentler (1988) 'Scaling Corrections for Chi-square Statistics in Covariance Structure Analysis', paper presented at the *Economic Statistics Section of the ASA*, Alexandria.

Sen, S., and C. Bhattacharya (2001) 'Does Doing Good Always Lead to Doing Better? Consumer Reactions to Corporate Social Responsibility', *Journal of Marketing Research* 38.2: 225-43.

Sethi, S.P. (1979) 'A Conceptual Framework for Environmental Analysis of Social Issues and Evaluation of Business Response Patterns', *Academy of Management Review* 4.1: 63-74.

Sirdeshmukh, D., J. Singh and B. Sabol (2002) 'Consumer Trust, Value, and Loyalty in Relational Exchanges', *Journal of Marketing* 66.1: 15-37.

Spreng, R.A., A.L. Dixon and R.W. Olshavsky (1993) 'The Impact of Perceived Value on Consumer Satisfaction', *Journal of Consumer Satisfaction, Dissatisfaction and Complaining Behaviour* 6: 50-55.

Swaen, V. (2003) 'Consumers' Perceptions, Evaluations and Reactions to CSR Activities' (IESEG working paper 2003-mar-7; Lille, France: IESEG).

Swan, J.E., and I.F. Trawick (1981) 'Disconfirmation of Expectations and Satisfaction with a Retail Service', *Journal of Retailing* 57.3: 49-67.

Van Marrewijk, M. (2003) 'Concepts and Definitions of CSR and Corporate Sustainability: Between Agency and Communion', *Journal of Business Ethics* 44.2–3: 95-105.

Webb, D.J., and L.A. Mohr (1998) 'A Typology of Consumer Responses to Cause-Related Marketing: From Skeptics to Socially Concerned', *Journal of Public Policy and Marketing* 17.2: 226-38.

Westbrook, R.A., and R.L. Oliver (1991) 'The Dimensionality of Consumption Emotion Patterns and Consumer Satisfaction', *Journal of Consumer Research* 18.1: 84-91.

Yang, Z., and R.T. Peterson (2004) 'Customer Perceived Value, Satisfaction, and Loyalty: The Role of Switching Costs', *Psychology & Marketing* 21.10: 799-822.

Yin, R.K. (2003) *Case Study Research: Design and Methods, Applied Social Research Methods Series* (Newbury Park, CA: Sage Publications, 3rd edn).

Zeithaml, V.A. (1988) 'Consumer Perceptions of Price, Quality, and Value: A Means–End Model and Synthesis of Evidence', *Journal of Marketing* 52.3: 2-22.

—— and M.J. Bitner (2002) *Marketing de servicios: un enfoque de integración del cliente a la empresa* (Mexico City: McGraw-Hill, 2nd edn).

# Appendix: measurement scales used

## TABLE 8.5 Measure of CSR association perceptions and expectations

| Item | Content |
|------|---------|
| | In my opinion a hotel chain to be considered as 'socially responsible' towards society . . . |
| CSRe1 | . . . should make financial donations to social causes |
| CSRe2 | . . . should help to improve the quality of life in the local community |
| CSRe3 | . . . should protect the environment |
| | In my opinion, [hotel chain name] is really . . . |
| CSRp1 | . . . trying to make financial donations to social causes |
| CSRp2 | . . . trying to help to improve the quality of life in the local community |
| CSRp3 | . . . trying to protect the environment |

Source: based on Brown and Dacin 1997

## TABLE 8.6 Measurement of perceived value

| Item | Content |
|------|---------|
| | I think that . . . |
| PV1 | . . . [hotel chain name[ has a good price–quality relationship |
| PV2 | . . . I stay in [hotel chain name] because it is the most economical option of its category |
| PV3 | . . . considering its price, [hotel chain name] offers excellent facilities to its guests |

Source: based on Oh 2003

**TABLE 8.7** Measurement of cognitive and affective satisfaction

| Dimension | Item | Content |
|---|---|---|
| | | In my opinion . . . |
| CS | CS1 | . . . staying in [hotel chain name] was a wise decision |
| | CS2 | . . . I did the right thing when I purchase the services of [hotel chain name] |
| | CS3 | . . . [hotel chain name] offers exactly what I need for my stay |
| AS | AS1 | . . . it's pleasurable to stay in a [hotel chain name] hotel |
| | AS2 | . . . I enjoy staying in a [hotel chain name] hotel |
| | AS3 | . . . the services offered by [hotel chain name] have positively surprised me |
| | AS4 | . . . it makes me happy to stay in a [hotel chain name] hotel |
| | AS5 | . . . staying in a [hotel chain name] hotel is gratifying |

Source: based on Cronin *et al.* 2000

# 9

# Strategic corporate social responsibility
## A brand–building tool

**Francisco Guzmán**
University of North Texas, USA

**Karen L. Becker–Olsen**
The College of New Jersey, USA

Corporate Social Responsibility (CSR) programmes have become an increasingly important and common element of business strategy for companies across a multitude of industries. Companies are recognising that CSR programmes not only improve overall quality of life; they also serve as a source of competitive advantage by attracting and retaining customers, employees and investors, potentially enhancing company performance and building more vibrant communities (Lichtenstein *et al.* 2004; Lafferty and Goldsmith 2005; Luo and Bhattacharya 2006; Porter and Kramer 2006; Pirsch *et al.* 2007). However, the proliferation of CSR programmes leads to increasing stakeholder expectations and the need for companies to strategically align their CSR programmes with their mission and position in the marketplace. As an example, Nestlé Corporation through a myriad of programmes, including an initiative for homeless pets, supplier diversity and employee matching grants, works to create shared value for employees, consumers, communities and shareholders, by ensuring that all of the programmes Nestlé operates and supports are strategically managed and coordinated to strengthen both the business and the community. These efforts are consistent with Nestlé's basic foundation, which is to develop a business that focuses on the ideas of fairness, honesty and a general concern for people (www.nestle.com, accessed 11 December 2009). However, as Nestlé and other brands build CSR into their business models, stakeholders will expect higher levels of commitment and engagement and will be less likely to deliver rewards for mediocre programmes.

CSR defines and describes the complex interrelationships between businesses and the larger society, including environmental protection and sustainability, employee well-being and human rights, and the community in general (Carroll 1999). According to both its original definition as 'the economic, legal, ethical and discretionary expectations that society has of organizations at a given point in time' (Carroll 1979: 500), and Maignan and Ferrell's (2004: 5) more modern characterisation that suggests 'CSR designates the duty . . . to meet or exceed stakeholder norms dictating desirable organizational behaviors', CSR is the way a company interacts with people and communities to create greater shared wealth, efficiencies and well-being for various stakeholder groups. Since the early 1990s, traditional views of CSR have focused more on the tension between business and society and programmes that might alleviate some of that tension. This programmatic approach is very reactionary in that companies respond to marketplace problems, issues or even requests. Many companies, through their corporate foundations or community relations departments, support a diverse set of programmes that build community relations and public image. It is only recently that more contemporary and progressive views of CSR have shifted the focus towards the interdependence between business and society and recognise CSR as a business model that can deliver innovative solutions for companies and communities. Gap Senior Vice President Dan Henkle espouses this notion and believes 'that acting in an ethical way is not only the right thing to do—it also unlocks new ways for us to do business better'. Gap and its affiliates are committed to improving factory conditions throughout the supply chain. It conducts inspections, helps set standards of conduct and works with foreign governments to reinforce basic human rights and raise safety standards. This business–society interdependence reflects Gap's renewed business approach, and has slowly moved CSR to a more strategic business model in which companies, organisations and communities act as partners all requiring and receiving some type of benefit.

By viewing the relationships between businesses and society as a zero-sum game (Porter and Kramer 2006), companies limit the potential and reach of CSR initiatives. In contrast, strategic CSR, the extent to which a company integrates social responsibility into the company's core value proposition in a way that is salient to the company's business operations and competitive context (cf. Porter and Kramer 2006), involves a win–win–win situation for society, businesses and customers (Laughlin and Ashan 1994; Gupta and Pirsch 2006) and implies a strategic alignment between the values of the company and the social and environmental issues that the company addresses (Guzmán *et al.* 2008). Furthermore, Husted and Allen (2007) argue that strategic CSR depends on the alignment between the company's social strategy and its internal and external environment. Strategic CSR promotes long-term business accountability to a wide range of stakeholders, including investors, employees, customers and community members (Snider *et al.* 2003). This wide-ranging concept goes beyond traditional philanthropy or marketing programmes and, because of the company's inherent responsibilities to various stakeholder groups, almost mandates the inclusion of business goals. US retailer Target Corporation, via its Leadership in Energy and Environmental Design programme, has committed to reduce its energy usage, use water resources more efficiently and improve indoor environmental air quality, which will not only reduce operational expenses but will also simultaneously conserve natural resources (www.target.com, accessed 11 December 2009). Similarly, Intel Corporation invests US$100 million annually in educational programmes to develop potential future employees and innovative technology initiatives that benefit both the company and the community (www.intel.com, accessed 11 December 2009).

In this chapter we explore the concept of strategic CSR and all its intricacies and implications for brand building. Our findings are based on a series of empirical research studies developed during the past five years in the United States, Spain and Mexico, as well as marketplace examples and case studies of specific companies. We explore the core business versus broader goals perspective in light of a strategic CSR framework (Heap 2000), and explain when and how it makes sense for a brand to adopt each of these perspectives according to the level of development of CSR in a determined market. This discussion leads to the introduction of the CSR life-cycle concept, an invaluable tool for making strategic CSR decisions and understanding marketplace details.

The chapter is organised as follows. First, we discuss how CSR and the market landscape have changed since the mid-1990s. Second, we discuss the singularities of strategic CSR. Third, we present the four key components of strategic CSR and summarise our research findings over the past five years which lead to the introduction of the CSR life-cycle concept. Finally, we present some international examples of strategic CSR and some conclusions.

## A changing landscape for CSR

As companies face an increasingly competitive marketplace, uncertain economic infrastructure, and growing pressure to behave responsibly towards society, they are seeking alternative ways to provide their brands with social meaning and values that differentiate them from their competitors while simultaneously increasing their connection with their consumers. To this end, many companies have integrated their marketing and corporate social responsibility strategies under the assumption that it will increase corporate performance (Barone *et al.* 2000; Ellen *et al.* 2006; Lichtenstein *et al.* 2004; Luo and Bhattacharya 2006; Sen *et al.* 2006) and brand equity (Guzmán and Montaña 2006; Simmons and Becker-Olsen 2006). Thus, over the past few years we have seen a growing number of companies develop sustainability and social responsibility policies and align themselves with causes, non-governmental organisations and philanthropic activities. In many cases these associations are not necessarily driven by the company's marketplace position, but are merely a responsive marketing tactic to temporarily satisfy consumer or governmental pressures. The programmes that have proved to be most successful are those that have fully integrated CSR into the very fabric of the organisation by developing initiatives and directions that reinforce the company mission.

The degree of understanding and adoption of CSR throughout the global marketplace is varied. CSR activity in developed markets such as Canada, the United States and Western Europe, has been characterised as running, while in other parts of the world, including Central and South America, it has been characterised as walking (Haslam 2004). Lower levels of CSR activity are normally indicative of a marketplace with low reward structures for CSR. Notwithstanding, the landscape is changing as global funding agencies such as the World Bank are tying loans to responsible citizenship, multilateral organisations such as the United Nations Development Programme are advocating Global Compact membership, and communities and consumers are beginning to see the impact of CSR programmes of large multinational enterprises (MNEs).

In the context of this changing system, if companies take a proactive stance and develop a strong CSR programme as part of the brand's identity, it will not only drive the brand's equity and consumer purchases, but also strengthen the company's reputation, help to build a more vibrant community, and create greater employee loyalty. In South Africa, multinationals such as Siemens, Vodafone, BMW and Airbus have integrated South African companies into their global supply chains leading to advances in technology and modernisation of facilities, higher wage levels and other social benefits for South Africans. Thus, even in markets where the rewards might currently appear low, the threshold for brand differentiation and stakeholder expectations are also low; therefore opportunities abound for companies to differentiate themselves on strong CSR programmes and build loyal customers in emerging as well as developed markets. In Peru, Pro Inversion, a private investment promotion agency, builds awareness and commitment to CSR by screening Peruvian state and private investment opportunities for level of CSR participation and commitment to Millennium Development Goals.

Although some business leaders embrace the notion of a triple bottom line (economic, environmental and social), many are still singly focused on the financial impact of corporate social responsibility. Previous research suggests a positive link between strong CSR programmes and improved financial performance, enhanced brand image and reputation, increased sales and customer loyalty, increased ability to attract and retain employees, reduced regulatory oversight and greater access to capital (McWilliams and Siegel 2001). In contrast, initiatives that are poorly conceived and communicated are not only less likely to improve the bottom line, but they are also likely to diminish reputation-related beliefs about the company as well as subsequent purchase intentions. While US consumers report a willingness to reward companies for strong social initiatives, they are also likely to punish companies for social infractions through boycott activities and product switching (Becker-Olsen *et al.* 2005). The *Corporate Social Responsibility Monitor 2001* corroborates and extends this perspective and reports that 42% of North American consumers surveyed rebuked companies with poor social performance by not buying their products, compared with only 23% of Latin American consumers. This contrast is likely to be indicative of a market in which there are lower levels of CSR advocacy, different definitional contexts for CSR and lower consumer expectations of corporate behaviour. However, increasing levels of CSR communication and advocacy are likely to bolster these numbers with consumers in developing countries, making companies with social infractions more vulnerable.

## Defining strategic CSR

Strategic CSR promotes a long-term vision of business accountability to a wide range of stakeholders, including investors, employees, customers and community members (Snider *et al.* 2003). This wide-ranging concept goes beyond traditional philanthropy and, because of the company's inherent responsibility to various stakeholder groups, mandates the inclusion of business goals such as profitability. Thus, the objective of strategic CSR is to identify ways in which companies can align business goals with consumer expectations to increase brand loyalty while simultaneously meeting larger societal demands. General managers have a uniquely broad perspective of the company and its goals and a parallel responsibility to the interests of various stakeholders, especially consumers, making them ideal candidates for overseeing CSR programmes. This multifaceted perspective needs to guide their decisions, as they face important social challenges and set the stage for strategic CSR programmes to positively influence business interactions, corporate reputation, customer loyalty and the larger community.

Within the framework of CSR, a continuum exists with the core business perspective securing one end and the broader goals perspective securing the other (Heap 2000). The core business approach suggests that companies need to act responsibly with regard to their core business, but do not need to engage in corporate social investment beyond the core business. Ford Motor Company, through a variety of programmes, supports its core mission by offering programmes in education related to driving safety (e.g. driver safety, car seat safety and drunk-driving prevention), environmental programmes related to climate change, energy efficiency and emissions, and diversity programmes aimed at employee empowerment. In contrast, the broader goals perspective suggests that companies should embrace goals beyond profit and core business operations, and include goals of sustainability, poverty reduction, education and other more philanthropic-based endeavours. Thus, their corporate social investment is not necessarily related to their core business operation. Nokia is one company that is highly committed to sustainability, poverty reduction and education around the world. Chief Executive Olli-Pekka Kallasvuo, believes that 'global issues cannot be removed from the business world', and Nokia seeks to set the standard for social investment and environmental sustainability through a set of corporate values that engage all stakeholders and create incentives for innovative solutions to global problems that may or may not relate directly to the telecommunications business.

Throughout our research we have observed that strategic fit plays a crucial role in the successful implementation of a CSR programme. Just as total quality management is a process that has moved beyond simple quality production, CSR has moved beyond simplistic marketing tactics or promotion. Therefore, it is our belief that the broader goals perspective, although not directly tied to a specific product or product line, should still be strategically integrated into the operating principles and practices of the company. For example, American Airlines, in support of the victims of the Myanmar Cyclone, the Wenchuan earthquake in China's Sichuan province, and of the Central US floods and tornadoes, donated all of its free cargo space available to transport supplies to the affected areas. By taking advantage of excess transportation capacity, American Airlines is capable of implementing a CSR programme by supporting a disaster relief effort that strengthens its brand image and helped the affected communities. Hence, even in the core business approach, we would advocate strategic alignment between the values of the company and the values of the CSR programme. The pet food brand Pedigree collaborated with the municipal government of Mexico City on a campaign called 'Responsible Owner' which sought to create consciousness around dog faeces. In order to help keep streets and parks clean, Pedigree installed special yellow wastebaskets to encourage dog owners to collect and dispose of their animals' waste. The wastebaskets resemble the company's 20 kg dog food bag; they carry a large logo and are emptied on a regular basis by a special cleaning crew.

Strategic CSR thus occurs only when a company adds a social dimension to its value proposition—its brand—making social impact a part of its overall business strategy (Porter and Kramer 2006). When a company truly engages in strategic CSR, issues of fit become void in that the term 'strategic' implies that the company develops a CSR programme that truly reinforces the brand's marketplace position. However, when CSR is more tactical, reactionary or programmatic, the lack of fit becomes relevant, given that consumers respond to the company's CSR message depending on the level of fit they perceive exists between the social dimension and the values of the brand (Bloom *et al.* 2006). We agree with Asongu (2007), in that CSR should be viewed from a strategic perspective all of the time.

# Four key components of strategic CSR

As noted above, in this chapter we make the case for strategic CSR in developing and emerging markets, articulating key lessons for developing, implementing and communicating a strong CSR programme that satisfies consumer needs and interests as well as the interests of the company and the community. Based on a series of empirical studies conducted in North America, Mexico and Spain over a multi-year time-frame, four key components have been identified as essential to the development of an effective strategic CSR programme (see Becker-Olsen *et al.* 2005; Guzmán *et al.* 2006, 2008; Simmons and Becker-Olsen 2006 for full details on the study methods, analysis and results): a **clear motivation** or strategic orientation that drives the CSR initiative, the selection of an **appropriate initiative**, and choosing the **right timing** and the **right communication** to explain the reach and objectives of the programme. Having the right perceived motivation allows consumers to view the company more favourably while selecting a high strategic fit initiative is critical in that strategic fit is a processing heuristic shown to alter stakeholder response to CSR communication. Lastly, timing and style are important consideration as they can further alter stakeholder responses.

## A clear strategic motivation

As mentioned above, corporate social responsibility is increasingly important for companies across a myriad of industries. However, the motivation for engaging in these programmes varies considerably. Some companies are intrinsically motivated and simply believe it is the right thing to do irrespective of the costs or rewards. These companies are highly committed to strategic CSR and have incorporated it as an integral part of their strategic plan. Other companies are motivated by outside sources, including governments, non-government organisations, consumer advocacy groups and investors. In such cases, compliance, and its associated rewards and costs, is the driving force. External pressure from national governments and multinational organisations such as OECD, World Bank and the Global Compact (GC) forces companies to become more responsible as they are required to document and report on their citizenship activities. Although reporting to the Global Compact is a voluntary activity for member companies, it is expected that companies will adhere to the guiding principles set forth by the GC (e.g. human rights, labour standards, environment and anti-corruption) and work to meet the Millennium Development Goals. Securing investors and employees is another reason companies engage in and promote CSR activities. Both investors and employees are increasingly interested in companies with strong CSR programmes. Many companies have responded with more visible investor relations material focused on CSR initiatives and employee/community engagement programmes. Lastly, strategic CSR programmes can serve a marketing purpose. In these instances companies may choose to engage in CSR programmes as public relations opportunities, reputational insurance that will help in times of crisis, or brand building.

In contrast to the preceding examples, the focus in this work is on using strategic CSR as a business management tool rather than a more short-term tactic to attract customers, investors or even employees. These short-term programmes and initiatives are generally not sustainable and do not create shared value for the company and various stakeholders. Thus, irrespective of motivation, companies need to understand the benefits of a strategic orientation to their CSR efforts so that they might create a win–win–win for the company, stakeholders and communities.

## An appropriate initiative

Although the evidence regarding the positive effects of CSR programmes is clear, care needs to be taken when designing and choosing CSR programmes and initiatives so that companies do not experience a boomerang effect or are not subject to greenwashing allegations. We find that programmes that do not strategically fit with the business or are perceived as reactionary can lead to brand equity dilution.

### Strategic fit

Strategic fit, as defined in a CSR context, is the perceived link between a particular cause, programme or initiative and the company's product line, brand image, position or target market. For example, an oil company might support certain environmental initiatives, while a women's apparel manufacturer might have a strong human rights programme focusing on women's educational development. Fit is important for a number of reasons, and has been shown to influence: (1) how much thought people give to a relationship (e.g. there is increased thought when perceived inconsistencies or low fit exist); (2) the specific types of thought that are generated (e.g. low fit generates more negative thoughts); and (3) evaluations of the two objects (e.g. low fit tends to garner lower evaluations).[1] Specifically, we find:

*Consumers realise that companies have business objectives as well as broader social goals and understand and appreciate when they are aligned.* Although consumers expect companies to be involved with the larger community, they do not require them to do so at the expense of their business goals and profitability. Consequently, consumers do not expect companies to engage in large-scale, purely philanthropic programmes. They understand and appreciate that companies have business goals and objectives and that social initiatives or programmes often provide an opportunity to align business goals with social or community objectives. Many consumers believe companies that are perceived as responsible and contribute to the development of the community create long-term economic growth options for both parties.

*Strategic fit between a social initiative and a company's product line or service offering has an important impact on subsequent thoughts.* When consumers cannot easily comprehend why a company might be involved with a given initiative, they automatically begin a process of cognitive elaboration or reflection in which they try to resolve the apparent discrepancy. This process often causes consumers to update their thoughts and beliefs related to the company. Research results demonstrate that company motive, programme efficacy and purchase intention are three key areas that are influenced negatively when the fit is deemed poor or unusual. Thus, low-fit CSR initiatives tend to engender more negative thoughts about companies' motives, strategic fit and purchase intentions, all diluting the company's potential benefits. Consumers instinctively question why companies would be involved in these initiatives and assume that they are merely public relations ploys designed to get people to buy particular products instead of those of competitors. Hence these more tactical promotional programmes may not deliver value to the company.

*Strategic fit influences overall attitude towards the company as well as beliefs related to credibility, commitment and position.* When strategic fit is high, thoughts about the company's credibility, reputation and commitment to the CSR programme are enhanced, whereas, when strategic fit is low, these factors are diluted, again attenuating potential CSR benefits.

*Strategic fit does not influence beliefs about the company's ability to deliver a quality product, but a lack of fit does dilute the company's competitive market position.* Interestingly, consumers are able to separate the more global impressions about a company's reputation from specific beliefs about product attributes and quality.

---

1 For a broader discussion, see Simmons and Becker-Olsen 2006.

This is important in that CSR programmes cannot make up for a bad product, but in a category where quality is relatively equal, CSR can be used as a point of differentiation. However, company and brand position are diluted when companies concentrate on CSR programmes that do not fit with their brands. This insight makes intuitive sense given that market position is defined primarily by perceptions of product offerings and their associated communications. Consider how consumers will react to a luxury goods marketer engaged in an initiative involving homelessness. They are likely to experience difficulty reconciling this programme with the company's offerings, target audience and position in the marketplace.

*Strategic fit influences purchase intentions.* This bottom-line result is one of the most important findings. If the fit is low and therefore deemed troublesome, consumers question company motivation and become less willing to purchase from the sponsoring brand. Historically, consumers who question companies' underlying motives are likely to distance themselves from such companies as well as their products.

*Strategic fit should be considered at both a functional and an emotional level.* Our research has tested strategic fit as a multidimensional concept—brand–value fit, and brand–function fit—and finds evidence for the differential effects of each dimension on consumer attitudes. Brand–function fit has a direct effect on attitude towards the brand, which in turn has a direct effect on brand equity. Therefore, brand–function fit should be considered in selecting the most effective social causes to associate with the brand. On the other hand, brand–value fit influences attitude towards the ad, and attitude towards the ad influences attitude towards the brand. Consequently, advertisements about strategic CSR programmes will be more effective when they emphasise the fit between the values of the brand and the values of the cause. Both functional fit (rational) and value fit (emotional) are important and complementary, and allow consumers to fully grasp the intent and logic of a CSR initiative.

In summary, we find that, when developing a CSR programme, fit matters. It simply does not make sense for an eyewear manufacturer to support an infant vaccination programme—a pharmaceutical manufacturer is a better choice for that type of programme. However, the eyewear manufacturer should support initiatives for glaucoma research, cornea transplants and UV awareness. Given what we know about CSR development in developing countries and the greater propensity for a core business approach to CSR, these findings related to fit are especially critical. However, even in the broader goals perspective, it does not make sense for the eyewear manufacturer to engage in an infant vaccination programme unless it was a vaccine to prevent some eye disease. The eyewear manufacturer could engage in a recycling programme for eyeglasses, hearing aids or other medical devices that might be recycled as part of a larger commitment to helping end healthcare inequality or increase recycling. If consumers expect companies to make social investments that are aligned to the core businesses and companies do not adhere to that, they are likely to find their social investment is a liability rather than an asset.

## The right timing

CSR initiatives that are perceived as proactive and unprovoked by outside sources are likely to be perceived differently from CSR initiatives that are a direct reaction to some corporate crisis. We have found that companies often engage in social initiatives as a reaction to natural disasters, consumer boycotts, NGO pressures, or a number of other corporate crises. It is likely that consumers' responses to these reactive CSR initiatives (e.g. McDonald's and its use of recyclable packaging material post consumer reaction or Starbucks' move for more fair-trade suppliers post consumer boycotts) will be different from responses to proactive initiatives (e.g. Yoplait and its ongoing support for the fight against breast cancer or Sabritas—PepsiCo's division of snacks in Mexico—and its efforts to create better eating and exercise habits in Mexican children). We have found that scepticism drives consumer response and lowers evaluations of the company when companies appear to be reactive rather than proactive in their CSR programmes. Specifically, we find:

*Scepticism negatively influences overall attitude towards the company as well as beliefs related to credibility, reputation and commitment to the cause.* When scepticism is high, as is the case for a CSR initiative that is in response to a human rights violation, global attitude towards the company and thoughts about the company's credibility, reputation and commitment to the CSR programme are diluted. When scepticism is low or the CSR programme is perceived as proactive, these factors are enhanced.

*Scepticism does not influence beliefs about the product quality, but does dilute perceptions of the company's managerial competence.* As was the case with strategic fit, consumers are able to separate the more global impressions about a company's reputation from specific beliefs about product quality. However, they do blame the company's management team for the infraction. This is important in that CSR programmes cannot make up for a poor managerial decision regarding human rights, environmental dumping, or other violations that consumers perceive as under the control of the company.

*Scepticism influences purchase intentions.* Again this bottom-line result is intuitive but one of the most important findings. Consumers are not willing to reward companies for 'correcting' a bad behaviour. In fact, they even report a willingness to select another brand. This raises the question: what should companies do? It is important to note that, in our research, the companies did not admit to a wrongdoing; they simply stated their CSR engagement. It is likely that consumers will respond less negatively if companies admit culpability, take corrective action and then move on swiftly and proactively. However, this is an area that needs further investigation.

## The right communication

Assuming that customers are ready to reward companies for high-fit proactive initiatives, companies need to make sure consumers can easily find the information they need to properly evaluate the social, environmental and ethical stance of the company and that the information is framed so it best aligns with customer expectations. Specifically we recommend the following:

*Make it easy for consumers to get positive CSR information.* Although consumers repeatedly report a willingness to support companies with strong CSR programmes, consumers are not willing to seek out that information. Thus, having CSR information available in the mass media, on packaging inserts, at point of purchase, on the package itself or easily accessible on company websites helps consumers to effortlessly integrate CSR information into their decision criteria. It is simply unrealistic to think that most consumers will seek CSR information on company websites or in annual reports. Companies can take a lesson from the consumer watchdog groups who are quick to disseminate non-compliance, pollution, child labour or other negative information. These groups effectively use the mass media and blogs to spread the message. By 2001 watchdog groups had assured that Nike was the poster company for sweatshop violations, disseminating information via Internet blogs and news reports. Yet, in 2008, Nike became the key supporter of the World Bank's Empowering Young Adolescence programme (now the Adolescent Girls Initiative) and very few customers or community activists are aware of its efforts.

*Make sure consumers understand why the company is engaged in the initiative.* Consumers want to know why companies are involved with a given programme especially when the strategic fit is low. Since consumers seem to instinctively leap to 'why', managers need to proactively share their programme rationale so the company's motives are less likely to receive negative scrutiny. Clearly communicating this link will help consumers understand the company's purpose for involvement and increase their willingness to reward the company. For example, US retailer Home Depot is engaged in several sustainability initiatives that help to limit habitat encroachment and protect endangered species. Although at first pass this seems to not fit with the mission or core business of the company, which is to assist consumers in their home improvement projects, it has been thinking more broadly in terms of sustainability given its impact on deforestation and the effect of real estate development on natural habitats. Thus, the company is a key sponsor of WWF and assists with the creation and building of protected spaces for endangered species with the notion that everyone deserves a home and sharing of the planet will lead to sustainable development.

*Share details regarding programme efficacy and community impact.* While consumers may continue to question why a company would choose a specific programme if they cannot instinctively find the fit, they are quick to remark on the positive outcomes of successful programmes. Although impact details do not alleviate thinking about *why*, they do leave consumers with more positive feelings about companies. The Product (Red) campaign is an excellent example. Over 2.5 million people in Africa have benefited from HIV/AIDS programmes through this campaign, and this information is readily available as one enters the campaign website. So, even though some of the nine select Product (Red) partners might not have a 'natural' fit with a cause such as the one this programme supports, people in the USA have understood the need for combating HIV/AIDS and value their efforts.

*When programme efficacy details are shared, consumers reading about high-fit programmes are more likely to integrate the company and the programme details.* In contrast, if there is high fit for the initiative and no programme details are shared, consumers are less likely to integrate the company and the programme in their thought structures, making it harder for them to recall the CSR information at point of purchase. While the thoughts are positive, they are very general in nature, indicating a limited amount of processing effort. However, when programme details are shared, the thoughts become more focused on programme details (in this case the positive outcomes) and their relation to the company, indicating a higher level of processing. This higher level of processing is more likely to lead to stronger memory traces and thus more likely to help guide purchase decisions.

*Not only do programme efficacy details tend to increase overall company attitude, they also increase feelings of company credibility, company trust, and perceptions of company commitment to the programme, irrespective of fit.* In the first phase of our research, global beliefs related to company reputation were diminished when strategic fit was low and enhanced when alignment was good. In the latter phases results have suggested that companies may further enhance these positive beliefs when fit is high and programme efficacy details are provided. This last finding may occur because consumers perceive the company as rising above their baseline expectation for corporate social responsibility. Equally important, positive programme details enhance the same set of beliefs even when strategic fit is low suggesting that the company may be able to overcome some of the negative effects of fit with a successful high impact programme.

*Program efficacy details also tend to increase purchase intentions even when strategic fit is low.* In contrast to our earlier research on fit where we found that purchase intentions were actually diminished under low-fit conditions and increased with proper alignment, in latter research we have found that purchase intentions were increased beyond the control level when programme efficacy details were shared. As expected, in the high-fit condition, purchase intentions also increase when programme efficacy details are shared.

In sum, programme efficacy details act as a signal both for the company's commitment to the programme as well as for the success of the programme, directing consumer beliefs about the brand and the initiative in a more positive direction.

# CSR life-cycle

The rise of CSR over the past 20 years has left many businesses, governments, NGOs, shareholders and consumers trying to understand how and why companies might act in a more socially responsible manner. Questions still abound: What role does CSR play in social, economic and environmental planning? Do stakeholders value CSR programmes across all contexts? How do we measure the social, environmental or business impact? Are companies sincere in their actions? How do we develop effective CSR programmes? Do the four components always play out the same? The development of a CSR life-cycle model helps companies understand the strategic decisions that need to be made at various stages in the model and help set some boundary conditions. For companies that are engaged in global operations, it may be that they are operating in an early stage in one market (e.g. Latin America) and in a later stage in a more developed market (e.g. United Kingdom). A tool such as this can help companies maintain a consistent strategic CSR programme while still meeting the needs of stakeholders in specific markets.

We find life-cycle models in many contexts, including product management, project management, economic development, and industry and market analysis. Although all of these models use different terms to identify various stages of development, they all assume that some entity, in this case corporate social responsibility, grows from its infancy to its eventual death. Generally the models help managers understand competitive context and market characteristics, and provide guidelines for which strategies and actions should be implemented in each stage. Thus, an evolutionary CSR model potentially helps managers better comprehend the CSR environment, likely stakeholder reactions, potential cost structures, and understand that a shift in perceived value is likely as CSR matures.

Life-cycle models, like most models, have underlying assumptions. One of the assumptions of life-cycle models is that key variables change as the unit of study (e.g. family, product, CSR . . .) changes. Specifically, in the product life-cycle (PLC), there is an underlying assumption that the competitive environment changes as the product moves through the stages of the life-cycle. In response to this change, alterations in both strategic and tactical plans may be warranted. Further, the model helps explain various cost/profit structures that emerge across the various stages. Similarly, the family life-cycle (FLC) helps consumer behaviour theorists to understand changes in family consumption as families move through the various stages and aids in predicting core motivations for family consumption based on the life-cycle stage. In the CSR life-cycle, model change revolves around stakeholder awareness and expectations.

We propose a CSR model that is reminiscent of market evolution and traditional product life-cycle models predicting four phases: **market crystallisation**, **market expansion**, **competitive turbulence and fragmentation**, and **absorption**. As noted, in contrast to most life-cycle models, we do not propose a terminal stage, rather an absorption phase in which CSR is absorbed into the strategic planning and fabric of companies and brands, not acting as an add-on activity with a life of its own. Our model is depicted in Figure 9.1.

**FIGURE 9.1** CSR life–cycle model

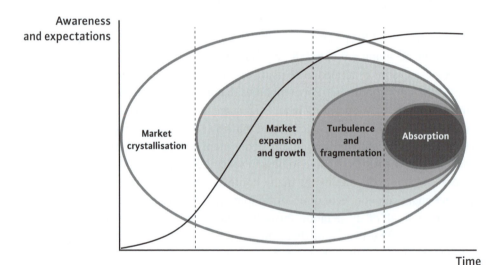

## Market crystallisation

In the market crystallisation phase we expect CSR will be introduced to the market through focused yet sporadic efforts of only a few companies attempting to spark interest in CSR and develop the market. CSR programmes are likely to be basic and offered as add-ons to product or brand strategy—not necessarily integrated into the brand or company's positioning strategy. As is typically the case in this early stage, consumers and other stakeholders have not clearly developed their preferences, thus companies tend to have CSR offerings that are managerially driven rather than market-driven. They are also likely to be a revenue drain and offer question-able financial value to the brand or company. Thus the 'price' is high with minimal rewards coming from small groups of stakeholders. Companies are likely to communicate their initiatives to these small groups of stakeholders in general terms. Thus, as with most life-cycle models, we propose that the introductory phase will be characterised by few companies, low profitability or return on the CSR investment, and relatively high costs. As an example, Africa is a region where there are only sporadic efforts related to CSR and a consumer and governmental culture where CSR is not necessarily valued. The African Institute of Corporate Citizenship is working to change the existing culture and encouraging both multinational corporations and locally owned businesses to go beyond charitable contributions and work with local community partners and governmental organisations to create sustainable programmes that strengthen businesses and improve quality of life.

## Market expansion and growth

As we move to the growth phase, we are likely to see a pattern of exponential diffusion. Thus, as more companies engage in CSR, it is likely that growth will be rapid and consumer awareness will increase exponentially. During this phase new companies are likely to reap the rewards of CSR as the first-movers to the CSR markets have paved the way for growth. Additionally, as the types of CSR programme diversify, and stakeholder experience with CSR increases, stakeholder preferences and expectations are likely to develop, with rewards accruing to companies that meet stakeholder demands. As an example, in China, CSR is in the early expansion phase and is influencing ever-increasing groups of consumers and investors. As companies begin to develop a critical base of knowledge regarding consumer and investor preferences, communications and programmes are likely to become more specific and begin to address these expectations. Later in this phase, CSR is also likely to have a greater impact on hiring. Potential and current employees are likely to have defined preferences for companies that encourage volunteerism, support environmental initiatives or encourage employee health and well-being. Employees may reward the company with their loyalty, thus reducing search costs and increasing the value of employee-directed CSR initiatives. Hence, this phase is characterised by rapid expansion of offerings, competitors and stakeholder interest as well as reduced costs and higher returns leading to an upward spiral. According to a recent survey developed by Times Foundation and TNS in India, 90% of the surveyed companies are involved in some kind of CSR initiative. The focus of these efforts, though, is still on general causes, not necessarily related to the companies' core values, such as microfinancing, environment, health education and women's empowerment, and has the goal of improving the public perception of the company.

## Competitive turbulence and fragmentation

It is the upward spiral, started in the growth phase (increase in number of companies offering CSR, leading to increased stakeholder awareness, leading to an increase in efficacy of CSR efforts and company profitability, thus making CSR more attractive to a greater number of companies and continuing the spiral), that propels CSR into the next stage of competitive turbulence. In this phase, stakeholder expectations are clearly developed with many stakeholder groups demanding more from companies and not necessarily rewarding programmatic efforts with minimal social impact. In fact, companies that fail to meet expectations or suffer perceived social infractions, are likely to be punished by various stakeholder groups. It is likely that only companies with exemplary CSR performance will continue to be rewarded. This is the case in the United States and many parts of Europe. Thus, the bar for financial rewards based on CSR activities goes higher, forcing some companies to consider 'dropping out'. However, these companies run the risk of losing customers, investors and employees. In essence, the price of CSR has dropped to zero, but the price of not engaging in CSR is high. In this phase new companies might lack the relevant base of knowledge regarding customer expectations, employee preferences or investor criteria to effectively design CSR programmes. Communication in this phase is likely to focus on specific preferences tailored to the various stakeholder groups and highlighting measurable results. For example, in August 2008, Grupo Bimbo became the first Mexican company to incorporate 100% biodegradable packaging to all of its product line. The bread manufacturing company's previous CSR efforts had focused on more general causes such as energy reduction, and nutrition and health education.

## Absorption

Interestingly, it is the raising of the bar or the increasing stakeholder expectations, that are the likely catalyst for companies to 'drop out', thus leading to what we call the absorption phase. As noted above, it is not likely that companies will stop acting socially responsibly in that the penalties by governments, stockholders and consumers are too high. However, it is likely that companies will take a more focused approach to CSR known as the core business approach. This style of CSR allows for CSR to be absorbed into planning and operations of the core business, rather than acting as a separate part of the brands or companies' strategic plan. For example, Stonyfield Farm—US organic yoghurt and dairy producer—has made its CSR pledge its business pledge. Stonyfield Farm's mission has a social responsibility focus:

> We're committed to healthy food, healthy people, a healthy planet, and healthy business.

**Healthy food.** We will craft and offer the most delicious and nourishing organic yogurts and dairy products.

**Healthy people.** We will enhance the health and wellbeing of our consumers and colleagues.

**Healthy planet.** We will help protect and restore the planet, and promote the viability of family farms.

**Healthy business.** We will prove that healthy profits and a healthy planet are not in conflict, and that in fact dedication to health and sustainability enhances shareholder value. We believe that business must lead the way to a more sustainable future.[2]

One of the underlying assumptions is that stakeholder interest will drive the diffusion rates for CSR through the introductory and growth phase; while increases in stakeholder expectations then act as the catalyst for the absorption phase. In the early stages, consumers, shareholders and governments are likely to reward companies (e.g. increased purchases and loyalty, tax incentives, positive word of mouth) for CSR activities. However, as more companies are engaged in CSR, stakeholder expectations increase while rewards tend to decrease thus diminishing the scope of many companies' CSR efforts. If a company cannot meet the high level demanded for rewards in the marketplace, they are likely to operate at a level which simply does not invite punishment.

In sum, it is crucial for a company to identify the current stage in the CSR life-cycle of the market in which it is trying to develop a strategic CSR programme. This is even more important for multinational companies that are trying to develop socially responsible global brands. Not only is it important to understand how the issue of fit might vary from one context to another, as we have found in our research, but also identifying the current stage of the CSR life-cycle will allow the company to adapt its CSR efforts effectively in order to fully benefit the brand.

# Examples of strategic CSR

Following are a set of examples of both strategic and traditional CSR initiatives. These examples are intended to illustrate in particular the importance of one of the four key components of strategic CSR described above: the appropriate initiative. Consumers are increasingly sceptical about these kinds of initiative because many companies have implemented social responsibility efforts in an irresponsible and non-strategic manner, primarily as a means of communication. As discussed

2 stonyfield.com/about_us/26_years_of_making_a_difference/yogurt_on_a_mission/index.jsp, accessed 24 March 2010.

earlier, finding the right fit between the social initiative and the values of the brand is what makes a strategic CSR initiative a strong brand-building tool. Businesses must associate their brands with social values that are consistent and complementary to their brand values, because not doing so will not only lead the consumer to believe that they are insincere, but they will also fall into the trap of using traditional philanthropy with little or no brand value creation.

To start off, we can illustrate the importance of fit between the cause and the brand with the following two examples:

- In 2002 Barcelona celebrated the Year of Gaudi. As part of the celebration, the city promoted the Modernism Route, a pedestrian route that passed by 100 of the most important modernist buildings in the city. The Spanish shoe brand Camper, whose designs are noted for being modern and in the vanguard, collaborated in the promotion of the celebration. Throughout the route one could see informative banners with images of some of the most well-known buildings accompanied by the Camper logo and its slogan 'Walk, don't run'

- In 2004, Mexico City's government began building the second floor of the principal highway running through its metropolitan centre. Because of the reduction of lanes from construction, they began diverting traffic to alternative routes. Throughout the main parallel route, traffic rules were modified and police booths were installed to ensure that drivers did not make once-legal left-hand turns. Pepsi, a brand that has always been considered young and alternative, collaborated in this effort. Each blue police booth that was installed along this avenue carried a large Pepsi logo

While in both cases the idea was to support a good cause, for Pepsi there was no real fit between the brand and the public service. In fact, the relationship between the company and the police force generated some confusion and the experience was quickly considered a failed promotional strategy. On the other hand, Camper's support of the Year of Gaudi was directly related to one of the central themes of its communication: in this case a lifestyle that promotes walking. Furthermore, this initiative was so successful that it became one of many between the brand and the city government which fell under an umbrella campaign called 'Walk through Barcelona'.

The following are other examples of low-fit initiatives. Starbucks Coffee Company has been the recipient of much negative publicity over fair-trade coffee and liveable wages. When the company announced a US$1.5 million three-year commitment to Jumpstart, an international education non-profit organisation that works with low-income preschoolers, consumers were likely to question the company's motives for supporting this cause. While most consumers may agree that the mission of the non-profit is worthwhile, they may be hard pressed to understand the strategic fit between Starbucks and Jumpstart, especially when the company could have addressed other citizenship issues more closely related to their everyday operations. Another example is Sabritas, which, with the help of Fundación Únete, an NGO devoted to making technology accessible to children of scarce resources, implemented a technology access programme. Sabritas helped install 20 media classrooms in different parts of Mexico. Although Sabritas's target consumers are children, education is not one of its basic business values.

Conversely, there are other examples of initiatives with high strategic alignment. Sabritas and Fundación Actívate, a not-for-profit organisation devoted to developing good eating and exercise habits in children, developed the programme *Activados* (activated) designed to raise awareness in children about the dangers of a sedentary lifestyle. With the repositioning of Sabritas and PepsiCo as a healthier food company, this type of programme is more strategically aligned with the companies' values and position. Another example is the Spanish company Gas Natural, which established a relationship with the city government and with the public transportation system (TMB) to power the city's bus fleet with natural gas. Gas Natural contributed 10% of the programme cost and offered TMB a preferential rate for natural gas, thus making buses more efficient and less polluting in terms of both emissions and sound. These buses carry a large Gas Natural logo not only as a means of advertising, but also to distinguish these buses from those that do not use the technology. As a result of this relationship, Gas Natural has gained recognition in Barcelona as a clean and environmentally responsible company. Since the beginning of the programme, 250 buses have been replaced and consumers have begun to relate the company name, which was traditionally linked only to the supply of gas for homes and businesses, to this new mode of transport. Home Depot, a retail store in the United Stated which sells building materials and other home products, and its commitment to support the NGO Habitat for Humanity, is another strong example of strategic CSR. Consumers instinctively understand the connection and respond more favourably to the company and are less likely to malign the company's underlying motivation. As mentioned above, our work has shown that consumers generate more positive overall thoughts when an initiative or programme fits strategically with the company.

This does not mean that companies cannot be flexible in their CSR initiatives and participate in programmes of sincere interest. It means that companies may need to be somewhat creative in establishing a strategic fit between the initiative and the core business. For example, Nokia Corporation runs a youth development programme with a network of local non-profit partners. Although the immediate fit between youth development and the company may not be intuitive, Nokia positions itself as a company that connects people and uses this notion of making connections between young people and the community for its youth development programmes.

## Conclusions

Consumers clearly are concerned about corporate social responsibility and do expect companies to be involved in CSR programmes and initiatives. However, consumers may need to know *why* companies selected particular programmes and initiatives, and how they fit with their strategic mission and brand values. Additionally, consumers are likely to respond more positively to programme descriptions that highlight efficacy, demonstrating companies' commitment to particular causes that lead to increased trust in and credibility of companies as well as purchase intentions. Although research findings identify strategic fit as a key variable in determining positive consumer responses, companies may still participate in initiatives that do not explicitly fit with their core product offerings or mission statements without detriment if they are able to demonstrate high programme efficacy. However, regardless of the relative alignment, managers should somehow create a connection between their programmes and their companies, communicate the viability of these connections to consumers, and develop appropriate metrics that quantify their CSR impact and support continuous improvement of initiatives. An important caveat is that corporate social responsibility is a long-term, broad-based strategic venture rather than a short-term, limited-product attribute, which requires a significant investment of resources.

In another investigation, ten global organisations that were headquartered in the United States and widely recognised for their socially responsible activities were studied (Hill *et al.* 2003). Their commitment to CSR was extensively integrated into the fabric of these public companies from their missions to their goals and objectives to their actions. Further, confirmation of this commitment went beyond their communications with various stakeholders to include media statements and published articles that corroborate their dedication to particular ideals. Managers identified so strongly with these social obligations that it was difficult to disentangle their business operations from their public service.

As evidenced by its number one ranking on the Dow Jones Sustainability Index European Technology and Global Communications Technology categories, Nokia is a company that exemplifies this strong, long-term commitment to societal outcomes without losing sight of its business objectives. The company makes significant social investments across a wide range of areas, with some programmes tied to and integrated with its core business operations (e.g. Bridge*it*, an educational initiative which uses mobile technology to bring learning materials to schools) while other programmes are not directly related to the company's core business and have a more subjective fit (e.g. Make A Connection, a youth life skills programme).[3] Nokia's motivation for engaging in these social initiatives is varied and complex and includes business and societal goals; yet its commitment to maximising the societal benefit is strong across all programmes. Irrespective of fit, Nokia takes a long-term perspective and is dedicated to business metrics such as brand tonality, employee satisfaction and customer satisfaction as well as social indicators which help to determine programme efficacy. (For example, how many people has this programme served? What is the human impact of this programme?) For Nokia, independent proof of societal impact and ongoing improvement are essential to the company's credibility, and to the effective communication of the programmes themselves. Additionally, Nokia has been forthright in explaining this position, for example tying its public reporting to outcomes rather than expenditure. Thus, although somewhat counterintuitive, by maximising societal impact and clearly communicating with its customers, Nokia is able to satisfy multiple stakeholders and provide a stronger business impact.

Strategic CSR in no way discredits more common methods of associating with social values, such as supporting NGOs, associating with causes or philanthropic donations, as all of these methods can also be part of a company's CSR programme. Furthermore, any of these methods can be part of a strategic CSR programme as long as the values of the cause are consistent with the values of the brand. Supporting a cause just to support it with no strategic connection to the brand may show social responsibility, but it will not necessarily contribute to brand building or to the bottom line, for that matter; and in highly developed CSR markets it might even invite scepticism. The takeaway is that the marketing tactics recommended in this chapter must be part of a more complete, long-term focus on strategic CSR in order to maximise the potential gains to companies, clients and the larger community.

---

3  Several interviews were conducted with members of Nokia's CSR team. Details of Nokia programmes are available at: www.nokia.com/corporate-responsibility and www.nokia.com/environment, both accessed 24 March 2010.

# References

Asongu, J.J. (2007) 'Sustainable Development as a Business Responsibility', *Journal of Business and Public Policy* 1.2: 1-30.

Barone, M., A.D. Miyazki and K.A. Taylor (2000) 'The Influence of Cause-Related Marketing on Consumer Choice: Does One Good Turn Deserve Another?', *Journal of the Academy of Marketing Science* 28.2: 248-62.

Becker-Olsen, K.L., B.A. Cudmore and R.P. Hill (2005) 'The Impact of Perceived Corporate Social Responsibility on Consumer Behavior', *Journal of Business Research* 59.1: 46-53.

Bloom, P.N., S. Hoeffler, K.L. Keller and C.E. Basurto Meza (2006) 'How Social-Cause Marketing Affects Consumer Perceptions', *MIT Sloan Management Review* 47.2: 49-55.

Carroll, A.B. (1979) 'A Three-dimensional Conceptual Model of Corporate Social Performance', *Academy of Management Review* 4.4: 497-505.

—— (1999) 'Corporate Social Responsibility: Evolution of a Definitional Construct', *Business and Society* 38.3: 268-95.

Corporate Social Responsibility Monitor (2001) 'Executive Report'; research.dnv.com/csr/PW_Tools/PWD/1/00/L/1-00-L-2001-01-0/lib2001/CSRpoll2001.pdf, accessed 24 March 2010.

Ellen, P.S., L.A. Mohr and D.J. Webb (2000) 'Charitable Programs and the Retailer: Do They Mix?', *Journal of Retailing* 76.3: 393-406.

——, D.J. Webb and L.A. Mohr (2006) 'Building Corporate Associations: Consumer Attributions for Corporate Socially Responsible Programs', *Journal of the Academy of Marketing Science* 34.2: 147-57.

Gupta, S., and J. Pirsch (2006) 'A Taxonomy of Cause-Related Marketing Research: Current Findings and Future Research Directions', *Journal of Nonprofit and Public Sector Marketing* 15.1–2: 25-43.

Guzmán, F., and J. Montaña (2006) 'Construir marcas mediante la asociación a servicios públicos', *Harvard Business Review (América Latina)* 84.4: 46-51.

——, J. Montaña and V. Sierra (2006) 'Brand Building by Associating to Public Services: A Reference Group Influence Model', *Journal of Brand Management* 13.4–5: 352-62.

——, K.L. Becker-Olsen and R.P. Hill (2008) 'Desarrollar un programa de RSC a la manera correcta', *Harvard Business Review (América Latina)* 86.4: 42-49.

Haslam, P.A. (2004) *The Corporate Social Responsibility System in Latin America and the Caribbean* (Focal Policy Paper FPP-04-1; Ottawa, Canada: Canadian Foundation for the Americas).

Heap, S. (2000) *NGOs Engaging with Business: A World of Difference and a Difference to the World* (Oxford University Press, UK: INTRAC).

Hill, R.P., D.L. Stephens and I. Smith (2003) 'Corporate Social Responsibility: An Examination of Individual Firm Behavior', *Business and Society Review* 108 (September 2003): 339-62.

Husted, B.W., and D.B. Allen (2007) 'Corporate Social Strategy in Multinational Enterprises: Antecedents and Value Creation', *Journal of Business Ethics* 74.4: 345-61.

Lafferty, B.A., and R.E. Goldsmith (2005) 'Cause-Brand Alliances: Does the Cause Help the Brand or Does the Brand Help the Cause?', *Journal of Business Research* 58.4: 423-29.

Laughlin, J.L., and M.B. Ashan (1994) 'A Strategic Model of Multinational Corporation Social Responsibility in the Third World', *Journal of International Marketing* 2.3: 101-15.

Lichtenstein, D.R., M.E. Drumwright and B.M. Braig (2004) 'The Effect of Corporate Social Responsibility on Customer Donations to Corporate-Supported Nonprofits', *Journal of Marketing* 68.4: 16-32.

Luo, X., and C.B. Bhattacharya (2006) 'Corporate Social Responsibility, Customer Satisfaction, and Market Value', *Journal of Marketing* 70.4: 1-18.

Maignan, I., and O.C. Ferrell (2004) 'Corporate Social Responsibility and Marketing: An Integrative Framework', *Journal of the Academy of Marketing Science* 32.1: 3-19.

McWilliams, A., and D. Siegel (2001) 'Corporate Social Responsibility: A Theory of the Firm Perspective', *Academy of Management Review* 26.1: 117-27.

Pirsch, J., S. Gupta and S. Landreth Grau (2007) 'A Framework for Understanding Corporate Social Responsibility Programs as a Continuum: An Exploratory Study', *Journal of Business Ethics* 70.2: 125-40.

Porter, M.E., and M.R. Kramer (2006) 'Strategy and Society: The Link between Competitive Advantage and Corporate Social Responsibility', *Harvard Business Review* 84.12: 78-92.

Sen, S., C.B. Bhattacharya and D. Korschun (2006) 'The Role of Corporate Social Responsibility in Strengthening Multiple Stakeholder Relationships: A Field Experiment', *Journal of the Academy of Marketing Science* 34.2: 158-66.

Simmons, C.J., and K.L. Becker-Olsen (2006) 'Achieving Marketing Objectives through Social Sponsorships', *Journal of Marketing* 70.4: 154-69.

Snider, J., R.P. Hill and D. Martin (2003) 'Corporate Social Responsibility in the 21st Century: A View from the World's Most Successful Firms', *Journal of Business Ethics* 48.2: 175-87.

In memory and gratitude to Alyssa Ruggieri who served as the research assistant for this project.

# 10

# Corporate social responsibility
## Risk managing for value creation in the housing sector in the UK

**Jyoti Navare**
Middlesex University, UK

New risks, uncertainties, corporate failures, market sector regulation and a growing focus on sustainable environments have meant pressure on corporations to develop and demonstrate socially responsible behaviour and enable a sustainable society. Corporations have been active in considering socially responsible strategies, yet there has been a growing interest from their stakeholder groups in considering corporate social responsibility (CSR) in terms of value creation.

The concept of 'housing association' (HA) is specific to the United Kingdom. They originated in the 19th century, post-Industrial Revolution. The intent of these HAs was to assist in the provision of affordable housing to special social groups such as those on low income, the disabled and pensioners together with supported accommodation for groups such as single parents. However, they became particularly important in the 1980s when government at that time imposed limitations on local (area sub-governments) authority housing. This enabled HAs to participate in a larger share of the social housing market providing both rental and shared-ownership schemes.

The key characteristic of an HA is that they are overseen by an appointed committee or board, which usually includes association directors, residents and independent directors, enabling a highly democratic management process. The regulation of these associations in England is by a body called the Housing Corporation, which is a non-departmental public body or quango (quasi-autonomous non-governmental organisation). There are other similar regulators for Scotland, Northern Ireland and Wales.

In recent years, HAs have been put under increased pressure to be accountable and to provide value for taxpayers' money, which has caused the government to come under criticism that their service is becoming more commercial and less beneficial to the poorest sectors of society.

HAs are by their very nature socially driven and stakeholder-oriented particularly in their attempt to develop affordable and sheltered housing for low-income and disadvantaged communities. Furthermore, their tie-ins with long-term loans and grant-providing establishments have required stakeholder strategies that are long-term (Murie 1997a, b; Van der Linden and Jonker 2004; Mullins 2006; Cobb 2006), requiring robust management and sustainable value outputs.

Determining risks and sustainable value outputs over a long period can be complex, yet without effective risk analysis it becomes difficult to establish value parameters. Risk management enables the integration of CSR by analysing the value chain (Porter and Kramer 2006) and enabling the shift from responsive CSR to proactive CSR.

The chapter considers the problems HAs in England have in identifying, prioritising and managing risks and uncertainties while at the same time ensuring that there are sustainable value determinants for the business and their stakeholders. In attempting the correlation between risk determination and value outputs a risk scorecard is created to test socially or stakeholder beneficial outcomes, with consideration predominantly given to the sustainability of operations and environment management. The scorecard tool communicates strategic objectives through performance metrics that are segmented into four organisational objectives: measurable excellence in service provision, performance, neighbourhoods and people. The metrics contain measures, targets and actions derived from strategic priorities based on the dual elements of risk (internal actions) and value (externally perceived performance and CSR). Scorecard metrics also consider value accumulation or reduction: for example, the growth and development of people acts as a catalyst for risk reduction and value creation for the other three objectives. A well-developed and motivated workforce has a direct impact on service provision, performance and, eventually, quality neighbourhoods. The implications translate towards a strong governance framework that enables effective and measurable CSR strategies—internal audit trails, responsiveness and sustainable values—for the organisation and stakeholders.

Evidence considers the risk factors that link to end-point outcomes and value creation. Although the link between risk management and value creation is not quantified, it can be measured by qualitative factors such as sustainable trends in satisfaction surveys and accessibility to capital linking to growth (staff, reputation and market) and higher excellence ratings by the UK Housing Corporation.

Following a brief introduction to HAs, a review of HA risks and performance indicators is undertaken enabling a platform for identifying sustainable value outcomes. A risk scorecard model is developed enabling the correlation of risk, performance indicators and values outcomes for the HA.

## The English housing association sector

England has seen rapid change in the housing market and particularly over the last three decades. The UK government has prioritised investment in new homes with new legislation formulated and acted on. Furthermore, a national funding agency and a regulator have been set up to ensure the governance of the provision of affordable housing. This has meant new systems and new focus on HA structures and management. As Mukhija (2001) explains, the role of government in enabling affordable housing provision is complex, involving models of public–private investment, supply as well as demand-driven initiatives.

At the same time as government-led initiatives, the parallel private sector role in the development and management of social housing has been expanding, although the recent recessionary economy has slowed down this expansion.

The other key set of changes already under way is in respect of the shape of the HA sector. There has been considerable sector consolidation, with the emergence of national and regional giants resulting in a new 'over 50,000 (homes) group', with the first 100,000-home HA not being far off.

HAs in England have been under continuing regulatory pressure to become more efficient, and to achieve 'best value' and continuous improvement. The concept of 'best value' is seen to be more than effective cost management; the concept seeks to consider both quality and reputation risks considered as risk surrogates: that is, those risks that are not operationally obvious but affect the end-point value. In other words, a risk surrogate is a factor that is not one of the key factors that are intrinsic to a risk but a factor that affects the overall outcome. As Sarkar *et al.* (2005) explain (albeit in an environmental context), surrogacy is a relationship between an indicator parameter (capable of quantitative measurement) and an objective parameter (end-point value). For example, a bank may be quantifiably high-risk (perhaps due to a high ratio of bad debts to revenue) but the reputation of the bank may create a perception of the bank being low-risk (the end value point). Reputation as a surrogate therefore is deceptive and can hide or increase in some instances the degree of riskiness perceived.

The power of risk surrogates has not been effectively considered in their link to value creation. Performance indicators tend to ignore end-point value outputs arising from this so-called risk surrogate category. The problem that arises is that organisations including HAs only consider incremental value declines based on current performance rather than shocks (Melendrez *et al.* 2005) which could arise by way of risk surrogates. Reputation can take a lifetime to build but one bad action can destroy it.

The value drivers reside within their organisational staffing structures and business processes. Successful organisations create innovative links between the use of their resources and the value outputs (De Miranda Santos *et al.* 2004). The value outputs are embedded in the relationships created between organisations and their stakeholders. There is need for a strong relationship of trust between a HA and each one of its tenants and residents, based on clarity of value outputs, and on mutual respect building and effective knowledge cascading. The value to individuals lies predominantly in the sound tenant–association relationship.

At the collective level, approaches seek to ensure the systematic and consistent devolvement of relevant decision-making, standard and target-setting, allocation of resources to the level within the organisation that is closest to tenants, and effective and professional front-line staff. Barnett (2006), however, argues that collective action (consensus) arises when benefits to the organisation outweigh the risks. Risks can be mitigated and strong value outputs could arise from the effective embedding of tenant and resident involvement in the organisation's decision-making. The embedding has its own risks in that there may be constrained information sharing and lack of effective governance of value measures (French *et al.* 2005).

A paradox, however, can arise in a sense that HAs in their attempt to grow and reap benefits of funding grants for development can be seen to be development-led rather than customer-led. This paradox, however, relates more to growth (De Wit and Meyer 2005; de Ruijter and van London 2006; Davis *et al.* 2008) than to value and hence the effective embedding of stakeholder participation and self-regulation is crucial to the management of risks and value outputs.

## The changing economic scenario: Implications for value

Housing associations, as other organisations, have not been immune to the national and global economic downturn beginning in 2008 and to specific conditions of their own sector such as the changing perceptions of financiers (Whitehead *et al.* 2008). The recent complex situation has meant that not only are there fewer traditional lenders to the sector because of withdrawals from the market but also there is less overall capacity for financing. The market for lending to the HAs has not only seen stringency in lending but also a lack of financial capacity to lend. With borrowing more difficult HAs have had to focus on their bottom lines more than value-added outcomes. Associations with less than one year of expenditure covered by loan facilities are subject to closer scrutiny and tend not to be able to bid for new grants and may become downgraded. Furthermore, the impact of falling house prices has been significant for the HAs in the UK. Lenders have no longer been offering 100% mortgages as before. Stricter underwriting of mortgages has a particular impact for the sale of new shared ownership units and the subsequent purchase of equity by leaseholders. There is also additional impact for sales of properties that are not viable for refurbishment. This has meant that the ripple effect of a hard market for lending affects not only the obvious service provision but also the wider stakeholder support services, making it difficult for HAs to balance service provision with funding constraints.

The sector has further been impacted by consumer price inflation rising over the official target. The increase in inflation is greater than planned increases in rent. However, this is a negative for tenants where rents stop becoming affordable, increasing the risk of void rentals (redundant properties). Offside costs such as employment costs, supplier costs and contractor costs can also creep upwards. Arguably a drop in the sector business can result in a soft market for contractors and suppliers as competition is on price (Chartered Institute of Housing in Scotland 2008).

Failing to sell redundant property has a dual impact for HA cash flow and surplus. The impact on surplus is twofold: first a potential loss on the sale of the property and, second, because cash from the sale is not received, borrowing and interest costs increase. Weak staircasing (the practice of purchasing additional percentages of a shared-ownership house) can result in an accumulation of risk and in turn reduces the capacity for organisations to cross-subsidise developments.

In such economic circumstances, both the Housing Corporation and lenders expect the associations to demonstrate robust financial action with minimum impact on services to residents. This has meant one of two things where there has not been prudential financial management: finding a more robust partner or closing operations.

## Risks faced by HAs

While governments pursue the policy for affordable housing, the tendency is to delegate the responsibility to 'close to the community' organisations such as local authorities and HAs. Kramer and van Welie (2001) identified that, in most European countries, governments were taking a back seat in allowing local housing groups to manage the operating risks of social housing, as they are seen as more efficient managers of the sector. The Smith Institute believes that governments that put housing central to their policy need to both take the driving seat and invest more and provide an integrated service enabling a 'system of progressive universalism and reforms that recognise the crucial intergenerational continuities of (social value [*sic*]) outcomes' (Feinstein *et al.* 2008).

Housing associations, by their very nature of being partly grant-assisted and partly rent-funded, take on a socio-market approach to managing social housing risks. The competitive and quality pressures on these associations have meant a significant strategic shift towards socially responsible and tenant management approaches. The underlying tensions between financial and social objectives exist and hence risk management becomes a crucial part of performance management.

By reason of the socio-market approach, HAs face both market risks and changing social risks (Liddle and Lerais 2007). This duality of risk creates a methodological problem: namely, how to categorise the risks that meaningfully demonstrate the impact on both value added (in terms of society and market needs for housing and HAs) and sustainability of strategies that diffuse the risks over a longer timeframe. The risks that affect the value to society and those that affect the value to market are systemic and complex. There is correlation between the accumulation of market risks and the impact on social housing risks (as seen in the case of recessionary trends). The complexity lies in the difficulty in estimating the end-point outcomes arising from the causal links between the social risks and the market risks that are intrinsic in a CSR strategy.

The risk implications in managing the internal economics of any HAs arise from social risk surrogates: reputation, improvement of quality of living and services supporting this (linked to Housing Corporation star ratings) and the management of sector risk as part of surviving the hard and soft market in the provision of affordable housing. For this reason social and organisational risks are grouped together from an end-point view rather than from a causal point of view.

In value terms, HAs face, in effect, two types of risk: **creeping value decline** and potentially **crippling value decline**. Creeping value decline is more insidious in the sense that negative values pervade cultural value and it becomes difficult to shift the values towards a positive outcome. This is an incremental progress towards decline. In the case of potentially crippling value decline, the shock is immediate with serious consequences to sustainability. In such circumstances the organisation indicates poor management including mismanaging financial and liquidity considerations. It could also mean that creeping value decline becomes so acute that it becomes a wider public issue result in a public outcry (Utting 2002).

There are, in effect, two different housing markets, characterised by different risks: tenancy agreements, which are fully determined by rental income; and tenants as share owners: these take on owner responsibility and hence are partly responsible for value determination. In the former case, tenants can decide to leave their current HA market and move from one rental accommodation to another based on what property value is on offer. This involves a nominal cost of attracting new tenants and loss of tenancy (void rentals). In void rentals HAs suffer a **productivity shock**. In the case of shared ownership (equity sharing) HAs suffer what is considered a **capital shock** where there is both a capital loss of mortgage plus a void rental. There are other accumulation losses such as early enfranchisement (where leaseholders buy their freehold before they have staircased up to 100% of the property under the terms of their shareholder lease). This would leave HAs with less funds to reinvest in affordable housing, and provide a disincentive for private investors to provide shared-ownership housing.

However, there is a diversification benefit of shared housing. The gradual amortisation of risk is attractive to HAs in the same way as mortgage lenders, although the critical difference is the additional value requirements demanded of HAs such as property and environment maintenance and renewal. The net cost value therefore is less for the HA than it is for a mortgage lender.

HAs also suffer from the disadvantage benefit of low rentals as opposed to open-market rentals. The low rentals factor is not in effect compensatory in reducing the value of risk for the HAs because they face the problem of adverse selection: that is, a high risk market for defaults. Hence the level of void rentals becomes a key risk score.

The chapter considers how risk factors, translated into risk scores, link to performance management and how value outcomes can be derived identifying value factors.

## Risk scores

There are two types of risk that make up the risk score: risks that have a direct impact on the value outcomes: for example, low response rate to calls from customers. These direct risks have been called simply **risk factors**. These factors make up the key risks and are related directly to the day-to-day operations: managing the customer, budget handling and financing, managing local environment and staff capability. The other risks are the **risk surrogates**. These produce end-point risk outcomes that contribute to a more sustainable value: housing sector risk, reputational risk and quality assurance risk.

### Risk factors: key methodological considerations

Based on the case study of one medium-sized HA, four risk factors have been identified (services, performance, neighbourhoods and people). These factors are compared with the Housing Corporation key lines of enquiry (KLOE) to benchmark with sector standards.

- **Tenant and stakeholder relations**. The level of participation of stake-holders can be critical to a HA for building long-lasting relationships and providing high-quality service and high standards. HAs have tried different models, from fostering strong links with the community through sponsorships and joint projects, enabling wider tenant inclusion, to active participation and development of new relationship cultures (Mitlin and Satterthwaite 1996: 31-33; Thaman 2002)

- **Performance management**. In a speech to the UK Chartered Institute of Housing, deputy chief executive of the Housing Corporation Peter Marsh recently claimed it important for housing associations to take steps to ensure they are able to ride out the impact of the credit crunch (June 2008). He further stated, 'The single most significant variable in housing association 30-year business plans is not interest rates or sale but operating cost inflation.' The demise of the London-based Ujima HA, which was also Europe's largest black-led social housing provider, sent shockwaves through the HA sector. This was an example of how quickly creeping value decline can become crippling. The need for a prudent and credible financial strategy in conjunction with strong performance and risk management controls is key to sustainability.

- **Neighbourhoods**. Thibodeau (2003) observed that house prices were influenced by housing market structure and liquidity characteristics of neighbourhood properties. Hills (2007) commented in the current research done on social housing: 'the evidence also shows that . . . in terms of general housing conditions, the obvious problems include: neighbourhood conditions and perceptions of safety'

- **People (internal service provider)**. Shriberg (2002) considered the role that staff play in filtering decisions of sustainability. HAs are focused on staff development and improving relations between staff and stakeholders. Thus enabling the development of socially responsible staff

Apart from these four key risk factors, three risk surrogates or end-point risk outcomes have been identified from the case study. The risk surrogate, although not an obvious operational key performance and sustainability indicator, manifests the intrinsic value to sustainability. The surrogates, however, are obvious as key outcome indicators, in the sense that ignoring these surrogates can lead to crippling value decline while operational performance indicators have a direct impact on creeping value decline.

## Risk surrogates (see Figure 10.1)

**Housing association sector risk.** According to Hill (2006), a UK social enterprise consultant, Housing Associations in light of current conditions remodel themselves as community businesses. In other words, they need to work closely with community stakeholders, using their socially based assets to ensure a competitive edge. The socially based assets include the power to purchase and borrow, housing management expertise, marketing of back office functions such as rent and payroll management, social networking and board level diversity groupings. These assets enable the embedding of CSR values.

**Reputation risk.** Turner (2004), of the UK Housing Corporation, stated that 'reputation is now often the single most valuable asset of a business or the one that differentiates it from the rest'. Converting into goodwill terms it has been estimated as worth around 82% of corporate assets. Interestingly, goodwill is one asset that does not feature in housing association balance sheets and hence remains outside the boundaries for scrutiny. Lenders of finance, on the other hand, are concerned with the quality of the management and reputational sustainability of HAs. Tenants too have increased choice of accommodation available to them and reputation of the HA is central to their decision-making. Most housing today is of a consistent standard; the advantage arises from the reputation of the association. Housing associations also need to use their reputations to influence negotiations, bid for preferred partner status, in entering new markets and recruiting top-level staff.

Reputation management is therefore crucial in the management of stakeholder expectations and reducing the gap between these expectations and actual performance of the organisation (Turner 2004). Managing reputation risk in parallel with performance management requires constant reassessment of operations linked to the dynamic shifts in shareholder expectations. For example, the growth of antisocial behaviour and its impact on tenancy expectations has meant that there is a greater need for dedicated resources to manage the changing expectations of the tenant and the wider stakeholder group in ensuring a safe and healthy living environment. The risk of not moving with the times can have accumulative outcomes such as loss of tenant rents, longer void rentals and harsher financing terms.

**Quality assurance risk.** All stakeholders, grant providers, administrators and tenants are clear that outcomes for tenants are a priority. The main areas for tenants as value-added outcomes are areas of affordability, appropriate (excellent homes and environment) housing, fair and equitable access to administration services, sustainability of tenancies, quality service and health and safety. Measures of tenant satisfaction have included instruments such as guarantees and policies on standards and customer service, satisfaction surveys (Turner 2004: 5) and operating standards and protocols.

**FIGURE 10.1** Risk surrogates

Value outputs are directly linked to risk management outputs which are directly linked to the performance indicators of financial viability and effective governance. According to the Audit Commission (2005), value for money essentially concerns efficiency and effectiveness (cost and quality).

The lack of empirical evidence makes it important to question how value is framed. The concept is key in performance management and also questions:

- The rationale for risk management and reporting systems in place to enable more pre-emptive action by management

- How quality assurance systems support continuous improvement in the housing sector

- How sustainability of value is measured

## Corporate social responsibility (CSR)

The key aspect of any business today is the impact of its actions on stakeholders, both internal to the organisation and external. Active and measurable CSR is seen to be more than a balance sheet snapshot of CSR strategies. There are demands that CSR activities are demonstrable as a high-profile strategy (such as board member representation for CSR; Davis *et al.* 2008) and that there is evidence of sustainable outcomes through constant attention to trends, and actions taken in support of the trends.

Margolis and Walsh (2003) suggest that CSR activities yield positive performance outcomes for the organisation. In the development of the risk scorecard, sustainability values imply stakeholder value outputs. CSR is therefore seen to be an implicit part of the overall end-point value outcomes.

## Developing risk scores and the risk scorecard

### Development of the risk scores

In the absence of a validated risk score for CSR, the scores developed are those developed internally by the HA in the case study that links the risk factors to the risk surrogate end-point value outcomes. The risk scorecard framework undertakes the triangulation of the management of the risk, performance measures and value outputs in general, and value outputs for investing in corporate social responsibility. The key focus lies on outcomes: value for continuous improvement, value factors in accountability and decision-making, and positive and negative indicators of the internal reporting systems. HAs undertake robust documentation of their operations but less so in respect of their deliverables and even less on risk.

**TABLE 10.1** Housing association case study: explicit key risks

| Risk factors | Risk surrogates |
| --- | --- |
| 1. Tenant and stakeholder relations (services) | Housing sector |
| 2. Performance management | Quality |
| 3. Neighbourhoods | Reputation |
| 4. People | (CSR) implicit |

Source: HA case study

Table 10.1 demonstrates the key factors that make up the value framework. Factor 1 is the value of the relationship with tenants, financiers (banks) and local authorities and the Housing Corporation. It is argued that, if the HA is more socially responsible, it will achieve a high rating and reduce restrictions in the firm's operations by the Housing Corporation and other stakeholders (Cornell and Shapiro 1987: 5-14).

Factor 2 seeks to consider the value of the social capital built up in performance outcomes or, in other words, the impact on creditability. Factor 2 considers issues arising out of areas such as tenant and staff satisfaction and a links with the stakeholders. Public perception towards the role of the HA in society shifts from seeing the business (of affordable housing provision) as a problem to being part of the solution (Pattberg 2006).

It is arguable that there exists a problem where CSR might entail a higher than normal emphasis on public relations than on actual value building (Frynas 2005). Hence there is a need to establish a factor determinant for the build-up of social capital by way of sustainable CSR. This factor would be the level of disclosure and governance applied and even social marketing (Gray et al. 1987) within the organisation. As Deegan (2002) stated, CSR disclosure is about providing information that enables social accountability. In corporate social responsibility determination, there is an assumption that organisations have different sets of information that constitute value determination. Woodruff and Gardial (1996) believe that organisations must evaluate their own information processes (and performance) to enable it to be benchmarked against their industry standard. Many HAs, as in the case study, are now undertaking benchmarking of their performance.

Factors 3 and 4 have direct links to the risk surrogates as both service and environment have impacts on the reputation of the HA and the sector. Neighbourhoods and their maintenance can be central to rental choice and in turn affects the relationship values with funders and grant providers. From the people point of view the efficacy of service provision contributes to the bottom line and the star ratings.

Table 10.3 (overleaf) demonstrates the working of the risk scorecard taking into consideration both the risk factors and the risk surrogates. The scorecard develops metrics for each operational activity and tolerance thresholds are developed which will flag up deviations. The scorecard considers the deviations in terms of no to high risk. Table 10.2 provides an example of the risk thresholds determined highlighting how the mechanism works. However, each operational manager will need to identify which of the key components make up the operational process and affect the overall risk.

**TABLE 10.2** Risk threshold example

| Example | No risk | Low risk | Medium risk | High risk |
|---|---|---|---|---|
| Tolerance level | Targeted tolerance or less than targeted tolerance | Up to 5% deviation | 6–15% deviation | > 16% deviation |
| Flags | Medium grey: no action | **Bold grey: keeping an eye on the situation** | Medium <u>underlined: action to be taken</u> | **<u>Bold underlined: high priority and urgent</u>** |

# Socially responsible strategic objectives and performance metrics

Most of the HAs relate their strategic priorities to four areas that demonstrate social responsibility: measurable excellence in service to tenants and other stakeholders, performance sustainability, management of the environment by way of managing neighbourhoods and people. There are three underlying considerations that

## TABLE 10.3 Risk scorecard (examples)

| Risks | Threshold | Actual | Performance | Average performance | Action |
|---|---|---|---|---|---|
| **RISK FACTORS** | | | | | |
| *Customer service risks (services)* | | | | | |
| Risk to customer service (e.g. level of satisfaction) | 92% | 95% | +3% | (94%) 1% up | None |
| *Financial (performance)* | | | | | |
| Risk of rental voids (rent collected) | 100% | 94% | −6% | (98%) 4% down | Medium risk |
| Stock investment (planned number) | 1,000 homes | 890 | −110 | (900) 1.1% down | Low/medium risk |
| Financial (spend vs. budget) | 100% | 140% | −40% | (100%) 40% down | Medium to high risk |
| *Environmental (neighbourhoods)* | | | | | |
| Level of decent homes | 99% | 99% | 0 | 99% unchanged | None |
| **Percentage complaining about antisocial offences** | **10%** | **28%** | **+180%** | **(10%) 180% up** | **High risk** |
| *Staff satisfaction risk (people)* | | | | | |
| Staff turnover | 15% | 22% | + 7% | (26% previously) 15% negative | Medium risk |
| **Average days per year lost per employee** | **4** | **10** | **+ 6** | **(5) 50% down** | **High risk** |
| **RISK SURROGATES** | | | | | |
| *Reputational risk* | | | | | |
| **Housing association rating** | **2 star** | **1 star** | **Down** | **(1 star) 0 star (up)** | **Medium/high risk** |
| *Sector risk* | | | | | |
| **Grants availability** | **80%** | **75%** | **Down** | **(90%) 17% down** | **High risk** |
| *Quality assurance/sustainability risks* | | | | | |
| **Sustainability measure Overall % of ups to down** | **100%** | **65%** | **Down** | **(100%) 35% down** | **High risk** |

link to the measures: (a) each measurement relates to an operational output with implications in terms of resource management and risk appetite; (b) the true risk is the variance from threshold (risk appetite); and (c) the sources that result in risk accumulation: that is, systemic impacts arising out of one risk area. For example, increased staff turnover is an increased risk for customer service provision and may lead to a higher level of customer complaints, or slower response rate to enquiries and so forth. From a governance viewpoint the key lines of enquiry become critical in monitoring the risks, operations and performance trends.

## Monitoring excellence

Responsible organisations seek value for their stakeholders: for example, provision of 'high quality and value for money systems' (retail industry); and 'excellence in teaching delivery' (universities). Similarly, housing excellence is measurable by performance and sustainability of performance. The performance indicators consider the key lines of operational enquiry (monitoring of risk factors) while the sustainability indicators consider the key aspects of end-point outcomes (monitoring of risk surrogates). Creeping value declines are monitored by way of trend analysis and managed, while the potential for crippling value decline (shock outcomes) is managed through the process of environmental scan measures (Aguilar 1967; Miller and Friesen 1977; Daft and Weick 1984) which also seeks to help prepare organisations against potential shocks or surprises (Sutton 1988).

### Monitoring performance trends

In considering measures, assumptions are built by Housing Associations about what constitutes a realistic target as outcome. Therefore, taking one example, it might be assumed that a call response rate of 97% is considered to be one strong indicator of service and socially responsible performance. This sort of measure can overlook a number of aspects which may result in failure of the measure.

First, it overlooks whether the response has resulted in a successful outcome. Returning a call may be a non-value outcome. Second, the measure does not indicate the correlation between the weighting of calls in terms of resource prioritisation. Hence just because a call is made does not mean that the call achieved the desired output. Third, there is no way of telling that the call is not systemic in the sense that one call results in a series of calls made by one tenant or a number of tenants on the same issue. There could be a situation where one response may be responding to a number of calls or vice versa or one response may open the gates to more calls.

Table 10.4 demonstrates how the problems can be circumvented. This measure brings in two new indicators: sustainability measures (closure of inquiry) and a forward outcome threshold desire (expected outcome).

**TABLE 10.4** Example of sustainability measure

| Required performance | 2007 | 2008 | % change since previous year | % of eventual threshold | average % of last five years | Expected outcome by 2013 |
|---|---|---|---|---|---|---|
| Calls | | | | | | |
| Response within 3 hours of call (92%) | 85% | 87% | +2.3% | 87% | 84%: calls need review | 100% |
| Number of calls where closure of inquiry happens within 24 hours (85%) | 60% | 65% | +8.3% | 68% | 61%: high risk needs action | 95% |

So, from the example in Table 10.4, performance area indicators need to be specifically defined to take into account systemic implications and to demonstrate a pattern of improvement and sustainable performance by 2013. If the response rate is higher than the closure rate this indicates that there is a need to take action.

## Key performance indicators (KPIs) and risk scores

Performance indicators therefore provide a measure against which HAs judge how well they are performing. Over time, they also form the basis for promoting and assessing continuous improvement as seen in Table 10.5. Different associations may have slightly different KPIs but in the main fall into the following areas: rental income, repair targets, re-let times, asset condition, voids, lettings and tenant satisfaction. These KPIs are based on end-point outcomes such as reputation evidence by star ratings. The risk scorecard reviews overall risks and progress against each key line of inquiry (KLOE). It enables instant visualisation of risk areas underlying the star ranking. Progress is checked against strategic priorities and scorecard outcomes (Table 10.5).

### Methodology for scoring

The KPIs are developed from KLOEs. KLOEs represent sets of questions and statements around each area of operational service which enable the identification and weighting of risk. KLOEs enable questions such as 'what is the risk of a particular service?' (risk factor) and 'what is the long-term risk of an inefficient service?' (risk surrogate).

For example, in Table 10.5, taking the first KPI, 'Customer care', the risk of an ineffective customer care strategy may result in high maintenance costs (a factor of two is provided for this risk). However, the greater risk is the end-point risk and that could be a credibility loss and potential impact on the star rating of the

**TABLE 10.5** Risk scores 1–3 (low–high)

| KPI | KLOE | Risk factors | Risk surrogate |
|---|---|---|---|
| Customer care | • What is the impact/outcome for customers?<br>• What are the levels of complaints that arise out of service provision? | 2 | 3 |
| Financial performance | • How has the organisation demonstrated that there is a clear relationship between costs and the level and quality of services provided?<br>• Are resources and policy aligned? | 3 | 3 |
| Neighbour-hoods | • What is the take-up rate of lettings?<br>• What is the environmental safety of the neighbourhoods? | 2 | 3 |
| People | • How efficient are the people at the operational level?<br>• Is the response to complaints efficiently handled? | 1 | 2 |

association. Hence a factor of three would intimate that the risk in effect was high and customer care as a KPI should be given high priority. Similarly for lettings, the end-point risk of greater void rentals could result in crippling value decline.

Once these KLOEs enable the assessment of risk, the actions can be prioritised. Table 10.6 exemplifies the prioritisation process.

**TABLE 10.6** Prioritisation of risks

| | | Risk factor | |
|---|---|---|---|
| | | Low | High |
| **Risk surrogate** | High | 3 x 1<br>High importance/low urgency (time to develop strategy for long-term quality processes—value impact medium/high) | 3 x 3<br>High importance/high urgency (time is short—need to dedicate all resources to ensure that risk does not materialise; value impact very high) |
| | Low | 1 x 1<br>Low importance/low urgency (none or minimal resources dedicated; value impact low) | 1 x 3<br>Low importance/high urgency (none or minimal resources dedicated; value impact low) |

## Measuring CSR value within the risk score

Hillman and Keim (2001) and Verschoor and Murphy (2002) found that increased CSR led to enhanced financial performance and vice versa. Hillman and Keim consider the CSR value determinants to relate to two aspects of organisational business: enhancement of stakeholder value (for HAs this would be ensuring value to tenants, Housing Corporations and funders) and social issues participation (which would be 'duty of care' issues such as working with other stakeholders to develop a more effective living environment).

Most of the CSR issues have chronic implications resulting in creeping value decline if not detected early. The shock of crippling outcomes are not common and may only arise in the event of large-scale catastrophe, which could be financial, fraud or some extraneous impact on the institution (such as in the case of September 11). The result could be suspension or closure of business (see Table 10.7).

Balvers *et al.* (1988) and earlier Booth and Smith (1986) suggest that organisational reputation has a positive effective on productivity and social status. Reputation measure is by the grading made by the Housing Corporation (no star to three star); hence an assumption is made that a three-star-rated association will be demonstrating high social responsibility and additional value while a non-star-rated organisation will need to develop a significant strategy to improve value to the stakeholders.

The Housing Corporation's key value parameter is tenant-centric, based on the level of tenant satisfaction (measurable by satisfaction surveys and other accepted customer feedback tools). Other value parameters have been the continuous improvement and innovation of current stock and the purchase of future stock; continuous improvement of standards; developing and empowering people; innovation; efficient utilisation of resources; commitment to stakeholders (such as improved communications); regeneration of environment; reducing antisocial behaviour in the neighbourhoods; development of policies for ethical behaviour, health and safety and equal opportunities; and effective risk management—in effect, socially responsible parameters.

## Conclusion

A value-added evaluation of sustainable corporate responsible strategies emphasises the monitoring and implementation of key performance indicators. Key concerns were:

**TABLE 10.7**  CSR factors, sustainable value parameters and creeping and crippling value systems

| | Risk | |
| --- | --- | --- |
| | *Creeping* | *Crippling* |
| *Stakeholder value* | | |
| Reduction of operational risks | ✓ | |
| Meeting threshold requirements for grants and other funding | ✓ | |
| Reduction of financial risk | ✓ | |
| Increasing quality of neighbourhoods | ✓ | |
| Increasing surplus | ✓ | |
| Reducing staff turnover and absences | ✓ | |
| Greater level of tenant participation in CSR practices | ✓ | |
| Less void rentals | ✓ | |
| *Social issue impact* | | |
| Enabling diversity of tenants | ✓ | |
| Enabling access to equal opportunities | ✓ | |
| Reducing litigation/claims by working more closely with interest groups | ✓ | |
| Increased support for disabled tenants | ✓ | |
| Helping tenants overcome social and financial exclusion | ✓ | |
| Enabling regeneration | ✓ | |
| *Catastrophes* | | |
| Financial crisis (housing sector risk) | | ✓ |
| Mismanagement (quality risk) | | ✓ |
| Tenant and external stakeholder impacts (CSR risk) | | ✓ |
| Public outcry and media intervention (CSR/reputation risk) | | ✓ |

- Creeping value decline factors based predominantly on operational performance indicators

- Crippling value decline (or shock) factors based on the performance indicators linked mainly to environmental/stakeholder effects

The methodology of the risk scorecard manifests three important considerations. The need to:

- Audit and monitor value and sustainability of processes and actions taken by way of evaluating key performance indicators

- Identify and evaluate risk factors (operational KPIs) and risk surrogates (end-point values linked to socially responsible actions) impacts

- Use the scorecard method to identify and manage risks of creeping and crippling value decline

The determination of risk factor and risk surrogate indicators is not only a risk identification tool, but also a risk management and governance tool to the extent that the stakeholder community can be involved directly in the measurement and analysis of risk and to consider the end-point values.

Before a value analysis can be achieved, management has to define its key lines of enquiry (KLOEs) surrounding the key performance indicators (KPIs). The KLOEs arise out of operational strategies. The scorecard sets out the risk tolerance thresholds which enable the action points for value end-points in respect of services (tenant and stakeholder management), performance management, neighbourhood (environmental management) and people (internal service provider management).

In summary, CSR in HAs is more than action taken. It is a culture of management that requires the identification of appropriate indicators which can determine the relationships between performance, value outcomes and socially responsible definitions of management action.

# References

Aguilar, F.J. (1967) *Scanning the Business Environment* (New York: McGraw-Hill).

Audit Commission (2005) *Value for Money within Housing: Supplementary Guidance* (London: HMSO).

Balvers, R., B. McDonald and R. Miller (1988) 'Underpricing of New Issues and the Choice of Auditor as a Signal of Investment Banker Reputation', *The Accounting Review* 63.4: 605-22.

Barnett, M.L. (2006) 'Waves of Collectivizing: A Dynamic Model of Competition and Cooperation over the Life of an Industry', *Corporate Reputation Review* 8.4: 272-92.

Booth, J.R., and R.L. Smith, II (1986) 'Capital Raising, Underwriting, and the Certification Hypothesis', *Journal of Financial Economics* 15.1–2: 261-81.

Chartered Institute of Housing in Scotland (2008) *Better Value for Housing Associations: Changes to Grant 2008/9 Consultative Response* (Edinburgh: CIH, March 2008).

Cobb, N. (2006) 'Patronising the Mentally Disordered? Social Landlords and the Control of "Anti-social Behaviour" under the Disability Discrimination Act 1995', *Legal Studies* 26.2: 238-66.

Cornell, B., and A.C. Shapiro (1987) 'Corporate Stakeholders and Corporate Finance', *Financial Management* 16: 5-14.

Daft, R.L., and K.E. Weick (1984) 'Toward a Model of Organizations as Interpretation Systems', *Academy of Management Review* 9.2: 284-95.

Davis, G.F., M.V.N. Whitman and M.N. Zaid (2008) 'The Responsibility Paradox', *Stanford Social Innovation Review*, Winter 2008: 31-37.

Deegan, C. (2002) 'The Legitimising Effect of Social and Environmental Disclosures: A Theoretical Foundation', *Accounting, Auditing and Accountability Journal* 15.3: 282-312.

De Miranda Santos, M., D.M. Dos Santos, L.F. Filho, G.M. Coelho and M. Zackiewicz (2004) 'Adding Value to Information in the Process of Promoting Technological Innovation', paper presented at the *EU-US Seminar: New Technology Foresight, Forecasting and Assessment Methods*, Seville, 13–14 May 2004.

De Ruijter, A., and S. van Londen (2006) 'Trust as a Condition for Corporate Social Responsibility in a Multicultural Context', paper presented at the *First Core Conference*, Italy, 2006.

De Wit, B., and R. Meyer (2005) *Strategy Synthesis: Resolving Strategy Paradoxes to Create Competitive Advantage* (London: Thomson Learning, 2nd edn).

Feinstein, L., R. Lupton, C. Hammond, T. Mujtaba, E. Slater and A. Sorhaindo (2008) *The Public Value of Social Housing: A Longitudinal Analysis of the Relationship between Housing and Life Chances* (London: The Smith Institute).

French, S., A.J. Maule and G. Mythen (2005) 'Soft Modelling in Risk Communication and Management: Examples in Handling Food Risk', *Journal of the Operational Research Society* 56: 879-88.

Frynas, J.G. (2005) 'The False Developmental Promise of Corporate Social Responsibility: Evidence from Multinational Oil Companies', *International Affairs* 81.3: 581-98.

Gray, R., D. Owen and K. Maunders (1987) *Corporate Social Reporting: Accounting and Accountability* (London: Prentice-Hall).

Hill, C. (2006) *Enterprise Associations: The Potential for Social Enterprise amongst Housing Associations in Yorkshire and Humber* (Social Enterprise Link Report).

Hillman, A., and G. Keim (2001) 'Shareholder Value, Stakeholder Management, and Social Issues: What's the Bottom Line?', *Strategic Management Journal* 22: 125-39.

Hills, J. (2007) *Ends and Means: The Future Roles of Social Housing in England* (London: ESRC Research Centre for Analysis of Social Exclusion).

Kramer, B., and T. van Welie (2001) 'An Asset Management Liability Model for Housing Associations', *Journal of Property Investment and Finance* 19.6: 453-71.

Liddle, R., and F. Lerais (2007) *Europe's Social Reality: A Consultation Paper from the Bureau of European Policy Advisers* (Brussels: Bureau of European Policy Advisers).

Margolis, J.D., and J.P. Walsh (2003) 'Misery Loves Companies: Rethinking Social Initiatives by Business', *Administrative Science Quarterly* 48: 265-305.

Melendrez, K.D., W.C. Schwartz and M.A. Trombley (2005) 'How Does the Market Value Accrual and Cash Flow Surprises?' (Working Paper; Tucson, AZ: University of Arizona).

Miller, D., and P.H. Friesen (1977) 'Strategy-making in Context: Ten Empirical Archetypes', *Journal of Management Studies* 14.3: 253-80.

Mitlin, D., and D. Satterthwaite (1996) 'Sustainable Development and Cities', in C. Pugh (ed.), *Sustainability, the Environment and Urbanisation* (London: Earthscan): 23-62.

Mukhija, V. (2001) 'Enabling Sum Redevelopment in Mumbai: Policy Paradox in Practice', *Housing Studies* 18.4: 213-22.

Mullins, D. (2006) 'Exploring Change in the Housing Association Sector in England Using the Delphi Method', *Housing Studies* 21.2 (March 2006): 227-51; www.ingentaconnect. com/content/routledg;jsessionid=4dmfrn9wqpfv.alice.

Murie, A. (1997a) 'Linking Housing Changes to Crime', *Social Policy and Administration* 31.5: 22-36.

—— (1997b) 'The Social Rented Sector, Housing and the Welfare State in the UK', *Housing Studies* 12.4: 437-62.

Pattberg, P. (2006) 'The Transformation of Global Business Regulation' (Global Governance Working Paper; Amsterdam: The Global Governance Project).

Porter, M.E., and M.R. Kramer (2006) 'Strategy and Society: The Link between Competitive Advantage and Corporate Social Responsibility', *Harvard Business Review* 85.12: 78-92.

Sarkar, S., J. Justus, T. Fuller, C. Kelly, J. Garson and M. Mayfield (2005) 'Effectiveness of Environmental Surrogates for the Selection of Conservation Area Networks', *Conservation Biology* 19.3 (June 2005): 815-25.

Shriberg, M. (2002) 'Toward Sustainable Management: The University of Michigan's Housing Division's Approach', *Journal of Cleaner Production* 10: 41-45.

Sutton, H. (1988) *Competitive Intelligence* (New York: The Conference Board).

Thaman, K.H. (2002) 'Shifting Sights: The Cultural Challenge of Sustainability', *Higher Education Policy* 15.2 (June 2002): 133-42.

Thibodeau, T. (2003) 'Marking Single-Family Property Values to Market', *Real Estate Economics* 31.1: 1-22.

Turner, M. (2004) 'Reputation, Risk and Governance' (Risk Management Topic Paper No. 6; London: Housing Corporation).

Utting, P. (2002) 'Regulating Business through Multistakeholder Initiatives: A Preliminary Assessment', in NGLS/UNRISD (eds.), *Voluntary Approaches to Corporate Responsibility: Readings and a Resource Guide* (Geneva: NGLS Development Dossier).

Van der Linden, B., and J. Jonker (2004) 'Corporate Social Responsibility through Communicational Discipline: A Theoretical Inquiry', *Ethical Space: The International Journal of Communication Ethics* 1: 30-36.

Verschoor, C., and E. Murphy (2002) 'The Financial Performance of Large US Firms and Those with Global Prominence: How Do the Best Corporate Citizens Rate?', *Business and Society Review* 107: 371-80.

Whitehead, C., G. Burgess and F.L. Grant (2008) *Low Cost Home Ownership, Affordability Risks and Issues* (Cambridge, UK: Cambridge Centre for Housing and Planning Research).

Woodruff, R.B., and S.F. Gardial (1996) *Know your Customer: New Approaches to Customer Value and Satisfaction* (Cambridge, MA: Blackwell Publishers).

# 11
# Healthcare provision of a multinational company operating in emerging markets
## Ethical motivations, benefits of healthcare investment and the impact on socially responsible investors

**Katinka C. van Cranenburgh, Daniel Arenas and Laura Albareda**
ESADE (Universitat Ramon Llull), Spain

The financial community's interest in extra-financial aspects such as environmental, social and governance issues (ESG) is growing rapidly. Socially responsible investment communities originating from faith-based or spiritual backgrounds have matured from mainly excluding 'sin' stocks such as alcohol, tobacco or weapons into organisations with extensive ESG databases ranging from 100 to 250 ESG criteria in order to refine their investment decision-making processes. Some mainstream investors, such as pension funds and institutional investors, are also integrating ESG aspects into their portfolio analysis.

One of the reasons for the mainstream financial community's interest in socially responsible investment (SRI) comes from the prospects of positive financial results, despite the lack of any conclusive empirical evidence. In their view, corporations that conduct their operations from a complex stakeholder view rather than a short-term shareholder view are regarded as more sustainable and therefore less of an investment risk. Following the banking industry crash of September 2008, this line of socially responsible investing could now find a more receptive market.

Of the range of ESG practices, the social aspect is the least quantifiable and therefore the hardest to measure or use for benchmarking. Environmental results, for example, are presented in the form of $CO_2$ emissions, water or energy use and other measurable factors, as well as having clearer regulation. Governance practices are similarly solid; a board member also being a member of the supervisory board sets off loud alarm bells among governance auditors. But valuing social aspects, including labour issues such as health and safety and employee healthcare, is still very much a grey area for many business managers, investors, NGOs and activists.

The lack of quantifiability of the 'S' in ESG becomes obvious when making a link to economic performance. Can healthcare provision by the private sector lead to employee and consumer bonding? Can it lead to increased returns, and therefore more investors?

Another point is that when embarking on social initiatives or even designing their social strategies, companies do not always prioritise the interests of the financial community, or maximise value for the company. How do social strategies arise? What are the motivators and the dilemmas facing companies? There are ethical issues involved that play a role at different stages of social strategy development, which are essential to a full understanding of the context and background of the situation.

In this chapter, the authors will attempt to give an insight into the benefits of healthcare investment by using a case study of the international beer brewer Heineken. An understanding of the Heineken healthcare provision system, the motivators and the boundaries of responsibility are presented in the following section. The main input for this section comes from the experience of one of the authors, who has been part of the Heineken Health Affairs Department for over eight years. The next two sections focus on the effects the global healthcare situation has on the private sector, and the effects that a healthcare system has on employees, managers and consumers. An extensive review of existing literature was used in this section. The impact of Heineken's healthcare system on the financial community, including mainstream, socially responsible and faith-based investors, is described using input from a survey conducted by the authors in 2007. The final section covers the authors' general considerations.

## Heineken's healthcare strategy: motivators and boundaries

Dutch beer brewer Heineken has the widest global presence of all international brewers, with 125 breweries in more than 70 countries, employing over 65,000 people worldwide. With total sales of over 150 million hectolitres in 2008, Heineken is also among the largest brewers in the world. Heineken's sustainability agenda consists of seven components: energy (consumption and $CO_2$ emission); water (consumption and wastewater discharge); safety (of employees and installations); agriculture (quality and availability of raw materials); supply chain responsibility; responsible beer consumption; and impact on developing markets.

Heineken has a long history of operating in many sub-Saharan countries such as Congo, Democratic Republic of Congo, Rwanda, Burundi, Nigeria and Sierra Leone. Heineken's ongoing growth in these countries is based on strong local operations selling local brands to local bars and restaurants. The local operations have either been acquired over the last 70 years, or built up by the brewer itself. And the acquisition and development of new breweries is ongoing (2009 in Congo and South Africa).

In these sub-Saharan countries, the public healthcare system deteriorated rapidly during the two decades following decolonisation. Currently the public healthcare system is very limited. Heineken runs its own clinics with a staff of doctors, nurses, lab technicians, midwives and pharmacists. Heineken employees and their family members are entitled to various types of healthcare, ranging from treatment of work-related illnesses and accidents, to treatment of complex diseases such as malaria, tuberculosis and HIV/AIDS (Van der Borght *et al.* 2006). In sub-Saharan Africa alone, almost 35,000 people have access to the services offered by Heineken. Healthcare has grown into an HR benefit and increasingly a key priority on Heineken's global corporate responsibility agenda. The motivators for starting up the healthcare system differ from current motivations for maintaining the system. The boundaries of the healthcare system are constantly in need of review, based on various stakeholder and social issues. Investors understand the need for a healthy workforce in order to run a (financially) healthy business. With the growth of faith-consistent investing (FCI) and socially responsible investing (SRI), healthcare provision in developing countries is a worthwhile topic for investigation.

## Heineken's motivations

So why is Heineken offering healthcare to employees and families? If labour is cheap and abundant, one could cynically argue that there is no economic need for healthcare provision. Is Heineken, then, a unique company in which managers conduct business according to high ethical standards? Motivations and intentions, and their status are, to say the least, complex subjects in the fields of psychology, ethics and management. There are usually several possible motivations and intentions involved when making a decision; there can be covert motives that decision-makers are unwilling to admit even to themselves, and intentions can change during the course of an action. Collection of suitable evidence and conclusive testing to determine which motivations were actually involved can be difficult or even impossible. Post-event questionnaires and interviews of players can be unreliable, as the players tend to rationalise what actually happened after the decision. This is particularly the case when the test of time has shown that decisions have been questionable, and have led to attack or criticism. Even pre-event views are not completely reliable. In our approach, we can do little more than put forward a few hypotheses supported by some preliminary evidence taken from the work experience of one of the authors of this article, who has spent eight years in the Heineken Health Affairs Department, combined with interviews[1] and analysis of speeches at a Heineken Health Symposium in 2007 (Rijckborst 2007; Van Boxmeer 2007).

At the most general level, Heineken's social strategy is related to the Universal Declaration of Human Rights. The Declaration states that:

> Everyone has the right to a standard of living adequate for the health and well-being of himself and of his family, including food, clothing, housing and medical care and necessary social services, and the right to security in the event of unemployment, sickness, disability, widowhood, old age or other lack of livelihood in circumstances beyond his control (Wynhoven and Senne 2006).

Through the Global Compact as well as the Millennium Development Goals, the United Nations has emphasised that business has a role in promoting human rights (including the above article on health and well-being), and that this role is particularly important in countries with limited state capacity to ensure human rights. The duties for the companies are, however, not completely clear, and mechanisms to enforce them are not in place. Developing countries have few national regulations concerning this that are clearly understood by the business community. There is also a lack of auditing compliance with the law. In most developing countries, Heineken follows better practices and has stronger policies than those set down in the legal and regulatory environment.[2] In particular, it gives formal rights to employees and their dependants on healthcare support, as part of the employee remuneration package. However, it is unclear just how far this right to healthcare extends, since the policies are based on global outlines that can be adapted locally.

---

1  Numerous interviews with H. Rijckborst conducted by Katinka van Cranenburgh, between May and September 2007
2  Heineken adheres to the OECD Guidelines, the Global Reporting Initiative (GRI) reporting guidelines, the Millennium Development Goals and the Global Business Coalition objectives among other standards. As well as all external guidelines, Heineken has set up a number of policies that are compulsory for all consolidated Heineken plants worldwide. These include the HIV/AIDS policy, the business code of conduct, the promotion girls policy and—not yet endorsed—medical principles. All these internal documents have a direct relation to the provision of healthcare.

A company's motivation for going beyond national standards and actually contributing to the expansion of human rights might lie in their focus on business opportunities and risks, then gaining competitive advantage and thereby accessing international capital markets. Despite extensive research on the connections between corporate social performance and corporate financial performance (Griffin and Mahon 1997; Roman *et al.* 1999; Margolis and Walsh 2003; Orlitzky *et al.* 2003; Allouche and Laroche 2005), the conclusions reached do not go much further than the fact that corporate social performance has a positive impact on corporate financial performance, but that this positive impact largely depends on geographical area and the type, disclosure and theme of the social action. In the case of healthcare provision by corporations, opportunities could include the reduced costs of replacing people who are off sick, training new people, hospitalisation fees, funerals, alternative doctors and many other costs involved when no action is taken. The reason for offering an in-house healthcare service might also be to avoid absenteeism due to long hours spent waiting at the national health doctor, counsellor or pharmacist.

But, apart from the instrumental considerations, was Heineken driven by any ethical considerations? A distinction can be made between starting up and continuing a healthcare system. Instrumental considerations seem to become prevalent when one needs to defend existing healthcare provisions. But, at the start, Heineken's expatriates in sub-Saharan countries simply felt that peace of mind was impossible when they had such enormous healthcare advantages compared with the local staff.[3] Heineken's managers saw the company at that time as morally responsible for delivering a minimal set of living standards to employees, which, in countries with limited public healthcare, automatically involved a certain level of company healthcare provision. These feelings and perceptions arose from moral considerations grounded in a number of ethical principles and theories. Thus, from a deontological perspective, they based their decisions on the ethical responsibility or obligation to 'do what is right, just and fair and avoid harm'. According to Doctor Rijckborst,[4] this moral duty argument for providing healthcare had been the main basis for starting clinics in Africa in the late 1980s. This initial reaction coincides with the view held by some proponents of the stakeholder theory of the firm (Evan and Freeman 1983) who have insisted on the need to take stakeholders as ends in themselves rather than merely as means. In this case, considerations about intrin-

---

3 Interview with H. Rijckborst conducted by Katinka van Cranenburgh, May 2007.

4 Dr Rijckborst MD was international medical adviser for Heineken International from 1986 to 2007 and was responsible for defining a healthcare strategy at Heineken Headquarters and for building an infrastructure that provides healthcare for employees and families in sub-Saharan Africa. He also integrated healthcare strategy into the company's business strategy.

sic human dignity, and what people are entitled to, seem to have played a role, quite apart from any instrumental considerations that there may have been.

Although it does not seem that Heineken managers formulated the idea in this way initially, it needs to be considered whether utilitarian ethics also played a role. If this is the case, providing healthcare for employees in emerging countries would be the alternative that maximised utility: that is, provided most welfare for most people, regardless of costs and difficulties. The problem in taking ethical utilitarianism as the basis of the initial decision to start up an in-house healthcare service is that it might lead to questioning why Heineken does not do more to increase the social welfare of more people, beyond employees and their families, in the areas where it operates, or even beyond that. In his public speeches, Heineken CEO Jean-François van Boxmeer (van Boxmeer 2007) showed acute awareness of the problem of limitations, which mainly came about through fear of intruding on governmental competences, the impossibility for a single company to tackle the immensity of the health problem in a whole country, and possible conflict with fiduciary responsibilities towards shareholders. In other words, one needs to take into account the environment of constraints in which actions take place: that is, how other stakeholders would be affected if Heineken went too far, how much they would be willing to accept, and where one can really be effective in one's efforts. It is possible that these types of calculation concerning the welfare of different groups and individuals affected by company decisions, as well as the total social welfare created, were taken into consideration by those people involved in the decision. But it is more likely that they began not long after the initial reaction, in a second step, after the actors' critical analysis of their own initial intuitions (Singer 2002).

Indeed, Heineken's managers did realise that they could engage in healthcare issues in the community, beyond employees and their families, but that this could best be done through partnerships with NGOs and governments. They also announced generous community healthcare support by Heineken through the Health Insurance Fund.[5]

At any rate, beyond ethical motivations, more was needed to develop a social strategy in a professional and integrated business system. Approaches based on economics or finance, corporate law, organisational theory and sociology all contributed to developing such a system. In the next section we will look at the consequences in the economic sphere which, after the initial considerations, currently set the tone for decision-making on healthcare in newly acquired Heineken operations. One can start by setting up clinics from a moral or ethical standpoint, but a business cannot run a full strategy of healthcare in developing countries based on ethical considerations alone.

5  The Health Insurance Fund is a foundation that provides private health insurance to low-income groups in sub-Saharan Africa. The insurance covers quality basic healthcare including treatment for HIV/AIDS (hifund.org).

## Boundary questions

Medical science and technology, expansion of multinationals in developing countries and increased communication and information technology have driven Heineken to consider the limitations of the healthcare it should provide and how the boundaries are to be determined. How far do the responsibilities of a company with respect to its own employees stretch? Does this include their dependants, families or extended families? Or does responsibility go beyond the employee and his or her family? Does the level of locally available public care set the standard? Does a budget made available to an individual or collective indicate the boundary? And who establishes that budget; or should the level of care that has been established over time be sustained? In the past, local management's actions towards their employees were based on best knowledge and a sense of enlightened paternalism. Local doctors also contributed to this development. They concentrated on the patients' interests rather than on anything else (finance/budgets). Medical provision gradually grew over the years. Developments in medical science as well as in patient access to information (mainly via the Internet) also played a part. A Heineken nurse in Congo made this obvious to Heineken's headquarters by asking for an IVF (*in vitro* fertilisation) fertility consultation in Amsterdam as she had read on the Internet that it was free. A human resources manager in Eastern Europe asked for HIV/AIDS medication for an HIV-positive colleague, as she understood Heineken was treating patients for AIDS in sub-Saharan Africa. Rapid access to local information on a global scale consequently means Heineken is continuously reconsidering the boundaries of the care it provides (Van der Borght *et al.* 2006).

As these new complexities arise, utilitarian ethics increasingly come into play. There are more concerns about the feasibility of new demands and the consequences of new programmes. Even before taking economics into account, managers need to evaluate the social costs and benefits of decisions for society overall and for the different stakeholders in particular. This does not contradict the ideal of impartiality that is at the basis of duty-based ethics. According to this ideal, our own kin, and those closest to us, should not take precedence over unrelated and unknown third parties. Anything we see as ethically correct should be applied equally to all situations without discrimination. Heineken follows this ideal insofar as it explicitly declares that it would like other companies, as well as governments, to do more in relation to healthcare as expressed by its CEO as well as the former head of health affairs (Rijckborst 2007; van Boxmeer 2007). In fact, it is Heineken's duty to encourage other companies and the government to do as Heineken does in relation to healthcare.

However, does the ethical demand for impartiality and universality make it Heineken's duty to expand its own healthcare programmes to non-employees, beyond family members? Is partiality towards one's own employees and their immediate families ethically justified? There are critics of impartialism who claim that we cannot be impartial in every aspect of life; that often the ethical thing to do as an individual is first to take care of those closest to you—your parents, spouse, children, friends. They contrapose two types of moral language, each with its own sphere (Walzer 1994): the thin language of impartiality and a thick language of partiality. From a company perspective, giving preference to one's employees can be understood as thick morality. However, according to utilitarian ethics it is also possible to find an impartial justification for partial preferences. Given the constraints in everyday life and the difficulties in foreseeing the consequences of all our decisions, it makes sense to privilege those on whom we have good reason to believe we can have more effect. Our contribution to general welfare is greater with some degree of partiality (Singer 2002).

Overall, the development of the Heineken healthcare system was initially not connected to the financial value of the company, and was not treated as a core factor for wealth maximisation. Moreover, it was not a one-off decision, but rather a gradual growth of investments. However, what do investors think about their money being spent on non-core business? They might adopt Milton Friedman's standpoint (Friedman 1970) that the only responsibility of business is to do business for the sake of the profits for shareholders. If so, they might think that Heineken is stealing from its investors by making expenditures that do not necessarily contribute to making profits. However, can healthcare provision also be a source of value for both the company and for its investors? What is the reaction of the rapidly growing number of faith-based and socially responsible investors? Will they rank Heineken higher among their investments? What Friedman in fact wrote in his article was a defence of profit maximisation while 'conforming to the basic rules of the society: both those embodied in law and those embodied in ethical custom' (Friedman 1970). So investors might feel that providing medical treatment to employees and their families affected by AIDS in sub-Saharan countries is today among 'the basic rules of the society . . . embodied in ethical custom', even if not required by law.

This chapter will analyse the possible sources of value, including the effects on employees in general, managers in particular and consumer appreciation. Before we get on to that, we will dedicate the next section to the external factors or 'outside-in linkages', which refer to external social conditions that influence businesses (Porter and Kramer 2006). They refer not necessarily to external stakeholders, but to the significant forces of external conditions. Some scholars also refer to 'triggers' (Grayson and Hodges 2004). Here, we investigate the 'triggering' global health burdens that affect society as a whole and corporations in particular.

# The global health burden

The worrying global healthcare situation needs to be taken into account by the private sector when setting up a business strategy for working in developing countries. What does this mean for private sector decision-making on healthcare provision, for its boundary setting and for its communication strategy? Can there be more opportunities taken from existing healthcare systems such as Heineken's? This section describes the global increase of chronic and infectious diseases and the expected consequences for businesses and management.

Chronic and infectious diseases spread through the world with enormous magnitude and speed. In both developing and developed countries the burden of global diseases is increasing rapidly. Chronic or non-communicable diseases such as cardiovascular disease, cancer, chronic respiratory disease and diabetes account for over half of the health problems in developing countries and almost 80% of the health burden in high-income countries. Infectious or communicable diseases such as HIV/AIDS, malaria and tuberculosis are the main burden in developing countries and to a lesser extent in the developed world (Suhrcke *et al.* 2006; WHO 2008). All studies on the impact of healthcare on micro, meso and macro levels reveal the global burden of diseases as a major challenge for world society. Africa is hit hardest (WHO 2008). Low household incomes, labour productivity and social mobility are resulting in lower labour supply and bringing forward retirement. According to Suhkre *et al.* (2006), employers absorb a significant portion of the economic burden of diseases through absenteeism, presenteeism, reduced productivity and increased employee turnover.

Several researchers have produced negative forecasts for the private sector. In Gupta and Taliento's 2003 report, entitled 'How Businesses Can Combat Global Disease', the authors not only highlight the effects, but also the role that businesses need to play: 'Multinationals are directly affected by the global epidemic. It can't be controlled without them.' This statement calls on corporations to take some responsibility in sharing the global burden of diseases. The essence of corporate involvement is approached from the ethical, deontological idea that one should use the means at one's disposal to do good. Gupta and Taliento refer to the fact that corporations could provide intellectual property, marketing skills and public relations channels, pharmaceutical development, distribution and project management. In addition to these in-kind donations, multinational corporations also provide natural platforms where large target audiences can be assembled and addressed. The workplace can provide a critical access point for healthcare, prevention messages and treatment clinics. As an extension to the workplace, families of workers could be reached by organising special family days or communicating directly with the family. For example, enclosing disease prevention messages with workers' wage slips would result in health messages going directly to the residential address of the employees' family. While in some countries places of worship such as churches, mosques or synagogues fulfil such a role, the workplace is far superior in terms of scale and bounded structure. Although the trend of corporations outsourcing workers is growing rapidly, the possibilities of reaching communities via corporations remains a very attractive one for healthcare workers.

However, most corporations are not collaborating with healthcare workers or opening up their doors to them. The reasons vary. Gupta and Taliento (2003) regard the passive position of managers towards healthcare workers as the result of managers being unaware of the impact that their companies could have on the public health sector. He accuses managers of, on the one hand, myopically trying to pursue the benefits of globalisation while, on the other hand, not accepting any responsibility for helping to manage the global health crisis. Being an actor in the global markets implicitly entails a moral, strategic and financial responsibility in combating global diseases. This insight is based on the assumption of long-term company strategies and visionary management. However, the performance management systems found in most corporations today lead to priority setting by managers based on targets that rarely exceed three-year periods. Managers 'rotate' jobs within companies at such a high speed (more than three or four years at one function is becoming less and less common) that, in combination with the bonus-performance structure and related evaluation systems, a manager is hardly ever called on to put any time or effort into disparate programmes such as contributing to disease control activities. Moreover, managers do not get the time to develop the necessary expertise that enables them to deal appropriately with non-core business matters. Even though it is highly likely that a large number of managers have a deontological background of 'wanting to do good', the top-down pressure for performance on volumes, sales and financials does not provide the manoeuvring space to fully take on these types of responsibility.

The impact of global epidemics on the private sector is increasing dramatically, correlating with the expansion of the private sector into the developing world and existing healthcare provision possibilities in the developed world. The impact of the burden of chronic diseases on the private sector is also increasingly alarming, correlating with the behaviour and expenditure patterns of workforces and the increasing technical possibilities in healthcare. The private sector, at least if it is to survive, cannot get away from a certain level of reaction and responsibility. The typical excuse of multinationals that they are not charitable organisations is simply not acceptable anymore. There is a growing awareness among global actors that dealing with global social misery is everyone's responsibility.

# Effects on employees, managers and consumers

While understanding the ethical considerations behind Heineken managers' investment in healthcare in the early 1980s, it is increasingly important to measure the value of private sector healthcare provision today and tomorrow. From among the various identifiable stakeholders, employees, managers in particular and consumers are being highlighted in this section. Although we realise a section could be written about all stakeholders, we have chosen employees, managers, consumers and—in a later section—investors, for the following reasons: employees have a huge personal stake as the public healthcare system in most emerging markets is poorly arranged and quality care is not widely available or comes at a high cost; managers are confronted more and more with responsibilities that go far beyond their core businesses, into activities that are more complex than what they were taught at universities or business schools;[6] lastly, consumers, certainly from Western countries, increasingly hold multinationals responsible for global catastrophes. Above all, consumers themselves are increasingly being held responsible for many of the world's disasters, and consumer groups for fair-trade products are growing rapidly.

## Employees and their dependants

As employees and dependants receive healthcare from Heineken, they obviously have an important stake in the valuation of the healthcare system. The question of whether the healthcare system will lead to increased company loyalty, or benefit recruitment for the local brewery, has been measured in several ways. The World Business Council for Sustainable Development (WBCSD 2006) refers to recent research which indicates that companies that invest in healthcare provision tend to benefit from increased productivity and morale, as well as from lower absenteeism and sickness costs. The WBCSD encourages corporations to provide healthcare for their employees by highlighting the positive experiences of Volkswagen, Unilever, Lafarge, Philips and others. Unpublished research carried out in the Heineken operating company in Pointe Noire, Congo (Van Mameren 2006), questioned employees and dependants on the importance of the healthcare system. This field research required both employees and their spouses to rank the reasons for working for the company. Respondents received a ten-point list to rank: (1) training

6 During the first decade of the 21st century, universities and business schools have been increasingly paying attention to sustainability in management education. The Principles of Responsible Management Education (PRME) reflect the importance a growing number of universities and business schools (243 in July 2009) place on educating future managers in such a way that they not only have positive impact on the business of their future employer, but also on society (www.unprme.org, accessed 16 December 2009).

and education possibilities; (2) salary; (3) healthcare; (4) status; (5) career perspectives; (6) other (specify); (7) international environment; (8) the product produced; (9) good working atmosphere; and (10) job security. The research showed that healthcare ranked first among spouses of employees, and second (after salary) among employees. Clearly provision of healthcare by Heineken is a major retention factor. Even if further research is also needed among trade unions—stakeholders who often have considerable power—this data seems to confirm the view that companies with a good reputation in social areas improve current employees' goodwill, which in turn may improve productivity and financial results.

## Managers

In their meta-analysis of the relation between corporate social performance (CSP) and corporate financial performance (CFP), Orlitzky *et al.* (2003) state that, first, market forces do not generally penalise companies that are high in corporate social performance, so managers can afford to be socially responsible. Furthermore, if managers believe that social performance leads to corporate financial performance, they may actively pursue social matters such as healthcare provision, because they think the market will reward them for doing so. Top managers would then have to learn to use social performance as a reputational lever and be aware of the perceptions of third parties, such as market analysts, public interest groups and the media. Lance Moir (2006) suggests that the connection between social and financial performance should be clear to managers because of its impact on value drivers. If managers understand the impact of ESG on sales growth, operating margins, cost of capital and competitive advantage, they will better understand the opportunities and risks of social involvement. They would then have the financial arguments to persuade shareholders to support acting in a responsible manner. This underlines the need to view business and society as being interdependent (Porter and Kramer 2006). This approach does not take the view of society solely as a group of various stakeholders, but emphasises the fact that there are triggers to incorporate ESG issues, both inside-out as well as outside-in (Grayson and Hodges 2004; Porter and Kramer 2006). The problem that a company such as Heineken faces is that managers are not trained or retained on aspects of ESG, or the effect ESG can have on the financial results. Also, the skills required to organise and implement this knowledge are not addressed by their training curriculum. Lastly, little attention is given to the relation between social and financial performance in the leadership programmes of middle and top management.

## Consumers

African or Asian consumers within the community of the Heineken breweries do not have access to the Heineken healthcare system and might not be aware of the fact that it exists. The stake they have may be defined as indirect; if they are impressed by the ethics of the company behind the brand, then they might also show a change in consumer behaviour. This is actually not expected, as the concept of corporate responsibility in general in developing regions has not proved to be correlated to consumer behaviour. However, for consumers in industrialised countries this might be different. In Western countries, research has demonstrated (GlobeScan 2009) that consumers' brand preference and brand loyalty is influenced by the company's ethics and social performance.

However, if one were to study the impact on Western consumer behaviour of Heineken's healthcare system in developing countries, the outcomes would most probably be nil. The reason for this is that consumers are not aware of Heineken's actions in this field; communication on this point has hardly ever been targeted to consumers. To measure if the healthcare system has value among Western consumers, they would first have to be informed.

Heineken's healthcare system will also affect stakeholders other than employees and consumers. Local communities, governments, non-governmental organisations, international institutions, project financers, shareholders in Heineken International and many more will also be interested in this aspect of the company's decision-making. In this section, we have chosen to highlight the stakes of employees, managers and consumers as these stakeholders are most directly connected with the financial performance of the company. In the next section we turn to the financial community: the shareholders.

## Impact of socially responsible investors

Socially responsible investment (SRI) has been an important trend in the financial markets since the 1970s when the first SRI mutual funds were created in the USA and later on in Europe. Some researchers point to the fact that SRI is one of the major drivers of CSR (Cowton and Sparkers 2004; Scholtens 2006). SRI allows investors to reflect their personal values in their financial choices (Eurosif 2003). The origin of SRI comes from ethical investment (Laufer 2003). The objectives of ethical investors are to screen 'sin industries' from portfolio management, and exclude sectors such as tobacco, alcohol and pornography.

Nevertheless, the evolution of the demands of socially responsible investors during recent years has moved SRI to a new pragmatic approach. This new approach comes from the embedding of accountability and sustainability into portfolio management and financial analysis (Eurosif 2003). As a consequence, SRI strategies have moved forward to promote the adoption of socially responsible and sustainable practices among firms (Prakash Sethi 2005).

SRI fund managers have based new strategies on seeking new criteria to analyse firms' value and risk management (Barnett and Salomon 2006). Among these new strategies are the best-in-class approach, company engagement and shareholder activism. During recent years, the maturing of SRI is related to the integration of the analysis of the impact of the external environment in which companies operate, including the culture of the local communities, and the social and legal aspects that affect its operation and influence the consequences of its actions and decision (Colle and York 2009).

These new approaches have also changed the way in which SRI investors and managers engage with alcohol firms. Historically alcohol was often seen as a 'sin stock' (Schwartz 2003). As mentioned above, when it comes to SRI, an immediate link with alcohol is made (Laufer 2003). In the past, alcohol-producing companies were often excluded from ethical portfolio management. Nevertheless, during recent years, alcohol firms have been analysed from a broader perspective. SRI managers evaluate the way a firm deals with the impacts of its product on its stakeholders and in the contingent environment in which they operate (Colle and York 2009). Beyond the exclusion, there have been efforts to justify and advance the financial results of those firms that are motivated by societal needs and concerns (Margolis and Walsh 2001).

In the Netherlands, the SRI issue in banking and financial markets dates back to the early 1960s (Scholtens 2007). Today, the Dutch financial market is built under a rich spectrum of SRI financial products and it is among the markets with the highest number of SRI products and services. Research shows how Dutch investment funds take a passive approach to firm engagement and screening policies. Just two out of seven SRI mutual funds had an active dialogue with senior management and executives of firms in their portfolios and they are predominantly engaged with Dutch firms.

Heineken is listed on the Dutch Stock Exchange AEX. Its shareholders comprise an extremely varied group of individuals and financial institutions: mainstream investors, socially responsible investors, active and passive shareholders, known and unknown shareholders and Heineken family member shareholders (through a holding company).

If alcohol were still a reason to exclude Heineken from the portfolios of investors, then there would be little point in considering the socially responsible investor as a stakeholder. Recently, however, a change has taken place. In the Netherlands, only two out of ten large SRI funds have alcohol as an exclusion criterion (van Cranenburgh 2007). As also indicated in the VBDO (Association of Investors for Sustainable Development) report (VBDO 2005), all socially responsible investment funds in The Netherlands require alcohol-producing companies to comply with a minimum set of standards. Fund managers and analysts only discarded alcohol as an exclusion criterion after companies met the minimum criteria imposed on them.

When alcohol production and sales are linked to Africa, the issue can become even more sensitive. According to Karnani (2007), alcohol consumption is a financial drain for the poor. He refers to research that indicates that poorer people spend a greater percentage of their income on alcohol than the better off. Aside from the direct financial cost, he mentions that alcohol abuse adds to other economic and social costs such as diminished work performance, health, accidents, domestic violence and child neglect. The criteria that alcohol beverage companies have to meet in order to be included in the previously mentioned Dutch SRI funds do not relate to geographical/GDP matters. In general, Heineken's Investor Relations Department perceives the alcohol sector as 'not an easy sector to begin attracting SRI' and this might explain the still limited growth of interest that Heineken takes in the SRI market.[7]

However, increased interest within Heineken for SRI has followed the inclusion of the company in the Dow Jones Sustainability Index (DJSI) in 2004. There was a consensus that SRI was important for risk reduction, and the strategy is therefore to ensure ranking in the DJSI World STOXX, FTSE4Good and other major SRI indexes.[8] Currently, within investor relations, SRI is being 'followed with interest' and, although this interest is not formalised, Heineken is weighing up the opportunities and risks of social performance for its financial community. The interest and related strategy of the investor relations department with regards to SRI is restricted to: (1) risk reduction; (2) ranking in the sustainability indexes; (3) sharing the index rankings with mainstream shareholders; (4) complying with CSR reporting crite-

---

7 These points of view were expressed in the interviews conducted with Mrs Bergamini, investor relations officer and Mr Van der Merbel, Head of Heineken Investor Relations Department, in March 2007.

8 The financial benefits of being included in these indexes cannot be quantified. Heineken lost its ranking in the DJSI in 2005 and retained it in 2006 but this cannot be directly connected to the low share price in 2005 and the high share price in 2006, as too many other factors contribute to the price of the shares. As with most aspects connected to ethical and social issues, costs can be calculated, but benefits are hardly quantifiable. For the Heineken investor relations (IR) department SRI is becoming somewhat more important. The IR department believes the reasons for SRI limited volumes is related to the high commission the SRI funds ask from their clients (approximately >3% compared with mainstream equity at about 1%), the lower liquidity (fewer companies to invest in due to social, ethical and environmental limitations) and the performance. IR notices an increase of performance by SRI funds but states that it remains below the performance of the mainstream and certainly the hedge funds averages.

ria; and (5) organising one or two SRI meetings per year. The number of investor meetings organised with the SRI sector is low compared with the 80–100 investor presentations and workshops held annually for standard investors. In addition to the increased interest in SRI as discussed above, the number of social questions raised during the AGM has grown over the last few years.

## Socially responsible investors and the impact of Heineken's healthcare system

As mentioned in the introductory part of this chapter, the social aspect of ESG is the least quantifiable and therefore the most difficult to measure and benchmark. Therefore, employee healthcare is not only a grey area for many business managers, NGOs or activists, but clearly also for investors. Given the impact healthcare provision has on stakeholders of the private sector (see section on the global health burden), combined with the expected and alarming impact the global health situation will have on corporations (see section on the effects on stakeholders, above), what are the risks, and what are the opportunities for investors in this field?

In formulating this question for the Heineken case, we focused our research on learning how healthcare provision developed by Heineken can lead to increased financial returns, attracting the financial communities that perceive the company as more reliable and less of an investment risk. In addition, we also focused on learning about the impact on SRI investors and faith-based organisations that strive to invest their money in businesses that serve their goals of creating a fair and sustainable world.

In 2007 the authors conducted a quantitative and qualitative research study among the SRI community. The research questions were divided into four areas. First, respondents were questioned on the existence of criteria for private sector healthcare provision in developing countries and were asked to share details. Second, a short description of Heineken's healthcare provision in developing countries was given and respondents were asked if they knew about the particular health programmes and how significant they thought they were compared with other health and safety aspects. They were also asked to put themselves in the position of investors in Heineken, and answer the following questions: 'If Heineken stops employee healthcare provision in developing countries, what would your reaction be?' and 'If Heineken's employee healthcare provision is conducted in some developing countries in which Heineken operates, but not in all of them, what would your reaction be?' A scale of possible answers ranged from 'disinvestment from Heineken' through 'shareholder activism' to 'no impact'. The third part of the questionnaire referred to the sources of information that the SRI community uses to understand private sector healthcare provision. The last part of the survey related to investing in alcoholic beverage companies, Heineken in particular.

The research covered 14 fund managers and analysts (12 from Dutch institutions, one from a UK institution and one from a Belgian institution), five large investment funds and five rating agencies in the Netherlands. Half of them stated they either owned Heineken shares or advised their clients to incorporate Heineken shares into their portfolio, 43% stated Heineken was not included in their portfolio and 7% did not want to disclose their status. To understand the value and the awareness of Heineken's healthcare system, 10 out of 13 respondents (77%) answered that they indeed were aware of the fact that Heineken has a programme for health in developing countries.

Respondents were asked to indicate their awareness of several aspects of Heineken's healthcare system in developing countries. Most of the respondents (69%) were aware of Heineken's health and safety programmes for employees, their employee healthcare provision and their employee health education programmes. Eight out of thirteen of the respondents (62%) were aware that Heineken discloses information on health and safety performance, and 54% knew that Heineken also provides healthcare for employees' families. Specific programmes covering selling beer safely for beer promoters[9] and the global Alcohol & Work programme[10] were known by fewer investors (38%) (see Figure 11.1).

When asked how significant the aspect of employee healthcare provision in developing countries was in relation to the other above-mentioned health and safety aspects, the respondents answered that Heineken should emphasise this programme (see Figure 11.2).

For Heineken it will be helpful to bear in mind these findings when setting up a healthcare strategy. The SRI community is very much aware of Heineken's healthcare system in general, and fund managers and analysts give high significance to Heineken's healthcare provision in developing countries. However, they are not aware of the specific employee programmes covering responsible alcohol use at work (Alcohol & Work) and health and safety while promoting and selling beer (Selling Beer Safely). If Heineken wishes to take the growing SRI community seriously, it needs to communicate its efforts in the field of health and safety in such a way that the SRI community is aware and constantly updated. As we will see later in this chapter, SRI fund managers use this information for industry benchmarks, the results of which are used in the investment decision-making process.

9  Selling Beer Safely (SBS) for beer promoters refers to a specific health and safety programme for (female) workers, either employed by Heineken or via a third party, to sell beer directly to consumers in bars, beer gardens and restaurants. The goal of SBS is to improve the working environment of beer promoters, to empower them and to educate them on health and safety matters.

10  Heineken's Alcohol & Work or Cool@Work programme is aimed at employees drinking responsibly, knowing the company's alcohol policy and understanding the (health) effects of alcohol.

**FIGURE 11.1** Awareness of Heineken's healthcare programmes

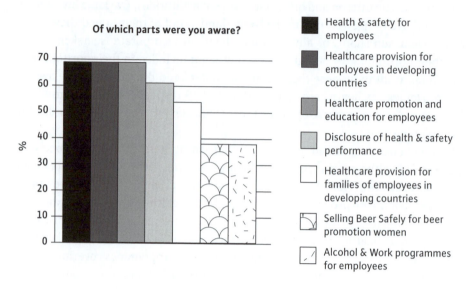

**FIGURE 11.2** Healthcare provision versus health and safety

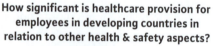

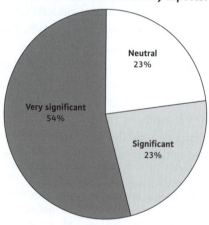

## SRI fund managers' decision-making strategies

The general tendency within financial institutions to regard ESG as profitability factors will most probably lead to healthcare considerations being included in their investment decisions. Although environmental and governance measurements are currently much more quantifiable and more easily benchmarked than social factors, the 'S' in ESG will gain ground. Bernstein's research (Bernstein 2008) shows the increased range of data sources dealing with corporate social behaviour. Goldman Sachs, RiskMetrics, KLD and other labour and human rights investment researchers are in the constant process of refining databases, looking out for improved sources to fill the databases, and interpreting the data. All investment researchers include health and safety and employee healthcare provision as a social indicator.

This led us to ask what might stop investors incorporating healthcare provision into their investment decisions. The research concluded that one of the most important criteria for companies in relation to SRI investors is to understand the way fund managers make decisions when investing in listed companies, and how analysts rate organisations on social and environmental aspects. Literature on SRI indicates that there are many common practices in decision-making methodology: in/exclusion, benchmarking, competitive advantage and so on (Eurosif 2008). Examples of individual SRI-related financial institutions from the USA, the UK and the European continent provide insight into the details and differences between decision-making methods. Although most decision-making is based on fixed procedures, in the end it is the clients of the financial institution who decide whether or not to include the highest-rated organisations in their portfolio. As well as procedural decision-making, some analysts use narrative information as input for their decisions. If a company communicates a certain 'best practice' in social performance, some analysts might then use this as a basis to create an industry benchmark on this particular issue.

Within SRI, health and safety is one of the major indicators in the various methods used and—mainly for companies working in developing countries—healthcare provision is a focus area for investors. Expectations from increasing external pressure from governments (e.g. investment transparency regulations) and international institutions (e.g. Millennium Development Goals) as well as the general health situation (considering epidemics such as HIV/AIDS) form a basis for financial institutions to further define and expand their healthcare criteria. All indicators show the need for private sector companies striving to financially out-perform others to have a solid social, ethical and environmental performance. Health and safety is one of the main priorities and—for companies working in the developing world—healthcare provision is growing in importance.

## Final considerations

The objectives of this chapter were: (1) to understand motivators and ethical boundaries of Heineken's development and maintenance of a healthcare provision system in emerging markets; (2) to provide an insight into the impact of the global health burden on the private sector; and (3) to explore the relationship between Heineken's healthcare system and investment decisions of socially responsible investors.

First, by studying this case we have seen that there are ethical motivators in the foundation of healthcare programmes in the developing world, and that these derive from a deontological ethics perspective more than a utilitarian ethics perspective. However, the utilitarian ethics perspective plays an important role in dealing with issues that arise once the healthcare programmes start, and once one needs to deal with boundary questions. From this perspective it could be argued that privileging one's own employees and their families is not necessarily against the ethical ideal of impartiality. A company facing constraints and uncertainty of consequences should focus on the alternative that produces the best outcomes in terms of benefits for society overall, while encouraging other actors to face up to their own responsibilities.

Second, we have seen that the impact of global epidemics on the private sector is growing dramatically in correlation with the expansion of the private sector into the developing world and existing healthcare provision possibilities in the developed world. The impact of the burden of chronic diseases on the private sector is also increasingly alarming, correlating with the behaviour and expenditure patterns of workforces and the increasing technical possibilities in healthcare. The private sector, at least if it is to survive, cannot escape certain reactions and responsibilities. It will be confronted with healthcare matters that will affect its bottom line. This situation, as we have seen, affects different stakeholders—employees, managers and consumers—in different ways.

Third, one of the most important stakeholder groups in this matter (as in many others) is investors. Because of the attention given to social, ethical and environmental issues by investors, corporate awareness of ESG may increase. As health and safety is a major aspect in the 'S' in ESG, attention to healthcare investments is also likely to grow. There is a need for more evidence that investing in healthcare can actually create value for the firm and lead to financially positive results. Although such data is not yet available, this qualitative example makes good business sense. It seems reasonable to presume that businesses will increase healthcare investments.

The results of our research on investors points to a correlation between Heineken's healthcare system and the potential market value of the company, which goes beyond the oft-mentioned considerable positive impact within the field of human resources (healthy employees, talent retention and employee motivation) and corporate relations (good reputation). In Heineken's case it has become clear that health and safety, and in particular healthcare provision, has an impact on stakeholders who are directly related to the company's financial performance: socially responsible investors. Although we cannot generalise, it makes good business sense to believe that this case can be a lesson for other companies.

The research concludes that there are two main challenges for a company such as Heineken in relation to SRI investors: first, to improve SRI investors' awareness of health and safety programmes for employees; and, second, to improve SRI fund managers' understanding of ESG decision-making processes. As we have seen, the general tendency within financial institutions to regard ESG as profitability factors will also lead to healthcare being included in their investment decisions. Although environmental and governance measurements are currently relatively much more quantifiable and more easily benchmarked than social factors, the 'S' in ESG will also gain ground, especially in terms of how to include health and safety and employee healthcare provision as a social indicator.

The combination of the worrying global healthcare situation, the increasing use of communication technology, the advance of medical science and shareholder knowledge and awareness of healthcare effects on business will lead to a growing need for business managers to include healthcare issues in their business strategy. Arguing the need and the justification for private sector healthcare provision may shift between utilitarian and duty-based dimensions but, in any case, it will increasingly become part of business practice.

# References

Allouche, J., and P. Laroche (2005) 'A Meta-analytical Investigation of the Relationship between Corporate Social and Financial Performance', *Revue de Gestion des Ressources Humaines* 57: 18-41.

Barnett, M.L., and R.M. Salomon (2006) 'Beyond Dichotomy: The Curvilinear Relationship between Social Responsibility and Financial Performance', *Strategic Management Journal* 27.11: 1,101-22.

Bernstein, A. (2008) 'Incorporating Labor and Human Rights Risk into Investment Decisions' (Harvard Law School, Pensions and Capital Stewardship Project Labor and Worklife Program, Occasional Paper Series, No. 2, September 2008).

Colle, S., and J.G. York (2009) 'Why Wine is not Glue? The Unresolved Problem of Negative Screening in Socially Responsible Investing', *Journal of Business Ethics* 85.1: 83-95.

Cowton, C., and R. Sparkers (2004) 'The Maturing of Socially Responsible Investment: A Review of the Developing Link with Corporate Social Responsibility', *Journal of Business Ethics* 52.1: 45-57.

Eurosif (2003) *Socially Responsible Investment among European Institutional Investors* (Paris: Eurosif).

—— (2008) *European SRI Study 2008* (Paris: Eurosif).

Evan, W., and R.E. Freeman (1983) 'A Stakeholder Theory of the Modern Corporation: Kantian Capitalism', in T. Beauchamp and N. Bowie (eds.), *Ethical Theory and Business* (Englewood Cliffs, NJ: Prentice Hall): 75-93.

Friedman, M. (1970) 'The social responsibility of business is to increase its profits', *New York Times Magazine*, 13 September 1970.

GlobeScan (2009) *The Corporate Social Responsibility Monitor* (Toronto: GlobeScan).

Grayson, D., and A. Hodges (2004) *Corporate Social Opportunity! Seven Steps to Make Corporate Social Responsibility Work for your Business* (Sheffield, UK: Greenleaf Publishing).

Griffin, J., and J. Mahon (1997) 'The Corporate Social Performance and Corporate Financial Performance Debate', *Business & Society* 36: 5-31.

Gupta, R.K., and L. Taliento (2003) 'How Businesses Can Combat Global Disease', *The McKinsey Quarterly* 4 (special edition, 'Global Directions').

Karnani, A. (2007) 'The Mirage of Marketing to the Bottom of the Pyramid: How the Private Sector Can Help Alleviate Poverty', *California Management Review* 49.4: 23.

Laufer, W.S. (2003) 'Social Screening of Investment: An Introduction', *Journal of Business Ethics* 43.3: 163-65.

Margolis, J.D., and J.P. Walsh (2001) *People and Profits? The Search for a Link between a Company's Social and Financial Performance* (Mahwah, NJ: Lawrence Erlbaum Associates).

—— and J.P. Walsh (2003) 'Misery Loves Companies: Rethinking Social Initiatives by Business', *Administrative Science Quarterly* 48: 268-305.

Moir, L. (2007) 'Measuring the Business Benefits of Corporate Responsibility', *Management Services*, August 2007.

Orlitzky, M., F.L. Schmidt and S.L. Srynes (2003) 'Corporate Social and Financial Performance: A Meta-analysis', *Organization Studies* 24.3: 403-41.

Porter, M., and M. Kramer (2006) 'Strategy and Society: The Link between Competitive Advantage and Corporate Social Responsibility', *Harvard Business Review* 84: 68-92.

Prakash Sethi, S. (2005) 'Investing in Socially Responsible Companies is a Must for Public Pension Funds? Because there is no Better Alternative', *Journal of Business Ethics* 56.2: 99-129.

Rijckborst, H. (2007) *What are the Responsibilities of the Private Sector in Health Care? International Visions on the Future of Health Care in Resource-Poor Settings* (Amsterdam: Heineken International Health Affairs).

Roman, R., S. Hayibor and B. Agle (1999) 'The Relationship between Social and Financial Performance', *Business & Society* 38: 109-25.

Scholtens, B. (2006) 'Finance as a Driver of Corporate Social Responsibility', *Journal of Business Ethics* 68.1: 19-33.

—— (2007) 'Financial and Social Performance of Socially Responsible Investments in the Netherlands', *Corporate Governance: An International Review* 15.6: 1,090-105.

Schwartz, M.S. (2003) ' "Ethics" of Ethical Investment', *Journal of Business Ethics* 43.3: 195-213.

Singer, P. (2002) *One World: The Ethics of Globalization* (New Haven, CT: Yale University Press).

Suhrcke, M., R.A. Nugent, D. Stuckler and L. Rocco (2006) *Chronic Disease: An Economic Perspective* (London: Oxford Health Alliance).

Van Boxmeer, J.F. (2007) *What are the Limits of Health Care Responsibilities?* (Amsterdam: Heineken NV).

Van Cranenburgh, K.C. (2007) *Private Sector Healthcare Provision and Socially Responsible Investors* (Vol. MBA; Amsterdam: HES Amsterdam School of Business/University of Amsterdam).

Van der Borght, S., T.F. Rinke de Wit, V. Janssens, M.F. Schim van der Loeff, H. Rijckborst and J.M. Lange (2006) 'HAART for the HIV-Infected Employees of Large Companies in Africa', *The Lancet* 368: 547-50.

Van Mameren, J. (2008) 'Aids-voorlichting door Heineken in Pointe Noire, Republiek Congo', master's thesis, University of Groningen, June 2008.

VBDO (2005) *Socially-Responsible Savings and Investments in the Netherlands 1987–2004* (Culemborg, Netherlands: VBDO).

Walzer, M. (1994) *Thick and Thin: Moral Argument at Home and Abroad* (Notre Dame, IN: University of Notre Dame Press): 120.

WBCSD (World Business Council for Sustainable Development) (2006) *The Business of Health—The Health of Business: Building the Case for Health, Safety and Wellness* (Geneva: WBCSD, March 2006).

WHO (World Health Organisation) (2008) *The Global Burden of Disease, 2004 Update* (Geneva: World Health Organisation Press).

Wynhoven, U., and J. Senne (2005) *Embedding Human Rights in Business Practice* (Joint Publication of the United Nations Global Compact and the Office of the United Nations High Commissioner for Human Rights; New York: The Global Compact).

# 12

# A rose by any other name?
## The Case of HIV/AIDS interventions among South African SMEs

**Karla A. Duarte and Maeve Houlihan**
University College Dublin, Ireland

Corporate social responsibility (CSR) contributes to sustainable development when it is creative, innovative and adds value. However, if CSR is truly to shift away from risk management and towards value creation, it must make the conceptual leap from neat rhetoric to messy realities, and a fundamentally pluralist approach.

In this chapter, we examine social responsibility *in action* in small and medium-sized enterprises (SMEs), taking the case of workplace responses to HIV/AIDS in South Africa. In the context of HIV/AIDS as a serious national crisis, we describe the choices some employers are making to get involved—largely without the language and rhetoric of CSR. We report on research among eight diverse, indigenous SMEs, describing what sort of initiatives were and were not under way, the responses of employees, and the external, internal, cultural and societal factors influencing both.

The chapter makes three contributions: first, the location of this case in a transitioning economy makes this case unique and particular. Country and culture play a role in defining what CSR means and there continues to be a need to investigate CSR activity in specific country contexts.

Second, it underscores that CSR does not always come with a label attached, and its remit is not confined to the traditional corporate environment. Small and medium-sized organisations can and do exercise corporate social responsibility, even when they don't describe it as such. SME CSR is an area that remains under-examined within academic research and this knowledge gap is critical, given that small business remains the dominant organisational form within the member countries of the OECD (Organisation for Economic Cooperation and Development) (Perrini 2006).

Third, however, and drawing on the ideas of Lewin (1951) in relation to the dynamics of change, this study maps a force field of driving and resisting factors surrounding such practices. This force field draws attention to the challenges of CSR, especially with regard to employer initiatives around employee health and welfare, and concerning HIV/AIDS in the South African context in particular. Its findings challenge assumptions about what employees need and want, and how they respond to such interventions, raising the questions 'what benefits?', 'whose benefit?' and 'why?'. They suggest the need for fresh thinking about the individual and his or her context when it comes to management strategies and CSR.

## The CSR proposition

Corporate social responsibility is a topic of growing interest for policy-makers and academics alike. Described as 'the way through which a company achieves a balance of economic, environmental and social imperatives, while at the same time addressing the expectations of shareholders and stakeholders' (UNIDO 2008), or 'the business contribution to sustainable development' (European Commission 2002: 347), debates on CSR go to the heart of the relationship between business and society. To what degree is the well-being of society a responsibility of business? While traditional views of business see its contribution as being restricted to wealth and employment creation, there is increasing evidence of the role businesses can play in social life beyond these two metrics. Contemporary CSR debate has thus largely circled around two perspectives: the **business case**, which appeals to self-interest in arguing that there are meaningful and tangible benefits to be had for organisations that choose to play such a role; and the **social justice case**, which argues that businesses, by virtue of their concentration of power in society and their reliance on it, owe a debt to society. While the business case focus has been the dominant one among contemporary research (Margolis and Walsh 2003), there is a growing consensus through social pressure, regulation and firm best practice towards some measure of social engagement. However, debates concerning the extent and meaningfulness of such initiatives continue (Griffin and Mahon 1997; Margolis and Walsh 2001; McWilliams and Siegel 2000). Furthermore, there is often considerable disjunction between the strategies and *realities* of

CSR (Kakabadse and Kakabadse 2007), and between espoused and actual behaviours.

## CSR, SMEs and developing economies

An implicit assumption prevails that CSR is a position of the privileged. Big business and advanced economies are seen as the beacons by which best practice is developed, and the paternalistic but also pragmatic assumptions that to a large degree underpin CSR, operate to suggest that an organisation (and economy) needs to reach a level of well-being and prosperity before such concerns become its responsibility. Reflecting on this implicit assumption, the major emphasis and attention of CSR researchers has focused on the actions and 'shoulds' of big business, particularly multinational corporations. However, small and medium-sized firms make up the majority of businesses worldwide and, as UNIDO (2008) argues, are critical 'pathways out of poverty' for developing and transitioning economies in particular. Can such organisations be expected to adhere to increasingly demanding lines of 'triple bottom line' reporting? Organisations such as UNIDO point out the restrictiveness that is occasioned by such expectations, particularly as they are often driven by powerful corporations prevailing on much less powerful supplier organisations in the supply chain. The debate on CSR in developing and transitioning economies has therefore focused on policy and expectation around reporting, responsible employment practice and environmental sustainability practices.

Yet smaller organisations can and do play innovative roles in their social environments beyond these arenas, and there is much to learn from those that have independently chosen to undertake initiatives that they might themselves not classify as CSR, but nevertheless demonstrate the capacity of business to contribute socially and with constructive effect. While there is a small body of literature on SME experiences in industrialised countries (Bond 1988; Lansing and Kuruvilla 1988; Di Norcia 1989), there is a very limited amount of research on SME CSR activity in developing economies (Visser *et al.* 2005).

The case of HIV/AIDS in South Africa is a compelling example; typically HIV/AIDS protection and intervention has been tackled from an institutional perspective, through national health and education agencies, and NGOs. The workplace, however, is another alternative, and, in a country such as South Africa where there has been mixed support at the national level, employer initiatives could provide an alternative platform for meaningful intervention. This chapter seeks to shed light on the spontaneous actions of small indigenous firms in consciously or unconsciously navigating social contribution. Such a practice-based understanding of

CSR, though not without difficulties, illustrates the capacity for small organisations to make a difference to society.

## The context: HIV/AIDS and South Africa

South Africa has the sixth highest prevalence of HIV in the world at 18.8% of the population (UNAIDS 2006) and, as of the end of 2006, 5.5 million South Africans were living with the virus (UNAIDS 2007). This makes South Africa the country with the second largest number of HIV infections in the world. To put this in context, 320,000 people died of AIDS-related disease in South Africa during 2005 (UNAIDS 2006) and 1.8 million people have died of AIDS-related disease since the epidemic began (UNAIDS 2007). New infections are still increasing and there are no signs of this crisis reaching a natural limit. Various global reports have stressed the need for interventions at local, as well as policy levels, and the importance of the involvement of all stakeholders, including, specifically, the business community (UNAIDS 2006).

This need for the involvement of all stakeholders is especially relevant in the South African situation. Government efforts to tackle the problem of HIV/AIDS have been the subject of much criticism. Though the South African government has a national strategy on paper and is legally required to provide treatment to HIV-infected individuals, in reality the roll-out campaign has encountered many obstacles and has helped only a small percentage of the infected population while failing to reach those most in need. As this chapter explores, some business owners and managers have responded by creating and implementing various CSR-driven HIV/AIDS initiatives, not least in an effort to minimise the impacts of HIV/AIDS on their organisations. But efforts to respond to the national epidemic by tackling it in the workplace have raised many challenges that require exploration.

That said, such employer responses take on a particular complexion in South Africa, a country with a chequered history on human rights, and sometimes hostile employment relationships rooted in a history of apartheid and white ownership. South Africa is a country of multiple and contested traditions—none more obvious than the overt distinction between white South African and black South African culture. The painful history of struggle between these cultures plays out in all arenas of life, not least work practice and employment relations.

There are nine main African groups (Ndebele, Xhosa, Zulu, Pedi, Sotho, Tswana, Swazi, Tsonga and Venda) and two main European groups (English and Afrikaaners) in South Africa. Their differences manifest in overt ways (for example, there are 11 official languages), and less obviously, but just as importantly, in people's varying behaviours and attitudes, not least how each perceived the issue of HIV/ AIDS. Throughout this study, we saw how varying cultural assumptions and cultural myths operated among different racial groups, and the degree to which this had been inscribed by social structure, educational opportunity, and cultural and material history. No element is more significant in material terms, than the legacy of the apartheid era (1948–1991), throughout which governments enforced a policy of white domination and racial separation. Among other things, the legacy of apartheid was skewed skills distribution and economic, political and educational disempowerment of the black majority (Bowmaker-Falconer *et al.* 1998). Although post-apartheid South African organisations are multicultural in workforce composition, ownerships of business remain almost entirely in the hands of the white minority, while non-white groups and women suffer disadvantage and discrimination in compensation, hiring and other staffing practices (Bowmaker-Falconer *et al.* 1998). Thus, still today, many employees in South Africa have and expect little by way of employment rights, and though it is illegal, for example, to be fired for being ill, large numbers of employees are unaware of their rights and many employers do not follow or enforce them. It is within this fractured context that understanding the actions and restrictions of organisations seeking to make a difference are of particular relevance.

## Methodological approach

As part of her PhD research, the first author undertook nine months of ethnographic fieldwork in South Africa with the specific goal of understanding the impetus to, variety, and success of efforts of small and medium-sized (and particularly) indigenous organisations with regards to HIV and AIDS. Research time was divided between volunteering with an NGO in order to become familiar with the sociopolitical issues around HIV and AIDS in South Africa, and collecting field data. Research focused on indigenous, geographically dispersed businesses across a range of sectors and this chapter reports on eight in-depth case studies, conducted via semi-structured interviews with at least three different stakeholders (owner, managers and employees), coupled with more informal conversations and extensive observation. These data were collated as transcripts, field notes and archive material and examined through a grounded, thematic approach through which the force field analysis offered here emerged. As an exploratory study, the objective was not representativeness or hypothesis testing, but rather through focus on context and contradictions, to tease out depth of understanding of what was happening and why.

# A glimpse into the lives of eight South African organisations

In the following sections we present pen pictures of these eight organisations: what they were doing, what they were not doing and how things worked out for them. As will be seen, some were more actively involved in addressing the issue of HIV/AIDS in the workplace than others. However, each of these cases provides a particular insight into the motivations and challenges of taking the initiative. They show that many had the impetus to strive to do something, and yet some felt powerless, ineffective or even antagonistic in trying. Where initiatives were undertaken, we get a glimpse of the barriers and complications they encountered. Significantly, these accounts draw attention to the impact of South Africa's cultural, economic, historical, political and social context as shaping forces. All of this presents a deeply realist context in which to consider the role, potential and challenges—effectively a force field of driving and resisting factors—for small and medium-sized organisations in undertaking these, and by extension broader, CSR-led initiatives.

## Lodge and Safaris

Lodge and Safaris was a medium-sized enterprise employing 70 people. It was located in Limpopo and its owner-manager, Jason, was a white Dutch male who had lived and worked in South Africa for many years. Jason was passionately concerned about HIV/AIDS and believed that he had a duty as an employer to help the community and his workforce. He was already significantly involved in the local community where he had helped build a crèche and had begun to assist with the building of an orphanage. But Jason had begun to recognise that he had a responsibility to his 'family' (staff) within the organisation as well. It was apparent that both he and his employees saw Lodge and Safaris as a family unit and there was much love and respect visible among staff and management. Both acknowledged this relationship and the responsibilities each role entailed.

Though Jason was feeling various effects of HIV/AIDS in his organisation, such as the death of staff members, ill workers, loss of skills (from workers who had died), low employee morale, an increase in absenteeism, and an increase in replacement and training costs, there were two events that prompted Jason to respond to HIV/AIDS in his workplace. First, a long-time friend and employee of more than ten years died of AIDS and, second, another long-time employee discovered he had AIDS and left the organisation.

Lodge and Safaris was responding to HIV/AIDS in small ways. It offered prevention and awareness workshops to selected employees, provided jobs with lesser duties for weak and ill staff members, and chose not to fire people with HIV or

AIDS. However, Jason saw this merely as a starting point and was looking for help and guidance to start implementing more extensive and comprehensive initiatives. Though he had energy, determination, interest and many ideas, he was at a loss about where to start and needed help executing initiatives. He had made previous efforts to response to HIV/AIDS in the workplace but had not managed to implement these efforts successfully. For example, he had purchased hundreds of condoms to distribute to staff and clients (tourists) but he was unsure of how and where to display them so he placed the boxes of condoms in the freezer until he could make a decision, where they remained unused.

As this case suggests, deciding what is the correct thing to do and how to do it are key challenges, even when the intention is there. These challenges are all the more intense when the issue is contentious, sensitive and surrounded by value judgements as is the case with HIV/AIDS. This sharp contextual reality exposes any initiatives employers might take to a high risk of misconception and distrust. For example, Lodge and Safaris employees believed an HIV-infected colleague had been dismissed on discovery of his HIV status, although this was not the case. The reason for his dismissal had not been communicated to staff and rumours developed that negatively affected both employees' trust in management and employee morale.

## Cattle and Pig Farm

Cattle and Pig Farm was a small and fascinating farm business located in the outskirts of KwaZulu-Natal. It employed 23 black South Africans and was run by a barefoot, Zulu-speaking white male and his wife. Paul and Nancy were honest and frank about the vast impact that HIV/AIDS was having on their business. Paul gave an account of the high number of employee deaths related to HIV/AIDS, a high number of ill workers, an increase in funeral leave and funeral cost coverage, an increase in absenteeism, a decrease in productivity, an increase in staff turnover, an increase in cost and time to replace lost workers, a loss of skills (from those people who had died or had left), and a decrease in morale of workers.

In the face of these significant impacts, Paul and Nancy took some specific steps to respond: they provided immune-boosting tablets to selected loyal employees as well as food rations, funeral leave and funeral cost coverage. However, trustworthiness was an extremely important factor for both owners. They were prepared to help out particular workers although it was noticeable these efforts only extended to those they deemed loyal and worthy. Employees selected for assistance made use of the services; however, most employees did not have a choice whether to use particular service offerings or not since the services were not universally available. In addition, Paul and Nancy were undecided on whether to promote particular employees whom they thought to be HIV-positive.

The owners described concern for their staff, and believed they had a moral duty to help them, but they were also pragmatic about the business demands they faced. For example, they chose not to dismiss workers who were unfit to work hard because of the financial costs of replacing staff and a requirement that they re-house any staff let go.

To better understand the conflicting stances these owners seemed to take, it was helpful to learn more about them. A number of contextual issues played on their minds which tell much about the realities of running a business in South Africa: they were in constant fear of losing their farm to land claims; they were having difficulty adapting to their new roles under a non-apartheid government whereby their previous paternalistic management style was now frowned on; and they described themselves as struggling with the management of a workforce that, they argued, was not used to having to act independently and in many instances, they felt, just did not want to work. In fact, a large part of farm duties had been mechanised because of worker inability to perform labour-intensive tasks—owing to a high rate of HIV/AIDS infection—and plans to mechanise further in the future were taking place.

## Horse Stud Farm

The white South African owner of Horse Stud Farm (a medium-sized enterprise with approximately 40–45 employees located in KwaZulu-Natal) was an amusing and energetic character. Mitch seemed to be bullied by his workers and was unable to communicate with the vast majority of them as he spoke English and Afrikaans but his staff spoke Zulu. He was constantly frustrated because work was not being completed, yet he would not consider firing any employees.

Though Mitch admitted that HIV/AIDS was having a huge impact on his organisation (for example, he had lost six workers to AIDS, estimated that 50% of his workforce was infected, and said people were often too sick to come to work or too weak to perform the tasks assigned to them), he believed that HIV/AIDS had reached its peak and would shortly start to lessen. It is hard to say why he believed this, but nevertheless he intended to continue responding somewhat in the workplace. He provided jobs with lesser duties for those workers infected with HIV/AIDS, offered transport to medical facilities, and assisted with funeral coverage for employees whose family members had died from AIDS. He had also given a large plot of land over to his workers for them to own, live on and farm.

Mitch also organised HIV/AIDS mobile clinic visits to Horse Stud Farm so that workers could test for HIV/AIDS; however, as was the case in other organisations, few workers wanted to take this test. He realised that employee unwillingness to test was in part a legacy of the apartheid era and believed that: 'They [workers] have attitudes in head that the white man will do them dirties [take advantage of them] so if I tell them something they won't believe it and can't accept that a white man would want to help' (Mitch, owner-manager, Horse Stud Farm).

It is important to state that Mitch (as well as other managers and owners in this sample) was and continues to be a product of the apartheid era. Though the legal practice of apartheid has been condemned and no longer exists, the colonial mentality of many people still does. Owners and managers, often white South Africans, at times conveyed a very negative and racist view of black South Africans, while black South Africans equally frequently indicated distrust of their employers. It is fair to say that, despite his initiatives, Mitch was disillusioned and demotivated with regard to his workers and his capacity to make a difference in relation to HIV/AIDS.

## Used Car Sales and Repairs

Used Car Sales and Repairs was an automobile retail and repair company located in Pretoria, Gauteng, and run by a white South African man, Lenny—who was also a peer educator in another organisation. He ran his business, fixing up and selling old cars, from a house he had purchased across the road from his own.

Lenny employed seven black South African males. He provided them with accommodation on the property and gave them the opportunity to own a car by fixing up an old and unworkable vehicle during their spare time. At the time of interviewing one employee had recently died from AIDS, and he was employing some workers who were frequently ill and whom he suspected of having the virus. He was also coping with high levels of absenteeism so that staff could attend funerals of loved ones. Lenny described how he was trying to find ways to 'get through' to his workers and make them take the threat of HIV/AIDS seriously. He brought his training as a peer educator into his own work environment—bringing home pamphlets and condoms, and trying out discussion techniques he had learned in workshops. However, he was encountering great resistance from his staff, especially in respect to testing for HIV/AIDS.

He found that his employees were uncomfortable discussing the subject of HIV/AIDS, an issue that was mirrored in many of the case studies and pointed to the deep cultural sensitivities and, often, misconceptions around HIV in South Africa. At the same time, staff were responding not only from a cultural context, but also from the context of an employment relationship. Lenny had offered health and life insurance (towards which he agreed to contribute half) but when staff discovered that they would be required to take a blood test they each declined, saying they did not want to know if they were HIV-positive. Not wishing to know is a widespread cultural norm/superstition, but also no doubt partly due to fear of implications for their employment were their status to be positive. Lenny described how he was at a loss of what to do next. He had good intentions and wanted to help but had begun to think that nothing he could do would make a difference. He was frustrated and deeply concerned because he saw his business in the future losing its skilled workforce.

## Lodge and Game Farm

Lodge and Game Farm was a game farm that primarily offered holiday accommodation to South African tourists. It was located in Mpumalanga, and run by Gale, a white South African female. Lodge and Game Farm was a small organisation that relied on 11 staff to keep the workings of the farm moving smoothly. In a now familiar story, Gale described how HIV/AIDS was impacting on her small business. She had had staff members die, several were currently ill, staff regularly needed time off for funerals and there was a high turnover as ill employees left.

Gale believed that it was her duty to help her workers and she tried to implement various initiatives even though they were sporadic and infrequent. She had held an education workshop, provided funeral leave and offered transportation for employees who wanted to attend local clinics for HIV/AIDS testing or to obtain HIV/AIDS-related information. Outside of HIV/AIDS initiatives she also offered support for retirees, accommodation and food rations for workers, and was helping to build a preschool for children in the local village.

Though this employer wanted to do more in the future, she was uncertain where to start and was conscious of not wanting to create a relationship of dependence between her and staff that would be reminiscent of the relationship between blacks and whites during apartheid. She wanted to help her staff by giving them the means and tools to make their own decisions and therefore give them the autonomy necessary to break away from the apartheid mentality of having everything decided and done for them. This theme of uncertainty about the right actions to take, and for the right reasons, is a resonant one across many cases, and points to the need for greater external support, information and guidance for employers seeking to make a social difference.

## Guest House

Guest House was a micro enterprise run by Helen, a white South African woman. It employed seven women and was located in Johannesburg, Gauteng. Though Helen was not feeling as many impacts of HIV/AIDS as other organisations, for over ten years she had provided free HIV/AIDS testing and condoms for her staff. Helen believed deeply in the benefits of knowing one's HIV status. She acknowledged that the average black South African's life was fraught with survival issues far beyond that of HIV/AIDS.

In an effort to make staff more comfortable with this service offering, she and her black head of housekeeping had gone for an HIV/AIDS test together and then returned to the workplace and, while doing a little dance, told staff of their personal experiences and results. They hoped that by going themselves and talking about it then the event would stimulate discussion and interest from staff.

Some staff did go for a test but none ever revealed his or her status to Helen or the head of housekeeping. Staff were not required to state their HIV/AIDS status and legally management could not ask about it; however, this lack of knowledge (of who was HIV-positive or who had AIDS) prevented Helen from being able to help staff in need of treatment or assistance. In fact, Helen believed that the protection of confidentiality exacerbated the problem of secrecy around the disease.

However, this initiative, as minor as it might seem, was not without controversy. In one instance an employee took Helen to court, claiming she had been forced to test and was subsequently discriminated against at work because of the test results. The employee was found to be HIV-negative and the case was thrown out of court. In another instance, an employee found that she was HIV-positive and pregnant. The employee had just begun working with Guest House. A lawyer then called Helen and demanded that she provide antiretrovirals (ARVs). The lawyer eventually withdrew her support from the case. Both events served to damage Helen's morale. By her own account, she was finally getting tired and disheartened about her staff and her HIV/AIDS efforts. She spoke of planning to reduce the number of staff she employed and, though she said she would continue with the testing offer, she did not feel any desire to increase or expand her efforts.

## Private Game Reserve

Private Game Reserve was a medium-sized enterprise and a newly open exclusive game and safari reserve located in a remote area hundreds of kilometres away from the nearest city in the province of KwaZulu-Natal. It employed 100 mainly black South Africans, for whom also it provided accommodation and food, as was the norm.

Private Game Reserve was not doing very much with regard to HIV/AIDS internally. There was some minimal prevention and awareness efforts—such as HIV/AIDS awareness posters in the cafeteria—and the general manager stated that people with AIDS would not be fired if discovered to be infected but would instead be put on jobs with lesser duties; however, as no one had ever disclosed their HIV status, this position had never been tested.

And yet, what is interesting about Private Game Reserve is that it was quite active externally in respect to HIV/AIDS. Private Game Reserve had initiated and was, at the time of interviews, carrying out an HIV/AIDS awareness and prevention campaign in secondary schools in the local villages. The owner of Private Game Reserve was the driving force behind this. The general manager, Stephen, explained that he felt that he had a responsibility to look after communities surrounding the reserve. Most of his staff came from the local communities and the organisation wanted to make sure that young people (and possibly future staff members) were educated about HIV/AIDS and able to protect themselves from the virus. Though this community focus was admirable, it is very interesting that the reserve was concerned about the future generation of workers but not the present one. While internally there were some minimal initiatives in place, these were disorganised and half-hearted. There was a lack of communication between management and staff about the initiatives and unsurprisingly a lack of awareness among staff of what was available to them.

## Financial Services Company

Financial Services Company was a medium-sized financial services firm employing 100 mainly skilled employees in Johannesburg, Gauteng. Although one employee had died of HIV-related causes, it is striking that management at this company believed that HIV/AIDS was not a pressing issue because employees were well educated and thus were seen as able to tackle the issue on a personal level, independent of the organisation. This perception underlines the strong cultural, racial and class biases around perceptions of HIV in South Africa.

Other than providing employees with funeral leave, Financial Services Company did not really do much to respond to HIV/AIDS in the workplace. However, the company was in the midst of creating an HIV/AIDS policy and had already circulated a draft policy to managers for approval and feedback. There was a great sense of urgency in finalising and completing this policy and on further discussion it emerged that the impetus for this was so people with AIDS could legally be let go. By way of explanation, Financial Services Company was concerned about having to retain employees (infected with HIV or AIDS) who were unproductive; its view was if a person could no longer perform the job he or she was hired to do then that person was no longer needed in the organisation. Therefore the intent behind the creation of an HIV/AIDS policy was to provide management with clear guidelines and procedures when supervising and terminating a person (with HIV/AIDS) who could no longer perform his or her duties. While not a positive example, this case serves to highlight the counter-context to initiatives in support of HIV/AIDS intervention, a shadow side that is always there and reinforces the fact that organisations face a spectrum of choices in the CSR debate.

# Analysis

As the foregoing pen pictures recount, most of these eight organisations were responding, though often in ad hoc ways, to HIV/AIDS in their work environments. Not least, these pen pictures underscore the uniqueness and individuality of each organisation's situation and experience. Where efforts were under way, these were most often preventive in orientation (e.g. awareness workshops, condom provision) although in some cases a more in-depth response was evident (for example HIV testing, and provision of light duties and other forms of support). Very notably, the managers and owners by their own account did not really see themselves as proactively tackling the problem of AIDS but rather as reacting and responding to circumstances and management concerns as they arose. Most responses were explained by a combination of practical need and moral concern. Yet too, in several cases, owners or managers felt their efforts were futile or inadequate, and some indeed ceased to try.

Nevertheless, although the actions may have been small, these cases show that action was taking place among SMEs that extended beyond the traditional remit of employer. These organisations did not use the language of CSR to describe their actions, and their actions were not without problems. However, these efforts still demonstrate the capacity of small businesses in developing economies to innovate socially, and this is an important contribution of this chapter.

What is of further interest for this chapter, however, and the point we go on to develop now in analysis, is the embattled outcomes that most of these initiatives faced, however worthy they might seem on face value. A closer examination of the cases reveals a range of significant driving and resisting factors surrounding these interventions, at the employee, employer and societal levels.

For example, one could assume that it would be in employees' interests to avail themselves of employer initiatives, in cases where they were at risk or infected and in need of assistance. They were not receiving sufficient help from the government and had no other real alternative. However, as these cases show, this assumption is too simplistic. Superstitious beliefs and overt stigma, resulting fear of testing and their concern for survival often were strong disincentives pulling employees against actively engaging with the various initiatives. Moreover, the climate of low-trust employment relations meant employees had little faith that, if they were diagnosed HIV-positive, this would not be used against them, putting them in an even further disadvantaged position.

Employers, on the other hand, had various emotional, practical, voluntary and compulsory concerns that encouraged them to respond to the problem of HIV/ AIDS in their workplaces. Humanitarian duty, moral obligation and retention of skilled workers all acted independently and sometimes together to drive managers and owners to become active in CSR. However, these encouraging factors were often hindered by various obstacles. Lack of guidelines for employers, lack of company resources, lack of employee usage or interest, occasions of employee abuse of programmes, and resulting loss of employer motivation worked to discourage these employers from becoming or remaining active in helping employees. Moreover, a cultural backdrop of frustration with and negative beliefs about employee work motivation played a significant role in several cases.

But employee and employers are not the only actors in this force field. Society itself also plays an important role. South Africa's traditional practice of paternalism combined with the extent and magnitude of the national crisis and the government's call for help all worked together to encourage society to take an active role in the fight against HIV/AIDS. However, societal denial of HIV/AIDS, the extensive stigma and discrimination around the disease, and the lack of individual education all worked to counter the efforts being made. In addition, apartheid plays both a encouraging and discouraging role. The era of apartheid left a legacy of guilt for many people and this guilt has transformed itself into a desire (especially in people more fortunate such as managers and owners of organisations) to help people in need. Though this has a positive dimension, apartheid has also left a legacy of resentment and distrust in people who were wronged during that era. As such, though the apartheid legacy encourages many employers to help their staff, it also discourages staff from trusting managers or making use of workplace initiatives.

## Conceptualising the force field

While the authors puzzled to make sense of the data collected during the analysis phase, we began to think about the actions undertaken by these organisations as analogous to the introduction of behavioural change. Kurt Lewin (1951) describes the context of any change as a force field of driving and resisting forces: driving forces are incentives to change/engage (i.e. the various advantages, motivations and incentives perceived in relation to the introduction of workplace initiatives around HIV/AIDS), while resisting forces are disincentives, or reasons to remain the same (i.e. dynamics pushing against or causing resistance to the introduction, use or effectiveness of such initiatives).

Each factor is shaped by the choices of key actors as stakeholders to the change. The choices of both employers and employees in this case are strongly influenced, contextualised and, in many senses, constrained by the broader social and cultural context. Such a view introduces a notion of **constrained choice**, and is an important empathic point in considering individual agency and seeking to understand actions that may at times seem misguided or even to be acting against one's own best interest in a rational sense. This perspective thus introduces an important area of nuance around human subjectivity, at once celebrating the agency of the individual, and yet recognising dynamics that create its contextualised constraint. Thus a force field emerges, mapped at three levels (society, employer and employee).

In Figure 12.1, we sketch the dimensions of this force field that together serve to create a series of tensions that shape the success and failure of CSR-based initiatives around HIV/AIDS in the workplace.

**FIGURE 12.1** Driving and resisting factors shaping the context of HIV/AIDS responses in the workplace

| | Drivers | Resistors |
|---|---|---|
| **Society** | • Paternalistic culture<br>• Context of national crisis<br>• Government and NGO encouragement | • Societal denial of HIV/AIDS<br>• Cultural stigma and discrimination<br>• Lack of education<br>• Social practice of multiple partners<br>• Female disempowerment<br>• Use of *Sangomas* (traditional healers)<br>• Distrust |
| **Employers** | • Obligation-led actions<br>• Voluntary actions<br>• Emotional concerns<br>• Practical concerns | • Magnitude of issue<br>• Lack of employe usage/interest<br>• Lack of guidance/guidelines<br>• Cost/lack of resources<br>• AIDS is not core duty of business<br>• Loss of programme synergy<br>• Problems with peer educators and HIV/AIDS |
| **Employees** | • High infection rate<br>• Need for assistance<br>• Lack of alternatives | • Taboo topic<br>• Belief in superstitions<br>• Fear of testing<br>• Fear of consequences<br>• Lack of organisational commitment<br>• Survival concern takes precedence over AIDS concern |

Society as an actor in this case is no incidental factor. Structure and, particularly, race emerged as key issues shaping the relationship between employer and employees, their attitudes and beliefs, and their choices. Managers and owners found that their efforts did not take place in a vacuum; it was not a case of 'build it and they will come'. In striving to understand the differing perspectives of organisations, managers and employees, it is inadequate to rely on prescription and idealised management tools.

Thus we suggest that CSR activity takes place within a force field of driving and resisting forces. These forces, operating at employer, employee and societal levels, together interact to complexify the undertaking and success of initiatives around HIV/AIDS in the workplace, and by extension, CSR activities more generally.

It is true that the case of workplace interventions towards HIV/AIDS in South Africa is quite a specific form of CSR. However, looking though the lens of this unique issue has revealed much about the dynamics of corporate social responsibility, the relationship between work and society, and the employment relationship itself. This case brings the role of employee agency, constrained as it might be, into the foreground. For too long, employee choices and actions, and the factors that shape them, have been unseen and unconsidered in the CSR picture.

This simple joining of two ideas—CSR and the force field theory of change— offers an important departure in the context of a literature on corporate social responsibility which largely neglects the emotional and cultural undertow of organisations, and which fails to give equivalence to the input of employees. By introducing this perspective, this chapter focuses attention on the practical challenges and limitations facing organisations seeking to make interventions of this nature, and CSR actions more generally.

## Discussion

In the foregoing accounts it was seen that, although many organisations were taking action, their actions were struggling to thrive and, in some cases, when the surface was scratched it became clear that they were less active than first appeared. There is a tension here in drawing conclusions: while many of these organisations were active in surprising ways towards the AIDS crisis, it would be difficult to claim they were actively trying to combat the problem of HIV/AIDS. Perhaps the fairest conclusion is that they were engaged in trying to survive as a business, and instigating these CSR efforts was done in an effort to retain loyal employees and not have the business go under.

The existing literature on SMEs tends to present two stereotypes of small businesses. First is the 'small is beautiful' scenario where small firms facilitate close and harmonious working relationships (Bolton 1971). The second view is the 'bleak house' scenario where small firms are run autocratically with little regard for employees as individuals. These two polarised views present a very black and white image of the firm, and this initial overview of these eight organisations' involvement or abstinence in CSR initiatives could be seen as evidence to support both views. However, analysis of data reveals that the organisations examined do not fit into either category easily. Rather, they occupy a space between the two. It is fair to say that the situation of SMEs regarding CSR is not black or white.

Overall then, this chapter strives to contribute to academic debate on social responsibility in the organisational context by mapping a practice-led understanding of CSR. Focusing on the specific case of HIV/AIDS, this research identifies factors that not only employers but also policy researchers must take into account if they are to be effective.

These cases allow us to understand a little more about how and why organisations—most especially small, independent organisations—do 'good things'. More importantly perhaps, in the spirit of not only doing things right but doing the right things, this analysis suggests cause for pause to explore the appropriateness and tenor of what those good things are. The intentions of these programmes can scarcely be criticised when there is such a crisis of help and intervention around HIV/AIDS. And yet the paternalistic nature of these interventions in many ways sowed the seeds of their own failure by failing to see the perspective of the individual employee or the force field of resisting factors at play. These cases draw us closer to understanding the mismatch or void that can sometimes exist between employer and employee perspectives, and how little, sometimes, we take into consideration the circumstance, context and role of the 'recipient' in designing such interventions.

The sometimes counterintuitive responses that employees in South Africa demonstrated in respect to actions to help minimise or stem the threat of HIV/AIDS gives us pause to consider just how poorly we understand and engage with the idea of the individual. This case and its conclusions highlight how unidirectional the view of employees truly is within mainstream management literature, and point to the fundamental limitations of a unitaristic view of employee needs. As a particular subset of the management literature, CSR literature reflects this same unidirectionality and flags how 'missing' the employee is—as a real person with real context—in ideas of what constitutes socially responsibly employer behaviour.

This case also builds evidence of the role CSR plays within small and medium-sized organisations. Little has been understood about the various ways small and medium-sized organisations in deliberate and unplanned ways become involved in what equates to (though at times is not even labelled as) social initiative.

The uniqueness of South Africa is also expressed in this chapter. South Africa is a country caught between growing industrialisation and sophistication in management and more traditional, reactive practices. With an economy mirroring the same dynamics, how can CSR initiatives among its SMEs be understood? In this emergent, situated and unfolding context, we see the interplay of two sets of ideas—social activism on one the hand, and instrumentalism on the other. The South African case tells us much about what we need to understand about both of these drives, for a more rounded and, ultimately, more honest view of CSR.

# References

Bolton, J.E. (1971) *Bolton Report: Report on the Committee of Enquiry on Small Firms* (Cmnd 4811; London: HMSO).

Bond, K.M. (1988) 'To Stay or to Leave: The Moral Dilemma of Disinvestment of South African Assets', *Journal of Business Ethics* 7.1–2: 9-18.

Bowmaker-Falconer, A., F.M. Horwitz, H. Jain and S. Taggar (1998) 'Employment Equality Programmes in South Africa: Current Trends', *Industrial Relations Journal* 29.3: 222-33.

Di Norcia, V. (1989) 'The Leverage of Foreigners: Multinationals in South Africa', *Journal of Business Ethics* 8.11: 865-71.

European Commission (2002) *European SMEs and Social and Environmental Responsibility* (Brussels: Enterprise Publications).

Griffin, J., and J. Mahon (1997) 'The Corporate Social Performance and Corporate Financial Performance Debate: Twenty-five Years of Incomparable Research', *Business & Society* 36.1: 5-31.

Kakabadse, A., and N. Kakabadse (2007) 'Introduction', in A. Kakabadse and N. Kakabadse (eds.), *CSR in Practice: Delving Deep* (Basingstoke, UK: Palgrave Macmillan): 1-8.

Lansing, P., and S. Kuruvilla (1988) 'Business Development in South Africa: In Whose Best Interest?', *Journal of Business Ethics* 7.8: 561-74.

Lewin, K. (1951) *Field Theory in Social Science; Selected Theoretical Papers* (New York: Harper & Row).

Margolis, J.D., and J.P. Walsh (2001) *People and Profits: The Search for a Link between a Company's Social and Financial Performance* (Rahway, NJ: Erlbaum Associates).

—— and J.P. Walsh (2003) 'Misery Loves Companies: Rethinking Social Initiatives by Business', *Administrative Science Quarterly* 48: 268-305.

McWilliams, A., and D. Siegel (2000) 'Corporate Social Responsibility and Financial Performance: Correlation or Misspecification?', *Strategic Management Journal* 21.5: 603-609.

Perrini, F. (2006) 'SMEs and CSR Theory: Evidence and Implications from an Italian Perspective', *Journal of Business Ethics* 67: 305-16.

UNAIDS (2006) *Report on the Global AIDS Epidemic* (Geneva: UNAIDS).

—— (2007) *AIDS Epidemic Update 2007* (Geneva: UNAIDS).

UNIDO (2008) 'What is CSR? Defining the Concept', www.unido.org/index.php?id=o72054, accessed 11 October 2008.

Visser, W., C. Middleton and M. McIntosh (2005) 'Corporate Citizenship in Africa', *Journal of Corporate Citizenship* 18 (Summer 2005): 18-20.

# 13

# Innovation in corporate social responsibility: how innovative is it?

## An exploratory study of 129 global innovative CSR solutions[1]

**Céline Louche**
Vlerick Leuven Gent Management School, Belgium

**Samuel O. Idowu**
London Metropolitan University Business School, UK

**Walter Leal Filho**
Hamburg University of Applied Sciences, Germany

Innovation is considered to be one of the main drivers of competitiveness although it is not always easy to achieve (Hoffman *et al.* 1998). It is a general understanding that firms that fail to innovate would survive in their market and industry only for a limited period of time.

To date, little attention has been paid to the fit between corporate social responsibility (CSR) and innovation. The reason for this may not be too obvious even to

1 We would like to thank Maren Lewinski for her help in analysing the data.

the most astute practitioner of the field. We therefore set out in this chapter some of the interrelationships between the two. Our reason for wanting to explore this area is to start the arduous journey of the discourse by academics, practitioners and others who might be interested in the fit between CSR and innovation, and consequently set the scene for scholars' understanding of this fit, perhaps leading to further studies in the area.

This timely shift is regarded as a positive and necessary development for CSR to remain and continue to permeate the business community. But, more importantly, CSR as 'do no harm' is no longer sufficient (Louche and Dodd 2009). There is a compelling need to move beyond this approach in order to embrace a more strategic perspective on CSR. Sustainable development means new partners of consumption and production which necessitates in-depth changes where innovation and creativity are key components (Roome 2006).

Over the last couple of years, corporate social responsibility seems to have embarked on a new journey. While previously CSR was addressed and understood as a way to avoid scandals and bad press, recently it is increasingly being perceived as an innovation driver. This new development provides a whole new perspective to CSR and facilitates a shift from risk management towards a more progressive and entrepreneurial approach that seeks not only to create value to the entity and its stakeholders but also to identify sustainable opportunities for strategic innovation for all interested parties.

The chapter is structured as follows. It first discusses corporate social responsibility and innovation, then explains the methodology used in the study, analyses the data available, provides the results and concludes with some discussions on its implications.

## CSR and innovation

Corporate social responsibility is a highly debated concept. It has been criticised for having unclear boundaries (Lantos 2001), a vague and intangible definition (Frankental 2001; McWilliams and Siegel 2001) and for meaning different things to different people (Kakabadse *et al.* 2005; Idowu 2009). In fact there is still no generally accepted definition of CSR (Carroll 1991; Idowu and Papasolomou 2007). Nonetheless, there is a consensus that CSR includes aspects that are related to economic, social and environmental spheres (the triple bottom line) (Elkington 1997; Carroll 1999). McWilliams and Siegel (2001) define CSR as a set of 'actions that appear to further some social good, beyond the interests of the firm and that which is required by law'.

'Where is innovation in all that?' one may ask. Hart and Milstein (2003) have, for example, argued that innovation is one of the key factors that must be present to facilitate the achievement of CSR objectives and for ensuring a company's continuity (Hart and Milstein 2003). Indeed, the adoption of CSR practices involves a necessary organisational but also cultural change within companies. It requires integrating social and environmental criteria into all their actions. Therefore CSR requires innovation.

Innovation is said to be one of the main vehicles used by corporations for gaining and maintaining competitive advantage. Innovation is usually associated with changing the way things have been previously done, creating something new and/or transforming the environment around in order to facilitate an improvement for the better.

In the literature there is compelling evidence to suggest the emergence of a concept such as 'social innovation', which refers to improvements in the CSR process, and 'eco-innovation', which focuses especially on clean technology (Hockerts and Morsing 2007). Hockerts and Morsing (2007) identify four themes around CSR and innovation: first, 'corporate social innovation'—a concept that was first introduced by Kanter (1999). This concept is based on the argument that firms should use social issues as their learning laboratory for identifying unmet societal needs and for developing solutions that create new markets (Kanter 1999). Second, and closely related to corporate social innovation, is the notion of the 'bottom of the pyramid' (BoP). The BoP premise suggests that, by focusing on the unmet needs of the low-income citizens, firms can create profitable markets while simultaneously contributing to the development of the poor (Prahalad and Hart 2002). The third theme is the concept of 'social entrepreneurship', which is about 'the discovery and sustainable exploitation of opportunities to create public goods' (Hockerts 2007, cited in Hockerts and Morsing 2007). And fourth is the idea of eco-innovation or sustainability innovation which focuses on environmental innovation.

Recently, many businesses have started to engage in CSR as a core aspect of their innovation, taking social and/or environmental concerns beyond mere decency and strategically including them in the core business model (Midttun 2009). However, CSR integration into business processes has been very uneven. The dominant model remains the conceptualisation of CSR primarily as a tool to reduce risks and operational costs (Hockerts 2008). According to Hockerts (2008), only a minority of firms are considering CSR as a factor of innovation. This chapter investigates a large sample of CSR solutions presented as innovative by 72 companies. The objectives are to facilitate a better understanding of the types of innovation that are CSR-related, to identify what sustainability issues are targeted by innovation, and to assess their degree of innovation.

# Methodology

In this section, the methodologies used to select the sample and analyse the data are presented including some concrete examples of CSR solutions and a description of the three-step approach to investigate the solutions.

## CSR solutions: the sample

Our study was based on the analysis of 129 cases. The cases were selected from the CSR Europe Solutions database.[2] CSR Europe is a not-for-profit organisation established in 1996 to encourage European businesses to embed the requirements of corporate social responsibility into their operations. Between 2005 and 2007, CSR Europe collected a database of CSR solutions consisting of CSR actions, initiatives or practices developed by companies in response to sustainability challenges. The solutions were voluntarily submitted by these companies. Each submission follows a standard format and is classified according to themes; 'innovation' is one of the themes. In total 663 CSR solutions are available in the database, among which 137 are classified under the theme of 'innovation'. The analysis focuses on these solutions.

For the purposes of this study, NGOs have been excluded from the analysis in an attempt to focus on profit-seeking companies. In total, six CSR solutions under the theme of 'innovation' were submitted by NGOs. In addition two of the 137 preselected CSR solutions were submitted twice. After withdrawing the solutions provided by NGOs and those submitted twice, we ended up with 129 CSR solutions in the study sample. Examples of the CSR solutions investigated are shown below.

- Development of a range of low-cost products that are fortified with micronutrients and affordable by people on extremely low incomes

- Providing safe drinking water in developing countries at very low cost

- Supporting young people without economic backing to develop their business ideas

- Redesigning a production process to lower its environmental impact

- Develop a new business model that contributes to reducing poverty by creating jobs as well as providing healthy food to the poor

- Contributing to local development by providing remote areas with access to telecommunication

2  For more information see www.csreurope.org (accessed 18 December 2009).

- Investing in research and development to develop new devices to provide water solutions

- Supporting the development of micro-enterprises

- Developing more energy efficient server systems

- Empowering women entrepreneurs in developing and emerging countries

- Changing the business model to provide new services responding to societal challenges

- Rethinking the relationship with suppliers to foster sustainability through the whole supply chain

- Providing access to medicines

- Converting a coal plant into a biomass unit

## Analysing the CSR solutions

The 129 solutions were analysed through a three-step approach, each step of which had a specific purpose and focus. The completion of the three steps led to the completion of the database that has been used for the study.

### Step 1: the company

The first step involves compiling basic information on the company, including sector activity, headquarters country, size, and whether it is a listed company.

### Step 2: the solution

The second step involves describing the solutions, including:

- **The year of submission to CSR Europe**

- **The stakeholder group that benefited from the solution.** After an analysis of all the targeted stakeholders, we classified them into four categories: minority groups, poor or people in need, primary stakeholders, secondary stakeholders and the company itself. Appendix 13.1 on page 304 provides a detailed list of the stakeholder groups

- **The geographical scope of the solution**. Six regions were identified: Australia, Europe, Africa, Asia, North America and rest of the world

- **The involvement of partnership(s) with stakeholders.** The range of stakeholders involved in the partnerships was very broad, from commercial partners to NGOs or governments/local authorities

- **The issues addressed by the solution.** The issues addressed by the different initiatives have been divided into eight dimensions, from G1 to G8, building on the Millennium Development Goals (MDGs). Each dimension focuses on a specific issue such as hunger and poverty (G1) or environmental sustainability (G7). Appendix 13.2 on page 304 provides the complete list of the eight dimensions and compares each with the eight MDGs

## Step 3: the innovative dimension

To assess the innovation dimension, we looked at three different aspects, discussed below.

**Innovativeness of the solution with regard to a societal/sustainability issue.** The objective was to evaluate the extent to which the solution provides a new approach or offers a new solution to a societal problem. We have used and adapted the scale developed by the Schwab Foundation (Kramer 2005), ranging from 'A' to 'D', with an explanation of what each represents, shown in Table 13.1.

**TABLE 13.1** Innovative solution scale

| Scale | Type of solution |
| --- | --- |
| A | The solution is not new |
| B | The solution is new to the area or this region of the world or population, but similar ones are already in place or practised |
| C | The solution was unknown prior to the initiative, but the innovation represents only a minor departure from earlier practice |
| D | The solution brings a truly unique discovery to the social problem it addresses |

Source: adapted from Kramer 2005

**The strategic dimension of the solution: exploration versus exploitation.** The objective was to evaluate whether the solution protects the current assets (exploiting) or develops solutions for the future (exploring). Exploitation and exploration are two very different strategic trajectories. 'Exploitation includes such things as refinement, choice, production, efficiency, selection, implementation, execution . . . The essence of exploitation is the refinement and extension of existing competences, technologies, and paradigms' (March 1991). In contrast, exploration focuses on the discovery of new capabilities and opportunities for the future. 'Exploration includes things captured by terms such as search, variation, risk taking, experimentation, play, flexibility, discovery, innovation . . . The essence of exploration is experimentation with new alternative' (March 1991).

**Type of innovation**. To identify the type of innovation brought by the solution, we have used and adapted the **innovation radar** developed by Sawhney *et al.* (2006). The innovation radar is a comprehensive model for identifying innovation dimensions (Sawhney *et al.* 2006). Anchored in four key dimensions—the offerings a company creates, the customers it serves, the processes it employs, and the points of presence it uses to take its offerings to markets—the radar expands these four axes with eight other related factors. We have adapted these factors to include particular CSR characteristics: we have combined presence and branding into one factor and added two new dimensions—stakeholders and research & development. In total our radar consists of 13 dimensions which are described in Table 13.2.

**TABLE 13.2** The 13 dimensions of innovation

| Dimension | Description |
| --- | --- |
| Offering | Develop innovative new products or services |
| Platform | Use common components or building blocks to create derivative offerings |
| Solution | Create integrated and customised offerings that solve end–to–end customer problems |
| Customers | Discover unmet customer needs or identify under–served customer segments |
| Customer experience | Redesign customer interactions across all touch points and all moments of contact |
| Value capture | Redefine how a company gets paid or create innovative new revenue streams |
| Processes | Redesign core operating processes to improve efficiency and effectiveness and internal processes such as HR |
| Organisation | Change form, function or activity scope of the firm |
| Supply chain | Think differently about sourcing and fulfilment |
| Presence | Create new distribution channels or innovative points of presence, including the places where offerings can be bought or used by customers and brand leverage |
| Networking | Create network-centric intelligent and integrated offerings |
| Stakeholders | Create new ways to engage and involve stakeholders |
| R&D | Think differently about R&D |

Source: adapted from Sawhney *et al.* 2006

# Data analysis

In this section we present the results of our analysis of the data. We first provide information on the sample with some insights on the solutions: the stakeholders and issues targeted by the solutions and the innovative assessment of the solutions.

## The sample

The 129 CSR solutions investigated covered 72 companies headquartered in 15 countries (see Figure 13.1). All the companies are large companies but not all have their stock quoted: 86% of the companies in the sample were stock quoted and 14% were not stock quoted at the date of the submission of the CSR solutions.

**FIGURE 13.1** Distribution of the companies according to the country of the headquarters

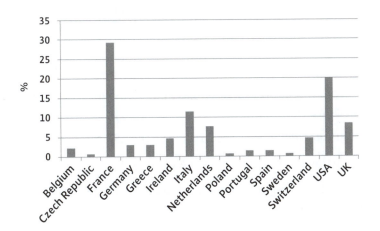

Companies from the sample were drawn from various sectors. The most frequently represented were information technology, financials and consumer staples (see Table 13.3).

The submissions of the CSR solutions are rather well distributed between the three years: 32% in 2005, 29% in 2006 and 39% in 2007. But it is interesting to note that the spread of the year of implementation is very broad: from 1965 to 2007. The two oldest solutions (implemented in 1965 and 1968) are, respectively, about microfinance and building employee engagement in education. Some of the submitted CSR solutions had been implemented for several years, but the majority of the solutions were implemented between 2002 and 2006.

**TABLE 13.3** GICS (Global Industry Classification Standard) sector of the companies from the sample

| GICS sector | % |
| --- | --- |
| Information technology | 17.1 |
| Financials | 16.3 |
| Consumer staples | 14.7 |
| Utilities | 10.8 |
| Consumer discretionary | 10.1 |
| Materials | 8.5 |
| Healthcare | 6.2 |
| Telecommunication services | 6.2 |
| Industrials | 5.4 |
| Energy | 3.1 |
| Other | 1.6 |

## Results

The data analysis was organised around five questions which are presented in the paragraphs below:

- Which stakeholder groups are targeted by the CSR solutions?
- What are the issues addressed by the solutions?
- What are the strategic dimensions of the innovation (exploitation versus exploration)?
- How innovative are the solutions?
- What types of innovation are covered by the solutions?

### Which stakeholder groups are targeted by the CSR solutions?

The CSR solutions have targeted a wide range of stakeholders from the company itself (meaning, for example, its production processes or its building) to some specific groups such as blind or disabled people, temporary workers, older people or a specific region in a specific country (see Figure 13.2). But more than 30% of the solutions have targeted the primary stakeholders of the company: that is, employees, clients and suppliers. These solutions are about customised products to respond to a specific need of clients, or technology development often related to environmental issues such as energy efficiency, climate change or water, but are also about setting up fair-trade systems in the supply chain, stimulating diversity and inclusion in the company or providing enhanced healthcare systems for the employees.

**FIGURE 13.2** Distribution of the stakeholder groups targeted by the CSR solutions

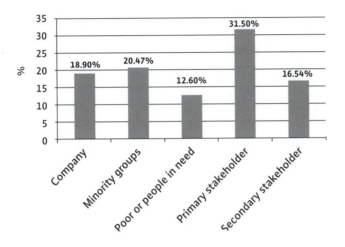

Minority groups—specific groups such as children, drivers, farmers, blind people or people with disabilities (see complete list in Appendix 13.1 on page 304)—constitute about 20% of the targeted stakeholders. Those solutions are mainly about social issues such as diversity, empowerment, demography, human capital but also poverty and solidarity. Although a majority of the CSR solutions target populations or stakeholder groups that are in emerging or developing regions such as India, Africa and Indonesia, quite a number target marginal groups in the country of their headquarters either in Europe or North America. Possibly overlapping with the minority groups is the 'poor or people in need' category. This group focuses only on G1: that is poverty reduction and solidarity or extreme or crisis situations such as earthquakes, hurricanes or floods. All but one of the solutions targeting this category are in developing countries; one targets poor people in Italy. Together, these two categories represent 57% of the solutions.

Finally, 19% of the solutions target companies and are almost entirely related to environmental concerns such as energy, waste, $CO_2$ emissions, transportation or sustainable buildings; 17% target the secondary stakeholders such as local authorities, local communities, governments and others. These solutions are predominantly related to social issues.

It is also interesting to note that about 40% of the solutions are applied in the country of the headquarters. This shows the importance of first managing those stakeholders closer to home before going further afield.

## What are the issues addressed by the solutions?

As shown in Figure 13.3, more than a third of the CSR solutions address environmental issues. A large majority of them are about energy and climate change challenges. Water and waste are also issues that are frequently addressed in these solutions. Others are about reducing, measuring and monitoring their environmental impacts. Five of the environmental solutions also address social or/and economic issues by, for example, providing easy access to environmentally friendly energy to the poor or excluded people or by developing projects around green supply chains in developing countries and thereby contributing to the economic development of the area.

**FIGURE 13.3** Environmental and social issues addressed by the CSR solutions

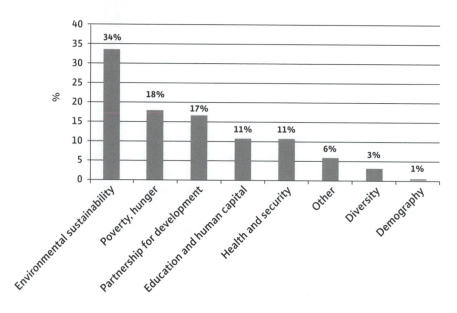

The theme of poverty reduction accounts for 18% of the solutions: contributing to basic needs such as food and water, providing access to technology, finance, and education to remote populations. Some others are about the implementation of fair trade.

Global or local partnership development is the concern of 17% of the solutions. Part of these solutions involves strong partnerships with local or global communities or authorities: for example, a partnership between government and the company to establish electrification programmes to remote communities at an affordable price. Another example is a project that aims to revive the community spirit and thereby reduce a number of social problems such as drugs, crime and prostitution in some specific areas in the UK.

Other partnership development solutions are about facilitating connections between communities or organisations to provide answers to specific problems: for example, a solution that provides platforms or 'meeting places' for connecting donors and aid organisations all over the world. Another one focuses on harnessing the computational power of computer idle time to undertake important scientific investigations. Another solution provides supporting platforms to facilitate collaborative solutions between governments and businesses.

A further 11% of the solutions tackle issues about human health and disease, terrorism and security, such as obesity, children's online safety, local security and development or access to medicine. And the same number of solutions (11%) cover education, among which one concerns compensation and benefits measures.

Our results suggest that only a small minority of these companies address issues relating to diversity and demographic challenges. Finally, it is worth noting that many of the solutions address more than one issue.

### What are the strategic dimensions of the innovation (exploitation versus exploration)?

Over half (56%) of these CSR solutions relate to exploitation while 44% relate to exploration. This means that a small number of the solutions are about exploring new avenues and possibilities. Companies tend to develop solutions that adapt to existing systems rather than change the systems; solutions that are more focused on refinement and efficiency rather than experimentation and risk taking. Of course, it is impossible to draw any conclusion from this as it would require analysis of the entire CSR solution portfolio of all the companies to establish whether they are of the exploitative or explorative type. However, it gives an indication since these solutions are presented as representative of the CSR approach (March 1991) of the companies in the sample.

Although there are more exploitative types of solution than explorative, the distribution is not far from equal. March (1991) argued that it is essential to maintain an appropriate balance between the two types for the survival and prosperity of these companies and the system as a whole. If companies focus their efforts mainly on exploitation they may not be ready to face changes in the environment and similarly not able to react in a timely and appropriate manner to the changes. On the other hand, when a company or a system excludes exploitation in order to concentrate on exploration it is 'likely to suffer the costs of experimentation without gaining many of its benefits' (March 1991) since it is more likely to lose the benefits which could accrue from the learning curve process.

## How innovative are the solutions?

Less than 7% or nine of the initiatives can be regarded as 'really' innovative: that is, bringing in a solution that leads to a unique discovery or a unique way of addressing a societal or environmental problem (category D on our scale; see Table 13.1). Four of these address environmental issues (energy, natural resources depletion and environmental impacts); five are concerned with social and economic issues (poverty, food issues, access to drinkable water, access to finance). Four of the D solutions are applied in the home country of the headquarters; five are applied outside (mainly in emerging or developing countries). Six are executed in partnership with one or several organisations (such as NGOs, governments or commercial partners); three did not involve a partnership. Eight are of an explorative type; one is about exploitation. It is therefore possible to suggest that the characteristics that distinguish the most innovative solutions from the others are the involvement of a partnership and the exploration orientation of the solutions used.

On the other side, the solutions that have been classified as not at all innovative—marked 'A' on our scale—represent 36% of our sample, which is a significant number. This is not to say that those 'A' solutions have no societal benefits, but they have nothing new or unique either in terms of objective or in the structure or process. These solutions are well known and widespread initiatives such as corporate donations, raising awareness among consumers or implementing fair-trade policies. Among those solutions, 20% or seven have involved a partnership and only 8% or three of them are of an explorative type. A solution can be non-innovative within the whole field of CSR but explorative in terms of a single company.

Finally, the in-between solutions—the 'B' solutions (those new to an area or region) and the 'C' solutions (those representing only a minor departure from current practice)—together represent 67% of the CSR solutions.

Figure 13.4 provides an overview of the distribution of the 129 solutions according to their innovation levels.

We have also looked at the repartition of the solutions according to their level of innovation and the issues they address (see Tables 13.4 and 13.5). Table 13.4 provides a summary of G1–G8 and their areas of focus. Table 13.5 shows that G1 (poverty, hunger, wealth distribution) is the issue with by far the highest percentage of innovative solutions followed by G6 (environmental sustainability). On the other side, almost 89% of the solutions in G8 (others) are not innovative ('A' type) while 11% are of the 'B' type. G2 (education and human capital), G5 (health and security), G6 (environmental sustainability) and G7 (partnership for development) have solutions that range from very innovative to not innovative. Interestingly, G3 (diversity) and G4 (demographic issues) are concentrated around the 'B' and 'C' types of solution.

**FIGURE 13.4** Distribution of the 'A', 'B', 'C' and 'D' solutions (degree of innovation)

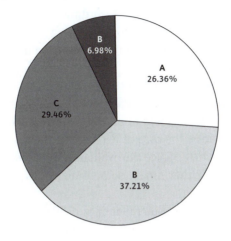

**TABLE 13.4** A summary of G1–G8

| Scale | Areas of interest |
| --- | --- |
| G1 | Poverty, hunger, and wealth distribution |
| G2 | Education and human capital |
| G3 | Diversity |
| G4 | Demographic issues |
| G5 | Health and security |
| G6 | Environmental issues |
| G7 | Partnership for development |
| G8 | Others |

**TABLE 13.5** Cross table: level of innovativeness and issue addressed (%)

|  | G1 | G2 | G3 | G4 | G5 | G6 | G7 | G8 |
| --- | --- | --- | --- | --- | --- | --- | --- | --- |
| A | 7.41 | 31.25 | 0.00 | 0.00 | 37.50 | 16.00 | 28.00 | 88.89 |
| B | 48.15 | 43.75 | 60.00 | 100.00 | 43.75 | 34.00 | 36.00 | 11.11 |
| C | 25.93 | 18.75 | 40.00 | 0.00 | 12.50 | 42.00 | 32.00 | 0.00 |
| D | 18.52 | 6.25 | 0.00 | 0.00 | 6.25 | 8.00 | 4.00 | 0.00 |
| Total | 100.00 | 100.00 | 100.00 | 100.00 | 100.00 | 100.00 | 100.00 | 100.00 |

## What types of innovation are covered by the solutions?

In terms of solutions, innovation is far broader in scope than product or technological innovation (Sawhney *et al.* 2006). According to Sawhney *et al.* (2006), business innovation is about 'new value not new thing', as creating new things may not be sufficient to create value. It is about creating value to the customers, other stakeholders and the firm by creatively changing one or more dimensions of the business system. Therefore, following the innovation radar of Sawhney *et al.*, we have examined the dimensions through which the CSR solutions have potentially brought opportunities for business to innovate and consequently create value to all concerned. One needs to be careful with the use of words here; therefore, the word 'potentially' is preferred since the evaluation is based on a limited amount of information which may either hinder some dimensions or over-emphasise other dimensions.

Figure 13.5 shows the innovation radar of the 129 CSR solutions analysed in this study. The solutions consider not only offerings and solutions but also strengthening stakeholder relationships with companies. A number of these solutions are about providing new types of product or service which are valuable for meeting sustainability challenges; developing customised, integrated combinations of products, services and information that solve a particular customer's problems or a group of customers or some other stakeholder groups' problems; which simultaneously lead to developing new and innovative partnerships with various stakeholder groups. The issues addressed also cover processes. A number of solutions addressed have changed the configuration of business activities that are used to conduct internal business operations. These solutions, for example, involve the redesign of production processes for greater energy efficiency or for reducing waste production.

**FIGURE 13.5** Innovation radar of the 129 CSR solutions

Looking at specific sub-groups from our sample, it became apparent to us that the solutions that are implemented in the home country of the headquarters tend to have a stronger influence on the offering dimension while the solutions implemented outside the home country tend to focus on the solutions and stakeholder relationship dimensions.

When looking at the place of implementation—headquarters country or outside—with the stakeholder group targeted, we notice some interesting differences as shown in Figures 13.6 and 13.7. It could be seen that the most important differences between these two sub-groups are in terms of the categories—poor or people in need and secondary stakeholders.

**FIGURE 13.6** Percentage and allocation of stakeholders groups where activities are allocated towards the country of the company's headquarters

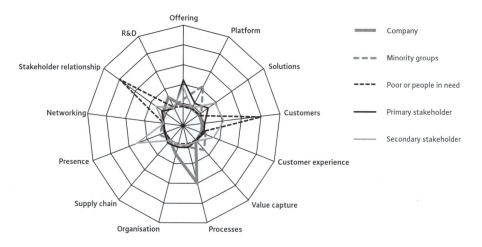

The innovation radar provides a valuable tool to assess the innovative dimension of the solutions. But it presents a severe limitation: it doesn't say anything about value creation for society. It requires corporations to change and adapt their existing strategy to refocus actions on customers and the firm. What about the other stakeholders? Of course, corporations are multi-stakeholder entities and will not survive for long unless they are aware of this fact in everything they do. To ignore the interests of any of their stakeholders could be fatal, if not straight away then certainly in the immediate future. Therefore, innovation for CSR should be more than only increasing the value proposition solely for customers and companies but should take into account society as a whole.

**FIGURE 13.7** Percentage and allocation of stakeholder groups where activities are allocated towards other countries

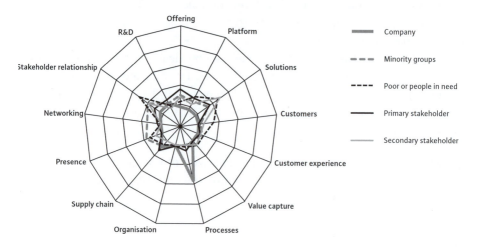

## Discussion and conclusion

Corporate social responsibility has been highly criticised for being too frag-
mented and disconnected from business and strategy (Idowu and Towler 2004;
Maignan and Ferrell 2004). Porter and Kramer (2006) also note that the prevailing
approaches to CSR are so disconnected from business as to obscure many of the
greatest opportunities for companies to benefit society (Porter and Kramer 2006).
Are these criticisms of CSR suggesting that it is an irrelevant activity? The answer is
certainly no, but scholars are suggesting that more innovation is required in order
to enable society to derive the greatest possible benefits from the field and all that
it stands for.

In this chapter, we have analysed 129 CSR solutions presented as 'innovative' by
these companies themselves. The solutions mainly address environmental issues
(most specifically those related to the energy challenge) and poverty. A significant
number of the solutions have led to a partnership either with civil society (governmental organisations) or commercial partners. But the degree of the innovative
aspect remains limited and a majority of it is related to either refining or exploiting
existing technologies or in some cases offering new avenues for exploring these
technologies. On the one hand we should recognise the efforts of companies to
come up with innovative solutions to respond to CSR-related challenges; however,

more is needed in order to bring about real change towards sustainable development.

Porter and Kramer (2006) have suggested that CSR can both be a source of good and a wellspring of innovation, competitive advantage and value creation for the firm (Porter and Kramer 2006). It seems that, as of today, CSR has not yet reached its full potential. How can firms derive these value-generating activities which Porter and Kramer (2006) were suggesting? One of the objectives of this chapter was to provide a framework that points to some of these value-adding innovative activities which the 129 CSR Europe solutions have in store for corporate entities. Grayson *et al.* (2008) argue that to achieve S²AVE (Shareholder and Social Added Value Environment) does not really require a re-engineering of the corporate structure but rather a new mind-set which requires corporate entities to take ten 'simple' steps (Grayson *et al.* 2008):

- Make innovating for sustainability a part of your company's vision

- Formulate a strategy with sustainability at its heart

- Embed sustainability in every part of your business

- Walk the talk: emphasise actions, not words

- Set up a body at board level with the power to make sustainability matter

- Set firm rules

- Bring your stakeholders on board

- Use people power

- Join the networks

- Think beyond reporting: align all business systems with the company's vision of sustainability

Firms that innovate in the field of CSR can soon discover that there are social opportunities to derive from taking this action. Both society and these firms would consequently benefit from the action.

While we recognise and accept that innovation must accelerate change towards sustainability, we also need to acknowledge that innovation has undesirable consequences that can produce the opposite effect to that intended (Roger 2003). As Roger (2003) wrote: 'Invention and diffusion are but means to an ultimate end: the consequences that result from adoption of an innovation'. But we cannot assume that the consequences of all the CSR-related innovation will produce beneficial results for society. Microfinance has been highly criticised for some of its negative consequences (Rogaly 1996; Buckley 1997; Ashta and Hudon 2009). Indeed, most of the reasons for current unsustainable patterns of production and consumption are the outcome of the unintended and undesirable consequences of innovation. It would be an illusion to believe that one can fully master and manage the consequences of innovation. However, one can monitor the consequences and correct trajectory when necessary. Therefore, innovation is a continuous and dynamic process which is perhaps an endless chain in the corporate arena.

# References

Ashta, A., and M. Hudon (2009) 'To whom should we be fair? Ethical Issues in Balancing Stakeholder Interests from Banco Compartamos Case Study' (Vol. CEB Working Paper No. 09/036; Brussels: Centre Emile Bernheim, Solvay Brussels School of Economics and Management).

Buckley, G. (1997) 'Microfinance in Africa: Is it Either the Problem or the Solution?', *World Development* 25.7: 1,081-93.

Carroll, A.B. (1991) 'The Pyramid of Corporate Social Responsibility: Towards the Moral Management of Organisational Stakeholders', *Business Horizons* 34.4: 39-48.

—— (1999) 'Corporate Social Responsibility: Evolution of a Definitional Construct', *Business & Society* 38.3: 268-95.

Elkington, J. (1997) *Cannibals with Forks* (Oxford, UK: Capstone Publishing).

Frankental, P. (2001) 'Corporate Social Responsibility: A PR Invention?', *Corporate Communication: An International Journal* 6.1: 18-23.

Grayson, D., Z. Jin, M. Lemon, M.A. Rodriguez, S. Slaughter and S. Tay (2008) 'A New Mindset for Corporate Sustainability' (white paper sponsored by BT and Cisco; SoM Working and Occasional Papers; https://dspace.lib.cranfield.ac.uk/bitstream/1826/4161/1/A_new_mindset_for_corporate_sustainability.pdf).

Hart, S.L., and M.B. Milstein (2003) 'Creating Sustainable Value', *Academy of Management Executive* 17.2: 56-69.

Hockerts, K. (2008) 'Managerial Perceptions of the Business Case for Corporate Social Responsibility' (cbsCSR Working Paper, Vol. No 03-2007; Copenhagen: Copenhagen Business School).

—— and M. Morsing (2007) *A Literature Review on Corporate Social Responsibility in the Innovation Process* (Copenhagen: Copenhagen Business School).

Hoffman, K., M. Parejo, J. Bessant and L. Perren (1998) 'Small Firms, R&D, Technology and Innovation in the UK: A Literature Review', *Technovation* 18.1: 3,956.

Idowu, S.O. (2009) 'Practicing Corporate Social Responsibility in the UK', in S.O. Idowu and W.L.F. Idowu (eds.), *Global Practices of CSR* (Berlin: Springer).

—— and I. Papasolomou (2007) 'Are the Corporate Social Responsibility Matters Based on Good Intentions or False Pretences? An Empirical Study of the Motivations behind the Issuing of CSR Reports by UK Companies', *Corporate Governance: International Journal of Business in Society* 7.2: 146-47.

—— and B.A. Towler (2004) 'A Comparative Study of the Contents of Corporate Social Responsibility Reports of UK Companies', *Management of Environmental Quality: An International Journal* 15.4: 420-37.

Kakabadse, N.K., C. Rozuel and L. Lee-Davies (2005) 'Corporate Social Responsibility and Stakeholder Approach: A Conceptual View', *International Journal of Business Governance and Ethics* 1.4: 277-302.

Kanter, R.M. (1999) 'From Spare Change to Real Change: The Social Sector as a Beta Site for Business Innovation', *Harvard Business Review* 77: 123-32.

Kramer, M.R. (2005) *Measuring Innovation: Evaluation in the Field of Social Entrepreneurship* (Palo Alto, CA: Skoll Foundation/Foundation Strategy Group).

Lantos, G.P. (2001) 'The Boundaries of Strategic Corporate Social Responsibility', *Journal of Consumer Marketing* 18.7: 595-632.

Louche, C., and T. Dodd (2009) 'Reframing Corporate Social Responsibility', *Reflets et perspectives de la vie économique* 4.18: 59-68.

Maignan, I., and O.C. Ferrell (2004) 'Corporate Social Responsibility and Marketing: An Integrative Framework', *Journal of the Academy of Marketing Science* 32.1: 3-19.

March, J. (1991) 'Exploration and Exploitation in Organizational Learning', *Organizational Science* 2.1: 71-87.

McWilliams, A., and D. Siegel (2001) 'Corporate Social Responsibility: A Theory of the Firm Perspective', *Academy of Management Review* 26.1: 117-27.

Midttun, A.E. (2009) 'Strategic CSR Innovation: Serving Societal and Individual Needs' (Research Report 2/2009; Oslo: Norwegian School of Management).

Porter, M.E., and M.R. Kramer (2006) 'Strategy and Society: The Link between Competitive Advantage and Corporate Social Responsibility', *Harvard Business Review* 84.12: 78-92.

Prahalad, C.K., and S.L. Hart (2002) 'The Fortune at the Bottom of the Pyramid', *Business & Strategy* 26: 54-67.

Rogaly, B. (1996) 'Microfinance Evangelism, "Destitute Women" and the Hard Selling of a New Anti-poverty Formula', *Development in Practice* 6.2: 100-12.

Roger, E.M. (2003) *Diffusion of Innovations* (New York: The Free Press, 5th edn).

Roome, N.J. (2006) 'Competitiveness, Corporate Responsibility and Innovation', presentation to the EU Conference on Competitiveness, Corporate Responsibility and Innovation under the Finnish Presidency, Brussels, 22 November 2006.

Sawhney, M., R.C. Wolcott and I. Arroniz (2006) 'The 12 Different Ways for Companies to Innovate', *MIT Sloan Management Review* 47.3: 75-81.

# Appendix 13.1 Classification of the stakeholder groups

| Minority groups | Poor or people in need | Primary stakeholders | Secondary stakeholders | Company |
|---|---|---|---|---|
| • Children | • Poor | • Employees | • Local authority | • Company |
| • Drivers | • People in need | • Clients | • Local communities | • Production |
| • Farmers | • Poor population | • Suppliers | • Local community | • Green building |
| • Students | • Distressed populations | • Consumers | • Local population | |
| • Temporary workers | • Emerging markets | | • Local entrepreneurship | |
| • Women | | | • Citizens | |
| • Young people | | | • Government | |
| • NGOs | | | • SMEs | |
| • Blind | | | • Micro-entrepreneurs | |
| • Disabled people | | | | |
| • Disadvantaged people | | | | |
| • Older people or people with disabilities | | | | |
| • People with disabilities | | | | |
| • Vulnerable customers | | | | |

# Appendix 13.2 Classification of the targeted issues

| | Classification used for the purpose of the study | Millennium Development Goals (MDGs) |
|---|---|---|
| G1 | Poverty, distribution of wealth, hunger, solidarity | Eradicate extreme poverty and hunger |
| G2 | Education, human capital, employees health and safety | Achieve universal primary education |
| G3 | Diversity, gender equality, empower women, equal opportunities | Promote gender equality and empower women |
| G4 | Demography, ageing population, growing and developing population, transparency | Reduce child mortality |
| G5 | Human health and diseases, nutrition and health, terrorism and security, health and safety | Improve maternal health |
| G6 | Environmental sustainability, climate change, energy, pollution, natural resources | Combat HIV/AIDS, malaria and other diseases |
| G7 | Global/local partnership for development | Ensure environmental sustainability |
| G8 | Other | Develop a global partnership for development |

# 14
# Towards a sustainable innovation model for small enterprises

**Steven P. MacGregor and Joan Fontrodona**
IESE Business School, Spain

**Jose Hernandez**
University of Strathclyde, UK

Innovation is one of the main drivers for competitiveness, yet it is far from easy to achieve. Evidence suggests that 'though innovative effort appears to be widespread, this does not translate directly into improved firm performance and, ultimately, greater profitability' (Hoffman *et al.* 1998). In addition, the expectations from customers and society have evolved, becoming extremely sensitive to the perceived ethical behaviour of organisations. Today, being a successful and innovative business requires consideration of the social and environmental impact of operational processes, stimulating employees to be creative and collaborating with customers, suppliers and other business partners in the design and development of new products and services.

Innovation is therefore hard to achieve and arguably even more so when having to address the increasing ethical expectations of society. Yet CSR and innovation have rarely been considered together, either in practice or theory. The RESPONSE project was a practical exploration that aimed to uncover some of the main issues for CSR and innovation, as applied to SMEs, a sector of industry that accounts for 98% of all European firms and which generates 66% of all the jobs.

In this chapter we present the RESPONSE project, which explored the relationship between innovation and CSR in 60 SMEs throughout Europe who were interviewed on-site, together with other informal discussions, analysis of the literature and model development over a 15-month period. We aimed to help SMEs add value to their business operations at the same time as behaving more responsibly. The chapter is structured as follows. First, a background section details the project context and motivation as well as a brief state of the art on CSR, SMEs and innovation. Research methodology is then presented followed by the project findings and main result: the RESPONSE model for sustainable innovation. This is followed by the presentation of a case study on a highly mature SME from the research—which the RESPONSE model may go some small way to producing. Finally a general discussion of the principal motivation of the research—mainstreaming of CSR in SMEs—concludes the chapter through reference to classic diffusion theory on innovation.

## Background

### CSR, innovation and SMEs

Although CSR is mostly a product of the 20th century, especially in the 2000s, the CSR movement has become a global phenomenon (Carroll 2008). The multiplicity of existing definitions and approaches makes it difficult to find a common base for defining what CSR is. Even the concept itself is far from being unanimous, and the attempts to classify CSR theories have been numerous (Spence 1999; Garriga and Melé 2004; Melé 2008). One of the most widely accepted definitions was coined by the European Commission (2001): 'A concept whereby companies integrate social and environmental concerns in their business operations and in their interactions with their stakeholders on a voluntary basis'.

CSR, as a broad concept that includes aspects related to economic, social and environmental spheres (Boatright 1993; Carroll 1999), introduces not only a change of philosophy in the business world, but, in more practical terms, means a new way of doing business, and requires that companies adapt their activities, organisational structures and processes (Castelo and Lima 2006; Lopez-Perez et al. 2007).

For that reason, a relation between CSR practices and innovation on products and processes seems to be clear, although some authors have demanded a more dynamic interpretation of CSR in order to accommodate a closer fit between CSR and innovation (Midttun 2007). There is also an open debate about the relation between CSR and competitiveness of companies (Vilanova et al. 2009). Grayson and Hodges (2004) maintained that innovation from non-traditional areas, such as those within the CSR agenda, is one of the drivers for business success. And Porter and Kramer (2006) have argued that there are opportunities for companies to benefit society by leveraging the firm's resources (Midttun 2007; Vilanova *et al.* 2009).

Furthermore, CSR has traditionally been associated with large companies. However, recognition of the importance of business ethics and social responsibility for the small- and medium-size enterprise sector has led to an increasing interest both at the researcher level and on the management side (Spence 1999; Fuller 2003; Spence *et al.* 2003, 2004; Jenkins 2004, 2009; Murillo and Lozano 2009). SMEs find their own internal and external drivers and barriers to social performance (Kusyk and Lozano 2007) and CSR could provide significant scope for competitive advantage for SMEs, not only a cost burden (Tilley 2003). Innovation, and specifically developing innovative products and services with CSR credentials, has been considered as one viable source of competitive advantage (Lefebvre and Lefebvre 1993; Jenkins 2009), although it has been acknowledged that sometimes SMEs do not have either the structure or the time to bring in all management innovations as they are created (Spence 1999; Baker 2003; Murillo and Lozano 2009).

## Project context and motivation

The RESPONSE project was a 15-month investigation conducted by partners with a diverse and complementary set of skills from Spain, the UK and Italy. Funded through a 'mainstreaming CSR in SMEs' grant from DG Enterprise & Industry, the initial aim of the research was to show that corporate social responsibility may not just be seen as an additional cost for the enterprise, rather something that could add value and, in our case, add value through innovation. The main output of the research was the RESPONSE model, presented later in the chapter, which can be used to diagnose or guide CSR and innovation activities in the enterprise.

To address European Commission aims and help mainstream CSR in SMEs the project counted on partner strengths as follows. IESE Business School provided academic expertise and rigour in CSR. Cluster Conocimiento, an association of public and private entities in the Basque Country, provided expertise in clusters and networks, and had previously developed a CSR network for SMEs. Network effects were also exploited by Politecnico Innovazione in Milan which functions as the Innovation Relay Centre (IRC) for Lombardia region. In its role as an IRC, Politecnico Innovazione also has many years of experience working with SMEs, something that is also at the core of the missions for the remaining two partners, University of Strathclyde in Glasgow, UK, and the University of Girona, Spain. The aim was therefore to develop a model that is rigorous but practical, taking account of the reality of the SME and the importance of building relationships, or social capital (Fuller and Tian 2006). To encourage ongoing development, a network was formed around the initial participants—the 60 SMEs interviewed and other intermediary agencies—who can also reference the freely available teaching and training material produced to disseminate the model and research.[1]

The challenge of mainstreaming CSR in SMEs is significant. The EC's call for 'mainstreaming CSR in European SMEs' aims to make CSR uptake a voluntary process instead of imposing a tranche of regulatory initiatives. The main aim is to effectively diffuse or 'mainstream' CSR in SMEs. Our own approach was to demonstrate the link with innovation, thereby showing SMEs that CSR implementation may lead to a more successful enterprise. Much of the existing development in Europe related to mainstreaming is framed within a discussion on 'scaling up'. An example of the scale of the challenge is the big-budget, Danish, People and Profit project, which aims to train 12,000 SME managers and employees, which still only represents 2% of the workforce in Danish private companies. Existing networks and structures should therefore be exploited together with a better understanding of what SMEs really need and how they are most influenced. The amount of field research completed on CSR and SMEs, at least at the time of the RESPONSE project, was very small, especially when also considering innovation. Most development can be traced to the community surrounding DG Enterprise's CSR team which has created a number of initiatives in recent years, including expert groups, newsletters and grant calls. Innovation, where mentioned, has been part of the limited discussion on the business case for CSR.

## Research methodology

Given the lack of an advanced knowledge base on CSR and innovation, the research was exploratory in nature. Development was advanced through case studies, based principally on in-company, semi-structured interviews across the four European regions where the project partners were based—Catalonia, the Basque Country, Lombardia and the West of Scotland (see Figure 14.1). An overview of the research methodology is presented in Table 14.1.

---

1 See project website for intermediate and final outputs: www.udg.edu/cid/response (accessed 19 December 2009).

**FIGURE 14.1** Project partner locations and focus

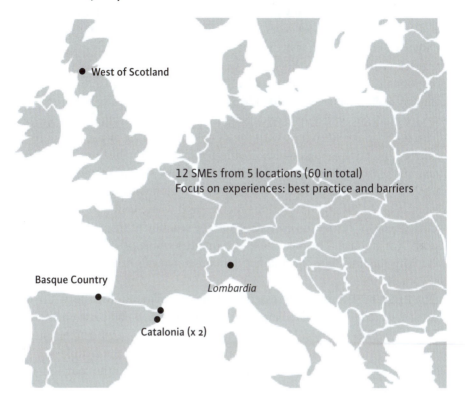

**TABLE 14.1** RESPONSE research methodology

|  | Preliminary interviews | Business cases | Sustainable network |
| --- | --- | --- | --- |
| Research focus | Descriptive: what do SMEs currently do regarding CSR and innovation? | Prescriptive: how can we improve current practice based on what we know? Experimental testing and evaluation | Prescriptive: scaling up support tools and methods based on previous evaluation stage |
| Number of companies | 60 (12 in each location) | 8 (2 in each location) | As many as possible |

Preliminary interviews were conducted with the 60 SMEs using two question-naires: a simple, quantitative-based questionnaire 'A' which uncovered basic activi-ties in innovation and CSR, and a more detailed, qualitative-based questionnaire 'B' which allowed the interviewer to probe more deeply into the content of part A and served as a basis for open discussion. Part A also served as a screen to filter only those companies with at least an interest or profile in either CSR or innovation. On average there was a two-week gap between data collection based on questionnaire A and B, and, in most cases, questionnaire A was completed by the company in advance of a research visit. The research visit, conducted by two members of the research team, in most but not all cases, began with a review of the answers to questionnaire A before the semi-structured interview based on questionnaire B. All company respondents were either the owner/managing director of the company or a senior manager with a deep understanding of company strategy and operations. These preliminary interviews with the sample of 60 SMEs focused on description of current practice though questionnaire B facilitated the beginning of investigation into the rationale associated with such practice. The next stage was to take a sample of the eight best SMEs (two from each region with 'best' meaning the biggest uptake of CSR and innovation practice, and where CSR and innovation were well aligned) for further investigation and the creation of short case studies showcasing best practice. The focus here was on prescribing practice that would work well, with the final focus an attempt to mainstream this practice through a wider network of SMEs.

The RESPONSE model progressed through several iterations. The first main version of the model was created after the literature review and basic understanding of the link between CSR and innovation. The second main version of the model was created after the completion of questionnaires A and B for the sample of 60 SMEs and the third and final version of the model was created after the completion of the eight case studies.

Although many definitions exist for CSR, we took a pragmatic approach, simply viewing CSR as positive social, environmental and economic actions in the following five areas: environment, community, customer, supply chain and employees. Table 14.2 details the main activities carried out by the project sample.

A definition of innovation is also necessary. Slowly but surely, the view that equates innovation exclusively with high technology and new products is being abandoned and innovation is at last coming to be understood as a broad, continuous and systematic activity that takes place throughout the enterprise (Sawhney et al. 2006; Hamel 2006; Vila and MacGregor 2007). However, such a view is still far from widespread and perhaps only practised by highly mature organisations. Enterprises, particularly SMEs, need to begin somewhere, often a narrow, departmentalised view of innovation such as NPD (new product development), or housed in the marketing function only. Narrow, departmentalised application has of course been the bugbear of the CSR field also, at times being manifested as a reactive phenomenon tied to the public relations department in a company. In its own evolution, such a notion is becoming less and less pronounced, as it is diffused throughout the company consciousness. With this background we took a very simple view of innovation in the sample SMEs, taking interest in anything that was

**TABLE 14.2** CSR classification and sample activities

| Environmental | Supply chain/business-to-business |
|---|---|
| • ISO 14001<br>• Waste minimisation, re-use and recycling schemes<br>• Reduction in use of harmful chemicals<br>• Reduction in atmospheric emissions<br>• Use energy from renewable sources<br>• Membership of environmental organisations<br>• Investment in new technology<br>• Environmental reporting<br>• Award-winning environmental schemes | • Open-house policy for customers, suppliers and competitors to look around<br>• Directors of business associations<br>• Seeking to develop long-term partnerships with customers and suppliers<br>• Supplier learning schemes<br>• Measurement of key performance indicators and feedback to staff, customers and suppliers<br>• Winners of industry awards, e.g. world-class manufacturing or service industry excellence<br>• Support and encouragement for suppliers to become more socially responsible<br>• Take part in industry best-practice programmes<br>• ISO 9001 quality standard |
| **Employees** | **Community/society** |
| • Investors in people<br>• Flat management structures<br>• Creation of good work–life balance and family-friendly employment<br>• Employee newsletters<br>• Social events for staff<br>• Employees sent to developing countries to undertake community projects<br>• Award-winning training and development programmes for employees<br>• Employment of older and disabled people<br>• One-to-one mentoring of employees<br>• 360° appraisal schemes<br>• Higher salaries<br>• Idea suggestion schemes | • Work with local schools on projects, e.g. working with children with learning difficulties<br>• Donate percentage of profits to charity/donations to local cultural and sporting events<br>• Supporting local homeless people<br>• Sponsorship of local sports teams<br>• Involvement in awards schemes for young people<br>• Time banks for employees to work in the community<br>• Social auditing<br>• Employ people from the local community<br>• Working on community projects in developing countries<br>• Work experience placements<br>• Award-winning community engagement programmes |
| **Customers** | |
| • Design for all<br>• Ecodesign<br>• Co-design<br>• Training programmes<br>• Open-door day | |

new in the enterprise and recording innovative activity as any new implemented activity in the areas of product, process or management. For example, the questions used to identify innovation activity in the primary questionnaire (A) pertained to the implementation of any new product, process or management innovation in the past five years. The details and effects of any action noted here were investigated more fully in the follow-up semi-structured interview.

## Main project findings

Examining the type of CSR in which enterprises engaged, we found the most common to be employee activities at 30%. One advantage that SMEs have over larger business is the fact that employees may feel more visible and better valued as part of a smaller workforce. With the right initiatives this can lead to a more multi-skilled, more highly motivated workforce with each employee playing a part in value creation. The most popular single employee activity was the Investors in People accreditation, which involves many other activities, including training and suggestion schemes. The next most popular category is involvement with the local community, found in over a quarter of all cases (26%). This is perhaps not surprising as many SMEs are family-owned businesses with a long history in the local area or created by entrepreneurs with a guiding set of values. Activities such as employing local workers, making donations to local events and facilities, and partnerships with local schools and universities are commonplace. Environmental activities were found in 23% of the cases (for example, the implementation of ISO 14001 and for a paper manufacturer involved in research certification for the Forest Stewardship Council) while the least popular categories were supply chain (14%) and customers (7%), indicating that recent concepts including co-innovation have still to take hold in many small companies, yet may represent a currently untapped source of potential growth.

We also found that the perception of CSR and its level of adoption varies depending on the size of the organisation, the sector in which it operates and the country of origin. It is too early to provide conclusions in this area though interesting points include the high relative use of the EFQM (European Foundation for Quality Management) model in the Basque Country, and implementation of the ISO standards for engineering-based businesses and also where health and safety is paramount. Additionally, in the home building and construction sector there is increased awareness of innovation and responsible entrepreneurship because of a combination of stringent regulations and the underlying opportunity to trade in international markets. As a result, firms in this sector pay increasing attention to health and environmental safety issues.

In many ways, CSR is a more natural proposition for small companies but the very essence of CSR for SMEs has to be acknowledged as being fundamentally different. Many companies implement CSR without viewing it as CSR, while others want to know more but lack the knowledge to implement a value-adding strategic approach. In general, the main obstacles to CSR implementation are as follows.

- **Lack of knowledge and awareness of CSR**. As there are many definitions it is often confusing and as a result companies undertake practices that are unsustainable—they lack the expertise for effective implementation. Some companies believe CSR is the new fad and something new will replace it. As such, they are not willing to invest in CSR as it is a long-term transformation

- **Poor view of cost versus benefit**. There is still not a sufficient belief in added value from CSR implementation. This can be partly attributed to a lack of adequate metrics that show the value of various CSR elements

- **People and time pressures**. Daily operational pressures result in a lack of integration of sustainable CSR policy. Part of this can be attributed to a lack of adequate tools and metrics, part to the lack of knowledge of how to best implement and often *where* to implement within the company

Regarding the uptake of CSR we found that SMEs in our sample had either a proactive or reactive approach to both CSR and innovation. Those companies with the greatest level of success were proactive in their approach and also, interestingly, had the highest level of CSR implementation. Yet we cannot say that implementing more CSR will lead to more success, or that it would happen every time. It could be that more CSR leads to a more successful or innovative enterprise, or that, once companies achieve a certain degree of success, they start to implement more responsible actions as a way of, say, 'putting something back'. We argue that proactive CSR is easier than proactive innovation. Innovation is an inherently risky activity with no guarantee of return, yet basic CSR actions, such as those related to legislation and stakeholder involvement, may be considered as risk reduction with a much clearer associated cost and return. CSR may serve as the starting point for proactive innovation and for those companies who want to improve their position in the industry but are generally risk-averse. Risk reduction CSR (see Figure 14.2) is sometimes criticised as an incremental, short-term view of CSR, yet the important aspect, in our view, is to get companies started on the process. As we show later, by starting on the process, companies may quickly realise the benefits and implement more long-term CSR.

**FIGURE 14.2** Reasons for CSR

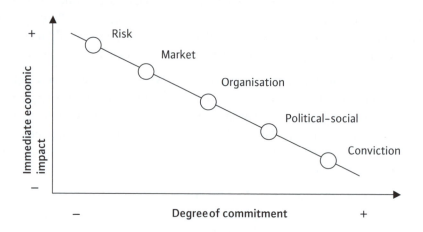

Source: adapted from Fontrodona 2006

In general, we found that the current uptake of CSR in European SMEs (at least in our sample) is good. However, the focus should be on integrating the different activities and tying them to the company strategy—this being the only way to generate real value. In general, many SMEs are eager to learn more about CSR, yet lack knowledge and become disillusioned with the poor results afforded by one-off, isolated initiatives. Yet there are several model firms, proactive in their CSR, and also highly innovative. CSR for SMEs isn't easy, yet innovation is even harder. For those aiming for added value, CSR could present a portal to a more innovative enterprise. For true mainstreaming of CSR, motivation should be closely examined. Many SMEs will be guided by founding values that are not centred solely on monetary reward, yet, for the some 23 million SMEs in Europe, showing how they can be more innovative, and therefore add value to their enterprise, will increase the chances of mainstreaming CSR.

In our entire sample we found that the main motivation was either values or the search for value. Values-based motivation focuses on the responsible action of the enterprise and the production of some social or environmental benefit, considered as, and usually more important than, economic value. This was often linked to some social entrepreneur with a close affinity with the local community or a deep-lying motivation to solve a social or environmental problem. Value-based motivation, the more conventional model of business, focuses on the economic growth of the enterprise and the generation of value for shareholders. Of course, when linked to the creation of employment this links closely to addressing a social need and the fulfilment of values. The distinction between each is rarely simple and clear yet we feel sufficiently differentiated to identify a CSR-centric motivation to CSR implementation (based on values) or an innovation-centric approach (based on value). Furthermore, to effectively mainstream CSR we believe it is necessary to focus on innovation and the search for value. CSR offers a framework for companies who want to innovate (sustainably and with less risk). This leads us to the final form of the RESPONSE model, presented below.

## RESPONSE: a model for CSR innovation

As noted in the research methodology, several iterations of the RESPONSE model were created, each advancing an understanding of the fit or space between CSR and innovation. Based on the research we have done, we conclude that a virtuous circle of CSR and innovation exists, as represented in Figure 14.3. Given the explanation above, SMEs may be driven by either *values* or the search for *value*: that is, either a CSR-centric motivation to CSR implementation or an innovation-centric approach. In terms of our CSR typology, *value* is arguably more closely linked to the workforce, supply chain and customer elements of CSR with *values* linked more to community and environment. Even though CSR may not be automatically considered in the value search, we believe it leads to a more sustainable, less risky approach through taking closer order of workforce, customer and supply chain actions.

**FIGURE 14.3** CSR elements according to value and values

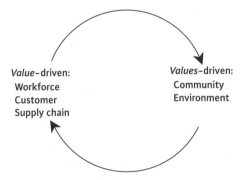

*Value–*driven:
Workforce
Customer
Supply chain

*Values–*driven:
Community
Environment

Our logic dictates that there is more than just CSR-driven innovation which is values-driven. For us to mainstream there has to be a bi-directional system for real sustainability. Yet where is the starting point? Although many SMEs are formed with a founding mission related to responsibility, we believe the majority of European SMEs will respond to a call for increasing value. We therefore need not even mention CSR. In many cases, the resource-stretched small enterprise does not have the time or even mental capacity to consider yet another business approach.

Indeed, many SMEs in our study believed that CSR was merely the latest business 'fad'. Simply put, we appeal to their need to be more competitive, through innovation, and we give them a CSR framework to do so. Essentially, we convert existing CSR theory into an innovation model, one that may best be described as sustainable (or even social) innovation. The final key concept to highlight is that we require this sustainable innovation process to be formalised within the enterprise. Many small companies actually do the right things, yet performance is often compromised through a lack of formalisation and control.

## CSR-driven innovation and innovation-driven CSR

This bi-directional system may be defined as CSR-driven innovation and innovation-driven CSR (shown in Figure 14.4).

**FIGURE 14.4** Virtuous circle of CSR and innovation

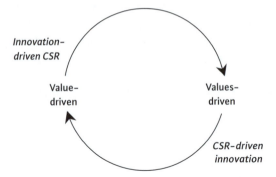

CSR-driven innovation has as its end result products and services that have some sort of social purpose. It is driven by values for the creation of social products and services. In our model we define these social products and services as being in the areas of design against crime, eco-design and design for all. Innovation-driven CSR, on the other hand, may be more aligned with creating social processes and is driven by value. The end result may not have a solely social rationale, yet the way that the output was developed, through, for example, employee or supplier actions, is more socially responsible. Furthermore, we can say that CSR-driven innovation is about 'doing the *right* things' with innovation-driven CSR about 'doing things *right*' (see Figure 14.5). We did find several high-performing SMEs in RESPONSE with an advanced profile of CSR and innovation and representative of this distinction. For example, Solas, a high-growth enterprise from Lombardia region, produces paints with no environmental impact through the use of biocompatible vegetal and mineral raw materials such as vegetable oils and resins. It has gained leadership through environmental-based CSR (including reducing energy consumption and producing 100% biodegradable waste), which is tied closely to the company strategy and quest for differentiation and value. This has resulted in enhanced revenues, visibility and brand image. Solas is innovative, yet the 'spark' was a values-centric motivation to solve an environmental issue and so the company is an example of innovation-driven CSR. Others implemented CSR unknowingly, or at least exclusively as a means of increasing competitiveness. JRG Group, an independent manufacturing company based in the west of Scotland, carries out CSR activities including building good relationships and collaboration with customers and suppliers which are essential to the organisation as a source of information and innovation. These relationships have led the organisation to establish itself as a 'one-stop shop' through the creation of an entirely new range of products. Unaware of its CSR implementation, the company's focus was on innovation and competitiveness, and so it is an example of CSR-driven innovation.

**FIGURE 14.5** CSR-driven innovation and innovation-driven CSR

Such a perspective on CSR and innovation necessitates the right tools and methods to aid development in each area. We have attempted to address the relative poverty of CSR support tools and methods (at least in comparison with innovation) by developing the RESPONSE model. On a basic level, the model (illustrated in Figure 14.6) is the end result of development regarding the virtuous circle concept. The reality of the bi-directional system is shown through the four spheres: social, relationship, organisation and process, which are populated in response to a series of questions.

The social sphere represents the capacity of an organisation to develop social products. The purpose of the social sphere is to show areas of opportunity in the design process that could potentially lead to product innovation, such as environmental paints in Solas, presented above. The relationship sphere represents the degree of interaction of an organisation with its stakeholders. Research suggests that the degree of innovation of an organisation is closely linked to the existing relationship between a company and its different stakeholders. The rationale behind this is that good stakeholder relationships open communication channels resulting in ideas that, if strategically selected and adequately resourced, could potentially lead to innovation. The organisational sphere represents an organisation in terms of its strategy, its culture and its structure. This sphere enables users to dissect the

## FIGURE 14.6  RESPONSE sustainable innovation model

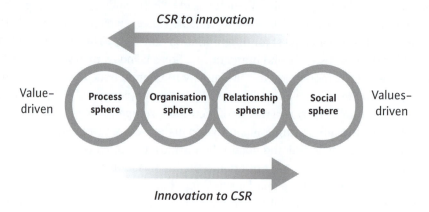

organisation and observe those areas of the business that have an effect on the uptake of CSR and innovation-related practices. Finally, the process sphere represents the life-cycle of a social product or service. It describes all of the operational processes undertaken during its manufacturing process from idea generation to its disposal. The purpose of this sphere is to enable users to visualise the relationship between the choices made during the product/service development process and the impact that these decisions have on the life-cycle of a product and the involved stakeholders.

The questions that serve as a guide for populating each sphere (either in a descriptive or prescriptive way) are presented in Figure 14.7. An organisation may define the current state, identify areas of opportunity and establish an action plan to undertake corrective actions. It is therefore both descriptive (or diagnostic) and prescriptive, and can be used in auditing or strategy design situations. However, it is essential that the users are aware of the motivation behind the organisation before undertaking the analysis. This then defines the starting point for the model. The questionnaire is divided into three sections as detailed below.

## FIGURE 14.7  Sustainable innovation model process

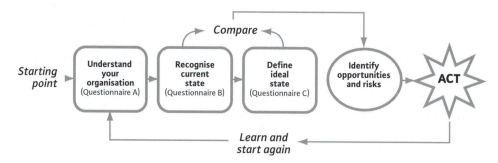

- **Section A**. The purpose of this questionnaire is to help the individuals undertaking the study to gain a better understanding of the organisation. The participants will be able to produce a more accurate diagnosis by identifying the unspoken goals of the organisation by recognising customer requirements and core organisational competences, as well as understanding the market and the long-term objectives of the organisation

- **Section B**. This questionnaire was designed as a diagnostic tool to help the user establish the current state of the organisation in relation to CSR. This questionnaire will enable the user to assess the capacity of the organisation to produce socially responsible products, observe the existing relationship with internal and external stakeholders and identify the attitude of the organisation towards CSR (i.e. proactive/reactive and inward/outward-looking)

- **Section C**. By undertaking this last questionnaire the users will be able to define the ideal state of the organisation. This is achieved by assessing the strategic importance of its processes, identifying the stance of the organisation towards innovation and recognising the strategic importance of key stakeholders

An example of a completed model is shown in Figure 14.8.

# Metalquimia: a CSR–innovation champion from RESPONSE

Some of the most valuable insights generated in the RESPONSE project proceeded from the identification of several 'champion' SMEs, highly developed in their approach to both CSR and innovation. One such firm is the Catalan SME Metalquimia. In essence, the RESPONSE model aims to formalise and accelerate CSR and innovation development that has evolved naturally in Metalquimia (over a period of nearly 40 years). It is particularly strong in company processes and culture and stakeholder involvement in innovation, and so the completed RESPONSE model could serve as best practice for less mature organisations.

Metalquimia was founded in the Northern Catalan town of Besalú in 1971 and is presently a world leader in meat-processing machinery, specifically for cured meats such as ham and sausage. It is still a family-run business and currently employs 100 people between its design and research plant (and headquarters) in Girona and production plant in nearby Figueres. It has a turnover of €18 million, of which 90% is from export markets, the company exporting to over 60 countries world-

**FIGURE 14.8** Final version of RESPONSE model with sample population

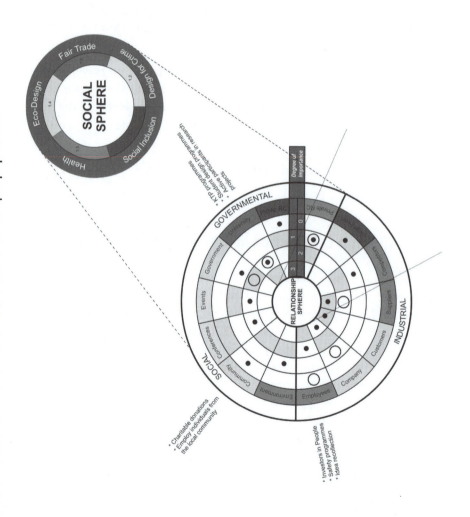

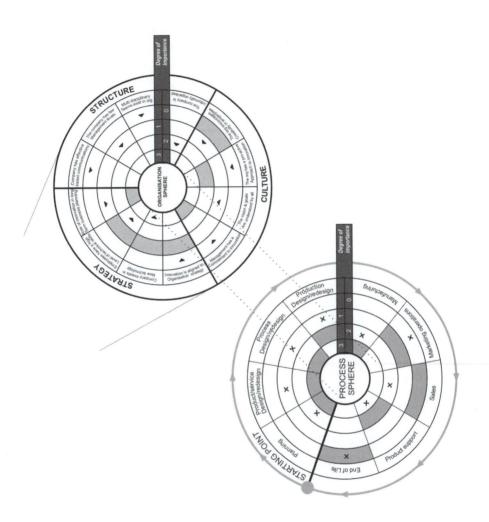

wide. It is situated within a strong regional cluster (pork production in Girona) which offers the opportunity for strategic alliances across the supply chain, and has helped ensure stability and favourable local conditions. The company has been studied from a variety of angles in recent years—innovation evolution, family business and CSR—and, in general, is very mature in all areas. The evolution towards this maturity is shown in Figure 14.9.

**FIGURE 14.9** Key steps in the evolution of Metalquimia

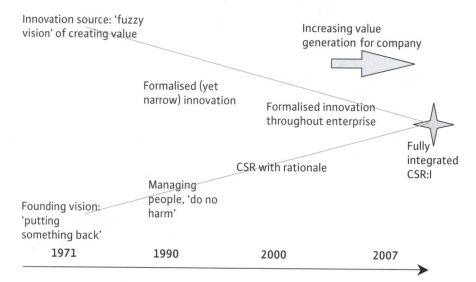

As shown in Figure 14.9, the company was founded on two disparate visions related to CSR and innovation, which could be viewed as romantic notions with little actual operational knowledge regarding how to achieve them. With time, both concepts have come closer together, as knowledge has improved, and importantly with formalisation, particularly of the innovation process. The current reality is that CSR and innovation overlap in several areas, so that each concept cannot be viewed in isolation from the other. Innovation is tightly tied to the overall strategic direction in the company. Strategy plans exist for innovation and people management, within which CSR plays a large role.

As stated by Josep Lagares, company CEO and son of company founder Narcis Lagares, 'I've been hearing more and more about CSR when talking to business school attendees, with customers and visiting luminaries, but this is what Metalquimia had been doing for years, without actually calling it that.' In Josep's view, people management and treating staff well is the cornerstone of the successful family business and, in Metalquimia, has served as a basis for all the other initiatives and change and improvement programmes that have driven growth. Further, company actions related to suppliers and customers also have sound business rationale for the company's systematic innovation process, and involvement with the local community is driven primarily by a creative and innovative rationale that identifies strongly with the vision and culture of the company. Environmental action, when related to the minimisation of waste, also derives greater value for the company. CSR is therefore present in different areas of the company, driving value generation, but requiring founding company values to make it function correctly.

The company is an extended family business and people are the key starting point for CSR to add value in the shortest term possible. Focus is placed on people growing as human beings, and not just professionals. The managing director, who is personally responsible for the management of the annual recreational activity plan, is a firm believer in being extremely open with workforce, letting them know as much as possible about what is going on, even at the highest levels of the company. They are also rewarded financially more than most private enterprises with 20% of the annual profits being distributed between the workforce. In many ways, the company operates like a small cooperative. Each employee is made to feel part of the family with the best example perhaps being the approach to recruitment. At a time when the length of time people spend at any one company is becoming shorter, and more people are less committed to their employer, when a new member of staff begins work at Metalquimia they are told that it could be a job for life, and indeed are encouraged to think that way. The use of simple information and communication technologies (ICTs) plays an important role. Josep comments,

> We put a lot of effort into the company Intranet in order to keep the workforce informed. I'm personally responsible for the company-wide activity plan which ensures the workforce spends some social time together in different activities outside of work.

Important company news is also publicised but is presented in such a way as to reduce information overload. Such responsible people management improves the motivation and creative capital of the company. The company has conducted internal research gauging the level of satisfaction of staff, finding that productivity has remained the same with fewer hours worked, more free time in addition to other measures improving that satisfaction, while fewer hours worked means lower overheads for the company (not to mention producing environmental value). Company culture often diffuses from the people in charge and here we can reference Josep's stated commitment to 'help to make the world a better place', at least on a relatively minor level. These are the personal values of Josep yet also evident in several of the strategies and plans of the company as a whole. The culture and values of Metalquimia are formalised in various strategy sub-plans, 12 in all, including sales, operations, innovation and internationalisation. Sub-plans for the family, people management and parts and servicing also exist. Talent capture is difficult and so strategic alliances and the dedicated attention and management of human capital are critical.

Since CSR is present within several areas of the company, as noted in the strategic sub-plans of people management, innovation and image and communication, ownership is spread between several key figures in senior management but championed by the person in charge, Josep. In the current climate of economic and financial crisis emphasis is put on relationships with staff and suppliers, assuring them that the company continues to thrive in difficult times. One of the key factors in Metalquimia's success is trust and confidence in what it does and where it is going. Examples include the activity plan detailed above, which grows year on year, and collaboration with suppliers on several innovative projects which add value to the core business, such as the recent QDS (Quick Dry Slice) process co-developed with a key customer, Casademont, and the AgroFood research and technology centre IRTA, which accelerates process time related to the drying and cutting of meat, from the typical 40–50 days when meat is hung in drying chambers, to the three days required in the QDS process. This patented process also helps reduce energy consumption as well as cost reduction and increased yield and is an example of a revolutionary innovation, arguably only possible through an open innovation approach in which the company believes strongly as it moves into the future.

Metalquimia's business is highly mechanised and technical in nature with constant pressures on technological innovation. CSR has acted as a stabilising factor in a rapidly changing environment, and provided through the company's focus on development of its human capital, the source of its competitive advantage. For a company that has experienced rapid change—technological innovation plays a big part in the core business, and the management of that innovation has gone through several ever-increasing change cycles in the past 30 years—CSR has been one of the constants. One interesting fact is the important implementation of lean philosophy, which looks at minimising waste and providing the basis for continuous improvement, which is first necessary before a company, especially a small enterprise, can innovate.

Even external CSR—that is, community-related initiatives most closely related to philanthropy—is integrated closely with innovation. Requests for assistance as well as personal goals of the management team are subjected to a series of filters, which evaluate their fit with the core principles of the company—creativity and innovation, and also satisfying specific aims of Metalquimia, such as the promotion of Catalonia and Catalan culture worldwide. Among other things, this helps to deal with the large volume of requests that the company receives on a continual basis. There is a type of potential return on investment measured for all requests, with the focus on the sustainable benefit to the people or institution receiving the help, the key being to try to help people help themselves in the longer term.

For Metalquimia, CSR and innovation are intertwined, value-adding mechanisms at the core of the company's global competitive advantage. The founding vision for both areas may start far apart, with few ideas on how both areas connect, yet with development, first implementing a formalised, narrow view before spreading throughout the company and beyond, both areas move closer together, and become bound by key strategic actions. For example, responsible people management improves the creative capital of the company while CSR actions with a creative or business rationale add to the overall value of the enterprise.

One of the key insights of the Metalquimia story was the formalisation of CSR and innovation over time, and with increasing maturity. In essence the RESPONSE model aims to formalise innovation for small enterprises, which, as we found in the research, often carry out many CSR and innovation-related actions but which are informal, sometimes chaotic and rarely measured, albeit important to the success and direction of the company. The trigger for this increasing formalisation in Metalquimia was the costly market failure of a large-scale project, which convinced the management team that a new approach to innovation was required—innovation that first had to be socialised, not over-relying on key creative individuals, and also formalised, so that innovative products could be produced time and again. In essence, CSR has provided the sustainable energy for this innovation to endure and succeed.

## Further research for mainstreaming CSR in SMEs

The RESPONSE model is our contribution to the challenge, which is a significant one, of mainstreaming CSR in SMEs. Given the scale of the challenge a wider discussion of CSR mainstreaming, in light of our findings, is valuable in concluding the chapter. We have framed this discussion within classical innovation diffusion theory which we believe offers some valuable insights into CSR diffusion and future policy guidance. It is important to note that we do not consider CSR as an innovation per se, yet within the context of mainstreaming it may encounter the same difficulties in being adopted by the 'target market' in being something new, and sometimes hard to understand in terms of value.

The diffusion of innovation is a classic view of social systems (Rogers 1962) which has been revisited in recent years (Moore 1991, 2006) as we advance through an age of rapidly changing technology. Yet the real challenge should not to be to diffuse an increasing amount of products and services but to ensure that these follow a more responsible and sustainable approach throughout their life-cycle, from conception to disposal.

Diffusion theory looks at how innovations spread within a social system. According to Rogers the 'tipping point' is the point at which a trend catches fire—spreading exponentially through the population. Crucially, for most members of a social system, the innovation decision depends heavily on the decision of others. This is reflected in our research which showed the behaviour of both proactive and reactive firms. Reactive firms (the majority) implement CSR practices only once they view that the market leaders (proactive firms) have done so. Within standard diffusion theory, relatively rapid adoption of the innovation takes place once 10–25% of system members adopt it. So, assuming that some of the similar dynamics could be at play in the diffusion of CSR, how do we get that initial 10–25% to lead the way? Here, a closer look at the dynamics of diffusion is necessary. The classic bell curve of diffusion is shown in Figure 14.10.

**FIGURE 14.10** Diffusion curve showing the 'crossing the chasm' concept

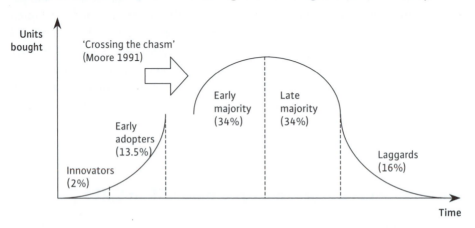

The classification shows five types of adopter group, with leaders classified as 'innovators' and 'early adopters'. Based on this classical model, Moore (1991) presents a contemporary analysis for the information age, highlighting the difficulty encountered in the space between 'early adopters' and 'early majority', this significant hurdle for many innovations being termed 'crossing the chasm'. An example offered by Moore is the Apple Newton PDA (personal digital assistant), which, although having promising early sales, failed to 'cross over' to the mass market.

According to Rogers the innovation decision is made through a cost–benefit analysis where the major obstacle is uncertainty. In the RESPONSE project we found that one of the main barriers to CSR adoption in SMEs was a poor view of cost versus benefit, something we hope to address through linking CSR with innovation. Yet Moore states that this perception is very different for the first two adopter groups than for the 'early majority'. It could therefore be the case that a radically different approach is also required after the initial adoption of CSR takes place.

Examining the rate of diffusion, two main factors are at play: mass media and opinion leaders. First, the mass media spreads knowledge of innovations to a large audience rapidly, yet this alone does not affect real change. Opinion leaders strongly influence the rest of the social system, and persuading those opinion leaders is the easiest way to engender positive attitudes toward an innovation. A discussion on diffusion is therefore appropriate in an age of increasing speed of awareness. The Internet and tools including blogs, wikis and other Web 2.0 social movements are changing the dynamics of countless industries forever.

Rogers explains that the types of opinion leader that change agents should target depend on the nature of the social system—those that tend to encourage change from system norms and those that tend toward current norms. These types (heterophilous and homophilous as termed by Rogers) depend to a large extent on the diversity of the members and their resultant attitude to change. We may match this type of behaviour to different industrial sectors in Europe. For example, the oil and gas industry has traditionally been viewed as innovation-averse while sectors such as electronics are viewed as the opposite. Rogers states that, for highly diverse and innovation-accepting systems, change agents can concentrate on targeting the most elite and innovative opinion leaders and the innovation will trickle down to non-elites. If an elite opinion leader is convinced to adopt an innovation, the rest will exhibit excitement and readiness towards adoption. For more traditional systems the task is far more difficult. Change agents must target a wider group of opinion leaders, including some of the less elite, because innovations are less likely to trickle down. Opinion leaders here are more likely to be regarded as suspicious and/or dismissed from their opinion leadership. Generally, in these types of system, opinion leaders do not control attitudes as much as pre-existing norms do. If we accept Rogers' theory for the diffusion of CSR it is necessary to first focus more attention and policies on those sectors considered to be highly diverse and open to change and innovation. More traditional sectors may require more investment, targeting a broader sample of the population, something that may best be tackled after innovation-open sectors lead the way, with even cross-sectoral benefits possible. That is, sectors traditionally opposed to change may see the benefit, and even risk-reduction of implementing CSR within more innovation-accepting sectors.

## Towards better policy

Successful efforts to diffuse an innovation therefore depend on the characteristics of the situation and involve a number of stages. To eliminate a deficit of awareness of an innovation, mass media channels are most appropriate. To change prevailing attitudes about an innovation, it is best to persuade opinion leaders. Further, what we find is that homophilous social systems are likely to frustrate change agents with their resistance to innovation. It is only for heterophilous social systems that pushing an innovation to the elusive tipping point is a relatively easy thing to do.

Recent awareness raising, by the European Commission and others, does seem to be having an effect, and so the identification of opinion leaders and sectoral analysis should constitute the next area of focus. Within the European Commission to date, capacity building in the form of new tools and methods has been the focus alongside awareness raising, and so the hope is that change agents will have the necessary tools at their disposal to affect change. We believe we have identified the model of the opinion leader, or change agent for SMEs, at least in heterophilous systems: the proactive, outward-looking enterprise.

Proactive, outward-looking SMEs identified in the RESPONSE project were leaders in their market. As discussed in the findings section, those leaders had the highest level of CSR implementation. Evidence suggests that social innovation requires a proactive attitude. Melé (2001) states that the responses by companies to social responsibility and sustainability range from inactive through reactive to interactive and proactive. Reactive approaches are of low value since there is little time to respond to the rapid changes of society. A reactive attitude could be described as catching opportunities as and when they occur (innovation) or responding to legislation (CSR), whereas a proactive stance requires a forward-looking and anticipatory mind-set that derives from the formulation of a long-term, planned strategy on CSR. Leaders, or best-practice firms, have a proactive approach to innovation: for example, in fulfilling customer demand before it manifests itself, or at least very early in the communication of those demands. Proactivity is usually a characteristic of innovating firms, which do not wait for competitors or external pressures to surface but that continuously strive to find and create breakthrough solutions. If other firms then see the potential benefits of a proactive approach they may be more likely to follow these 'opinion leaders' and move closer to the tipping point, and true mainstreaming.

## Conclusion

This chapter has presented the RESPONSE model, a means of adding value or innovating in the small enterprise based on the key aspects of CSR. We believe there exists a virtuous circle of innovation and CSR and that the majority of enterprises will be driven by value, which represents a valid starting point for greater CSR implementation as long as the right roadmap is available. Classic innovation diffusion theory is presented as a useful basis for considering longer-term mainstreaming, and the story of Metalquimia shows that CSR and innovation have an opportunity to co-evolve in the enterprise, with better connectivity able to create greater value and sustainability in the long term. One of the keys is formalising the innovation process, which shows us the most probable application for the RESPONSE model. We can say that the tool is primarily for companies who want to innovate but who don't have a highly formalised process (like Metalquimia in the mid-1970s), and may have had some experience of implementing innovation as a chaotic activity, with a high generation of ideas but leaving much to chance.

The key idea of the RESPONSE model is that we do not appeal to responsibility directly, rather the pursuit of value and particularly a more innovative firm. CSR is presented *as* an innovation process, where small enterprises are often held back by the lack of formalisation and proactive behaviour. For SMEs that want to transform innovation chaos into formalised, sustainable value creation across the enterprise, we believe that CSR can act as an effective delivery mechanism for small-company value generation in the 21st century and that, for innovation, SMEs should be proactive in CSR.

# References

Baker, M. (2003) 'Doing it Small', *Ethical Corporation Magazine*, 20 August 2003.

Boatright, J.R. (1993) *Ethics and the Conduct of Business* (Englewood Cliffs, NJ: Prentice-Hall).

Carroll, A.B. (1999) 'Corporate Social Responsibility: Evolution of a Definitional Construct', *Business & Society* 38: 268-95.

—— (2008) 'A History of Corporate Social Responsibility: Concepts and Practices', in A. Crane (ed.), *The Oxford Handbook of Corporate Social Responsibility* (Oxford, UK: Oxford University Press): 19-46.

Castelo, M., and L. Lima (2006) 'Corporate Social Responsibility and Resource-Based Perspectives', *Journal of Business Ethics* 69: 111-32.

European Commission (2001) *Promoting a European Framework for Corporate Social Responsibility* (Green Paper; Luxembourg: Office for Official Publications of the European Communities).

Fontrodona, J. (2006) 'Turning Words into Action', *IESE Alumni Magazine*, January–March 2006.

Fuller, T. (2003) 'Small Business Futures in Society', *Futures* 35.4: 297-304.

—— and Y. Tian (2006) 'Social and Symbolic Capital and Responsible Entrepreneurship: An Empirical Investigation of SME Narratives', *Journal of Business Ethics* 67.3: 287-304.

Garriga, E., and D. Melé (2004) 'Corporate Social Responsibility Theories: Mapping the Territory', *Journal of Business Ethics* 53:1–2, 51-71.

Grayson, D., and A. Hodges (2004) *Corporate Social Opportunity! Seven Steps to Make Corporate Social Responsibility Work for Your Business* (Sheffield, UK: Greenleaf Publishing).

Hamel, G. (2006) 'The Why, What, and How of Management Innovation', *Harvard Business Review* 84.6: 72-84.

Hoffman, K., M. Parejo, J. Bessant and L. Perren (1998) 'Small Firms, R&D, Technology and Innovation in the UK: A Literature Review', *Technovation* 18.1: 39-55.

Jenkins, H. (2004) 'A Critique of Conventional CSR Theory: An SME Perspective', *Journal of General Management* 9.4: 55-75.

—— (2009) 'A "Business Opportunity" Model of Corporate Social Responsibility for Small- and Medium-sized Enterprises', *Business Ethics: A European Review* 18.1: 21-36.

Kusyk, S., and J.M. Lozano (2007) 'SME Social Performance: A Four-Cell Typology of Key Drivers and Barriers on Social Issues and their Implications for Stakeholder Theory', *Corporate Governance: The International Journal of Effective Board Performance* 7.4: 502-15.

Lefebvre, L.A., and E. Lefebvre (1993) 'Competitive Positioning and Innovative Effort in SMEs', *Small Business Economics* 5.4: 297-305.

Lopez-Perez, M.V., M.C. Pérz-López and L. Rodríguez-Ariza (2007) 'The Opinions of European Companies on Corporate Social Responsibility and its Relation to Innovation', *Issues in Social and Environmental Accounting* 1.2: 276-95.

Melé, D. (2001) *Corporate Social Performance* (IESE Technical Note TDN-114-E; Barcelona: IESE Business School).

—— (2008) 'Corporate Social Responsibility Theories', in A. Crane (ed.), *The Oxford Handbook of Corporate Social Responsibility* (Oxford, UK: Oxford University Press): 47-82.

Midttun, A. (2007) 'Corporate Responsibility from a Resource and Knowledge Perspective. Towards a Dynamic Reinterpretation of C(S)R: Are Corporate Responsibility and Innovation Compatible or Contradictory?', *Corporate Governance* 7.4: 401-13.

Moore, G.A. (1991) *Crossing the Chasm* (New York: HarperBusiness).

—— (2006) *Dealing with Darwin: How Great Companies Innovate at Every Phase of Their Evolution* (Chichester, UK: Capstone Publishing).

Murillo, D., and J.M. Lozano (2009) 'Pushing Forward SME CSR through a Network: An Account from the Catalan Model', *Business Ethics: A European Review* 18.1: 7-20.

Porter, M.E., and M. Kramer (2006) 'Strategy and Society: The Link between Competitive Advantage and Corporate Social Responsibility', *Harvard Business Review*, December 2006: 78-92.

Rogers, E.M. (1962) *Diffusion of Innovations* (New York: The Free Press).

Sawhney, M., R.C. Wolcott and I. Arroniz (2006) 'The 12 Different Ways for Companies to Innovate', *MIT Sloan Management Review* 47.3: 74-81.

Spence, L.J. (1999) 'Does Size Matter? The State of the Art in Small Business Ethics', *Business Ethics: A European Review* 8.3: 163-74.

——, R. Schmidpeter and A. Habisch (2003) 'Assessing Social Capital: Small and Medium-sized Enterprises in the UK and Germany', *Journal of Business Ethics* 47.1: 17-29.

——, A. Habisch and R. Schmidpeter (2004) *Responsibility and Social Capital: The World of Small and Medium Sized Enterprises* (Basingstoke, UK: Palgrave Macmillan).

Tilley, F. (2003) 'Sustainability and Competitiveness: Are There Mutual Advantages for SMEs?', in O. Jones and F. Tilley (eds.), *Competitive Advantage in SMEs: Organising for Innovation and Change* (Chichester, UK: John Wiley): 71-84.

Vila, J., and S.P. MacGregor (2007) 'Business Innovation: What it Brings, What it Takes', *IESE Alumni Magazine*, July–September 2007.

Vilanova, M., J.M. Lozano and D. Arenas (2009) 'Exploring the Nature of the Relationship between CSR and Competitiveness', *Journal of Business Ethics* 87: 57-69.

# 15
# Barriers to innovative CSR
## The impacts of organisational learning, organisational structure and the social embeddedness of the firm

**Lutz Preuss**

Royal Holloway, University of London, UK

A discussion of innovative CSR brings together two terms—corporate social responsibility (CSR) and innovation—that clearly have an impact on each other. On the one hand, innovation and the application of new technological options by the private sector are increasingly perceived as having fundamental implications for consumption choices and living standards of individuals across the globe (Matten *et al.* 2007). Consumption patterns are shaped, for example, through such novel technologies as mobile telephony or genetic engineering (Frewer *et al.* 1997; Griesse 2007). Through deploying such innovation, companies not only provide new products but they actually shape, in a fundamental way, people's quality of life. On the other hand, innovation can make a contribution to achieving the aims of CSR. Through concepts such as design for environment (Fiksel 1996; Lenox *et al.* 2008) or sustainable design (Carrano and Thorn 2006), innovative solutions to product and process design can contribute to a reduction of the social and environmental externalities of economic activity.

However, the two terms, CSR and innovation, are more often discussed in isolation from each other (MacGregor and Fontrodona 2008). As a contribution to closing this gap, this chapter discusses what barriers companies are likely to experience on their journey towards innovative forms of CSR. The chapter begins with a brief overview of the nature of innovation. On this basis a framework is presented that characterises innovation as being shaped by knowledge generation and application processes, control and coordination structures within the innovating organisation as well as factors that arise from the social embeddedness of the firm (Lam 2000). The framework is then applied to draw out what barriers to innovative CSR arise in these three areas. Following this, the chapter explores how innovative CSR relates to neighbouring concepts, such as strategic CSR or the business case for CSR. Finally, implications for future research and managerial practice are discussed.

Being positioned at the intersection of academic writing on innovation and CSR, this chapter makes three contributions to the literature. First, it provides a definition of innovative CSR, which the literature has so far omitted to do. Second, it generates—on the basis of a framework derived from the innovation literature—a catalogue of barriers to innovative CSR, which can serve as a starting point for future empirical research on this question. Third, by presenting innovative CSR as an alternative concept to strategic CSR, arguments are put forward to explain why the former is capable of providing a potentially more encompassing conceptualisation than the latter has been able to do thus far.

## On the nature of innovation

The Organisation for Economic Cooperation and Development (OECD) (OECD and Eurostat 1997) defines innovation as technological or organisational novelties. Technological innovation can comprise either novel or improved products or production processes, while organisational innovation concerns changes in organisational structure, corporate strategy or management techniques. Both technological and organisational innovation can be gradual or radical changes of the status quo (Murphy and Gouldson 2000; Utterback and Acee 2005). Innovation has been conceptualised from a multitude of directions, such as the role of individual creativity (Amabile *et al.* 1996) and the interaction processes within an innovating organisation (Burns and Stalker 1961; Van de Ven *et al.* 1999; Christiansen 2000) as well as the interactions across organisational boundaries (Pavitt 1984; von Hippel 1988). Combining (1) a focus on internal organisational changes as a key strategy for promoting innovative capabilities of a firm with (2) an emphasis on organisational coordination mechanisms and routines which (3) are heavily influenced by societal factors such as education systems, labour market structures and social relationships between different occupational groups, Lam (2000) proposed an integrated framework of innovation that consists of three elements.

The first element builds on work regarding the nature of knowledge and organisational learning (Nonaka and Takeuchi 1995; Spender 1996). A key distinction here is the one made by Polanyi (1966) between explicit and tacit types of knowledge. Explicit knowledge can be processed by a computer, transmitted electronically or stored in a database, whereas tacit knowledge is personal and context-specific and hence difficult to formalise and communicate (Nonaka and Takeuchi 1995). Another distinction has been made between learning processes that operate at the level of the individual and those at the level of the organisation (Spender 1996). While individual knowledge is discrete and self-contained, collective knowledge refers to the ways in which knowledge is distributed and shared among members of the organisation, forming a kind of 'organizational memory' (Walsh and Ungson 1991). The dynamic interaction and combination of these types of knowledge is crucial for the ability of an organisation to create new knowledge (Nonaka and Takeuchi 1995).

Second, the resource-based theory of the firm can be used to explain how a firm can become dominated by one knowledge type rather than another (Lam 2000). Following Penrose (1959), the resource-based theory sees the firm as a social community that specialises in the creation and internal transfer of knowledge (Grant 1996; Kogut and Zander 2003). In particular, the structure of the organisation—whether it applies hierarchical or decentralised coordination and control structures—determines the degree to which it can make use of different types of knowledge (Mintzberg 1979). For example, a bureaucratic structure depends on standardised knowledge, while a task force structure brings together representatives from different units on an intensive and flexible basis and is hence much more able to tap into tacit knowledge (Nonaka and Takeuchi 1995).

Third, processes of knowledge generation and application do not proceed in a social vacuum; rather, they are powerfully shaped by broader societal factors (Lam 2000). These can be captured through the national business systems approach, which stresses the lasting impact of historically grown patterns in the institutional context of business (Whitley 1999; Hall and Soskice 2001). Specifically concerning innovation, the work on 'national innovation systems' seeks to understand the link between national institutions, such as education systems, industrial relations, technical and scientific institutions, government policies, cultural traditions and many others, to the innovative performance of firms and national economies (Nelson 1993; Freeman 1995; Fagerberg and Srholec 2008).

This integrated framework of innovation as being shaped by organisational learning, organisational structures and the social embeddedness of the firm shall in the following be applied to innovative CSR, in particular to identify barriers to innovative CSR. Before this, however, the next section will clarify what is meant here by innovative CSR. Addressing this question is important as many concrete CSR initiatives are criticised for being static and without sufficient attention to their context (Beaulieu and Pasquero 2003). A related recurring criticism of CSR is that such initiatives often are not integrated into company strategy and operations but remain bolted on (Grayson and Hodges 2004; Schaltegger and Wagner 2006).

## Defining innovative CSR

CSR is often undertaken for economic reasons—the business case for CSR—according to which companies can reap significant benefits from differentiating themselves from competitors through their CSR activities (Salzmann *et al.* 2005; Porter and Kramer 2006; Laszlo 2008). Adapting Porter's (1985) distinction between cost reduction and niche strategies, CSR can lead to cost savings from environmental and social initiatives, such as increased product recyclability, greater energy efficiency or reduced emissions. Alternatively, companies can apply a CSR differentiation strategy, which aims to improve the public perception of the company and its products in order to generate greater sales, higher prices or an early-mover advantage (Welford 2000). Extending these arguments to the developing world, Prahalad and Hammond (2002) suggested that business could become a solution to global poverty through paying attention to the 'bottom of the pyramid', the huge unmet demand among the world's poorest consumers. A variant of the business case is the risk management approach to CSR, where companies aim to stave off unwelcome attention from key stakeholders, such as governments or NGOs (Werther and Chandler 2005).

Some firms address social and environmental externalities, because they perceive they have an obligation to important stakeholders to do so. Such thinking can be linked to a range of ethical theories, such as Kantian deontology (Bowie 1999), virtue ethics (Solomon 1992) or social contract theory (Donaldson and Dunfee 1999). Due to the increasing financialisation of the modern market economy, an ethical approach to CSR is likely only where entrepreneurs can insulate themselves from short-term financial pressures to maximise returns on investment (Vogel 2005). Empirically, such an ethical orientation towards CSR has been found in some family-run businesses or in small firms, where the owner-manager has discretion to integrate personal values into the management of the business (Hemingway and Maclagan 2004; Jenkins 2006). However, the distinction between economic and ethical arguments for engaging in CSR does not yet tell us whether such initiatives can claim to be innovative.

One avenue that seeks to more closely address this question is the strategic approach to CSR (Burke and Logsdon 1996; Gardberg and Fombrun 2006; Porter and Kramer 2006; Husted and Allen 2007). This concept applies to CSR the basic tenet of strategic management: the company should seek to manoeuvre itself into a unique position through doing things differently from competitors in a way that lowers costs or better serves customer needs. Since no business can solve all CSR issues, a company should select issues that are closely aligned with its business objectives. Turning the business case argument back to front, the touchstone of good CSR is then 'not whether a cause is worthy but whether it presents an opportunity to create . . . a meaningful benefit for society that is also valuable to the business' (Porter and Kramer 2006: 84). CSR programmes should hence be seen as strategic investment in very much the same way as R&D and advertising, as they can create assets that help firms to outcompete their rivals. In particular, such investment can aid multinational enterprises (MNEs) to operate effectively across diverse local markets and hence contribute to a better a fit between the external environment and the firm's strategic actions (Gardberg and Fombrun 2006).

However, as valuable as an overlap of corporate and societal value creation is, strategic CSR does not yet address the question of whether such projects are indeed of an innovative nature. Hence a number of authors have sought to explicitly link CSR to innovation. For example, Grayson and Hodges (2004: 9) argue that the 'driver for successful business is entrepreneurialism, opportunity and the competitive instinct . . . a willingness to look for creativity and innovation from non-traditional areas—including CSR'. They go on to suggest that successful CSR has three dimensions: namely, innovation in products and services, finding unserved markets and building new business models. Halme and Laurila (2009) suggest that CSR projects differ along three dimensions: the relationship of CSR to the core business, the target of the initiative and the anticipated benefits (similarly Kourula and Halme 2008). On this basis, they classify CSR projects into:

- **Philanthropy**. Engage in charity, sponsorship and employee volunteering

- **CSR integration**. Conduct existing business operations in a more responsible fashion

- **CSR innovation**. Develop new business models for solving social and environmental problems

On closer inspection, these approaches are again rooted in strategic thinking rather than in innovation. Note that Grayson and Hodges (2004) speak of CSR, as an example of a non-traditional area, becoming a driver for business success. Furthermore, developing novel products and services, finding unserved markets and building new business models (Grayson and Hodges 2004; Halme and Laurila 2009) makes sense from a strategic point of view—but is this already innovative CSR? Take the example of providing financial support for a dance company, the most 'uninnovative' category in the typology by Halme and colleagues: this would be unrelated to the core business for both a manufacturer and a credit card firm. In contrast to the manufacturer, the project would, however, make strategic sense for the financial services firm as it depends much more on entertainment, hospitality and tourism (Porter and Kramer 2006). Irrespective of this, engaging in such a project may be a new endeavour—and hence an innovative one—for both companies.

Thus developing new business models for solving social and environmental problems (Grayson and Hodges 2004; Kourula and Halme 2008; Halme and Laurila 2009) appears to be a further variation on the theme of strategic CSR rather than necessarily a categorisation of CSR as innovative or otherwise. In other words, the starting point for defining a CSR project as innovative or otherwise should not be a categorisation of activities—however useful this is in strategic terms—but the status quo of the respective organisation. In line with the OECD definition presented above of innovation as technological or organisational novelties (OECD and Eurostat 1997), innovative CSR can now be defined as comprising:

- **Technological CSR innovation**. The development of novel or improved products or new production processes that offer a superior balance, from a societal point of view, of economic, social and environmental benefits

- **Organisational CSR innovation**. Changes to organisational structure, corporate strategy or management techniques that enable the firm to better achieve an integrated economic, social and environmental performance

As was mentioned above, technological and organisational innovation can be gradual or radical changes of the status quo (Murphy and Gouldson 2000; Utterback and Acee 2005). Hence both technological CSR innovation and organisational CSR innovation can proceed in gradual or radical fashion too. Supporting the dance company could thus be an example of gradual innovative CSR for both the manufacturer and the financial services firm if the company had not engaged in these activities before. From this perspective, CSR can clearly provide opportunities for innovation, but 'it is not a given that CSR innovation will either produce competitive advantage or value creation' (Husted and Allen 2007: 605). Furthermore, the definition of innovative CSR applies a subjective conceptualisation of innovation as being novel to a particular organisation—irrespective of whether it has been applied in a different organisation or not (see Pavitt 1984). This conceptualisation may blur the line between innovation and dissemination, yet pure diffusion is rare as it requires a process of adaptation to a novel context. In terms of innovative CSR it is furthermore desirable that best practice spreads quickly to reduce the social and environmental footprint of economic activity (Rennings *et al.* 2005).

Linking CSR more strongly to the innovation literature, rather than the strategic management one, offers the opportunity to link the concept to other themes in the innovation literature. For example, managers charged with the diffusion of CSR could learn from the diffusion of innovation (MacGregor and Fontrodona 2008). Here Rogers (1995) pointed to the bell curve of innovation diffusion of innovators—early adopters, early majority, late majority and laggards—where the step from early adopters to early majority presents a particularly formidable obstacle. Such a model finds its pendant in CSR studies that distinguish between proactive and reactive firms, with reactive ones only adopting a new CSR trend once they see that the innovation of the more proactive companies has become accepted. The mutual influences between the innovation literature and innovative CSR cannot be exhaustively covered in this chapter, yet the next section will make a small contribution to this by examining what barriers to innovative CSR firms might experience. This will be undertaken through the integrated framework of innovation developed by Lam (2000).

## Innovative CSR and organisational learning

The integrated framework presented above characterised innovation as being shaped by organisational learning processes, structural enablers and constraints within the organisation as well as the social embeddedness of the firm (Lam 2000). The first element of the framework was concerned with the nature of knowledge and organisational learning. It stressed that the knowledge held by a firm is multifaceted, complex and dynamic, while organisational learning requires a successful combination of explicit and tacit knowledge (Polanyi 1966; Nonaka and Takeuchi 1995) as well as of individual and organisational learning processes (Walsh and Ungson 1991; Spender 1996).

From a vantage point in knowledge management theory, two distinct but complementary types of knowledge have been identified: a static perspective of the elements that need to be developed to facilitate knowledge capture; and a dynamic view of the processes that lead to effective knowledge utilisation (Henderson and Clark 1990; Al-Ghassani *et al.* 2004). The element view sees knowledge as a resource that is to be captured, stored and connected to existing knowledge, whereas the process view sees knowledge as being inter-subjectively constructed. This distinction can be used to sketch a knowledge management perspective of CSR (Preuss and Córdoba-Pachon 2009). Here the element view points to the explicit knowledge an organisation needs when designing and implementing a CSR strategy, while the process view stresses the political skills required to generate organisational buy-in for CSR as well as achieving support from key external stakeholders.

Such a knowledge management perspective of CSR shows two distinct areas where barriers to innovative CSR could arise in an organisation. The element view highlighted the possibility of the organisation having insufficient knowledge on CSR: for example, concerning compliance and adherence to CSR standards. This may be caused by deficiencies in the way the organisation organises its knowledge-sharing processes, in particular the cooperation between CSR specialists and non-specialists. In environmental management, for example, many firms lack environmental performance data (e.g. on the composition of their waste streams or the recyclability of their products); in large firms such knowledge may exist but is usually dispersed throughout the organisation (Lenox et al. 2008). From the process view, a barrier to innovative CSR may arise from deficiencies in the political skills applied by organisational members which can lead to insufficient organisational buy-in and to an incomplete integration of stakeholder priorities into CSR strategy design and implementation. Barriers of this type are highlighted in the emphasis in the organisational greening literature on the need for policy entrepreneurs and converts to drive the innovative approach (Drumwright 1994).

From the perspective of organisational learning theory, learning has been conceptualised from two complementary perspectives. It can be understood as an adaptive process where the organisation is viewed as a goal-driven adaptive system that generates new learning through trial-and-error interactions with its environment (Cyert and March 1963; Levitt and March 1988) or as a process of cognitive change that involves questioning and rebuilding existing perspectives, interpretation frameworks or decision premises (Argyris 1993). This distinction can be used to explain the CSR performance of a company as the outcome of its learning processes (Benthoin Antal and Sobczak 2004; Gond and Herrbach 2006). CSR as corporate social adaptation sees the organisation achieve incremental progress in the adaptation to demands made by its stakeholders but the range of stakeholders and the organisation's value system are not questioned, whereas CSR as a process of cognitive change involves feedback processes from the outcomes of the firm's CSR activities that lead to a re-examination of the principles and values that underlie its CSR strategy (Gond and Herrbach 2006). As learning generally, organisational learning processes around CSR are thus unlikely to proceed in a linear fashion; at times even processes of unlearning may be necessary (Benthoin Antal and Sobczak 2004).

Organisational learning theory can identify two further barriers to innovative CSR. From the perspective of CSR as social adaptation, organisational routines are understood as outcomes of previous learning and these may lead a company to not engage with critics at all. Rather than building bridges to their external environment, the company may decide to buffer itself from the social and political environment (Meznar and Nigh 1995). For example, when confronted with NGO criticism over its involvement with the military junta in Burma, Unocal decided not to address the criticism but to insulate itself against future consumer pressure by selling its filling stations and concentrating on its wholesale business (Spar and La Mure 2003). CSR as process of cognitive change points to the possibility that the organisation does not question the values it brings to dealing with CSR and/or the range of stakeholders it listens to when designing its CSR strategy. Such barriers are well illustrated by the taken-for-granted discourses of scientific management and economic performance that dominated in Shell prior to its confrontation with Greenpeace in the mid-1990s (Livesey 2001).

## Innovative CSR and organisational structure

The second element of the integrated framework concerned the relationship between organisational structural forms and innovativeness (Lam 2000). Here Burns and Stalker (1961) presented a typology of 'mechanistic' versus 'organic' organisations to demonstrate how the effective organisation of resources alters in response to changes in the organisation's technological and market environments. The 'mechanistic organisation' utilises a hierarchical structure of control, authority and communication with a specialisation and differentiation in the organisation of individual tasks and is typically found where its environment is stable and predictable. By contrast, the 'organic organisation' has a network structure of control, authority and communication and individual tasks are subject to continuous adjustment and redefinition, which makes it a more appropriate form for changing environmental conditions that require innovative responses.

Mintzberg (1979) synthesised much of the work on organisational structure into five basic configurations, each with a different innovative potential: simple structure, machine bureaucracy, professional bureaucracy, divisionalised form and adhocracy. While bureaucratic structures work well in stable environments, they find it difficult to cope with unpredictable change. By contrast, adhocracies are highly flexible forms of organisation capable of radical innovation in a volatile environment, but their high communication costs make them rather inefficient and they are under constant pressure to bureaucratise. Teece (1998) expanded the discussion of organisational structure and innovation by linking these to firm strategy. Based on four classes of variables—firm boundaries, internal formal structure, internal informal structure and external linkages—he identified four archetypal governance modes for innovative firms: the multi-product integrated hierarchy, the highly flexible Silicon Valley-type firm, the virtual corporation and the conglomerate.

Thus four central features of organisational structure emerge from the literature that impact on the firm's innovativeness, namely:

- **Tasks of individual organisational members**. Specialisation and functional differentiation versus continuous adjustment and redefinition of individual tasks

- **Structures of control, authority and communication**. Hierarchy versus network

- **Scale of operations**. Small start-up versus large firm

- **External linkages**. Reliance on voice versus exit of a dissatisfied partner

All of these are also important indicators of potential barriers to innovative CSR.

Regarding the organisation of CSR activities within a firm, differentiation and specialisation can have significant consequences for the ability of the firm to engage in innovative CSR. Where CSR is delegated to a remote department or shared service centre, there is a danger that CSR activities remain bolted on to operational requirements (Schaltegger and Wagner 2006). In contrast, a US-based electronics MNE established a network of environmental stewards across all its operating units, which enabled the firm not only to keep pace with legal developments in various regions of the globe but also to tap into local and regional potential to improve its sustainability performance (Preuss 2005). The impact of specialisation on CSR innovation can be illustrated by the use of CSR management systems. The current generation of management systems, such as environmental management system ISO 14001 or health and safety management system OHSAS 18001, with their focus on 'doing things right first time' are important in preventative terms as they reduce the likelihood of industrial accidents. However, the rational approach that underlies them is less suited to developing and embedding organisational values that enable organisational members to 'do the right things' and do so in an innovative fashion (Zwetsloot 2003).

The argument of a mismatch between instrumental rationality and the value-based nature of CSR also extends to the structures of control, authority and communication that are used in the management of CSR. The dominant rational management approach, together with a centralised allocation of resources, responsibilities and accountabilities, overlooks the fact that it is particular people lower down the organisational hierarchy that can make important contributions to identifying and promoting opportunities for innovative CSR (Drumwright 1994). It is especially middle managers who can contribute to a bottom-up evolution of CSR as it is their responsibility anyway to translate corporate strategy into actions and results, while in particular the human resources profession emphasises the personal and interpersonal aspects of employment (O'Higgins and Kelleher 2005). At the same time, middle manager initiatives need top management support. There is indeed empirical evidence that the structure of the board of management, in particular the number of outside directors, is a crucial determinant of corporate social performance (Zahm 1989; Johnson and Greening 1999).

The impact of company size on CSR activities has been established by a number of studies (Aragón-Correa 1998). The larger the firm is, the more visible it tends to become and hence the more subject to pressure to demonstrate social and environmental responsibility (Aragón-Correa 1998; Sharma 2000; Preuss 2005). Large firms also tend to have better access to the resources required to meet CSR demands, in particular where these do not translate into an improved economic performance in the short run (Sharma 2000). Studies that focused more specifically on the relationship between innovation and CSR outcomes indeed found that the probability of innovation leading to a reduced social and/or environmental impact is positively associated with firm size but also industrial sector, where firms in industries such as oil, paper or consumer chemicals had the highest probability and those in financial services or real estate the lowest (Pavelin and Porter 2008). A related research stream has begun to assess the opportunities for and barriers to innovative CSR as they arise specifically in small and medium-sized firms (SMEs). On the one hand, many SMEs display a lack of human and financial resources that can be dedicated to CSR (Taylor *et al.* 2003) and they often lack formal practices to manage their social and environmental impact (Merritt 1998; Petts *et al.* 1999). On the other hand, SMEs were found to display a range of unique strategic characteristics that aid an innovative approach to CSR, such as shorter lines of communication, visibility of owner-manager values or flexibility in managing external relationships (Aragón-Correa *et al.* 2008; Jenkins 2009).

Among the external linkages of the company, the supply chain has received particular attention in the CSR literature (Preuss 2005; Seuring and Müller 2008). Many companies—in particular the global textile and toy value chains—have adopted a range of technological and organisational innovations, such as the introduction of safer production methods or the application of codes of conduct (Mamic 2004; de Brito *et al.* 2008). They have thus engaged in innovative CSR as defined above. However, the study of CSR in supply chains has also unearthed significant structural barriers to innovative CSR that arise from the diversity and the complexity of the product chain as well as the power of the focal companies in the chain (Cramer 2008). For example, in the electronics industry, electronics contract manufacturers have to use vendors that are approved by their customers. A deviation from this list, even if it was in order to source from a supplier with a particularly innovative CSR profile, would not be possible without prior approval (Preuss 2005). In developing countries, the share of the labour force who work for multinationals or their key suppliers—and who benefit from pressure for improved labour standards in global supply chains—is often small. In India, for example, an estimated 35 million people out of a total workforce of 470 million are employed in the formal economy, of which foreign companies account for no more than 2 million (Luce 2006).

## Innovative CSR and societal context

The third element of the integrated innovation framework takes its starting point in the fact that all organisations exist in a particular institutional context (Lam 2000). Processes of innovation are thus not only shaped by organisational learning and structural constraints but also by the national institutional frameworks that surround business. As proponents of the 'varieties of capitalism' approach argue, differences between firms in innovative potential are caused by differences in the organisation of financial markets or education systems as well as in societal norms and values governing the role of business in society (Whitley 1999; Hall and Soskice 2001). The latter leads to the emphasis, in the institutionalism literature, on the normative embeddedness of organisations in their institutional context (DiMaggio and Powell 1983; Zucker 1987). A major focus by institutionalists has been on the ways in which norms, rules, values, beliefs and assumptions enable or constrain organisational change (e.g. Hinings *et al.* 1996). However, as the evolution of CSR shows, the institutional context may also become a driver for change that is then imposed on organisations.

The direction in which CSR should develop—that is, in which innovative CSR should head—is increasingly defined through a corporate dialogue with its stakeholders (Waddock 1988; Pedersen 2006; Burchell and Cook 2008; Seitanidi and Crane 2009). Such collaboration is proffered as a participatory approach to bring about mutually beneficial outcomes (Waddock 1988). In other words the locus of innovation now lies outside the firm boundaries (Holmes and Moir 2007), which is in itself an innovation in comparison with earlier phases of CSR (Vogel 2005). However, there are practical and theoretical limits to business–CSO (civil society organisation) collaboration, not least surrounding the motives for a dialogue and the need for a longer-term commitment on all sides (Waddock 1988; Burchell and Cook 2008). At a practical level, such a dialogue is likely to be shaped by a set of filters—regarding the selection of stakeholders, the interpretation of their voices or the formulation of a corporate response—that make the dialogue operational but also limit its benefits to participants (Pedersen 2006). There also lurks selectivity in the issues to which stakeholders draw attention, as campaigning stakeholders in particular, such as NGOs, have scarce resources. Hence the categories of stakeholder power, legitimacy and urgency (Mitchell *et al.* 1997) explain not only which stakeholders managers should listen to but also which issues stakeholders can successfully push.

Business–CSO collaborations gain their legitimacy from the claim that CSOs enable an alignment of business interests with the expectations of society (Seitanidi and Crane 2009). However, the representative role of CSOs is not an automatic one; they may end up serving their own interests rather than those of the wider society they claim to represent. Such a gap may be enhanced by the limited attention span of the public. Citizens—particularly in Europe—have shown a low level of interest in corporate social and environmental initiatives; as social and environmental standards are high, enforcement is on average strong and compliance is widespread (Steger 2006). Hence citizens think they can rest relatively assured that corporate misdeeds are kept in check through other means even if they themselves do not engage with these. This has its pendant in the varying degrees of voter apathy many democratic countries have experienced (Eliasoph 1998). The limited public attention span is thus another barrier to innovative CSR, as it can undermine efforts by societal elites to push for higher social and environmental standards.

The impact of institutional frameworks on innovative CSR can also be illustrated through the literature on the diffusion of innovation, which stresses that the diffusion of innovation depends on the social system and is influenced by two major factors: mass media and opinion leaders (Rogers 1995; MacGregor and Fontrodona 2008). While Rogers (1995) was primarily concerned with the diffusion of technological innovation, similar processes can be observed in the diffusion of CSR—and of innovative CSR. In many continental European societies, CSR has not been traditionally expected of business because of the high levels of taxation. The formerly 'implicit' emphasis on CSR became 'explicit' only when governments began to run out of funds to maintain the welfare state (Matten and Moon 2008). Such differences in expectations regarding the direction in which CSR should innovate are illustrated by the argument that voluntary corporate commitments that go beyond legal obligations, a mainstay of CSR in North America and Europe, are less suited to many developing countries where the enforcement of legal obligations is weak in the first place (Blowfield and Frynas 2005).

To summarise the discussion, the integrative framework of innovation as being shaped by organisational knowledge management and learning processes, organisational structures and the social embeddedness of the firm (Lam 2000) has been applied here to draw out what barriers might prevent companies from taking up more innovative approaches to CSR (see Table 15.1). The discussion of the role of knowledge management in CSR identified barriers in terms of an insufficient capacity to combine CSR knowledge or a lack of political skills among organisational members, as a result of which novel priorities may not get integrated into CSR strategy. In terms of organisational learning, barriers to innovative CSR may

**TABLE 15.1** Framework of barriers to innovative CSR

| Element | Key features | Barriers to innovative CSR |
| --- | --- | --- |
| Nature of knowledge and organisational learning | Forms of knowledge: element view and process view of knowledge | Insufficient organisational capacity to combine CSR knowledge |
| | | Lack of political skills leading to insufficient organisational support for CSR and/or to incomplete integration of stakeholder priorities into CSR strategy |
| | Forms of organisational learning: adaptive processes and processes of cognitive change | Company decision to buffer itself from external demands rather than build bridges |
| | | Failure to question organisational values and/or range of stakeholders that are consulted |
| Organisational structure | Specialisation and functional differentiation versus continuous adjustment and redefinition of individual tasks | Delegating CSR to remote department or shared service centre is likely to lead to bolted-on CSR |
| | Structures of control, authority and communication around CSR | Hierarchical control limits opportunities for organisational members to contribute to innovative CSR |
| | Impact of company size and sector on CSR strategy and performance | Limited resources for CSR in smaller companies and firms outside the public limelight |
| | Supply chain members as potential source of innovative CSR for the entire chain | Structural barriers relating to the complexity of the product chain and the power of focal companies within the chain |
| Societal embeddedness | Direction for innovative CSR derived from stakeholder dialogue | Practical and theoretical limits to business–CSO collaboration (selection of stakeholders, interpretation of their voices, formulation of response, etc.) |
| | | Limited public attention span |
| | Processes of diffusion of innovation and innovative CSR | Inertia to innovation in social system surrounding an industry |
| | | Differences between societies in terms of priorities for future CSR developments |

emerge from a decision to buffer the company from external demands rather than to build bridges as well as from a failure to question the values that underlie its CSR strategy. The impact of organisational structure on innovative CSR became clear in the barriers that can lurk in specialisation and functional differentiation of the CSR function, the structures of control, authority and communication around CSR, the impact of company size and sector on CSR strategy and performance as well as in structural limitations to tap into the potential of supply chain members to provide input for innovative CSR. Societal embeddedness pointed to practical and theoretical limits of stakeholder dialogues to give a direction for innovative CSR as well as the processes of diffusion of innovation, where differences in societal expectations may make particular forms of innovative CSR suitable for some societies but not for others.

## Conclusions

This chapter set out to develop a definition of innovative CSR. On the basis of the OECD definition of innovation as technological and/or organisational novelties (OECD and Eurostat 1997), innovative CSR was defined as consisting of technological CSR innovation and/or organisational CSR innovation. The former could entail changes to products or production processes that reduce environmental impact or enhance employee working conditions, while the latter may consist of the application of CSR tools—as long as they are novel for the implementing organisation. Such innovation differs from other types in two crucial aspects. On the one hand, innovative CSR has the ability to address external stakeholder demands; in particular it offers stakeholders the opportunity to play an active role in the innovation process, which is not usually the case in conventional forms of innovation. On the other hand, the payback period of innovative CSR may need to be longer than that of conventional innovation, as the emergent nature of demands for socially and environmentally responsible products and manufacturing processes makes the calculation of benefits from the innovation less reliable (Pavelin and Porter 2008).

The concept of innovative CSR can serve as an alternative conceptualisation to strategic CSR, which in turn builds on the business case for CSR. This has important practitioner and theoretical implications. For practitioners, the starting point for CSR would then lie not in stakeholder demands (Waddock 1988; Mitchell *et al.* 1997; Cragg and Greenbaum 2002) nor in the tangible benefits of strategic CSR (Salzmann *et al.* 2005; Porter and Kramer 2006; Laszlo 2008); rather, the status quo of CSR activities in their firm would determine which technological and/or organisational CSR activities they should tackle. Offering a different rationale from the business case for engaging in CSR would be useful CSR rhetoric to convince managers in firms that see little tangible benefit from CSR. The major advantage of innovative over strategic CSR would thus lie in its ability to generate greater buy-in among a greater number of firms, such as firms in capital goods industries or SMEs that find it difficult to achieve tangible benefits from their CSR activities. From a public policy perspective, innovative CSR would offer the possibility that the uptake of CSR would proceed faster and hence its social and environmental benefits would be realised more quickly than through foregrounding strategic CSR.

From a theoretical perspective, the relationship between financial and social performance in innovative CSR still needs discussion, as no firm will engage in innovation for innovation's sake. Moving the CSR debate beyond the zero-sum game, where social and environmental improvements had been assumed to impact negatively on financial performance, proponents of strategic CSR pointed to an ability of CSR to generate both societal and company benefits through improved products and services, tapping into unserved markets or designing new business models (Grayson and Hodges 2004; Halme and Laurila 2009). The notion of innovative CSR, however, stresses a wider conceptualisation of benefits the company can reap. Innovation in the field of CSR, particularly the philanthropic type, may be easier to undertake than other forms of innovation—innovative CSR may be of the stand-alone rather than the systemic type (Teece 1998)—and in view of the generally risky nature of innovation, innovative CSR may provide an experimenting ground where the risks are relatively controlled, precisely because they are not closely linked to the company's core business (MacGregor and Fontrodona 2008). If the innovative CSR project works, the company will have improved its standing in society and perhaps innovative CSR could even become a crystallisation point for other forms of innovation.

Another theoretical implication of the concept of innovative CSR concerns the nature of innovation, in particular where innovation does not proceed in a gradual but in a disruptive fashion. The 'creative destruction' Schumpeter (1980) described hardly reflects the types of social concern that are traditionally associated with CSR (Midttun 2007). Future research thus needs to establish to what extent innovation and CSR are complementary or antithetic (but see here the work of Midttun 2007). From a managerial perspective, managers may perceive the unpredictability of new technologies to be a threat to their job or the operations of their firm and hence select options that seek to minimise risk rather than maximise gains (Kahneman and Tversky 1979). Future research should thus establish whether managers are unlikely under such conditions to search for innovative solutions to social and environmental challenges—as predicted by Sharma (2000)—or whether the fact that innovative CSR is only loosely coupled to the firm's operational core would offer managers an experimental ground from which they may venture into other forms of innovation—as suggested above. However, these are question that go beyond the scope of this chapter.

# References

Al-Ghassani, A.M., J.M. Kamara, C.J. Anumba and P.M. Carrillo (2004) 'An Innovative Approach to Identifying Knowledge Management Problems', *Engineering, Construction and Architectural Management* 11.5: 349-57.

Amabile, T.M., R. Conti, H. Coon, J. Lazenby and M. Herron (1996) 'Assessing the Work Environment for Creativity', *Academy of Management Journal* 39.5: 1,154-84.

Aragón-Correa, J.A. (1998) 'Strategic Proactivity and Firm Approach to the Natural Environment', *Academy of Management Journal* 41.5: 556-67.

——, N. Hurtado-Torres, S. Sharma and V.J. García-Morales (2008) 'Environmental Strategy and Performance in Small Firms: A Resource-Based Perspective', *Journal of Environmental Management* 86.1: 88-103.

Argyris, C. (1993) *On Organizational Learning* (Cambridge, MA: Blackwell).

Beaulieu, S., and J. Pasquero (2003) 'Reintroducing Stakeholder Dynamics in Stakeholder Thinking: A Negotiated-Order Perspective', in J. Andriof, S. Waddock, B. Husted and S. Rahman (eds.), *Unfolding Stakeholder Thinking: Theory, Responsibility and Engagement* (Sheffield, UK: Greenleaf Publishing): 101-18.

Benthoin Antal, A., and A. Sobczak (2004) 'Beyond CSR: Organisational Learning for Global Responsibility', *Journal of General Management* 30.2: 77-98.

Blowfield, M., and J.G. Frynas (2005) 'Setting New Agendas: Critical Perspectives on Corporate Social Responsibility in the Developing World', *International Affairs* 81.3: 499-513.

Bowie, N.E. (1999) *Business Ethics: A Kantian Perspective* (Oxford, UK: Blackwell).

Burchell, J., and J. Cook (2008) 'Stakeholder Dialogue and Organisational Learning: Changing Relationships between Companies and NGOs', *Business Ethics: A European Review* 17.1: 35-46.

Burke, L., and J.M. Logsdon (1996) 'How Corporate Social Responsibility Pays Off', *Long Range Planning* 29.4: 495-502.

Burns, T., and G.M. Stalker (1961) *The Management of Innovation* (London: Tavistock Publishing).

Carrano, A.L., and B.K. Thorn (2006) 'A Multidisciplinary Approach to Sustainable Product and Process Design', *Journal of Manufacturing Systems* 24.3: 209-14.

Christiansen, J.A. (2000) *Building the Innovative Organization* (Basingstoke, UK: Macmillan).

Cragg, W., and A. Greenbaum (2002) 'Reasoning about Responsibilities: Mining Company Managers on What Stakeholders Are Owed', *Journal of Business Ethics* 39.3: 319-35.

Cramer, J.M. (2008) 'Organising Corporate Social Responsibility in International Product Chains', *Journal of Cleaner Production* 16.3: 395-400.

Cyert, R., and J. March (1963) *A Behavioral Theory of the Firm* (Englewood Cliffs, NJ: Prentice Hall).

De Brito, M.P., V. Carbone and C.M. Blanquart (2008) 'Towards a Sustainable Fashion Retail Supply Chain in Europe: Organisation and Performance', *International Journal of Production Economics* 114.2: 534-53.

DiMaggio, P.J., and W.W. Powell (1983) 'The Iron Cage Revisited: Institutional Isomorphism and Collective Rationality in Organizational Fields', *American Sociological Review* 48: 147-60.

Donaldson, T., and T.W. Dunfee (1999) *Ties That Bind: A Social Contracts Approach to Business Ethics* (Boston, MA: Harvard Business School Press).

Drumwright, M.E. (1994) 'Socially Responsible Organizational Buying: Environmental Concern as Noneconomic Buying Criterion', *Journal of Marketing* 58 (July 1994): 1-19.

Eliasoph, N. (1998) *Avoiding Politics: How Americans Produce Apathy in Everyday Life* (New York: Cambridge University Press).

Fagerberg, J., and M. Srholec (2008) 'National Innovation Systems, Capabilities and Economic Development', *Research Policy* 37.9: 1,417-35.

Fiksel, J. (1996) *Design for Environment: Creating Eco-efficient Products and Processes* (New York: McGraw-Hill).

Freeman, C. (1995) 'The "National System of Innovation" in Historical Perspective', *Cambridge Journal of Economics* 19: 5-24.

Frewer, L.J., C. Howard and R. Shepherd (1997) 'Public Concerns in the United Kingdom about General and Specific Applications of Genetic Engineering: Risk, Benefit, and Ethics', *Science, Technology, and Human Values* 22.1: 98-124.

Gardberg, N.A., and C.F. Fombrun (2006) 'Corporate Citizenship: Creating Intangible Value across Institutional Environments', *Academy of Management Review* 31.2: 329-46.

Gond, J.-P., and O. Herrbach (2006) 'Social Reporting as an Organisational Learning Tool? A Theoretical Framework', *Journal of Business Ethics* 65.4: 359-71.

Grant, R.M. (1996) 'Toward a Knowledge-Based Theory of the Firm', *Strategic Management Journal* 17 (Special Issue): 109-22.

Grayson, D., and A. Hodges (2004) *Corporate Social Opportunity! Seven Steps to Make Corporate Social Responsibility Work for your Business* (Sheffield, UK: Greenleaf Publishing).

Griesse, M. (2007) 'Developing Social Responsibility: Biotechnology and the Case of DuPont in Brazil', *Journal of Business Ethics* 73.1: 103-18.

Hall, P., and D. Soskice (eds.) (2001) *Varieties of Capitalism* (Oxford, UK: Oxford University Press).

Halme, M., and J. Laurila (2009) 'Philanthropy, Integration or Innovation? Exploring the Financial and Societal Outcomes of Different Types of Corporate Responsibility', *Journal of Business Ethics* 84.3: 325-39.

Hemingway, C.A., and P.W. Maclagan (2004) 'Managers' Personal Values as Drivers of Corporate Social Responsibility', *Journal of Business Ethics* 50.1: 33-44.

Henderson, R.M., and K.B. Clark (1990) 'Architectural Innovation: The Reconfiguration of Existing Product Technologies and the Failure of Established Firms', *Administrative Science Quarterly* 35.1: 9-30.

Hinings, C.R., L. Thibault, T. Slack and L.M. Kikulis (1996) 'Values and Organizational Structure', *Human Relations* 49.7: 885-916.

Holmes, S., and L. Moir (2007) 'Developing a Conceptual Framework to Identify Corporate Innovations through Engagement with Non-profit Stakeholders', *Corporate Governance: International Journal of Business in Society* 7.4: 414-22.

Husted, B.W., and D.B. Allen (2007) 'Strategic Corporate Social Responsibility and Value Creation among Large Firms', *Long Range Planning* 40.6: 594-610.

Jenkins, H. (2006) 'Small Business Champions for Corporate Social Responsibility', *Journal of Business Ethics* 67.3: 241-56.

—— (2009) 'A "Business Opportunity" Model of Corporate Social Responsibility for Small- and Medium-sized Enterprises', *Business Ethics: A European Review* 18.1: 21-36.

Johnson, R.A., and D.W. Greening (1999) 'The Effects of Corporate Governance and Institutional Ownership Types on Corporate Social Performance', *Academy of Management Journal* 42.5: 564-76.

Kahneman, D., and A. Tversky (1979) 'Prospect Theory: An Analysis of Decisions under Risk', *Econometrica* 47.2: 263-91.

Kogut, B., and U. Zander (2003) 'Knowledge of the Firm and the Evolutionary Theory of the Multinational Corporation', *Journal of International Business Studies* 34.6: 516-29.

Kourula, A., and M. Halme (2008) 'Types of Corporate Responsibility and Engagement with NGOs: An Exploration of Business and Societal Outcomes', *Corporate Governance: The International Journal of Business in Society* 8.4: 557-70.

Lam, A. (2000) 'Tacit Knowledge, Organizational Learning and Societal Institutions: An Integrated Framework', *Organization Studies* 21.3: 487-513.

Laszlo, C. (2008) *Sustainable Value: How the World's Leading Companies are Doing Well by Doing Good* (Sheffield, UK: Greenleaf Publishing).

Lenox, M., A. King and J. Ehrenfeld (2008) 'An Assessment of Design-for-Environment Practices in Leading US Electronics Firms', *Interfaces* 30.3: 83-94.

Levitt, B., and J. March (1988) 'Organizational Learning', *Annual Review of Sociology* 14: 319-40.

Livesey, S.M. (2001) 'Eco-identity as Discursive Struggle: Royal Dutch/Shell, Brent Spar, and Nigeria', *Journal of Business Communication* 38.1: 58-91.

Luce, E. (2006) *In Spite of the Gods: The Strange Rise of Modern India* (London: Little, Brown).

MacGregor, S.P., and J. Fontrodona (2008) 'Exploring the Fit between CSR and Innovation' (IESE Business School Working Paper WP 759; Barcelona: IESE Business School, University of Navarra).

Mamic, I. (2004) *Implementing Codes of Conduct: How Businesses Manage Social Performance in the Global Supply Chain* (Sheffield, UK: Greenleaf Publishing).

Matten, D., and J. Moon (2008) ' "Implicit" and "Explicit" CSR: A Conceptual Framework for a Comparative Understanding of Corporate Social Responsibility', *Academy of Management Review* 33.2: 404-24.

——, A. Crane and J. Moon (2007) 'Corporate Responsibility for Innovation: A Citizenship Framework', in G. Hanekamp (ed.), *Business Ethics of Innovation* (Berlin: Springer): 63-87.

Merritt, J.Q. (1998) 'EM into SME Won't Go? Attitudes, Awareness and Practices in the London Borough of Croydon', *Business Strategy and the Environment* 7: 90-100.

Meznar, M.B., and D. Nigh (1995) 'Buffer or Bridge? Environmental and Organizational Determinants of Public Affairs Activities in American Firms', *Academy of Management Journal* 38.4: 975-96.

Midttun, A. (2007) 'Corporate Responsibility from a Resource and Knowledge Perspective. Towards a Dynamic Reinterpretation of C(S)R: Are Corporate Responsibility and Innovation Comparative or Contradictory?', *Corporate Governance: The International Journal of Business in Society* 7.4: 401-13.

Mintzberg, H. (1979) *The Structure of Organizations: A Synthesis of the Research* (Englewood Cliffs, NJ: Prentice Hall).

Mitchell, R.K., B.R. Agle and D.J. Wood (1997) 'Toward a Theory of Stakeholder Identification and Salience: Defining the Principle of Who and What Really Counts', *Academy of Management Review* 22.4: 853-86.

Murphy, J., and A. Gouldson (2000) 'Environmental Policy and Industrial Innovation: Integrating Environment and Economy through Ecological Modernisation', *Geoforum* 31.1: 33-44.

Nelson, R. (1993) *National Innovation Systems: A Comparative Analysis* (Oxford, UK: Oxford University Press).

Nonaka, I., and H. Takeuchi (1995) *The Knowledge Creating Company* (New York: Oxford University Press).

O'Higgins, E., and B. Kelleher (2005) 'Comparative Perspectives on the Ethical Orientations of Human Resources, Marketing and Finance Functional Managers', *Journal of Business Ethics* 56.3: 275-88.

OECD and Eurostat (1997) *Oslo Manual: Proposed Guidelines for Collecting and Interpreting Technological Innovation Data* (Paris: OECD).

Pavelin, S., and L.A. Porter (2008) 'The Corporate Social Performance Content of Innovation in the UK', *Journal of Business Ethics* 80.4: 711-25.

Pavitt, K. (1984) 'Sectoral Patterns of Technological Change: Towards a Taxonomy and Theory', *Research Policy* 13: 343-73.

Pedersen, E.R. (2006) 'Making Corporate Social Responsibility (CSR) Operable: How Companies Translate Stakeholder Dialogue into Practice', *Business and Society Review* 111.2: 137-63.

Penrose, E.T. (1959) *The Theory of the Growth of the Firm* (New York: John Wiley).

Petts, J., A. Herd, S. Gerrard and C. Horne (1999) 'The Climate and Culture of Environmental Compliance within SMEs', *Business Strategy and the Environment* 8: 14-30.

Polanyi, M. (1966) *The Tacit Dimension* (New York: Anchor Day Books).

Porter, M.E. (1985) *Competitive Advantage: Creating and Sustaining Superior Performance* (New York: The Free Press).

—— and M.R. Kramer (2006) 'Strategy and Society: The Link between Competitive Advantage and Corporate Social Responsibility', *Harvard Business Review* 84.12: 78-92.

Prahalad, C.K., and A. Hammond (2002) 'Serving the World's Poor, Profitably', *Harvard Business Review* 80.9: 48-57.

Preuss, L. (2005) *The Green Multiplier: A Study of Environmental Protection and the Supply Chain* (Basingstoke, UK: Palgrave).

—— and J.-R. Córdoba-Pachon (2009) 'A Knowledge Management Perspective of Corporate Social Responsibility', *Corporate Governance: The International Journal of Business in Society* 9.4: 517-27.

Rennings, K., K. Ankele, E. Hoffmann, J. Nill and A. Ziegler (2005) *Innovationen durch Umweltmanagement: Empirische Ergebnisse zum EG-Öko-Audit* (Heidelberg: Physica-Verlag).

Rogers, E.M. (1995) *Diffusion of Innovations* (New York: The Free Press, 4th edn).

Salzmann, O., A. Ionescu-Somers and U. Steger (2005) 'The Business Case for Corporate Sustainability', *European Management Journal* 23.1: 27-36.

Schaltegger, S., and M. Wagner (2006) 'Introduction: Managing and Measuring the Business Case for Sustainability', in S. Schaltegger and M. Wagner (eds.), *Managing the Business Case for Sustainability: The Integration of Social, Environmental and Economic Performance* (Sheffield, UK: Greenleaf Publishing).

Schumpeter, J.A. (1980) *Theory of Economic Development* (New Brunswick, NJ: Transaction Publishers).

Seitanidi, M.M., and A. Crane (2009) 'Implementing CSR through Partnerships: Understanding the Selection, Design and Institutionalisation of Nonprofit-Business Partnerships', *Journal of Business Ethics* 85.S2: 413-29.

Seuring, S., and M. Müller (2008) 'From a Literature Review to a Conceptual Framework for Sustainable Supply Chain Management', *Journal of Cleaner Production* 16: 1,699-1710.

Sharma, S. (2000) 'Managerial Interpretations and Organizational Context as Predictors or Corporate Choice of Environmental Strategy', *Academy of Management Journal* 43.4: 681-97.

Solomon, R.C. (1992) *Ethics and Excellence: Cooperation and Integrity in Business* (New York: Oxford University Press).

Spar, D.L., and L.T. La Mure (2003) 'The Power of Activism: Assessing the Impact of NGOs on Global Business', *California Management Review* 45.3: 78-101.

Spender, J.-C. (1996) 'Making Knowledge the Basis of a Dynamic Theory of the Firm', *Strategic Management Journal* 17 (Winter Special Issue): 45-62.

Steger, U. (2006) *Inside the Mind of the Stakeholder: The Hype behind Stakeholder Pressure* (Basingstoke, UK: Palgrave).

Taylor, N., K. Barker and M. Simpson (2003) 'Achieving "Sustainable Business": A Study of Perceptions of Environmental Best Practice by SMEs in South Yorkshire', *Environment and Planning C* 21: 89-105.

Teece, D.J. (1998) 'Design Issues for Innovative Firms: Bureaucracy, Incentives and Industrial Structure', in A.D. Chandler, P. Hagstrom and Ö. Sölvell (eds.), *The Dynamic Firm: The Role of Technology, Strategy, Organization, and Regions* (Oxford, UK: Oxford University Press): 134-65.

Utterback, J.M., and H.J. Acee (2005) 'Disruptive Technologies: An Expanded View', *International Journal of Innovation Management* 9.1: 1-17.

Van de Ven, A.H., D.E. Polley, R. Garud and S. Venkataraman (1999) *The Innovation Journey* (New York: Oxford University Press).

Vogel, D. (2005) 'Is there a Market for Virtue? The Business Case for Corporate Social Responsibility', *California Management Review* 47.4: 19-45.

Von Hippel, E. (1988) *The Sources of Innovation* (New York: Oxford University Press).

Waddock, S.A. (1988) 'Building Successful Partnerships', *Sloan Management Review* 29.4: 17-23.

Walsh, J.P., and G.R. Ungson (1991) 'Organizational Memory', *Academy of Management Review* 16: 57-91.

Welford, R. (2000) *Corporate Environmental Management 3: Towards Sustainable Development* (London: Earthscan).

Werther, W.B., and D. Chandler (2005) 'Strategic Corporate Social Responsibility as Global Brand Insurance', *Business Horizons* 48.4: 317-24.

Whitley, R. (1999) *Divergent Capitalisms: The Social Structuring and Change of Business Systems* (Oxford, UK: Oxford University Press).

Zahm, S.A. (1989) 'Boards of Directors and Corporate Social Responsibility Performance', *European Management Journal* 7.2: 240-47.

Zucker, L.G. (1987) 'Institutional Theories of Organizations', *Annual Review of Sociology* 13: 443-64.

Zwetsloot, G.I.J.M. (2003) 'From Management Systems to Corporate Social Responsibility', *Journal of Business Ethics* 44.2: 201-207.

# 16
# How consultants contribute to CSR innovation
## Combining competences and modifying standards

**Magnus Frostenson**
Uppsala University, Sweden

Consultants have come to play an increasingly important role within the evolving field of corporate social responsibility (CSR) (Windell 2006; Dubbink *et al.* 2008). One reason for this is that consultants have benefited from the vagueness and flexibility of the concept of CSR. The possibility of framing the concept according to business logic—making it a necessary condition for better and more profitable business—has been central for the acceptance of CSR as a management idea (Sahlin-Andersson 2006; Kurucz *et al.* 2008). As such, it has been developed and diffused by consultants on the basis of knowledge and expertise. As Windell (2006: 135) notes, CSR has become 'a proactive management idea that would not only minimise the risks of corporations being scrutinised by their stakeholders, but would also contribute to increased profitability'. In this sense, CSR has come to resemble other management ideas such as total quality management or business process re-engineering (Ghobadian *et al.* 2007; Sahlin and Wedlin 2008).

Consultants can be seen as carriers of general management ideas that are materialised and implemented in business through concrete models, processes or solutions (Sahlin-Andersson and Engwall 2002; Ernst and Kieser 2002). Consultants are active counterparts to corporations. They redevelop ideas and play an active role in diffusing them (Czarniawska 1990; Sahlin-Andersson and Engwall 2002; Fincham 2006). So far, however, knowledge on how this is done within the field of CSR is poor. One reason for examining how consultants contribute with ideas and knowledge on CSR is that there is a strong tradition of 'outsourcing' CSR services to consultants (Borglund *et al.* 2008). New knowledge on CSR, frequently conveyed by consultants, tends to spur new activities, tools and frames of reference in corporations as their awareness of the expectations for responsible behaviour increases.

The aim of the chapter is to analyse how consultants contribute with ideas, knowledge and tools within the field of CSR. This is done by an empirical study of how consultants treat, communicate and package their knowledge of CSR in their offers to clients. In other words, the chapter analyses how consultants 'translate' CSR to clients. From a theoretical point of view, the chapter connects to the 'travel of ideas' literature within the wider framework of neo-institutional theory. This theoretical perspective facilitates an understanding of how overarching ideas can travel and establish themselves in different settings with sometimes contrasting meanings.

The innovation focus of the chapter lies on the capacity of consultants to develop new knowledge that materialises into products or tools useful for clients in their development of responsible business. It treats CSR innovation from the supply side, which means that it highlights the role of consultants when it comes to spreading CSR as a management idea. At the end of the chapter, some tentative ideas on the significance of consultants for innovation within corporations are formulated.

## Consultants and innovation

One of the striking aspects of business in recent decades is the tendency to adopt new management ideas, concepts or tools that diffuse rapidly across the globe (Fincham 2006). Several studies have suggested that consultants have played an important role as carriers of such ideas or concepts. As noted by Sahlin-Andersson and Engwall (2002) and Sahlin-Andersson (2006), the expansion and flow of management techniques and models is not primarily a demand-driven process. Rather, the active role of consultants tends to create a supply-driven expansion of management knowledge. Consultants, for this reason, contribute strongly to expanding management knowledge by producing concepts, methods and tools as well as selling them (Berglund and Werr 2000; Sahlin-Andersson and Engwall 2002; Werr and Stjernberg 2003).

The process where consultants are active in expanding and diffusing new knowledge shows some characteristics that are highly relevant in the discussion about innovation. Basically, two elements tend to be seen as central for innovation. The first element is novelty. As the concept of innovation has been treated in the literature, it always seems to contain an element of novelty compared with what has existed before. The novelty can be a feature of an idea, object or practice (Rogers 1995; Valiente 2006). Innovation involves the creation of something that is new in itself or constitutes a new combination of existing phenomena (Mölleryd 1999).

The second element in an elaborated understanding of innovation is what one could call applicability. The condition of applicability is what separates innovation from invention. Invention refers to the generation of a concept that may or may not lead to an innovation. An invention becomes an innovation when it is applied to a product or a production process (Zander 1991). Another way of framing the applicability condition is to connect it to the acceptance within a certain social system. By means of a diffusion process the invention is communicated and reaches acceptance over time and among members of a particular social system (Rogers 1995; Valiente 2006). On such an understanding, innovation becomes the outcome of a process application of something that is invented.

Consultants can be seen as drivers of innovation if they promote novelty and play an active role in the process of diffusing, implementing or developing ideas that are new to the clients. They provide management with 'advice, expertise, project management, change programme coordination, or process skills in facilitating change' (Caldwell 2003: 140). Facilitating choice of action and reducing confusion in 'over-complex' situations (Hagenmeyer 2007) is part of traditional consulting activity. Since their solutions are believed to contribute to long-term profitability by improving productivity and cutting costs, consultants are seen as legitimate problem-solvers (Windell 2006). According to Kieser (2002), an ideal strategy for risk-averse managers is to innovate through the implementation of new management concepts under the guidance of consultants. Innovation, in this case, is considered to arise with the use and implementation of the new concept, while, at the same time, the concept is not a novelty within the actual management discourse, where it has already found approval. This increases the legitimacy of the concept and reduces the risk of failure.

Czarniawska (1990) suggests that the major contribution of consultants is symbolic. They infuse new meanings to practices within the organisation. Even though problem-solving is a central task, the activity that consultants engage in when solving problems is, according to this view, 'the manipulation of symbolic values' (Fincham 2006: 17). To a large extent, consultants are active in constructing the service that they offer, which also, owing to the intangibility of the service, implies construction of the success criteria of their own offers. For this reason, consultants often engage in a sort of dramatisation of persuasive character (Clark and Salaman 1998; Berglund and Werr 2000).

Whatever approach one prefers, one conclusion is that consultants seem to be active in the process of both constructing and promoting management concepts

(Kieser 2002). They 'commodify' such concepts, which means that they transform unstructured problems and solutions into standardised problems and solutions, which also implies structuring the problems within understandable and communicable frames of meaning. Through the knowledge that consultants convey, managers are promised a higher capacity to control their organisations (Ernst and Kieser 2002), for example through new instruments, new frames of reference, and by providing concepts that managers can connect to well-known management problems (Kieser 2002). This phenomenon also makes itself known in the field of CSR, for example in attempts to link the concept to quality and business excellence (van Marrewijk *et al.* 2004).

# The expansion and nature of the CSR consulting field

Even though research on the topic is scarce, it is clear that consultants have been active in constructing and diffusing the management idea of CSR in recent years (Frostenson and Borglund 2006; Borglund *et al.* 2008). Windell (2006) describes the CSR consulting expansion as going through two phases. The ideology-driven phase of the 1990s was characterised by strongly motivated 'world saviours' who tried to establish CSR as a concept for business for moral and ideological reasons, basically with the objective of creating a better world. At the turn of the millennium, this ideological approach was challenged by a business-driven expansion of CSR consultants in the wake of corporate scandals, increased media coverage, increased soft regulation and protests against globalisation. This development coincided with the active market extension of traditional consulting firms towards the field of CSR. Following the increased popularity of socially responsible investment, screening companies and ethical investment specialists also emerged. The number of consultancies working with CSR grew rapidly, not least because CSR specialists working at larger firms started their own businesses. For example, the number of CSR consulting firms in Sweden grew from zero in 1990 to around 50 in 2003, and has continued to rise after 2003 (Windell 2006). The 'weak professionalization' (Fincham 2006) of the consulting industry—implying low entry barriers, lack of common work ethics and few accreditation systems—facilitated the growth. Consulting firms have become an important job market for people interested in CSR. In late 2007, a study by Ellen Weinreb Recruiting and Consulting and Net Impact (2007) revealed a 37% annual growth in total CSR jobs from 2004 to 2007. The study confirmed that CSR is often outsourced. Service companies, including consulting firms, based in the UK or US had the largest number of job postings.

In addition to this, the cultural relativity and vagueness of the CSR concept (De Geer *et al.* 2009) has been a trigger of consulting activity as it has facilitated differentiation and unique service offers (cf. Furusten 2001). Culture, history, religion and other structural factors tend to condition the corporate 'licence to operate' in a certain society (De Geer 2002; Urban 2006). An implication of this is that specific knowledge of how to adopt a 'new' macro idea in a particular cultural context is needed, which also means that the demand for consulting knowledge increases (cf. Czarniawska and Joerges 1996; Sahlin-Andersson 1996). Even though supernational CSR standards have developed extensively (Jutterström 2006), there is no clear-cut answer to the question of how to apply such standards in a particular national setting. Government decisions and new regulation have also triggered the need for CSR consultants (Moon and Vogel 2008).

The corollary of this development is a growing and strongly heterogeneous group of consultants with either ideological or business rationales for their activities (Windell 2006). To a large degree, the antagonism between ideologically and business-driven consultants has circled around the power to define the concept of CSR. CSR can be defined as an ethical concept or a construct building on instrumental financial rationality (Kurucz et al. 2008). In other words, one can say that the history of CSR consulting has been marked by the struggle between two 'master ideas' (Czarniawska and Joerges 1996; Berglund and Werr 2000): the idea of goodness versus the idea of efficiency. In theoretical terms, there was and still is a contest between competing logics within the field (Lounsbury 2008). However, the consulting expansion has implied a clear tendency towards commercialisation of the CSR consulting industry (Windell 2006), which suggests that the business case for CSR has gained ground in recent years (Kurucz et al. 2008). A sign indicating this has been that the early network structures—where small consultancies often worked together and everyone knew each other—have been challenged by larger consultancies entering the scene with more established consulting models (Windell 2006). A new feature of the CSR consulting market is that NGOs such as the Amnesty Business Group offer services that can be seen as consultative rather than oriented towards monitoring or activism, and that commercial ethics analysts providing socially responsible investors with information have come to play an increasingly important role (Borglund et al. 2008).

Today, the CSR consulting industry covers a wide range of activities. While consultants within accounting, communication and environmental affairs have added CSR services to their traditional offers, there are also a number of newly established firms riding on the CSR wave, focusing on specific issues such as stakeholder dialogues, information or screening (Borglund et al. 2008). A typical example of how traditional consulting firms approach the CSR field could be auditing firms that assist corporations in verifying sustainability reports or include CSR issues in their due diligence work (Dubbink et al. 2008). Producing sustainability reports is to a large degree the work of communication consultants, while the formulation of ethical codes and codes of conduct may be activities performed by, for example, management consultants. Consultants may, for example, assist corporations in handling investor pressure to conform to CSR standards (Borglund *et al.* 2008). In addition to this, a central task for CSR consultants is to assist clients in navigating between the many initiatives and guidelines in the field. A well-informed choice about what sort of soft regulation one should follow and what initiatives one should support requires knowledge (Windell 2006).

## Innovation through translation of ideas and knowledge

A theoretically based understanding of the role of consultants that has been described above suggests that they have the capacity to translate overarching ideas and knowledge to their clients. Translation is a theoretical concept deeply rooted in the Scandinavian approach to neo-institutional theory (Czarniawska and Joerges 1996; Sahlin-Andersson 1996; Sahlin and Wedlin 2008). The concept has been used to explain the heterogeneity of practices that tends to follow the diffusion of overarching macro ideas in society. Such ideas, according to traditional neo-institutional theory, tend to diffuse across fields and sectors creating relative uniformity of structures and practices (DiMaggio and Powell 1983). Basically, organisations conform to and institutionalise certain behaviours and practices for legitimacy reasons. Meyer and Rowan (1977) claim that organisations accept and adapt to 'symbolic myths' that condition legitimacy in a certain institutional context. Recent developments within institutional theory, however, have devoted much attention to issues such as the heterogeneity of practices at a micro level as well as the influence of multiple logics within a particular field (e.g. Lounsbury 2008). In these attempts, a stronger focus on actors and agency has emerged (e.g. Boxenbaum and Battilana 2005; Lounsbury and Crumley 2007). One idea in present research is that individual agency serves as a catalyst for organisational innovation and is required to establish knowledge-based structures (Anand *et al.* 2007).

When ideas or practices are translated, they are 'edited' in order to make sense in the new context (Czarniawska and Joerges 1996; Sahlin-Andersson 1996; Sahlin and Wedlin 2008). Without meaningfulness, the idea or practice will become void or even irrational or immoral. This means that the capacity to reconceptualise the practice and to infuse it with meaning is central to an idea's diffusion capability. Practices, this position would claim, are always enacted at a local level, and such enactment takes on different forms, not least since the internal dynamics of organisations tends to create different responses to external institutional pressure (Fiss 2008). Within a certain field, or 'communities of organisations that participate in the same meaning systems . . . defined by similar symbolic processes, and . . . subject to common regulatory processes' (Scott 1994: 71), competing logics tend to create different practice solutions that partly undermine the homogeneity of practices that is often emphasised in institutional theory (Lounsbury 2008).

Translation is often considered to be an element of a vertical process where an idea such as CSR comes from 'above' and then trickles down to lower spheres (Kieser 2002). There is also, however, the possibility of a certain practice to be transposed horizontally from one context or institutional field to another. Importing a practice from one field to another is a means of innovation in the receiving field (Boxenbaum and Battilana 2005). When a practice is 'moved' or transposed from one field to another, translation is required. The new practice must be made relevant in the new context. One example given by Boxenbaum and Battilana (2005) is the practice of diversity management, a practice that had not previously been applied to integration of immigrants. They find that individuals play an important role in transposing the practice. A reason for this is their embeddedness in various social contexts. The more contexts that individuals or organisations are embedded in, the more options they have to transpose practices or ideas. This means that multiple embeddedness is an important precondition for transposition, since it increases the capacity to absorb ideas and practices across fields. A higher innovative capacity should, according to this idea, be based on an ability to understand logics of different fields, because such an understanding gives the consultant a role as a carrier of knowledge from other contexts.

## The study

To examine the immersion of CSR in consulting offers, a choice was made to focus on firms in 12 different consulting subfields. Within the larger field of consulting, subfields can be constructed on the basis of services provided (cf. Boxenbaum and Battilana 2005). Such subfields are communities of action within a larger system of professional advisory services. The categorisation of subfields follows the database *Konsultguiden* (*The Consulting Guide*), administered by the Swedish business journal *Affärsvärlden*. This database documents facts and figures about the 12 different subfields of consulting in Sweden every year. The fields are described in Table 16.1.

Within each subfield, the ten largest firms were chosen for further examination. It should be noted, however, that eight consulting firms were represented in two categories: for example, Accenture, which is among the ten largest consulting firms within both management and IT services, and Deloitte, which is represented in the accounting/auditing field as well as within management consulting. As a consequence, the total number of consultancies included in the study was 112 rather

**TABLE 16.1** Consulting subfields and examples of types of service

| Consulting field | Types of service (examples) |
| --- | --- |
| Accounting/auditing | Accounting, auditing, management advisory services, strategy |
| Advertising agencies | Advertising services, branding |
| Education | Education on different levels, corporate education, public education, rehabilitation |
| IT | IT systems development and maintenance, outsourcing services |
| Law | Legal advice |
| Management | Advisory services, strategy |
| Market research | Market surveys, counselling, brand reputation issues, customer and employee loyalty |
| Patent | Patent procedures, immaterial rights protection |
| PR | Communication strategies, PR, profiling of firms |
| Recruitment/outplacement | Headhunting, job market placement services, training |
| Staffing | Job matching, recruitment, staffing services |
| Technology | Technological development and maintenance, outsourcing services |

than 120 (12 times 10). There are two reasons for focusing on the larger firms in terms of annual revenue: first, the tendency for decreasing amounts of information the smaller the consulting firms get; and second, the fact that only ten accounting and auditing firms are registered in the database *Konsultguiden*, from which the information was taken.

Information available on the Internet was used. The Internet is a source of information that is becoming increasingly important as a broad-based tool for informing stakeholders about official corporate policy and standpoints (Bondy *et al.* 2004). Content analysis is often used for CSR research (Sweeney and Coughlan 2008). As a research technique, it focuses on the presence of certain words, expressions or concepts in a certain text. Not only quantitative but also qualitative conclusions can be drawn from analyses of texts, however. As noted by Buhr and Grafström (2007), content analysis is useful when one tries to unfold values and meanings of texts in order to get a more profound understanding of the meaning and significance of messages contained in texts.

CSR in client offers was examined with regard to frequency and content. Three categories were created to facilitate comparison. Firms were registered as having explicit, implicit or non-existing CSR offers to clients. Explicit CSR offers implies actively using the concepts CSR, CR or sustainability as components of the knowledge content offered to clients. Implicit CSR offers were deemed to exist in cases where firms did not talk specifically about CSR, CR or sustainability, but used or talked about other strategic measures often included in CSR discourse, such as stakeholder analyses or social risk management. No mention of any of those concepts implied that the firm was classified as having no CSR offers.

It should be noted that the firms under study are active on the Swedish consulting market. This may imply a national bias that reduces the possibility of international comparison and relevance. To mitigate this bias, national ownership was taken into consideration. In cases where the consulting firms had non-Swedish ownership, the websites of the parent company (usually the dot.com domains) were scanned for information on CSR offers at an international level. The national ownership clusters are shown in Figure 16.1.

**FIGURE 16.1** Percentage of consulting firms included in the study with Swedish, US/UK or other national ownership

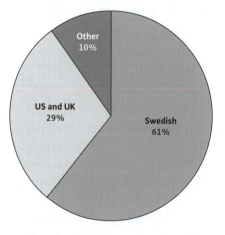

While most of the consulting firms (61%) have Swedish owners, some 29% are owned by larger American or British firms (primarily in the subfields of management consulting, accounting/auditing and market research). The third category consists of a smaller number of firms with owners from different countries (Denmark, Norway, Finland, France, the Netherlands, Germany and Switzerland). This complementary scanning of international CSR offers does not completely eliminate the potential national bias, but at least it tends to widen the sphere of the study to a Scandinavian/US/UK context. It is also the case that many firms with Swedish owners are active on international markets, which means that their CSR offers are directed towards an international audience.

The second part of the study involved a deeper analysis of the self-presentations of the firms with explicit CSR offers to clients. According to Bäcklund (2003), consultants approach their clients with different strategies depending on what they consider to be the needs, characteristics and knowledge of clients. Referring to the theoretical concept of translation, the different strategies can be seen as different ways of translating knowledge to clients. Through their strategies, consultants contribute to innovation in different ways or modes. Depending on the strategy chosen, different kinds of contribution to innovation in the client firms can be found. The strategies are illustrated in Table 16.2.

**TABLE 16.2** Adaptation strategies in consulting tenders

| Elements of adaptation | Adaptation strategies | | |
| --- | --- | --- | --- |
| | *Tailor-made solutions* | *Combined competences* | *Modified standard solutions* |
| How to meet client needs? | Clients represent unique demands and solutions. Consultants must use idiosyncratic and cooperative approaches to solve problems | Client specificity implicitly de-emphasised. Consultants create individual solutions to problems by combining competence areas | Client needs met by adapting prefabricated standardised models and tools. Best-practice approach (experiences can be transferred and reapplied) |
| What characteristics do clients have? | Organisations are different. Clients know their own situation and must actively participate to perceive, identify and solve problems | Organisations share common features. Consultant experience and expertise help the client identify relevant problems | Organisations are similar. Consultants have the expert knowledge needed to modify standardised models and tools for clients. Client involvement de-emphasised |
| Where is relevant knowledge situated? | Experience and knowledge is local and not directly transferable to other settings or organisations | Experience and knowledge is transferable. Possible re-use of consulting experiences and knowledge from other competence and business fields | Consulting experience from other settings manifested in standardised methods and tools that, with some local modification, can be used to solve problems at a local level |

Source: adapted from Bäcklund 2003: 152

Tailor-made solutions imply that clients represent unique demands and situations. According to this perspective, innovation is local and not transferable. The combined competences strategy emphasises the different competences that the consulting firm has in different fields as means to solutions of the client's problems. This means that the client's role in innovation is de-emphasised and the role of the consultancy's transposable intra-firm knowledge stressed. The modified standard solution approach relies on prefabricated standardised models and tools. This strategy suggests little involvement of the client when it comes to innovation since it implies that modest modifications or translations of models with successful applications elsewhere can be made to solve the client's problems.

By using this model as a basis for analysis, the second part of the study provides answers about the modes of innovation that consultants use in their interaction with clients. Such an analysis will show how consultants translate and develop new knowledge in the form of CSR services or tools useful for clients in their development of responsible business.

## Results

The study identifies three clusters of consulting firms that tend to include CSR in their client offers to a very different extent. Consulting fields marked by explicit CSR offers constitute one such cluster. Another cluster consists of fields that are to a lesser extent capitalising on CSR in their service offers but are at least implicitly tackling the issue of CSR, while the last cluster of firms does not seem to have integrated CSR at all in their service offers to clients. Figure 16.2 illustrates the findings.

**FIGURE 16.2** Percentage of firms with explicit, implicit or non-existent CSR content in client offers in different consulting subfields

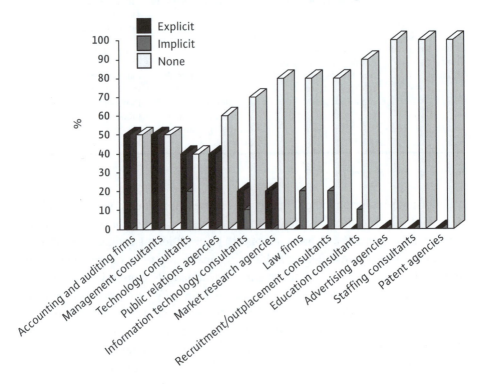

The first cluster consists of a number of fields that distinguish themselves when it comes to offering explicit CSR services to clients. Those fields are management consultants, consultants within accounting and auditing, PR consultants and the combined field of technology and IT consultants (combined in the sense that they are closely related; three consulting firms are present in both subfields). Among the top 50 firms representing these fields a total of 40% are explicit in presenting CSR as part of their client service offers. This figure indicates, of course, that the tendency within a field to include CSR in client offers does not mean that all firms within the field do so.

American management consultants such as Accenture, McKinsey, Boston Consulting Group and Booz Allen Hamilton tend to include CSR in a wider knowledge context of strategy, business development and risk analysis. In particular, CSR or sustainability is treated as a strategy issue. For example, the Boston Consulting Group claims to have the capacity of helping corporate clients to 'take a strategic approach to CSR in order to achieve competitive advantage and maximise social impact at the same time',[1] while Accenture can 'guide organisations toward high performance by integrating sustainability into their operating models, business strategies and critical processes'.[2] In emphasising the strategy perspective, McKinsey develops 'strategies for sustainability, including those focused on environmental responsibility and green growth'.[3]

The larger international firms within accounting and auditing perform activities within the CSR field. The main focus of these firms lies on CSR as an advisory or auditing service, primarily related to sustainability reporting. But internal and external responsibility structures, such as codes of ethics or codes of conduct, also lie within the professed competence range of the larger firms. For example, KPMG assists clients in a number of areas. Its CSR-related activities include producing sustainability reports based on GRI (Global Reporting Initiative) criteria, auditing of sustainability reports based on recommendations from the national association of accountants and auditors (FAR-SRS), architecture and quality assurance of the internal process for sustainability reporting, follow-up of the internal work with environmental issues, ethics and social responsibility as well of codes of conduct in the value chain, and due diligence in mergers and acquisitions. In addition to this, accounting and auditing firms such as PricewaterhouseCoopers play an important role within knowledge diffusion: for example, through education and seminars on

---

1 'Social impact'; www.bcg.com/about_bcg/social_impact/default.aspx, accessed 1 March 2010.
2 'Sustainability'; www.accenture.com/Global/Consulting/Strategy/Sustainability/default. htm, accessed 1 March 2010.
3 'Climate Change Special Initiative'; www.mckinsey.com/clientservice/Social_Sector/ our_practices/Climate_change.aspx, accessed 1 March 2010.

CSR and climate change, and through integration of sustainability-related issues into coherent business strategies. One example is the linking of corporate governance to sustainable development. Another example is the claim that new regulation prompts challenges that must be tackled from a corporate strategic point of view: for instance, the international emissions trading system. One further role that consultants within this field play is to actively participate in the standardisation procedures of soft regulation. For example, representatives from PricewaterhouseCoopers and Ernst & Young are active in the elaboration of practical and analytical standards: for example, standards for CSR analysis for financial analysts. It is clear, however, that size matters. Smaller accounting firms do not have the same kinds of elaborated service to offer their clients.

The activity of sustainability reporting is also the terrain of PR consultants in their attempts to position their clients as responsible businesses. Substantial reference is made to strategy. For example, Kreab Gavin Anderson offers strategic advice with regard to CSR while Hallvarsson & Halvarsson 'offers consultancy on strategies for CSR and ethics'.[4] This means that PR consultants are acting not only as communication consultants, producing reports and other publications that explain the standpoints and activities of the client, but also as carriers of strategic knowledge on issues such as sponsoring and charity as well as the company's position in relation to competitors, NGOs and other stakeholders. Another aspect of social responsibility stressed by PR consultants is knowledge development and crisis management. Framing CSR as an investor relations tool involves guidance on ethical indexes and what Hallvarsson & Halvarsson call 'Investor Intelligence on Socially Responsible Investments (SRI)'.[5]

IT consultants such as IBM also link CSR strategy to growth opportunities. This involves model and tool construction for assisting clients in achieving objectives. The IBM Green Sigma™ model is a typical example of this, being part of IBM Global Business Services' growing offer within CSR. IBM claims that, by applying the 'Lean Six Sigma' principles to virtually every aspect of corporate operations and facilities, it is possible to reduce negative environmental consequences and costs as well as increase efficiency. A firm such as Semcon signals that the rising focus on social and environmental issues creates pressure to adapt to new regulation, such as the regulatory demands on vehicle emissions under way in the EU. Knowledge on such issues is important and something that the consultant can provide.

More outspoken technology consultants such as WSP and Vattenfall Power Consultant tend to focus on technological environmental solutions that they contextualise as CSR. Vattenfall Power Consultant claims to assist clients with strategic analyses including social aspects, environmental management, strategic advice,

4 'CSR'; www.halvarsson.se/en/Services/CSR, accessed 1 March 2010.
5 *Ibid.*

environmental communication and business development, and other services. Two aspects stand out: the references to environmental codes and agreements such as the Kyoto Protocol, and the strong focus on the ability of the consultant to system-ise work with regard to environmental management and CSR in general. A similar approach is taken by WSP, focusing on the consequences of climate change and pressure to systematically deal with environmental challenges. To help clients, the firm offers sustainable management system services, including strategy support, auditing, communication and models for stakeholder dialogue and participation.

The next cluster defines CSR as a major competence offered to clients only to a limited extent. In principle, its CSR offers are of a more implicit kind. It includes consulting firms within market research, law, recruitment/outplacement and edu-cation. In this cluster, CSR knowledge is less frequently referred to, and the CSR knowledge that the firms claim to have is of a more indirect character, which means that it is not directly referred to as a core competence. Rather, it is something that some firms claim to have as a small knowledge component within a much larger competence frame. For example, CSR can be a minor component of a much wider curriculum for an education consultant, or law firms such as Mannheimer Swart-ling can arrange a seminar where CSR-related issues are discussed. Other examples are outplacement firms that have done research showing that CSR is important in employer branding or market research firms that include CSR as a parameter when measuring corporate image or corporate reputation. This is knowledge that is com-municated but not directly included in client offers. What is evident, however, is the fact that, even though these consulting firms do not position themselves as CSR consultants, there is a tendency towards professing awareness of the role that the CSR concept plays today.

While the second cluster reveals some awareness of CSR issues, patent, staff-ing and advertising agencies are part of a third cluster that does not seem to have capitalised on CSR in the sense that they have included the concept in their client offers. There may be explanations for this. For patent firms, it may be evident that CSR is much more of a process innovation than a product innovation, rendering services from professional patent agencies less relevant. CSR is not trademarked in the same way as other management models either, reducing the need for immate-rial rights. Even though PR and communication consultants are active in expand-ing knowledge on CSR, advertising agencies—a subfield that is hardly distant from PR and communication—do not profess knowledge on CSR. One reason for this may be advertising agencies' reliance on the marketing paradigm (4Ps: product, price, place and promotion), a thought model of the advertising industry that may not have been affected by the increased awareness of CSR issues in business in gen-eral (Oppewal *et al.* 2008; Gupta and Pirsch 2008). Compared with recruitment and outplacement firms, consultants in the subfield of staffing may focus less on abstract image issues such as employer branding where the need to prove socially responsible can be assumed to be higher.

## Modes of innovation

The basic model elaborated from Bäcklund (2003) contains different ways of approaching the client. Three strategies are suggested in the model, each representing different ways of translating or developing knowledge in the relationship to the client. As noted above, tailor-made solutions suggest that clients represent unique demands and situations. According to this perspective, innovation is local and not transferable. The combined competences strategy suggests that knowledge from other fields is a means to solving the client's problems, while the modified standard solutions strategy rests on prefabricated standardised models and tools.

The content analysis of the explicit CSR offers of the consultancies reveals that not all approaches are used to the same extent. **Tailor-made solutions** are clearly de-emphasised. In the CSR offers, references to tailor-made solutions are scarce. Idiosyncratic and collaborative approaches are not put forward as typical solutions, probably since the needs of the clients are not treated as unique. Clients from many fields of business may benefit from the competences and experience of the consultant. Even though the local knowledge of clients is not explicitly denied, it is the consultants' knowledge and experience from other fields that are the key to solving problems. Since the focus is on the capacities and experience of the consultants, the unique aspects and differences of each client do not get much attention.

Rather, a clear use of the **combined competences** strategy can be identified. Consultants actively combine competences. For example, they connect general business strategy competence to CSR strategy (management consultants), communication knowledge to sustainability reporting (PR), accounting knowledge to sustainability reporting (accounting/auditing), or emphasise their competence from other business fields. One example could be the use of general strategy competence applied elsewhere. The re-use of consulting competence from other business fields is seen as possible since organisations share many features and client specificity is not so striking that it undermines the relevance of consulting competence gained from other fields. CSR knowledge, on this stance, is transferable.

The strategy of **modified standard solutions** is also applied to a large extent. The use of standardised tools or models is widespread. Such tools or models can be self-invented, for example the Green Sigma™ model of IBM, or general standards that the consultants have knowledge of, for example the accounting standards of the GRI or the principles of the UN Global Compact. What is suggested here is that frameworks and models can be applied to fit all, which also means that clients in all fields can benefit from them. Apart from certain modifications that each client needs, no client involvement is necessary when it comes to applying the established and standardised methods or models. This is because the methods and models are designed to fit all, which they are believed to do because clients have many similar features. The expert knowledge of consultants needed to adapt the methods or models to the client seems to be enough. There is hardly any evidence in the material that there is client involvement in establishing standardised methods or models. The methods and models tend to already exist.

An implication of the fact that CSR offers are constructed according to the combined competence strategy or the modified standard solution strategy is that the consulting contribution to CSR innovation gets a special character. Three features stand out. As suggested earlier in this chapter, it seems to be supply-driven, elements of transposition are strong, and the role of standardised tools and models is evident.

The **supply-driven tendency** supports the contention (Sahlin-Andersson and Engwall 2002) that consultants are active in co-creating, developing and diffusing the idea of CSR. But at the same time this tendency downplays the client contribution to CSR innovation. It would be too much to say that the consultants claim that clients are ignorant about the CSR context that they are in. The local knowledge of the clients is not unimportant, but this does not mean that their personal knowledge is so specific that consultants' experiences from other fields do not enhance CSR service quality. Rather, consultants claim to have the ability to create awareness of CSR issues, and to structure local knowledge into and according to relevant CSR frameworks.

Along with this, **strong elements of transposition** exist. Consultants re-use experiences and knowledge from different business fields and competence areas. Clients are not considered to be so unlike one another that their differences are obstacles to re-using competences or practices from other fields. For example, communication consultants mostly working with investor relations of industrial multinationals do not have any problems writing sustainability reports for companies within gambling. Since the CSR problems of the clients are not presented as field specific (even though there is hardly a denial of the fact that field-specific problems may exist), consultant experience from working with clients in other business fields is considered relevant.

**Standardised tools and models** can be seen as a response to a need for support structures, or a traditional way of 'commodifying' (Kieser 2002) ideas and knowledge. Standardisation has not only to do with self-generated models or tools. It also refers to the use of the ever-increasing amount of soft regulation. By utilising and creating products and services based on normative guidelines and principles, consultants are able to offer CSR knowledge in a coherent form. Models, standards and soft regulation are in a sense obstacles to local innovation and tailor-made solutions. When consultants create the models or tools themselves, the supply-driven tendency of CSR innovation is obvious. But when they convey knowledge of soft regulation they are carriers of knowledge more than innovators.

## Conclusions and reflections

The study has shown that consultants within certain sectors—management consulting, accounting and auditing, PR, IT and technology—have embraced the idea of CSR and translated it into client offers. Clear tendencies in these offers are that the consultants are active in constructing CSR (the supply-driven tendency), that transposition is frequent (consultants re-use or apply competences or practices from other fields), and that standardised models and tools are used to a large extent.

Some conclusions can be drawn from these observations. From an innovation perspective, consultants contribute with *newness* in the sense that they convey knowledge from other fields and experiences rather than inventing CSR 'anew' within the existing field of business. This is possible since organisations and organisational problems tend to be treated as similar or at least exhibiting certain common features. As far as *applicability* is concerned, the other important aspect of innovation, a connection to established models or frameworks exists. Knowledge on CSR is basically believed to reside with consultants. The consultants claim to have the capacity to transfer CSR knowledge by means of models that they have created themselves or imported from other fields where they are active. Another option is to use their competence on soft regulation, which they can transfer to clients to support their CSR work.

The use of combined competences and modified standard solutions suggests a relative homogeneity of practices in the CSR field, perhaps more coherent with traditional ideas within neo-institutional theory (Meyer and Rowan 1977; DiMaggio and Powell 1983) than with other strands of the theory emphasising heterogeneity. The supply-driven active elaboration of ideas, concepts and models into commercially viable entities (Sahlin-Andersson and Engwall 2002) is part of the construction of the business case for CSR (Kurucz *et al.* 2008). It is clear that the innovative capacity of CSR consultants is not just a matter of creating tangible products or distinct services, but also a matter of providing a more general meaning or logic that it is possible for business to understand (Czarniawska 1990). In the study, the logic referred to by the consultants is financial rationality, the foundation of the business case for CSR. However, the construct of the business case is made against a background where the consultants suggest that clients encounter increased pressure from different constituents in society, belong to specific stakeholder contexts, are challenged by climate change and other environmental factors, just to mention a few aspects. By drawing up a situation marked by external forces and threats, the self-preserving, profit-maximising corporation must acquire the knowledge that the consultants can offer in order to protect its interests and minimise risks. This means that consultants are active in creating and structuring the logic of the field where they are active.

Consultants that are multiply embedded (Boxenbaum and Battilana 2005) seem to have advantages when it comes to such constructions since the condition of multiple embeddedness facilitates transposition. Consultants can benefit from understanding facts, contextual circumstances and institutional logics of different spheres since they can capitalise on 'input' from fields other than their traditional one. By combining competences acquired in different settings, consultants transfer ideas to other fields. To do so, receptivity is needed as well as 'limited omnipresence', implying a capacity to identify and make use of relevant knowledge by participating in different societal and economic discourses. Of course, this presence is not limited to professional discourses, but also includes the moralised context of CSR itself as well as national scenes where particular understandings of these moralised contexts develop.

The use of standardised tools, models and the reference to soft regulation are signs of the need to conceptualise the vague concept of CSR. At least when it comes to self-generated models, one may question whether consultants develop them as a consequence of a compelling idea of CSR or whether CSR becomes a concept adapted to already existing thought patterns of consultants. For example, CSR may become a management idea through becoming integrated into the wider sense of strategy. In this case it is reasonable to say that the novelty—the idea of CSR—is applied in another context where tools and concepts are malleable and able to capture the novelty, incorporating it into the logics of the already existing field of business. The use of the combined competence and modified standard solution strategies is probably possible because of the vagueness of the CSR concept. The field of CSR opens up for handy products, tools or methods proved to function in other fields.

The chapter has analysed how consultants contribute with ideas, knowledge and tools within the field of CSR. The contribution of the study is twofold. First, it gives a clue to how CSR practices are created, developed and diffused. Second, it further illustrates the role of consultants when it comes to spreading the idea of CSR. A couple of limitations of the study should be mentioned, though. It does not focus on the interaction between consultants and clients (cf. Faust 2002), and it does not cover CSR innovation within client firms. Because of this, it is important to ask whether consulting firms have the capacity to encourage, stimulate or create change and innovation within firms in a more genuine sense, or if the consulting expansion in the field of CSR is just a classic way of extending markets without stimulating change among clients in any deeper sense of the word.

Even though this aspect has not been examined empirically, some final reflections are necessary. It has been suggested above that a prerequisite for the flourishing of consultants on the CSR market is the lack of knowledge on CSR (Borglund *et al.* 2008). Larger firms tend to accumulate such knowledge to increasingly higher degrees, partly through frequent interaction with consultants, thereby reducing the demand for 'simpler' CSR services. One aspect of organisational learning is that knowledge on CSR is disseminated within client firms. More people tend to be aware of the importance of CSR, which reduces the gap between different streams of management. For example, as CSR knowledge increases in firms, it becomes an issue for investor relations, information units, human resources or other units of the firm that have traditionally not been 'CSR territory' (Grafström *et al.* 2008). Because of their initial role as knowledge providers, consultants play at least an implicit role in this knowledge-based development of CSR issues within firms as more units adopt the idea of CSR. Developments such as health balance sheets or fund managers' adoption of the UN's Principles for Responsible Investment may be seen as a result of increased internal knowledge on the value of CSR. Of course, such developments frequently presuppose consulting involvement but can also be seen as innovative implicit effects of the importation of CSR knowledge into firms. This process can be seen as a knowledge—or even market—extension within client firms, which is usually to the benefit of CSR consulting firms since they frequently experience tensions within client firms. Some managers are interested in CSR while others discard the entire concept (Borglund *et al.* 2008). For this reason, the knowledge absorption of client firms is not just a bad thing for consulting firms. More business opportunities may be created as a result of such knowledge dissemination.

Another factor that seems to be important for the lasting effects of consulting activities in client firms is the nature of the consulting assignment. If CSR is treated like a project or programmatic solution, the outcome may be different (Caldwell 2003). If CSR is a relatively isolated project, it can be assumed to be an activity that does not generate many effects within the organisation. If, however, it is the result of a programmatic approach to CSR, it may involve cultural change and other more ground-breaking changes within the organisation. This means that it is not only the particular project or product that is a sign of innovation in the firm (it may very well, according to the findings of this chapter, have a standardised character); rather, programmatic approaches open up for more basic process innovations without necessarily having the 'output' defined beforehand.

# References

Anand, N., H.K. Gardner and T. Morris (2007) 'Knowledge-Based Innovation: Emergence and Embedding of New Practice Areas in Management Consulting Firms', *Academy of Management Journal* 50.2: 406-28.

Bäcklund, J. (2003) *Arguing for Relevance: Global and Local Knowledge Claims in Management Consulting* (Uppsala, Sweden: Department of Business Studies at Uppsala University).

Berglund, J., and A. Werr (2000) 'The Invincible Character of Management Consulting Rhetoric: How One Blends Incommensurates While Keeping them Apart', *Organization* 7.4: 633-55.

Bondy, K., D. Matten and J. Moon (2004) 'The Adoption of Voluntary Codes of Conduct in MNCs: A Three-Country Comparative Study', *Business & Society Review* 109.4: 449-77.

Borglund, T., H. De Geer and M. Hallvarsson (2008) *Värdeskapande CSR: Hur företag tar socialt ansvar* (Stockholm: Norstedts).

Boxenbaum, E., and J. Battilana (2005) 'Importation as Innovation: Transposing Managerial Practices across Field', *Strategic Organization* 3: 355-83.

Buhr, H., and M. Grafström (2007) 'The Making of Meaning in the Media: Corporate Social Responsibility in the Financial Times, 1988–2003', in F. den Hond, F.G.A. de Bakker and P. Neergaard (eds.), *Managing Corporate Social Responsibility in Action: Talking, Doing and Measuring* (Burlington, VT: Ashgate Publishing): 15-32.

Caldwell, R. (2003) 'Models of Change Agency: A Fourfold Classification', *British Journal of Management* 14: 131-42.

Clark, T., and G. Salaman (1998) 'Creating the "Right" Impression: Towards a Dramaturgy of Management Consultancy', *The Service Industries Journal* 18.1: 18-38.

Czarniawska, B. (1990) 'Merchants of Meaning: Management Consulting in the Swedish Public Sector', in B. Turner (ed.), *Organizational Symbolism* (Berlin: Walter de Gruyter): 139-50.

—— and B. Joerges (1996) 'Travels of Ideas', in B. Czarniawska and G. Sevón (eds.), *Translating Organizational Change* (Berlin: Walter de Gruyter): 13-48.

De Geer, H. (2002) 'Business and Society', in L. Zsolnai (ed.), *Ethics in the Economy: Handbook of Business Ethics* (Bern, Switzerland: Peter Lang AG): 59-80.

——, T. Borglund and M. Frostenson (2009) 'Reconciling CSR with the Role of the Corporation in Welfare States: The Problematic Swedish Example', *Journal of Business Ethics* 89: 269-83.

DiMaggio, P., and W.W. Powell (1983) 'The Iron Cage Revisited: Institutional Isomorphism and Collective Rationality in Organizational Fields', *American Sociological Review* 48: 147-60.

Dubbink, W., J. Graafland and L. van Liedekerke (2008) 'CSR, Transparency and the Role of Intermediate Organisations', *Journal of Business Ethics* 82: 391-406.

Ellen Weinreb Recruiting and Consulting and Net Impact (2007) *CSR Jobs Report* (Report; Berkeley, CA, December 2007).

Ernst, B., and A. Kieser (2002) 'In Search of Explanations for the Consulting Explosion', in K. Sahlin-Andersson and L. Engwall (eds.), *The Expansion of Management Knowledge* (Stanford, CA: Stanford University Press): 47-73.

Faust, M. (2002) 'Consultancies as Actors in Knowledge Arenas: Evidence from Germany', in M. Kipping and L. Engwall (eds.), *Management Consulting: Emergence and Dynamics of a Knowledge Industry* (Oxford, UK: Oxford University Press): 146-63.

Fincham, R. (2006) 'Knowledge Work as Occupational Strategy: Comparing IT and Management Consulting', *New Technology, Work and Employment* 21.1: 16-28.

Fiss, P.C. (2008) 'Institutions and Corporate Governance', in R. Greenwood, C. Oliver, K. Sahlin and R. Suddaby (eds.), *The SAGE Handbook of Organizational Institutionalism* (Thousand Oaks, CA: SAGE Publications): 389-410.

Frostenson, M., and T. Borglund (2006) *Företagens sociala ansvar och den svenska modellen* (SIEPS report, 2006:9; Stockholm: SIEPS).

Furusten, S. (2001) *Consulting in Legoland: The Jazz of Small-Scale Management Consultation in the Improvisation of Standards* (Score Report 2001:3; Stockholm: Stockholm School of Economics).

Ghobadian, A., D. Gallear and M. Hopkins (2007) 'TQM and CSR Nexus', *International Journal of Quality and Reliability Management* 24.7: 704-21.

Grafström, M., P. Göthberg and K. Windell (2008) *CSR: Företagsansvar i förändring* (Malmö, Sweden: Liber).

Gupta, S., and J. Pirsch (2008) 'The Influence of a Retailer's Corporate Social Responsibility Program on Re-conceptualizing Store Image', *Journal of Retailing and Consumer Services* 15.6: 516-26.

Hagenmeyer, U. (2007) 'Integrity in Management Consulting: A Contradiction in Terms?', *Business Ethics: A European Review* 16.2: 107-13.

Jutterström, M. (2006) 'Corporate Social Responsibility: The Supply Side of CSR Standards' (Score Working Paper 2006-2; Stockholm: Stockholm School of Economics).

Kieser, A. (2002) 'Managers as Marionettes? Using Fashion Theories to Explain the Success of Consultancies', in M. Kipping and L. Engwall (eds.), *Management Consulting: Emergence and Dynamics of a Knowledge Industry* (Oxford, UK: Oxford University Press): 167-83.

Kurucz, E.C., B.A. Colbert and D. Wheeler (2008) 'The Business Case for Corporate Social Responsibility', in A. Crane, A. McWilliams, D. Matten, J. Moon and D.S. Siegel (eds.), *The Oxford Handbook of Corporate Social Responsibility* (Oxford, UK: Oxford University Press): 83-112.

Lounsbury, M. (2008) 'Institutional Rationality and Practice Variation: New Directions in the Institutional Analysis of Practice', *Accounting, Organizations and Society* 33: 349-61.

—— and E.T. Crumley (2007) 'New Practice Creation: An Institutional Approach to Innovation', *Organization Studies* 28: 993-1,012.

Meyer, J.W., and B. Rowan (1977) 'Institutionalized Organizations: Formal Structure as Myth and Ceremony', *American Journal of Sociology* 83: 340-63.

Mölleryd, B.G. (1999) *Entrepreneurship in Technological Systems: The Development of Mobile Telephony in Sweden* (Stockholm: EFI).

Moon, J., and D. Vogel (2008) 'Corporate Social Responsibility, Government, and Civil Society', in A. Crane, A. McWilliams, D. Matten, J. Moon and D.S. Siegel (eds.), *The Oxford Handbook of Corporate Social Responsibility* (Oxford, UK: Oxford University Press): 303-23.

Oppewal, H., A. Alexander and P. Sullivan (2008) 'Consumer Perceptions of Corporate Social Responsibility in Town Shopping Centres and their Influence on Shopping Evaluations', *Journal of Retailing and Consumer Services* 13.4: 261-74.

Rogers, E.M. (1995) *Diffusion of Innovations* (New York: The Free Press, 4th edn).

Sahlin, K., and L. Wedlin (2008) 'Circulating Ideas: Imitation, Translation and Editing', in R. Greenwood, C. Oliver, K. Sahlin and R. Suddaby (eds.), *The SAGE Handbook of Organizational Institutionalism* (Thousand Oaks, CA: SAGE Publications): 218-42.

Sahlin-Andersson, K. (1996) 'Imitating and Editing Success: The Construction of Organiza-tion Fields and Identities', in B. Czarniawska and G. Sevón (eds.), *Translating Organiza-tional Change* (Berlin: Walter de Gruyter): 69-92.

—— (2006) 'Corporate Social Responsibility: A Trend and a Movement, but of What and for What?', *Corporate Governance* 6.5: 595-608.

—— and L. Engwall (2002) 'Carriers, Flows and Sources of Management Knowledge', in K. Sahlin-Andersson and L. Engwall (eds.), *The Expansion of Management Knowledge* (Stan-ford, CA: Stanford University Press): 3-32.

Scott, W.R. (1994) 'Institutions and Organizations: Towards a Theoretical Synthesis', in W.R. Scott and J.W. Meyer (eds.), *Institutional Environments and Organizations: Struc-tural Complexity and Individualism* (Thousand Oaks, CA: SAGE Publications): 55-80.

Sweeney, L., and J. Coughlan (2008) 'Do Different Industries Report Corporate Social Responsibility Differently? An Investigation through the Lens of Stakeholder Theory', *Journal of Marketing Communications* 14.2: 113-24.

Urban, S. (2006) 'Introductory Reflections', paper presented at the *IV Simposio Europeo dei Docenti Universitari: L'impresa e la costruzione del nuovo umanesimo*, Rome, Italy, 22–25 June 2006.

Valiente, P. (2006) *Re-innovating the Existing: A Study of Wireless IS Capabilities to Support Mobile Workforces* (Stockholm: EFI).

Van Marrewijk, M., I. Wuisman, W. De Cleyn, J. Timmers, V. Panapanaan and L. Linnanen (2004) 'A Phase-wise Development Approach to Business Excellence: Towards an Inno-vative, Stakeholder-Oriented Assessment Tool for Organizational Excellence and CSR', *Journal of Business Ethics* 55: 83-98.

Werr, A., and T. Stjernberg (2003) 'Exploring Management Consulting Firms as Knowledge Systems', *Organization Studies* 24.6: 881-908.

Windell, K. (2006) *Corporate Social Responsibility under Construction: Ideas, Translations, and Institutional Change* (Uppsala, Sweden: Department of Business Studies at Uppsala University).

Zander, U. (1991) *Exploiting a Technological Edge: Voluntary and Involuntary Dissemination of Technology* (Stockholm: Institute of International Business).

# 17
# Strategic CSR in the Japanese context
## From business risk to market creation

**Scott Davis**
Rikkyo University, Japan

The Japanese public mind is currently filled with images of corporate duplicity, greed and callousness. The Japanese public are bombarded with a seemingly endless series of reports in the media of deaths or injury due to manufacturers failing to recall appliances they knew to be faulty, cheap imports fraudulently sold as expensive domestic produce, the sale of foodstuffs known to contain out-of-date or contaminated ingredients, and most recently the appalling story of groups of corporations having setting up dummy companies supposedly staffed by disabled employees in order to fraudulently obtain government subsidies and discounts on public services. The social responsibility of Japan's corporations is again currently under question.

Japan's corporations are facing ever-increasing demands by consumers, trading partners, social groups and government agencies to behave in a responsible manner. In response to this, many of Japan's corporations are declaring their commitment to acting in a socially responsible manner and implementing corporate social responsibility (CSR) initiatives to translate their words into action. Despite the resulting abundance of newly socially minded corporations and the increasing volume of CSR reports, stakeholder dialogues, CSR officers and offices, CSR rankings and training programmes being implemented, judging from the almost daily reports of corporate misconduct, there seems to be little progress being made in increasing the actual number of corporations conducting their business in a socially responsible manner. In short, there seems to be lots of CSR in Japan, but not much good business coming out of it.

This chapter will briefly review the landscape of CSR in Japan today and build up a typology of corporate approaches to meeting the prevailing demands for greater social responsibility. Legitimated by concepts of what it means to be an 'ethical business' largely borrowed from some part of Japan's rich tradition of social thought on what constitutes a responsible business, it will be argued that, in their haste to answer their critics, most CSR initiatives today are oriented towards passive, risk-avoiding structures for aligning corporations with social demands and are therefore of limited effect in actually creating value for society as businesses.

Using the work on 'sense-making' by Basu and Palazzo (2008), a process-based typology of CSR initiatives will be applied to reclassify these approaches and evaluate their utility for integrating social betterment within strategic business objectives in a manner that makes innovative CSR initiatives possible.[1] The last part of this chapter will introduce and describe a process-based CSR initiative implemented by a retailer in Japan. The innovative capacity of the processes constituting this initiative will be explored using an 'active-transformational model' of CSR. The main contention of this chapter is that a process-based approach to CSR, which enables the members of a corporation to integrate social needs (opportunities for the betterment of society) into their business strategies and operations, is essential for the realisation of an innovative and value-creating CSR initiative.

## A descriptive typology of approaches to CSR

Corporate approaches to CSR can be divided into one of four types using a descriptive typology based on two dimensions (see Figure 17.1), where social responsibility is defined as a result of the way in which a corporation locates its strategic goals for responsible business as either 'managing risk' or 'creating value', and how it manages and conceives of the organisational resources that it commits in order to achieve this goal as either a 'cost' or an 'investment'. In this typology the management of risk is the reduction or amelioration of a potentially unfavourable effect on the performance of business. Value creation is the enrichment of the business by

---

1  This distinction between alignment and integration was explained in a comment by Dr Kiyoshi Kasahara, Professor of the Graduate School of Social Design at Rikkyo University, when he noted in a recent discussion with the author that 'compared to the inherent limits of corporate initiatives based on the alignment of business with social demands, CSR based on the integration of social awareness into strategic business process promises huge potential'.

the generation of profits, increasing net worth, or otherwise increasing the value of the corporation and its assets. Cost is taken as meaning an expenditure of resources in a manner that excludes an expectation of potential gain in the future and the (eventual) loss of the resources committed. In contrast, investment presumes a potential gain or at least the preservation of the value of the resources committed.

**FIGURE 17.1** A descriptive typology of CSR initiatives

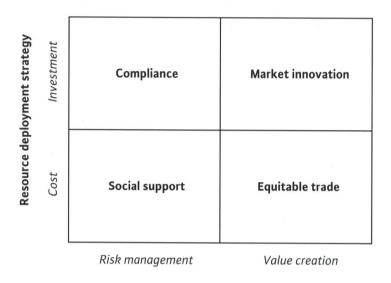

Strategic objectives

Amid the current scandals involving business misconduct and the resulting decline in the public's trust of corporations, many social commentators and business leaders are calling for a return to the traditions of responsible business that have marked different periods in Japan's commercial history (Suenaga 2004; Hirata 2005; Onuki 2006). All but the last approach in the framework is legitimated by a conceptualisation of what a corporation must do in order to be socially acceptable.

In the **value/cost** quadrant, corporations seek to align their businesses with the expectations of society by avoiding opportunities for profit-taking that disadvantage others. In this approach to CSR the ideal of 'good' business harks back to the *Sanpo Yoshi* or 'triple win principle' (Kawaguchi 2006: 147), the pragmatic code of fair trade of the Omi Merchants—a group of itinerant merchants who traded during the Middle Ages in Japan (Sheldon 1973: 7; Tonomura 1992: 96; Arata 2006) According to this formula, a transaction could not be considered fair if it disadvantaged either of the parties directly involved in the trade (buyer or seller) or if it negatively influenced the interests of indirectly involved third parties (the wider community). This code required merchants to regulate themselves and forgo profits only attainable by unacceptable trade opportunities. In an interesting parallel with the present, the merchants at this time occupied the lowest social rank, were looked on with suspicion and thought to be dishonourable because they created no value and merely sold the goods of others. Despite its current popularity as the 'original Japanese CSR' (Suenaga 2004; Kawaguchi 2004), the *Sanpo Yoshi* formula gives business today no guidance other than the maxim that business should not profit at the expense of society. Like the itinerant Omi merchants, corporations following this approach often expend considerable resources in the search for individual business opportunities that suit their definition of an equitable trade as they tend to 'seek' rather than 'create' opportunities.

In the **cost/risk** quadrant, corporations tend to approach CSR as a means to align themselves with society by making amends for the negative externalities resulting from the conduct of their businesses. Social condemnation is deflected by a corporation's willingness to support social causes—to pay back to society what it has gained at their expense. The actor in this approach is often the members of the organisation, not the organisation or corporation itself. Social responsibility is a matter of individual morality and integrity. Rather than attributing blame to faults in business models, ill-designed supply chains and irreconcilable conflicts of interest, in Japan as elsewhere, it is easier to explain the negative impact of management on society as a moral shortcoming in corporate executives and employees.

This approach to CSR is largely justified by reference to ethicists from the Edo and later periods. The recent renewal of interest in Japan regarding the thoughts of these ethicists is in part driven by the perception that greed among business leaders is responsible for the numerous acts of corporate misconduct today. Nostalgia for the days when hard work and self-sacrifice were the mark of a good businessperson is a common popular sentiment in Japan today.

During the Edo period the ethicists Suzuki Shosan (1579–1655), Ishida Baigan (1685–1744) and Ninomiya Sontoku (1787–1856) promoted hard work, self-sacrifice and fairness to legitimise the taking of profit from trade. Despite the prevailing opinion of the day, these social thinkers maintained that merchants benefited society by redistributing its products and resources into more effective configurations according to demand (Hirata 2005). Suzuki urged the merchants of the time to 'renounce desires and pursue profit single-heartedly. But you should never enjoy profits. You should instead, work for the good of all the others' (quoted in Nakamura 1968: 159). Perhaps the most vocal proponent of this view was Ninomiya who is famous for his statement that 'Commerce without ethics is crime: Ethics without commerce is nonsense' (Onuki 2006). The importance of the businessperson's own personal integrity was later further refined by Shibusawa Eiichi (1840–1931) who insisted that 'commercial undertaking without a moral basis borders on deceit, dilettantism; it is chicanery, sophistry, but not truly great commercial talent' (quoted in Tai 1993: 47). In the period leading up to the Second World War, Matsushita Konosuke argued that:

> possessing material comforts in no way guarantees happiness. Only spir-
> itual wealth can bring true happiness. If that is correct, should business
> be concerned only with the material aspect of life and leave the care of
> the human heart to religion or ethics? I do not think so. Businessmen
> too should be able to share in creating society that is spiritually rich and
> materially affluent (Matsushita 1984: 87-88).

Initiatives in the **invest/risk** quadrant approach CSR largely as a matter of compliance. Here the actor is the corporation. Corporations invest resources in governance, legal compliance training for employees, CSR reporting and other mechanisms in order to ensure their credibility as responsible organisations. While creating negligible value, these investments result in an infrastructure by which risk can be managed effectively. Social responsibility as compliance is a perception that has increasingly prevailed during post Second World War Japan.

After the Second World War the role of the state shifted from being that of the defender of the national interest to being that of the defender of the public interest. As such, along with the task of physically rebuilding the industrial infrastructure, the process of rebuilding the legal framework in which corporations operated was also commenced. As the protector of the public welfare, the state initiated a series of legal reforms to the commercial, labour and anti-monopoly laws effectively cod-ifying the social responsibility of corporations in terms of minimum legal obliga-tions. As a result of this, the post-war, modernised corporation (as opposed to the business leader) came to be the principal actor in CSR (Morimoto 1994: 78).

Morimoto has characterised the development of the concept of the social respon-sibility of corporations in Japan since the Second World War as a series of 'pas-sive' reactions to changing external demands (Morimoto 1994: 79). The cost of the high rates of economic growth enjoyed in Japan during the 1960s were felt in the early 1970s in the form of pollution and contamination caused by the steel and chemical industries, environmental damage caused by the construction and lei-sure industries, hazardous and contaminated products sold by the automobile and processed food industries, and false advertising and misleading product labelling by the pharmaceutical and real estate industries. This, combined with the effect of wild speculation in land and commodities by trading companies after the 'Nixon Shock' of 1971, which resulted in shortages in land and resources, severely under-mined the public's trust in corporations. Symbolic of these incidents was the indus-trial mercury contamination that came to be known as Minamata disease after the city in which its victims lived (Oiwa *et al.* 2001). The social criticism in response to these scandals prompted a highly instrumental approach to CSR. Corporations invested in introducing systems to ameliorate risk such as corporate codes of con-duct and behaviour, internal audit and monitoring systems. The primary motivation here is to achieve sufficient self-management so as to prevent the risk of future misconduct and avoid further regulation by the government.

The **invest/value** quadrant is problematic. Corporations operating within this quadrant would ideally approach CSR as an investment to create value as a business. Unfortunately, this quadrant is only sparsely populated because the current conceptualisation of the means for realising socially responsible business is largely seen in terms of systems and structures for alignment with social demands, rather than of the processes that are needed to discern opportunities to invest resources in order to initiate value-creating innovations.

Addressing this scarcity, in May 2008 the Japan Association of Corporate Executives (Keizai Doyukai) published a report entitled *Social Change by Value-Creating CSR: Towards a CSR that Builds Social Trust and Deals with Social Issues*. In the report the association called for corporations to:

> go beyond simply responding to increasingly strict [government] regu-
> lations and to bring to bear their initiative and power as independent
> entities in order to demonstrate the way in which the market within a
> market-based economy should function effectively and thereby accom-
> plish the urgent task of winning back the trust of society (Japan Associa-
> tion of Corporate Executives 2008: 1).

The Keizai Doyukai is effectively calling on corporations to engage in CSR from an invest/value approach. This is a call for corporations to go beyond efforts to align their businesses with the demands of society and instead to actively integrate CSR as a part of their business strategies—to change the processes by which social betterment is integrated into corporate objectives and formed into strategies for the implementation and further development of responsible business. In order to respond to the Keizai Doyukai's call, corporations must reconsider their CSR initiatives in terms of business processes.

## A process–based typology of CSR in Japan

If the descriptive typology of CSR is redrawn in terms of perceptions and interactions, it results in a process-based typology which can be used to show the extent to which prevailing approaches to CSR can be effective in strategically integrating social responsibility into business and thereby achieving a 'value-creating CSR' (see Figure 17.2). This process-based typology is based on a dimension of the initiative for engagement as being either active or passive. The initiative for engagement sets the course for the engagement between two entities—in this case the corporation and the groups that constitute its context (its market). Where active, the course is influenced to a considerable extent by the corporation. Where passive, the initiative for setting the course is mainly set by an entity other than the corporation. The second dimension is that of the level of engagement between the corporation and its actors comprising its context. Engagement ranges from transaction to transformation. Transaction is where two actors interact and, while influencing each other to a certain degree, retain their original identity intact after the interaction. Transformation is the process of engagement whereby the identities (their perceptions of themselves and their reasons for existence) of the actors involved in the interaction are altered as a result of the interaction. Compared with transformation, transaction holds little scope for learning and innovation.

**FIGURE 17.2** A process–based typology of CSR initiatives

| | **Compliance**<br>Conformity with external codifications of responsibility | **Market innovation**<br>Innovating business relationships to realise new opportunities for social value creation |
|---|---|---|
| | **Social support**<br>Seeking moral legitimacy by exchanging resources for social support and approval | **Equitable trade**<br>Searching for business opportunities acceptable within existing relationships |

*Transformational* / *Transactional* — Level of engagement

*Passive* — *Active*

**Initiative for engagement**

In the **active/transactional** approach the actors engage in an interaction defined in terms of the core business activity of the firm in a way that leaves both parties unchanged. Here a favourable interaction is one that benefits both actors as a result of the interaction. Again, this process is the *Sanpo Yoshi* of the Omi merchants who engage in trade with a partner within a particular social context where the outcome of that transaction can be determined to be good for seller, buyer and the community at large. However, when seen in terms of processes the shortcomings of this approach become apparent. Roles remain the same after as before the deal and the deal may be repeated as independent acts at the discretion of the merchant for as long as the benefit derived from the transaction can be maintained. To be successful, the merchants must be able to discern in advance whether or not an opportunity is compatible with their own resource set and goals. There is no impetus to rectify problems or further develop opportunities here—the point is merely to choose an acceptable opportunity. Poorly managed systems of fair trade and social labelling protocols often display a similar limitation.

In the **passive/transactional** approach an interaction occurs according to an agenda defined outside the control of the corporation and leaves all actors involved basically unchanged on its conclusion. An example of this process would be the merchant who seeks to legitimise his or her accumulation of wealth from trade by adopting a moral code which is defined as acceptable by the community. This often involves a corporation sharing its profits with the community. A survey by the Japan Business Federation showing that philanthropy is a major component of many corporate CSR initiatives suggests that many Japanese corporations subscribe to this approach (see Figure 17.3). To be successful in this the business leader must be able to determine the trends shaping the demands expressed by a community regarding the acceptable behaviour of a businessperson as the ideals and ambitions of that community change.

**FIGURE 17.3** Average corporate expenditure on social contribution, 1990– 2006

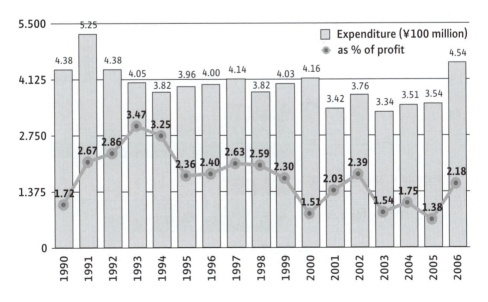

Source: Japan Business Federation Committee for Promotion of Corporate Social Contribution 2008: 18

In the **passive/transformational** approach an agenda for change is set, or prima-rily defined, by actors outside the corporation. Unlike the preceding two approaches where the transaction is based on a definition of the common good, here the issue is that of finding common ground. The process involved here is the modification (innovation) of a corporation's internal systems and processes in order to ensure that it remains compatible with the changing interpretation of what is considered by society as a responsible business. The capacity to learn, change and communi-cate the transformation deemed necessary becomes the competences required in order for a corporation to qualify as being socially responsible. However, because this process occurs without the initiative of the corporation shaping the course of action within the context of its business, it fails to produce a unique contribution based on the knowledge and resources of a particular corporation.

A study by the Japan Association of Corporate Executives has shown that, while almost 70% of Japanese corporations see CSR as a critical issue at the centre of their businesses, over 50% still consider CSR to be nothing more than a cost of doing business (see Figure 17.4). Furthermore, when asked about the content of their CSR initiatives, most corporations replied that they were mainly involved in establishing systems for legal compliance and only about 16% were actually plan-ning or implementing value-creating CSR initiatives as a part of their businesses (see Figure 17.5).

**FIGURE 17.4** 'What meaning does CSR have for your business?'

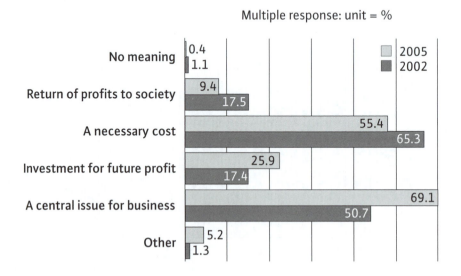

Source: Japan Association of Corporate Executives 2006: 8

**FIGURE 17.5** 'How advanced is your CSR initiative?'

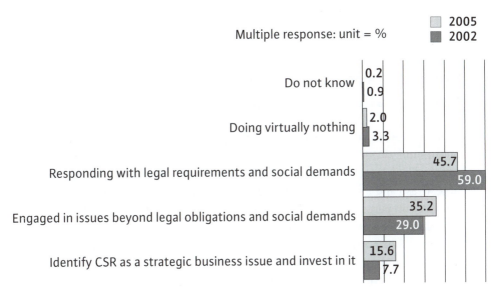

Source: Japan Association of Corporate Executives 2006: 8

In this approach corporations are playing a game of catch-up by trying to integrate CSR tools into their existing strategies and improve their CSR ratings. The result is a strategy of defensive CSR (Ibuki 2005) where the form of a responsible corporation is being given precedence over function. The corporate resources of innovation are being applied to create new systems whereby the organisation can attain compliance with legal and social demands set according to agendas controlled by external entities. Resources are increasingly being invested to minimise externally defined risk. This has led some social critics to conclude that Japanese corporations are currently experiencing an identity crisis (Adachi and Kanai 2004: 12).

In the **active/transformational** approach the corporation actively identifies an area of common ground (see Wenger *et al.* 2002: 35) where, by engaging in a process of mutual transformation with partners it specifically identifies, it may generate both a means and an end (outcome) of doing business that will benefit all involved. This is the area that the Japan Association of Corporate Executives refers to in its call for the promotion of value-creating CSR initiatives. Again, CSR initiatives of this type are rare.

The point of this classification, however, is not to suggest that there exists four phases in an inevitable evolutionary process of development towards a value-creating CSR. The point is to identify the processes that distinguish these different approaches. The following section will examine the processes—the perceptions and interactions—essential for realising the innovation necessary for an active/transformational model of CSR.

## Towards a process–based model of active/transformational innovation

Basu and Palazzo (2008) have stated that we need to go beyond 'analyzing CSR by examining CSR', and instead study the processes that guide an organisation's sense-making 'as they pertain to relationships with stakeholders and the world at large' (Basu and Palazzo 2008: 123-24). By focusing on the processes by which an organisation perceives its strategic position and potential opportunities for creating value, CSR initiatives can be located within the active context of managerial decision-making and not simply within the passive context of a given agenda. Basu and Palazzo identify three dimensions in this sense-making process: cognitive, linguistic and conative. Basically how a corporation thinks, communicates and behaves.

Following the framework proposed by Basu and Palazzo (2008: 126-30), implementing an active/transformational approach requires:

1. A **collectivistic identity** which locates it as a member of larger groups that transcend its immediate business ties (see Brickson 2007)

2. A **moral legitimacy** by which it 'co-creates acceptable norms of behavior with relevant stakeholders' (see Schuman 1995)

3. An **ethical justification** based on normative values that transcend immediate social issues and guide it in setting its own agenda

4. An **open posture** based on learning by listening to others and thinking using the perspectives of others

5. An **internally consistent** strategic approach to evaluating options and making decisions

6. A **normative commitment** to integrate and regulate actions throughout the organisation and its partners

These six processes can be organised into three categories of principles, processes and partners—a new '3P' model for innovative CSR (see Table 17.1). In order to bring these sense-making processes closer to a more pragmatic framework—one more closely aligned to the management of a business—they can also be reorganised into three categories which follow the 'domain, shared practice and community' spheres as identified as constituting a community of practice by Wenger (Wenger 1998; Wenger *et al.* 2002).

**TABLE 17.1 Process–based model of active/transformational innovation**

| Categories | Processes |
|---|---|
| Principles (mode of identity) | • Ethical justification<br>• Normative commitment |
| Processes (mode of decision–making) | • Internally consistent<br>• Open posture |
| Partners (mode of interaction) | • Collectivistic identity<br>• Moral legitimacy |

An active/transformational approach requires that a corporation can identify itself in terms of both its reason for existence and its mode of existence. This is the function of principles. Principles enable an organisation to maintain an identity that locates it in a unique position within its current context, as well as a perception of purpose that enables it to transcend its current context by enabling it to set goals for the future—an identity makes sense of its current position, while a purpose defines its direction for action.

To be active requires coordination and objectivity—coordination within the organisation to allow the smooth flow of information for creating learning opportunities and the effective use of resources, and objectivity in order to enable the evaluation of alternative courses of action and thereby effective decision-making.

Achieving a deep level of interaction with other actors is necessary in order to achieve a meaningful degree of transformation. Successful partnership depends on an articulation of long-term shared interests, an appreciation of different capabilities and perspectives, and a sense of a 'common ground' or motive.

The following section will give an illustration of an innovative CSR initiative based on this active/transformational approach model—a CSR initiative developed as a part of the core business of the Ito-Yokado Corporation, one of Japan's largest supermarket chains. The sense-making processes that define the organisation and its management will then be analysed in order to explain how these processes have enabled the corporation to reframe the relationships that shape their business and thereby achieve innovative CSR using an active/transformational approach.

# An example of active/transformational innovation

Currently one of Japan's largest retailers, the Ito-Yokado Corporation (hereafter IY) operates 176 general merchandise superstores throughout Japan.[2] IY is a wholly owned subsidiary of Seven & I Holdings—Japan's largest retail conglomerate—and the core of Seven & I Holdings' domestic superstore business.[3] IY reported total annual sales of ¥1,464,094,000,000 for the year ending February 2008, and employment of 43,137 people.

Founded in 1958 by Ito Masatoshi—widely recognised as being responsible for modernising the retail industry in Japan—IY is still well known throughout the industry today as a highly innovative retailer. It has developed and re-engineered the convenience store business model, the online banking industry, and the use of information technology in managing distribution and retailing logistics. The innovation that concerns us here, however, is a less-well-known innovation in retailing called the 'Vegetables with Faces' project.

The Vegetables with Faces project was commenced by IY in 2002. 'Vegetables with Faces' is a convenient translation of the Japanese term 'Kao ga mieru yasai'—which translates more accurately into English as 'vegetables where the faces can be seen'. The 'faces' here are a reference to the identity of the farmers who produce the vegetables. The term is actually a somewhat sophisticated pun in the Japanese language. It is fashionably vague and can be interpreted in several different ways. 'Vegetables you can get to know', 'vegetables with an identity', and 'vegetables who are not strangers to you' are all possible interpretations of the phrase. Suffice it to note that the phrase is an example of good copywriting and is suitably intriguing to serve as a brand.

In sharp contrast to its naming, the Vegetables with Faces (hereafter 'Faces') project is a very clear and carefully designed innovation in retailing. Put simply, it is a branded system for product traceability. The Faces project consists of a branded line of vegetables produced by farmers participating in a closely organised network of contracted suppliers managed by IY, monitored by external testing agencies, and integrated by an Internet-based tracking system which gives customers access to information on products and producers, the farming standards demanded of products and producers, and the future goals of the project.

The Faces initiative consists of three processes:

---

2  This case study is based entirely on publicly available sources of information.
3  Disclosure: at the time of writing, the Ito-Yokado Corporation is a wholly owned subsidiary of the Seven & I Holdings Corporation. The author has previously served as an independent member of the board of directors of the Ito-Yokado Corporation and currently serves as an independent member of the board of directors of the Seven & I Holdings Corporation.

- Standardisation of farm management and produce quality assurance

- Administration of quality checks by independent testing agencies

- Open relationship building based on information disclosure

Behind these three processes are the 'Five Promises of the Vegetables with Faces' on which the initiative is based. As publicly stated on the Faces homepage, these principles are:

1. All Faces vegetables must be grown in Japan

2. Information about who grew the vegetables and how they were farmed must be given on the Faces homepage

3. Good vegetables come from good farmland. Only farmers who practice good farmland management may participate as Faces farmers

4. Pesticide use must be less than 50% of the volume officially permitted for each type of vegetable by region

5. In order to ensure trust, checks (tests of soil, farming methods and products in stores) must be administered by independent agencies[4]

Farmers who wish to participate in the Faces project and supply produce to be sold under the Faces brand in the IY stores must first apply to IY and be inspected before acceptance as a responsible producer. For the farmer, participation in the Faces initiative involves compliance with farming standards set by IY which include the restriction of pesticides as noted above, the prohibition of such practices as the use of genetically modified seeds and plants, and the use of radiation to extend the shelf-life of produce. Farmers are encouraged to participate in local study groups with Faces farmers from their region where innovations in farming and best practices are studied and discussed. Farmers are also organised into regional teams including other farmers, vegetable processors and distribution carriers that become units for optimising logistics and effective information sharing. IY representatives also visit the farms regularly to share information and inspect farms. Reports of these visits are released on the Faces homepage. Faces farmers also gain access to a huge volume of information on the day-by-day trends in the vegetable market, along with interpretation of this information and advice from merchandising specialists from IY.

Modern commercial farming in Japan can be described as being shaped by a play-off between the two forces of cooperation and competition between producers. Cooperation has been promoted among farmers for decades by the *Nokyo*, the Japan Agricultural Cooperatives (Moore 1990; Mulgan 2000), but, despite their

4 look.itoyokado.co.jp/yasai/main.html (in Japanese, accessed 6 January 2010).

efforts, some counterproductive competitive trends mark the industry. One such trend is the boom-and-bust cycle which characterises the introduction of new produce to the market (Jonker and Takahashi 2002). Following the introduction of a new product to the market, or a revival in popularity for an existing product, rapid growth in demand and good prices encourage many farmers to 'follow the trend' and start producing the same product. The subsequent rapid increase in supply, combined with an inability to see emerging trends that potentially eclipse the current boom, create an oversupply and result in low, if any, returns to farmers for their investments.

The Faces project ameliorates this 'swinging effect' to a considerable extent by guiding farmers in their investment and production plans. Faces farmers effectively work within IY's marketing framework, which is based on ongoing analysis of consumption patterns extending far beyond the vegetable market. Faces farmers are therefore able to protect their businesses from swings in the market by basing their planning on evolving lifestyle trends, and need not rely on past sales results for individual products. By October 2007 over 2,500 farmers in approximately 260 regions throughout Japan were participating in the initiative.

**FIGURE 17.6** Vegetables with Faces products

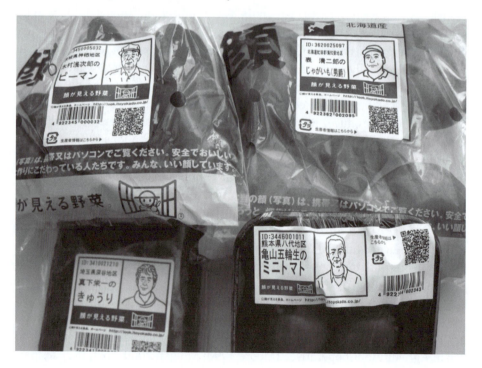

For the customer, the Faces initiative means access to product information. Basically, this consists of telling the customer the name of the producer of each vegetable and providing the customer with ready access to information about the farmer, the location of the farm, the particular type of vegetable, the farming process used in its production, the reason for this particular product being chosen for sale, and messages from the farmer as well as ideas and recipes for preparing the vegetable. As shown in Figure 17.6, the vegetables are packed in a branded Faces package (either a closed or open-ended plastic container as suited to the vegetable) and has an individually printed label affixed to the front. Each label shows the name of the farmer, a line drawing of the farmer's face, the farmer's Faces identification number, the area address of the farm (prefecture, region and town or village), the URL of the Faces homepage on the Internet, and a Quick Reference barcode (QR code).

The customer can access information on the product by entering the Faces identification number into the search section of the Faces homepage from any computer connected to the Internet, or they can use the camera on a mobile phone to take a picture of the QR code which will give them access to the same information via a homepage designed for display on the web browser of a mobile phone. The QR code allows customers to rapidly access the product information from within the store as they examine the products while actually shopping.

Customers can send messages to the store regarding particular products. These range from complaints, to requests and very frequently to complementary letters and requests to the farmers. The farmers are sent information from customers regarding their produce and often respond to these comments on their own pages within the Faces homepage.

For many businesses in Japan, product traceability is seen as an onerous burden and a logistical challenge imposed on them by the demands and threats of non-profit organisations (NPOs) and consumer protection groups. In marked contrast, IY has interpreted these same demands into a system that goes beyond ensuring traceability and also promotes increased satisfaction and value for customers, provides management and technical resources for farmers to improve their businesses, and creates a competitive advantage for IY. The Faces initiative actually reverses a long-standing dynamic of the large-scale retail industry in Japan. Instead of pressing producers for lower prices, the initiative pushes instead for better quality from producers, greater efficiency in the use of data on consumption trends, and more feedback from customers based on a comprehensive re-engineering of production, distribution, marketing and retail relationships from the perspective of the enhanced welfare of each of the respective parties involved.

Farmers gain access to stable markets with good prices, information on effective farming and farm management innovations, interaction with their end-users (the customers) and technical and specific marketing support from IY. In return they are expected to comply with rigorous production standards, plan their production according to the system, and take pride and responsibility for their work.

Customers gain a supply of fresh produce that is safe, good and responsive to their needs. In return they pay a premium over the price of non-Faces vegetables because of the higher costs of domestic production. The importance to the Japanese consumer of a source of safe and wholesome vegetables cannot be overemphasised at present given the frequency of media reports of sales of contaminated or fraudulent produce.

IY gains control over a supply of safe, fresh vegetables, access to a source of knowledge and innovation in farming, increased feedback from customers about their demands for vegetables which goes beyond immediate issues such as cost, and the image of being a retailer that operates in the interest of the customer and the future. Again, given current public anguish over scandals in the produce industry, access to a supply of fresh and wholesome vegetables is a considerable competitive advantage. In return IY assumes the cost of maintaining and developing the Faces IT infrastructure, managing the production network, planning production and promoting awareness and understanding of the brand.

At the same time, the Faces project exerts a force for change. Farmers feel compelled to further improve their products and production processes—claiming responsibility, where responsibility is measured in terms of expertise, demands proof of ongoing innovation. Customers feel a responsibility to support domestic production and to practise responsible consumption; awareness has developed among some that demanding cheap products effectively undermines responsible producers. Perhaps the greatest pressure is on IY itself. IY must expand the initiative and continue innovating by introducing new projects in order to avoid criticism that its acts are superficial: that it only innovates where it must and will ignore its responsibilities where profits can be realised with less effort.

IY has subsequently expanded the Faces project to include meat, fish and fruit with a total of 135 products offered under the Faces brand in 2007 with combined sales of over ¥16 billion. Similar innovations exist in other nations, and other retailers and cooperatives have developed their own versions of related strategies. The point here is not to extol the merits of the Faces initiative as an innovation in retailing, but to explain how IY identified the strategic potential of Faces when it did, and how it was able to design the initiative as a set of relationships based on an internal dynamic of sustainable innovation. In other words, how IY was able to reframe product traceability from being a tool for risk-mitigation into an opportunity to develop an entirely new value-creating market.

# Analysis of IY innovation

It is impossible to present a comprehensive analysis of a large corporate group such as IY within the limits of this chapter. Moreover, such an exposition is not the goal here. IY's capacity for, and record of, innovation in the retail industry has already been made the subject of numerous studies (Sparks 1995; Johansson and Nonaka 1996; Czinkota and Kotabe 2000; Rapp 2002; Barfield *et al.* 2003). At this point, the task is to identify the sense-making processes that enable IY to conceptualise and plan active/transformational innovation and thereby realise a contribution to a sustainable enhancement of the standard of living as a business engaged in retail. Analysing IY's business philosophy and management practices according to this model shows that there are in fact processes in place that fill the roles necessary for an active/transformational approach to innovative CSR.

## Principles (mode of identity)

### Ethical justification

IY's ethical justification is encapsulated in its mission statement. Almost as old as the company itself, it fits well with the current 'age of CSR'. It states that:

> We strive to be a sincere company, worthy of our customers' trust. We strive to be a sincere company, worthy of the trust of our trading partners, shareholders and communities. We strive to be a sincere company, worthy of the trust of our employees (Ito-Yokado 2007).

In its mission statement IY defines itself in the most basic terms for a merchant: integrity for trust. In the Japanese original the word *seijitsu* is used. *Seijitsu* means integrity, sincerity, to be principled, incorruptible, virtuous and pure. In contrast, most other retailers in Japan state their desire to be the best, strongest or most innovative retailer in the industry. With this simple formula of striving to become a corporation with integrity, IY takes the responsibility for success upon itself as defined by its ability to earn trust through its own actions. This mission is constantly repeated in stories. IY revels in stories of employees whose actions have embodied this ideal. Internal communications inevitably contain stories of employees whose actions have generated trust. Surprisingly, however, these acts are rarely heroic; usually the smallest actions are given the most attention. As a result, IY abounds in examples of how this mission is put into action on a day-to-day basis across all its functions and businesses.

### Normative commitment

Suzuki Toshifumi is the Chairman of IY and of the parent company Seven & I Holdings. Suzuki is a remarkably charismatic figure: forceful in character and concise in speech. When asked to explain the social responsibility of IY, Suzuki responded 'to think and act from the perspective of the customer [customer's welfare]'. When asked to explain the most important thing for IY as a business, Suzuki responds, 'the customer'. The response that 'the customer is our highest priority' is common among Japanese corporations. What is different about IY is Suzuki's explanation of how the customer should be prioritised: 'Reject the logic of the seller, follow the logic of the buyer' (Akiba 2003).

Suzuki has observed that there are two ways to plan and operate a retail business—one from the perspective of the retailer and the other from the perspective of the customer. The retailer's perspective is based on an understanding of accepted industrial practices and internal logistics, a confidence in past achievements and performance measurement using indicators abstracted from the market. In contrast, the customer's perspective is based on a perception of lifestyle expectations, the quality and value of products and service within the context of aspirations and plans for the future. For Suzuki and IY, the retailer's perspective is myopic and reactionary, compared with the customer's perspective which is expansive and dynamic. For Suzuki, only the retailer who understands the perspective of the customer and manages in order to promote the customer's interests can find opportunities for innovation and growth. It is interesting to note here that throughout the company the word 'customer' (*okyakusama*, the 'honoured guest' in Japanese) is used to refer to the buyer. The word 'consumer' (*shohisya* in Japanese) is actively discouraged at IY where its use is considered a sign of a company where the buyer is defined according to the logic of the seller.

The normative commitment is embodied in the concept of welfare of the customer. IY envisages its mission as being one of constantly improving the standard of living by developing and applying its knowledge of products, commercialisation and distribution in order to innovate the business of retailing. IY makes its contribution to society as a supermarket, and its contribution is uniquely that of a supermarket.

## Processes (mode of decision-making)

### Internally consistent

The processes here are numerous and varied: it is beyond the scope of this chapter to properly describe them all; instead only one representative example will be introduced. Since 1984 IY has held a biannual business policy meeting where all employees of middle management level and above gather to hear the chairman explain the corporate strategy for the next year and review recent developments. Lasting for half a day and attended by thousands of people, these meetings are used to convey strategic plans, the decisions behind their development, and the use of resources for their implementation. After the meeting the participants return to their workplaces—this may be a single shop floor or a vast distribution centre—and hold a meeting with their own team members to explain and discuss the strategy first-hand. IY calls this 'immediate communication' and considerable resources are invested in promoting it.

### Open posture

Learning about and acting from the perspective of others is, as already mentioned, a hallmark of IY's management philosophy. This open stance is not restricted to the customer, but includes all of IY's partner corporations (members of Seven & I Holdings group), suppliers and service contractors. The process for sharing information and developing and reviewing business plans from the perspective of others is embodied in IY's *Gyokakukaigi*, the Business Process Innovation Committee. Commenced in February 1982 and held weekly ever since, the *Gyokakukaigi* has been used as an open forum for debating plans and analysing situations from multiple perspectives. Proposals are made and discussed by representatives of departments, product lines, suppliers and related corporations. The purpose of the meeting is to evaluate and rethink business plans and their implementation from the perspective of different departments, functions, group companies and even suppliers. Again, the *Gyokakukaigi* is well known in Japan and is the subject of numerous studies.

## Partners (mode of interaction)

### Collectivistic identity

Japanese corporations have traditionally formed groups or conglomerates. IY is no exception. As a part of Seven & I Holdings, IY is a unit in a network of over 100 corporations that belong to the group and many more that deal with the group as strategic partners. A retailer is by definition a partner, measured by the strength of its partnerships and its ability to perform as a partner to others. Because the resources IY must rally in order to accomplish its goals are often the abilities and assets of the corporations with which they collaborate, it is necessary to constantly locate these goals as part of the common interest binding these partners together. IY refers to the companies that it deals with as its strategic partners. The importance of partnership and their resultant synergies for ensuring successful business is emphasised throughout the company.

### Moral legitimacy

The legitimacy of IY is grounded on acceptance of the fact that IY does not monopolise the moral high ground in the industry. IY maintains a pragmatic dialogue with partners where the legitimacy of IY as a 'good business' is constantly tested and redefined. In more pragmatic terms, this takes the form of governance structures, all-inclusive codes of conduct, monitoring, hotlines both in-house and for suppliers, and other balances and checks which it maintains for self-regulation and reassessment. IY uses its compliance and monitoring infrastructure as a vehicle for maintaining and identifying acceptable norms of behaviour with its relevant stakeholders—not just as a tool to ensure compliance with externally imposed standards.

## Conclusion

IY's solution to securing a supply of fresh, safe vegetables goes beyond simply investing in a product traceability system in order to mitigate the potential risk to its business of selling produce that may be contaminated. In going beyond such a reactionary response, and by redefining the roles and relationships of the actors involved in the produce market, IY has created what is arguably a fundamentally new market which produces and trades streams of value not previously possible using a network of partnerships not previously existent.

Faced with the same situation, however, most retailers in Japan have sought to comply with the social demands for safe produce by introducing standard product traceability systems to increase their control over their existing supply chains, and implementing testing protocols to detect contaminated produce within established production systems. These retailers also attempt to reassure their customers with advertisements and promises that their produce is 'safe', which, given the current level of anxiety generated by ongoing reports of instances of sales of contaminated food, only heightens consumers' concern for their safety, focuses their attention on risk, and gives rise to ever more strident calls for stricter controls. The result is a vicious circle where consumer anxiety prompts more risk management, and more risk management leads to the identification of more problems, which again exacerbate the anxiety of the consumer. Considering the fact that consumers prefer to base their produce purchase decisions on such factors as taste and nutritional value, this is a remarkable situation.

Despite the absurdity of the situation, however, corporations find themselves trapped in these vicious cycles as they attempt to respond to the demands of a society that is itself reacting to the dysfunctions of an outdated way of doing business. Increasing attempts to quantify and measure social responsibility within the context of existing relationships has put huge pressure on corporations to conform and align their actions to immediate social demands. Rather than preoccupying themselves with efforts to prove their responsibility in terms of the various standard-ised measures that have come to constitute the mechanics of the CSR movement, corporations need to innovate using their unique configurations of knowledge and resources.

Why in this instance was IY able to interpret this same situation as an opportu-nity to reconfigure its business relationships and to initiate an innovation to cre-ate new sources of value? IY was able to perceive an opportunity to create new value-creating relationships, rather than being overwhelmed by the risks of an out-moded, established market because of its process-based approach to CSR.

In order to implement innovative CSR a corporation requires:

- A set of principles that enables it to objectively identify itself within the context of existing relationships, and yet also guide it by indicating a wider sense of purpose

- Internal processes that allow information to flow throughout the organi-sation and be evaluated objectively from a variety of perspectives both within and beyond the organisation

- Processes that enable the corporation to identify a common ground with its partners and thereby inform plans to reconfigure interactions into increasingly more beneficial relationships

Combined, these processes enable a corporation to perceive and integrate social opportunities within their strategic objectives. While most CSR initiatives today are designed by corporations to respond to public demands by aligning business activities to what is seen as being socially acceptable norms, IY was able (at least in this instance) to integrate opportunities for social betterment into its strategic objectives. Instead of designing their CSR initiatives as transactions of resources for legitimacy in certain areas of short-term importance (the passive/transactional approach), or as internal restructurings according to the specifications of those with power to condone a business (the passive/transformational approach), or as a search for current business opportunities that fit current social expectations of good business (the active/transactional approach), corporations in Japan need to develop these processes of strategic integration by which they can identify oppor-tunities to create value by reframing relationships to achieve their own unique social contributions as value-creating businesses (the active/transformational approach).

# References

Adachi, E., and T. Kanai (2004) *CSR Management and SRI* (Tokyo: Kinyuzaiseijijyo Kenkyu-kai; in Japanese).

Akiba, Y. (2003) *The ItoYokado Business Innovation Committee* (Tokyo: Kodansha; in Japanese).

Arata, K. (2006) *Lessons of the Family Codes of the Merchants of Edo: The Origins of Trade* (Tokyo: Subarusha; in Japanese).

Barfield, C., G. Heiduk and P. Welfens (eds.) (2003) *Internet, Economic Growth and Globalization: Perspectives on the New Economy in Europe, Japan, and the US* (Berlin: Springer).

Basu, K., and G. Palazzo (2008) 'Corporate Social Responsibility: A Process Model of Sensemaking', *Academy of Management Review* 33.1: 122-36.

Brickson, S. (2007) 'Organisational Identity Orientation: The Genesis of the Role of the Firm and Distinct Forms of Social Value', *Academy of Management Review* 32.3: 864-88.

Czinkota, M., and M. Kotabe (2000) *Japanese Distribution Strategy: Changes and Innovations* (London: Cengage Learning EMEA).

Hirata, M. (2005) *What are Corporate Ethics? The Spirit of CSR as Learnt from Ishida Baigan* (Tokyo: PHP Shinsho; in Japanese).

Ibuki, E. (2005) *Managing for Corporate Social Responsibility* (Tokyo: Toyokeizai Shinposha; in Japanese).

ItoYokado Corporate History Committee (2007) *Change and Adaptation: Ongoing Challenge to Create* (Tokyo: ItoYokado).

Japan Association of Corporate Executives (2006) *Survey of Executive Perceptions of the Social Responsibility of Corporations* (Tokyo: Keizai Doyukai, in Japanese).

Japan Association of Corporate Executives—Keizai Doyukai (2008) *Social Change by Value Creating CSR: Towards a CSR that Builds Social Trust and Deals with Social Issues* (Tokyo: Keizai Doyukai, in Japanese).

Japan Business Federation Committee for Promotion of Corporate Social Contribution (2008) *Social Contribution in the Age of CSR* (Tokyo: Keidanren Publishing; in Japanese).

Johansson, J., and I. Nonaka (1996) *Relentless: The Japanese Way of Marketing* (New York: HarperBusiness).

Jonker, T.H., and I. Takahashi (2002) 'Public Concerns and Consumer Behaviour in Japan', in F. Brouwer and D. Ervin (eds.), *Public Concerns, Environmental Standards, and Agricultural Trade* (New York: CABI Publishing).

Kawaguchi, M. (2004) 'The Quality of a Genuinely Good Company: What Financial Results Alone can not Measure', in Nikkei CSR Project, *CSR: Enhancing Corporate Value* (Tokyo: Nikkei Shuppan; in Japanese).

—— (2006) 'CSR: Examples of Relevant Practices in Japanese SMEs', in M.E. Contreras (ed.), *Corporate Social Responsibility in the Promotion of Social Development: Experiences from Asia and Latin America* (Washington, DC: Inter-American Development Bank).

Matsushita, K. (1984) *Not for Bread Alone: A Business Ethos, a Management Ethic* (Tokyo: PHP Institute).

Moore, R. (1990) *Japanese Agriculture: Patterns of Rural Development* (Boulder, CO: Westview Press).

Morimoto, M. (1994) *Managerial Research in Corporate Social Responsibility* (Tokyo: Hakuto-Shobo; in Japanese).

Mulgan, A. (2000) *The Politics of Agriculture in Japan* (London: Routledge).

Nakamura, H. (1968) 'Basic Features of the Legal, Political, and Economic Thought of Japan', in C.A. Moore and A.V. Morris (eds.), *The Japanese Mind: Essentials of Japanese Philosophy and Culture* (Honolulu, HI: University of Hawaii Press).

Oiwa, K., M. Ogata and K. Colligan-Taylor (2001) *Rowing the Eternal Sea: The Story of a Minamata Fisherman* (Lanham, MD: Rowman & Littlefield).

Onuki, A. (2006) *The Management Wisdom to be Learnt from Ninomiya Sontoku* (Tokyo: Nihonnoritsu Daigaku Shuppan; in Japanese).

Rapp, W. (2002) *Information Technology Strategies: How Leading Firms Use IT to Gain an Advantage* (Oxford, UK: Oxford University Press).

Schuman, M. (1995) 'Managing Legitimacy: Strategic and Institutional Approaches', *Academy of Management Review* 20.3: 571-610.

Sheldon, C.D. (1973) *The Rise of the Merchant Class in Tokugawa Japan, 1600–1868: An Introductory Survey* (New York: Russell & Russell).

Sparks, L. (1995) 'Reciprocal Retail Internationalization: The Southland Corporation, Ito-Yokado and 7-Eleven Convenience Stores', *Services Industry Journal* 15.4: 57-96.

Suenaga, K. (2004) *An Introduction to the Study of Omi Merchants: 'Sanpo Yoshi' the Origins of Corporate Social Responsibility* (Tokyo: Sunrise Shuppan; in Japanese).

Tai, K. (1993) 'Confucianism and Japanese Modernization: A Study of Shibusawa Eiichi', in S. Durlabhji, N.E. Marks, E. Norton and S. Roach (eds.), *Japanese Business: Cultural Perspectives* (Albany, NY: SUNY Press).

Tonomura, H. (1992) *Community and Commerce in Late Medieval Japan: The Corporate Villages of Tokuchin-Ho* (Stanford, CA: Stanford University Press).

Wenger, E. (1998) *Communities of Practice: Learning, Meaning and Identity* (Cambridge, UK: Cambridge University Press).

——, R. McDermott and W. Snyder (2002) *Cultivating Communities of Practice* (Boston, MA: Harvard Business School Press).

# 18

# CSR, the mining industry and indigenous peoples in Australia and Canada

## From cost and risk minimisation to value creation and sustainable development

**Ciaran O'Faircheallaigh**

Griffith University, Australia

The global minerals industry is characterised by two features that are highly germane to its adoption and pursuit of CSR policies and activities. First, with few exceptions (historically, diamond and bauxite mining) the industry is ruthlessly competitive, with firms competing on international markets where supply regularly exceeds demand, and with those that fail to minimise costs and maximise profits going out of business or facing takeover by more profitable rivals. This point is well illustrated by the fate of six resource companies used by the author as a basis for a study of human rights and CSR, completed in 2002 (O'Faircheallaigh and Kelly 2002). Three of them, Western Mining Corporation, Mount Isa Mines and Normandy Ltd, have since been taken over by BHP Billiton, Xstrata and Newmont, respectively. A fourth, Pasminco Ltd, ceased trading in 2004 as a result of depressed zinc prices and foreign currency losses. A fifth, Rio Tinto, might also have ceased to exist as a separate entity if the sixth company, BHP Billiton, had not abandoned its recent takeover attempt for Rio because of the global economic downturn. In such a competitive environment, cost minimisation is not just important or even critical. It is a matter of survival.

The second feature involves the level and nature of risks (other than competition from rivals) faced by the mining industry. As the industry has become more concentrated and competitive and as smaller, richer and more accessible mineral deposits have been exhausted, mining increasingly involves the exploitation of huge, low-grade deposits in areas that are geographically remote and often encompass the ancestral lands of indigenous peoples. For instance, Dowie (2009: 24) estimates that 70% of the world's uranium resources lie below indigenous land. Many of the regions in which mining is now concentrated are also characterised by (at least relatively) pristine environments and hold much of the world's biodiversity, while at the same time the potential for the industry to cause environmental damage, always substantial, has escalated with the scale of its operations (Ali and O'Faircheallaigh 2007: 9-11).

This combination of factors creates major risks for mining companies. New projects may be delayed or abandoned because of opposition from indigenous or environmental groups and/or as a result of government regulatory processes. For instance in 2005 Rio Tinto ceased developing the Jabiluka uranium deposit in Australia's Northern Territory because of opposition from the Mirrar Aboriginal traditional owners of the lease area. Another example involves the Voisey's Bay nickel project in Canada, where indigenous opposition resulted in long project delays and contributed to a decision by the developer, Inco, to write off C\$2 billion of its investment in the project (Gibson 2006). This example highlights the fact that project delays or abandonment can be very expensive, given the large costs involved in developing modern mining projects and the fact that delay may mean that vital market opportunities are missed.

Operating projects may be closed temporarily or have to be abandoned entirely because of action by indigenous groups. For example, in 1972 Rio Tinto began operating what was then one of the world's largest copper mines on Bougainville Island in Papua New Guinea. In 1988 and 1989 the mine was subject to sustained military action by the Bougainville Revolutionary Army, incensed at the environmental damage caused by the project and what it saw as Rio's failure to deliver substantial economic benefits to Bougainvilleans. Rio Tinto permanently closed the mine in 1989, abandoning a US\$1.5 billion investment.

Numerous other examples of project delays and company losses are documented in the literature (Humphreys 2000; Gao *et al.* 2002; Day and Affum 2005; Richards 2006; Trebeck 2007). This context provides strong incentives for mining companies to use CSR to secure their 'social licence to operate', by creating benefits for communities affected by their projects and by winning support among environmental and other lobby groups, government policy-makers and the wider public. Many companies, with the strong support and encouragement of industry bodies, have adopted extensive and, in some cases, costly CSR policies and activities (see for example BHP Billiton 2006; ICMM 2008). However, I argue in the next section that an analysis of these policies and activities in the context of relations with indigenous communities in Australia and Canada indicates that in many cases they are characterised by a preoccupation with cost minimisation, and by an emphasis on risk management which is short-term and focused on securing initial project approvals rather than on building positive, long-term relationships with affected communities. This approach can be explained partly in terms of competitive pressures to contain costs. Also important is company resistance to what is seen as demands by external stakeholders to share control over key operational areas, particularly environmental management, and the impact of ideas and modes of operating that are deeply entrenched in many mining corporations.

In the following sections I discuss a number of major problems associated with this risk and cost minimisation approach. One is that it can result in accumulated resentment and opposition which, ironically, increases precisely those risks that CSR policies are designed to address. Another and fundamental problem is that the approach militates against a more strategic and positive view of CSR as a means of *creating* value, rather than reacting to threats to the *existing* value of projects and investments. It also detracts from mining's capacity to contribute to sustainable development, a serious drawback given that the industry is increasingly being assessed in terms of that contribution (Veiga *et al.* 2001; Gibson 2006; Richards 2006). Two specific areas are examined to illustrate these points. The first concerns indigenous employment in mining, which, over the longer term, can cut labour costs and increase productivity. The second involves indigenous participation in the environmental management of major projects, which can help reduce the negative environmental impacts of mining and enhance its overall contribution to sustainability.

The final section considers what is needed to develop a different approach to CSR that is less reactive to short-term risk and recognises the potential for creating value and contributing to sustainable development. Substantial innovation is required in company organisational structures, skill sets and resource allocation systems, and deeply entrenched views both in industry and among indigenous peoples must be challenged. New approaches to negotiation are also required; in particular a shift away from approaches that emphasise short-term gains and focus on obtaining indigenous consent on a 'once off' basis, rather than on ongoing implementation and relationship building.

## CSR in the mining industry

The international mining industry is large and diverse. Despite the tendency to concentration it still includes small, nationally based companies operating only one or two mines, as well as large, diversified multinationals. In addition the industry operates within a variety of national and sub-national policy contexts which can influence the form and focus of CSR (Matten and Moon 2008). As such the industry is likely to encompass considerable diversity in CSR policies and activities, cautioning against over-generalisation. Yet there is substantial evidence to suggest that there is a strong general orientation towards the risk and cost minimisation approach outlined above.

This does not mean that some companies do not make substantial, long-term commitments to building relationships with affected communities. Telewiak (2001) outlines the efforts of Falconbridge Ltd to develop and maintain positive engagement with Inuit communities over more than 15 years. For instance, the company modified standard operating procedures to enhance Inuit employment opportunities and minimise the impact of ship movements on Inuit hunting, and spent C\$2 million to remediate another mine, not owned by Falconbridge, that had earlier operated in the area and been abandoned without being properly rehabilitated (see also Harvey and Gawler 2003). However the overall emphasis is on managing immediate risks to the corporate 'social licence to operate'.

Such a conclusion is certainly supported by the literature on CSR in the mining industry. Labonne (1999: 320-21) states that, at a global level, the 'mining and oil industries are struggling to reduce what they regard as social risk'. Kemp *et al.* (2006: 397-98) also note the focus on risk, and state that 'a risk focus does not necessarily assist an operation identify and maximise community development opportunities that are unrelated to specific, current risks, or pre-emptive actions that would reduce future extreme risks'. They recommend moving from the 'traditional risk-dominated model to a more balanced approach, which focuses on opportunities as well as risks and also incorporates a relationship focus' (Kemp *et al.* 2006: 399). Banerjee (2001: 46-47) reports one manager as saying that his company's engagement with indigenous communities 'is really about our licence to operate . . . we see Aboriginal people as an important component of maintaining our licence and providing security for our investment'. Cragg and Greenbaum (2002: 238) report that, while managers in a Canadian mining company recognised the need to address the capacity of disaffected aboriginal groups to interfere with company projects, they tended to see engagement with aboriginal and other stakeholders as an obstacle to 'getting the job done'. Crawley and Sinclair (2003: 372) concluded on the basis of a study of five mining companies that, while they were increasingly seeking to build better relations with indigenous communities, the justification for doing so was primarily to obtain 'a "licence to operate" or to build a better public profile' (for other similar findings see Kapelus 2002; Rajak 2008).

One limitation with this literature, and one shared by much other research on CSR, is its heavy reliance on company sources of information. As Campbell (2007:

950) notes, much literature in the field focuses on 'the rhetoric of socially responsible corporate behaviour [as expressed] in corporate reports, advertising, websites and elsewhere', and fails to address the question of whether 'corporations are actually behaving in socially responsible ways or simply making hollow claims to that effect'. Such a focus is especially problematic given that a recent, extensive review of mining company reporting on CSR concluded that it provides 'no real measure . . . of whether policy statements are applied in practice in any meaningful way' (Jenkins and Yakovleva 2006: 282).

For a number of reasons, agreements negotiated between mining companies and indigenous peoples on whose lands they wish to develop projects, which are now standard in industrialised countries such as Australia and Canada, offer an important source of independently verifiable empirical information on company CSR *behaviour*, as opposed to policy and rhetoric. First, while Australia and a number of Canadian jurisdictions require the *fact* of an agreement with indigenous landowners as a precondition for the grant of project approvals, the content of agreements is generally not specified by law. Thus their negotiation offers considerable latitude for the operation of CSR policies. Second, they represent an important component of companies' risk minimisation strategies. Formally, they involve the consent of aboriginal representatives for a project to proceed, and often require aboriginal groups to refrain from delaying or interfering with project development, providing financial and legal sanctions if they fail to do so (Kennett 1999: 45-46; Sosa and Keenan 2001: 10). More broadly, they can help deflect criticism by groups critical of the mining industry, and create a favourable impression with policy-makers and the wider public. Thus if company executives are serious about CSR, one would expect to find this commitment evident in agreement-making. Finally, agreements involve binding company commitments to specific actions, and as such provide a sound basis for assessing the extent to which companies 'take [CSR] seriously and dedicate significant resources to it' (Campbell 2007: 950).

The most comprehensive study of agreements to date is that by O'Faircheallaigh and his colleagues (O'Faircheallaigh 2004, 2008; O'Faircheallaigh and Corbett 2005). The 45 Australian agreements included in the study allow a broadly based analysis as they include numerous commodities (diamonds, gold, coal, iron ore, copper, zinc, nickel, bauxite, silica and heavy mineral sands); projects whose annual turnover ranges from as little as A\$20 million a year to in excess of A\$1 billion a year; and a variety of company types from one-mine Australian companies to the world's two largest multinational mining companies. In addition, the sample includes five agreements negotiated by a single company and three by another, allowing a comparison of outcomes negotiated by individual companies in different political and indigenous contexts.

How can the 'CSR performance' of companies that negotiate agreements be assessed? O'Faircheallaigh (2004) developed a set of numerical scales for evaluating agreement provisions in terms of the extent to which they address indigenous interests, and dealing with eight substantive issues that tend to be central to company–indigenous agreements. These are environmental management; cultural heritage protection; financial compensation; indigenous participation in employment and training; indigenous participation in business opportunities; indigenous consent and support for project development; recognition of indigenous rights in land; and support for agreement implementation. The provisions of each agreement were assessed using these scales. (See O'Faircheallaigh 2004 for a detailed discussion of the evaluative criteria and how they were developed; and O'Faircheallaigh 2008 on the methodological issues involved in applying specific scales to agreement provisions.)

A major finding of the study was that a substantial majority of the agreements scored poorly on most criteria. For instance, many agreements did not include substantial financial compensation, relative to the size and expected revenues of the project. About three-quarters of agreements offered little additional protection to Aboriginal cultural heritage beyond that already available under general legislation. Only one in four agreements provided for substantive Aboriginal participation in environmental management of the projects involved. Two agreements actually reduced opportunities for Aboriginal participation, by requiring the Aboriginal signatories to refrain from exercising rights (such as to object to the level of environmental impact proposed for a project) enjoyed by Australian citizens under environmental legislation. In the minority of cases where agreements did offer major benefits to indigenous groups, the latter had access to additional legal rights because of the applicability of specific state legislation, and/or were represented by strong Aboriginal political organisations with the capacity to threaten to delay or halt projects (O'Faircheallaigh 2006a, 2008).

This pattern of outcomes indicates that mining companies did not see agreements as an opportunity to proactively build long-term relationships by providing substantial benefits to indigenous communities. Only where Aboriginal groups had the political leverage to pose a risk to their projects did companies negotiate substantial benefits. This interpretation is strongly supported by an analysis of the two companies with multiple agreements in the sample. Despite espousing a single set of CSR policies at the corporate level, the content of each company's agreements varied greatly from case to case. For instance one company negotiated cultural heritage provisions that achieved a score of only 2 on a scale of 0–6 in one case, but in another agreed provisions that scored 5 on that scale. Again, these differences appear to reflect companies' assessment of the political strength of the Aboriginal groups involved (O'Faircheallaigh 2008: 45).

Why would Aboriginal landowners willingly sign agreements that offer them few benefits? Under Australian federal legislation (the Native Title Act 1993), in the absence of agreement with indigenous landowners, a government tribunal determines whether a company should be permitted to develop a mining project. In all 19 cases determined by the tribunal between introduction of the legislation in 1994 and 2007, the project was allowed to proceed (Corbett and O'Faircheallaigh 2007). Thus Aboriginal landowners may believe their only choice is between the limited benefits offered by a negotiated agreement, and no benefits at all. This allows companies the opportunity to use agreements as part of their risk minimisation strategies, but to do so at little cost. The Australian evidence strongly suggests that, except where Aboriginal people can exercise countervailing political power, mining companies adopt such a risk and cost minimisation approach.

No comparable study of agreements has been undertaken in Canada. However, the author's review of 20 Canadian agreements for a study of implementation provisions in Australia and Canada (O'Faircheallaigh 2003) and relevant Canadian literature (see for example Kennett 1999; Sosa and Keenan 2001: 20-21) reveals the same sort of variability in outcomes as occurs in Australia. For instance, some agreements contain no financial compensation, while others provide for payments totalling millions of dollars annually. Certain agreements include only vague commitments to increasing aboriginal employment and devote no specific resources to training programmes. Others establish firm employment targets and fund initiatives aimed at creating all the essential requirements to recruit, train and promote aboriginal employees. In this case also, aboriginal political strength appears to be a key determinant. For example, one of Canada's most favourable agreements from an aboriginal perspective, that for the Voisey's Bay nickel mine in Labrador, was concluded after the Innu and Inuit groups on whose land the project lies used direct action and litigation to cause repeated delays to project development (Gibson 2006).

The negotiating behaviour of individual companies in Canada also reveals a cost minimisation approach. For instance, in 1996 BHP Billiton negotiated separate agreements with two aboriginal groups with interests in lands affected by the company's Ekati diamond project. There was no legal requirement for the company to negotiate agreements. The relevant federal minister did require 'significant progress' on negotiation of agreements before he would issue relevant regulatory approvals, but he said nothing about the content of the proposed agreements, leaving this to be negotiated with the two groups. One group was better resourced and more experienced in negotiations than the other, and, according to participants, BHP Billiton negotiators also felt that, in the absence of the 'stronger' group's consent, it might not be politically feasible to proceed. The company negotiated agreements with the two groups that differed in significant ways, with the stronger group securing, for example, more favourable financial compensation, and targets for employment of its members, an outcome sought but not achieved by the other group (Bielawski 2004). Again, BHP Billiton's behaviour reflects an emphasis on achieving project approval at the lowest possible cost, rather than an emphasis on building sustainable relationships. Indeed the outcome resulted in ongoing resentment towards BHP Billiton by members of the aboriginal groups that received the less favourable outcome, some of whom expressed the belief, a decade later, that the company was 'sneaky' and 'tricked' the community (Weitzner 2006: 9-10).

## Failure to manage long-term risk

An obvious problem with a risk and cost minimisation approach to CSR is that it may not in fact allow risks to be managed, especially in the longer term, because it fails to provide a basis for establishing and maintaining positive relationships with groups and communities affected by mining. Cost minimisation, combined with too heavy a focus on overcoming obstacles to initial project approvals, may mean that the benefits offered to communities from CSR initiatives are inadequate to achieve their ongoing support for mining activities. In relation to negotiated agreements, a further and specific problem is a failure to provide the resources required to put agreements into effect, and a lack of ongoing attention and commitment by senior company managers once projects are approved. The result is chronic implementation failure, and the benefits potentially offered by agreements are not actually delivered.

In recent decades numerous company–indigenous agreements in Australia, Canada and other countries have failed to deliver promised benefits, as revealed by the author's macro-analysis of a large sample of agreements in the two countries (O'Faircheallaigh 2003) and by detailed case studies of specific agreements (AMSI 1992; NEDGI 1993; Kapelus 2002: 292; O'Faircheallaigh 2002; Weitzner 2006). For example, employment and training programmes have often not been delivered and employment targets have not been achieved. Structures such as joint implementation and coordination committees designed to ensure community involvement in project management have failed to operate for more than a few years after an agreement is signed. Commitments to incorporate indigenous knowledge into environmental management have not been met.

Such failures can threaten a company's ongoing social licence to operate and, as illustrated above, may ultimately lead to loss of investment. They can also destroy the social sustainability of mining on a regional basis. Both this wider risk and the specific problems associated with implementation failure are illustrated by the recent history of uranium mining in the Alligator Rivers Region of Australia's Northern Territory. In the late 1970s one of the world's largest uranium mines, Ranger, was established on the traditional lands of the Mirrar people. Agreements negotiated between the project developer, Energy Resources of Australia (ERA), the Australian government, and representatives of the Mirrar people promised substantial economic benefits, especially in the form of access to employment and training opportunities. They also promised a major initiative to monitor and address adverse social impacts potentially associated with the Ranger mine. However, ERA did not deliver on many of its commitments in relation to employment and training. For example, it failed to develop an Aboriginal employment and training policy; to provide appropriate accommodation for potential Aboriginal recruits; and to provide resources to company staff responsible for employment and training initiatives. The result was that few jobs were created for Aboriginal people, and that the large majority of those that were, other than casual labouring positions, were monopolised by Aborigines from outside the region (O'Faircheallaigh 2002: 89-95). The social monitoring initiative was discontinued in 1984, and partly for that reason little was done to address the major social problems, including alcohol abuse and youth suicide, that escalated during the late 1980s and the 1990s (Supervising Scientist 1997).

In the late 1990s ERA began developing another large uranium deposit, Jabiluka, also located on Mirrar land. Convinced that establishment of a second mine would spell the social destruction of her people, the senior Mirrar traditional owner, Yvonne Margarula, initiated a national and international legal and political campaign to prevent development of Jabiluka. After numerous protests and the arrest of Margarula and scores of traditional owners and their supporters, ERA agreed to delay development of the project. ERA's parent company, North Ltd, was subsequently taken over by Rio Tinto. In response to ongoing pressure by the Mirrar, in 2005 Rio signed a binding agreement with the Mirrar that Jabiluka would not be developed without their consent. Margarula has indicated that this will not be forthcoming (Environment News 2005).

Thus an approach focused on cost minimisation and on obtaining an initial 'licence to operate' can both create longer-term risks for investors in a specific project, and result in a complete prohibition of mining on indigenous lands.

## CSR, value creation and sustainable development

A risk and cost minimisation approach also prevents companies from taking advantage of opportunities to create value and to enhance the industry's contribution to sustainable development. The opportunities forgone can be illustrated by looking at two specific areas. The first, aboriginal employment and training, represents an area where there are clear opportunities to add value to the enterprise. The second, aboriginal participation in environmental management, also offers such opportunities, and in addition has the potential to enhance the industry's ability to demonstrate that it can contribute to sustainability. But, as outlined below, industry has to date been strongly resistant to indigenous involvement in environmental management, indicating the need for significant innovation if this potential is to be realised.

## Aboriginal employment and training

Mining executives often regard the obligation to employ aboriginal people both as a burden on their companies and as a 'benefit' to aboriginal people which should help earn companies a 'licence to operate' (Cragg and Greenbaum 2002: 321-23; ABARE 2003; Crawley and Sinclair 2003: 367). In reality, proactive, sustained initiatives to maximise aboriginal employment and training can yield significant value for mining companies themselves and enhance their contribution to sustainable development.

Unlike many non-indigenous mining employees who migrate to or 'commute' to remote mine sites, local aboriginal people have a long-term commitment to live in the regions where mines are located. If they can be recruited and retained by mining companies, this can significantly reduce workforce turnover, which in turn can reduce company expenditure on staff recruitment, relocation and severance, and enhance workforce cohesion and morale. In addition, resources committed to upgrading the skills of aboriginal workers can generate higher returns for the corporation, as they are less likely to move elsewhere, taking their new skills with them. Use of local labour can also reduce the costs involved in transporting workers into remote sites and providing them with 'camp' accommodation. Companies must incur additional upfront costs in recruiting and training aboriginal workers but, especially if a longer time-frame is adopted in assessing returns, this investment can generate significant gains (SIWGMI 1996: 20-21; Harvey and Gawler 2003; NWT and Nunavut Chamber of Mines 2005: 11; Barker 2008: 144).

Wider considerations are also involved. Recruiting substantial numbers of aboriginal workers can give local communities a strong stake in a mining project, reducing the chances that opposition to mining will emerge, and increasing the likelihood that companies can rely on community support in meeting economic and political challenges they face. A company's aboriginal workforce can also constitute a source of valuable information for company managers, giving them 'early warning' of any issues likely to cause conflict between the project and neighbouring communities, and providing advice on how to avoid problems and how to resolve conflict if it does arise.

In addition, employing and training aboriginal workers can significantly enhance a mining project's contribution to sustainable development. While individual mining projects are finite, the skills and experience gained by aboriginal workers can greatly enhance their employment prospects more generally. For instance, a survey of former Aboriginal employees and trainees of Argyle Diamonds Ltd in Western

Australia found that the vast majority (91%) were working at the time of the survey, a strongly positive outcome given the high levels of Aboriginal unemployment in the Kimberley region (Taylor 2006). The survey also found that Argyle's training programmes had helped Aboriginal people find new jobs both in other mining projects and in other economic sectors. For instance, while 29% of trainees and apprentices were not in the workforce before being recruited by Argyle, only 14% of them were unemployed at the time of the survey (CSRM 2007: 14-17). Similarly, Barker and Brereton (2005) report that 66% of Aboriginal respondents who had worked for Century Zinc believed that the skills and experience they acquired helped them to find other work.

## Aboriginal participation in environmental management

Managing the environmental impacts of its activities represents an issue of critical importance to the mining industry. This reflects both legal and political realities. Environmental impacts are the subject of extensive legislation and regulation in most jurisdictions. Failure to secure environmental approvals means that projects cannot proceed, while breach of environmental conditions imposed by government authorities can result in fines, in suspension of operations and, ultimately, in withdrawal of operating permits. In recent years, even satisfying domestic authorities does not necessarily protect companies from litigation, as illustrated by the success of Papua New Guinea villagers in taking legal action against BHP Billiton in Australian courts because of the environmental effects of waste disposal from the company's Ok Tedi mine (Gao et al. 2002). At a political level, many of the mining industry's public relations disasters in recent years have been associated with its perceived failure to adequately protect the environment (Warhurst and Mitchell 2000; Veiga et al. 2001; IIED 2002: 346-49). It is not surprising therefore that the industry as a whole and individual company managers, including those that are reluctant to address the social and cultural impacts of their projects, take environmental management very seriously (Cragg and Greenbaum 2002; Guerin 2006; ICMM 2008: 5).

Aboriginal peoples are often in a unique position to assist mining companies in minimising negative environmental impacts and in returning mine sites to acceptable environmental standards. One critical resource possessed by aboriginal people is time depth in relation to information on the existing environment (baseline data). Typically, mining companies only start collecting baseline data (which they use in assessing likely project impacts, in establishing acceptable impacts, and in designing environmental monitoring and management systems) some 2–3 years before project construction is planned to commence. The difficulty is that environmental conditions can be highly variable over time, and a few years' data may not provide a sufficient basis on which to develop an understanding of environmental dynamics. Indigenous landowners draw not only on decades of experience in observing environmental conditions, an understanding of which is vital to their subsistence activities, but also on generations of experience handed down to them. Thus their participation is essential in achieving a full and accurate understanding of existing environmental dynamics, which in turn is the foundation for effective environmental protection (Usher 2000; Nadasdy 2003).

A second area involves the intimate and ongoing contact that many indigenous people have with their ancestral lands and waters and which allows them to quickly detect ecological changes that may signal problems with a mine's environmental management system, helping to avoid potential damage. On one occasion, the author, while travelling across country with traditional owners of a major mine in north Australia, encountered a small area of lush vegetation in a place that elders said would normally be dry at that time of year. They alerted mine management to what they believed was a leak of water from the mine's open pit into subsurface drainage channels. The mine's environmental section initially rejected this possibility, stating that its extensive water monitoring system had not picked up any sign of water moving out of the open pit. After a subsequent visit to the area revealed a further increase in vegetation, the traditional owners insisted that the mine undertake additional investigations. These revealed that water was indeed leaving the open pit, and the company was able to take remedial action.

A range of more specific indigenous knowledge can also greatly assist effective environmental management. This can include understanding of animal and bird behaviour essential in devising effective wildlife monitoring and management regimes; and knowledge of the soil and drainage conditions required for specific plants to thrive, critical for successful rehabilitation of areas disturbed by mining and associated activities.

Despite the obvious contribution indigenous people could make in addressing a matter of enormous economic and political significance to the mining industry, in general few attempts have been made by companies to take advantage of indigenous environmental knowledge. As noted above, an extensive analysis of negotiated agreements in Australia indicates that the opposite is the case, with few companies using the opportunity agreements provide to secure indigenous participation and with some seeking to use agreements to reduce indigenous input below that allowed by environmental legislation. This impression is strongly supported by the author's own experience in agreement negotiations (see also Cragg and Greenbaum 2002: 321-22). Even where companies are prepared to accept provisions strongly favourable to aboriginal landowners in areas such as financial compensation, cultural heritage protection, and employment and training, they tend to strongly resist sharing control over environmental management. This reluctance creates fundamental problems for aboriginal traditional owners, because in aboriginal law and custom they have duties to look after their land and waters which they cannot abrogate (O'Faircheallaigh 2008: 31-32).

The reluctance to incorporate aboriginal traditional ecological knowledge (TEK) into environmental management is evident even in situations where there is a legal requirement for this to occur. For instance in Canada's Northwest Territories, separate environmental management agreements involving government, mining companies and aboriginal groups have been negotiated to govern environmental management of three diamond mines developed by BHP Billiton, Diavik Diamond Mines Ltd and De Beers. Each of these agreements contemplates aboriginal involvement in environmental management, and specifically calls for the integration of TEK into company environmental management systems. For example, the parties to the agreement for the Ekati mine undertake to 'fully consider both traditional knowledge and other scientific information' in managing Ekati. A key goal of the Independent Environment Monitoring Agency (IEMA) established under the agreement is to secure 'the integration of traditional knowledge and experience of Aboriginal Peoples into Ekati's environmental plans and programs' (Government of the Northwest Territories *et al.* 1997).

BHP Billiton has funded a number of TEK studies and has invited aboriginal community members, especially elders, to visit Ekati each year to observe caribou migration on its project area and to inspect and comment on environmental management issues. It has involved aboriginal people in wildlife monitoring and sought their advice in relation to activities with a high potential to affect wildlife (O'Faircheallaigh 2006b: 23-24). However, aboriginal people maintain that the relative priority attached to application of TEK is low, as indicated by the difficulty they encounter securing funding for its documentation and application, a situation they contrast with the large amounts allocated to environmental work undertaken by scientists and consultants. Aboriginal people see consultation with them as ad hoc and lacking coordination (Terra Firma Consultants 2004: 13, 19). A recommendation from a 2003 workshop on application of TEK that a TEK Panel be established to ensure that TEK was being incorporated actively and effectively into environmental monitoring (IEMA 2003: 9) has not been acted on. The extent to which the expertise of aboriginal people is integrated into environmental decision-making is also an issue. According to one observer, both the IEMA and BHP Billiton tend to obtain information or views from aboriginal people and then proceed to make their own decisions, rather than integrate aboriginal people and aboriginal perspectives into the decision-making process (O'Faircheallaigh 2006b: 24; see also IEMA 2003: 20).

In 2005 the IEMA reached the following general conclusion: 'Neither BHPB nor the regulators have made much progress in incorporating TEK effectively with western science in the environmental monitoring, management and regulation of Ekati. This is a serious, ongoing issue that we continue to highlight' (IEMA 2005: 24).

# Requirements for a new approach to CSR

A more strategic and positive approach to CSR in the mining industry is necessary if risk is to be effectively managed over the longer term, and if enterprise value and the industry's contribution to sustainable development are to be maximised through engagement with indigenous people. But existing practices are deeply entrenched, and substantial innovation is required to support a fundamentally different approach.

An essential prerequisite involves changes in attitudes and values. Industry leaders and managers must *see* their engagement with indigenous peoples as a source of potential value. For example, indigenous employment programmes must not be perceived as a burden that must be shouldered to help gain a licence to operate, but as part of a human resource development strategy designed to enhance productivity and a project's contribution to sustainable development over the longer term. Indigenous attempts to play a role in environmental management must not be seen as a threat to corporate control and capacity to comply with legal obligations, but both as a legitimate exercise of responsibility by indigenous landowners and an opportunity to enhance a project's environmental performance and so its contribution to sustainability.

Such changes in attitudes and values can occur only by enhancing communication between indigenous people and company personnel, allowing each group to appreciate the motives, constraints and capacities of the other. Critical in this regard is the establishment of cross-cultural training initiatives, not just as part of a short, one-off induction provided for new employees and managers, but as an ongoing system of information exchange and learning activities. For instance, at the Argyle diamond mine in Western Australia, each week Aboriginal elders conduct a traditional *manthe* ceremony that is intended both to welcome outsiders to their traditional lands and protect them while they reside there. All new employees and contractors participate in the ceremony but, more importantly, its weekly occurrence is a regular reminder to non-indigenous staff that they are living and working on Aboriginal land and in an Aboriginal cultural domain. In addition, new managers are required to undertake cross-cultural training that includes spending time camping with elders, and traditional owners undertake regular tours of the mine with company environmental staff (Argyle Diamonds *et al.* 2004).

Opportunities for company personnel and aboriginal people to undertake projects jointly are especially valuable in building mutual trust and understanding. These have been rare in the past, but innovative practices are starting to emerge. For example, during 2008 teams consisting of Aboriginal landowners and scientists worked together in undertaking cultural and environmental surveys designed to identify a suitable location for the establishment of a liquefied natural gas (LNG) processing plant along the Kimberley coast of Western Australia. This process created unique opportunities for each group to gain insights into the other's knowledge base, methodologies and understandings of how ecosystems come into existence and function. In August 2008 a series of meetings allowed a sharing of the knowledge gained with a wider group of company managers, regulators and Aboriginal organisational leaders. It is significant that, while the assumptions, perspectives and methods of scientists and Aboriginal landowners were often fundamentally different, they came to similar conclusions about the relative desirability of alternative sites; three of the four potential sites shortlisted by each group were the same (KLC 2008; NDT 2008). This example provides a good illustration of the concrete benefits associated with a more proactive and engaged approach to CSR. Aboriginal opposition to development and resultant project delays are much less likely to occur given that the site selection process has incorporated aboriginal cultural and ecological frameworks.

Organisational considerations are also relevant. Careful organisational design is required to achieve a balance between allowing operational units the flexibility required to respond to local opportunities for engagement (Labonne 1999: 319-20), while maintaining sufficient central control to ensure that operational units do not downgrade CSR functions in favour of their own priorities (Carter 1999: 356-58). CSR functions must be located within corporate structures in a way that ensures they receive ongoing attention from senior executives, and are allocated the attention and resources required for effective implementation throughout the project life-cycle. Responsibility for engagement with aboriginal communities, for instance, is frequently subsumed within organisational units that are also responsible for community or public affairs generally and for environmental management, with the result that it does not attract the priority and resources it requires (Crawley and Sinclair 2003: 365-66; Kemp *et al.* 2006: 392-93). The seniority and reporting lines of responsible staff must also be considered. Szablowski (2002), for instance, reports that what he terms 'social specialists' within resource companies often report to production managers whose main priority is not community engagement, severely limiting the capacity of the former to influence project development and operations so as to recognise community needs (see also Rajak 2008).

Another major issue involves the human skills required to support community engagement and innovative approaches to CSR, especially in an industry where engineering and financial skills may be highly valued and social skills involved in cross-cultural communication, for instance, much less so (Carter 1999: 363, 367; Kemp *et al.* 2006: 400; Richards 2006). It is essential for senior managers to insist on, and support, professional training for CSR staff, and not assume that the skills required can be obtained 'on the job' by employees whose formal training lies in other areas. One of the few surveys of community relations staff in mining companies, for instance, found that in Australian companies 90% had previously worked in technical or natural science areas, and only 27% had any qualifications in the humanities or social sciences (Kemp 2004).

Funding is also a key issue. Many CSR initiatives wither because responsible company staff are unable to obtain the resources required to bring them to fruition (Carter 1999: 362-63; O'Faircheallaigh 2002: 105-106; Rajak 2008: 307-308). This raises a broader question about corporate resource allocation and decision-making. While some of the benefits associated with innovative CSR are immediate and easily quantifiable—for instance, lower recruitment costs resulting from use of local aboriginal labour—in other cases they are not easy to quantify and only accrue over the long term. Corporate resource allocation systems must recognise this reality; otherwise the resources allocated to CSR will be suboptimal and subject to attrition when economic conditions deteriorate. Mineral industries already utilise long-term horizons in certain resource allocation decisions. For instance, large sums are invested in 'green fields' prospecting activity which may not add to mineral production capacity for many decades. The same long-term view must be applied to CSR.

New approaches are also needed in relation to the more specific area of agreement negotiation. As mentioned earlier, in many existing negotiations the emphasis is on minimising corporate financial exposure in the short term, leading companies to resist, for instance, aboriginal proposals for more ambitious employment and training initiatives. For their part, negotiators for aboriginal groups, who are often specialist consultants hired on a short-term basis, may also emphasise clearly quantifiable gains such as financial compensation, as this allows them to easily demonstrate their 'success' in negotiations and so helps build reputations and careers. But this also may result in a failure to sufficiently emphasise the long-term, hard-to-quantify benefits achievable, for instance, from cooperative environmental management regimes. Both companies and aboriginal groups need to ensure, through regular oversight and review by senior decision-makers, that negotiations are driven by a determination to realise the full range of benefits available from a long-term approach to maximising value. Emphasising the interrelationship between the various points discussed in this section, such an approach is much more likely where there is an emphasis on improving cross-cultural understanding, and where CSR policies are developed and CSR initiatives are managed through appropriate organisational structures.

Finally, realising the value inherent in CSR requires a strong and consistent effort to address the chronic implementation failures that have plagued CSR initiatives in the mining industry. Company and community negotiators must maintain a strong focus on implementation throughout negotiation of agreements or other mechanisms used to 'deliver' on CSR policies. This is not easy to achieve given that negotiations often occur under pressure of time and in the shadow of potential conflicts over project development, and so negotiators tend to be preoccupied with reaching agreement rather than with what will happen after agreement is reached. Yet such an approach is almost certain to dissipate the gains potentially available from CSR. Thus negotiators must work together to maintain a focus on implementation, and company–community agreements must contain within them the prerequisites for effective implementation. These include: adequate resources; joint company–community structures the primary purpose of which is to focus on implementation; clearly specified goals, and measures for gauging progress towards these; incentives and sanctions to encourage all parties involved to achieve agreement goals; and properly resourced processes to review implementation on a regular basis (see O'Faircheallaigh 2003 for a full discussion).

## Conclusion

The dominant cost and risk minimisation approach to CSR in the international mining industry may help control CSR costs and achieve an initial licence to operate for new projects, by generating short-term benefits for local communities and creating an impression among policy-makers and the wider public that the industry takes the interests of stakeholders into account. But in many cases this approach, while ostensibly focused on risk management, is in fact failing to effectively manage risk over the longer term, because it is not creating a basis for lasting, positive relationships with communities affected by mining. This is certainly the case in relation to indigenous peoples, from whose ancestral lands a larger and larger proportion of mineral output will come in future years. The result is costly delays, interruptions to production and abandonment of projects. In addition, the approach to CSR adopted by many mining companies lacks the capacity to create value and contribute to sustainable development.

Developing an approach to CSR that focuses more on value creation, sustainability and management of long-term risk requires substantial innovation by the mining industry. Examples of innovative practice certainly exist and some have been discussed above. However, the industry as a whole needs, for instance, to greatly enhance its cross-cultural communication in order to develop an accurate understanding of the available opportunities and how to pursue these, and to foster the trust that is at the heart of long-term, productive relationships. It is also essential to find better ways not only to communicate with indigenous groups, but also to work with them in pursuit of shared goals; to support CSR policies with appropriate organisational structures and decision-making systems that focus on the longer term and on intangible as well as tangible benefits; and to achieve a strong emphasis on sustained implementation of CSR initiatives, so that their potential can actually be realised.

More broadly, the mining industry is increasingly being assessed in terms of its contribution to sustainable development. Particularly given that mining exploits non-renewable resources and so is by definition finite, its contribution will be judged on its capacity to minimise its negative environmental impacts, and to promote the economic and social sustainability of communities it affects. The industry will be found wanting in this regard if it continues to pursue the current cost and risk minimisation approach to CSR. In the long term, pursuit of a different approach is a matter of survival.

# References

ABARE (Australian Bureau of Agricultural and Resource Economics) (2003) 'Indigenous People in Mining', Commonwealth of Australia, Canberra; www.abare.gov.au/publications_html/research/research_03/er_indigenouspeople.pdf, accessed 25 March 2010.

Ali, S., and C. O'Faircheallaigh (2007) 'Extractive Industries, Environmental Performance and Corporate Social Responsibility', *Greener Management International* 52: 5-16.

AMSI (Andersen Management Services Inc) (1992) *Evaluation of the Dona Lake Agreement: Final Report* (Thunder Bay, ON: AMSI).

Argyle Diamonds Ltd, Traditional Owners and Kimberley Land Council Aboriginal Corporation (2004) 'Argyle Diamond Mine Participation Agreement: Indigenous Land Use Agreement'; www.atns.net.au/objects/Agreements/Argyle%20ILUA.pdf, accessed 25 March 2010.

Banerjee, S.B. (2001) 'Corporate Citizenship and Indigenous Stakeholders: Exploring a New Dynamic of Organizational-Stakeholder Relationships', *Journal of Corporate Citizenship* 1: 39-55.

Barker, T. (2008) 'Indigenous Employment Outcomes in the Australian Mining Industry', in C. O'Faircheallaigh and S. Ali (eds.), *Earth Matters: Indigenous Peoples, the Extractive Industries and Corporate Social Responsibility* (Sheffield, UK: Greenleaf Publishing): 143-62.

—— and D. Brereton (2005) 'Survey of Local Aboriginal People Formerly Employed at Century Mine', Centre for Social Responsibility in Mining (CSRM), University of Queensland, Brisbane; www.csrm.uq.edu.au/docs/CSRM%20Research%20Paper%204.pdf, accessed 20 January 2009.

BHP Billiton (2006) 'Sustainable Development', www.bhpbilliton.com/bb/sustainableDevelopment.jsp, accessed 18 September 2006.

Bielawski, E. (2004) *Rogue Diamonds: Northern Riches on Dene Land* (Vancouver: Douglas & McIntyre).

Campbell, J.L. (2007) 'Why Would Corporations Behave in Socially Responsible Ways? An Institutional Theory of Corporate Social Responsibility', *Academy of Management Review* 32.3: 946-67.

Carter, A.S. (1999) 'Mining Companies as Agents of Development? Corporate Social Responsibility, Participation and Local Community at Mining Projects' (PhD thesis; Bath, UK: University of Bath).

Corbett, T., and C. O'Faircheallaigh (2007) 'Unmasking Native Title: The National Native Title Tribunal's Application of the *NTA*'s Arbitration Provisions', *University of Western Australia Law Review* 33.1: 153-77.

Cragg, W., and A. Greenbaum (2002) 'Reasoning about Responsibilities: Mining Company Managers on What Stakeholders are Owed', *Journal of Business Ethics* 39: 319-35.

Crawley, A., and A. Sinclair (2003) 'Indigenous Human Resource Practices in Australian Mining Companies: Toward an Ethical Model', *Journal of Business Ethics* 45: 361-73.

CSRM (Centre for Social Responsibility in Mining) (2007) 'Survey of Aboriginal Former Employees and Trainees of Argyle Diamond Mine', CSRM, University of Queensland; www.csrm.uq.edu.au/docs/Argyle%20former%20employees%20final%20report.pdf, accessed 20 January 2009.

Day, J.C., and J. Affum (1995) 'Windy Craggy: Institutions and Stakeholders', *Resources Policy* 21.1: 21-26.

Dowie, M. (2009) 'Nuclear Caribou: On the Front Lines of the New Uranium Rush with the Inuit of Nunavut', *Orion*, January/February 2009: 20-28.

Environment News (2005) 'Aboriginal People Win Right to Limit Australian Uranium Mine'; www.ens-newswire.com/ens/feb2005/2005-02-28-03.asp, accessed 15 January 2009.

Gao, Z., G. Akpan and J. Vanjik (2002) 'Public Participation in Mining and Petroleum in Asia and the Pacific: The Ok Tedi Case and its Implications', in D.N. Zillman, A.R. Lucas and G. Pring (eds.), *Human Rights in Natural Resource Development* (New York: Oxford University Press): 679-93.

Gibson, R. (2006) 'Sustainability Assessment and Conflict Resolution: Reaching Agreement to Proceed with the Voisey's Bay Nickel Mine', *Journal of Cleaner Production* 14.3–4: 334-48.

Government of the Northwest Territories, BHP Diamonds Inc (1997) *Environmental Agreement* (Yellowknife, Northwest Territories: Government of the Northwest Territories).

Guerin, T.F. (2006) 'A Survey of Sustainable Development Initiatives in the Australian Mining and Minerals Industry', *Minerals & Energy* 20.3–4: 11-44.

Harvey, B., and J. Gawler (2003) 'Aboriginal Employment Diversity in Rio Tinto', *International Journal of Diversity in Organisations, Communities and Nations* 3: 197-209.

Humphreys, D. (2000) 'A Business Perspective on Community Relations in Mining', *Resources Policy* 26: 127-31.

ICMM (International Council on Mining & Metals) (2008) *Annual Review 2007: Essential Materials, Produced Responsibly* (London: ICMM).

IEMA (Independent Environmental Management Agency) (2003) *Technical Annual Report 2002–2003* (Yellowknife, Northwest Territories: IEMA).

—— (2005) *Technical Annual Report 2004–2005* (Yellowknife, Northwest Territories: IEMA).

IIED (International Institute for Environment and Development) (2002) *Breaking New Ground: Mining Minerals and Sustainable Development* (London: IIED).

Jenkins, H., and N. Yakovleva (2006) 'Corporate Social Responsibility in the Mining Industry: Exploring Trends in Social and Environmental Disclosure', *Journal of Cleaner Production* 14: 271-84.

Kapelus, P. (2002) 'Mining, Corporate Social Responsibility and the "Community": The Case of Rio Tinto, Richards Bay Minerals and the Mbonambi', *Journal of Business Ethics* 39.3: 275-96.

Kemp, D. (2004) 'The Emerging Field of Community Relations: Profiling the Practitioner Perspective', CSRM, University of Queensland; commdev.org/content/document/detail/2314, accessed 19 January 2009.

——, R. Boele and D. Brereton (2006) 'Community Relations Management Systems in the Minerals Industry: Combining Conventional and Stakeholder Driven Approaches', *International Journal of Sustainable Development* 9.4: 390-403.

Kennett, S.A. (1999) *A Guide to Impact and Benefits Agreements* (Calgary, Alberta: Canadian Institute of Resources Law, University of Calgary).

KLC (Kimberley Land Council) (2008) 'Traditional Owners Announce Shortlist for Gas Development Hub', Media Release, 10 September 2005, www/klc/org/au/media/080910_HUB_shortlist.pdf, accessed 19 January 2009.

Labonne, B. (1999) 'The Mining Industry and the Community: Joining Forces for Sustainable Social Development', *Natural Resources Forum* 23: 315-22.

Matten, D., and J. Moon (2008) ' "Implicit" and "Explicit" CSR: A Conceptual Framework for a Comparative Understanding of Corporate Social Responsibility', *Academy of Management Review* 33.2: 404-24.

Nadasdy, P. (2003) *Hunters and Bureaucrats: Power, Knowledge and Aboriginal-State Relations in the Southwest Yukon* (Vancouver: University of British Columbia Press).

NDT (Northern Development Taskforce) (2008) 'Northern Development Taskforce: Final Site Evaluation Report', Department of Industry and Resources, Government of Western Australia; www.dsd.wa.gov.au/documents/000269V04.GARY.SIMMONS.pdf, accessed 19 January 2009.

NEDGI (New Economy Development Group Inc) (1993) *Evaluation of the Golden Patricia Agreement* (Ottawa, Ontario: NEDGI).

NWT and Nunavut Chamber of Mines (2005) 'Sustainable Economies: Aboriginal Participation in the Northwest Territories Mining Industry 1990–2004'; www.miningnorth.com/docs/Aboriginal%20Participation%202005%20(2).pdf, accessed 19 January 2009.

O'Faircheallaigh, C. (2002) *A New Approach to Policy Evaluation: Mining and Indigenous People* (Aldershot, UK: Ashgate Press).

—— (2003) 'Implementing Agreements between Indigenous Peoples and Resource Developers in Australia and Canada', Griffith University, Brisbane; www.griffith.edu.au/business/griffith-business-school/pdf/research-paper-2003-implementing-agreements.pdf, accessed 19 January 2009.

—— (2004) 'Evaluating Agreements between Indigenous Peoples and Resource Developers', in M. Langton, M. Tehan, L. Palmer and K. Shain (eds.), *Honour Among Nations? Treaties and Agreements with Indigenous People* (Melbourne: Melbourne University Press): 303-28.

—— (2006a) 'Aborigines, Mining Companies and the State in Contemporary Australia: A New Political Economy or "Business as Usual"?', *Australian Journal of Political Science* 41.1: 1-22.

—— (2006b) *Environmental Agreements in Canada: Aboriginal Participation, EIA Follow-up and Environmental Management of Major Projects* (Calgary, Alberta: Canadian Institute of Resources Law, University of Calgary).

—— (2008) 'Negotiating Protection of the Sacred? Aboriginal–Mining Company Agreements in Australia', *Development and Change* 39.1: 25-51.

—— and A. Corbett (2005) 'Indigenous Participation in Environmental Management of Mining Projects: The Role of Negotiated Agreements', *Environmental Politics* 14.5: 629-47.

—— and R. Kelly (2002) 'Corporate Social Responsibility and Native Title Agreement Making', in Human Rights and Equal Opportunity Commission and Griffith University (eds.), *Development and Indigenous Land: A Human Rights Approach* (Sydney: Human Rights and Equal Opportunity Commission): 9-16.

Rajak, D. (2008) ' "Uplift and Empower": The Market, Morality and CSR on South Africa's Platinum Belt', *Research in Economic Anthropology* 28: 297-324.

Richards, J. (2006) 'The Application of Sustainable Development Principles in the Minerals Industry', *International Journal of the Interdisciplinary Social Sciences* 1.3: 57-68.

SIWGMI (Sub-Committee of the Intergovernmental Working Group on the Mineral Industry) (1996) 'Aboriginal Participation in the Mining Industry in Canada 1996: Seventh Annual Report'; www.publications.gov.sk.ca/details.cfm?p=7169, accessed 19 January 2009.

Sosa, I., and K. Keenan (2001) 'Impact Benefit Agreements between Aboriginal Communities and Mining Companies: Their Use in Canada', Canadian Environmental Law Association, www.cela.ca/publications/cardfile.shtml?x=1021, accessed 19 January 2009.

Supervising Scientist (1997) 'Kakadu Region Social Impact Study: Report of the Aboriginal Project Committee', Commonwealth of Australia; www.environment.gov.au/ssd/publications/krsis-reports/project-committee/index.html, accessed 21 April 2009.

Szablowski, D. (2002) 'Mining, Displacement and the World Bank: A Case Analysis of Compania Minera Antamina's Operations in Peru', *Journal of Business Ethics* 39.3: 247-53.

Taylor, J. (2006) *Indigenous People in the West Kimberley Labour Market* (Canberra: Centre for Aboriginal Economic Policy Research, Australian National University).

Telewiak, R. (2001) 'Keys to Building Successful Relationships with Inuit Communities at Raglan', paper presented at the *Prospectors and Developers Conference*, Toronto, 13 March 2001 (www.pdac.ca/pdac/publications/papers/2001/pdf/Telewiak(T-24).pdf, accessed 20 January 2009).

Terra Firma Consultants (2004) *An open door exists and . . . we need to change and improve from what we've learned: Aboriginal Caucus Workshop on Environmental Monitoring of Diamond Mines: Final Report* (Yellowknife, Northwest Territories: Terra Firma Consultants).

Trebeck, K. (2007) 'Tools for the Disempowered? Leverage Over Mining Companies', *Australian Journal of Political Science* 42.4: 541-62.

Usher, P. (2000) 'Traditional Ecological Knowledge in Environmental Assessment and Management', *Arctic* 53.2: 183-93.

Veiga, M.M., M. Scoble and M.L. McAllister (2001) 'Mining with Communities', *Natural Resources Forum* 25: 191-202.

Warhurst, A., and P. Mitchell (2000) 'Corporate Social Responsibility and the Case of the Summitville Mine', *Resources Policy* 26: 91-102.

Weitzner, V. (2006) *'Dealing Full Force': Lutsel K'e Dene First Nation's Experience Negotiating with Mining Companies* (Ottawa: North South Institute and Lutsel K'e Dene First Nation).

# Innovative corporate social responsibility in the 21st century

## Some thoughts

**Walter Leal Filho**
Hamburg University of Applied Sciences, Germany

**Céline Louche**
Vlerick Leuven Gent Management School, Belgium

**Samuel O. Idowu**
London Metropolitan University Business School, UK

Modern corporate social responsibility (CSR) has been strongly influenced by both economic and political developments that have occurred globally over the last two decades, in particular its increased influence on the capital and financial markets and private investment in the business sector. More recently, it has been suffering as a result of the impacts of the global credit crunch. At present, businesses are under increasing pressure to review their business models and strategies, in order to address responsibly their adverse impact on the environment, economy and society. In this context, it has become apparent that society not only expects corporate entities to play a key role in addressing these issues but also expects consumers, employees, supply chain operators and national and international government agencies to take positive actions in regard to these matters.

There are many directives and guidelines on CSR (e.g. European Commission 2000) and a widespread awareness of its relevance worldwide (Idowu and Leal Filho 2009), but the real basis of CSR is the fact that businesses have now realised that they have a broader responsibility, not only towards their own shareholders but also to the community as a whole (SustainAbility 2004; Demirag 2005; Derickson and Henley 2008). Many companies have learned to take advantage of this trend (Kotler and Lee 2004) and *The A to Z of Corporate Social Responsibility* by Visser *et al.* (2007) provides a detailed description of the elements this entails.

As an attempt to document and disseminate current practice, this book has provided a wealth of case studies and wide range of examples on the innovative dimension of CSR as it is seen and practised today. In this context, it may be useful, on the basis of the trends experienced today, to make some forecast on what may be expected in the future—in other words, how the practice of CSR would transform its own outlook in the remaining 90 years of the 21st century and perhaps beyond that.

## Some future trends

Three main future trends have been identified: the convergence of international CSR standards; the management of costs related to the implementation of CSR; and opportunities for innovation. These are analysed in turn below.

The first trend, the convergence of international CSR standards, seems to be on the increase. There are at present generally accepted CSR practices, which are finding their way into enterprises both large and small. Chapter 2, by Williamson, Lynch-Wood and Dragneva-Lewers, explores the regulatory preconditions for business advantage in CSR and illustrates the need for a long-term approach, while Baden has shown the relevance of CSR to SMEs (Chapter 4). Some experiences distilled from the practice of CSR leaders are documented by Arnold in Chapter 5, where CSR practices and relationships to stakeholders are analysed.

As far as the links between CSR and strategies are concerned, Galbreath and Benjamin have, in Chapter 1, illustrated how prioritisation of issues in an industry context can be achieved while Misani describes the differences between convergent and divergent CSR in Chapter 3. Further, Del Bosco presents in Chapter 6 the strategic and social opportunities offered by CSR, especially but not exclusively in respect of energy saving and environmental protection.

Indeed, CSR has moved away from being an area of marginal interest, towards becoming a mainstream activity. With the globalisation of the world economy, enterprises are shifting actions from ad hoc initiatives to corporate plans which illustrate their social responsibilities and commitments in this important field. This is certainly line with what Griffin (2007) describes as a new move towards reputation management.

The second trend identified in this book, the management of costs related to the implementation of CSR, is also a sign of an emerging field. Also called 'strategic cost management', the idea here is that CSR can be included in virtually all aspects of an organisation's processes and activities. Chapter 9, by Guzmán and Becker-Olsen, illustrates the fact that strategic CSR can be a brand-building tool in the context of which the views of stakeholders in strategic management should be taken into account. The question of whether CSR offers value to consumers was analysed by Alvarado-Herrera, Bigné-Alcañiz, Currás-Pérez and Aldás-Manzano (Chapter 8), while a multi-level perspective was presented by Maas and Boons (Chapter 7). Costs are also one of the main elements considered behind the HIV/AIDS intervention among South African SMEs, as outlined by Duarte and Houlihan in Chapter 12.

Ethical motivations, return on investment and the impact on socially responsible investors were the subject of the analysis performed by van Cranenburgh, Arenas and Albareda in Chapter 11. The management of risk for value creation in a specific sector—housing—was explored by Navare in Chapter 10.

Regardless of whether one is raising issues from either management or an accounting perspective, the management of costs associated with the implementation of a CSR strategy involves selecting some vital best performance measures, customer profitability and value-creation reporting. It also entails advanced budgeting that includes funding for the agreed strategic initiatives within an enterprise.

The third trend is related to innovation. Chapter 13, by Louche, Idowu and Leal Filho, deals with this and shows the relevance of a strategic dimensional approach, including the involvement of non-accountants in CSR, while Chapter 17, by Davis, shows the approach used in Japan where strategic CSR includes due consideration to business risk and market value creation. MacGregor, Fontrodona and Hernandez discuss the issues to be considered in heading towards a sustainable innovation model for small enterprises (Chapter 14), a line of thinking that also applies to the mining industry as indicated by O'Faircheallaigh in Chapter 18.

Further, Preuss describes in Chapter 15 some of the barriers to innovative CSR and outlines the impacts of organisational learning, organisational structure and social embeddedness of the firm in the process, while the role of consultants and how they contribute to innovation in the field of CSR was described by Frostenson in Chapter 16.

A fact that has also become clear is that the marketplace does play a key role in encouraging companies to operate in an ethical way. Should the pool of consumers who make decisions based on ethical criteria (where ethics is a primary decision factor or is at least high on their agendas) become limited, CSR may not survive and will simply become easy prey to the usual budget cuts. One hopes that if the reverse were to be the case and consumers continue to praise and value CSR, then the future of CSR is probably secure.

## Conclusions

The experiences and case studies presented in this book reinforce the fact that future practices of CSR will be more closely related to entrepreneurial practices than they have ever been before. Moreover, there are many elements that indicate that the shifts seen in CSR thus far are no longer limited to comfortable board-rooms; these issues are now finding their way into various sectors of society and different industries. As stated by McWilliams *et al.* (2006), the strategic implications of CSR are manifold and both multinationals and SMEs are increasingly being expected to seek suitable strategies and find new ways to respond to the challenges posed by addressing social issues as part of *entrepreneurial* practice. The tensions that have existed and will continue to exist between economic and social objectives need to be continuously monitored in order to allow them to be properly dealt with.

Critically speaking, there are numerous voluntary CSR initiatives undertaken by companies across the world. Most, but by no means all of them, engage in activities that have contributed positively towards improvements in local living conditions and quality of life and this book has documented a number of them. In many cases, their work has been instrumental towards establishing an enabling environment for the private sector, to which they belong, in order for them to function in an efficient way—thus fostering democracy, human rights awareness and local economic development.

An important question one may wish to ask in the future is: will companies continue to value their socially responsible work in the light of the current global recession? The answer to this question may not be easy to find as things stand currently but it will determine whether the practice of CSR turns out to be a trend of the 'good days' or a way of thinking that prevails regardless of the state of the economy.

# References

Demirag, I. (ed.) (2005) *Corporate Social Responsibility, Accountability and Governance: Global Perspectives* (Sheffield, UK: Greenleaf Publishing).

Derickson, R., and K. Henley (2008) *Awakening Social Responsibility: A Call to Action* (Cupertino, CA: Happy About).

European Commission (2000) *Green Paper: Promoting a European Framework for Corporate Social Responsibility* (Brussels: Commission of the European Communities).

Griffin, A. (2007) *New Strategies for Reputation Management: Gaining Control of Issues, Crises and Corporate Social Responsibility* (London: Kogan Page).

Idowu, S.O., and W. Leal Filho (eds.) (2009) *Global Practices of Corporate Social Responsibility* (Berlin: Springer).

Kotler, P., and N. Lee (2004) *Corporate Social Responsibility: Doing the Most Good for Your Company and Your Cause* (Chichester, UK: John Wiley).

McWilliams, A., D.S. Siegel and P.M. Wright (2006) 'Corporate Social Responsibility: Strategic Implications', *Journal of Management Studies* 43.1: 1-18.

SustainAbility (2004) *Gearing Up, from Corporate Responsibility to Good Governance and Scalable Solutions* (London: SustainAbility).

Visser, W., D. Matten, M. Pohl and N. Tolhurst (eds.) (2007) *The A to Z of Corporate Social Responsibility: A Complete Reference Guide to Concepts, Codes and Organisations* (Chichester, UK: John Wiley).

# About the contributors

## About the editors

**Céline Louche** is Assistant Professor at Vlerick Leuven Gent Management School, Belgium. She teaches and researches in the area of corporate social responsibility and sustainability. In her work, she explores the way processes of change take place. Céline's major research interests are in CSR as a factor of innovation and value creation; socially responsible investing (SRI) and stakeholder processes.

Before joining Vlerick, Céline worked for five years as a sustainability analyst for socially responsible investment at the Dutch Sustainability Research institute.

Céline received her PhD from the Rotterdam Erasmus University. She is a recipient of the 2005 FIR award for the best European PhD thesis in finance and sustainability. She is the author of several articles in both academic and non-academic journals, has contributed chapters to several books on the subject of responsible investment, stakeholder management, corporate governance and CSR and has attended and presented papers at several international conferences.

She is a member of the academic board of the European Academy for Business in Society, the scientific committee of the International Network for Research on Organisations and Sustainable Development, and the SRI advisory committee of Dexia Asset Management.

**Samuel O. Idowu** is a senior lecturer in accounting at the city campus of London Metropolitan Business School, London Metropolitan University, where he was course organiser for accounting joint degrees and currently the course leader/personal academic adviser (PAA) for students taking accounting major/minor and accounting joint degrees. He is a fellow member of the Institute of Chartered Secretaries and Administrators, a fellow of the Royal Society of Arts, a Liveryman of the Worshipful Company of Chartered Secretaries and Administrators and a named freeman of the City of London. Samuel has published over 30 articles in both professional and academic journals and contributed chapters to edited collections. Samuel has been in academia for 23 years winning one of the Highly Commended Awards of the Emerald Literati Network Awards for Excellence in 2008. He has examined for the Chartered Institute of Bankers (CIB) and the Chartered Institute of Marketing (CIM) and has marked examination papers for the Association of Chartered Certified Accountants (ACCA).

His teaching career started in November 1987 at Merton College, Morden, Surrey; he was a lecturer/senior lecturer at North East Surrey College of Technology (Nescot) for 13 years where he was the course leader for BA (Hons) Business Studies, ACCA and CIMA courses. He has also held visiting lectureship posts at Croydon College and Kingston University. He was a senior lecturer at London Guildhall University prior to its merger with the University of North London in August 2002, when London Metropolitan University was created. He is currently an external examiner at the University of Sunderland, University of Ulster, Belfast, and Anglia Ruskin University, Chelmsford. He is also a trustee/treasurer for Age Concern, Hackney in East London, and he is on the Editorial Advisory Board of the *Management of Environmental Quality* journal. He has been researching in the field of CSR since 1983 and has attended and presented papers at several national and international conferences and workshops on CSR.

Professor **Walter Leal Filho** has a PhD and a DSc in environmental technology, plus a honorary doctorate (DL) in environmental information. He is head of the Research and Transfer Centre 'Applications of Life Sciences' at the Hamburg University of Applied Sciences, where he is in charge of a number of European projects. He has authored, co-authored or edited over 40 books on the subjects of environment, technology and innovation and has in excess of 130 published papers to his credit.

Professor Walter Leal Filho teaches environmental management at many European universities. He is also the editor of the journal *Management of Environmental Quality* and founding editor of the *International Journal of Sustainability in Higher Education*, *International Journal of Climate Change Strategies and Management* and *Environment and Sustainable Development*. He is a member of the editorial board of *Biomedical and Environmental Sciences*, *Environmental Awareness* and *Sustainable Development and World Ecology*. His work on CSR has primarily focused on institutional aspects and tools for benchmarking within industry.

## The contributors

**Laura Albareda** is a Post-doc Fellow at Carroll School of Management and at the Center for Corporate Citizenship of Boston College. She is also a researcher at the Institute for Social Innovation of ESADE Business School, Spain. Her lines of research are: the role of business in global governance; CSR and social innovation; and SRI. She is co-author of *Governments and Corporate Social Responsibility* (Palgrave, 2008).

**Joaquín Aldás-Manzano** (PhD in Business and Economics, University of Valencia, Spain) is associate professor of marketing in the Department of Marketing, Faculty of Economics at the University of Valencia and Associate Researcher of Valencia Economics Research Institute (IVIE). His research interest is focused on advertising media planning, consumer behaviour and quantitative methods in marketing research and his work has been published in the *European Journal of Marketing*, *Journal of Product & Brand Management*, *Online Information Review*, *Qualitative Marketing Research*, *European Journal of Innovation Management*, *Sex Roles*, *Equal Opportunities International* and in the best Spanish refereed journals. He has presented numerous papers at AM (Academy of Marketing), EMAC (European Marketing Academy) and AMS (Academy of Marketing Science) conferences.

**Alejandro Alvarado-Herrera** is associate professor of marketing at the University of Quintana Roo, Mexico. He obtained his PhD in Marketing from the University of Valencia, Spain. His research interests include CSR, non-lucrative marketing, sports marketing and consumer behaviour. His research results have been published in the *Journal of Business Ethics*, the *International Review on Public and Nonprofit Marketing*, as well as in some of the Spanish and Latin American refereed academic journals. He is Head of the Division of Sustainable Development at the University of Quintana Roo.

**Daniel Arenas** is associate professor at ESADE Business School-Universitat Ramon Llull, Spain, where he teaches business ethics, CSR and sociology. He is also the head of research at the Institute for Social Innovation at ESADE and a member of the management committee of the European Academy of Business in Society (EABIS).

**Malcolm Arnold** has held several senior management, director and consultant positions in the telecommunications industry in the UK, other EU countries and the USA. He completed his PhD in 2007 on the effects of UK competition regulation on mergers and shareholder value. His research interests lie in corporate responsibility, corporate value creation and managerial behaviour.

**Denise Baden** achieved her PhD at the University of Southampton, UK, in the School of Psychology and spent a number of years teaching and doing research in the area of social psychology. She joined the School of Management in 2005 working in the area of entrepreneurship. She is currently involved in research into CSR and SMEs and teaches in the areas of business ethics, CSR, work psychology and entrepreneurship.

**Karen L. Becker-Olsen** is an assistant professor of marketing and interdisciplinary business at the School of Business of the College of New Jersey, USA. Her research focuses on branding, consumer behaviour, marketing strategy, CSR, non-profit marketing and sponsorship. Her work is published in journals including *Journal of Marketing, Journal of Business Research, Journal of Advertising* and the *Harvard Business Review América Latina*.

**Kim Benjamin** is a researcher with the Curtin Business School, Curtin University of Technology, Australia. She has a PhD in botanical eco-physiology, and has taught numerous undergraduate courses in botany. Current research interests are focused on corporate social responsibility and sustainability.

**Enrique Bigné-Alcañiz** is professor of marketing and market research at the University of Valencia, Spain, since 2001. He previously occupied the same position at Jaume I University (1996–2001). He has lectured in the area of marketing, tourism and market research in undergraduate, master and PhD programmes, and has published eight books and over 120 articles in national and international publications. He is director of an inter-university doctoral programme in marketing.

**Frank Boons** is senior researcher at the Department of Public Administration, Erasmus University Rotterdam, The Netherlands. His work centres on the way in which firms deal with ecological and social impacts in the context of production and consumption systems. Recently, he published *Creating Ecological Value* (Edward Elgar, 2009) in which he presents an evolutionary approach to business strategies and the natural environment.

**Rafael Currás-Pérez** is currently assistant professor in the Department of Marketing at the University of Valencia, Spain. He is a graduate of the Polytechnic University of Valencia, and obtained his PhD from the University of Valencia in 2007. Research interests include CSR, corporate communication, non-lucrative marketing and online consumer behaviour. His research has appeared in *Journal of Business Ethics, International Review on Public and Nonprofit Marketing, International Journal of Internet Marketing and Advertising, Corporate Reputation Review*, and the best Spanish refereed journals.

**Scott Davis**, originally from Australia, has lived and worked for over 25 years in Japan. Previously a researcher at the Japan Institute of Labour (at that time the research body of the Japanese Ministry of Labour), and a professor at the School of Management at Reitaku University, Davis currently holds the position of Professor of Strategic Corporate Social Responsibility at the College of Business at Rikkyo University in Tokyo. Davis currently serves as a member of the board of directors of the Seven & I Holdings Corporation, a statutory auditor of the Nissen Holdings Corporation, and a permanent director of the Japanese Academy of Social Design. Davis consults for many of Japan's major corporations, industrial associations, government and international agencies on strategic and organisational issues.

**Barbara Del Bosco** is Assistant Professor of Management at the University of Bergamo, Italy. She received her PhD in Business Administration from the University of Pavia. Her research interests are in corporate social responsibility, entrepreneurship and growth strategies.

**Rilka Dragneva-Lewers** was previously a lecturer at the Faculty of Law, University of Leiden, The Netherlands. At the University of Manchester Rilka has developed her research interests in corporate governance and development by being a member of the Institute for Law, Economy and Global Governance and a Faculty Associate of the Brooks World Poverty Institute. Rilka has acted as a consultant in a number of legal reform projects in Eastern Europe for the IFC (International Finance Corporation), the World Bank and the EBRD (European Bank for Reconstruction and Development), and is a member of the editorial board of the *Review of Central and East European Law*.

**Karla Duarte** holds an MBA from the University of Windsor, Canada, and was recently awarded a PhD in Organisational Behaviour from the Michael Smurfit Graduate School of Business at University College Dublin, Ireland. Her research concerns CSR-driven HIV/AIDS initiatives within indigenous, mainly small and medium-sized enterprises in South Africa.

**Joan Fontrodona Felip** is an associate professor and chairman of business ethics at IESE as well as academic director of the IESE Center for Business in Society, University of Navarra, Spain. He holds a PhD in Philosophy and an MBA in Management. He is the chairman of Etica, Economía y Dirección (the Spanish branch of the European Business Ethics Network), and member of the executive committee of the Association of Spanish Entities adhering to the United Nations Global Compact (ASEPAM). He also serves on the academic board of the European Academy of Business in Society (EABIS).

**Magnus Frostenson** holds a PhD in Business Ethics from the Stockholm School of Economics. He currently works as a researcher and assistant professor at Uppsala University, Sweden. His main research interests include organisational ethics, management consulting, and media issues related to business.

**Jeremy Galbreath** is a senior lecturer at the Graduate School of Business, Curtin University of Technology, Australia. He is the author of over 60 articles and has written chapters for strategic management, business ethics and corporate sustainability texts. Dr Galbreath conducts research in strategy, corporate governance and sustainability.

**Francisco Guzmán** is an assistant professor of marketing at the University of North Texas, USA. His research focuses on branding, corporate social responsibility and new product development. His work has been published in journals such as *Journal of International Marketing, European Journal of Marketing, Journal of Marketing Management, Journal of Brand Management* and the *Harvard Business Review América Latina*. He is a visiting professor both at ESADE in Barcelona and Monterrey Tec in Mexico.

**Jose Luis Hernandez** holds an MSc in Engineering Design from the Department of Design, Manufacture and Engineering Management (DMEM) at the University of Strathclyde, Glasgow, UK, and a BSc in Mechanical Engineering and Management from the Technological Institute of Superior Studies of Monterrey in Mexico (ITESM). He currently works for the Strathclyde Institute for Operations Management (SIOM) at DMEM and is currently working with Blairs of Scotland on a Knowledge Transfer Partnership programme.

**Maeve Houlihan** lectures in organisational behaviour at UCD Business Schools, University College Dublin, Ireland. Her research focuses on working lives, management practices and their links with society. She recently co-edited two books with Sharon Bolton on *Work Matters: Critical Reflections on Contemporary Work* (Palgrave, 2009) and *Searching for the Human in Human Resource Management* (Palgrave, 2007).

**Gary Lynch-Wood** lectures on a range of undergraduate and postgraduate programmes, at the University of Manchester, UK, and has recently developed courses on corporate environmental and social responsibility. In addition to this Gary is director of the Sustainability, Policy and Regulation Research Centre, where he conducts research on the relationship between sustainability and regulation.

**Karen Maas** is Assistant Professor at the Department of Business Economics and the Erasmus Centre for Philanthropy, Erasmus University Rotterdam. She worked for 12 years as a (senior) consultant in the field of environmental economics, sustainability and CSR. Since September 2007 she has been working at the Erasmus School of Economics and presented her thesis 'Corporate Social Performance: From Output Measurement to Impact Measurement' in December 2009.

**Steven MacGregor** is a researcher at IESE and was the scientific coordinator for the RESPONSE project presented in this volume. He is managing partner at Macstrong Sustainable Innovation, a management research and consultancy firm based in Girona, Spain, and also teaches at the University of Girona. Dr MacGregor completed his post-doctoral research at Ikerlan, part of the Mondragón Cooperative in the Basque Country, and holds a PhD in Engineering Design Management from the University of Strathclyde in Glasgow.

**Nicola Misani** is an assistant professor of management at Università Bocconi, Italy, and he is a research fellow at the SPACE Research Centre, Università Bocconi. His current research interests revolve around the strategic implications of corporate social responsibility, its effects on consumers, and the financing of sustainable ventures. His academic work has appeared in national and international refereed journals, including the *Journal of Business Ethics*, *Business Strategy and the Environment* and *Business Ethics: A European Review*.

**Jyoti Navare** is a reader and head of department, Marketing and Enterprise at Middlesex University Business School, UK. She is also a non-executive director of Swale Housing Association UK (overseeing the risk and performance management portfolio) and member of the Professional Standards and Ethics Board of the Chartered Insurance Institute, London.

**Ciaran O'Faircheallaigh** has published extensively on the interrelationship between mineral development and indigenous peoples; negotiation; social impact assessment; and CSR. In 2008 he edited, with Saleem Ali, *Earth Matters: Indigenous Peoples, the Extractive Industries and Corporate Social Responsibility* (Greenleaf Publishing). For over 15 years he has assisted indigenous communities in Australia and Canada to undertake negotiations with mining companies.

**Lutz Preuss** is Senior Lecturer in International Business Policy at the School of Management of Royal Holloway, University of London, UK, where he is also programme director of the MSc Sustainability and Management. His research focuses on the input into corporate social responsibility by various corporate functions, such as supply chain, innovation or human resource management. Dr Preuss has published in a range of academic journals, such as *Journal of Business Ethics*, *International Journal of Human Resource Management*, *International Journal of Innovation Management*, *Supply Chain Management: An International Journal*, *Business Ethics: A European Review*, *Business Strategy and the Environment* and *Journal* *of Cleaner Production.* He is also the author of *The Green Multiplier: A Study of Environmental Protection and the Supply Chain,* which was published by Palgrave in 2005.

**Katinka C. van Cranenburgh** is secretary general of 3iG, the International Interfaith Investment Group, visiting scholar at ESADE Business School, Spain, associate director of the European Academy of Business in Society (EABIS) and coordinator of the Heineken Africa Foundation. For over eight years she has contributed to Heineken's healthcare strategy for developing countries.

**David Williamson** is the director of the Sustainability, Policy and Regulation Research Centre in the School of Law at the University of Manchester, UK. David coordinates and conducts research on regulation and CSR. He is particularly interested in CSR in small and medium-sized businesses, CSR in law firms, civil regulation and corporate citizenship.

# Index

Page numbers in *italic figures* refer to illustrations;
'n' following a page number refers to a footnote.